Building Oracle XML Applications

Steve Muench

O'REILLY®

Beijing · Cambridge · Farnham · Köln · Paris · Sebastopol · Taipei · Tokyo

Building Oracle XML Applications
by Steve Muench

Published by O'Reilly & Associates, Inc., 101 Morris Street, Sebastopol, CA 95472.

Editor: Deborah Russell

Production Editor: Madeleine Newell

Cover Designer: Ellie Volckhausen

Printing History:

September 2000: First Edition.

Library of Congress Cataloging-in-Publication Data

Muench, Steve
Building Oracle XML applications/Steve Muench.
p. cm.
ISBN 1-56592-691-9
1. XML (Document markup language) 2. Oracle (Computer file) 3. Application software--Development. I. Title.

QA76.76.H94 M75 2000
005.7'2--dc21 00-062358

ISBN: 1-56592-691-9
[M]

Table of Contents

Preface

This book is a hands-on, practical guide that teaches you the nuts and bolts of XML and the family of Internet standards related to it and shows how to exploit XML with your Oracle database using Java™, PL/SQL, and declarative techniques. It's a book *for* Oracle developers *by* an Oracle developer who has lived the technology at Oracle Corporation for over ten years and has directly catalyzed the company's XML technology direction and implementation. As you read this book, I hope you will come to appreciate the wide variety of tools Oracle provides to enable you to combine the best of XML with the best of Oracle to build flexible, database-powered applications for the Web.

This book abounds with tested, commented, and fully explained examples because—in the unforgettable words of a high school mentor of mine—"you only get good at something by working through an ungodly number of problems." The examples include a number of helper libraries and utilities that will serve to jump-start your own Oracle XML development projects (see "About the Examples" later in this Preface for details).

If this book has one main goal, it is to educate, excite, and thoroughly convince you that by combining:

- The speed, functionality, and reliability of the Oracle database
- The power of XML as a universal standard for data exchange
- The flexibility to easily transform XML data into any format required

we can accomplish some pretty amazing things, not to mention saving ourselves a lot of work in the process.

Audience for This Book

This book is aimed mainly at Java and PL/SQL developers who want to use the XML family of Internet standards in conjunction with their Oracle databases. I also expect that this book may catch the eye of existing Oracle database administrators who want to update their skills to learn how to apply Java, PL/SQL, and XML to their daily work. In addition, the in-depth coverage of Oracle's template-driven XSQL Pages technology should prove useful to non-programmers as well.

This book assumes no prior knowledge of XML on your part, but it does assume a basic working knowledge of SQL and familiarity with either Java or PL/SQL as a programming language.

Which Platform and Version?

Much of this book applies to Oracle8 and Oracle8*i* (and even Oracle7 in some cases). In general, if you want to use XML outside the database, you can use any Oracle version. However, if you want to use XML features inside the database (and take full advantage of the features I describe here), you must use Oracle8*i*. Wherever relevant, I note whether a particular XML feature is specific to Oracle8*i* or can be used with earlier Oracle versions as well.

The examples for this book were developed and tested on a Windows NT 4.0 platform using JDeveloper 3.1 as a development environment and Oracle8*i* Release 2 Enterprise Edition for NT (version 8.1.6) as the database. However, none of the examples, tools, or technologies covered in the book are Windows-specific. The JDeveloper 3.1 product—included on the CD-ROM that accompanies this book—is certified to run on Windows NT and Windows 2000.

Structure of This Book

This book is not divided strictly by individual tool and function. Instead, it begins in Part I with an overview of fundamental XML standards and concepts. Part II covers all core Oracle XML technologies, presenting increasingly detailed discussions of various Oracle XML capabilities. Part III describes combining the technologies we've learned to build applications and portals. Finally, Part IV includes four useful appendixes with installation and reference information.

The book uses extensive examples—in both PL/SQL and Java—to present material of increasing sophistication.

The following list summarizes the contents in detail.

Part I, *XML Basics*, introduces the basics of XML and provides a high-level overview of Oracle's XML technology. It consists of the following chapters:

- Chapter 1, *Introduction to XML*, provides a gentle introduction to XML by describing what it is, what you can do with it, why you should use it, and what software Oracle supplies to work with it.
- Chapter 2, *Working with XML*, describes how to build your own "vocabularies" of tags to represent the information *you* need to work with, as well as how to use XML namespaces and entities to modularize your documents and XPath expressions to search them.

Part II, *Oracle XML Fundamentals*, describes the core development activities that Oracle XML developers need to understand when using XML with an Oracle database. It consists of the following chapters:

- Chapter 3, *Combining XML and Oracle*, provides a typical "day-in-the-life" scenario illustrating the power of combining XML with an Oracle database.
- Chapter 4, *Using JDeveloper for XML Development*, describes how you can use Oracle's JDeveloper product to help with XML development.
- Chapter 5, *Processing XML with PL/SQL*, explains how you can use PL/SQL to load XML files, parse XML, search XML documents, post XML messages, and both enqueue and dequeue XML messages from queues.
- Chapter 6, *Processing XML with Java*, explains how you can combine Java and XML both inside and outside Oracle8*i* to load XML files, parse XML, search XML documents, and post XML messages, as well as enqueue and dequeue XML messages from queues.
- Chapter 7, *Transforming XML with XSLT*, explains the fundamentals of creating XSLT stylesheets to carry out transformations of a source XML document into a resulting XML, HTML or plain text output.
- Chapter 8, *Publishing Data with XSQL Pages*, explains how to build dynamic XML datagrams from SQL using declarative templates to perform many common tasks.
- Chapter 9, *XSLT Beyond the Basics*, builds on the fundamentals from Chapter 7 and explores additional XSLT functionality like variables, sorting and grouping techniques, and the many kinds of useful transformations that can be done using a variation on the identity transformation.
- Chapter 10, *Generating Datagrams with PL/SQL*, gives Java developers a whirlwind introduction to PL/SQL and describes how to use PL/SQL to dynamically produce custom XML datagrams containing database information.

- Chapter 11, *Generating Datagrams with Java*, describes numerous techniques for programmatically producing XML datagrams using Java by using JDBC™, SQLJ, JavaServer Pages™, and the Oracle XML SQL Utility.
- Chapter 12, *Storing XML Datagrams*, explains how to store XML datagrams in the database using the XML SQL Utility and other techniques, as well as how to retrieve them using XSQL pages and XSLT transformations.
- Chapter 13, *Searching XML with interMedia*, describes how you can use Oracle8*i*'s integrated interMedia Text functionality to search XML documents, leveraging their inherent structure to improve text searching accuracy.
- Chapter 14, *Advanced XML Loading Techniques*, describes the techniques required to insert arbitrarily large and complicated XML into multiple tables. It also covers using stylesheets to generate stylesheets to help automate the task.

Part III, *Oracle XML Applications*, describes how to build applications using Oracle and XML technologies. It consists of the following chapters:

- Chapter 15, *Using XSQL Pages as a Publishing Framework*, builds on Chapter 8, explaining the additional features that make XSQL Pages an extensible framework for assembling, transforming, and delivering XML information of any kind.
- Chapter 16, *Extending XSQL and XSLT with Java*, describes how to extend the functionality of the XSQL Pages framework using custom action handlers, and how to extend the functionality of XSLT stylesheets by calling Java extension functions.
- Chapter 17, *XSLT-Powered Portals and Applications*, builds further on Chapter 11 and on earlier chapters, describing best-practice techniques to combine XSQL pages and XSLT stylesheets to build personalized information portal and sophisticated online discussion forum applications.

Part IV, *Appendixes*, contains the following summaries:

- Appendix A, *XML Helper Packages*, provides the source code for the PL/SQL helper packages we built in Chapter 3: `xml`, `xmldoc`, `xpath`, `xslt`, and `http`.
- Appendix B, *Installing the Oracle XSQL Servlet*, describes how to install the XSQL Servlet that you can use with any servlet engine (Apache JServ, JRun, etc.).
- Appendix C, *Conceptual Map to the XML Family*, graphically summarizes the relationships between key XML concepts and the family of XML-related standards that supports them.
- Appendix D, *Quick References*, provides "cheat sheets" on XML, XSLT, and XPath syntax.

About the Examples

This book contains a large number of fully working examples. Many are designed to help you build your own Oracle XML applications. To that end, I've included all examples on the O'Reilly web site (*http://www.oreilly.com/catalog/orxmlapp*). The site includes full source code of all examples and detailed instructions on how to create the sample data required for each chapter. I'll try to keep the code up to date, incorporating corrections to any errors that are discovered, as well as improvements suggested by readers.

In order to run the *complete* set of examples yourself, you will need the following software:

- Oracle 8*i* Release 2 (version 8.1.6) or greater
- Oracle JDeveloper 3.1 or greater

From the Oracle XML Developer's Kit for Java:

- Oracle XML Parser/XSLT Processor for Java, Release 2.0.2.9 or greater
- Oracle XSQL Pages and the XSQL Servlet Release 1.0.0.0
- Oracle XML SQL Utility

From the Oracle XML Developer's Kit for PL/SQL:

- Oracle XML Parser/XSLT Processor for PL/SQL Release 1.0.2 or greater

All of this software is downloadable from the Oracle Technology Network (OTN) web site for Oracle developers at *http://technet.oracle.com* and is available free of charge for single-developer use. For information on runtime distribution of the Oracle XML Developer's kit components, read the license agreement on the download page of any of the components. For your convenience, all of the software listed—with the exception of the Oracle8*i* database itself—is available on the CD-ROM accompanying this book and is automatically installed as part of the JDeveloper 3.1 installation.

About the CD-ROM

We are grateful to Oracle Corporation for allowing us to include the JDeveloper 3.1 for Windows NT software (developer version) on the CD-ROM accompanying this book. This product provides a complete development environment for Java developers working with Oracle and XML. Chapter 4 covers the details of significant JDeveloper 3.1 features that are of interest to XML application developers. You'll find full product documentation and online help on the CD-ROM as well.

Conventions Used in This Book

The following conventions are used in this book:

Italic
: Used for file and directory names and URLs, menu items, and for the first mention of new terms under discussion

`Constant width`
: Used in code examples and for package names, XML elements and attributes, and Java classes and methods

`Constant width italic`
: In some code examples, indicates an element (e.g., a filename) that you supply

`Constant width bold`
: Indicates user input in code examples

UPPERCASE
: Generally used for Oracle SQL and PL/SQL keywords

lowercase
: Generally used for table names in text and for table, column, and variable names in code examples

The following icons are used in this book:

The owl icon indicates a tip, suggestion, or general note related to surrounding text.

The turkey icon indicates a warning related to surrounding text.

Comments and Questions

I have tested and verified the information in this book to the best of my ability, but you may find that features have changed (or even that I have made mistakes!). Please let me know about any errors you find, as well as your suggestions for future editions, by writing to:

O'Reilly & Associates
101 Morris Street
Sebastopol, CA 95472
800-998-9938 (in the U.S. or Canada)
707-829-0515 (international or local)
707-829-0104 (FAX)

You can also send O'Reilly messages electronically. To be put on the mailing list or request a catalog, send email to:

info@oreilly.com

To ask technical questions or comment on the book, send email to:

bookquestions@oreilly.com

We have a web site for this book, where we'll include examples (see "About the Examples" earlier in the Preface), errata, and any plans for future editions. You can access this page at:

http://www.oreilly.com/catalog/orxmlapp/

For more information about this book and others, see the O'Reilly web site:

http://www.oreilly.com

Acknowledgments

I owe an unrepayable debt of gratitude to my wife Sita. For over a year, she juggled our two active youngsters on nights and weekends while Daddy "disappeared" to work on his book—a true labor of love. She did not understand what demon drove me to write this book, but she felt I might regret *not* writing it for the rest of my life. I'm happy to say to her, Emma, and Amina, "Daddy's home."

Thanks to my mother-in-law, Dr. Nila Negrin, who assisted me in finding the perfect XML insect to grace the cover of this book, *Xenochaetina Muscaria Loew*. Regrettably, O'Reilly couldn't find a print of this Tennessee-native fly, so we had to go for plan B.

Many thanks to the technical reviewers for this book: Adam Bosworth, Terris Linenbach, Don Herkimer, Keith M. Swartz, Leigh Dodds, Murali Murugan, Bill Pribyl, and Andrew Odewahn. I owe Keith a special thank you for his amazingly detailed review.

Garrett Kaminaga, a key developer on Oracle's interMedia Text product development team, wrote the lion's share of Chapter 13, for which I am very grateful. In addition, thanks go to MK, Visar, and Karun in Oracle's Server Technology XML development team for answering questions when I bumped into problems, and for always having an open mind to new ideas.

Norm Walsh, coauthor of *DocBook: The Definitive Guide* (O'Reilly & Associates), offered early encouragement for my then-crazy idea of authoring this entire book in XML, and he answered many questions at the outset about using the DocBook DTD for technical manuals.

Many thanks to Tony Graham at Mulberry Technologies for giving us permission to include the helpful XML, XSLT, and XPath quick references in Appendix D and to Oracle Corporation for allowing us to include JDeveloper 3.1 on the accompanying CD-ROM.

Thanks to the entire O'Reilly production team, especially to Madeleine Newell, the project manager and copyeditor, whose keen questions about wording and XML enhanced the book.

Finally, thanks to Debby Russell, my editor at O'Reilly, for believing in my initial idea and more importantly for not rushing me to finish. The book you're now reading is everything I envisioned at the outset for a one-stop-shop book for developers using Oracle and XML. No compromises were made and thankfully, none was ever asked of me.

I

XML Basics

This part of the book introduces the basics of XML and provides a high-level overview of Oracle's XML technology. It consists of the following chapters:

- Chapter 1, *Introduction to XML*, provides a gentle introduction to XML by describing what it is, what you can do with it, why you should use it, and what software Oracle supplies to work with it.
- Chapter 2, *Working with XML*, describes how to build your own vocabularies of tags to represent the information *you* need to work with, as well as how to use XML namespaces and entities to modularize your documents and XPath expressions to search them.

In this chapter:
- *What Is XML?*
- *What Can I Do with XML?*
- *Why Should I Use XML?*
- *What XML Technologies Does Oracle Provide?*

1 Introduction to XML

The Internet is driving an unprecedented demand for access to information. Seduced by the convenience of paying bills, booking flights, tracking stocks, checking prices, and getting everything from gifts to groceries online, consumers are hungry for more. Compelled by the lower costs of online outsourcing and the ability to inquire, day or night, "What's the status?," businesses are ramping up to reap the rewards. Excited by improved efficiency and universal public access, governments are considering how all kinds of raw data, from financial reports to federally funded research, can be published online in an easily reusable format.

More than ever before, database-savvy web application developers working to capitalize on these exciting Internet-inspired opportunities need to rapidly acquire, integrate, and repurpose information, as well as exchange it with other applications both inside and outside their companies. XML dramatically simplifies these tasks.

As with any new technology, you first need to understand what XML is, what you can do with it, and why you should use it. With all the new terms and acronyms to understand, XML can seem like a strange new planet to the uninitiated, so let's walk before we run. This chapter introduces "Planet XML" and the "moons" that orbit it, and provides a high-level overview of the tools and technology Oracle offers to exploit the combined strengths of XML and the Oracle database in your web applications.

What Is XML?

First, let's look at some basic XML definitions and examples.

Extensible Markup Language

XML, which stands for the "Extensible Markup Language," defines a universal standard for electronic data exchange. It provides a rigorous set of rules enabling the structure inherent in data to be easily encoded and unambiguously interpreted using human-readable text documents. Example 1-1 shows what a stock market transaction might look like represented in XML.

Example 1-1. Stock Market Transaction Represented in XML

```
<?xml version="1.0"?>
<transaction>
  <account>89-344</account>
  <buy shares="100">
    <ticker exch="NASDAQ">WEBM</ticker>
  </buy>
  <sell shares="30">
    <ticker exch="NYSE">GE</ticker>
  </sell>
</transaction>
```

After an initial line that identifies the document as an XML document, the example begins with a **<transaction>** tag. Nested inside this opening tag and its matching **</transaction>** closing tag, other tags and text encode nested structure and data values respectively. Any tag can carry a list of one or more named ***attribute*="*value*"** entries as well, like **shares="*nn*"** on **<buy>** and **<sell>** and **exch="*xxx*"** on **<ticker>**.

XML's straightforward "text with tags" syntax should look immediately familiar if you have ever worked with HTML, which also uses tags, text, and attributes. A key difference between HTML and XML, however, lies in the kind of data each allows you to represent. What you can represent in an HTML document is constrained by the fixed set of HTML tags at your disposal—like **<table>**, **<img>**, and **<a>** for tables, images, and anchors. In contrast, with XML you can invent any set of meaningful tags to suit your current data encoding needs, or reuse an existing set that someone else has already defined. Using XML and an appropriate set of tags, you can encode data of any kind, from highly structured database query results like the following:

```
<?xml version="1.0"?>
<ROWSET>
  <ROW num="1">
    <ENAME>KING</ENAME>
    <SAL>5000</SAL>
  </ROW>
  <ROW num="2">
    <ENAME>SCOTT</ENAME>
    <SAL>3000</SAL>
  </ROW>
</ROWSET>
```

to unstructured documents like this one:

```
<?xml version="1.0"?>
<DamageReport>
  The insured's <Vehicle Make="Volks">Beetle</Vehicle> broke through
  the guard rail and plummeted into a ravine. The cause was determined
  to be <Cause>faulty brakes</Cause>.  Amazingly there were no casualties.
</DamageReport>
```

and anything in between.

A set of XML tags designed to encode data of a particular kind is known as an XML *vocabulary*. If the data to be encoded is very simple, it can be represented with an XML vocabulary consisting of as little as a single tag:

```
<?xml version="1.0"?>
<OrderConfirmed/>
```

For more complicated cases, an XML vocabulary can comprise as many tags as necessary, and they can be nested to reflect the structure of data being represented:

```
<?xml version="1.0"?>
<Planet Name="Earth">
  <Continent Name="North America">
    <Country Name="USA">
      <State Name="California">
        <City Name="San Francisco"/>
      </State>
    </Country>
  </Continent>
</Planet>
```

As we've seen in the few examples above, an XML document is just a sequence of text characters that encodes data using tags and text. Often, this sequence of characters will be the contents of a text file, but keep in mind that XML documents can live anywhere a sequence of characters can roost. An XML document might be the contents of a string-valued variable in a running computer program, a stream of data arriving in packets over a network, or a column value in a row of a database table. While XML documents encoding different data may use different tag vocabularies, they all adhere to the same set of general syntactic principles described in the XML specification, which is discussed in the next section.

XML Specification

The XML 1.0 specification became a World Wide Web Consortium (W3C) Recommendation in February 1998. Before a W3C specification reaches this final status, it must survive several rounds of public scrutiny and be tempered by feedback from the early implementation experience of multiple vendors. Only then will the W3C Director declare it a "Recommendation" and encourage its widespread, public adoption as a new web standard. In the short time since February 1998, hundreds of vendors and organizations around the world have delivered support for XML in their products. The list includes all of the big-name software vendors like Oracle, IBM, Microsoft, Sun, SAP, and others, as well as numerous influential open source organizations like the Apache Software Foundation. XML's apparent youth belies its years; the W3C XML Working Group consciously designed it as a simplified subset of the well-respected SGML (Standard Generalized Markup Language) standard.

In order to be as generally applicable as possible, the XML 1.0 specification does not define any particular tag names; instead, it defines general syntactic rules enabling developers to create their own domain-specific vocabularies of tags. Since XML allows you to create virtually any set of tags you can imagine, two common questions are:

- How do I understand someone else's XML?
- How do I ensure that other people can understand my XML?

The answer lies in the document type definition you can associate with your XML documents.

Document Type Definition

A *document type definition* (DTD) is a text document that formally defines the lexicon of legal names for the tags in a particular XML vocabulary, as well as the meaningful ways that tags are allowed to be nested. The DTD defines this lexicon of tags using a syntax described in the DTD specification, which is an integral part of the XML 1.0 specification described earlier. An XML document can be associated with a particular DTD to enable supporting programs to validate the document's contents against that document type definition; that is, to check that the document's syntax conforms to the syntax allowed by the associated DTD. Without an associated DTD, an XML document can at best be subjected to a "syntax check."

Recall our transaction example from Example 1-1. For this transaction vocabulary, we might want to reject a transaction that looks like this:

```
<?xml version="1.0"?>
<transaction>
  <buy>
    <ticker exch="NASDAQ">WEBM</ticker>
    <sell shares="30">
      <ticker exch="NYSE">GE</ticker>
    </sell>
  </buy>
</transaction>
```

because it's missing an account number, doesn't indicate how many shares to buy, and incorrectly lists the `<sell>` tag inside the `<buy>` tag.

We can enable the rejection of this erroneous transaction document by defining a DTD for the transaction vocabulary. The DTD can define the set of valid tag names (also known as element names) to include `<transaction>`, `<account>`, `<buy>`, `<sell>`, and `<ticker>`. Furthermore, it can assert additional constraints on a `<transaction>` document. For example, it can require that:

- A `<transaction>` should be comprised of exactly one `<account>` element and one or more occurrences of `<buy>` or `<sell>` elements
- A `<buy>` or `<sell>` element should carry an attribute named `shares`, and contain exactly one `<ticker>` element
- A `<ticker>` element should carry an attribute named `exch`

With a `<transaction>` DTD such as this in place, we can use tools we'll learn about in the next section to be much more picky about the transaction documents we accept. Figure 1-1 summarizes the relationships between the XML specification, the DTD specification, the XML document, and the DTD.

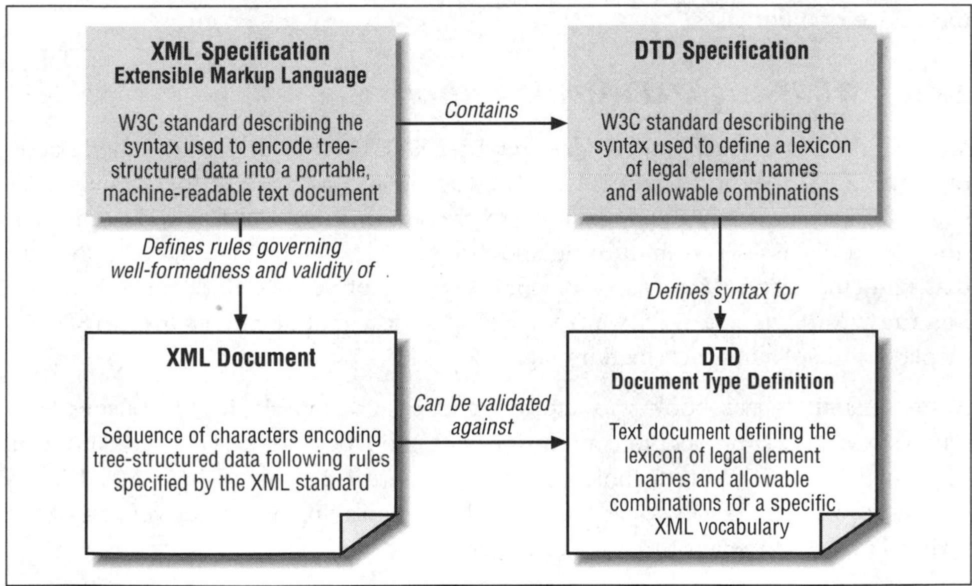

Figure 1-1. Relationship between the XML spec, XML document, DTD spec, and DTD

If an XML document passes the strict XML syntax check, it is known as a *well-formed* document. If in addition, its contents conform to all the constraints in a particular DTD, the document is known as "well-formed and *valid*" with respect to that DTD.

What Can I Do with XML?

Beyond encoding data in a textual format, an XML document doesn't do much of anything on its own. The true power of XML lies in the tools that process it. In this section, we take a quick tour of the interesting ways to work with XML documents using tools and technologies widely available today from a number of different vendors.

Work with XML Using Text-Based Tools

Since an XML document is just text, you can:

- View and edit it with vi, Emacs, Notepad, or your favorite text editor
- Search it with *grep*, *sed*, *findstr*, or any other text-based utility
- Source-control it using systems like CVS, ClearCase, or RCS

These and other tools can treat an XML file the same as any other text file for common development tasks.

Edit XML Using DTD-Aware Editors

More sophisticated XML editing tools read an XML DTD to understand the lexicon of legal tag names for a particular XML vocabulary, as well as the various constraints on valid element combinations expressed in the DTD. Using this information, the tools assist you in creating and editing XML documents that comply with that particular DTD. Many support multiple views of your XML document including a raw XML view, a WYSIWYG view, and a view that augments the WYSIWYG display by displaying each markup tag.

As an example, this book was created and edited entirely in XML using SoftQuad's XMetal 1.0 product in conjunction with the DocBook DTD, a standard XML vocabulary for authoring technical manuals. Figure 1-2 shows what XMetal looks like in its WYSIWYG view with tags turned on, displaying an earlier version of the XML source document for this very chapter.

If the XML documents you edit look more like a data structure than a technical manuscript, then a WYSIWYG view is likely not what you want. Other DTD-aware editors like Icon Software's XML Spy and Extensibility's XML Instance present hierarchical views of your document more geared toward editing XML-based data structures like our transaction example in Example 1-1, or an XML-based purchase order.

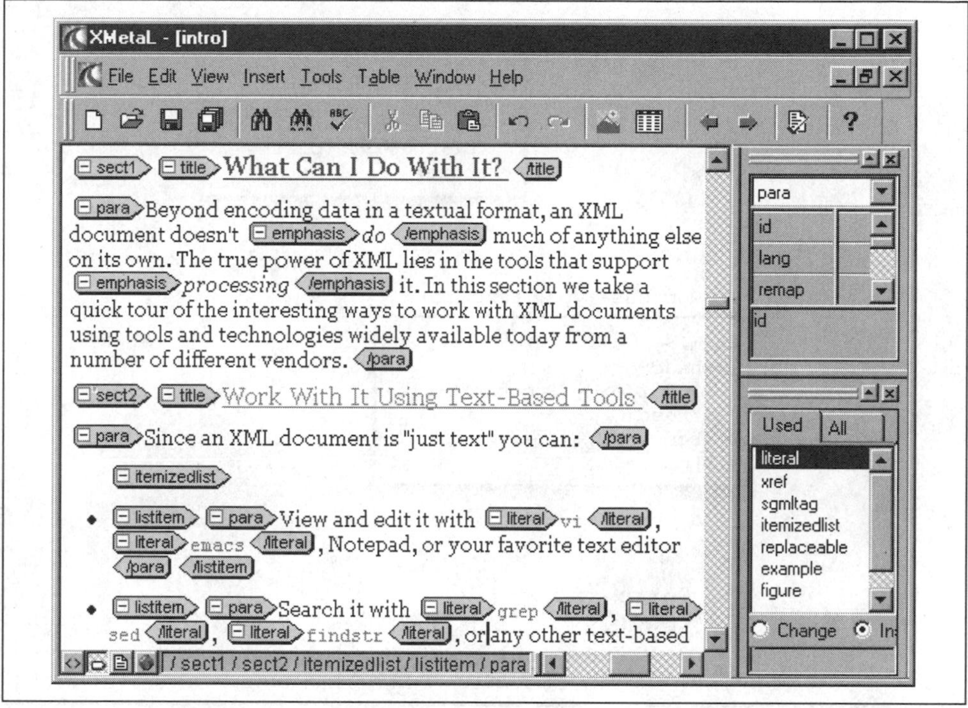

Figure 1-2. Editing a chapter in this book with XMetal

Send and Receive XML over the Web

An XML document can be sent as easily as any other text document over the Web using any of the Internet's widely adopted protocols, such as:

FTP
: The File Transfer Protocol, used for sending and receiving files

SMTP
: The Simple Mail Transfer Protocol, used for exchanging documents in email

HTTP
: The HyperText Transfer Protocol, used for exchanging documents with web servers

By convention, when documents or other resources are exchanged using such protocols, each is earmarked with a standard content type identifier that indicates the kind of resource being exchanged. For example, when a web server returns an HTML page to a browser, it identifies the HTML document with a content type of `text/html`. Similarly, every time your browser encounters an `<img>` tag in a page, it makes an HTTP request to *retrieve* the image using a URL and gets a binary document in response, with a content type like `image/gif`. As illustrated in

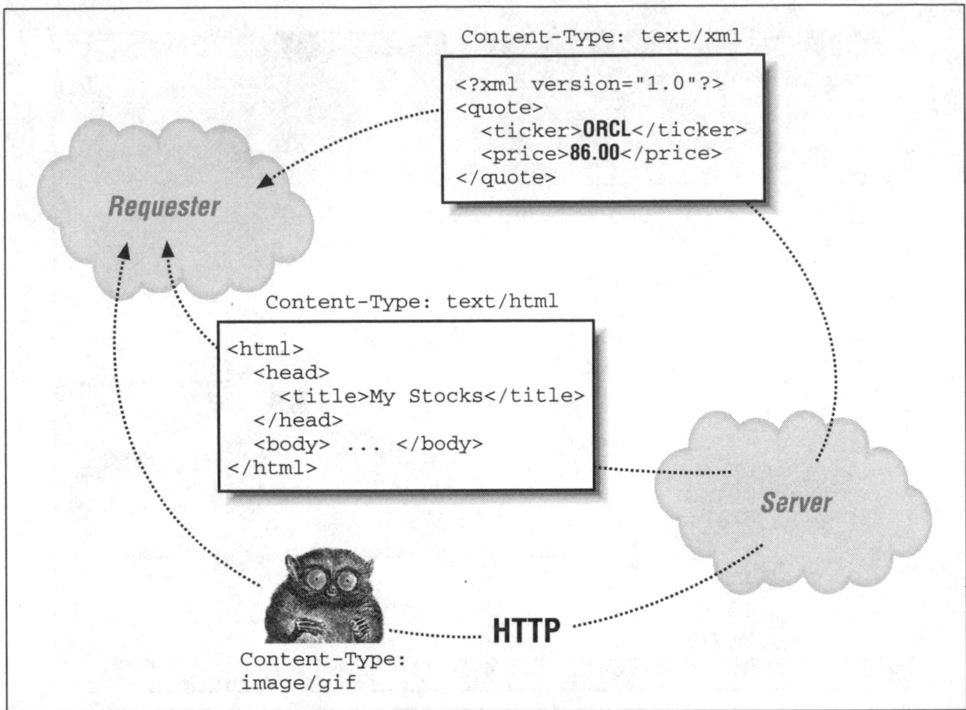
Content-Type: text/xml
<?xml version="1.0"?>
<quote>
<ticker>ORCL</ticker>
<price>86.00</price>
</quote>
Requester
Content-Type: text/html
<html>
<head>
<title>My Stocks</title>
</head>
<body> ... </body>
</html>
Server
HTTP
Content-Type:
image/gif

Figure 1-3. The Web already supports XML document exchange

Figure 1-3, you can easily exchange XML documents over the Web by leveraging this same mechanism. The standard content type for XML documents is `text/xml`.

The act of exchanging XML documents over the Web seems straightforward when XML is viewed as just another content type, but it represents something very powerful. Since any two computers on the Web can exchange documents using the HTTP protocol, and since any structured data can be encoded in a standard way using XML, the combination of HTTP and XML provides a vendor-neutral, platform-neutral, standards-based backbone of technology to send any structured data between any two computers on the network. When XML documents are used to exchange data in this way, they are often called *XML datagrams.* Given the rapid increase in the number of portable electronic devices sporting wireless Internet connectivity, these XML datagrams can be easily shuttled between servers and cell phones or personal data assistants (PDAs) as well.

Generate XML with Server-Side Programs

The XML datagrams exchanged between clients and servers on the Internet become even more interesting when the content of the XML datagram is generated *dynamically* in response to each request. This allows a server to provide an interesting web service, returning datagrams that can answer questions like these:

What are the French restaurants within one city block of the Geary Theatre?

```
<?xml version="1.0"?>
<RestaurantList>
  <Restaurant Name="Brasserie Savoy" Phone="415-123-4567"/>
</RestaurantList>
```

When is Lufthansa Flight 458 expected to arrive at SFO today?

```
<?xml version="1.0"?>
<FlightArrival Date="06-05-2000">
  <Flight>
    <Carrier>LH</Carrier>
    <Arrives>SFO</Arrives>
    <Expected>14:40</Expected>
  </Flight>
</FlightArrival>
```

What is the status of the package with tracking number 56789?

```
<?xml version="1.0"?>
<TrackingStatus PackageId="56789">
  <History>
    <Scanned   At="17:45" On="06-05-2000" Comment="Williams Sonoma Shipping"/>
    <Scanned   At="21:13" On="06-05-2000" Comment="SFO"/>
    <Scanned   At="04:13" On="06-06-2000" Comment="JFK"/>
    <Scanned   At="06:05" On="06-06-2000" Comment="Put on truck"/>
    <Delivered At="09:58" On="06-06-2000" Comment="Received by Jane Hubert"/>
  </History>
</TrackingStatus>
```

Since XML is just text, it is straightforward to generate XML dynamically using server-side programs in virtually any language: Java, PL/SQL, Perl, JavaScript, and others. The first program you learn in any of these languages is how to print out the text:

```
Hello, World!
```

If you modify this example to print out instead:

```
<?xml version="1.0"?>
<Message>Hello, World!</Message>
```

then, believe it or not, you have just mastered the basic skills needed to generate dynamic XML documents! If these dynamic XML documents are generated by a server-side program that accesses information in a legacy database or file format, then information that was formerly locked up in a proprietary format can be liberated for Internet-based access by simply printing out the desired information with appropriate XML tags around it.

Work with Specific XML Vocabularies

As we saw above, an XML document can use either an ad hoc vocabulary of tags or a formal vocabulary defined by a DTD. Common questions developers new to XML ask are:

What are some existing web sites that make XML available?
: The nicely organized *http://www.xmltree.com* site provides a directory of XML content on the Web and is an interesting place to look for examples. The *http://www.moreover.com* site serves news feeds in XML on hundreds of different news topics.

How do I find out whether there is an existing standard XML DTD for what I want to publish?
: There is at present no single, global registry of all XML DTDs, but the following sites are good places to start a search: *http://www.xml.org*, *http://www.schema.net*, and *http://www.ebxml.org*.

If I cannot find an existing DTD to do the job, how do I go about creating one?
: There are a number of visual tools available for creating XML DTDs. The XML Authority tool from Extensibility (see *http://www.extensibility.com*) has proven itself invaluable time and time again during the creation of this book, both for viewing the structure of existing DTDs and for creating new DTDs. An especially cool feature is its ability to import an existing XML document and "reverse engineer" a DTD for it. It's not always an exact science—since the example document may not contain occurrences of every desired combination of tags—but the tool does its best, giving you a solid starting point from which you can easily begin fine-tuning.

Parse XML to Access Its Information Set

We've seen that XML documents can represent tree-structured data by using tags that contain other nested tags as necessary. Because of this nesting, just looking at an XML document's contents can be enough for a human to understand the structured information it represents:

```
<?xml version="1.0"?>
<transaction><account>89-344</account><buy shares="100"><ticker
exch="NASDAQ">WEBM</ticker></buy><sell shares="30"><ticker
exch="NYSE">GE</ticker></sell></transaction>
```

This is especially true if the document contains extra whitespace (line breaks, spaces, or tabs) between the tags to make them indent appropriately, as in Example 1-1. For a computer program to access the structured information in the document in a meaningful way, an additional step, called *parsing*, is required. By reading the stream of characters and recognizing the syntactic details of where elements, attributes, and text occur in the document, an *XML parser* exposes the hierarchical set of information in the document as a tree of related elements, attributes, and text items. This logical tree of information items is called the XML document's *information set*, or *infoset* for short. Figure 1-4 shows the information set produced by parsing our `<transaction>` document.

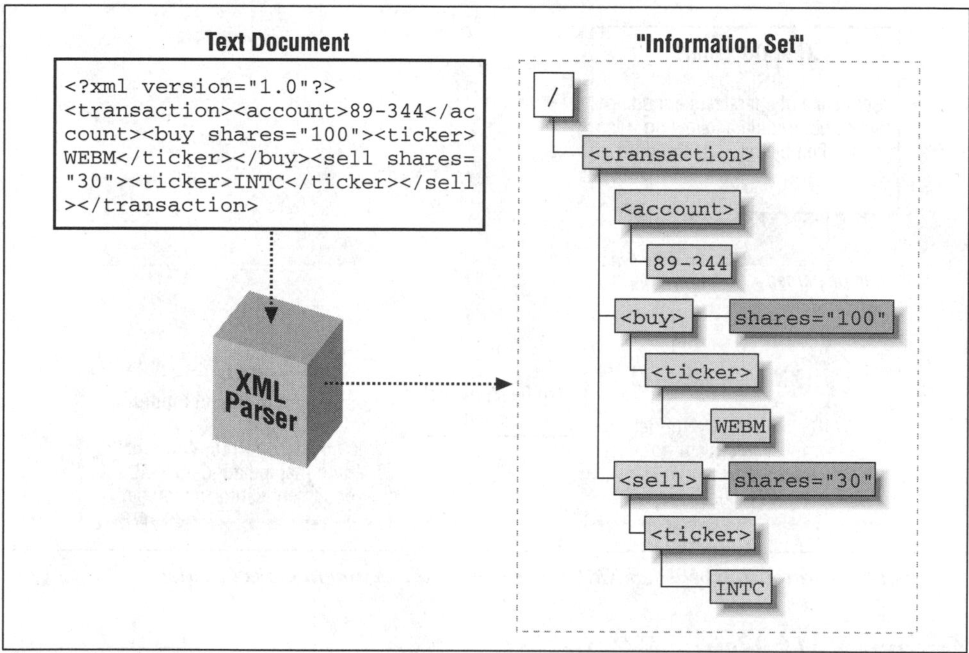

Figure 1-4. Parsing to access the transaction datagram's information set

When you work with items in the logical, tree-structured infoset of an XML document, you work at a higher level of abstraction than the physical "text and tags" level. Instead, you work with a tree of related nodes: a root node, element nodes, attribute nodes, and text nodes. This is conceptually similar to the "tables, rows, and columns" abstraction you use when working with a relational database. Both abstractions save you from having to worry about the physical "bits and bytes" storage representation of the data and provide a more productive model for thinking about and working with the information they represent.

Manipulate XML Using the DOM

Once an XML document has been parsed to produce its infoset of element, attribute, and text nodes, you naturally want to manipulate the items in the tree. The W3C provides a standard API called the Document Object Model (DOM) to access the node tree of an XML document's infoset. The DOM API provides a complete set of operations to programmatically manipulate the node tree, including navigating the nodes in the hierarchy, creating and appending new nodes, removing nodes, etc. Once you're done making modifications to the node tree, you can easily save, or *serialize* the modified infoset back into its physical text representation as text and tags again. Figure 1-5 illustrates the relationship between an XML document, the infoset it represents, and the DOM API.

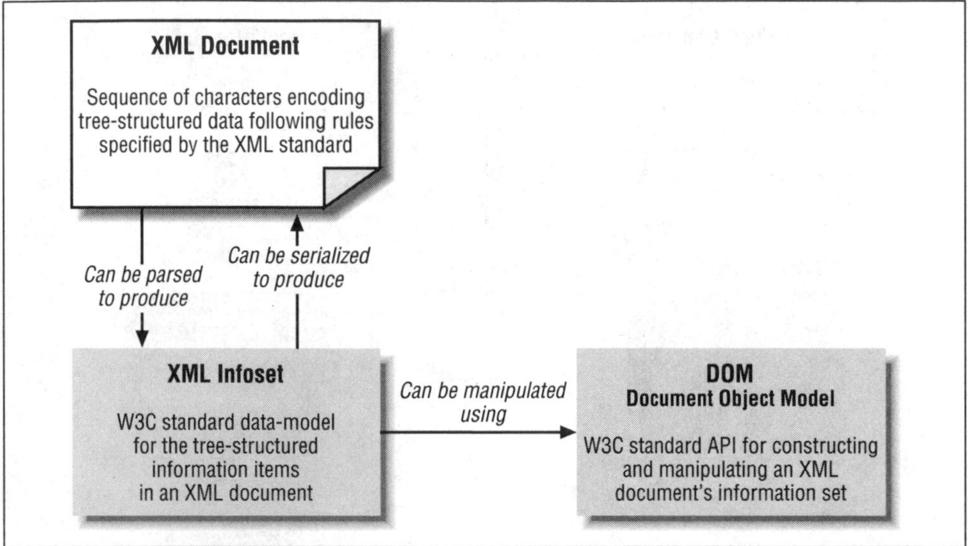

Figure 1-5. Relationship between XML document and Document Object Model

Query XML Using XPath

Often you will want to interrogate an XML document to select interesting subsets of information. The W3C standard XML Path Language (XPath) provides a simple, declarative language to accomplish the job. Let's look at some simple examples of this declarative syntax using our `<transaction>` document from Example 1-1.

Leveraging your familiarity with the hierarchical path notation for URLs and files in directories, an XPath expression allows you to select the `<ticker>` symbol of the `<buy>` request in the `<transaction>` by using the expression:

```
/transaction/buy/ticker
```

To select the number of `shares` in the `<sell>` request in the `<transaction>`, you can use the expression `/transaction/sell/@shares`, prefixing the name of the attribute you want with an at-sign. Filter predicates can be added at any level to refine the information you will get back from the selection. For example, to select the ticker symbol for `<buy>` requests over 50 shares, you can use the expression `/transaction/buy[@shares>50]/ticker`.

As illustrated in Figure 1-6, XPath queries select information from the logical tree-structured data model presented by an XML document's infoset, not from its raw text representation.

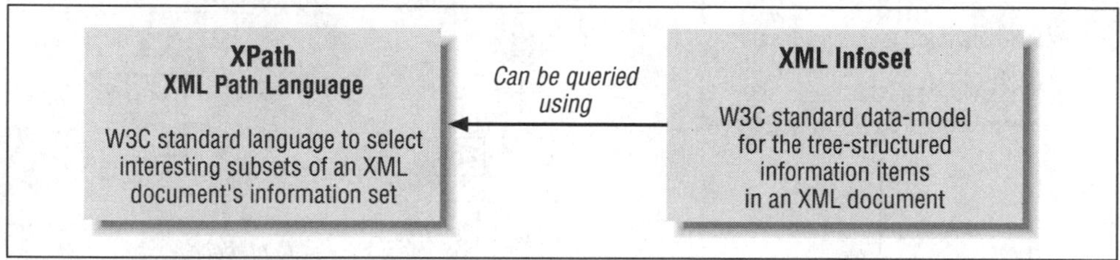

Figure 1-6. Relationship between XML infoset and XPath language

Transform XML Using XSLT

One of the most useful things you can do with XML is transform it from one tree-based structure to another. This comes in handy when you want to:

- Convert between XML vocabularies used by different applications
- Present an XML document's data by transforming it into HTML or another format that's appropriate to the user or device requesting the data

Fortunately, the W3C has again provided a companion standard called XSLT (the XML Stylesheet Language for Transformations) to make this task declarative. XSLT was originally conceived as a language to transform any XML document into a tree of *formatting objects* from which high-quality printed output could be easily rendered. The W3C XSL Working Group recognized early that this XML transformation facility would be an important subset of functionality in its own right, so they formally separated the XSLT language from the XSL formatting objects specification. This allowed the XSLT language to perform any useful XML-to-XML transformation. These origins help explain why the definition of an XML transformation is known as a *stylesheet.*

An XSLT stylesheet is an XML document that uses the XSLT language's vocabulary to describe the transformation you want to perform. The stylesheet consists of transformation instructions, which use XPath expressions to select interesting information items from the infoset of a *source document* and specify how to process the results of these selections to construct an infoset for a *+++result document* with a different structure. Figure 1-7 highlights this relationship between XSLT and XPath and illustrates how the transformation is carried out on the logical source tree and result tree.

Let's assume that on receiving our transaction datagram, our application needs to turn around and send an appropriate datagram to the NASDAQ trading system to complete the trade. Of course, the datagram we send to NASDAQ must use the

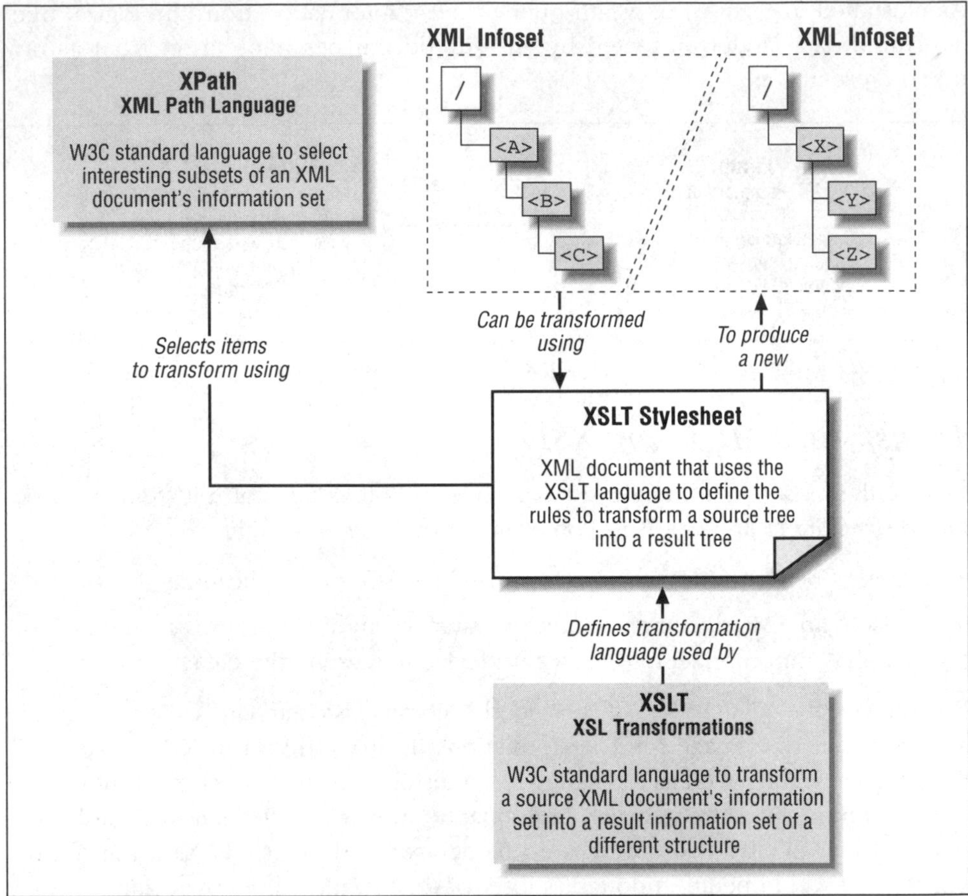

Figure 1-7. Relationship between XSLT, XPath, and the infoset

XML vocabulary that the NASDAQ trading system understands. The relevant datagram using the <nasdaq-order> vocabulary might look like this:

```
<?xml version="1.0"?>
<nasdaq-order clientid="123">
   <trans type="buy">
      <security>WEBM</security>
      <shares>100</shares>
   </trans>
</nasdaq-order>
```

We can create an XSLT stylesheet that selects any <buy> requests in the <transaction> for stocks on the NASDAQ exchange and constructs the appropriate <trans>, <security>, and <shares> elements as nested "children" of a <nasdaq-order> in the result. Example 1-2 shows what this stylesheet looks like.

Example 1-2. XSLT Stylesheet to Transform Between XML Vocabularies

```
<?xml version="1.0"?>
<xsl:stylesheet version="1.0" xmlns:xsl="http://www.w3.org/1999/XSL/Transform">
  <xsl:output indent="yes"/>
  <xsl:template match="/">
    <nasdaq-order clientid="123">
      <!-- Use XPath to select buy transactions for stocks on the NASDAQ -->
      <xsl:for-each select="/transaction/buy[ticker/@exch='NASDAQ']">
        <trans type="buy">
          <security><xsl:value-of select="ticker"/></security>
          <shares><xsl:value-of select="@shares"/></shares>
        </trans>
      </xsl:for-each>
    </nasdaq-order>
  </xsl:template>
</xsl:stylesheet>
```

Notice that we use the XPath expression `/transaction/buy[ticker/@exch='NASDAQ']` to select the <buy> elements that satisfy our criteria as part of the transformation. Given a source tree structure like the one for our incoming transaction document and an XSLT stylesheet like Example 1-2 describing the transformation, an *XSLT processor* carries out the transformation to produce the result tree as illustrated in Figure 1-8.

Appendix C, *Conceptual Map to the XML Family*, illustrates how all the basic standards in the XML family relate to one another. It's a summary of what we've seen in this chapter, all in a single diagram for easy reference.

Why Should I Use XML?

Why have vendors like Oracle, IBM, Microsoft, Sun, SAP, and many others moved so fast to support XML? After all, these companies have worked for many years to fine-tune the efficiency of their proprietary data formats and tools. The reason is simple: as a vendor-neutral, platform-neutral, language-neutral technology for web-based data exchange, the XML family of standards solves a key problem for these companies' customers. In a nutshell, XML simplifies the task of connecting applications and services over the Web.

XML Enables a Data Web of Information Services

Proprietary data formats undoubtedly represent data in a more efficient way, but what XML sacrifices in compactness, it gains many times over in flexibility. If you can publish an XML datagram on the "wire," anyone connected to the Internet can

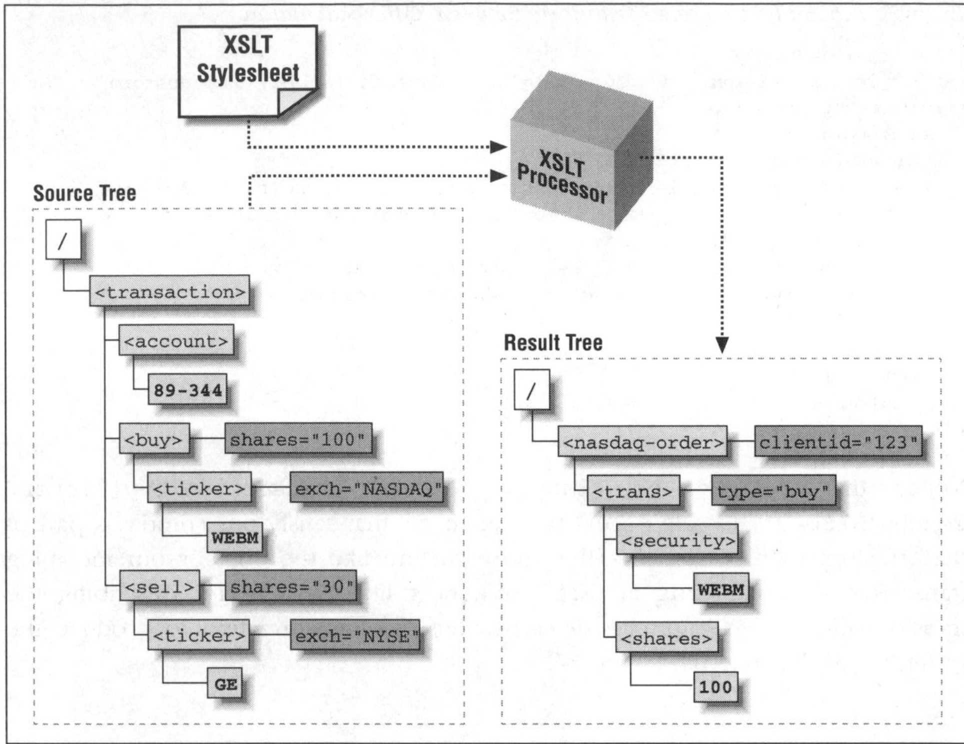

Figure 1-8. XSLT processor transforms source tree to result tree

receive the datagram, parse it, manipulate it, search it, and transform it using a wide selection of freely available tools that implement the XML family of standards. Skeptics who dwell on XML's apparent inefficiencies ("It's more tags than data, for heaven's sake!," they say), haven't yet understood how its usefulness grows when it is combined with the Internet's universal reach. The HTML standard and the essentially free cost of HTML-savvy browsers sparked the creation of the Web as we know it today: a sea of information available 24 hours a day for a pair of human eyeballs focused on a browser to exploit. The XML family of standards and the low cost of many XML-savvy tools have already begun to spark an analogous "data web" of Internet-based machine-to-machine information exchanges. XML is on track to have an even greater impact on the computing landscape than HTML has had.

Critics are correct to point out that XML is no magic bullet, noting that companies still need to agree on common XML vocabularies for application data exchange. However, market forces are already quickly resolving these concerns. Due to the tremendous opportunities presented by business-to-business e-commerce, a burgeoning sector whose key players are already leveraging this new XML-based data web, the number of XML-based standards for domain-specific business messages is growing exponentially. By tapping into the XML data web, you can save money by leveraging outsourced business content and services, and generate new revenue by publishing slices of your own valuable data as web services to be "consumed" by other partners.

XML Simplifies Application Integration

It is not uncommon for a company to have:

- Machines running operating systems from Sun, HP, IBM, Microsoft, and others
- Databases from Oracle, IBM, Microsoft, and others
- Packaged applications from Oracle, SAP, and others

An XML-based representation of data and the HTTP protocol might be the only things these various systems can ever hope to have in common! More and more, these systems must be integrated over the Internet and across firewalls, so XML over HTTP or secure HTTPS is the data exchange mechanism of choice to connect these heterogeneous applications.

Figure 1-9 illustrates a sample architecture for XML-based application integration. It shows how an SAP system using a Microsoft SQL Server database sends an XML datagram over the Web to a server that acts as a message hub. The hub server routes the datagram to a particular target application, say an Oracle Applications installation using an Oracle8*i* database. In doing this, it may need to transform the incoming XML datagram into an appropriate XML vocabulary for the target application before sending the datagram to its destination.

Adopting an architecture like this does not require invasive, dramatic changes to existing systems. Data in the SAP and Oracle Applications systems is still stored in its original relational tables, exactly as it was before the integration. The XML datagram is materialized from information in the source system by dynamically generating an XML document. Upon arrival at the target system, the datagram is parsed, searched, and programmatically manipulated to enable appropriate information from the datagram to be inserted into the target application's database. While SAP and Oracle Applications use completely different database schemas to support their respective application suites, these physical storage details are not a roadblock to integration when the two systems communicate using XML datagrams.

XML Simplifies Information Publishing and Reuse

The same strengths that make XML good for application integration also deliver benefits to other areas of application development. Leveraging the dynamic duo of XML (to represent rich data structures independent of presentation details) and

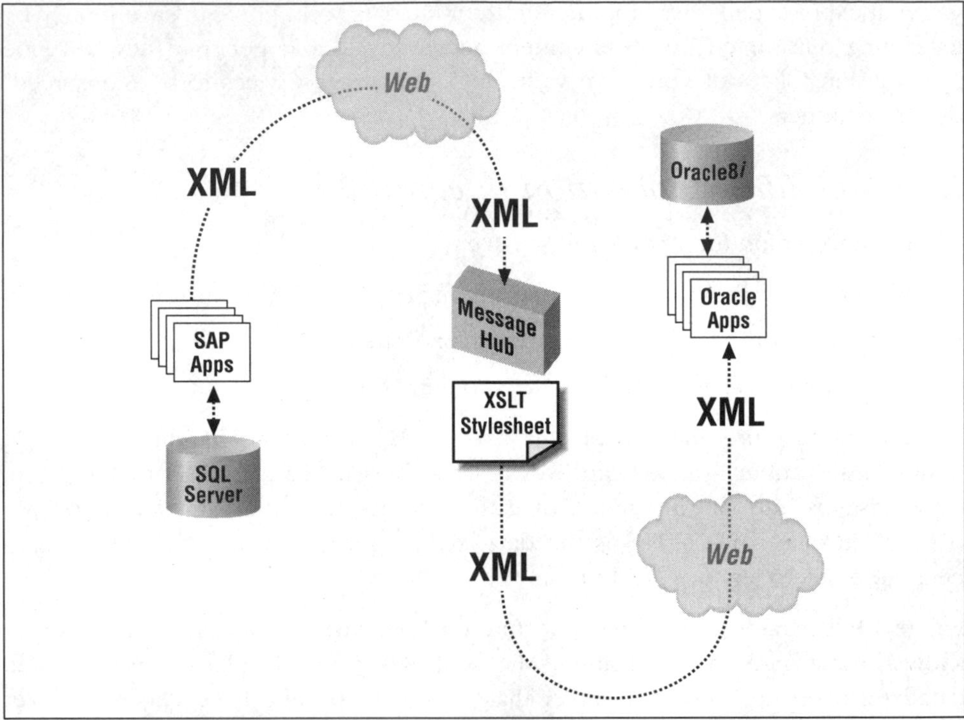

Figure 1-9. XML and HTTP can connect different applications

XSLT (to transform the data into any other XML, HTML, or text-based output format), you can easily:

- Separate data from presentation, allowing you to change the *look* of the information without affecting application code
- Publish the same data using output styles specific to each kind of requesting device: browser, cell phone, PDA, another computer, etc.

With the exploding number of web-enabled devices and the increasing number of XML-based standards emerging, the ability to assemble information from multiple sources and transform it for delivery into any format required by the target device is extremely valuable.

As any database-savvy developer knows, SQL is a highly effective tool for finding, filtering, shaping, and summarizing the data required by any application task. Using XML to publish SQL-based query results packs an even stronger punch, making the information in the query results easy to transform, transport, and transcribe. Figure 1-10 shows the high-level architecture for the combination of SQL, XML, and XSLT. By representing SQL query results as XML, we can assemble a "data page" from multiple queries and external XML information sources. Then we can use XSLT to transform this assembled XML data page into any desired output format (like HTML) for presentation in a browser or any of a number of XML-based formats, such as:

WML
: The Wireless Markup Language, for cell phones and PDAs

SVG
: The Scalable Vector Graphics language, for rendering rich, data-driven images

XSL Formatting Objects
: For high-quality printed output

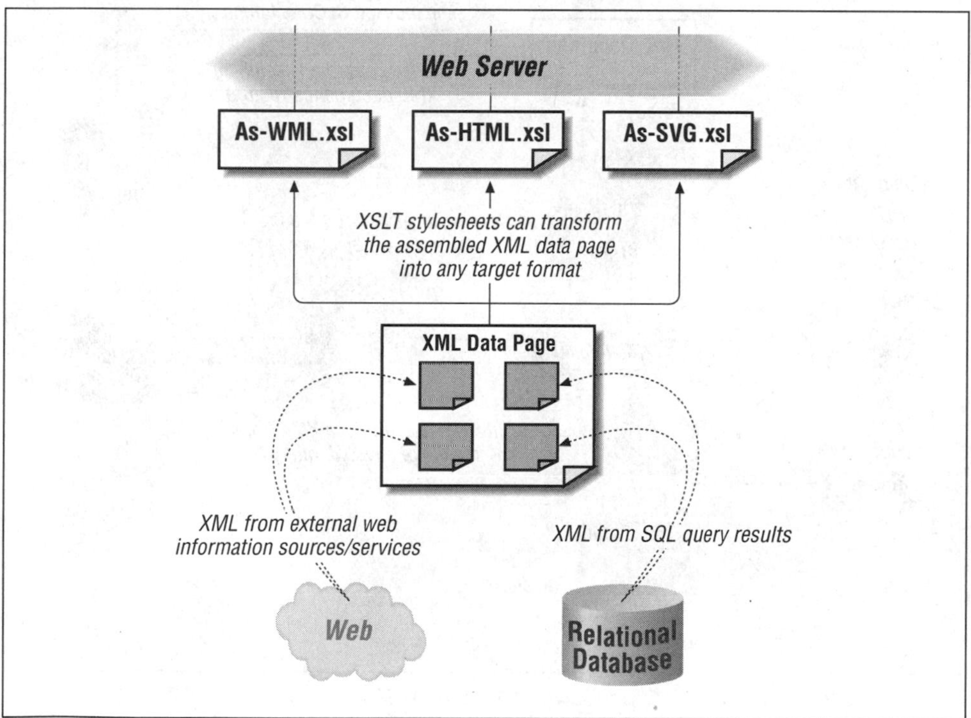

Figure 1-10. Assembling and transforming XML "data pages"

Publishing XML datagrams from relational databases and storing the information from XML datagrams you receive in the database as tables and columns offer you the best of both worlds. You retain the proven scalability, reliability, manageability, and performance of today's mature relational databases and the tools and applications that work with them. You also gain the newfound ability to exchange information with anyone, anywhere over the Web. As we will see throughout this book, the combination of SQL, XML, and XSLT is powerful stuff.

What XML Technologies Does Oracle Provide?

Now that we understand what the XML family of standards is, what we can do with it, and why it is interesting to apply to database-driven web applications, let's get an overview of the tools and technologies that Oracle provides to implement Oracle XML applications. Figure 1-11 shows an example of the key Oracle XML components and how they relate to the XML standards we've discussed earlier.

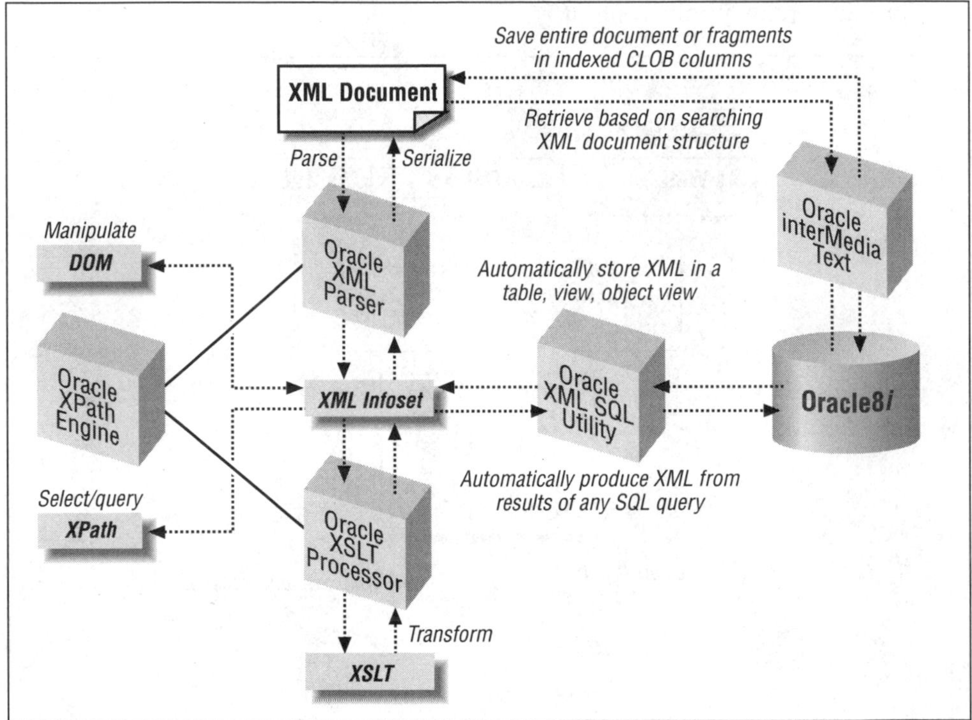

Figure 1-11. Overview of key Oracle technologies for XML

Using the Oracle XML Parser, you can parse XML documents into their infoset, manipulate their contents, and return the modified infoset back into XML format. Using the Oracle XSLT processor, you can transform XML into XML, HTML, or text of another structure. Both the Oracle XML Parser and the Oracle XSLT processor share the common Oracle XPath Engine that enables querying an XML document's infoset to select interesting subsets of its information. The Oracle XML SQL Utility automates the tasks of producing XML from SQL query results and storing XML documents into tables in the database. Oracle interMedia Text enables indexing and querying of XML documents or document fragments, with rich support for leveraging the structure of the XML in the query criteria. These core components are used by more than 40 of Oracle's own internal development teams, so their quality, performance, and conformance to W3C standards are very high.

Building on these core Oracle XML technologies, the Oracle XSQL Pages system is an extensible XML publishing framework that makes combining the strengths of SQL, XML, and XSLT a declarative walk in the park. It simplifies the job of assembling XML data pages from multiple sources and transforming their information content for delivery using XSLT. Table 1-1 provides a summary of key Oracle XML technologies and the chapters that cover each one.

Table 1-1. Key Oracle XML Technologies and Chapters That Cover Them

Oracle Technology	Description	Chapter(s)
XML Parser	Parses, constructs, and validates XML documents	5, 6
XPath Engine	Searches in-memory XML documents declaratively	2
XSLT Processor	Transforms XML documents	3, 5, 6, 7, 8, 9, 12, 14,16, 17
XML SQL Utility	Produces XML from SQL and inserts XML into tables	5, 6, 11, 12
XSQL Pages	Assembles XML data declaratively and publishes with XSLT	3, 8, 12, 15, 17
interMedia Text	Indexes and searches XML documents using their structure	13
Object views	Serve rich XML-enabled views of flat relational data	12
JServer Java VM[a]	Reduces network traffic by running Java in the database	6
JDeveloper	Creates, syntax-checks, and debugs Java, XML, XSLT, and XSQL	4, 6
Advanced Queuing	Queues and dequeues XML messages	5, 6
PLSXML utilities	Produce XML datagrams in Oracle7	10

[a] In Oracle8*i* Release 3, JServer has been renamed Oracle8*i* JVM.

In the sections that follow, I will summarize the Oracle XML tools and technologies described in this book, noting which chapters describe them and which Oracle releases support them. Many of these Oracle technologies are installed as part of the JDeveloper 3.1 development environment, which comes on the CD-ROM that accompanies this book; I'll note which technologies are included in JDeveloper 3.1 and give their version numbers.

By the time you read this book, updated releases of some of these components may be available. It's best to check for the latest versions on the Oracle Technology Network (OTN) at *http://technet.oracle.com/software*, where all of the technologies described here, including the Oracle8*i* database, are available for download.

You will need to sign up for a free OTN membership before getting to the download page. See the OTN web page for details.

Oracle XML Parser

The Oracle XML Parser fully supports the W3C XML 1.0 Recommendation as well as the Document Object Model (DOM) for processing and constructing XML. Using its companion support for the Simple API for XML (SAX), you can process XML datagrams of arbitrary size with low memory usage. Using the supplied `oraxml` tool, you can parse and validate XML files from the command line or in scripts. The parser supports integrated XPath searching on in-memory XML documents using the integrated Oracle XPath Engine, an embedded component shared by the Oracle XML Parser and the Oracle XSLT processor. The Oracle XPath Engine fully supports the W3C XPath 1.0 Recommendation.

I cover all of the key XML Parser capabilities, both inside and outside the database, in Chapter 5, *Processing XML with PL/SQL*, and Chapter 6, *Processing XML with Java.* We'll learn about using XPath expressions in Chapter 2, *Working with XML*, and we'll use them throughout the book in our XSLT transformations.

The Oracle XML Parser is available for Java, PL/SQL, and C/C++ on all popular platforms. The Java, C, and C++ versions can run outside the database, but exploiting the PL/SQL and Java versions inside the database requires Oracle8*i*. Version 2.0.2.7 of the Oracle XML Parser for Java is included with JDeveloper 3.1 on the CD-ROM.

Oracle XSLT Processor

The Oracle XSLT processor fully supports the W3C XSLT 1.0 Recommendation. Using the supplied `oraxsl` tool, you can perform XSLT transformations on XML files from the command line or in scripts. Of course, you can also use the XSLT processor in your own programs.

I cover extensive examples of XSLT in Chapters 3, 5, 6, 7, 8, 9, 12, 14, 16, and 17.

You can use the Oracle XSLT processor both inside the database using PL/SQL or Java, and outside the database using Java, C, or C++. Using the processor inside the database requires Oracle8*i*. Version 2.0.2.7 of the Oracle XSLT processor for Java is included with JDeveloper 3.1 on the CD-ROM.

Oracle XML SQL Utility

The Oracle XML SQL Utility provides a rich layer of services to work with the results of SQL statements as XML documents and to process incoming XML documents for inserting their information into database tables, views, and object views.

I explore using the Oracle XML SQL Utility in PL/SQL in Chapter 5, and using it in Java in Chapters 6, 11, and 12.

The Oracle XML SQL Utility can be used outside the database in any Java program, or inside the database in Oracle8*i*. Version 1.1 of the XML SQL Utility is included with JDeveloper 3.1 on the CD-ROM.

Oracle XSQL Pages XML Publishing Framework

Using declarative templates called *XSQL pages*, you can assemble any kind of dynamic XML information and transform it for delivery using XSLT stylesheets, as illustrated in Figure 1-12. The Oracle XSQL Pages framework includes an XML template processing engine called the XSQL page processor. This processor manages the assembly of XML fragments based on SQL queries and external XML resources and coordinates transformation of the assembled data page using the Oracle XSLT processor. Also included as part of the framework are the XSQL Servlet, for web-based publishing of XSQL pages, and the XSQL command-line utility for offline batch publishing.

You'll see a preview of using XSQL Pages in Chapter 3, *Combining XML and Oracle*, and learn how to use it in Chapters 8, 12, 15, and 17.

Oracle XSQL Pages works against any version of Oracle and can run outside the database on your favorite servlet engine (Apache JServ, JRun, ServletExec, Tomcat, and so on) as well as inside the database on the Oracle Servlet Engine in Oracle8*i* Release 3 (version 8.1.7). Version 1.0.0.0 of Oracle XSQL Pages comes preinstalled with Oracle Internet Application Server 1.0, Oracle8*i* Release 3, and is installed with JDeveloper 3.1 on the CD-ROM that accompanies this book.

Oracle8 XML-Enabled Object Views

Leveraging Oracle's investment in object-relational technology, object views defined over relational data provide a powerful technique to superimpose one or more richly structured, logical views on top of your existing database data. Data queried from object views can be automatically rendered as XML documents, and XML documents can be inserted automatically into the database using object views of an appropriate structure.

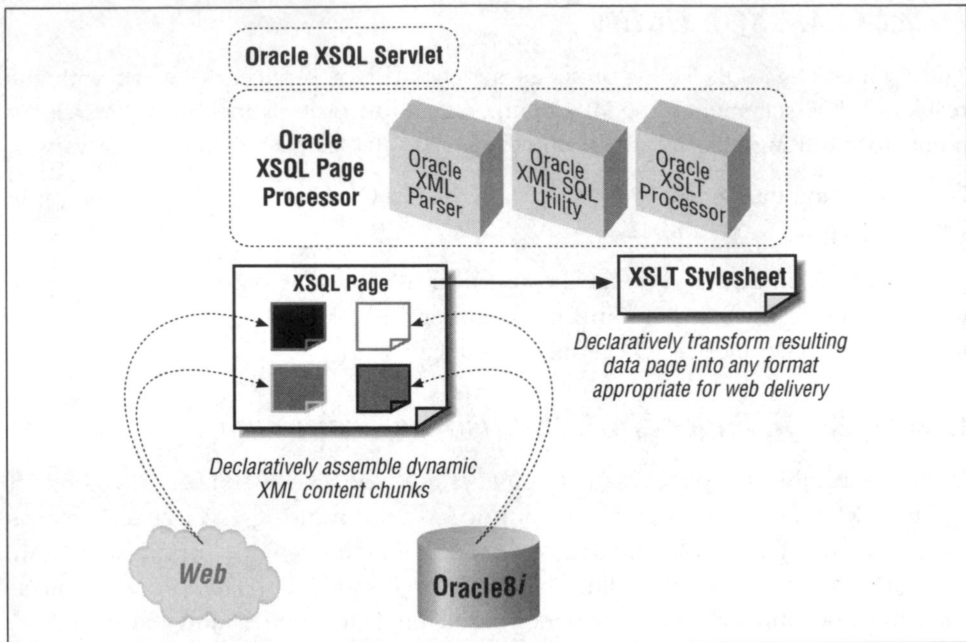

Figure 1-12. Oracle XSQL Pages framework simplifies XML publishing

You'll learn how to define and use object views for XML in Chapter 12, *Storing XML Datagrams*. You can exploit this feature outside the database using any version of Oracle8, but using it inside the database requires Oracle8*i*.

Oracle8i JServer Java Virtual Machine

Java and PL/SQL are now peer languages for the Oracle8*i* database. Any standard Java and JDBC™ code can execute in the same process as the database server, reducing network traffic of data-centric Java code. PL/SQL and Java can interoperate using Java stored procedures.

You'll learn the ins and out of developing, deploying, and debugging Java-based XML application code with JServer in Chapter 6. JServer is an integrated feature of Oracle8*i*.

Oracle interMedia

Using interMedia's Text component's XML document indexing, you can perform queries over millions of XML documents, leveraging the structure of the XML document for razor-sharp search precision. XML document searching is fully integrated with Oracle SQL, so you can easily exploit it in combination with other SQL query predicates to find your "needle" in a "haystack" of XML documents.

You'll learn how to create XML indexes and use XML searching in Chapter 13, *Searching XML with interMedia.*

XML searching with interMedia Text is available only in Oracle8*i*, and Oracle8*i* Release 2 or later is recommended because of the many functional improvements over Release 1 in this area.

Oracle JDeveloper IDE

With its built-in support for color-coded XML editing, indenting, and syntax checking, the JDeveloper Integrated Development Environment (IDE) makes common XML development tasks easier. Its native support for running servlets, XSQL Pages, and JavaServer™ Pages, combined with robust remote debugging support for Apache JServ, Tomcat, and JServer, makes a big difference in development productivity.

You'll learn how to use JDeveloper for XML development in Chapters 4 and 6.

JDeveloper 3.1 can be used to work with Java, XML, and Oracle with any database version, but Java stored procedures and JServer debugging are only relevant when using it with Oracle8*i*. JDeveloper 3.1 can be installed from the CD-ROM accompanying this book on any Windows NT or Windows 2000 machine.

Oracle Advanced Queuing

Oracle's persistent queuing mechanism is perfect for asynchronously processing XML messages. I cover both PL/SQL and Java techniques for enqueuing and dequeuing XML messages in Chapters 5 and 6.

Advanced queues are available in any version of Oracle8 and can be used with Java APIs outside the database; however, dequeuing, parsing, and searching XML messages inside the database require Oracle8*i*.

Oracle PLSXML Utilities

Implemented in PL/SQL, the PLSXML utilities (including the DBXML package) are available to customers using Oracle7 or Oracle8 to automatically produce XML from SQL statements. While the Oracle XML Parser and the XML SQL Utility have superseded the functionality provided by these utilities, using these new components inside the database requires Oracle8*i*.

We explore using the PLSXML utilities in Chapter 10, *Generating Datagrams with PL/SQL*. Because they consist of pure PL/SQL, the PLSXML utilities work with any current production version of Oracle.

2

In this chapter:
- *Creating and Validating XML*
- *Modularizing XML*
- *Searching XML with XPath*

Working with XML

In this chapter, I cover the essential technical details you will need to work with XML documents. I also devote a section to learning the powerful XPath language, which you can use to flexibly search XML documents.

Creating and Validating XML

Building on the high-level overview in Chapter 1, *Introduction to XML*, here we drill down in more detail to some of the specifics of working with XML documents.

Creating Your Own XML Vocabularies

As we saw in the examples in Chapter 1, XML can represent virtually any kind of structured information. A coherent set of elements and attributes that addresses a particular application need is called an *XML vocabulary*. The elements and attributes are the "words" in the vocabulary that enable communication of information on a certain subject. An XML vocabulary can be as simple as a single element—for example a **<Task>**, or can contain as many elements and attributes as you need. An example document that uses the **<Task>** vocabulary looks like this:

```
<Task Name="JDeveloper 3.1">
   <Task Name="Improved XML Support">
     <Task Name="Syntax-Check XML/XSL" Dev="Steve"/>
     <Task Name="Color-Coded Editing"  Dev="Yoshi"/>
     <Task Name="Run XSQL Pages"       Dev="Bret"/>
   </Task>
   <Task Name="Improved Debugging Support">
     <Task Name="Remote Debugging">
       <Task Name="JServer Debugging"       Dev="Jimmy"/>
       <Task Name="Apache JServ Debugging" Dev="Liz"/>
     </Task>
   </Task>
</Task>
```

One of the big attractions about working with XML is its low cost of admission. The specification is free to be used by anyone, and you only need a text editor to get started. One way to begin creating your own XML vocabulary is to simply start typing tags in a text file as they come to your mind. For example, if you've been assigned the task of managing a "Frequently Asked Questions" (FAQ) list, you might open up vi or Emacs and start typing the example shown in Figure 2-1.

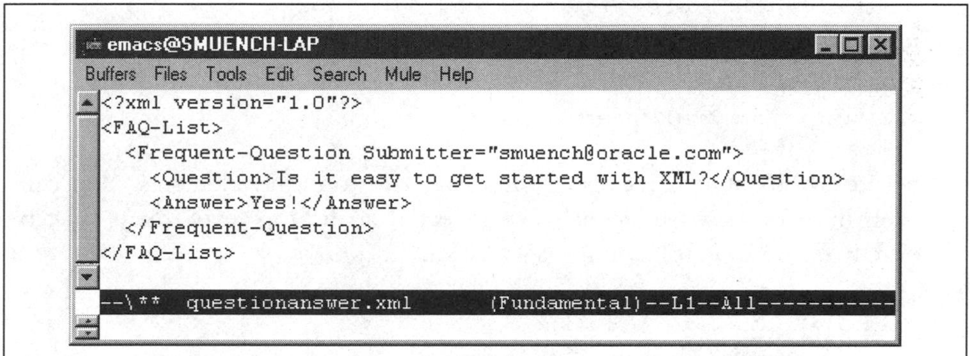
emacs@SMUENCH-LAP
Buffers Files Tools Edit Search Mule Help
<?xml version="1.0"?>
<FAQ-List>
<Frequent-Question Submitter="smuench@oracle.com">
<Question>Is it easy to get started with XML?</Question>
<Answer>Yes!</Answer>
</Frequent-Question>
</FAQ-List>
--** questionanswer.xml (Fundamental)--L1--All----------

Figure 2-1. Creating a new XML document using Emacs

It's very useful to just prototype your vocabulary of tags by working directly on an example document. It makes the process easy to think about. As ideas pop into your head—for example, "I'm going to need to keep track of who *submitted* each question"—just type the necessary element or attribute in your file. You don't have to get it right the first time; just get it down and get it in there. You can make corrections later. If you decide you like the look of a `<FAQ>` element more than `<Frequent-Question>`, go right ahead and change it! You're the boss. Just do a global search and replace in your editor, and you're done.

In honor of the eminently pragmatic William Strunk, Jr., and E. B. White (authors of the classic writing handbook, *The Elements of Style*), we present the XML elements of style, outlining the rules you must follow as you create your own documents:

1. *Begin each document with an XML declaration.*

   The first characters in any XML document should be an XML declaration. The declaration is case-sensitive and looks like this in its simplest form:

   ```
   <?xml version="1.0"?>
   ```

   The special tag delimiters of `<?` and `?>` distinguish this declaration from other tags in the document. The `<?xml` characters in the XML declaration must be the very first characters in the document. No spaces or carriage returns or *anything* can come before them.

2. *Use only one top-level document element.*

   The first, outermost element in an XML document is called the *document element* because its name announces what kind of document it encloses: `<FAQ-List>`, `<Book>`, `<transaction>`, `<TrackingStatus>`, and so on. You must only have one document element per document. So the following is legal:

```
<?xml version="1.0"?>
<Question>Is this legal?</Question>
```

   But the following is not:

```
<?xml version="1.0"?>
<Question>Is this legal?</Question>
<Answer>No</Answer>
```

   because both `<Question>` and `<Answer>` are top-level elements. You can't even have the *same* element name repeated at the top level: there must be exactly one. So the following is also illegal:

```
<?xml version="1.0"?>
<Question>Is this legal?</Question>
<Question>Is that your final answer?</Question>
```

   You need to pick a single name and use that element to enclose the others, like this:

```
<?xml version="1.0"?>
<FAQ-List>
  <Question>Is this legal?</Question>
  <Question>Is that your final answer?</Question>
</FAQ-List>
```

3. *Match opening and closing tags properly.*

   XML is case-sensitive, so the following are not considered matching tag names:

```
<Question>Is this legal?</question>
<QUESTION>Is this legal?</Question>
```

   You'll find that XML syntax is rigid and unforgiving. You cannot get away with being sloppy about the order of closing tags. The following is illegal:

```
<Question><Link href="http://qa.com/">Is this legal?</Question></Link>
```

   You need to close `</Link>` before closing `</Question>`, like this:

```
<Question><Link href="http://qa.com/">Is this legal?</Link></Question>
```

   Simply keeping your tags neatly indented helps you avoid this mistake:

```
<Question>
  <Link href="http://qa.com/">Is this legal?</Link>
</Question>
```

   Note that adding extra spaces, carriage returns, or tabs between nested tags to make an XML document look indented to the human eye does not affect its structural meaning when working with datagrams, although clearly whitespace increases the document's size slightly.

4. *Add comments between* `<!--` *and* `-->` *characters.*

   You can include comments anywhere after the XML declaration as long as they are not inside attribute values and don't occur in the middle of the < and > boundaries of a tag. So the comments in the following document are legal:

```
<?xml version="1.0"?>
<!-- Comment Here ok -->
<FAQ-List>
  <!--
   | And here, multiple lines are fine
   +-->
  <Question>Is this legal?<!-- Here is fine --></Question>
  <!-- Here too -->
  <Answer>Yes</Answer>
</FAQ-List>
<!-- Even Here -->
```

   but all four comments in this example are not:

```
<!-- NOT before XML declaration -->
<?xml version="1.0"?>
<FAQ-List>
  <FAQ Submitter="<!-- NOT in an attribute value -->" >
    <Question <!-- NOT between < and > of a tag --> >Is this legal?</Question>
    <Answer>Yes</Answer>
    <!-- Illegal for comment to contain two hypens -- like this -->
  </FAQ>
</FAQ-List>
```

5. *Start element and attribute names with a letter.*

   An element or attribute name must be a contiguous sequence of letters and cannot start with a digit or include spaces. The following are not allowed:

```
<2-Part-Question>       <!-- Error: element name starts with a digit   -->
<Two Part Question>     <!-- Error: has spaces in the name             -->
<Question 4You="Yes">   <!-- Error: attribute name starts with a digit -->
```

   Some punctuation symbols (like underscore and hyphen) are allowed in names, but most others are illegal:

```
<_StrangeButLegal>Legal</_StrangeButLegal>
<More-Normal-Looking>Legal</More-Normal-Looking>
<OK_As_Well>Legal</OK_As_Well>
```

6. *Put attributes in the opening tag.*

   Attributes are listed inside the opening tag of the element to which they apply. The following is correct:

```
<FAQ Submitter="smuench@oracle.com">
   <!-- etc. -->
</FAQ>
```

while the following is illegal:

```
<FAQ>
  <!-- etc. -->
</FAQ Submitter="smuench@oracle.com">
```

7. *Enclose attribute values in matching quotes.*

   Either of the following is fine:

   ```
   <FAQ Submitter="smuench@oracle.com">
   <FAQ Submitter='smuench@oracle.com'>
   ```

   but the following two are not:

   ```
   <FAQ Submitter=smuench@oracle.com>
   <FAQ Submitter='smuench@oracle.com">
   ```

   You can't forget the quotes or be sloppy about using the same closing quote character as your opening one.

8. *Use only simple text as attribute values.*

   Elements are the only things that can be nested. Attributes contain only simple text values. So the following is illegal:

   ```
   <Task Subtasks="<Task Name='Learn XML Syntax'>"/>
   ```

9. *Use* `<` *and* `&` *instead of* `<` *and* `&` *for literal less-than and ampersand characters.*

   The less-than and ampersand characters have a special meaning in XML files, so when you need to use either of these characters *literally*, you should use `<` and `&` instead:

   ```
   <Company>AT &amp; T</Company>               <!-- AT & T   -->
   <Where-Clause>SAL &lt; 5000</Where-Clause>  <!-- SAL < 500 -->
   ```

   On occasion, `"` and `'` also come in handy to represent literal `"` and `'` in attribute values:

   ```
   <Button On-Click="alert('Print a &quot; and &apos;'); " ></Button>
   ```

10. *Write empty elements as* `<ElementName/>`.

    Elements that do not contain other nested elements or text can be written with the more compact "empty element" syntax of:

    ```
    <Task Name="Learn XML Syntax">
      <Task Name="Use Empty Elements"/>  <!-- Empty Element -->
    </Task>
    ```

    As shown here with the `Name` attribute on the empty `<Task>` element, attributes on empty elements are still legal.

If your XML document follows these ten basic rules, it is called a *well-formed* XML document.

Unicode Character Encoding

One level below the characters you see in an XML document lies their numerical representation. The XML specification defines XML documents as sequences of characters, as defined by the Unicode standard.

Quoting the *unicode.org* web site, "Unicode provides a unique number for every character, no matter what the platform, no matter what the program, no matter what the language." Given the unique 16-bit number Unicode assigns to a character, there are different approaches for representing that number physically as bytes on the disk. These different approaches are called *character encoding schemes.*

One encoding scheme, named UTF-16, is the most straightforward. It uses two bytes (16 bits) to represent each character. This can be inefficient, however, if the document consists largely or entirely of ASCII characters that need only values in the range of 0–127 to be represented.

Another, more clever scheme, named UTF-8, takes a different approach, using a single byte to represent ASCII characters and a sequence of from two to five bytes to represent other characters. UTF-8 is the default encoding scheme for an XML document if one is not specified. If the default UTF-8 character encoding is not appropriate, include an `encoding` attribute that says what encoding your document is using. For example, an XML document containing Japanese data might use:

```
<?xml version="1.0" encoding="Shift_JIS"?>
```

If the default UTF-8 encoding is what you want to use, you can even legally leave off the XML declaration entirely, although it is good practice to always include one. To save trees where we can, many of the XML documents in the examples will leave off the XML declaration to shorten this book a little.

Checking Your XML Document's Syntax

It's easiest to learn the rules if you have a program that will quickly point out your errors while you are learning. There are three tools that will identify problems.

First, as illustrated in Figure 2-2, you can use JDeveloper 3.1's built-in XML syntax checking by selecting *Check XML Syntax...* on any XML file in your project. In the blink of an eye, JDeveloper finds any problems, prints out the offending error messages in the *XML Errors* tab, and positions your cursor in the file at the location of the first error.

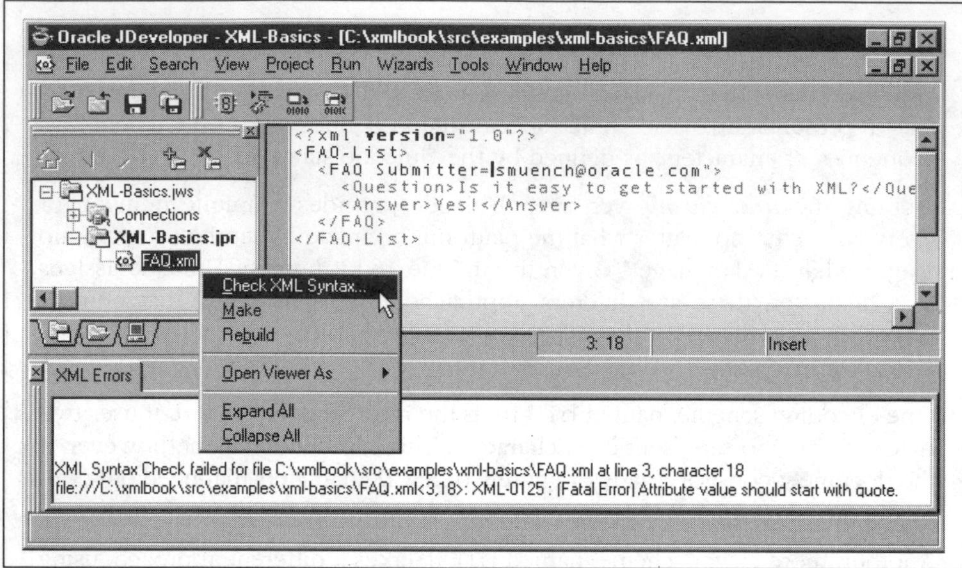

Figure 2-2. Checking the syntax of your XML files with JDeveloper 3.1

Second, if you are a fan of command-line tools, you can use the `oraxml` command-line utility that comes with the Oracle XML Parser to check your XML syntax, as shown in Figure 2-3. Just type:

```
oraxml filename
```

and either you'll be told that your file is well-formed, or the offending errors will print out to the console.

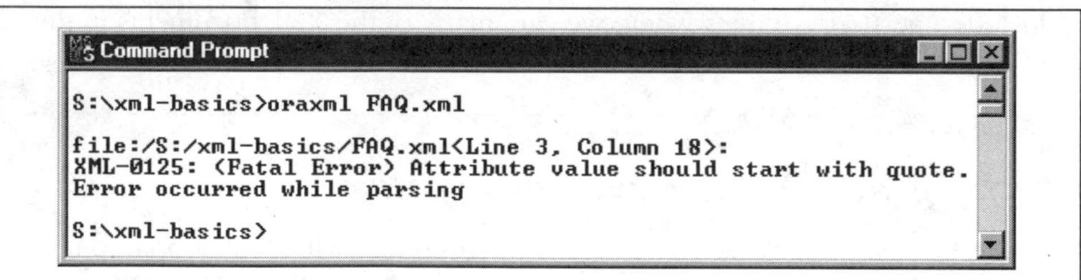

Figure 2-3. Checking XML syntax with the oraxml command-line utility

If the `oraxml` command does not work, try the following instead:

```
java oracle.xml.parser.v2.oraxml filename.xml
```

to explicitly run the `oraxml` command-line utility as a Java class. If this also fails, make sure you have done the following:

1. You must have a Java runtime environment properly set up.
2. You must list the fully qualified Java archive containing the Oracle XML Parser for Java in your `CLASSPATH` environment variable.

If you have installed JDeveloper 3.1 from the CD-ROM, for example, into the *C:\JDev* directory, you can do the following to properly set up your Java environment to run `oraxml`. Run the following command to set up your Java runtime environment:

```
C: \> c:\jdev\bin\setvars c:\jdev
```

then run:

```
C: \> set CLASSPATH=
    c:\jdev \lib\xmlparserv2_2027.jar;%CLASSPATH%
```

to add the Oracle XML Parser for Java to your CLASSPATH.

Third, you can simply attempt to browse your file with Microsoft's Internet Explorer version 5.0 or later. IE5 features built-in support for visualizing the structure of any XML document. Simply type its URL or filename in the *Address* bar. Figure 2-4 shows the effect of starting up IE5 and browsing our *FAQ.xml*. If there are any syntax errors, they show up immediately in your browser window.

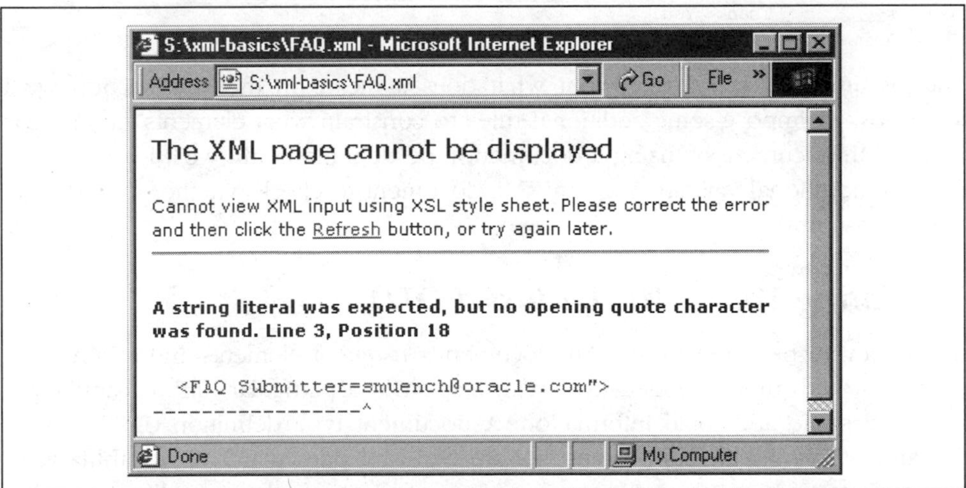

Figure 2-4. Checking XML syntax by browsing a file with IE5

While initially presenting us with a few new rules to get used to, XML's unforgiving syntax is actually one of its core strengths. It means that an XML file is either well-formed or ill-formed. There is no gray area. Programs needing to process XML documents are easy to write because they don't have to account for lots of loopholes, endless exceptions to the rules, or oodles of optional features. They check the ten elements of style I presented earlier, and don't waste their time processing the document if any of the rules is broken.

In practice, the ten elements of style are the main things you need to know. For an exhaustive list of all XML syntax arcana, you can refer to the XML 1.0 specification at:

http://www.w3.org/TR/1998/REC-xml-19980210

or to Tim Bray's helpful annotated version at:

http://www.xml.com

However, sometimes you'll be interested in knowing more about an XML document than the fact that all of its tags match up properly. Consider the following document:

```
<Animal>
  <Couch Currency="Rumblefish">
    <Draft Raindrops="15">
      <Stunning/>
    </Draft>
  </Couch>
  <__________Thank__You__________/>
</Animal>
```

The document is well-formed, but what does it mean? In the next section we'll learn how to impose some additional rules to constrain what elements can appear in an XML document by using a document type definition, and we'll learn how to perform additional validation on an XML document to check whether it abides by these constraints.

Validating Your XML Against a DTD

If we want to be sure that an XML document's *usage* of elements and attributes is consistent with their intended use—with respect to a particular XML vocabulary—we need some additional information. A document type definition (DTD) specifies all of the valid element names that are part of a particular XML vocabulary. In addition, it stipulates the valid combinations of elements that are allowed—what can appear nested within what, and how many times—as well as what attributes each element is allowed to have. While it's beyond the scope of this book to delve into the finer points of DTD design, we will study a simple example. It will suffice for us to understand:

- How to associate an XML document with a DTD
- How to validate the document by that DTD

Since JDeveloper does not include built-in support for *visually* creating or inspecting DTDs, we can use a tool like XML Authority from Extensibility. Figure 2-5 illustrates the document type definition for the frequently asked questions document we saw earlier. We get a graphical view of the element structure that it defines.

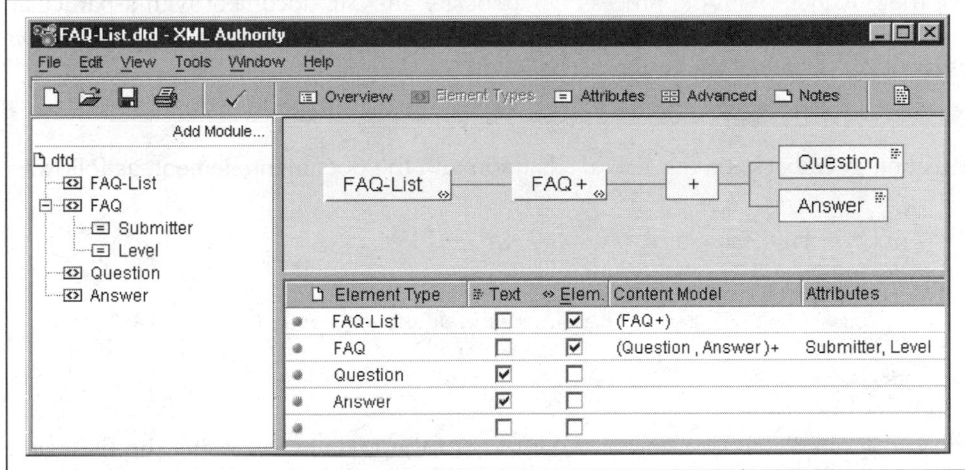

Figure 2-5. Viewing DTD element structure with XML Authority

The diagram in the figure illustrates that:

- The `<FAQ-List>` element is comprised of one or more `<FAQ>` elements.
- A `<FAQ>` element is comprised of one or more pairs of `<Question>` followed by `<Answer>`.
- A `<FAQ>` element has attributes named `Submitter` and `Level`.
- The `<Question>` and `<Answer>` elements contain text.

Using another view, the tool shows us some additional information about the attributes, as shown in Figure 2-6.

Attribute Name	Element	Data Type	Constraints	Default	Required
Level	FAQ	enumeration	Beginner | Intermediate | Advanced	Intermediate	☐
Submitter	FAQ	string			☐

Figure 2-6. Viewing DTD attribute definitions with XML Authority

Here we can see that the **Level** attribute has a default value of **Intermediate**, and must be one of the values **Beginner**, **Intermediate**, or **Advanced**. If you open the DTD file in vi, Emacs, or JDeveloper, you'll see this text document:

```
<!ELEMENT FAQ-List  (FAQ+ )>
<!ELEMENT FAQ  (Question , Answer )+>
<!ATTLIST FAQ  Submitter CDATA  #IMPLIED
               Level (Beginner | Intermediate | Advanced )  'Intermediate' >
<!ELEMENT Question  (#PCDATA )>
<!ELEMENT Answer  (#PCDATA )>
```

Even a cursory read of this very simple DTD makes you happy that there are tools out there to help with the process! To associate an XML document with a particular DTD we add one extra line to the top of the XML document, called the *Document Type Declaration*, which looks like this:

```
<!DOCTYPE DocumentElementName SYSTEM "DTDFilename">
```

This line goes between the XML declaration and the document element, as follows:

```
<?xml version="1.0"?>
<!DOCTYPE FAQ-List SYSTEM "FAQ-List.dtd">
<FAQ-List>
  <FAQ Submitter="smuench@oracle.com">
    <Question>Is it easy to get started with XML?</Question>
    <Answer>Yes!</Answer>
  </FAQ>
</FAQ-List>
```

We can immediately see one of the effects of the DTD by browsing the file again with Internet Explorer 5.0, as shown in Figure 2-7. Notice that even though our document does not specify a **Level** attribute on the FAQ element, IE5 shows **Level="Intermediate"**. This happens because the DTD defined a *default* value for **Level**. An XML processor that conforms to the XML 1.0 standard treats the document as if it had specified the attribute with its default value. So default attribute values are one effect a DTD can have on an XML document that refers to it in its **<!DOCTYPE>** declaration.

Let's look at an example of the other kind of effect: validation errors. Suppose we extend our file to have a couple of questions like this:

```
<?xml version="1.0"?>
<!DOCTYPE FAQ-List SYSTEM "FAQ-List.dtd">
<FAQ-List>
  <FAQ Submitter="smuench@oracle.com">
    <Question>Is it easy to get started with XML?</Question>
    <Answer>Yes!</Answer>
  </FAQ>
  <FAQ Submitter="derek@spinaltap.com" Level="Silly">
    <Question>Are we going to play Stonehenge?</Question>
  </FAQ>
</FAQ-List>
```

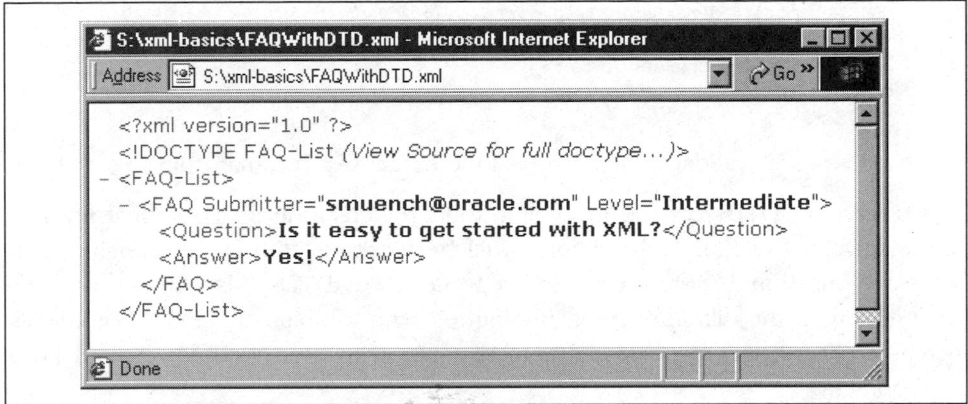

Figure 2-7. DTD-declared default attributes appear automatically

If we try the **oraxml** command on this file we get the message:

```
The input file parsed without errors
```

So the file is well-formed, but is it valid with respect to the DTD? Let's find out. We can use the **oraxml** command-line tool again—this time with the -v flag—to validate the document against its DTD:

```
oraxml -v FAQWithTwoQuestions.xml
```

We immediately get two errors:

```
FAQWithTwoQuestions.xml <Line 8, Column 53>
XML-0141: (Error) Attribute value 'Silly' should be one of
                  the declared enumerated values.

FAQWithTwoQuestions.xml <Line 10, Column 9>
XML-0150: (Error) Element FAQ not complete, expected elements '[Answer]'.

Error occurred while parsing
```

The **oraxml** tool consulted the rules in the associated *FAQ-List.dtd* file and validated the contents of *FAQWithTwoQuestions.xml* to find two inconsistencies. We can correct them by:

1. Changing the attribute value Silly to a valid value like Advanced
2. Adding the expected <Answer> element to go with the <Question> inside the second <FAQ> element

This produces the modified document:

```
<?xml version="1.0"?>
<!DOCTYPE FAQ-List SYSTEM "FAQ-List.dtd">
<FAQ-List>
  <FAQ Submitter="smuench@oracle.com">
    <Question>Is it easy to get started with XML?</Question>
    <Answer>Yes!</Answer>
  </FAQ>
```

```
  <FAQ Submitter="derek@spinaltap.com" Level="Advanced">
    <Question>Are we going to play Stonehenge?</Question>
    <Answer>But of course</Answer>
  </FAQ>
</FAQ-List>
```

which now passes validation if we repeat the `oraxml-v` command on it.

As we've seen, DTDs can be invaluable tools for ensuring an additional level of consistency in the XML information you'll be working with or exchanging with others. As more and more web-based repositories of DTDs (also known as *schemas*) emerge, the likelihood of finding existing domain-specific vocabularies increases. This bodes well for a future of reuse with less need for custom DTD development.

Modularizing XML

XML entities and namespaces provide two techniques to modularize the contents of XML documents. In this section we study simple examples of both.

Including Text and External Resources

Entities are a mechanism for defining named string substitution variables in your XML file. They can save typing repetitive text in your documents. For example, if the Frequently Asked Questions document that we're working on is for the Oracle JDeveloper 3.1 product, the text `Oracle JDeveloper` and the current version number of the product might appear in many of the questions and answers. We can define two entities to represent this repetitive text using the syntax:

```
<!ENTITY jdev "Oracle JDeveloper">
<!ENTITY ver  "3.1">
```

With these in place we can refer to the entities by name in the contents of our *FAQ.xml* document with the syntax:

```
<Question>What is the current version of &jdev;?</Question>
<Answer>The current version is &jdev; &ver;</Answer>
```

The syntax for user-defined entities is identical to that of the built-in entities we saw earlier (`<`, `>`, `'`, and `"`). References to user-defined entities like `&jdev;` start with an ampersand character and end with a semicolon, with the entity name in between. Like the default attribute values we saw earlier, these entities can be defined in an external DTD file, or right in the current document by including them in the local DTD section known as the *internal subset*. The syntax for including these entity definitions in the document you're working on (when you do not control the DTD or when the entities are not interesting enough to be placed there for global use) looks like this:

```
<?xml version="1.0"?>
<!DOCTYPE FAQ-List SYSTEM "FAQ-List.dtd"[
  <!-- Internal subset adds local definitions -->
  <!ENTITY jdev "Oracle JDeveloper">
  <!ENTITY ver  "3.1">
]>
<FAQ-List>
  <FAQ Submitter="smuench@oracle.com">
    <Question>Is it easy to get started with XML?</Question>
    <Answer>Yes!</Answer>
  </FAQ>
  <FAQ Submitter="smuench@oracle.com" Level="Beginner">
    <Question>What is the current version of &jdev;?</Question>
    <Answer>The current version is &jdev; &ver;</Answer>
  </FAQ>
</FAQ-List>
```

Notice that when we browse the file with Internet Explorer 5.0 again, as shown in Figure 2-8, the values of the entities are expanded by the XML processor inside IE5. The same process will occur when any XML processor reads the document.

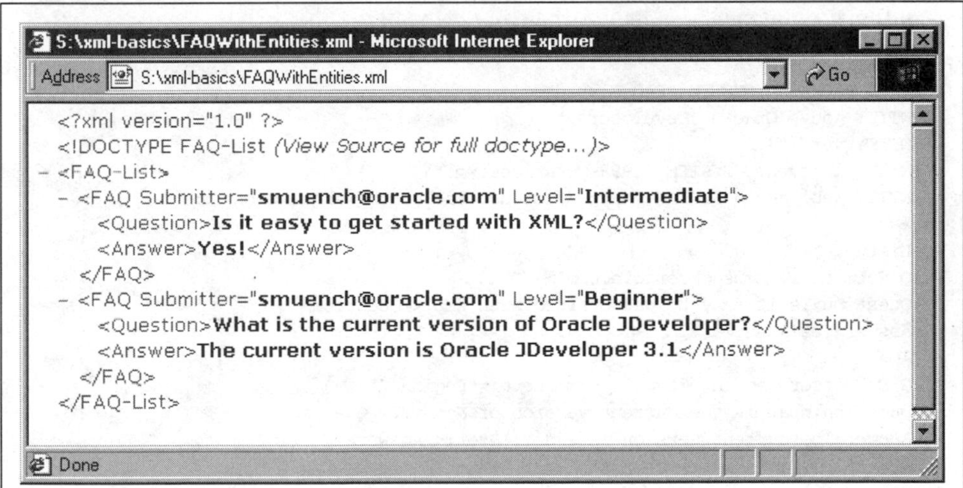

Figure 2-8. XML processor expands the text of entities

When we upgrade the *FAQ.xml* document for the 4.0 release of JDeveloper, or, heaven forbid, if the product gets renamed, with our entities in place, we can just edit the text in one place. References to entities can go anywhere in an XML document where text content is legal, including inside attribute values. Note that entities are expanded before well-formedness checking and validation occur on the document, so their text can contain XML tags as well.

In addition to representing useful chunks of substitution text, entities can also refer to external resources by URL. For example, there might be a file full of questions from 1999 named *1999-Questions.xml*:

```
<FAQ Submitter="ppuddle@za.oracle.com" Level="Advanced">
  <Question>Can I remotely debug servlets and stored procedures?</Question>
  <Answer>Yes.</Answer>
</FAQ>
```

and a file full of questions from our web site named *webquestions.xml*:

```
<FAQ Submitter="rcardena@pr.oracle.com">
  <Question>Does JDeveloper support XML?</Question>
  <Answer>Yes.</Answer>
</FAQ>
```

By including the additional keyword **SYSTEM** in our entity definition, followed by a relative or absolute URL to the text resource we'd like to include, we can pull in these external document fragments and make them appear as part of our single XML document, *FAQWithMultipleEntities.xml*, as shown in Example 2-1.

Example 2-1. Using Entities to Include Text and External Resources

```
<?xml version="1.0"?>
<!DOCTYPE FAQ-List SYSTEM "FAQ-List.dtd"[
  <!ENTITY jdev "Oracle JDeveloper">
  <!ENTITY ver  "3.1">
  <!ENTITY lastyears SYSTEM "1999-Questions.xml">
  <!ENTITY webq_and_a SYSTEM "http://xml.us.oracle.com/webquestions.xml">
]>
<FAQ-List>
  <FAQ Submitter="smuench@oracle.com">
    <Question>Is it easy to get started with XML?</Question>
    <Answer>Yes!</Answer>
  </FAQ>
  <FAQ Submitter="smuench@oracle.com" Level="Beginner">
    <Question>What is the current version of &jdev;?</Question>
    <Answer>The current version is &jdev; &ver;</Answer>
  </FAQ>
  &webq_and_a;
  &lastyears;
</FAQ-List>
```

When we browse the *FAQWithMultipleEntities.xml* file again with IE5, its XML processor substitutes the entities, and the browser (as would any program processing the file) "sees" the contents with all of the entities expanded.

Using Namespaces to Mix XML Vocabularies

If thoughtfully designed XML vocabularies already exist for a particular problem domain, it's a natural instinct of a good developer to want to reuse the existing vocabulary instead of inventing a new one. However, when attempting to combine the elements from two or more different XML vocabularies in a single document, name clashes can occur for common element names. *XML namespaces* provide a solution to this problem by specifying a mechanism to uniquely qualify elements from different vocabularies.

Consider a fictitious tax advice company called Tax Time. A customer named Tina Wells calls to set up an appointment to discuss her income tax return with one of Tax Time's consultants, named Jim. Suppose that Tax Time uses an XML document like the following to represent Tina's <Appointment> with Jim:

```
<Appointment>
  <Name>Tina Wells</Name>
  <Schedule For="04/20/2000">
    <Consult With="Jim" Time="10:00am">
      <Regarding>
         <UnknownSubject/>
      </Regarding>
    </Consult>
    <ArrangePayment With="Ella" Time="11:00am"/>
  </Schedule>
</Appointment>
```

As part of a routine pre-visit screening, Jim's administrative assistant Ella calls Tina to get more details about the subject of her visit. She learns that Tina needs some advice on her Federal income tax Form 1040. Ella asks Tina to post her 1040 Form over secure HTTP to Tax Time's web site so Jim can review it before their meeting. Since Tina's tax preparation software supports the new XML-based IRS tax <Form> format:

```
<Form id="1040">
  <Filer EFileECN="12345">
    <Name>Tina Wells</Name>
    <TaxpayerId>987-65-4321</TaxpayerId>
    <Occupation>Vice President</Occupation>
  </Filer>
  <Schedule id="B">
    <Dividend Amount="12358.74">
      <Payer>Bank of America</Payer>
    </Dividend>
  </Schedule>
</Form>
```

Tina exports her tax <Form> and posts it to Tax Time. After combining Tina's income tax <Form> into the <Appointment> datagram, Ella ends up with the XML document shown in Example 2-2.

Example 2-2. Combining Appointment and Form Vocabularies in One Document

```
<Appointment>
  <Name>Tina Wells</Name>
  <Schedule For="04/20/2000">
    <Consult With="Jim" Time="10:00am">
      <Regarding>
        <Form id="1040">
          <Filer EFileECN="12345">
            <Name>Tina Wells Johnson</Name>
            <TaxpayerId>987-65-4321</TaxpayerId>
            <Occupation>Vice President</Occupation>
          </Filer>
          <Schedule id="B">
            <Dividend Amount="12358.74">
              <Payer>Bank of America</Payer>
            </Dividend>
          </Schedule>
        </Form>
      </Regarding>
    </Consult>
    <ArrangePayment With="Ella" Time="11:00am"/>
  </Schedule>
</Appointment>
```

The document is now ambiguous, since the element `<Schedule>` appears twice, meaning two different things, as does the `<Name>` element. This is precisely the ambiguity that XML namespaces are designed to remedy.

We need some way to distinguish the elements in the `<Appointment>` vocabulary from those in the tax `<Form>` vocabulary. Suppose we could just qualify the element names in the `<Appointment>` vocabulary with some kind of prefix that would uniquely identify its elements, like this:

- `<[TaxTimeAppointmentVocabulary]:Appointment>`
- `<[TaxTimeAppointmentVocabulary]:Schedule>`
- `<[TaxTimeAppointmentVocabulary]:Name>`

And, similarly, some unique identifier for the IRS tax `<Form>` vocabulary:

- `<[IRSTaxFormVocabulary]:Form>`
- `<[IRSTaxFormVocabulary]:Schedule>`
- `<[IRSTaxFormVocabulary]:Name>`

Then the elements would be easy to combine since they are impossible to confuse. But that sure means a lot of extra characters in our document. Who comes up with the unique names? Couldn't two clever people who think alike potentially come up with the same unique name?

The designers of XML namespaces have standardized the answers to these concerns. They decided that Internet domain names were a great way to come up with unique names for things. As long as companies or organizations use their Internet domain names as part of the unique names for the XML vocabularies they design, they need only to pick a unique name within their own organization and the name will be globally unique. So we use standard Internet URLs as the unique names for XML vocabularies.

The XML Namespaces specification talks about using URIs, not URLs. URI, or *Uniform Resource Identifier*, is a generic term for all types of names and addresses that refer to resources on the World Wide Web. A URL is by far the most widely used kind of URI in practice. The other kind of URI used on occasion is a URN, a *Uniform Resource Name*. URNs look like this:

```
urn:oracle-xsql
```

instead of *http://somesite/somename*. For the curious, more details are available at *http://www.w3.org/Addressing/*.

Since these unique URL-based namespace names can be long, the XML Namespaces specification allows document authors to coin a short nickname, called a *prefix*. This namespace prefix represents its associated globally unique vocabulary name, which saves a lot of typing.

To define a namespace, you include a special attribute named `xmlns` on any element with the following syntax:

```
<SomeElement xmlns:prefixname="uniqueURLForTheNamespace">
```

So we can define an `appt` prefix for the `http://www.taxtime.com/Appointment` vocabulary with the syntax:

```
<appt:Appointment xmlns:appt="http://www.taxtime.com/Appointment">
```

and an `irs` namespace prefix for the `http://www.irs.gov/Form` vocabulary:

```
<irs:Form xmlns:irs="http://www.irs.gov/Form">
```

The presence of a URL like *http://www.irs.gov/Form* in a namespace definition does *not* mean that the program processing your XML document attempts to contact that URL over the Web using that URL. It's just a convenient unique string that's a little easier for humans to remember than the other common scheme for globally unique names (called GUIDs), which look like this:

```
BDC6E3F0-6DA3-11D1-A2A3-00AA00C14882
```

With the `appt` and `irs` namespace prefixes defined, we can unambiguously represent Ella's XML document about Tina's appointment as shown in Example 2-3.

Example 2-3. XML Namespaces Allow Mixing Different XML Vocabularies

```
<appt:Appointment xmlns:appt="http://www.taxtime.com/Appointment">
  <appt:Name>Tina Wells</appt:Name>
  <appt:Schedule For="04/20/2000">
    <appt:Consult With="Jim" Time="10:00am">
      <appt:Regarding>
        <irs:Form id="1040" xmlns:irs="http://www.irs.gov/Form">
          <irs:Filer EFileECN="12345">
            <irs:Name>Tina Wells Johnson</irs:Name>
            <irs:TaxpayerId>987-65-4321</irs:TaxpayerId>
            <irs:Occupation>Vice President</irs:Occupation>
          </irs:Filer>
          <irs:Schedule id="B">
            <irs:Dividend Amount="12358.74">
              <irs:Payer>Bank of America</irs:Payer>
            </irs:Dividend>
          </irs:Schedule>
        </irs:Form>
      </appt:Regarding>
    </appt:Consult>
    <appt:ArrangePayment With="Ella" Time="11:00am"/>
  </appt:Schedule>
</appt:Appointment>
```

Keep in mind that the prefix is a shortcut name chosen at the discretion of each author of any document that uses a given vocabulary, so all of the following are equivalent:

- `<irs:Form xmlns:irs="http://www.irs.gov/Form">`
- `<i:Form xmlns:i="http://www.irs.gov/Form">`
- `<Form xmlns="http://www.irs.gov/Form">`

The so-called *qualified name* of each example shown is logically the fully qualified name `<[http://www.irs.gov/Form]:Form>`, regardless of the prefix used. The third example in this list uses a further convenient feature of the XML Namespaces recommendation to define a namespace URL as the default namespace. When a default namespace has been defined, the *absence* of a namespace prefix on an element associates it with the default namespace. This is especially handy when large sections of a document use the same namespace. Using default namespaces, you can further simplify the document syntax without sacrificing clarity.

Example 2-4 shows Ella's document using `http://www.taxtime.com/Appointment` as the default namespace, while using the `irs` prefix for the `http://www.irs.gov/Form` namespace.

Example 2-4. Using the Default Namespace for the Appointment Vocabulary

```
<Appointment xmlns="http://www.taxtime.com/Appointment">
  <Name>Tina Wells</Name>
  <Schedule For="04/20/2000">
    <Consult With="Jim" Time="10:00am">
      <Regarding>
        <irs:Form id="1040" xmlns:irs="http://www.irs.gov/Form">
          <irs:Filer EFileECN="12345">
            <irs:Name>Tina Wells Johnson</irs:Name>
            <irs:TaxpayerId>987-65-4321</irs:TaxpayerId>
            <irs:Occupation>Vice President</irs:Occupation>
          </irs:Filer>
          <irs:Schedule id="B">
            <irs:Dividend Amount="12358.74">
              <irs:Payer>Bank of America</irs:Payer>
            </irs:Dividend>
          </irs:Schedule>
        </irs:Form>
      </Regarding>
    </Consult>
    <ArrangePayment With="Ella" Time="11:00am"/>
  </Schedule>
</Appointment>
```

Each namespace definition has a *scope* in which it is effective. By defining a namespace on a given element, that namespace is in scope and available for use for that element and all of the elements it contains. One of the contained elements can *redefine* a namespace prefix to be bound to a different namespace—including redefining the default namespace—and as before, the new namespace is in effect for that new element and any elements *it* contains. It is also legal to qualify individual attributes by a namespace prefix, although this usage is less common.

We end with Example 2-5, which shows how Ella's document would look if she uses `http://www.taxtime.com/Appointment` as the default namespace and redefines the default namespace to be `http://www.irs.gov/Form` for the `<Form>` element and its children.

Example 2-5. Redefining the Default Namespace for a Subtree

```
<Appointment xmlns="http://www.taxtime.com/Appointment">
  <Name>Tina Wells</Name>
  <Schedule For="04/20/2000">
    <Consult With="Jim" Time="10:00am">
      <Regarding>
        <Form id="1040" xmlns="http://www.irs.gov/Form">
          <Filer EFileECN="12345">
            <Name>Tina Wells Johnson</Name>
            <TaxpayerId>987-65-4321</TaxpayerId>
            <Occupation>Vice President</Occupation>
          </Filer>
          <Schedule id="B">
```

Example 2-5. Redefining the Default Namespace for a Subtree

```
          <Dividend Amount="12358.74">
            <Payer>Bank of America</Payer>
          </Dividend>
        </Schedule>
      </Form>
    </Regarding>
  </Consult>
  <ArrangePayment With="Ella" Time="11:00am"/>
</Schedule>
</Appointment>
```

In this book, one of the most frequent examples of namespaces that we will see is the namespace for XSLT. We will work with many examples of XSLT stylesheets that use this vocabulary, whose unique namespace name is **http://www.w3.org/1999/XSL/Transform**. Now that you've seen the examples with namespaces above, the simple XSLT stylesheet in Example 2-6 should look familiar from a syntactical point of view with its namespace-qualified element names like **<xsl:stylesheet>**, **<xsl:template>**, **<xsl:for-each>**, and **<xsl:value-of>**.

Example 2-6. To Write XSLT Stylesheets, XML Namespaces Are Required

```
<xsl:stylesheet version="1.0" xmlns:xsl="http://www.w3.org/1999/XSL/Transform">
  <xsl:output indent="yes"/>
  <xsl:template match="/">
    <OscarFavorites Year="2000">
      <xsl:for-each select="/MovieList/Movie[Award/@From='Oscar']">
        <Winner Category="{Award/@Category}">
          <xsl:value-of select="@Title"/>
        </Winner>
      </xsl:for-each>
    </OscarFavorites>
  </xsl:template>
</xsl:stylesheet>
```

This stylesheet transforms an XML **<MovieList>** that we'll see in the next section into the output:

```
<?xml version = '1.0' encoding = 'UTF-8'?>
<OscarFavorites Year="2000">
  <Winner Category="Best Film">American Beauty</Winner>
</OscarFavorites>
```

To reiterate our point that a prefix is just a shortcut name, observe that the following stylesheet, which picks **x** as the convenient prefix instead of **xsl**, is functionally identical to the previous one:

```
<x:stylesheet version="1.0" xmlns:x="http://www.w3.org/1999/XSL/Transform">
  <x:output indent="yes"/>
  <x:template match="/">
    <OscarFavorites Year="2000">
      <x:for-each select="/MovieList/Movie[Award/@From='Oscar']">
```

```
        <Winner Category="{Award/@Category}">
          <x:value-of select="@Title"/>
        </Winner>
      </x:for-each>
    </OscarFavorites>
  </x:template>
</x:stylesheet>
```

It's clear that without the ability to unambiguously combine elements from the `http://www.w3.org/1999/XSL/Transform` namespace with the unqualified elements in the stylesheet like `<OscarFavorites>` and `<Winner>`, we would have a tough time writing a stylesheet.

Searching XML with XPath

When you organize files into directories on a disk, you use the directories to give some meaningful structure to your files. Familiar commands like `dir` or `ls` allow you to search for matching files that have been organized into those nested directories. Consider the directory hierarchy of drive `M:` as shown in Figure 2-9 using the Windows Explorer.

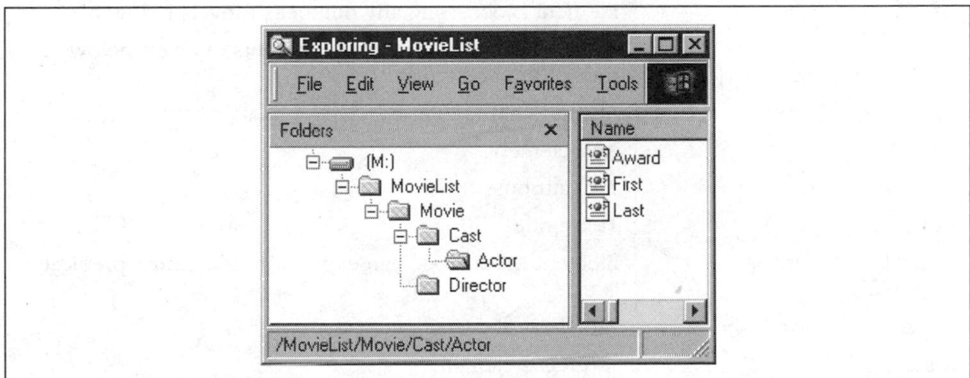

Figure 2-9. Browsing hierarchical directory structure

In order to search this hierarchy, you use a *path notation* to indicate what files you are trying to find. The path notation for searching a Unix filesystem, for example, allows you to use the notation */MovieList/Movie/Cast* to refer to the *Cast* subdirectory under the *Movie* subdirectory of *MovieList*, or */MovieList/Movie/Cast/** to refer to *any* file in that directory.

To list all the files in the *Actor* subdirectory, you can issue the command:

```
ls /MovieList/Movie/Cast/Actor/*
```

which produces this list of matching files:

```
/MovieList/Movie/Cast/Actor/First
/MovieList/Movie/Cast/Actor/Last
/MovieList/Movie/Cast/Actor/Award
```

As we saw in Chapter 1, XML documents also have an industry-standard path notation for searching their content, called XPath. You'll find its syntax easy to understand because of its basic similarity to what we saw earlier for files in directories. We'll see with several examples (and throughout this book) that the searches you can do with the XPath notation over an XML document are much more powerful than the simple file listings illustrated above.

Table 2-1 summarizes the syntax for the most common XPath expressions.

Table 2-1. Syntax Summary for the Most Common XPath Expressions

XPath Expression Syntax	Matches
Name	Element named Name
/*Name*	Element named Name at the root of the document
a/*b*	Element b occurring as a direct child of element a
a//*b*	Element b occurring any number of levels below a
//*Name*	Element Name occurring any numbers of levels below the root of the document.
@*Name*	Attribute named Name
*	Any element
@*	Any attribute
text()	Text node
Name [*BoolExpr*]	Element Name if boolean expression *BoolExpr* predicate is true
Name [position() = *n*]	*n*th Name element
Name [*n*]	*n*th Name element
(*ListExpr*) [*n*]	*n*th node in list of nodes matching *ListExpr*
Name1 | *Name2*	Elements Name1 or Name2
(*ListExpr*) [*BoolExpr*]	Nodes in *ListExpr* where predicate *BoolExpr* is true.
.	The current node
.//*Name*	Element Name that occurs any number of levels below the current node
..	The parent node

Let's put some of these to work. Consider the <MovieList> document in Example 2-7. It contains a hierarchy of elements conceptually similar to a hierarchy of directories and files. Elements that contain other elements are analogous to directories, and elements that don't contain other elements are like files.

Example 2-7. MovieList Document to Search XPath Expressions

```
<MovieList>
  <Movie Title="American Beauty" RunningTime="121" Rating="R">
    <Director>
      <First>Sam</First>
      <Last>Mendes</Last>
      <Award From="Oscar" Category="Best Director"/>
    </Director>
    <Cast>
      <Actor Role="Lester Burnham">
        <First>Kevin</First>
        <Last>Spacey</Last>
        <Award From="Oscar" Category="Best Actor"/>
        <Award From="BAFTA" Category="Best Actor"/>
      </Actor>
      <Actress Role="Carolyn Burnham">
        <First>Annette</First>
        <Last>Bening</Last>
        <Award From="BAFTA" Category="Best Actress"/>
      </Actress>
    </Cast>
    <Award From="Oscar" Category="Best Film"/>
    <Award From="BAFTA" Category="Best Film"/>
  </Movie>
  <Movie Title="The Talented Mr.Ripley" RunningTime="139" Rating="R">
    <Director>
      <First>Anthony</First>
      <Last>Minghella</Last>
    </Director>
    <Cast>
      <Actor Role="Tom Ripley">
        <First>Matt</First>
        <Last>Damon</Last>
      </Actor>
      <Actress Role="Marge Sherwood">
        <First>Gwyneth</First>
        <Last>Paltrow</Last>
      </Actress>
      <Actor Role="Dickie Greenleaf">
        <First>Jude</First>
        <Last>Law</Last>
        <Award From="BAFTA" Category="Best Supporting Actor"/>
      </Actor>
    </Cast>
  </Movie>
</MovieList>
```

`/MovieList/Movie/Cast/Actor/*` is the XPath notation used to find any of the elements in the document located under `Actor` on a `Cast` of a `Movie` in the `MovieList`. We can use the handy **`testxpath`** command-line tool that is supplied with the example files for this chapter (available on the O'Reilly web site) to

any step in the path. You filter a search using an XPath expression that returns a boolean result, enclosed in square brackets `[`*Expr*`]`. The expression in a predicate is evaluated relative to the node to which it is applied, so you can use relative paths in a predicate like the following to find the `RunningTime` of any `Movie` whose `Director`'s `Last` name is `'Minghella'`:

```
/MovieList/Movie[Director/Last='Minghella']/@RunningTime
```

Using our `testxpath` tool to test this we get:

```
RunningTime="139"
```

The expression can include multiple conditions with `and` and `or` operators. For example, to select the `Cast` of any movies directed by Minghella with a running time greater than 130 minutes you can use:

```
/MovieList/Movie[Director/Last='Minghella' and @RunningTime > 130]/Cast
```

A predicate can appear on any number of the steps in a path. The following example uses two predicates, one qualifying `Movie` and the other qualifying `Actor`, and illustrates that you can use whitespace like carriage returns between steps in a pattern to make it more readable when it gets long:

```
//Movie[Award/@Category='Best Film']
  //Actor[Award/@Category='Best Actor']
    /Last
```

This finds the `Last` name of any `Actor` who won a `Best Actor` award in a `Movie` that won an award for `Best Film`. Trying this expression at the `testxpath` command line, we get:

```
<Last>Spacey</Last>
```

To return just the *text* that's included in an element, we can use the `text()` expression. If we tack on an additional `text()` at the end of the previous example, like this:

```
//Movie[Award/@Category='Best Film']
  //Actor[Award/@Category='Best Actor']
    /Last/text()
```

we get just the text:

```
Spacey
```

and not the `<Last>` element *containing* the text `'Spacey'`.

Frequently, you'll want to select the first matching element or the first three matching elements or the *n*th matching element. You can use the `position()` function in a predicate to achieve this. It returns the position of a matching element among all elements that match the expression in the current step. Note that the position numbering starts with one. So to find only the first `Award` listed at any level in the

`MovieList`, excluding second and subsequent `Awards` that a `Movie`, `Director`, `Actor`, or `Actress` might have received, you can use:

```
//Award[position()=1]
```

which returns:

```
<Award From="Oscar" Category="Best Director"/>
<Award From="Oscar" Category="Best Actor"/>
<Award From="BAFTA" Category="Best Actress"/>
<Award From="Oscar" Category="Best Film"/>
<Award From="BAFTA" Category="Best Supporting Actor"/>
```

If, instead, you want the first `Award` that occurs anywhere in the document, you can use parentheses to cause `//Award` to be evaluated first and then filter this list of all matching `Award` elements to return only the first one. The syntax for this is:

```
(//Award)[position()=1]
```

As expected, this returns only the first `Award` element in document order:

```
<Award From="Oscar" Category="Best Director"/>
```

To retrieve the first three `Awards` anywhere in the document, we can use a predicate that tests for elements with `position() < 4` as in:

```
(//Award)[position() < 4 ]
```

which returns:

```
<Award From="Oscar" Category="Best Director"/>
<Award From="Oscar" Category="Best Actor"/>
<Award From="BAFTA" Category="Best Actor"/>
```

As a convenience, instead of using `[position()=` *n*`]`, we can just use the array-like subscript notation of `[`*n*`]`. So to find the `Role` played by the second `Actor` in the second `Movie` in the `MovieList` you can use `Actor[2]` and `Movie[2]` in the expression `/MovieList/Movie[2]/Cast/Actor[2]/@Role`. This gives the result:

```
Role="Dickie Greenleaf"
```

In addition to the `position()` function, XPath defines numerous other useful string, number, and set functions to use in path expressions. The following are some examples:

Find the directors of movies that won more than four awards of any kind

XPath expression using the `count()` function:

```
/MovieList/Movie[count(.//Award)>4]/Director
```

Result:

```
<Director>
   <First>Sam</First>
   <Last>Mendes</Last>
   <Award From="Oscar" Category="Best Director"/>
</Director>
```

Find the last actor in a movie whose name contains the word "Talented"

XPath expression using the `last()` and `contains()` functions:

```
//Movie[contains(@Title,'Talented')]/Cast/Actor[last()]
```

Result:

```
<Actor Role="Dickie Greenleaf">
   <First>Jude</First>
   <Last>Law</Last>
   <Award From="BAFTA" Category="Best Supporting Actor"/>
</Actor>
```

Find the actors or actresses who won a BAFTA award

XPath expression (which uses the union operator | to combine the results of two expressions):

```
//Actress[Award/@From='BAFTA'] | //Actor[Award/@From='BAFTA']
```

Note that the combined results appear in document order, regardless of the order in which the expressions were unioned.

Result:

```
<Actor Role="Lester Burnham">
   <First>Kevin</First>
   <Last>Spacey</Last>
   <Award From="Oscar" Category="Best Actor"/>
   <Award From="BAFTA" Category="Best Actor"/>
</Actor>
<Actress Role="Carolyn Burnham">
   <First>Annette</First>
   <Last>Bening</Last>
   <Award From="BAFTA" Category="Best Actress"/>
</Actress>
<Actor Role="Dickie Greenleaf">
   <First>Jude</First>
   <Last>Law</Last>
   <Award From="BAFTA" Category="Best Supporting Actor"/>
</Actor>
```

Find the role played by any actor with more than one award

XPath expression:

```
/MovieList/Movie/Cast/Actor[count(Award) > 1]/@Role
```

Result:

```
Role="Lester Burnham"
```

Find any actor who did not win an award

XPath expression:

```
/MovieList/Movie/Cast/Actor[not(Award)]
```

Result:

```
<Actor Role="Tom Ripley">
   <First>Matt</First>
   <Last>Damon</Last>
</Actor>
```

Find the title of any movie with a cast member or director whose last name starts with "D"

XPath expression:

```
/MovieList/Movie[.//Last[starts-with(.,'D')]]/@Title
```

Result:

```
Title="The Talented Mr.Ripley"
```

The XPath expression language is much more extensive and powerful than what we've seen in this section, but these are the fundamental concepts you'll use every day. In several later chapters, we'll learn about additional XPath syntax and features as we need them (rather than providing an exhaustive list here to remember). You can refer to the XPath quick-reference in Appendix D, *Quick References*, for a complete list that you're sure to find handy.

Since the **testxpath** tool we used in this chapter is useful for testing XPath expressions against XML documents from any file or URL, you may find it handy in later chapters; you may also find it useful to experiment with XPath in your daily work.

II

Oracle XML Fundamentals

This part of the book describes the core development activities that Oracle XML developers need to understand when using XML with an Oracle database. It consists of the following chapters:

- Chapter 3, *Combining XML and Oracle*, provides a typical "day-in-the-life" scenario illustrating the power of combining XML with an Oracle database.
- Chapter 4, *Using JDeveloper for XML Development*, describes how you can use Oracle's JDeveloper product to help with XML development.
- Chapter 5, *Processing XML with PL/SQL*, explains how you can use PL/SQL to load XML files, parse XML, search XML documents, post XML messages, and both enqueue and dequeue XML messages from queues.
- Chapter 6, *Processing XML with Java*, explains how you can combine Java, JDBC, and XML both inside and outside Oracle8*i* to load XML files, parse XML, search XML documents, and post XML messages, as well as enqueue and dequeue XML messages from queues.
- Chapter 7, *Transforming XML with XSLT*, explains the fundamentals of creating XSLT stylesheets to carry out transformations of a source XML document into a resulting XML, HTML, or plain text output.
- Chapter 8, *Publishing Data with XSQL Pages*, explains how to build dynamic XML datagrams from SQL using declarative templates to perform many common tasks.

- Chapter 9, *XSLT Beyond the Basics*, builds on the fundamentals from Chapter 7 and explores additional XSLT functionality like variables, sorting and grouping techniques, and the many kinds of useful transformations that can be done using a variation on the identity transformation.
- Chapter 10, *Generating Datagrams with PL/SQL*, gives Java developers a whirlwind introduction to PL/SQL and describes how to use PL/SQL to dynamically produce custom XML datagrams containing database information.
- Chapter 11, *Generating Datagrams with Java*, describes numerous techniques for programmatically producing XML datagrams using Java by using JDBC, SQLJ, JavaServer Pages, and the Oracle XML SQL Utility.
- Chapter 12, *Storing XML Datagrams*, explains how to store XML datagrams in the database using the XML SQL utility and other techniques, as well as how to retrieve them using XSQL pages and XSLT transformations.
- Chapter 13, *Searching XML with interMedia*, describes how you can use Oracle8*i*'s integrated interMedia Text functionality to search XML documents, leveraging their inherent structure to improve text searching accuracy.
- Chapter 14, *Advanced XML Loading Techniques*, describes the techniques required to insert arbitrarily large and arbitrarily complicated XML into multiple tables. It also covers using stylesheets to generate stylesheets to help automate the task.

In this chapter:
- *Hosting the XML FAQ System on Oracle*
- *Serving XML in Any Format*
- *Acquiring Web-based XML Content*

3
Combining XML and Oracle

In this chapter, we'll get a taste for what the rest of the book is about: making XML a lot more interesting by combining it with the power of your Oracle database. We explore a scenario of a growing company that needs to integrate and share information for a frequently asked questions "knowledge bank" and put the information to use in a variety of formats.

Don't worry if we move quickly through a lot of the details here. You'll learn how to do everything we cover in this rapid-fire walkthrough—and much, much more—in the numerous examples throughout the rest of the book. This chapter is meant as a preview. So buckle yourself in—the ride is about to start.

Hosting the XML FAQ System on Oracle

Recall the frequently asked questions document from Chapter 2, *Working with XML*:

```
<?xml version="1.0"?>
<!DOCTYPE FAQ-List SYSTEM "FAQ-List.dtd">
<FAQ-List>
  <FAQ Submitter="smuench@oracle.com">
    <Question>Is it easy to get started with XML?</Question>
    <Answer>Yes!</Answer>
  </FAQ>
  <FAQ Submitter="derek@spinaltap.com" Level="Advanced">
    <Question>Are we going to play Stonehenge?</Question>
    <Answer>But of course</Answer>
  </FAQ>
</FAQ-List>
```

Let's assume that we're working at a small Internet startup company. We start out with a single, small XML file using the *FAQ-List.dtd* vocabulary similar to the one described earlier. In the beginning, only a single person is in charge of editing the

FAQ file; the number of questions is small, and the number of products we sell is tiny, too. Then, as we develop and ship newer products, we naturally hire more people to help in the process, and now each product team wants to manage its *own* XML FAQ file. So we split up the frequently asked questions into one XML FAQ file per *product* team—all still sharing the *FAQ-List.dtd* format. But inevitably:

- Our products get more and more popular.
- Our list of frequently asked questions begins to grow.
- Our customers begin demanding to search FAQs across *all* products.
- Our customers insist on flexible, fast searching on multiple criteria.
- Our competition launches a personalized FAQ portal page for web developers.

Help! We need a powerful database to go with our XML. So we create a faq_table to hold all of our frequently asked questions:

```
create table faq_table(
  category     VARCHAR2(30),
  question     VARCHAR2(4000),
  answer       VARCHAR2(4000),
  qlevel       NUMBER,
  submitted_by VARCHAR2(80)
);
```

and we decide to store the difficulty level of the question as a NUMBER so we can sort the questions numerically by how difficult they are. It's kind of unfortunate that "Advanced" sorts before "Beginner," but it's not a problem if we treat each level as a number. In order to store all the questions for *all* the products, we add a CATEGORY column to the table as well. By querying the faq_table, we should be able to search for questions across all products or, simply by adding an appropriate WHERE clause, for just questions in a particular category.

On the Oracle Technology Network (OTN) web site we read about Oracle XSQL Pages. The release notes claim that people who know SQL can get started quickly combining SQL, XML, and XSLT to easily publish database information in a variety of formats, so we decide to give it a try. We create our first XSQL page by pasting a SELECT statement over the faq_table into an XML file between a `<xsql:query>` and a closing `</xsql:query>` tag. We specify the name of a database connection to use at the top of the page, and provide a default value of "`%`" for the `cat` parameter in the query, representing the name of the frequently asked question category to retrieve. The *FAQ.xsql* file we came up with is shown in Example 3-1.

Example 3-1. XSQL Page to Query FAQ Data from faq_table

```
<?xml version="1.0"?>
<!-- FAQ.xsql: Return the results of faq_table query as XML Information -->
<xsql:query connection="xmlbook" cat="%" xmlns:xsql="urn:oracle-xsql">
```

Example 3-1. XSQL Page to Query FAQ Data from faq_table (continued)

```
  SELECT category, question, answer, submitted_by,qlevel,
         DECODE(qlevel,1,'Beginner',
                       2,'Intermediate',
                       3,'Advanced') as "LEVEL"
    FROM faq_table
   WHERE category LIKE UPPER('{@cat}')
  ORDER BY category, qlevel

</xsql:query>
```

We save the *FAQ.xsql* file to disk and try to request the page through our browser. To our surprise, we immediately see the results of our SQL query as XML in the browser. That was pretty easy: we just had to specify the name of the database `connection` we wanted to use, paste in our SQL statement, and save the file. We reference a parameter in the query called `cat` using the `{@cat}` syntax right where we want the value of the category to be substituted. So if we try to request the page by passing a particular category value in the URL as follows:

```
http://localhost/xml-basics/FAQ.xsql?cat=jdev
```

We instantly see XML for only the frequently asked questions in the `jdev` category, as shown in Figure 3-1, from our IE5 browser.

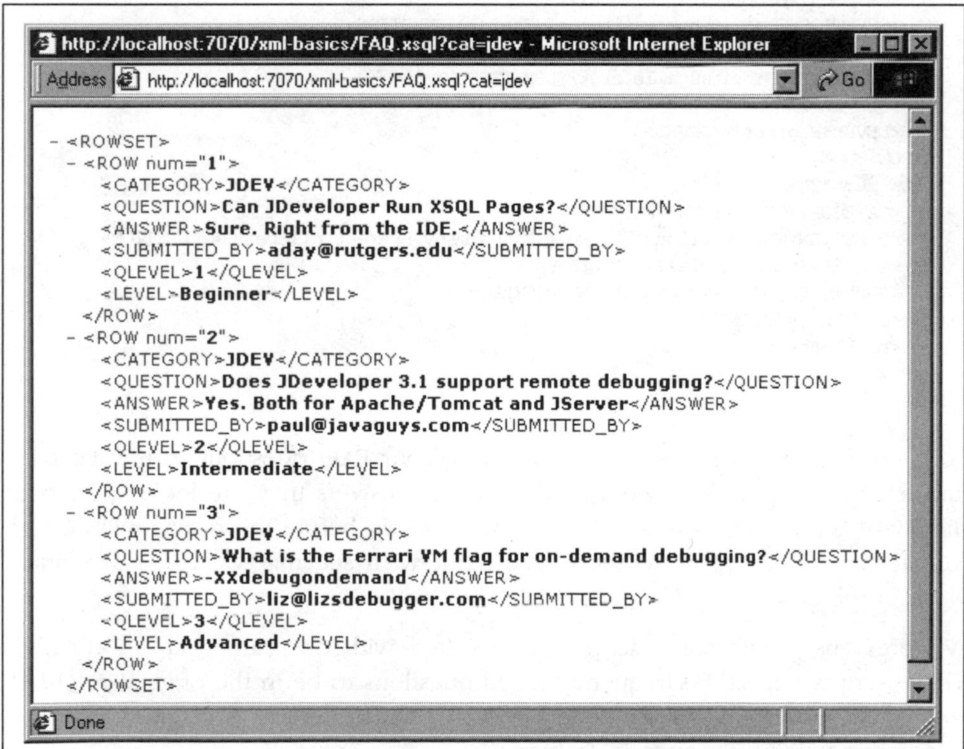

Figure 3-1. XML from SQL query displayed in IE5

The results don't *look* that pretty, but we'll see shortly how we can transform this canonical <ROWSET>/<ROW> structure into something more useful—in fact, into many different useful target formats.

We learn that in addition to the XSQL Servlet that comes with the XSQL Pages distribution from Oracle, there's also a command-line **xsql** tool that lets us do offline processing of any XSQL pages in command scripts. On a whim a few weeks back, we began featuring frequently asked questions for trivia categories like "famous people" and "geography." So let's try out one of those categories.

We use the same *FAQ.xsql* page we created above, but this time use the **xsql** command-line tool and pass **geography** as the category:

```
xsql FAQ.xsql cat=geography
```

And right out on the console appears the dynamic XML shown in Example 3-2 for the frequently asked questions in the **geography** category.

Example 3-2. Results of Processing FAQ.xsql for the Geography Category

```
<?xml version = '1.0'?>
<!-- FAQ.xsql: Return the results of faq_table query as XML Information -->
<ROWSET>
   <ROW num="1">
      <CATEGORY>GEOGRAPHY</CATEGORY>
      <QUESTION>What is the capital of Italy?</QUESTION>
      <ANSWER>Rome</ANSWER>
      <SUBMITTED_BY>sita@gallo.org</SUBMITTED_BY>
      <QLEVEL>1</QLEVEL>
      <LEVEL>Beginner</LEVEL>
   </ROW>
   <ROW num="2">
      <CATEGORY>GEOGRAPHY</CATEGORY>
      <QUESTION>What perilous obstacle stops many Everest climbers?</QUESTION>
      <ANSWER>Khumbu Icefall</ANSWER>
      <SUBMITTED_BY>desio@crn.it</SUBMITTED_BY>
      <QLEVEL>3</QLEVEL>
      <LEVEL>Advanced</LEVEL>
   </ROW>
</ROWSET>
```

So it seems that it will be easy to host all of our FAQ questions in the database and leverage SQL to let users quickly find the answers they are looking for over the Web. We clearly have a little more work to do before the results will be in a format suitable for users to see directly, but we'll see that we can make quick work of the task.

We previously built some scripts that worked with our earlier XML FAQ files. Those scripts expect the frequently asked questions to be in the original *FAQ-List.dtd* format, but it appears the default way that Oracle returns XML query results is in a generic <ROWSET> and <ROW> format.

Since XSLT stylesheets let us to transform XML information from one format to another, we should be able to transform the <ROWSET>/<ROW>–based information into the *FAQ-List.dtd* vocabulary fairly easily. We come up with the XSLT stylesheet in Example 3-3 to handle the job.

Example 3-3. Stylesheet to Transform ROWSET/ROW into FAQ-List

```
<?xml version="1.0"?>
<!-- FAQ-In-XML.xsl: Transform ROWSET/ROW format to FAQ-List.dtd vocabulary -->
<xsl:stylesheet version="1.0" xmlns:xsl="http://www.w3.org/1999/XSL/Transform">
  <xsl:output doctype-system="FAQ-List.dtd" indent="yes"/>
  <xsl:template match="/">
    <FAQ-List>
      <xsl:for-each select="ROWSET/ROW">
        <FAQ Submitter="{SUBMITTED_BY}" Level="{LEVEL}">
          <Question><xsl:value-of select="QUESTION"/></Question>
          <Answer><xsl:value-of select="ANSWER"/></Answer>
        </FAQ>
      </xsl:for-each>
    </FAQ-List>
  </xsl:template>
</xsl:stylesheet>
```

We found the stylesheet pretty straightforward to create because XSLT stylesheets use XPath expressions like the **ROWSET/ROW** expression you see in Example 3-3 to find, iterate over, and plug information from the source XML document into a template that describes what we want the target XML to look like. We used JDeveloper 3.1 to create and syntax-check the stylesheet as we were building it, so that caught our mistakes and made things go faster.

After saving the output of processing the XSQL page in Example 3-1 in a file named *GeographyROWSETFromXSQL.xml*, we transform the <ROWSET>/<ROW> structure using the *FAQ-In-XML.xsl* stylesheet by using the command-line **oraxsl** tool:

```
oraxsl GeographyROWSETFromXSQL.xml FAQ-In-XML.xsl
```

to produce:

```
<?xml version = '1.0' encoding = 'UTF-8'?>
<!DOCTYPE FAQ-List SYSTEM "FAQ-List.dtd">
<FAQ-List>
   <FAQ Submitter="sita@gallo.org" Level="Beginner">
      <Question>What is the capital of Italy?</Question>
      <Answer>Rome</Answer>
   </FAQ>
   <FAQ Submitter="desio@crn.it" Level="Advanced">
      <Question>What perilous obstacle stops many Everest climbers?</Question>
      <Answer>Khumbu Icefall</Answer>
   </FAQ>
</FAQ-List>
```

```
    <Query-Frequently-Posed By="paul@javaguys.com" Difficulty="Intermediate">
      <Query>Does JDeveloper 3.1 support remote debugging?</Query>
      <Reply>Yes. Both for Apache/Tomcat and JServer</Reply>
    </Query-Frequently-Posed>
    <Query-Frequently-Posed By="liz@lizsdebugger.com" Difficulty="Advanced">
      <Query>What is the Ferrari VM flag for on-demand debugging?</Query>
      <Reply>-XXdebugondemand</Reply>
    </Query-Frequently-Posed>
</Frequently-Posed-Queries>
```

Next we tackle our web site. Our users want to see the results of their frequently asked questions searches in a nice HTML format in their browser. We ask our web design department to provide us with the HTML source of the "look and feel" they want the FAQ web site to have. They give us something that looks like Figure 3-3.

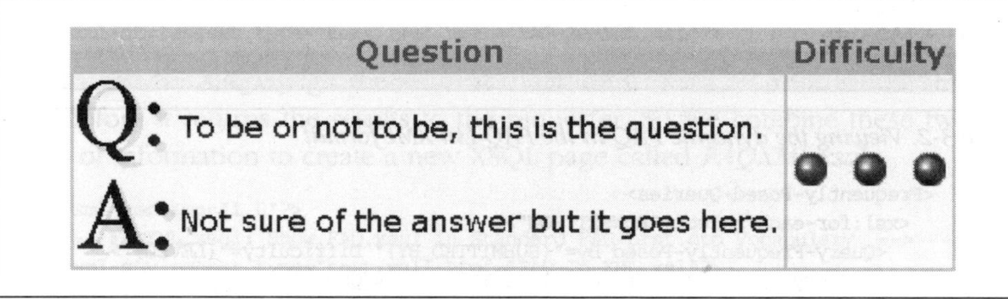

Figure 3-3. Mockup of HTML page to display FAQs

The web designers at our place work with Dreamweaver, so in order to turn their mockup into well-formed XML that we can quickly use as the basis for an XSLT stylesheet, we run Dave Raggett's free Tidy utility* over the *HTMLMockup.html* file they gave us:

```
tidy -asxml -indent HTMLMockup.html > HTMLMockup.xml
```

and produce the indented, well-formed XML you see in Example 3-4.

Example 3-4. Output of Using the Tidy Utility on an HTML File

```
<?xml version="1.0"?>
<!DOCTYPE html PUBLIC "-//W3C//DTD XHTML 1.0 Transitional//EN"
    "http://www.w3.org/TR/xhtml1/DTD/xhtml1-transitional.dtd">
<html xmlns="http://www.w3.org/1999/xhtml">
  <head>
    <meta name="generator" content="HTML Tidy, see www.w3.org" />
    <title>
      Frequently Asked Questions
    </title>
```

* This very helpful utility corrects many of the most common mistakes made by HTML designers, producing a well-formed XML document from a messy HTML page. You can obtain it from *http://www.w3.org/People/Raggett/tidy*. See the documentation available there for a full explanation of the utility, including its flags.

Example 3-4. Output of Using the Tidy Utility on an HTML File (continued)

```
    <style type="text/css">
          td {font-family:verdana,arial; font-size:18;
              background-color:#f7f7e7; color:#000000 }
          th,table {font-family:verdana,arial; font-size:18;
              background-color:#cccc99; color:#336699 }
    </style>
  </head>
  <body>
    <center>
      <table border="0">
        <tr>
          <th>
            Question
          </th>
          <th>
            Difficulty
          </th>
        </tr>
        <tr>
          <td>
            <table border="0" cellspacing="0">
              <tr>
                <td>
                  <img src="images/Question.gif" />
                </td>
                <td valign="middle">
                  To be or not to be, this is the question.
                </td>
              </tr>
              <tr>
                <td>
                  <img src="images/Answer.gif" />
                </td>
                <td valign="middle">
                  Not sure of the answer but it goes here.
                </td>
              </tr>
            </table>
          </td>
          <td>
            <img align="absmiddle" src="images/Advanced.gif" />
          </td>
        </tr>
      </table>
    </center>
  </body>
</html>
```

The careful reader will recognize the `xmlns="http://www.w3.org/1999/xhtml"` default namespace declaration on the `<html>` document element in the tidied-up XML output. This refers to the XML vocabulary called XHTML, the next generation version of HTML that uses XML syntax with all of the familiar HTML tags. An HTML page that has been tidied up to be compliant with the strict XML syntax rules discussed earlier in this chapter is known as *well-formed HTML.*

Notice that Tidy has tidied up the HTML `<img>` tags to be XML empty elements `<img/>` so the HTML page will be well-formed HTML. We can rename *HTMLMockup.xml* to *FAQ-In-HTML.xsl* and begin turning this tidied-up HTML mockup into the XSLT stylesheet that plugs in our dynamic query information.

We can easily evolve this well-formed HTML into an XSLT stylesheet by adding the `xsl:version="1.0"` attribute to the `<html>` element, adding the appropriate namespace declaration for the XSLT vocabulary, and adding a `<xsl:for-each>` element to loop over the results of the `ROWSET/ROW` XPath expression. Doing so loops over each `<ROW>` element in the XML output of the original *FAQ.xsql* page. We replace the static text the web designers gave us with `<xsl:value-of>` elements to plug in the dynamic data from our *FAQ.xsql*, using the XPath expressions `QUESTION` and `ANSWER` that are interpreted relative to the current `<ROW>` elements our `<xsl:for-each>` loop is processing.

Finally, we use the XSLT *attribute value template* syntax of putting XPath expressions between curly braces to plug dynamic information into the `href` attribute of the `<img>` tag to appropriately refer to *Beginner.gif, Intermediate.gif,* or *Advanced.gif* images that the graphic art department created for us to show the difficulty level. We end up with the XSLT stylesheet in Example 3-5.

Example 3-5. HTML Mockup Converted to an XSLT Stylesheet

```
<!-- FAQ-In-HTML.xsl: Transform ROWSET/ROW format into HTML Format -->
<html xsl:version="1.0" xmlns:xsl="http://www.w3.org/1999/XSL/Transform">
  <head>
    <title>Frequently Asked Questions</title>
    <style>
       td {font-family:verdana,arial; font-size:18;
           background-color:#f7f7e7; color:#000000 }
       th,table {font-family:verdana,arial; font-size:18;
           background-color:#cccc99; color:#336699 }
    </style>
  </head>
  <body>
    <center>
      <table border="0">
```

Example 3-5. HTML Mockup Converted to an XSLT Stylesheet (continued)

```
        <tr>
          <th>Question</th>
          <th>Difficulty</th>
        </tr>
        <xsl:for-each select="ROWSET/ROW">
          <tr>
            <td>
              <table border="0" cellspacing="0">
                <tr>
                  <td>
                    <img src="images/Question.gif"/>
                  </td>
                  <td valign="middle">
                    <xsl:value-of select="QUESTION"/>
                  </td>
                </tr>
                <tr>
                  <td>
                    <img src="images/Answer.gif"/>
                  </td>
                  <td valign="middle">
                    <xsl:value-of select="ANSWER"/>
                  </td>
                </tr>
              </table>
            </td>
            <td>
              <img align="absmiddle" src="images/{LEVEL}.gif"/>
            </td>
          </tr>
        </xsl:for-each>
      </table>
    </center>
  </body>
</html>
```

Let's again create a little XSQL page to reuse our original *FAQ.xsql* and associate it with our new *FAQ-In-HTML.xsl* stylesheet:

```
<?xml version="1.0"?>
<!-- FAQHTML.xsql: Show FAQ.xsql in HTML Format for browsers -->
<?xml-stylesheet type="text/xsl" href="FAQ-In-HTML.xsl"?>
<xsql:include-xsql href="FAQ.xsql" xmlns:xsql="urn:oracle-xsql"/>
```

We then can request the *FAQHTML.xsql* page through any browser (Netscape 6 is shown in Figure 3-4) to see the results. We've taken our web designer's HTML mockup, turned it into an XSLT stylesheet, associated it with an XSQL page, and are now delivering our frequently asked question information dynamically from faq_table in an eye-catching HTML format.

Our DBA comes up to us and asks, "Any chance I could get a SQL script to insert the geography questions in your faq_table into an Oracle8*i* Lite database I'm setting up?" We think for a second and tell him, "Sure. Come back in five minutes."

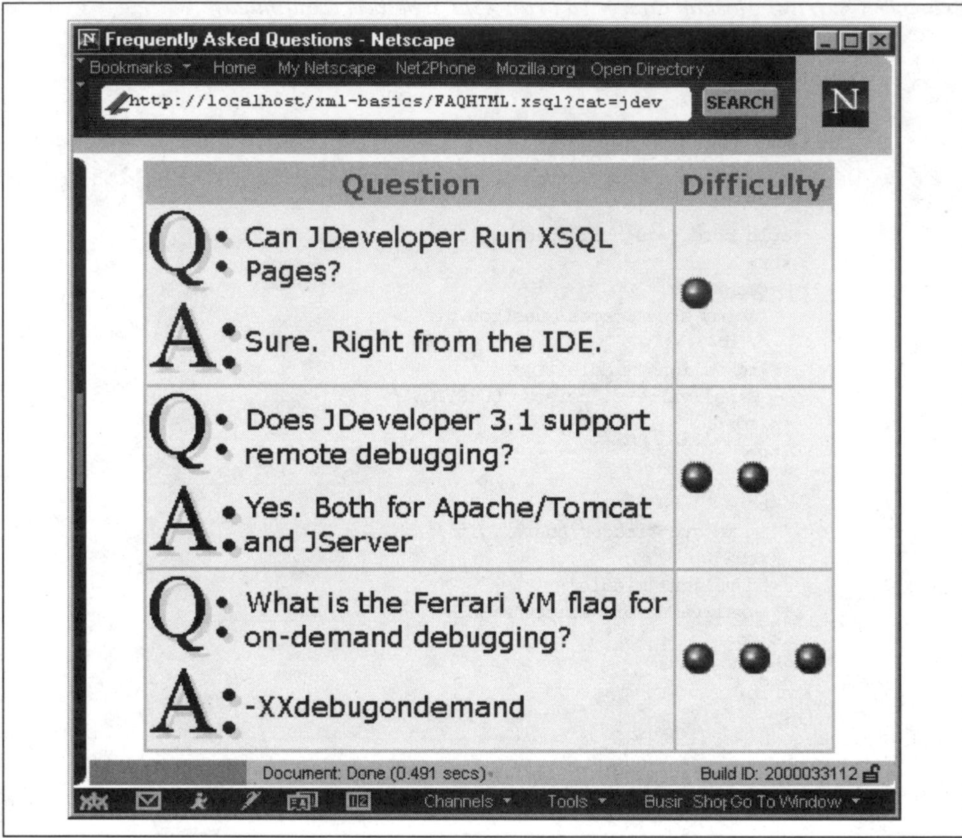

Figure 3-4. Dynamic XML transformed with XSLT into HTML

The surprised look on his face says to us, "Five minutes? Wow." He leaves to get a cup of coffee and we're already in JDeveloper creating another XSLT stylesheet to transform the output of *FAQ.xsql.xsl* into a SQL script that inserts the data.

We create a stylesheet like *FAQ-As-Insert.xsl*:

```
<?xml version="1.0"?>
<xsl:stylesheet version="1.0" xmlns:xsl="http://www.w3.org/1999/XSL/Transform">
<xsl:output method="text"/>
<xsl:template match="/">
<xsl:for-each select="ROWSET/ROW">
INSERT into faq_table values(
  /* category  */ '<xsl:value-of select="CATEGORY"/>',
  /* question  */ '<xsl:value-of select="QUESTION"/>',
  /* answer    */ '<xsl:value-of select="ANSWER"/>',
  /* qlevel    */ '<xsl:value-of select="QLEVEL"/>',
  /* submitter */ '<xsl:value-of select="SUBMITTED_BY"/>'
);
</xsl:for-each>
</xsl:template>
</xsl:stylesheet>
```

using the familiar tags from the XSLT vocabulary to loop over and plug data into the text template of an INSERT statement. We create another XSQL page—*FAQExport.xsql*—to reuse our *FAQ.xsql* XML output from faq_table and associate it with the *FAQ-As-Insert.xsl* stylesheet:

```
<?xml version="1.0"?>
<!-- FAQExport.xsql: Export FAQ.xsql results as INSERT statements -->
<?xml-stylesheet type="text/xsl" href="FAQ-As-Insert.xsl"?>
<xsql:include-xsql href="FAQ.xsql" xmlns:xsql="urn:oracle-xsql"/>
```

Then we go out to a command prompt and use the **xsql** command-line tool to process our new page:

```
xsql FAQExport.xsql cat=geography
```

to get the results the DBA needs:

```
insert into faq_table values(
  /* category  */ 'GEOGRAPHY',
  /* question  */ 'What is the capital of Italy?',
  /* answer    */ 'Rome',
  /* qlevel    */ 1,
  /* submitter */ 'sita@gallo.org'
);
insert into faq_table values(
  /* category  */ 'GEOGRAPHY',
  /* question  */ 'What perilous obstacle stops many Everest climbers?',
  /* answer    */ 'Khumbu Icefall',
  /* qlevel    */ 3,
  /* submitter */ 'desio@crn.it'
);
```

We copy the SQL script to a floppy and move on to our next challenge. Next, our boss asks us to set up a system to email frequently asked questions to developers who have purchased our products. By now, we know the drill. He budgeted two weeks to have us set up the system, but we're done with the bulk of the work in a few minutes because we are working with XML to separate our data from the format we need to deliver it in. We simply create yet another XSLT stylesheet to produce the results of the XML information from *FAQ.xsql* as the body of an email:

```
<?xml version="1.0"?>
<!-- FAQ-In-Email.xsl: Transform ROWSET/ROW format into email body text -->
<xsl:stylesheet version="1.0" xmlns:xsl="http://www.w3.org/1999/XSL/Transform">
  <xsl:output method="text"/>
  <xsl:template match="/">
    <xsl:text>Hello,&#xa;&#xa;</xsl:text>
    <xsl:text>Here is your daily email dose of FAQ...</xsl:text>
    <xsl:for-each select="ROWSET/ROW">
      <xsl:text>&#xa;&#xa;Question </xsl:text>
      <xsl:value-of select="position()"/>
      <xsl:text>: </xsl:text>
      <xsl:value-of select="QUESTION"/>
      <xsl:text>&#xa;    Answer: </xsl:text>
```

```
        <xsl:value-of select="ANSWER"/>
      </xsl:for-each>
    </xsl:template>
  </xsl:stylesheet>
```

Next we create another familiar XSQL page to reuse *FAQ.xsql* and associate it to our *FAQ-In-Email.xsl* stylesheet:

```
<?xml version="1.0"?>
<!-- FAQEMail.xsql: Format FAQ.xsql results as an Email -->
<?xml-stylesheet type="text/xsl" href="FAQ-In-Email.xsl"?>
<xsql:include-xsql href="FAQ.xsql" xmlns:xsql="urn:oracle-xsql"/>
```

Now our new notification system can use the XSQL page processor *programmatically* through its `XSQLRequest` Java API to incorporate this dynamic, data-driven email based on our FAQ table. Write a couple of lines of code in the middle of our mailer program to process the *FAQEmail.xsql* page—passing in a `cat` parameter value of `jdev` to the routine programmatically—and out pops our customized email for FAQ questions in the `jdev` category:

```
Hello,

Here is your daily email dose of FAQ...

Question 1: Can JDeveloper Run XSQL Pages?
    Answer: Sure. Right from the IDE.

Question 2: Does JDeveloper 3.1 support remote debugging?
    Answer: Yes. Both for Apache/Tomcat and JServer

Question 3: What is the Ferrari VM flag for on-demand debugging?
    Answer: -XXdebugondemand
```

At this point, we're smiling a pretty wide smile. Suddenly, we're told we have to come up with a solution for pulling in dynamic FAQ content from Sun's web site, where tons of Java-related FAQ content lives. Sun's just made it available in XML format and published it to the world, and our boss got the clever idea that it just might be useful to our customers as well. Once we heard that the information on Sun's site was available in XML, we started smiling again.

Acquiring Web-based XML Content

We check out the *ServletsFAQ.xml* file on Sun's site, which they update periodically, and notice that it has a format like this:

```
<?xml version = '1.0' encoding = 'UTF-8'?>
<Servlets-FAQ>
  <FAQ>
    <Q>What's the next major release of the Servlet API?</Q>
    <A>Servlet API 2.2</A>
  </FAQ>
```

```
  <FAQ>
    <Q>How do I set the age of a cookie?</Q>
    <A>yourCookie.setAge(120);</A>
  </FAQ>
  <FAQ>
    <Q>How do I save a variable in a per-user session?</Q>
    <A>request.getSession(true).putValue('varname','value');</A>
  </FAQ>
</Servlets-FAQ>
```

We want this Servlet FAQ content and others like it from Sun's site to reside in our database so we can search over it together with all of our own content. We learn that the Oracle XML SQL Utility can insert XML documents automatically into our faq_table if they have the canonical `<ROWSET>`/`<ROW>` structure, so we create another XSLT stylesheet to transform a document in Sun's `<Servlets-FAQ>` vocabulary into a `<ROWSET>`/`<ROW>` document:

```
<ROWSET xsl:version="1.0" xmlns:xsl="http://www.w3.org/1999/XSL/Transform">
  <xsl:for-each select="/Servlets-FAQ/FAQ">
    <ROW>
      <CATEGORY>SERVLETS</CATEGORY>
      <QLEVEL>1</QLEVEL>
      <QUESTION><xsl:value-of select="Q"/></QUESTION>
      <ANSWER><xsl:value-of select="A"/></ANSWER>
      <SUBMITTED_BY>Sun</SUBMITTED_BY>
    </ROW>
  </xsl:for-each>
</ROWSET>
```

This time, the tables are turned and our XPath expressions in `<xsl:for-each>` are looping over Sun's XML format and constructing the `<ROWSET>`, `<ROW>`, and column-name elements required for the automatic insert. As in all of our other stylesheets, we use `<xsl:value-of>` to plug in the `Q` and `A` children element values from the current `/Servlets-FAQ/FAQ` element as the values of our `<QUESTION>` and `<ANSWER>` elements. Note that because Sun doesn't keep track of the difficulty level in the FAQ format, we're using a constant value of `1` in our stylesheet to default to a value that makes sense to our system. Also, we use a constant value of `SERVLETS` for the category to make sure that the information from FAQs for Servlets is placed in an appropriate category for searching through our faq_table.

We suspect that the XSQL Pages system offers some quick way to take advantage of this facility declaratively, so we look at the online help and notice an `<xsql:insert-request>` element that allows us to transform and insert any XML document that's posted as input to the page. We create another little XSQL page, *InsertSunJavaFAQ.xsql*:

```
<?xml version="1.0"?>
<!-- InsertSunJavaFAQ.xsql : Transform and insert XML in Sun FAQ Format -->
<xsql:insert-request connection="xmlbook" xmlns:xsql="urn:oracle-xsql"
                     transform="SunJavaFAQ-to-FAQTABLE.xsl"
                         table="faq_table"  />
```

This provides the name of our *SunJavaFAQ-to-FAQTABLE.xsl* stylesheet as the value of the `transform` attribute and faq_table as the value of the `table` attribute. We run the page using the `xsql` command-line utility—providing the URL to Sun's *ServletsFAQ.xml* file as the `posted-xml` to handle:

```
xsql InsertSunJavaFAQ.xsql posted-xml=http://java.sun.com/faqs/ServletsFAQ.xml
```

In processing this page, the XSQL page processor retrieves the XML from Sun's web site, transforms it using our indicated stylesheet into `<ROWSET>/<ROW>` format, and inserts it into the faq_table with the help of the Oracle XML SQL Utility under the covers. We see the status message on the console:

```
<?xml version = '1.0'?>
<!-- InsertSunJavaFAQ.xsql : Transform and insert XML in Sun FAQ Format -->
<xsql-status action="xsql:insert-request" rows="3"/>
```

indicating that all of Sun's servlet content is now in our database. Just to confirm, we point our browser at the *FAQHTML.xsql* page we built earlier and pass `servlets` for the value of the `cat` parameter. Lo and behold, we're now serving up dynamic FAQ content to our users that we acquired by permission from Sun's site using XML as an exchange format.

At the end of the day, we retrace our steps. By combining SQL, XML, and XSLT transformations using Oracle XML technology we were able to:

- Transition our static XML-based solution to dynamic, database-driven XML
- Reuse the dynamically produced XML as an interim data abstraction
- Leverage the flexibility of XSLT transformations to make our database-driven FAQ content available in numerous XML, HTML, and text formats:
  - — The *FAQ-List.dtd* format for our U.S. office
  - — The *Frequently-Posed-Queries.dtd* format for our U.K. office
  - — Eye-catching HTML for our web developer's portal page
  - — SQL scripts for our DBA
  - — Email for our developer outreach program
- Acquire XML-based information over the Web and store it in our database

The overview in this chapter is just the appetizer course of the bountiful feast of solutions you can build by exploiting Oracle's many XML facilities. In fact, Oracle's XSQL Pages technology itself is a shining example of what can be built using Oracle's other XML-enabling technologies, like the Oracle XML Parser, the Oracle XSLT processor, and the XML SQL Utility. As we've seen here, the XSQL Pages technology provides a declarative approach to solve common problems easily, but it does so by tapping into the power these other layers provide. We cover all of Oracle's XML technologies from the ground up starting in the next chapter. So what are you waiting for? Turn the page!

In this chapter:
- *Working with XML, XSQL, and JSP Files*
- *Working with Database Objects*
- *Using JDeveloper with Oracle XDK Components*

4
Using JDeveloper for XML Development

Whether you want to just work with XML and XSL files or you are a hardcore Java or PL/SQL developer, you'll find that JDeveloper 3.1 has lots of features to make your life easier. A few of the features that I personally use every single day of my life are:

- Color-coded syntax highlighting for XML/XSLT editing
- Auto-indenting and block indent/unindent to keep XML looking nice
- Built-in XML syntax checking
- Native support for running XSQL pages
- Ability to browse all Oracle8*i* schema objects, including Java classes
- Context-sensitive help as you type for methods and arguments
- Fast jumping to source and JavaDoc for any class that pops into your head
- Robust remote debugging support for Apache JServ, Tomcat, and others
- Robust remote "in-the-database" debugging support for JServer

We'll cover what you need to know to exploit these JDeveloper 3.1 features in this chapter.

JDeveloper 3.1 ships with a number of helpful XML samples. These include sample XSQL pages, Java programs, and servlets to help you make sure your environment is properly set up to run all the examples in this book. Open the *JDeveloperXMLExamples.jws* workspace in the *.\samples\xmlsamples* subdirectory of your JDeveloper installation home directory to take a look.

Working with XML, XSQL, and JSP Files

This section describes the many ways JDeveloper helps you work with XML, XSQL and JavaServer Pages.

Performing Basic Project and File Manipulation

JDeveloper allows you to create workspaces to facilitate working on many different projects at once. The contents of all the projects in your current workspace are always visible and organized in alphabetical order in the project navigator, as shown in Figure 4-1. At any time, you can click your mouse in the project navigator and begin typing the initial letters of a file you are looking for—for example, the letters `myi`—and a *Search for* pop-up appears. JDeveloper incrementally jumps you to the first file matching the letters you've typed in so far, as illustrated in the figure, so typically only a few letters are required to jump to the file you want.

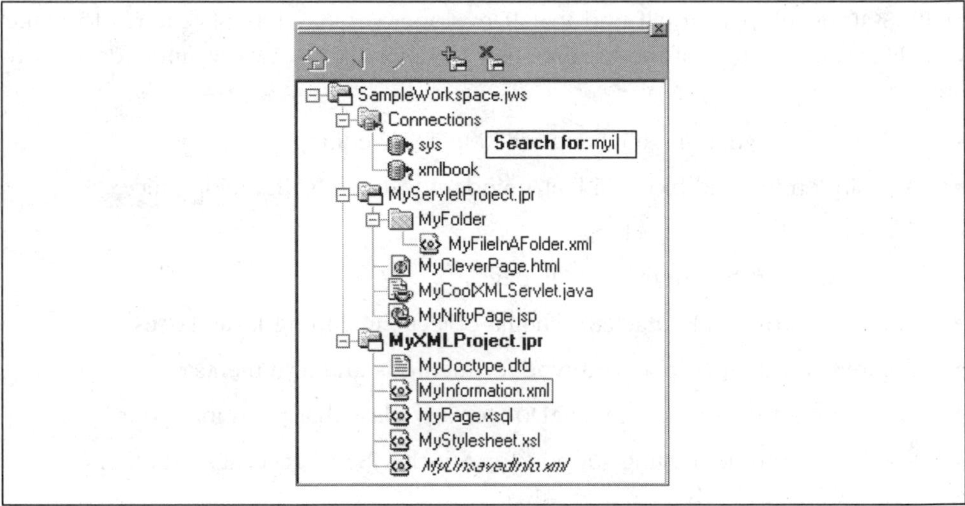

Figure 4-1. Incrementally search for a file in a project

By selecting a project in the navigator and choosing *Add Folder...* from the right mouse button menu, you can create additional folders to further organize your files within a project.

To add new or existing files to a project, select the target project to make it active (displayed in bold in the navigator). Then click the Add File icon—the folder with a plus sign—at the top of the navigator pane. The *File Open/Create* dialog appears. Select an existing file or type the name of a new file you want to create, and click the *Open* button to dismiss the file dialog and add the file to your project.

If you select an existing file in your project before clicking the Add File icon, the file dialog will use the existing file's directory as the current directory for the *File Open/Create* dialog. This is handy if you'll be adding a file from the same directory as another file in your project.

To delete a file from your project, select the file in the project navigator. Then click the Delete File icon—the folder with a minus sign—at the top of the navigator pane. Confirm the *Save changes to file?* alert box, if appropriate.

Files that have been edited show up with italic names in the navigator. You can save the current file with Ctrl-S, or use the menu or toolbar to *Save All* files.

Doing Color-Coded XML, XSL, XSQL, and JSP Editing

JDeveloper 3.1 supports the editing of any XML-based file with color-coded syntax highlighting and automatic indenting assistance to make it easier to work with XML and HTML source code. Table 4-1 shows the list of file types and extensions that JDeveloper 3.1 recognizes by default as XML/HTML file formats.

Table 4-1. Default File Extensions for Syntax Highlighting

File Extension	Description
.xml	XML files
.xsl	XSLT stylesheets
.xsql	XSQL pages
.dtd	Document type definitions
.xsd	XML schema definitions
.htm, .html	HTML files
.jsp	JavaServer pages

Figure 4-2 illustrates the different XML editing syntax constructs that the JDeveloper 3.1 code editor recognizes.

```
<!-- Comment -->
<Identifier Identifier="String" href="String">
  <TD> Plain Text </TD>
</Identifier>
```

Figure 4-2. Syntactic elements that can be highlighted

You can change the syntax highlighting colors for any of these constructs by following these steps:

1. Select *Tools* → *IDE Options...* from the JDeveloper 3.1 menu.
2. Select the *Fonts* tab in the *IDE Options* dialog that appears.

From the *Fonts* tab, you can set the color, font, foreground color, and background color of any syntactic element by selecting its name in the *Element* list and:

- Clicking the left mouse button in a colored square to set the foreground (FG) color
- Clicking the right mouse button in a colored square to set the background (BG) color
- Checking the *Foreground* or *Background* checkbox in the *Use defaults for* group to reset the respective color to the default setting

In addition, as shown in Figure 4-3, you can set the font name, size, and style for any syntax element.

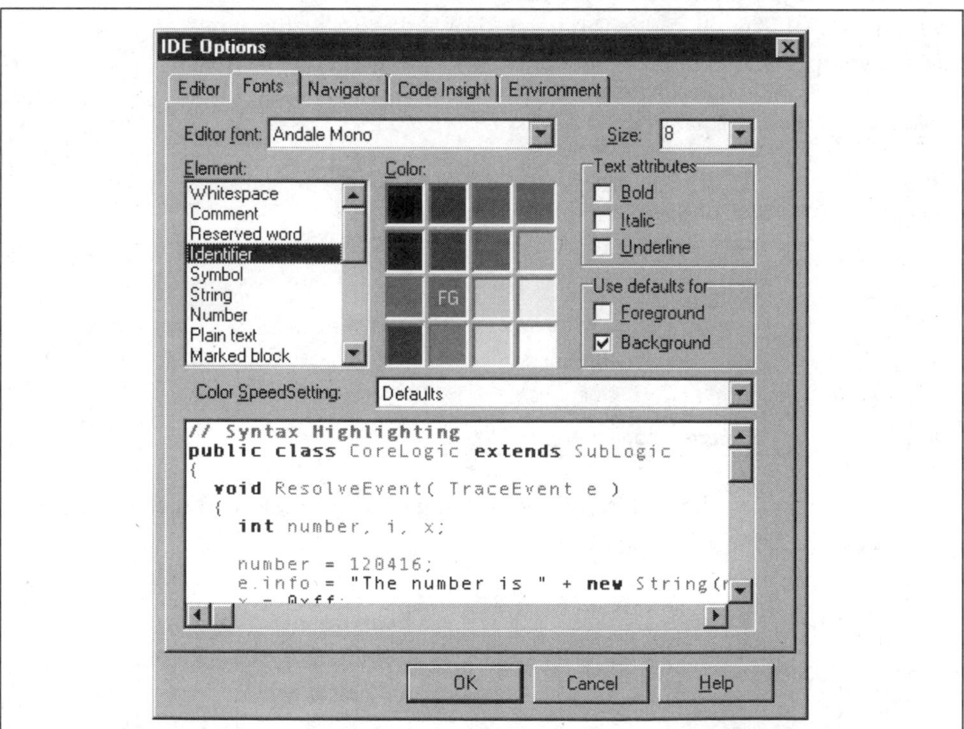

Figure 4-3. Customize color syntax highlighting on the Fonts panel

Table 4-2 describes the correspondence between the name of the syntactic element in the *Element* list and the context it affects for XML editing.

Table 4-2. Syntax Elements and the Contexts They Affect

Syntax Element Name	Controls Color For
Whitespace	Space between elements and attributes
Comment	XML comments
Reserved word	Names of recognized names of HTML elements and attributes
Identifier	XML element and attribute names
Symbol	< , >, and /> characters
String	Attribute values
Plain text	Text content of elements

Changes you make to colors for the code editor take effect immediately and can be changed at any time.

If you work with other XML-based file types and would like JDeveloper to syntax-highlight these files as well, you can teach the product about your new files. For example, if you want files with an **.xyz* extension to be syntax-highlighted, then do the following:

1. Add **.xyz* as a file extension that JDeveloper should treat as a text file, as follows:
   - Select the *Tools* → *Treat as text...* menu option.
   - Type in `*.xyz` in the *File pattern to be treated as text* field, and click the *Add* button.
   - Dismiss the *Treat as text...* dialog by pressing the *OK* button.
2. Add *xyz* to the list of file extensions that should be syntax-highlighted like HTML/XML files, as follows:
   - Select the *Tools* → *IDE Options...* menu option.
   - Click on the *Editor* tab of the *IDE Options* dialog.
   - Choose "Cursor/Search/Display options" from the *Settings for:* pop-up list.
   - In the *Display Options* frame, add `xyz` to the end of the current list of file extensions displayed in the *HTML File Extensions* field, separated by a semicolon.
   - Click the *OK* button to dismiss the *IDE Options* dialog.

Make sure to see the instructions in the next section for enabling XML syntax checking on your **.xyz* file extension, if this is desirable. The next time you open your workspace or restart the JDeveloper product, these new settings will be in effect.

You'll find that JDeveloper's automatic indenting helps a lot in keeping your XML elements nicely aligned. If you add elements or remove elements, however, often you'd like to quickly fix the indenting for whole blocks of elements at a time to make the file look nice again. In these cases, you will find that JDeveloper's block indent and block unindent support come in handy over and over again. To indent a block of text by two spaces, select the desired lines and type Ctrl-Shift-I. To unindent a block of text by two spaces, select the desired lines and type Ctrl-Shift-U.

To change the number of spaces used for each block indent, choose the *Tools → IDE Options...* menu, select the *Editor* tab in the *IDE Options* dialog, and set the value of *Block Indent* to the value you prefer.

Interactively Syntax Checking XML-based Files

In addition to XML syntax highlighting, JDeveloper 3.1 supports XML syntax checking of any file in your project that is not read-only and that has one of the file extensions listed in Table 4-3.

Table 4-3. Default File Extensions Recognized for XML Syntax Checking

File Extension	Description
.xml	XML files
.xsl	XSLT stylesheets
.xsql	XSQL pages
.xsd	XML schema definitions

At any time, you can select the *Check XML Syntax...* option from the right mouse button menu after selecting the desired file to check in the project navigator. JDeveloper checks the syntax of the file based on the current state of its editor buffer, even if you have pending changes that have not been saved to disk. If any XML well-formedness errors are detected, appropriate error messages appear in the *XML Errors* tab of the *Message View* and your cursor is brought to the position of the first error in your file, as Figure 4-4 illustrates.

To quickly jump to a line by number in the current buffer, type Ctrl-O+Ctrl-G and type in the line number you want to jump to in the *Go to Line Number* dialog that appears.

Note that the *Check XML Syntax...* menu option does just that: it checks syntax. It does not perform validation of the XML file against its associated DTD. As we saw in Chapter 2, *Working with XML*, you can use the `oraxml` command-line tool with the `-v` flag to perform DTD validation of an XML file.

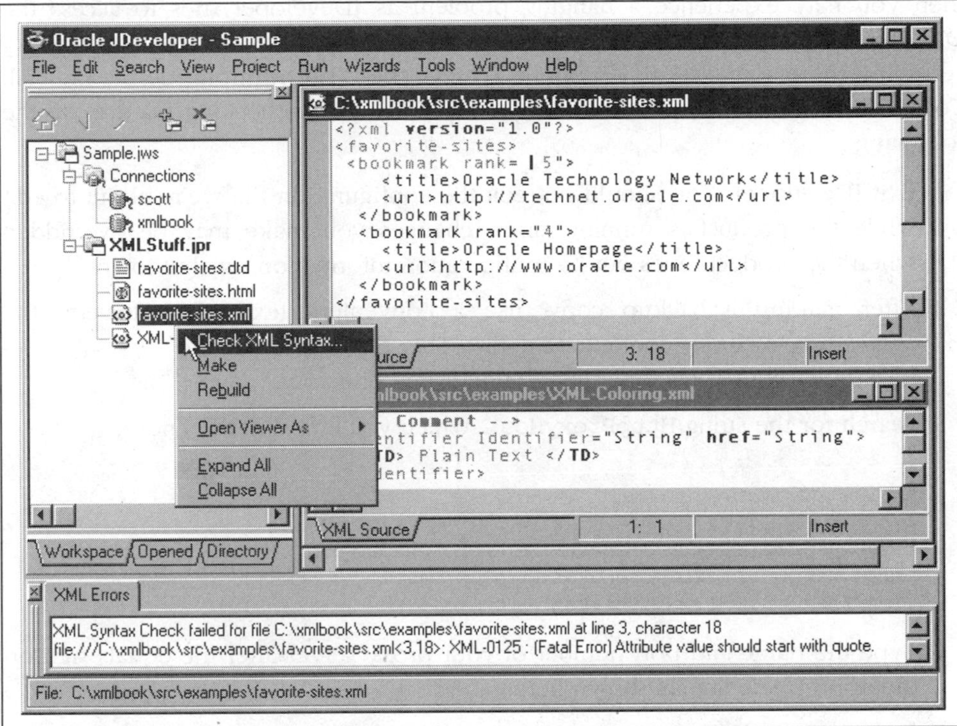

Figure 4-4. Checking the XML syntax of a file

Note, however, that JDeveloper 3.1's *Check XML Syntax...* feature still must read the DTD if your XML file has an associated `<!DOCTYPE>`, even though it does not perform full DTD validation. Be aware that if you work on a computer that is behind a firewall, and if the XML file you are attempting to syntax-check uses an external DTD with an HTTP-based URL, as in the following example:

```
<?xml version="1.0" encoding="iso-8859-1"?>
<!DOCTYPE moreovernews SYSTEM "http://w.moreover.com/xml/moreovernews.dtd">
<moreovernews>
   <article id="_6721342">
      <url>http://c.moreover.com/click/here.pl?x6721341</url>
      <headline_text>U.S. Officers Seize Cuban Boy, Reunite Him With Father
      </headline_text>
      <source>New York Times</source>
      <media_type>text</media_type>
      <cluster>Top stories</cluster>
      <tagline> </tagline>
      <document_url>http://www.nytimes.com/yr/mo/day/front/</document_url>
      <harvest_time>Apr 23 2000  2:19AM</harvest_time>
      <access_registration>http://www.nytimes.com/auth/login?Tag=/&amp;Url=
      </access_registration>
      <access_status>reg</access_status>
   </article>
</moreovernews>
```

then you may experience a hanging problem as JDeveloper tries to access the DTD over the Web. The solution is to teach JDeveloper the name of your proxy server machine so that it may properly retrieve the DTD from outside the firewall. To set the name of the proxy server for the XML syntax-checking feature, do the following:

1. Exit JDeveloper. You should not edit the configuration file we're about to edit while the product is running, since changes you make may be overridden when the product saves out its configuration information on shutdown.
2. After making a backup copy, use a convenient text editor to edit the *jdeveloper.properties* configuration file. This file resides in the *./lib* subdirectory under your JDeveloper installation home directory.
3. Search for the string `HttpProxyHost`, which you'll find in the lines:

```
#
# Check XML Syntax... Addin
#
jdeveloper.xml.XmlFileParserAddin.XmlFileExtensions=xml,xsl,xsql,xsd
jdeveloper.xml.XmlFileParserAddin.HttpProxyHost=
jdeveloper.xml.XmlFileParserAddin.HttpProxyPort=
```

4. Type the name and port number of your proxy server after the equals sign on the appropriate line as shown here:

```
#
# Check XML Syntax... Addin
#
jdeveloper.xml.XmlFileParserAddin.XmlFileExtensions=xml,xsl,xsql,xsd
jdeveloper.xml.XmlFileParserAddin.HttpProxyHost=yourproxyserver.you.com
jdeveloper.xml.XmlFileParserAddin.HttpProxyPort=80
```

5. Save the file and restart JDeveloper.

Now you should be able to syntax-check any XML file without incident.

If you work with other XML-based file types and would like JDeveloper to syntax-check these additional file types as XML, you can teach the product about your new XML-based files. For example, if you want files with an **.xyz* extension to allow XML syntax checking, do the following:

1. First, make sure you've followed the instructions in the previous section, "Doing Color-Coded XML, XSL, XSQL, and JSP Editing," to register files with extension **.xyz* to be treated as text files and optionally registered as files to syntax-color as XML.
2. Exit JDeveloper. You should not edit the configuration file we're about to edit while the product is running, since changes you make may be overridden when the product saves out its configuration information on shutdown.

3. After making a backup copy, edit the *jdeveloper.properties* file found in the *./lib* subdirectory of your JDeveloper installation home directory.
4. Search for the line:

```
jdeveloper.xml.XmlFileParserAddin.XmlFileExtensions=xml,xsl,xsql,xsd
```

5. Add `xyz` to the end of the list of file extensions, separated by a comma.

The next time you start JDeveloper the *Check XML Syntax...* menu item should appear for the **.xyz* files in the project.

Developing XSQL Pages and JSPs Using JDeveloper

JDeveloper has built-in support for working with both JavaServer Pages and Oracle XSQL Pages. While editing JSP and XSQL pages, you get color-coded syntax highlighting as we've described in the previous section. In addition, since XSQL pages are XML-based templates, they also benefit from the *Check XML Syntax...* feature. At any time during development, you can test a JSP or XSQL page in your browser by running it directly from your project. To run either a JSP or XSQL page, do the following:

1. Select *YourFile.xsql* or *YourFile.jsp* in the project navigator.
2. Select *Run* from the right mouse button menu.

If the *Run* item in the right mouse button menu is disabled, make sure that your project is set up to debug files as a "Normal Java Class" and not as "Remote Debugging". To verify this, select the *Project → Project Properties...* menu, click on the *Run/Debug* tab, and look at the value of the *Debug Files as* pop-up list. This value needs to be set to "Normal Java Class"—the default—to run JSP or XSQL pages.

In order to run JSP or XSQL pages from your project, you must include the appropriate JSP and/or XSQL Runtime libraries in your project's library list. To check the contents of your project's library list, select *Project → Project Properties...* from the main menu and click on the *Libraries* tab of the *Project Properties* dialog. You'll see something like the display shown in Figure 4-5.

To properly run XSQL pages from the JDeveloper environment, you need the *XSQL Runtime* library in your library list. For JSP pages, you need the *JSP Runtime* library. If the appropriate library is not in the list for your current project, click the *Add...* button and select it from the list of defined libraries. Note that each project in a workspace has its own project property settings, so you might have to perform this operation for each project.

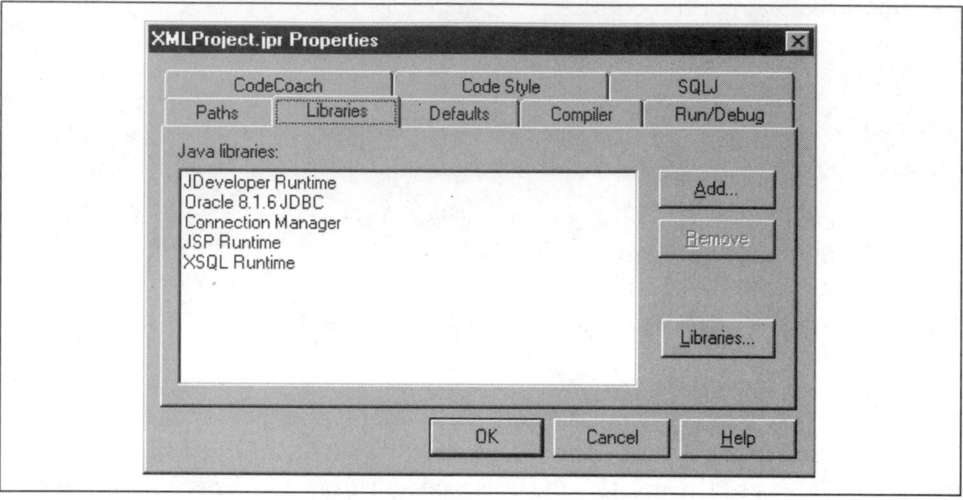

Figure 4-5. List of libraries for a project

When you run a JSP or XSQL page from your project, JDeveloper does the following for you:

1. Starts—or automatically restarts—the Oracle JSP Runner or the Oracle XSQL Servlet as appropriate using the Oracle Web-to-go web server on port 7070
2. Sets the web server's virtual filesystem to map onto your project's HTML path
3. Launches your default browser if one is not currently running
4. Requests the page you're running in your browser using the URL *http://yourmachine:7070/YourCurrentProject/YourFile.xsql*

While you are running your XSQL or JSP page from your project, you can make edits to:

- XSQL pages, to change any aspect of their functionality
- XSLT stylesheets being used by your XSQL pages
- JSP page source

You can see the effects of your changes instantaneously by refreshing your browser. Before refreshing your browser, you should use the *Check XML Syntax...* feature on your edited files and make sure your XSQL pages and XSLT stylesheets are well-formed to avoid getting an error from the XSQL Servlet complaining about their syntax. Note that the JSP pages you've edited while running require on-the-fly recompilation. This is handled automatically by the Oracle JSP Runner but may cause a noticeable delay on the first request of the changed JSP page. Since XSQL pages and associated XSLT stylesheets are *templates* and not compiled Java classes, no recompilation delay for edited XSLT stylesheets or XSQL pages is necessary.

If after editing your XSQL, XSLT, or JSP files you refresh your browser and do *not* see the changes you are expecting, typically it is because you have forgotten to save the edited files to disk in JDeveloper. If you notice that their names are italicized in the project navigator, just select *File* → *Save All...* from the menu and try refreshing your browser again.

Note that for JSP pages, it is also possible to select the *Debug* menu from a page's right mouse button menu in the project navigator to debug the JSP page locally. This means that as you request pages through your web server, you can hit breakpoints and step through the Java code in your JSP pages.

When running XSQL pages from within the JDeveloper 3.1 environment, the XSQL Servlet picks up its configuration information from the *XSQLConfig.xml* file in the *.\lib* subdirectory of your JDeveloper installation home. To add or change the properties related to the named database connection definitions used by the XSQL page processor, edit this file and modify the `<connectiondefs>` section as indicated by the comments in the file.

Understanding Project Path Settings

If you receive an error message like:

```
J:\myprojects\MyPage.xsql must reside in the
HTML root directory or a subdirectory beneath it.
```

when you attempt to run an XSQL or JSP page, this means your page's source file is not located under the HTML root directory defined for the project. All of your project's path settings are visible on the *Paths* tab of the *Project Properties* dialog as shown in Figure 4-6.

To allow for multiple projects in a workspace to share the same virtual root directory when running JSP or XSQL files, each JDeveloper project has the following two HTML-related path settings:

HTML root directory

This is the physical directory to use as the Web-to-go server's "virtual root" while running JSP or XSQL pages in your project. While running pages inside the JDeveloper environment, this directory corresponds to the URL:

```
http://yourmachine:7070/
```

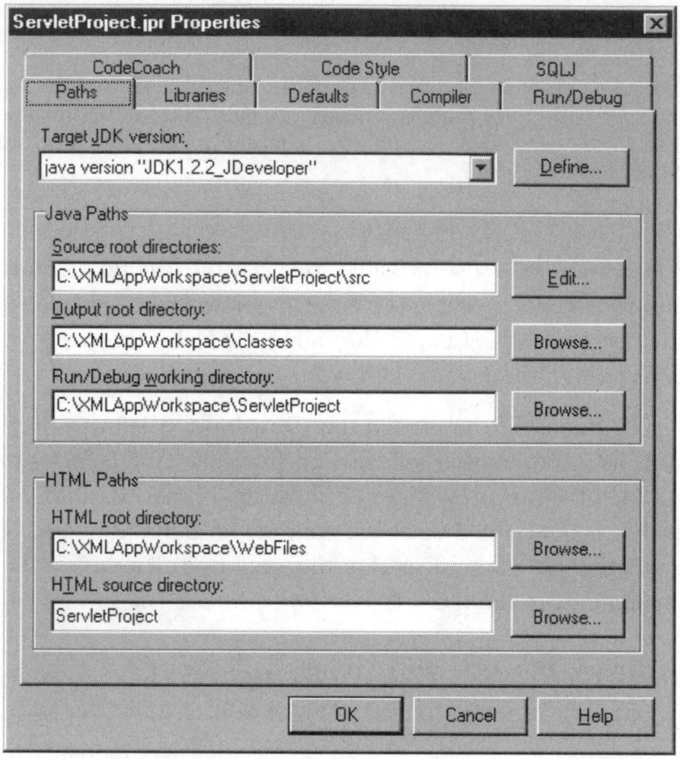

Figure 4-6. HTML root directory in the Project Properties Paths tab

HTML source directory

This is a physical subdirectory of the directory. It contains the current project's web-related files: *.jsp*, *.xsql*, *.html*, *.gif*, etc. While running pages inside the JDeveloper environment, this directory corresponds to the URL:

```
http://yourmachine:7070/HTMLSourceDirectoryName/
```

By setting the HTML root directory to the same physical directory for multiple projects in the workspace, you can refer to web-related files *across* projects while running a page from any one of them. So if you have a workspace with projects named `ServletProject` and `XMLProject`, and you have their respective HTML paths set like this:

- HTML Paths for `ServletProject:`

```
HTML Root Directory   = C:\XMLAppWorkspace\Webfiles
HTML Source Directory = ServletProject
```

- HTML Paths for `XMLProject:`

```
HTML Root Directory   = C:\XMLAppWorkspace\Webfiles
HTML Source Directory = XMLProject
```

then while running any XSQL or JSP page from `ServletProject` using the URL:

```
http://yourmachine:7070/ServletProject/SomePage.xsql
```

you can refer to files from the `XMLProject` using a URL like:

```
http://yourmachine:7070/XMLProject/AnotherPage.xsql
```

without restarting the web server.

In addition to the HTML path settings, each project also has Java-related path settings for:

Source root directories
: A semicolon-separated list of one or more root directory names containing Java source code files for the project

Output root directory
: The root directory where Java *.class* files are written during compilation

Run/Debug working directory
: The directory that a Java program being run or debugged will "see" as the current operating system directory during execution

Figure 4-7 shows the filesystem structure of a typical JDeveloper workspace with multiple projects related to XML application development.

Source code root directories for the `ServletProject` and `XMLProject` can be organized under a single physical directory or not, as you wish. However, it is important that both `ServletProject` and `XMLProject` have the *same* directory path settings for the following directories:

HTML root directory
: So their web-related files can be cross-referenced while running pages in the JDeveloper environment

Output root directory
: So any classes that they share at runtime will be found in the CLASSPATH

Following these suggestions should further simplify your Java/XML-related development using JDeveloper 3.1.

Working with Database Objects

All of the examples in this book use a database account named XMLBOOK that you'll need to create to follow along and try out any code we discuss. In this section, we create an XMLBOOK user and explore JDeveloper 3.1's features for working with database objects in the development environment.

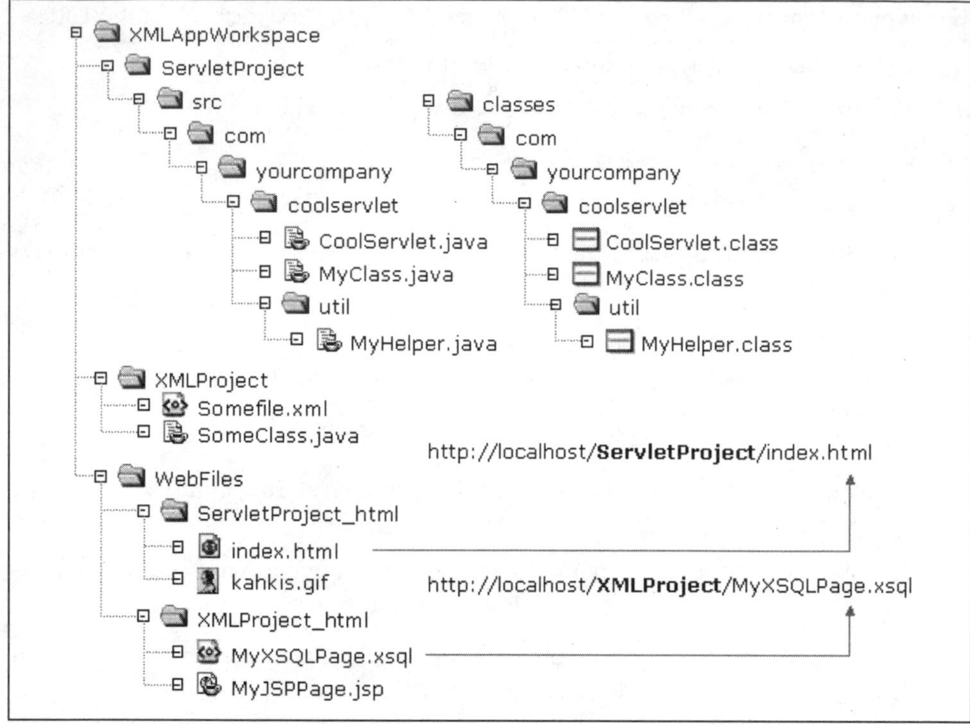

Figure 4-7. Sample directory structure of a typical Java/XML project

Creating the XMLBOOK User to Run the Examples

To create the XMLBOOK user, connect to your Oracle database as a DBA account like SYS or SYSTEM using the SQL*Plus tool and issue the following commands:

```
SQL> CREATE USER xmlbook IDENTIFIED BY xmlbook;
User created.
SQL> GRANT connect, resource, query rewrite TO xmlbook;
Grant succeeded.
```

Then try to connect as the new XMLBOOK user and try a simple SELECT statement by doing the following:

```
SQL> CONNECT xmlbook/xmlbook
Connected
SQL> SELECT sysdate FROM dual;
SYSDATE
---------
23-APR-00
```

If this works, then you're ready to go create a named connection for XMLBOOK inside the JDeveloper 3.1 environment.

Defining and Browsing Database Connections

JDeveloper 3.1 has a number of built-in features for working more easily with Oracle database objects. You can define any number of commonly used database connections that are then available for all workspaces and projects. After starting JDeveloper 3.1, you'll notice a *Connections* folder at the top of the project navigator. Double-clicking on this folder or selecting *Connections...* from the right mouse button menu option on the folder brings up the JDeveloper *Connection Manager* dialog. From here you can create, edit, delete, import, and export connection definitions for databases you frequently work with during development. Click the *New...* button to define a new connection to work with our XMLBOOK user. The *Connection* dialog shown in Figure 4-8 appears.

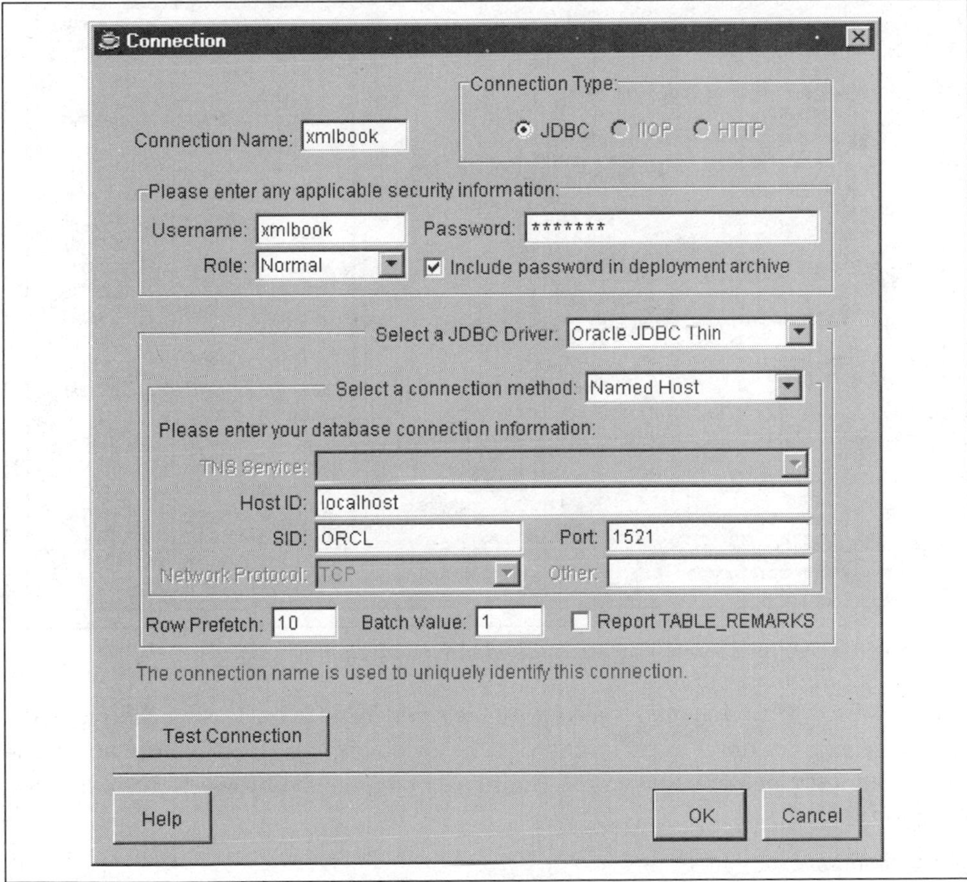

Figure 4-8. Defining a new named connection

Enter the username of XMLBOOK and password of XMLBOOK and click on the *Test Connection* button to see if the JDBC connection information is correct for your database. The default values typically work for a local Oracle database running on the same machine as JDeveloper, but if you are working with a database on another machine, set the host, SID, and port values appropriately until clicking on *Test Connection* gives you a `Success!` message. Click *OK* on the *Connection* dialog and *Done* on the *Connection Manager* and we're ready to go.

You can use JDeveloper's built-in database browsing facilities by selecting your named `xmlbook` connection in the *Connections* folder of the project navigator and selecting the *Open Viewer As → Database Browser* option off the right mouse button menu as shown in Figure 4-9.

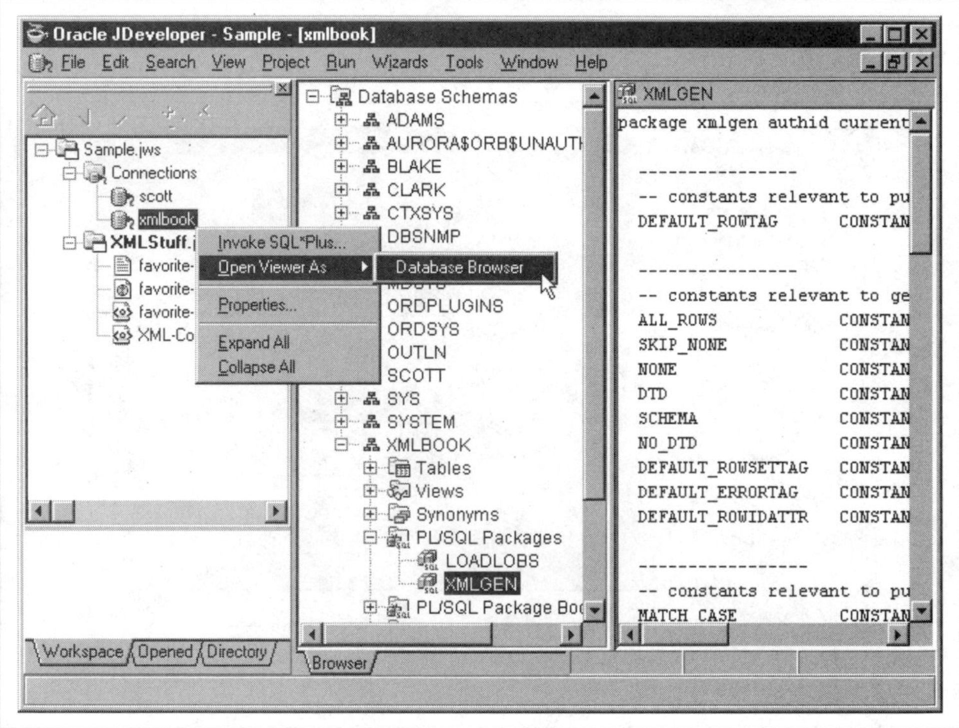

Figure 4-9. Browsing schema objects for a database connection

You can browse all schema objects to which you have access using the database browser's tree control. For each kind of schema object you select, where appropriate, additional details appear in the right-hand pane of the browser. For example, selecting a:

Table or View
: Displays information on its columns

PL/SQL Package, Package Body, Procedure, Function, or Trigger
: Displays its PL/SQL source code

Sequence

Displays its last value, and minimum, maximum, and increment values

Object Type

Displays the source code of its type specification

By expanding the *Deployed Java Classes* folder in the browser, you can inspect the Java package hierarchy of all Java classes (to which you have access) that have been loaded into JServer. In Figure 4-10, we can see that the Oracle XML Parser for Java has been loaded into JServer by the presence of the `oracle.xml.parser.v2` packages.

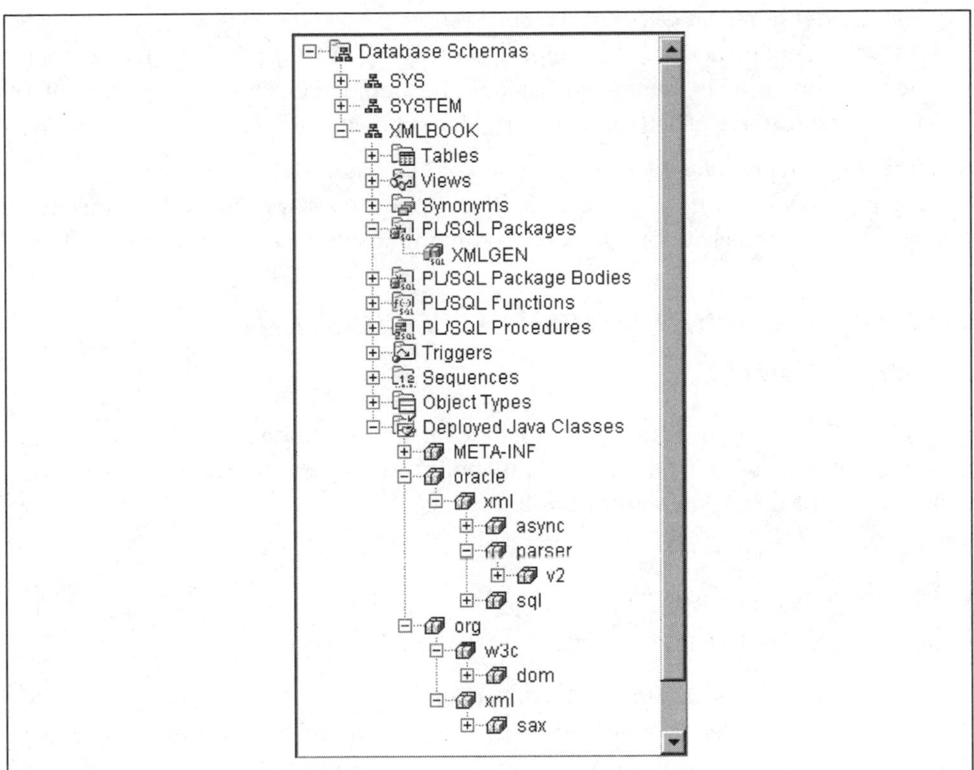

Figure 4-10. Browsing schema objects for a connection

Expanding a package node in the browser displays all classes in that package as well as subpackages. Clicking on a specific class shows its decompiled method signatures in the details panel.

In addition to browsing the contents of a named connection that you've defined, connections are also used by JDeveloper 3.1 for automatically:

*Launching SQL*Plus on a connection*
: Just select the connection in the navigator and choose *Invoke SQL*Plus*... from the right mouse button menu.

Running any SQL script on a connection
: Just select the SQL script in your project and select *Invoke SQL*Plus*... from the right mouse button menu. A submenu allows you to pick which connection you'd like to run the script under.

Deploying Java stored procedures to a connection
: As we'll see in detail in Chapter 6, *Processing XML with Java*, JDeveloper's deployment profiles feature automates the deployment and redeployment of Java code to the Oracle8*i* server using named connections.

Starting the JServer remote debug agent on a connection
: Again, as we'll see in Chapter 6, JDeveloper uses the named connections when you remotely debug Java code running inside Oracle8*i*'s JServer VM.

Using JDeveloper with Oracle XDK Components

Oracle's XML Developer's Kit (XDK) includes many of the enabling XML technologies that we'll be using in the rest of this book. Among other components, it contains Java and PL/SQL versions of the following:

- Oracle XML Parser
- Oracle XSLT Processor
- Oracle XML SQL Utility

In addition, it includes an Oracle XSQL Servlet that comes with a Java API for adding your own so-called *action handlers* and programmatically processing XSQL Pages templates. In the following sections, we'll discuss the basics of setting up JDeveloper to work with these Oracle XDK components in Java. While JDeveloper 3.1 does offer color-coded syntax editing of PL/SQL and the ability to browse stored procedures and run the SQL scripts against a named database connection, most of the true developer productivity features in the product target Java development (as you'd assume from the "J" in JDeveloper).

Adding Oracle XDK Libraries to Your Project

To dramatically simplify working with libraries of Java code in your projects, JDeveloper 3.1 has a facility called *named libraries.* Each library consists of:

- A user-friendly library name like "Oracle XML Parser 2.0."
- A Class path comprising one or more *.jar* files, *.zip* files, or directories separated by semicolons, containing the executable classes to support the library; for example, *J:\lib\xmlparserv2.jar.*
- An optional Source path comprising one or more *.jar* files, *.zip* files, or directories containing the Java source code for the library.
- An optional Doc path comprising one or more *.jar* files, *.zip* files, or directories containing the JavaDoc HTML files for the library.

To use the functionality provided by a library in your project, do the following:

1. Select *Project → Project Properties...* from the main menu.
2. Click on the *Libraries* tab in the *Project Properties* dialog.
3. Click on the *Add...* button on the *Libraries* tab to select a library to add to your project's library list.
4. Select a library to add from the list that appears.
5. Click *OK.*

In the *Libraries* tab of the *Project Properties* dialog, notice the *Java libraries* list. This is an ordered list of the libraries your project depends on. The order of the library names in this list is very significant because their order directly controls the order of the *.jar* files, *.zip* files, and directories in the Java CLASSPATH of the compilation and runtime environment for the current project. You can use drag-and-drop to rearrange the order of the libraries in the library list.

So, rather than fighting with CLASSPATH settings—one of the biggest frustrations of Java developers the world over—you simply pick the libraries you need and they, in turn, are used by JDeveloper to control the CLASSPATH.

JDeveloper 3.1 comes preconfigured with Java libraries to work with the principal Oracle XML Developer's Kit components: Java SDKs and JDBC libraries. This means that building custom XML applications in Java using the Oracle XDK is a matter of simply picking the library you want to work with and adding it to your project's library list. Table 4-4 shows the most common tasks you might want to perform and which built-in named libraries you add to your project to accomplish them.

Table 4-4. Built-in Libraries for XML Application Development

If you want to do this	Add this library to your project
Connect to an Oracle database	Oracle 8.1.6 JDBC
Produce XML from SQL queries	Oracle XML SQL Utility
Save XML documents into tables/views	Oracle XML SQL Utility
Parse XML documents using DOM or SAX	Oracle XML Parser 2.0
Transform XML documents using XSLT	Oracle XML Parser 2.0
Searching XML documents using XPath	Oracle XML Parser 2.0
Construct XML documents using DOM	Oracle XML Parser 2.0
Build servlets to process or return XML	Servlet SDK
Run XSQL Pages	XSQL Runtime
Build custom XSQL action handlers	XSQL Runtime
Process XSQL pages programmatically	XSQL Runtime
Compile/run JSP from your project	JSP Runtime

You can use JDeveloper's library facility to create your own libraries as well to complement the built-in library names. To create your own library to manage code you frequently need to use in other projects, do the following:

1. Select *Project → Project Properties...* from the main menu.
2. Click on the *Libraries* tab in the *Project Properties* dialog.
3. Click on the *Libraries...* button on the right edge of the *Libraries* tab to call up the *Available Java Libraries* dialog.
4. Click on the *New* button.

An Untitled library entry appears, as shown in Figure 4-11, and you can enter the new library Name, Class path, and optional Source and Doc paths, then click *OK*.

If you find yourself using a library in almost every project you create, you can add the library to the *Default Project Properties* library list so that every new project will contain that library upon creation. For example, to add your new "My Really Useful XML Code" library to the *Default Project Properties* library list, follow these steps:

1. Select *Tools → Default Project Properties...* from the main menu.
2. Select the *Libraries* tab.
3. Click on the *Add...* button to add your library to the list, as shown in Figure 4-12.

Now any subsequently created projects will have your library by default. You can add built-in libraries as well as any libraries you create yourself to this list.

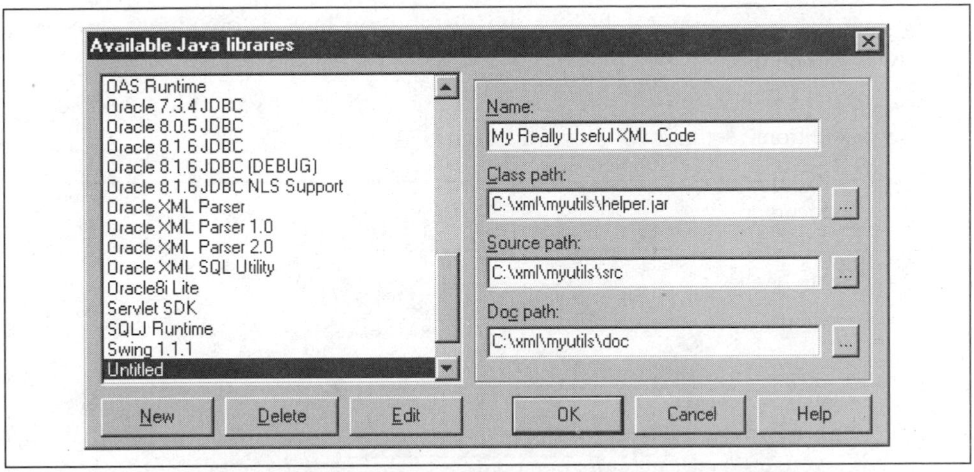

Figure 4-11. Creating a new library definition

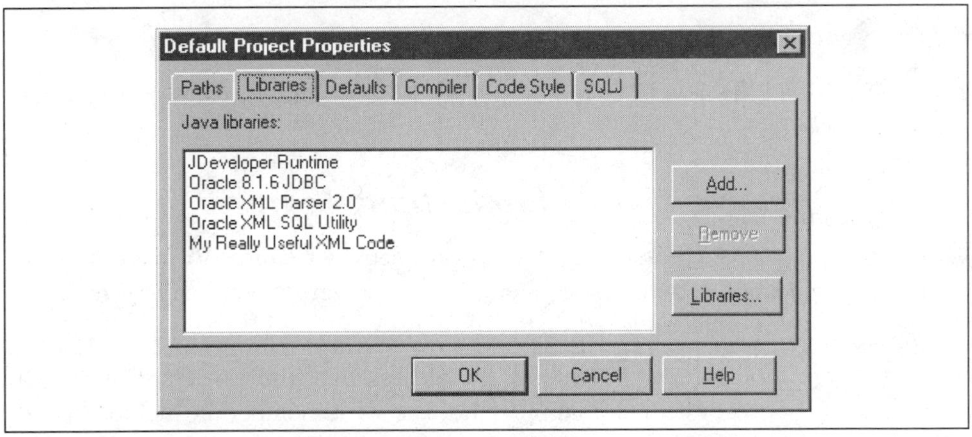

Figure 4-12. Defining default libraries for all new projects

Updated versions of the Oracle XDK Components for Java are released frequently on the Oracle Technology Network (OTN) web site. As a result of this rapid release pace, it is very possible that the version of the XDK libraries that ships with the JDeveloper 3.1 release on the accompanying CD-ROM is no longer the most current version available. You should check the XML home page at OTN at the following URL:

> *http://technet.oracle.com/tech/xml*

to see if more recent versions are available for any of the Oracle XDK Java components. If you find that a new version is available, simply do the following:

1. Download the latest release of the XDK component from OTN. Let's say, for example, that you discover that a new version 2.0.2.9 of the Oracle XML Parser for Java is now available.

2. Extract the *.tar.gz* or *.zip* file for the distribution into a convenient directory; for example, into *C:\xmlparserv2_2.0.2.9*.
3. Create a new library in JDeveloper to work with it; for example, we'd set up the new library settings as shown in Figure 4-13.

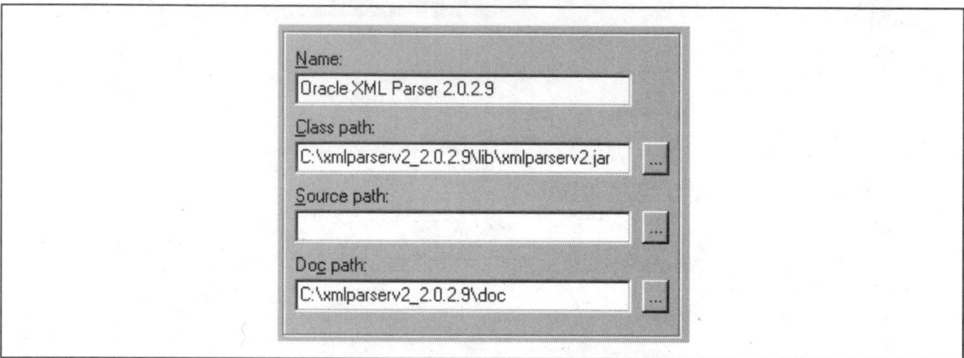

Figure 4-13. Defining path information for a new library

Then we can add the new "Oracle XML Parser 2.0.2.9" library to any project where we want to use it.

Using JDeveloper Coding Productivity Features

JDeveloper 3.1 offers a number of coding productivity features to make building your XML application code in Java easier. Here we cover the key features to which you will quickly become addicted.

While you are typing code, JDeveloper's Code Insight feature watches what you are doing and is ready to help simplify the task of remembering method names and method arguments for any class you work with. Any time you type a dot between an object and a method name, JDeveloper pops up a context-sensitive list of the methods that are relevant to call on the object, as shown in Figure 4-14.

After typing just enough of the leading letters of the method name you want—or alternatively, using the up/down arrow keys—you can hit Return and JDeveloper fills in the rest of the method name for you. As soon as you type the opening parenthesis to pass the arguments to the method, the Code Insight feature pops up another context-sensitive list of all overloadings, arguments, and their datatypes that are relevant as shown in Figure 4-15.

If there are multiple arguments, Code Insight will step through the arguments in the pop-up help, keeping the current argument required and its datatype in bold.

```
C:\xmlbook\src\examples\xml-basics-java\XPathValidator.java
import java.net.URL;
import oracle.xml.parser.v2.*;
import org.w3c.dom.*;

public class XPathValidator {
  public static void main(String[] args) throws Exception {
    if (args.length == 2) {
      XPathValidator xpv = new XPathValidator();
      xpv.validate(args[0],args[1]);
    }
    else errorExit("usage: XPathValidator xmlfile rulesfile");
  }
  //Validate an XML Document against a set of XPath Validation Rule
  public void validate(String filename, String rulesfile) throws Ex
    // Parse the file to be validated and the rules file
    XMLDocument source = XMLHelper.parse(URLUtils.newURL(filename))
    XMLDocument rules  = XMLHelper.  Method   formatParseError : String
    // Get the name of the Ruleset   Method   parse : XMLDocument
    String ruleset = rules.valueOf(
    if (ruleset.equals("")) errorExit("Not a valid ruleset file.");
    System.out.println("Validating "+filename+" against " +ruleset+
    // Select all the <rule>'s in the ruleset to evaluate
    NodeList ruleList = rules.selectNodes("/ruleset/rule");
    int rulesFound    = ruleList.getLength();
    if (rulesFound < 1) errorExit("No rules found in "+rulesfile);
Source  Design  Class  Doc    16: 36    Modified    Insert
```

Figure 4-14. Code Insight assists with methods as you type

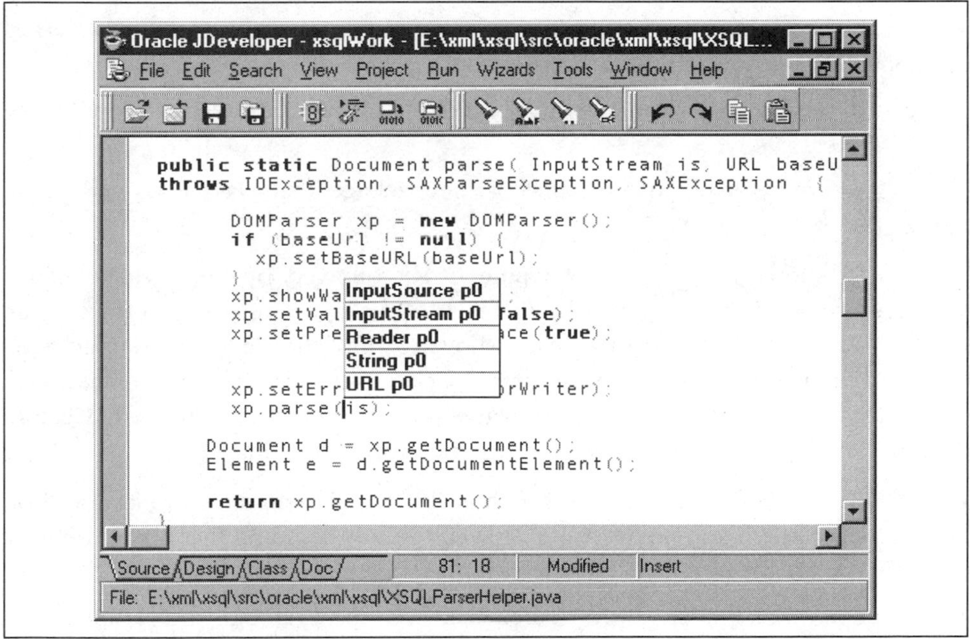

Figure 4-15. Code Insight assists with method arguments

If you find that the Code Insight feature is not working for you, it's probably for one of the following reasons:

- JDeveloper cannot deduce what type your object is because of a typo or because your code has not yet declared the object. To resolve this, check for typos and/or define the variable properly in your code.
- You're using a class that you have not imported. To resolve this, add an appropriate `import` statement to the top of your class.
- You've forgotten to add the appropriate library to your project's library list that contains the current class. To resolve this, add the appropriate library to your project's library list.
- Your code contains some horrible syntax error and JDeveloper's Code Insight parser gets confused by it. To resolve this, try compiling your class to find the culprit.

To browse the source code of any class you have two choices:

- If it's the class for an object your code is currently working with, click the right mouse button over the class or variable in your code and select *Browse Symbol at Cursor.*
- If it's a class that just pops into your head, press Ctrl-/ and a *Goto:* box appears in the status line at the very bottom of the JDeveloper window. Then:
  - — If you remember the fully qualified name of the class, type it in and press Enter.
  - — Otherwise, type in the name of the package that class is in and press Enter.

Figure 4-16 shows an example of typing Ctrl-/ followed by the package name `javax.servlet.http`, followed by Enter. The package appears for browsing in the *Opened* tab of the project navigator, showing all of the classes in the package. Single-clicking on any of the classes in the package shows a structural breakdown of all of its members in the "Structure Pane" located below the project navigator. Double-clicking on any class summons up one of the following:

- The class's source code in a code editor, if it is a class in the current project or if it is a class in a library on your project's library path and that library defines a "Source path" so JDeveloper can find the source.
- A decompiled version of the source which is good enough to see the methods and arguments.

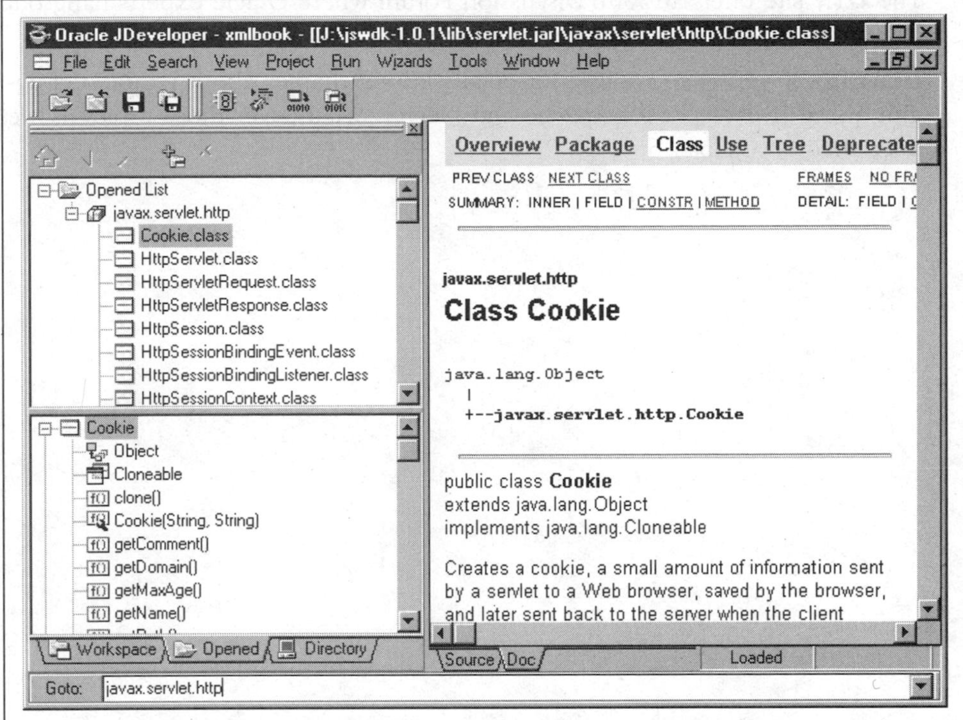

Figure 4-16. Quickly jump to the source code and JavaDoc of any class

Clicking on the *Doc* tab of any code editor causes one of two things to occur:

- The class's JavaDoc appears if it is a class in a library on your project's library path and that library defines a "Doc path" so JDeveloper can find the JavaDoc.
- Otherwise, JDeveloper shows a blank page with "No JavaDoc found".

So you can very quickly refer to the structure, source, and JavaDoc for any class in any library you use. Each of these features is small in and of itself, but put together they "nickel and dime" their way to saving you lots and lots of time.

Final Observations

I'll close this chapter with a few final observations:

- Don't underestimate the power of the Oracle Technology Network web site. If you do nothing else, try searching its online "Documentation" archive. This archive has every manual of every product Oracle has shipped in the last ten years indexed using Oracle and interMedia for fast searching and fewer dead trees. Reference information right at your fingertips!

- The OTN site offers an XML Discussion Forum where Oracle experts hang out and answer questions. It's a great resource.
- Don't fret if you were waiting for details in this chapter about remote debugging using JDeveloper for Apache and JServer. We'll cover those topics as we need them in Chapter 6.

In this chapter:

- *Loading External XML Files*
- *Parsing XML*
- *Searching XML Documents with XPath*
- *Working with XML Messages*
- *Producing and Transforming XML Query Results*

5 *Processing XML with PL/SQL*

PL/SQL is Oracle's procedural language extension to SQL, and is the database programming language familiar to nearly all Oracle DBAs and application developers. In this chapter, we'll study lots of examples that illustrate how to perform basic XML processing using PL/SQL. In particular, we'll learn how to:

- Load external XML files into the database
- Parse XML using the Oracle XML Parser for PL/SQL
- Search XML documents in memory using XPath expressions
- Post an XML message to another server and get an XML response back
- Enqueue and dequeue XML messages from Oracle Advanced Queuing (AQ) queues

In addition, in this chapter we'll cover the basic mechanics of producing XML automatically from SQL queries and transforming the results into any desired XML format using XSLT stylesheets. Both of these topics are covered in full in their own chapters later in the book. For an abbreviated overview of PL/SQL itself, see Chapter 10, *Generating Datagrams with PL/SQL*.

Along the way, we'll build up several useful PL/SQL packages that you can use to simplify basic XML processing from within your own PL/SQL stored procedures, functions, packages, and database triggers. The full source code for these XML helper packages appears in Appendix A, *XML Helper Packages*, and is available on the O'Reilly web site. Let's dive right in.

Loading External XML Files

When a developer is setting out to store the contents of an XML document in the database to perform queries over its content and structure, one of the first questions that arises is, "How do I get XML files in there?" While in Chapter 12, *Storing XML Datagrams*, we explore numerous techniques available for storing XML in the database, here we'll start simple and work through the steps of loading an existing XML file into a CLOB column.

CLOB (pronounced "klob" or "see-lob") stands for *C*haracter *L*arge *OB*ject. You can think of a column of type CLOB as a very, very large VARCHAR2. It can hold character-based data like XML documents as large as four gigabytes (4GB).

Assume that we have an XML document like *claim77804.xml* below in a directory named *C:\XMLFILES* on the filesystem of the machine where our database is installed:

```
<!-- claim77804.xml -->
<Claim>
  <ClaimId>77804</ClaimId>
  <Policy>12345</Policy>
  <Settlements>
    <Payment Approver="JCOX">1000</Payment>
    <Payment Approver="PSMITH">1850</Payment>
  </Settlements>
  <DamageReport>
    The insured's <Vehicle Make="Volks">Beetle</Vehicle>
    broke through the guard rail and plummeted into a ravine.
    The cause was determined to be <Cause>faulty brakes</Cause>.
    Amazingly there were no casualties.
  </DamageReport>
</Claim>
```

Since operating systems differ in their file and directory naming conventions, Oracle abstracts these details with a logical directory object. You create a logical directory with the command:

```
CREATE DIRECTORY directoryname AS 'OS-Specific-Dirname';
```

You then use the logical directory name `directoryname` when working with files inside PL/SQL. In order to create a logical directory, use SQL*Plus to connect to the database as a user with the CREATE ANY DIRECTORY privilege. The SYS and SYSTEM users have this privilege by default, so the easiest way to proceed is to connect as SYS or SYSTEM and create the directory with:

```
CREATE DIRECTORY xmlfiles AS 'C:\xmlfiles';
```

Once the logical directory name exists, you can grant READ permission on the directory to another user like XMLBOOK with the command:

```
GRANT READ ON DIRECTORY xmlfiles TO xmlbook;
```

This enables the XMLBOOK user to read files from the *XMLFILES* directory. To verify this, you can connect to the database as XMLBOOK and issue the SELECT statement:

```
SELECT directory_name,directory_path
  FROM all_directories;
```

which gives a list of all the directories to which XMLBOOK has access:

```
DIRECTORY_NAME                 DIRECTORY_PATH
------------------------------ --------------------
XMLFILES                       C:\xmlfiles
```

Any time you want to refer to an operating system file in PL/SQL, you use the built-in datatype for external files called a BFILE. To refer to our existing *claim77804.xml* file in the *XMLFILES* directory, we use the special **BFileName()** function, whose syntax is:

```
BFileName('logical-directory-name','filename').
```

Let's immediately put this file to use. For example, we can determine the length of the *claim77804.xml* file with the SELECT statement:

```
SELECT DBMS_LOB.getLength( BFileName('XMLFILES','claim77804.xml'))
       AS length
  FROM dual;
```

which uses one of the functions in the built-in **DBMS_LOB** package to determine the length of a BFILE object, returning the result:

```
LENGTH
----------
       488
```

Now we're ready to load the document into the database. We have two choices:

- Save a handle to the external file in a column of type BFILE
- Save a copy of the contents of the external file in a column of type CLOB

The BFILE column offers an option that occupies virtually no space inside the database (just a file pointer) but restricts the contents of the external document to be read-only. The CLOB column option takes up space in the database but is fully readable and writable. As we'll see in Chapter 13, *Searching XML with interMedia*, XML documents in both BFILEs and CLOBs can be indexed for fast XML document searching across millions of rows. The need for the document content to be writable and/or the desire to have the content completely inside the database (where it cannot be accessed by file-based tools) are the factors in deciding whether to use CLOBs over BFILEs.

Let's study the CLOB example. We can create a simple table named xml_documents having a "document name" as a primary key and the body of the XML document in a CLOB column:

```
CREATE TABLE xml_documents (
  docname     VARCHAR2(200) PRIMARY KEY,
  xmldoc      CLOB,
  timestamp   DATE
);
```

By adding a database trigger, we can have the table automatically maintain the last modified `timestamp` column on any XML documents stored in this table:

```
CREATE TRIGGER xml_documents_timestamp
BEFORE INSERT OR UPDATE ON xml_documents
FOR EACH ROW
BEGIN
  :new.timestamp := SYSDATE;
END;
```

With the xml_documents table in place, we're ready to start inserting XML documents into it. To store an external XML file into our xml_documents table, follow these steps:

1. Insert a new row into xml_documents with an empty CLOB for the `xmldoc` column.
2. Retrieve the empty CLOB into a variable.
3. Get a BFILE handle to the external file.
4. Open the file for reading.
5. Copy the contents of the file into the CLOB variable.
6. Close the file and COMMIT.

Example 5-1 shows a sample `insertXMLFile` stored procedure that accepts as arguments the directory name, the filename, and the name you'd like to associate with the document as its primary key. Then it performs the six steps above to store the external file into the xml_documents table.

Example 5-1. Inserting an External XML File into a CLOB

```
CREATE OR REPLACE PROCEDURE insertXmlFile( dir VARCHAR2,
                                           file VARCHAR2,
                                           name VARCHAR2 := NULL) IS
  theBFile    BFILE;
  theCLob     CLOB;
  theDocName VARCHAR2(200) := NVL(name,file);
```

Example 5-1. Inserting an External XML File into a CLOB (continued)

```
BEGIN
  -- (1) Insert a new row into xml_documents with an empty CLOB, and
  -- (2) Retrieve the empty CLOB into a variable with RETURNING..INTO

  INSERT INTO xml_documents(docname,xmldoc) VALUES(theDocName,empty_clob())
  RETURNING xmldoc INTO theCLob;

  -- (3) Get a BFile handle to the external file
  theBFile := BFileName(dir,file);

  -- (4) Open the file
  dbms_lob.fileOpen(theBFile);

  -- (5) Copy the contents of the BFile into the empty CLOB
  dbms_lob.loadFromFile(dest_lob => theCLob,
                        src_lob => theBFile,
                        amount  => dbms_lob.getLength(theBFile));

  -- (6) Close the file and commit
  dbms_lob.fileClose(theBFile);
  COMMIT;
END;
```

With the `insertXmlFile` procedure now in place, from the SQL*Plus command-line we can execute the stored procedure to load *claim77804.xml* from the *XMLFILES* directory using the syntax:

```
EXEC insertXmlFile('XMLFILES','claim77804.xml')
```

Directory names are case-sensitive and are created in uppercase by default, like other database object names. So this syntax:

```
CREATE DIRECTORY mydir AS 'F:\files\mydir';
```

creates a directory object named `MYDIR`, while:

```
CREATE DIRECTORY  "AnotherDir" AS 'W:\another\mydir';
```

creates a directory object named `AnotherDir`. When using the `BFileName()` constructor to refer to a file in a directory, the directory name is always case-sensitive, and the filename is case-sensitive if filenames on the operating system of your database server are case-sensitive. So if the directory object is named MYDIR, the function `BFileName('mydir','myfile.xml')` will fail because you referred to the directory object's name in lowercase.

Note this line in the example:

```
theDocName VARCHAR2(200) := NVL(name,file);
```

This ensures that if you do not pass in the optional third argument to assign a meaningful name to the file being stored, the value of `theDocName` will default to the name of the file being loaded and will be used during the insert as the value of the docname column in the xml_documents table.

Parsing XML

The Oracle XML Parser for PL/SQL provides PL/SQL developers with a set of APIs for parsing, manipulating, and transforming XML documents inside the database. As we'll see in Chapter 6, *Processing XML with Java*, these same APIs are available to Java programmers as well using the Oracle XML Parser for Java. As illustrated in Figure 5-1, in Oracle8*i* Releases 1, 2, and 3—server versions 8.1.5, 8.1.6, and 8.1.7, respectively—the Oracle XML Parser for PL/SQL is a set of PL/SQL packages that expose the underlying functionality of the XML Parser for Java. In the 8.1.7 release, the XML Parser for Java is natively compiled inside the server for better performance.

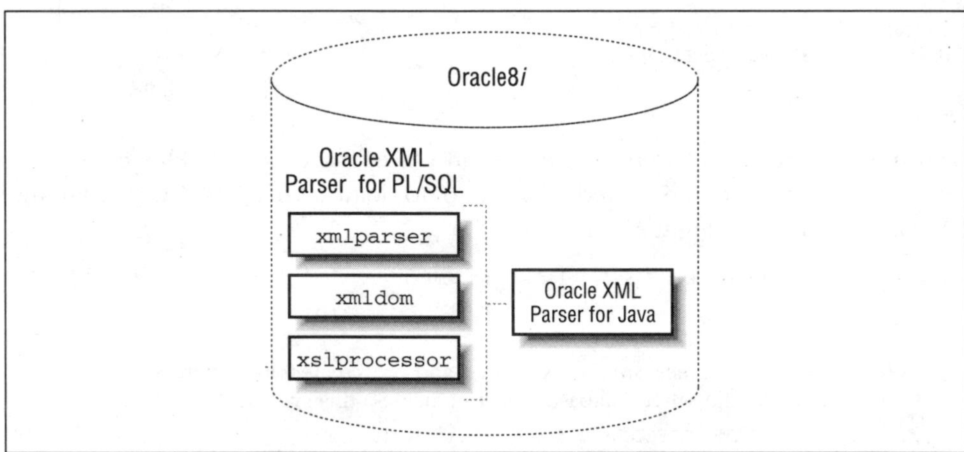

Figure 5-1. XML Parser for PL/SQL wraps the XML Parser for Java

The packages included in the Oracle XML Parser for PL/SQL are listed in Table 5-1.

Table 5-1. Key PL/SQL Packages for Working with XML

PL/SQL Package Name	Description
xmlparser	Contains datatypes, functions, and procedures for parsing XML
xmldom	Contains datatypes, functions, and procedures for creating and manipulating the members of an XML document's object model like elements, attributes, text, comments, etc.
xslprocessor	Contains datatypes, functions, and procedures for transforming XML documents using XSLT stylesheets and searching an in-memory XML document using XPath expressions

In this chapter, we build up various PL/SQL helper packages that centralize the key functionality from the `xmlparser`, `xmldom`, and `xslprocessor` packages. However, for your reference, full API documentation for these packages is available in the *./doc* subdirectory of the XML Parser for PL/SQL distribution that you can download from the Oracle Technology Network at *http://technet.oracle.com/tech/xml*.

By the end of this chapter we'll have made extensive use of all of these facilities. But before we can use the Oracle XML Parser for PL/SQL inside Oracle8*i*, we should check that it's installed properly.

We require the Oracle XML Parser for PL/SQL Release 1.0.2 or greater for the examples in this section. This is the default version that ships with Oracle8*i* Release 3 (8.1.7), but if you are using an earlier release of Oracle8*i*, you can download the appropriate release from the Oracle Technology Network web site.

Installing Oracle XML Parser for PL/SQL

We first need to make sure that the XML Parser for Java is properly installed, since the XML Parser for PL/SQL depends on it. You can verify proper installation by doing the following:

1. Connect to your Oracle8*i* database with SQL*Plus:

   ```
   sqlplus xmlbook/xmlbook
   ```

2. Check the status of the `oracle.xml.parser.v2.DOMParser` class by running the following SQL statement:

   ```
   SELECT SUBSTR(dbms_java.longname(object_name),1,30) AS class, status
     FROM all_objects
    WHERE object_type = 'JAVA CLASS'
      AND object_name = dbms_java.shortname('oracle/xml/parser/v2/DOMParser');
   ```

If you see the result:

```
CLASS                          STATUS
------------------------------ -------
oracle/xml/parser/v2/DOMParser VALID
```

then the Oracle XML Parser for Java is already installed and ready to be used.

If you see this result, but the status is `INVALID`, try the command:

```
ALTER JAVA CLASS "oracle/xml/parser/v2/DOMParser" RESOLVE
```

If the parser is installed, you do *not* need to complete any further installation steps.

If the verification procedure produces the SQL*Plus message `no rows selected`, complete the following steps to install the Oracle XML Parser for Java in your Oracle8*i* database:

1. Locate the *xmlparserv2.jar* file that contains the executable code for the XML Parser for Java. It is bundled with the XML Parser for PL/SQL download from OTN.
2. Go to the *./lib/java* subdirectory where the *xmlparserv2.jar* file that you'll be installing is located.
3. Load the *xmlparserv2.jar* file into your schema using the `loadjava` command:

```
loadjava -verbose -resolve -user xmlbook/xmlbook xmlparserv2.jar
```

If the `loadjava` command does not appear to work, make sure that the *./bin* subdirectory of your Oracle installation home is in your system path.

Repeat the test above to confirm that the status of the class is now `VALID`, meaning the XML Parser for Java is ready to be used in the server.

Next, check to see if the Oracle XML Parser for PL/SQL is already installed in your Oracle8*i* database by doing the following:

1. Connect to your Oracle8*i* database with SQL*Plus:

```
sqlplus xmlbook/xmlbook
```

2. Try to describe the `xmlparser` package from the SQL*Plus command line:

```
DESCRIBE xmlparser
```

If you see a description of the procedures and functions in the `xmlparser` package, the Oracle XML Parser for PL/SQL is already installed and ready to be used. You do not need to complete any further installation steps.

If instead you get an error like `ORA-04043: object xmlparser does not exist`, complete the following steps to install the Oracle XML Parser for PL/SQL in your Oracle8*i* database:

1. Download the latest release of the Oracle XML Parser for PL/SQL from *http://technet.oracle.com/tech/xml*.
2. Extract the *.zip* or the *.tar.gz* file into a convenient directory.
3. Change directory to the *./lib/java* subdirectory of the distribution.

4. Load the *xmlplsql.jar* file into your schema:

   ```
   loadjava -verbose -resolve -user xmlbook/xmlbook xmlplsql.jar
   ```

5. Change directory to the *./lib/sql* subdirectory of the distribution.
6. Run the *load.sql* SQL script to create the XML Parser for PL/SQL packages:

   ```
   sqlplus xmlbook/xmlbook @load.sql
   ```

Repeat the earlier test to confirm that you can now describe the **xmlparser** package, so the XML Parser for PL/SQL is ready to be used in the server. As with any PL/SQL packages, you can GRANT EXECUTE on the **xmlparser**, **xmldom**, and **xslprocessor** packages to other database users to give them privileges to access these components.

Parsing XML from a CLOB

The **xmlparser** package provides a very straightforward API for parsing XML documents from within PL/SQL stored procedures, functions, and packages. Given an XML document in text form, the XML Parser reads the document and constructs an in-memory tree of the elements, attributes, and text content of the document. In the process of accomplishing this task, the parser will identify any syntactic errors in the document that prevent it from correctly completing the job. One useful way to use the parser is to simply verify that the XML documents you've stored in your database are well-formed.

We can check that an XML document is well-formed in just three steps:

1. Call **xmlparser.newParser** to create a new XML Parser for the job.
2. Call one of the following to parse the document: **xmlparser.parse**, **xmlparser.parseBuffer**, or **xmlparser.parseCLOB**.
3. Call **xmlparser.freeParser** to free the instance of the XML Parser.

If any syntactic problems are encountered while parsing the XML document, the PL/SQL exception number –20100 will be raised. If we declare a user-defined exception (for example, **XMLParseError**) and use the PL/SQL PRAGMA EXCEPTION_INIT to associate the named exception with the error code –20100:

```
-- Associate the XMLParseError exception with the -20100 error code
PRAGMA EXCEPTION_INIT( XMLParseError, -20100 );
```

we can then handle the exception in a PL/SQL EXCEPTION block:

```
EXCEPTION
  WHEN XMLParseError THEN
     -- Some Error Handling Code Here
```

Example 5-2 shows a **checkXMLInCLOB** stored procedure that returns a boolean status indicating whether the XML document in the CLOB you pass in is well-formed. If the document is not well-formed, the parsing error message is also returned in the `error` argument.

Example 5-2. Checking the Well-Formedness of XML in a CLOB

```
CREATE OR REPLACE PROCEDURE checkXMLInCLOB(c CLOB,
                                          wellFormed OUT BOOLEAN,
                                          error      OUT VARCHAR2) IS
  parser        xmlparser.Parser;
  xmldoc        xmldom.DOMDocument;
  XMLParseError EXCEPTION;

  -- Associate the XMLParseError exception with the -20100 error code
  PRAGMA EXCEPTION_INIT( XMLParseError, -20100 );

BEGIN

  -- (1) Create a new parser
  parser := xmlparser.newParser;

  -- (2) Attempt to parse the XML document in the CLOB
  xmlparser.ParseCLOB(parser,c);

  -- (3) Free the parser.
  xmlparser.freeParser(parser);

  -- If the parse succeeds, we'll get here
  wellFormed := TRUE;
EXCEPTION
  -- If the parse fails, we'll jump here.
  WHEN XMLParseError THEN
    xmlparser.freeParser(parser);
    wellFormed := FALSE;
    error := SQLERRM;
END;
```

Now suppose we use our **`insertXMLFile`** procedure from the SQL*Plus command line to insert the *syntaxError.xml* file in the *XMLFILES* directory:

```
<!-- syntaxError.xml (Missing quote on Vehicle Element's Make attribute) -->
<Claim>
  <ClaimId>77804</ClaimId>
  <Payment>1000</Payment>
  <DamageReport>
    The insured's <Vehicle Make=Volks">Beetle</Vehicle>
    broke through the guard rail and plummeted into a ravine.
    The cause was determined to be <Cause>faulty brakes</Cause>.
    Amazingly there were no casualties.
  </DamageReport>
</Claim>
```

by using the syntax:

```
EXEC insertXMLFile('XMLFILES','syntaxError.xml')
```

The result is that the contents of the *syntaxError.xml* file will be inserted into the xml_documents table, with the document name that defaults to the name of the file, *syntaxError.xml.*

We can then try out our **checkXMLInCLOB** procedure on the newly loaded XML document in the xml_documents table with the following anonymous block of PL/SQL:

```
SET SERVEROUTPUT ON
DECLARE
  xmlClob CLOB;
  wellFormed BOOLEAN;
  parseError VARCHAR2(200);
BEGIN

  -- Select the CLOB for the document named 'syntaxError.xml' into a variable
  SELECT xmldoc
    INTO xmlClob
    FROM xml_documents
  WHERE docname = 'syntaxError.xml';

  -- Check it for XML Well-formedness
  checkXMLInCLOB(xmlClob,wellFormed,parseError);

  -- Print out an error if it was not well-formed.
  IF NOT wellFormed THEN
    dbms_output.put_line(parseError);
  END IF;
END;
```

Blocks of PL/SQL code can be part of a named procedure, function, or package, or can be executed directly in a block of code with no name. These so-called *anonymous blocks* of PL/SQL are frequently used in SQL scripts to run a sequence of PL/SQL commands without predefining them as part of a named stored procedure, function, or package.

This retrieves the XML document from the **xmldoc** CLOB column in the xml_documents table, calls **checkXMLInCLOB** to verify whether the document is well-formed, and prints out the returned error message if it is not. In this case, executing the anonymous block of code above generates the message:

```
ORA-20100: Error occurred while parsing:
           Attribute value should start with quote.
```

This is expected since the *syntaxError.xml* file is missing an opening quote for the value of the **Make** attribute on the **<Vehicle>** element.

Taking this simple idea a step further, let's say we want to create a stored procedure to periodically comb through the xml_documents table and move any documents that are not well-formed to another table called bad_xml_documents. We can start by creating a bad_xml_documents table in the image of the existing xml_documents table, and adjusting the new table's columns to fit our needs. We can accomplish this by:

1. Creating an empty table named bad_xml_documents with the same structure as xml_documents:

```
CREATE TABLE bad_xml_documents AS
  SELECT *
    FROM xml_documents
   WHERE ROWNUM < 1 /* Don't Select Any Data, Just Get the Structure */;
```

2. Dropping the `timestamp` column using the new ALTER TABLE . . . DROP COLUMN feature in Oracle8*i* Release 2:

```
ALTER TABLE bad_xml_documents DROP COLUMN timestamp;
```

3. Adding a column to store the error message that's causing the document not to parse correctly:

```
ALTER TABLE bad_xml_documents ADD (error VARCHAR2(4000));
```

Then we can use a stored procedure like `moveBadXmlDocuments` in Example 5-3 to complete the task. Note that it makes use of our `checkXMLInCLOB` procedure from Example 5-2 to automatically move "syntactically-challenged" XML documents into the bad_xml_documents table where they can be studied and corrected later.

Example 5-3. Moving Ill-Formed XML Documents to Another Table in Batch

```
CREATE OR REPLACE PROCEDURE moveBadXmlDocuments IS
  wellFormed BOOLEAN;
  errMessage VARCHAR2(200);
BEGIN
  -- Loop over all documents in the xml_documents table
  FOR curDoc IN ( SELECT docname,xmldoc FROM xml_documents ) LOOP

    -- Check the syntax of the current 'xmldoc' CLOB in the loop
    checkXMLInCLOB( curDoc.xmldoc, wellFormed, errMessage );

    IF NOT wellFormed THEN
      -- Move ill-formed xml document to a bad_xml_documents table
      INSERT INTO bad_xml_documents(docname,xmldoc,error)
           VALUES ( curDoc.docname, curDoc.xmldoc, errMessage);
      DELETE FROM xml_documents WHERE docname = curDoc.docname;
      COMMIT;
    END IF;
  END LOOP;
END;
```

Of course, since **moveBadXmlDocuments** is a PL/SQL procedure like any other, it can be run in a database job every night at 2 A.M. by using the standard Oracle facilities in the **DBMS_JOB** package like this:

```
SET SERVEROUTPUT ON
DECLARE
  jobId     BINARY_INTEGER;
  firstRun DATE;
BEGIN
  -- Start the job tomorrow at 2am
  firstRun := TO_DATE(TO_CHAR(SYSDATE+1,'DD-MON-YYYY')||' 02:00',
                      'DD-MON-YYYY HH24:MI');

  -- Submit the job, indicating it should repeat once a day
  dbms_job.submit(job       => jobId,
                  what      => 'moveBadXmlDocuments;',
                  next_date => firstRun,
                  interval  => 'SYSDATE + 1' /* Reschedule for 1 Day Later */
                 );
  dbms_output.put_line('Successfully submitted job. Job Id is '||jobId);
END;
```

So even after just a few simple examples, you can see that by making XML processing accessible to PL/SQL, the Oracle features you know and love are all you need to use XML in your database. There's no need to learn any new management, backup, and recovery techniques for applications to work with XML. Any place where PL/SQL is valid, now XML can play, too.

Parsing XML from a String

In addition to parsing XML stored in CLOBs, it's also possible to parse XML documents that reside in VARCHAR2 string variables. This is especially convenient if you want to write stored procedures or functions that take small XML datagrams as arguments and do some processing on them.

The **xmlparser** package has a **parseBuffer** function that parses a string buffer and returns an instance of **xmldom.DOMDocument** if it is successful. The **xmldom** package provides datatypes, functions, and procedures for working with the parsed XML document's complete "object model," allowing programmatic manipulation of all elements, attributes, text content, comments, etc., that appear in the file. Table 5-2 provides a short list of the of the most common Document Object Model (DOM) API methods you will use in practice.

The **xmldom** package provides a PL/SQL language binding to all of the functionality specified in the W3C's DOM Level-1 Core. We'll use a few of the most commonly used methods in the DOM API in the examples in this chapter, giving us a feeling for how they are used in PL/SQL. Complete details on these methods can be found at *http://www.w3.org/TR/REC-DOM-Level-1/level-one-core.html*.

Table 5-2. Highlighting Some Common DOM API Methods

DOM API Method Name	Description
`getDocumentElement`	Returns the document element, the top-level element in the XML document
`getAttribute`	Returns the value of a named attribute for an element
`getChildren`	Returns the list of child nodes of an element
`getNodeType`	Returns the numerical constant indicating the type of a node
`getNodeName`	Returns the name of a node
`getNodeValue`	Returns the string value of a node
`setNodeValue`	Sets the string value of a node
`createElement`	Creates a new element
`setAttribute`	Sets an attribute value on an element
`createText`	Creates a new text node
`appendChild`	Appends a node as a child of another
`removeChild`	Removes a child node of an element
`getElementsByTagName`	Returns a list of descendent elements with a given tag name
`getFirstChild`	Returns the first child node of any node

The **idAttributeOfDocElement** function in Example 5-4 illustrates a simple example of using the **xmlparser.parseBuffer** function and a few functions in the **xmldom** package to get the document element of the parsed XML document and return the value of its `id` attribute.

Example 5-4. Parsing XML from a String and Using DOM

```
CREATE OR REPLACE FUNCTION idAttributeOfDocElement(xmldoc VARCHAR2 )
RETURN VARCHAR2 IS

  theXmlDoc xmldom.DOMDocument;
  theDocElt xmldom.DOMElement;
  retval    VARCHAR2(400);
  XMLParseError EXCEPTION;
  PRAGMA EXCEPTION_INIT( XMLParseError, -20100 );

  -- Local parse function keeps code cleaner. Return NULL if parse fails
  FUNCTION parse(xml VARCHAR2) RETURN xmldom.DOMDocument IS
```

Example 5-4. Parsing XML from a String and Using DOM (continued)

```
    retDoc xmldom.DOMDocument;
    parser xmlparser.Parser;
  BEGIN
    parser := xmlparser.newParser;
    xmlparser.parseBuffer(parser,xml);
    retDoc := xmlparser.getDocument(parser);
    xmlparser.freeParser(parser);
    RETURN retdoc;
  EXCEPTION
    -- If the parse fails, we'll jump here.
    WHEN XMLParseError THEN
      xmlparser.freeParser(parser);
      RETURN retdoc;
  END;

BEGIN
  -- Parse the xml document passed in the VARCHAR2 argument
  theXmlDoc := parse(xmldoc);
  -- If the XML document returned is not NULL...
  IF NOT xmldom.IsNull(theXmlDoc) THEN
    -- Get the outermost enclosing element (aka "Document Element")
    theDocElt := xmldom.getDocumentElement(theXmlDoc);
    -- Get the value of the document element's "id" attribute
    retval    := xmldom.getAttribute(theDocElt,'id');
    -- Free the memory used by the parsed XML document
    xmldom.freeDocument(theXmlDoc);
    RETURN retval;
  ELSE
    RETURN NULL;
  END IF;
END;
```

The `idAttributeOfDocumentElement` function uses a lesser-known PL/SQL feature of declaring a nested, local function inside the outer function's DECLARE section. This makes the code cleaner and makes it easier to extract that function later as a standalone function if you begin to discover a wider need for its facilities.

To check whether a variable of type `xmldom.DOMDocument` is NULL, use the syntax:

```
-- Check if yourXmlDocVar is NULL
IF xmldom.IsNull(yourXmlDocVar) THEN
```

You need to do this because the normal:

```
IF yourXmlDocVar IS NULL THEN
```

syntax does not work for RECORD-type variables. If you look in the source code for the `xmldom` package specification—located in the *xmldom.sql* file supplied with the Oracle XML Parser for PL/SQL—you'll see that the `DOMDocument` and other `DOMXxxx` datatypes are declared as RECORD types.

Let's give our new function a try. Suppose we have a table of small XML-based messages, whose XML message bodies are less than 4000 characters defined with the command:

```
CREATE TABLE message(
  received    DATE,
  recipient   VARCHAR2(80),
  xml_message VARCHAR2(4000)
);
```

Since our `idAttributeOfDocumentElement` function has no side-effects that modify the database, we are free to use it in the middle of a SELECT statement like the following:

```
SELECT idAttributeOfDocElement(XML_MESSAGE) AS ID, RECIPIENT, XML_MESSAGE
  FROM message
 WHERE received > SYSDATE - 1
```

that produces the expected SQL result:

```
ID   RECIPIENT  XML_MESSAGE
---- ---------- -----------------------------------
101  wsmithers  <Message id="101">
                  <From>Montgomery Burns</From>
                  <Text>Release the Hounds!</Text>
                </Message>
```

Of course, we can also use the function within the body of any other PL/SQL program. Note that while using the `getAttribute()` function on an element makes it easy to retrieve any attribute value, retrieving the value of an element is less than obvious. For example, in the output just shown, to retrieve the text "Montgomery Burns" as the value of the `<From>` element, you need to realize that the string "Montgomery Burns" is actually a text node that is a child of the `<From>` element. An element doesn't technically have a value of its own. Retrieving an element's value requires a combination of using the `getFirstChild()` or `getChildNodes()` functions, followed by using the `getNodeValue()` function on the child text nodes.

Before moving on to the next section, make sure you understand the following points about using the XML Parser for PL/SQL packages:

- Since PL/SQL is not an object-oriented language like Java, the PL/SQL API for DOM is not object-oriented. In Java, you would call a `getDocumentElement` *method* on an instance of an XML document object; in PL/SQL, you pass the XML document object to the `xmldom.getDocumentElement` function as an *argument*, as shown here:

```
// Java syntax
theDocElt = theXMLDoc.getDocumentElement();

-- PL/SQL syntax
theDocElt := xmldom.getDocumentElement(theXmlDoc);
```

Understanding Maximum Sizes for VARCHAR2 Data

While SQL and PL/SQL share the ability to work with data of type VARCHAR2, they differ in the maximum allowed length. Within a PL/SQL program, local variables of type VARCHAR2 can be declared to contain up to 32,767 characters. However, when declaring a database column of type VARCHAR2, the maximum length is 4000 characters. This SQL VARCHAR2 limit of 4000 characters holds as well when VARCHAR2 values appear inside DML (Data Manipulation Language) statements like SELECT, INSERT, UPDATE, and DELETE. Keep this in mind when referencing PL/SQL functions inside DML statements, since their return values cannot exceed 4000 characters. To illustrate the problem, imagine a simple function like this:

```
CREATE OR REPLACE FUNCTION stars(how_many NUMBER)
RETURN VARCHAR2 IS
BEGIN
  -- Return a string with 'how_many' stars
  RETURN RPAD('*',how_many,'*');
END;
```

The statement **`SELECT stars(4000) FROM dual`** selects a string of 4000 stars, while the statement **`SELECT stars(4001) FROM dual`** produces the error:

```
ORA-06502: PL/SQL: numeric or value error:
           character string buffer too small
```

Use CLOB datatypes and the `DBMS_LOB` package to work with character data that is over 4K.

- Since the XML Parser for PL/SQL is a wrapper of the Java implementation, you have to explicitly call routines to free the XML documents you parse when you no longer need them. This means that whether you use XML documents for a brief moment inside a function or a procedure, or keep XML documents in PL/SQL package-level variables to cache them, you need to be diligent about freeing them when you're done using them. This ensures that the memory used by the underlying Java objects is properly reused. In Example 5-4, we see calls at appropriate points to:

  ```
  xmlparser.freeParser(parser);
  ```

  and to:

  ```
  xmldom.freeDocument(theXmlDoc);
  ```

  which free the XML Parser object and XML Document object, respectively.

Next we'll see how to reach out over the network to pull XML into the database by retrieving and parsing XML over a URL.

Parsing XML from a URL

The **xmlparser.parse** function allows you to parse XML documents from any URL. This is the easy part. The tricky parts of working with XML over the network from inside Oracle8*i* involve dealing with:

- Firewall machines that protect your intranet from the Internet
- Database permissions to enable a user to successfully open a connection to another server from inside the Oracle8*i* database

We'll learn how to deal with these issues by working through an example.

Moreover.com is an Internet startup that publishes news stories on the Web. Other sites can leverage the news that Moreover.com is constantly adding to gigantic databases in order to offer headline news features on their own sites. At the time of this writing, Moreover.com offers 253 different categories of news. Of particular interest to us is the category of news about XML-related technologies. The fact that the company deliver its news feeds in XML is particularly serendipitous. We'll use the live web-based news feed *on* XML *in* XML as the example for this section.

Browsing the following URL:

> *http://p.moreover.com/cgi-local/page?index_xml+xml*

will retrieve an XML datagram of news stories that looks like Example 5-5.

Example 5-5. Example Moreover.com News Feed Datagram

```
<?xml version="1.0" encoding="iso-8859-1"?>
   <!DOCTYPE moreovernews
      SYSTEM "http://w.moreover.com/xml/moreovernews.dtd">
   <moreovernews>
      <article id="_6331562">
         <url>http://c.moreover.com/click/here.pl?x6331558</url>
         <headline_text>IBM, Oracle Expand XML's Role</headline_text>
         <source>Internet Week</source>
         <media_type>text</media_type>
         <cluster>XML and metadata news</cluster>
         <tagline> </tagline>
         <document_url>http://www.internetwk.com/</document_url>
         <harvest_time>Mar 30 2000  3:50PM</harvest_time>
         <access_registration> </access_registration>
         <access_status> </access_status>
      </article>

      <!-- More <article>s here -->

      <article id="_6328106">
         <url>http://c.moreover.com/click/here.pl?x6328104</url>
         <headline_text>XML May Mark Spot for B2B Profits</headline_text>
         <source>ON24 Audio/Video</source>
         <media_type>audio</media_type>
```

Example 5-5. Example Moreover.com News Feed Datagram (continued)

```
        <cluster>XML and metadata news</cluster>
        <tagline> </tagline>
        <document_url>http://www.on24.com/newsline/top</document_url>
        <harvest_time>Mar 30 2000 12:00PM</harvest_time>
        <access_registration> </access_registration>
        <access_status> </access_status>
    </article>
  </moreovernews>
```

What we want to do is programmatically retrieve this XML by parsing the URL cited previously, and process the news story information that arrives. If you have to set a proxy server name in order to use your web browser, that's a good sign that your database machine will need to have the proxy server set correctly, too.

Even if you are parsing an XML document from a VARCHAR2 or CLOB value, that document *might* contain a `<!DOCTYPE>` that references its associated external DTD via an *http://*-based URL like this:

```
<!DOCTYPE moreovernews
  SYSTEM "http://w.moreover.com/xml/moreovernews.dtd">
```

Since the XML Parser will attempt to retrieve the external DTD, this is another situation when you need the HTTP proxy server name to be properly set to avoid network timeouts when the XML Parser tries to retrieve the DTD.

Since the XML Parser for PL/SQL is implemented in Java under the covers, we need to set the proxy server in the way that Java programs require, by setting the values of the three System properties in Table 5-3.

Table 5-3. Java System Properties to Control Proxy Server Settings

System Property Name	Description
`proxySet`	Has the value `true` or `false` to indicate whether the proxy server should be used. If unset, the default is `false`.
`proxyHost`	The name or IP address of the machine to be used as the HTTP proxy server for URL requests. No leading `http://` is required, just the machine name.
`proxyPort`	The port number to use for communication with the proxy server.

Since there is no built-in PL/SQL API to set Java System properties, we'll need to build one by:

1. Creating a Java class to call `System.setProperty(`*`name`*`,`*`value`*`)`
2. Compiling the class and loading it into Oracle8*i*
3. Creating a Java stored procedure specification for it

So let's do it. The tiny **PropertyHelper** class below will do the job for us:

```
public class PropertyHelper {
  public static void setSystemProperty(String name, String value) {
    System.setProperty(name,value);
  }
}
```

This class defines a single method named **setSystemProperty** that sets the value of a named System property to the value passed in. To compile this class, use JDeveloper or any command-line **javac** compiler:

```
javac PropertyHelper.java
```

This produces the compiled Java class file named **PropertyHelper.class**. To load this class into the database, do the following:

```
loadjava -verbose -resolve -user sys/password PropertyHelper.class
```

We're loading it into the SYS schema since SYS has privileges to set System properties (SYSTEM does not, by default). We'll control access to this capability by granting EXECUTE permission on the Java stored procedure wrapper we're just about to create.

Connect to the database using SQL*Plus as SYS and run the script:

```
CREATE OR REPLACE PROCEDURE setJavaSystemProperty(name VARCHAR2,value VARCHAR2)
AS LANGUAGE JAVA NAME
'PropertyHelper.setSystemProperty(java.lang.String, java.lang.String)';
```

The CREATE PROCEDURE command uses the following syntax that is new with Oracle8*i*:

```
AS LANGUAGE JAVA NAME 'classname.methodname(args)'
```

This allows you to create a PL/SQL procedure or function specification whose body is implemented by static methods of a Java class. Once a Java stored procedure specification like **setJavaSystemProperty** is created, both SQL and PL/SQL can call it exactly as if it were implemented in PL/SQL.

We can create an **http_util** package that exposes the ability to set the proxy server and port through a **setProxy** procedure with the code:

```
CREATE OR REPLACE PACKAGE http_util AS

  -- Set proxy server for any Java code running in the current session.
  PROCEDURE setProxy(host VARCHAR2, port NUMBER := 80);

END;
CREATE OR REPLACE PACKAGE BODY http_util AS
  PROCEDURE setProxy(host VARCHAR2, port NUMBER := 80) IS
  BEGIN
    setJavaSystemProperty('proxySet','true');
    setJavaSystemProperty('proxyHost',host);
```

```
    setJavaSystemProperty('proxyPort',TO_CHAR(port));
  END;
END;
```

So now, any user with permissions to invoke:

```
http_util.setProxy('somemachine');
```

can set the proxy server. As with any globally useful package, we'll create a public synonym for it:

```
CREATE PUBLIC SYNONYM http_util FOR http_util;
```

and then have SYS grant permission to the XMLBOOK user to use the new `http_util` package:

```
GRANT EXECUTE ON http_util TO XMLBOOK;
```

Finally then, we can connect again as XMLBOOK and set the HTTP proxy by issuing the command:

```
exec http_util.setProxy('proxyserver.you.com');
```

Whew! With all this machinery in place, let's get to the good stuff. Example 5-6 shows the code necessary to retrieve the top news stories about XML from Moreover.com. The code:

1. Sets the proxy server using our new `http_util.setProxy()`
2. Parses the XML "news feed" document retrieved from the URL
3. Searches for all `<headline_text>` elements using `getElementsByTagName`
4. Loops over all the found `<headline_text>` nodes, and for each node, gets the first text node child of `<headline_text>` and prints out the headline

Example 5-6. Retrieving an XML-based News Feed from Moreover.com

```
SET SERVEROUTPUT ON
DECLARE
  newsURL       VARCHAR2(80);
  parser        xmlparser.Parser;
  newsXML       xmldom.DOMDocument;
  titles        xmldom.DOMNodeList;
  titles_found NUMBER;
  curNode       xmldom.DOMNode;
  textChild     xmldom.DOMNode;
BEGIN
  dbms_output.put_line('Top Stories on XML from Moreover.com on '||
                       TO_CHAR(SYSDATE,'FMMonth ddth, YYYY'));
  -- This is the URL to browse for an XML-based news feed of stories on XML
  newsURL := 'http://p.moreover.com/cgi-local/page?index_xml+xml';

  -- Set the machine to use as the HTTP proxy server for URL requests
  http_util.setProxy('yourproxyserver.you.com');
```

Example 5-6. Retrieving an XML-based News Feed from Moreover.com (continued)

```
  -- Parse the live XML news feed from Moreover.com by URL
  parser  := xmlparser.newParser;
  newsXML := xmlparser.parse( newsURL );
  xmlparser.freeParser(parser);

  -- Search for all <headline_text> elements in the document we receive
  titles  := xmldom.getElementsByTagName(newsXML,'headline_text');

  -- Loop over the "hits" and print out the text of the title
  FOR j IN 1..xmldom.getLength(titles) LOOP
    -- Get the current <headline_text> node (Note the list is zero-based!)
    curNode    := xmldom.item(titles,j-1);
    -- The text of the title is the first child (text) node of
    -- the <headline_text> element in the list of "hits"
    textChild := xmldom.getFirstChild(curNode);
    dbms_output.put_line('('||LPAD(j,2)||') '||xmldom.getNodeValue(textChild));
  END LOOP;
  -- Free the XML document full of news stories since we're done with it.
  xmldom.freeDocument(newsXML);

END;
```

If you have no firewall or proxy server machine between you and the wild, woolly Internet, you can comment out the line:

```
http_util.setProxy('yourproxyserver.you.com');
```

If you do have a firewall, edit the example on the CD to reflect the name of your proxy server before running examples.

Executing the anonymous block of PL/SQL in Example 5-6 should produce output like this:

```
Top Stories on XML from Moreover.com on April 2nd, 2000
( 1) Oracle increases XML support
( 2) An object programming lesson on how you can be successful
( 3) Here's a vignette about how e-commerce platforms are shaking out
( 4) Vendors don't want you to sell used software as you would used books or CDs
( 5) SpaceWorks, WebMethods Ink OEM Alliance
( 6) XML Comes Of Age
( 7) IBM, Oracle Expand XML's Role
   :
(29) Pinacor Establishes XML-Based E-Business Inventory Pipeline
(30) Moving Home: Portable Site Information
```

If, instead, it produces an error like this:

```
Top Stories on XML from Moreover.com on April 2nd, 2000
DECLARE
*
ERROR at line 1:
```

```
ORA-29532: Java call terminated by uncaught Java exception:
java.security.AccessControlException: the Permission
(java.net.SocketPermission p.moreover.com resolve) has not been granted by
dbms_java.grant_permission to
SchemaProtectionDomain(XMLBOOK|PolicyTableProxy(XMLBOOK))
```

then we've found a good reason to talk about the other tricky part of parsing web-based XML by URL over HTTP: the permission to open a socket from inside the database.

Of course, you don't want all your database users to be able to write programs that run on your production server that can open up HTTP connections with other machines and send or receive information. To address this, Oracle8*i* provides fine control over the ability to open a communication socket with another machine.

We get this error because you don't have permission to open a socket of any kind, not to mention a socket to connect for an HTTP-based TCP/IP exchange with `p.moreover.com` to get your XML news feed. You can grant this "open-a-socket" permission on:

- Any machine name or IP address (`"*"`)
- Any machine in a given domain (`"*.moreover.com"`)
- A particular machine or IP address (`"101.123.208.104"` or `"stocks.xmlville.com"`)

We can resolve the problem by creating a useful PL/SQL procedure to `allow_url_access` to a particular server (or wildcard pattern for a server name). The code in Example 5-7 will do the trick.

Example 5-7. Controlling Security on URL Access Inside Oracle8i JServer

```
CREATE OR REPLACE PROCEDURE allow_url_access( to_user VARCHAR2,
                                              on_server VARCHAR2) IS
BEGIN

  -- Note "on_server" can include a leading asterisk (e.g. '*.oracle.com')
  -- See JavaDoc for the java.net.SocketPermission class for other legal values
  dbms_java.grant_permission(grantee           => to_user,
                             permission_type   => 'java.net.SocketPermission',
                             permission_name   => on_server,
                             permission_action => 'connect,resolve');
END;
```

This code should be created in the SYS or SYSTEM account and then access to open connections with particular servers can be granted to individual users by executing the `allow_url_access` procedure, like this:

```
EXEC allow_url_access('XMLBOOK','*.moreover.com');
```

This grants XMLBOOK the ability to open a connection and retrieve a resource from any URL with a domain name that ends in `.moreover.com`. By connecting again as XMLBOOK and executing the SQL statement:

```
SELECT name AS allowed_server_name
  FROM user_java_policy
 WHERE type_name = 'java.net.SocketPermission'
```

You should now see this heart-warming result:

```
ALLOWED_SERVER_NAME
--------------------
*.moreover.com
```

This granted permission will enable us to successfully retrieve:

- The "news feed" URL:

  `http://p.moreover.com/cgi-local/page?index_xml+xml`

- The DTD referenced in the XML news feed document:

  `http://w.moreover.com/xml/moreovernews.dtd`

Rerunning the code in Example 5-6 as the XMLBOOK user should now work fine.

PL/SQL Helper Packages for XML Parsing

Since we'll be parsing XML documents a lot, it makes sense to build a convenience package called `xml` that handles all of our common parsing needs with the simplest possible API. Example 5-8 shows the PL/SQL package specification of precisely the little helper package we need.

Example 5-8. The xml Helper Package Specification

```
CREATE OR REPLACE PACKAGE xml AS

  -- Set HTTP proxy server in case you reference documents
  -- or DTDs outside a corporate firewall

  PROCEDURE setHttpProxy(machinename VARCHAR2,
                         port        VARCHAR2 := '80');

  -- Parse and return an XML document

  FUNCTION parse(xml VARCHAR2) RETURN xmldom.DOMDocument;
  FUNCTION parse(xml CLOB)     RETURN xmldom.DOMDocument;
  FUNCTION parse(xml BFILE)    RETURN xmldom.DOMDocument;

  -- Parse and return an XML Document by URL

  FUNCTION parseURL(url VARCHAR2) RETURN xmldom.DOMDocument;
```

Example 5-8. The xml Helper Package Specification (continued)

```
  -- Free the memory used by an XML document

  PROCEDURE freeDocument(doc xmldom.DOMDocument);

END;
```

The `xml` package centralizes the key XML parsing functionality for:

- Setting the HTTP proxy server
- Parsing XML from a VARCHAR2
- Parsing XML from a CLOB
- Parsing XML from a BFILE
- Parsing XML from a URL
- Freeing an XML document when we're done using it

Internally, the helper package worries about creating and freeing the XML parser object needed to do the parsing, so already that's one less thing to think about. We'll see that creating helper packages like this will make future PL/SQL-based XML work a lot easier and will save us a lot of typing.

While we're at it, we can create a helper package called `xmldoc` for simplifying our life when working with useful chunks of XML we'd like to store in tables, such as our xml_documents table from earlier in the chapter.

The `xmldoc` package in Example 5-9 centralizes the basic, useful functionality of:

- Saving an XML document in the xml_documents table as a VARCHAR2, CLOB, BFILE, or `xmldom.DOMDocument`, with a given document name as its "key"
- Getting an XML document by document name as a CLOB, VARCHAR2, or `xmldom.DOMDocument` from the xml_documents table
- Removing an XML document by name from the table
- Testing whether a given document name exists in the table

Example 5-9. The xmldoc Helper Package Specification

```
CREATE OR REPLACE PACKAGE xmldoc AS

  -- Save an XML document (parsing it first if necessary) into the
  -- xml_documents table with a given document name.

  PROCEDURE save(name      VARCHAR2,
                 xmldoc    VARCHAR2,
                 docommit BOOLEAN := TRUE);
  PROCEDURE save(name      VARCHAR2,
                 xmldoc    CLOB,
                 docommit BOOLEAN := TRUE);
```

Example 5-9. The xmldoc Helper Package Specification (continued)

```
  PROCEDURE save(name      VARCHAR2,
                 xmldoc    BFILE,
                 docommit BOOLEAN := TRUE);
  PROCEDURE save(name      VARCHAR2,
                 xmldoc xmldom.DOMDocument,
                 docommit BOOLEAN:=TRUE);

  -- Get an XML document by name from the xml_documents table
  FUNCTION  get(name VARCHAR2) RETURN xmldom.DOMDocument;

  -- Get an XML document as a CLOB by name from the xml_documents table
  FUNCTION  getAsCLOB(name VARCHAR2) RETURN CLOB;

  -- Get an XML document as a VARCHAR2 by name from the xml_documents table
  FUNCTION  getAsText(name VARCHAR2) RETURN VARCHAR2;

  -- Remove an XML document by name from the xml_documents table
  PROCEDURE remove(name VARCHAR2, docommit BOOLEAN := TRUE);

  -- Test if a named document exists in the xml_documents table
  FUNCTION  docExists(name VARCHAR2) RETURN BOOLEAN;
END;
```

You'll find the full source code of the `xml` and `xmldoc` packages in Appendix A as well as instructions for installing them. We'll exploit these helper packages (as well as introduce a few more) later in this chapter.

In Example 5-6 we used some DOM techniques for:

- Finding all `<headline_text>` elements using `xmldom.getElementsByTagName`
- Getting the value of the `<headline_text>` element by using `xmldom.getFirstChild()` to get the text node child of the `<headline_text>` element

In the next section, we'll see how these raw DOM techniques will seem brute force, at best, in comparison with XPath.

Searching XML Documents with XPath

While processing XML documents and datagrams inside the database, you'll frequently find it necessary and convenient to search the content of the document you're processing. We've noted that the `xmldom` package provides a completely programmatic way of hunting through the entire tree of nodes of an XML document to find what you're looking for. We'll see in this section how XPath's searching of in-memory XML makes it all declarative and so much easier.

Basic Use of XPath in PL/SQL

We saw in Chapter 2, *Working with XML*, that XPath expressions provide a compact, declarative syntax to describe any parts of an XML document you would like to address. Let's explore what opportunities exist for the PL/SQL developer to exploit XPath expressions to search in-memory documents.

Let's look again at our simple insurance claim XML document:

```
<!-- claim77804.xml -->
<Claim>
  <ClaimId>77804</ClaimId>
  <Policy>12345</Policy>
  <Settlements>
    <Payment Approver="JCOX">1000</Payment>
    <Payment Approver="PSMITH">1850</Payment>
  </Settlements>
  <DamageReport>
    The insured's <Vehicle Make="Volks">Beetle</Vehicle>
    broke through the guard rail and plummeted into a ravine.
    The cause was determined to be <Cause>faulty brakes</Cause>.
    Amazingly there were no casualties.
  </DamageReport>
</Claim>
```

We might want to answer the following questions about this document:

What is the value of the policy number for this claim?

We may want to store the policy number for this XML-based insurance claim in its own database column so we can more easily search, sort, and group by that key piece of information. To do this, we need the ability to retrieve the value of the XPath expression:

```
/Claim/Policy
```

Does this claim have any settlement payments over $500 approved by JCOX?

If this XML document were arriving as a CLOB attribute of an object type in an Oracle8*i* AQ message queue, we might want to evaluate boolean tests based on XPath expressions like:

```
//Settlements/Payment[. > 500 and @Approver="JCOX"]
```

so we can properly route the message to the right department.

What is the XML document fragment contained by the `<DamageReport>` *element?*

We might be creating a data warehouse of millions of insurance claims to study trends in the kinds of claims we receive. We might want to extract the content of the `<DamageReport>` element as an XML fragment using the XPath expression:

```
/Claim/DamageReport
```

We can then store the fragment in a column that has been indexed for lightning-fast XML document searching using Oracle's interMedia Text product (described in Chapter 13).

Who approved settlement payments for this claim?

We might want to iterate over the `<Payment>` elements in the claim matching the XPath expression:

```
/Claim/Settlements/Payment
```

and then do some processing with the value of each `<Payment>` element's `Approver` attribute.

The Oracle XML Parser for PL/SQL provides the enabling APIs to answer all of these questions on in-memory XML documents in its `xslprocessor` package. Its powerful `valueOf` and `selectNodes` functions allow us to retrieve the value of an XPath expression and return a list of nodes matching an XPath expression, respectively. Using a combination of these functions, we can create an `xpath` helper package that puts all the most common XPath-related activities right at our fingertips, allowing us to:

- Easily retrieve the `valueOf` an XPath expression
- Quickly `test` whether an XPath expression is true or false
- Conveniently `extract` matching subtrees of a document matching an XPath expression
- Use `selectNodes` matching an XPath expression to process a list of matches

All four of these functions are provided in versions that work on an `xmldom.DOMDocument` that has already been parsed in memory, or directly on a VARCHAR2 or CLOB value. If you use the VARCHAR2 or CLOB versions, the implementations of these functions do the parsing for you internally by using the `xml.parse` routine from our `xml` helper package.

Example 5-10 shows the specification of our `xpath` helper package. As with the other helper packages, you can find the full source code for the `xpath` package in Appendix A.

Example 5-10. The xpath Helper Package Specification

```
CREATE OR REPLACE PACKAGE xpath AS

  -- Return the value of an XPath expression, optionally normalizing whitespace

  FUNCTION valueOf(doc        xmldom.DOMDocument,
                   xpath      VARCHAR2,
                   normalize BOOLEAN:=FALSE) RETURN VARCHAR2;

  FUNCTION valueOf(node       xmldom.DOMNode,
                   xpath      VARCHAR2,
                   normalize BOOLEAN:=FALSE)   RETURN VARCHAR2;
```

Example 5-10. The xpath Helper Package Specification (continued)

```
  FUNCTION valueOf(doc       VARCHAR2,
                   xpath     VARCHAR2,
                   normalize BOOLEAN := FALSE) RETURN VARCHAR2;

  FUNCTION valueOf(doc CLOB,
                   xpath     VARCHAR2,
                   normalize BOOLEAN := FALSE) RETURN VARCHAR2;

  -- Test whether an XPath predicate is true

  FUNCTION test(doc  xmldom.DOMDocument,xpath VARCHAR2) RETURN BOOLEAN;
  FUNCTION test(node xmldom.DOMNode,     xpath VARCHAR2) RETURN BOOLEAN;
  FUNCTION test(doc  VARCHAR2,           xpath VARCHAR2) RETURN BOOLEAN;
  FUNCTION test(doc  CLOB,               xpath VARCHAR2) RETURN BOOLEAN;

  -- Extract an XML fragment for set of nodes matching an XPath pattern
  -- optionally normalizing whitespace (default is to normalize it)

  FUNCTION extract(doc       xmldom.DOMDocument,
                   xpath     VARCHAR2:='/',
                   normalize BOOLEAN:=TRUE)   RETURN VARCHAR2;
  FUNCTION extract(doc       VARCHAR2,
                   xpath     VARCHAR2 := '/',
                   normalize BOOLEAN := TRUE) RETURN VARCHAR2;
  FUNCTION extract(doc       CLOB,
                   xpath     VARCHAR2 := '/',
                   normalize BOOLEAN := TRUE) RETURN VARCHAR2;

  -- Select a list of nodes matching an XPath pattern
  -- Note: DOMNodeList returned has a zero-based index

  FUNCTION  selectNodes(doc xmldom.DOMDocument,
                        xpath VARCHAR2) RETURN xmldom.DOMNodeList;

  FUNCTION  selectNodes(node xmldom.DOMNode,
                        xpath VARCHAR2) RETURN xmldom.DOMNodeList;

  FUNCTION  selectNodes(doc VARCHAR2,
                        xpath VARCHAR2) RETURN xmldom.DOMNodeList;

  FUNCTION  selectNodes(doc CLOB,
                        xpath VARCHAR2) RETURN xmldom.DOMNodeList;

END;
```

Using this new `xpath` helper package, let's see how we can easily answer all four of our previous questions. The PL/SQL script in Example 5-11 illustrates using the following functions:

`xml.parse`
: From our `xml` helper package; reads the contents of the *claim77804.xml* file in the *XMLFILES* directory into memory

`xpath.valueOf`
: Answers the first question

`xpath.test`
: Answers the second question

`xmldoc.save`
: Saves the document with the name of claim77804 to our xml_documents table

`xmldoc.get`
: Retrieves the document with the name of claim77804 from our xml_documents table

`xpath.extract`
: Answers the third question

`xpath.selectNodes`
: Answers the fourth question

`xml.freeDocument`
: Frees the XML document's parsed representation

Of course, saving the claim XML document to our xml_documents table and getting it back again are not at all required to answer the questions, but seeing a working example of how this helper package works doesn't do any harm. The sample appears in Example 5-11.

Example 5-11. Test, Extract, and Retrieve an XPath Expression Value

```
SET SERVEROUTPUT ON
DECLARE
  doc         xmldom.DOMDocument;
  approvers xmldom.DOMNodeList;
  PROCEDURE p(msg VARCHAR2, nl BOOLEAN := TRUE) IS BEGIN
    dbms_output.put_line(msg);IF nl THEN dbms_output.put(CHR(10)); END IF;
  END;
  FUNCTION yn(b BOOLEAN ) RETURN VARCHAR2 IS
  BEGIN IF b THEN RETURN 'Yes'; ELSE RETURN 'No'; END IF; END;
BEGIN
  doc := xml.parse(BFileName('XMLFILES','claim77804.xml'));

  p('What is the value of the Policy number for this claim?');
  p( xpath.valueOf(doc,'/Claim/Policy') );

  p('Does this claim have any settlement payments over $500 approved by JCOX?');
  p(yn(xpath.test(doc,'//Settlements/Payment[. > 500 and @Approver="JCOX"]')));

  -- Demonstrate Saving and Re-getting the XML document
  xmldoc.save('claim77804',doc);
  doc := xmldoc.get('claim77804');

  p('What is XML document fragment contained by the <DamageReport> element?');
  p(xpath.extract(doc,'/Claim/DamageReport'));
```

Example 5-11. Test, Extract, and Retrieve an XPath Expression Value (continued)

```
  p('Who approved settlement payments for this claim?');
  approvers := xpath.selectNodes(doc,'/Claim/Settlements/Payment');
  FOR j IN 1..xmldom.getLength(approvers) LOOP
    p(xpath.valueOf(xmldom.item(approvers,j-1),'@Approver'),nl=>FALSE);
  END LOOP;
  xml.freeDocument(doc);
END;
```

Running the script in the example produces the following output in the SQL*Plus command console window:

```
What is the value of the Policy number for this claim?

12345

Does this claim have any settlement payments over $500 approved by JCOX?

Yes

What is XML document fragment contained by the <DamageReport> element?

<DamageReport> The insured's <Vehicle Make="Volks">Beetle</Vehicle> broke
through the guard rail and plummeted into a ravine. The cause was determined to
be <Cause>faulty brakes</Cause>. Amazingly there were no casualties.
</DamageReport>

Who approved settlement payments for this claim?

JCOX
PSMITH
```

We're just scraping the surface of XPath here. Since Oracle's implementation of XPath is fully compliant with the W3C XPath 1.0 Recommendation (see *http://www.w3.org/TR/1999/REC-xpath-19991116*), you can use any legal XPath expression with the `xpath` helper package or the underlying `xslprocessor` package on which it depends. Even these simple examples demonstrate the power of XPath compared to tedious DOM node-navigation code; with XPath, you just say what you want and get it instantly.

Using XPath for Custom XML-to-Table Mapping

XPath expressions and the functions in the `xpath` helper package come in handy when trying to write custom routines to store XML documents into one or more database tables. Theoretically, you could use the `xmldoc.save` routine to store all XML documents as CLOBs into a single xml_documents table. Most likely, however, this is not what you want if your incoming XML documents are business documents and your business applications need to query, sort, search, and perform calculations using the full power of SQL on the information contained in the documents.

Rather than dump the incoming XML-based insurance claim datagrams into a single, generic xml_documents table, you might choose to store them in the combination of the two relational tables ins_claim and ins_claim_payment:

```
CREATE TABLE ins_claim (
  claimid       NUMBER PRIMARY KEY,
  policy        NUMBER,
  damagereport  CLOB
);
CREATE TABLE ins_claim_payment (
  claimid  NUMBER,
  amount   NUMBER,
  approver VARCHAR2(8),
  CONSTRAINT payment_for_claim
  FOREIGN KEY (claimid) REFERENCES ins_claim
  ON DELETE CASCADE
);
```

We can create a package like **xml_claim** in Example 5-12 to take in the XML insurance claim document as a CLOB or an in-memory DOM **Document** object and perform the required INSERTs into the ins_claim and ins_claim_payment tables. We store raw scalar data like the **claimid**, the **policy** number, the payment **amount**, and the payment **approver** into appropriate NUMBER and VARCHAR2 columns, and we store the contents of the <DamageReport> XML document fragment (all XML markup intact) into the **damagereport** CLOB column. In Chapter 13, we'll learn how to create an XML search index on the **damagereport** column to enable precise XML-based searches over millions of claims.

Example 5-12. Storing XML Insurance Claim in Multiple Tables with XPath

```
CREATE OR REPLACE PACKAGE xml_claim AS

  PROCEDURE store( doc xmldom.DOMDocument );
  PROCEDURE store( claimdoc CLOB );

END;
CREATE OR REPLACE PACKAGE BODY xml_claim AS

  PROCEDURE store( doc xmldom.DOMDocument ) IS
    claim    ins_claim%ROWTYPE;
    payment ins_claim_payment%ROWTYPE;
    damrep      CLOB;
    damrepText VARCHAR2(32767);
    payments xmldom.DOMNodeList;
    curNode  xmldom.DOMNode;
  BEGIN
    -- Use xpath.valueOf to retrieve values for INSERT
    claim.claimid := xpath.valueOf(doc,'/Claim/ClaimId');
    claim.policy  := xpath.valueOf(doc,'/Claim/Policy');

    -- Use xpath.extract to extract matching XML fragment
    damrepText     := xpath.extract(doc,'/Claim/DamageReport');
```

Example 5-12. Storing XML Insurance Claim in Multiple Tables with XPath (continued)

```
    INSERT INTO ins_claim(claimid,policy,damagereport)
         VALUES (claim.claimid, claim.policy, empty_clob())
    RETURNING damagereport INTO damrep;

    -- Write the damagereport xml document fragment into the CLOB column
    dbms_lob.writeappend(damrep,LENGTH(damrepText),damrepText);

    -- Process all the <Payment> elements in the <Settlements> section
    payments := xpath.selectNodes(doc,'/Claim/Settlements/Payment');
    FOR j IN 1..xmldom.getLength(payments) LOOP

      -- Recall that the Node List is zero-based!
      curNode := xmldom.item(payments, j-1);

      -- Use xpath.valueOf to retrieve the values for INSERT
      -- Note that Amount is the value of the current "Payment" element
      payment.amount   := xpath.valueOf(curNode,'.');
      payment.approver := xpath.valueOf(curNode,'@Approver');

      INSERT INTO ins_claim_payment(claimid, amount, approver)
           VALUES(claim.claimid,payment.amount,payment.approver);

    END LOOP;
  END;

  PROCEDURE store( claimdoc CLOB ) IS
    xmldoc xmldom.DOMDocument;
  BEGIN
    -- If we're called with a CLOB, parse it and pass it to the other store()
    xmldoc := xml.parse(claimdoc);
    store(xmldoc);
    xml.freeDocument(xmldoc);
  EXCEPTION
    WHEN OTHERS THEN xml.freeDocument(xmldoc); RAISE;
  END;

END;
```

The variable declarations:

```
claim   ins_claim%ROWTYPE;
payment ins_claim_payment%ROWTYPE;
```

in Example 5-12 use the *TABLENAME*%ROWTYPE as the datatype of a variable, which automatically declares a record variable with the same structure as a row in *TABLENAME*.

To prove that it works, we can try out the little test program in Example 5-13.

Example 5-13. Testing the xml_claim Package

```
DECLARE
  claimdoc xmldom.DOMDocument;
BEGIN

  -- Store an XML insurance claim into ins_claim and ins_claim_payment
  -- tables directly from an external XML BFILE

  claimdoc := xml.parse(BFileName('XMLFILES','claim77805.xml'));
  xml_claim.store(claimdoc);
  xml.freeDocument(claimdoc);

  -- To show another technique, first store the external XML file in
  -- the xml_documents "staging" table...

  claimdoc := xml.parse(BFileName('XMLFILES','claim77804.xml'));
  xmldoc.save('claim77804',claimdoc);
  xml.freeDocument(claimdoc);

  -- ...Then store the XML insurance claim into ins_claim and
  -- ins_claim_payments by reading the XML from the staging table.

  claimdoc := xmldoc.get('claim77804');
  xml_claim.store(claimdoc);
  xml.freeDocument(claimdoc);

END;
```

After executing this code to exercise our **xml_claim.store** procedure, we can immediately query our underlying tables to see its effect:

```
SELECT claimid,policy,damagereport
  FROM ins_claim
 WHERE claimid IN (77804,77805)
```

Using the SQL*Plus command **COLUMN damagereport FORMAT A60** to widen the display, we see the results:

```
CLAIMID POLICY DAMAGEREPORT
------- ------ ------------------------------------------------------------
  77804  12345 <DamageReport> The insured's <Vehicle Make="Volks">Beetle
               </Vehicle> broke through the guard rail and plummeted into a
               ravine. The cause was determined to be <Cause>faulty brakes
               </Cause>. Amazingly there were no casualties. </DamageReport>

  77805  12345 <DamageReport> The insured's <Vehicle Make="Audi">TT</Vehicle>
               hit a tree. The cause was determined to be a <Cause>missing bolt
               </Cause> in the wheel assembly. </DamageReport>
```

A query over the detail table ins_claim_payment:

```
SELECT claimid, amount, approver
  FROM ins_claim_payment
 WHERE claimid IN (77804,77805)
ORDER BY claimid,amount
```

shows that our routine correctly inserted both master claim information and detail payment information based on the insurance claim XML document given as input:

```
CLAIMID     AMOUNT APPROVER
------- ---------- --------
  77804       1000 JCOX
  77804       1850 PSMITH
  77805        498 JCOX
  77805       2000 DALLEN
```

Since we have versions of the `xpath` helper package functions that work directly on VARCHAR2 and CLOB datatypes, and since these functions return VARCHAR2, they are legal to use inside a SELECT statement. For example, we can combine the following:

- Regular columns like `claimid`
- SQL aggregate calculations for the `SUM` of settlement payments
- PL/SQL functions like `xpath.valueOf` to "dig in" to the `damagereport` XML fragment and pick out just the <Make> and <Cause> information

in the same SQL statement, as in this example:

```
SELECT c.claimid,
       s.total AS settlement_total,
       xpath.valueOf(c.damagereport,'//Vehicle/@Make') AS Make,
       xpath.valueOf(c.damagereport,'//Cause') AS Cause
  FROM ins_claim c, (SELECT claimid,
                            SUM(amount) AS TOTAL
                           FROM ins_claim_payment p
                          WHERE p.claimid in (77804,77805)
                         GROUP BY claimid) s
WHERE c.claimid = s.claimid
  AND c.claimid in (77804,77805)
```

This returns the result:

```
CLAIMID SETTLEMENT_TOTAL MAKE     CAUSE
------- ---------------- -------- ---------------
  77805             2498 Audi     missing bolt
  77804             2850 Volks    faulty brakes
```

These are all quite simple examples of using XPath, but the `xpath` helper package we've put in place works for any XML document and any valid XPath expression, so you can achieve quite sophisticated in-memory XML queries. However, keep in mind that all of the functions in the `xpath` helper package rely on having the parsed XML representation of the document in memory. This works great for doing XPath processing on a small number of small to medium-sized XML documents at a time. However, the xpath package is absolutely not the right tool for the job if you want to search through your huge claims table of one million insurance claims for a document matching a given XPath expression.

For example, the following is never a good idea if you have more than a handful of insurance claims in your ins_claim table:

```
/*
** Performance would be horrible with xpath helper
** functions in the WHERE clause
*/
SELECT claimid, xpath.valueOf(damagereport,'//Cause') AS Cause
  FROM ins_claim
 WHERE xpath.valueOf(damagereport,
                     '//Cause[contains(.,"brakes")]') IS NOT NULL
```

Given enough time and memory, this approach would end up parsing each XML document in your ins_claim table, perhaps to find that none of them matches! Yikes.

We'll see in Chapter 13 how searching through millions of XML documents is made both fast and easy using Oracle8*i*'s interMedia Text XML searching facilities. As a sneak preview of this functionality, instead of using `xpath` helper functions in the WHERE clause, let's leverage the interMedia Text `CONTAINS()` operator in our SQL statement's WHERE clause like this:

```
/*
** Performance is excellent with intermediaText
** CONTAINS() to narrow down the millions of
** documents to the few matching ones. Then,
** xpath.valueOf can be used in the SELECT
** statement to operate on the few matching documents.
*/
SELECT claimid, xpath.valueOf(damagereport,'//Cause') AS Cause
  FROM ins_claim
 WHERE CONTAINS(damagereport,'brakes WITHIN Cause') > 0
```

By using interMedia Text to locate the few matching documents out of a million, and our `xpath` helper package to extract XML subtrees from the few matching document fragments, we can have our cake and eat it, too.

Using XPath Expressions as Validation Rules

Next, let's take a closer look at how we can apply the `xpath.test` function to create a data-driven system of XPath-based validation rules. Imagine that we're building a system to manage the logistics of a large conference, like XML99 or JavaOne. Part of the Herculean task of organizing shows like these is the "Request for Submissions" process. Authors submit proposals for technical presentations they would like to deliver and, out of thousands of choices, the conference organizers have to pick a select few that make the cut.

Years ago, submitting a proposal involved filling out a paper form and mailing or faxing it in. These days, authors typically submit proposals online by sending in an email or filling out a web page. Some conferences have begun using an XML format for these proposals, imposing some structure on the incoming submissions so they can be machine-processed and automatically put into a database. Here's a simple example of such a proposal:

```
<Submission>
  <Title>Using XPath Expressions as Validation Rules</Title>
  <Author>
    <Name>
      <First>Steve</First>
      <Last>Muench</Last>
    </Name>
    <Email>smuench@yahoo.com</Email>
    <Company>Oracle</Company>
    <PreviousExperience>Yes</PreviousExperience>
  </Author>
  <Abstract>

     By storing XPath expressions in a database table, grouped
     into "rule sets", data-driven validation rules can be
     applied to any XML document by iterating over the list of
     rules in a rule set and testing whether each XPath expression
     is true or false.

  </Abstract>
</Submission>
```

While this sample seems complete, it turns out that many of the submissions sent in are frequently missing key information. This obviously complicates the lives of the conference organizers! We're going to build a system to automate the process of checking a set of validation rules for each XML-based submission to make sure each proposal contains the key information the conference organizers need.

Let's say that for a proposal to be valid, it must satisfy the following rules:

1. *The submission must have an abstract.*

   The organizers need to know a little more about the submission than just the title.

2. *The author must supply first name, last name, and email address.*

   The organizers need to know who's making the proposal and how to get back in touch with that person.

3. *The title must be longer than 12 characters.*

   The organizers have been burned in the past by presentations like "Webbing It!" and "XML: Cool!," so this year they want the title to have a little more substance.

4. *The presenter must have previous presentation experience.*

   The organizers are tired of dealing with stage fright. This year, only folks who have presented before will be considered.

Since our technical paper submissions are coming in as XML documents, it's natural to think of XPath as a language to express these rules. To ascertain whether the submission is valid, we just need to parse the submission's XML document and test whether the following four XPath expressions are true:

1. *The submission must have an abstract.*

   ```
   /Submission/Abstract
   ```

2. *The author must supply first name, last name, and email address.*

   ```
   /Submission/Author[Name/First and Name/Last and Email]
   ```

3. *The title must be longer than 12 characters.*

   ```
   string-length(/Submission/Title) > 12
   ```

4. *The presenter must have previous presentation experience.*

   ```
   //Author/PreviousExperience = "Yes"
   ```

If all of these expressions test true on our document, we'll consider it valid. If any of them tests false, we should notify the submitter of the proposal about the offending error so they can resubmit their proposal after making the necessary corrections. At the moment, the conference organizers have told us about four rules they need to check on each submission document; however, it is inevitable that they will:

- Change their minds or discover some additional rules later on
- Want to apply the system of validations against other XML documents besides the `<Submission>` documents for which they will initially use the system

Given this foregone conclusion, it is best if we design our solution to be generic and reusable so the same XPath-based rules-validation system can have its rules changed or extended easily and can be applied to any kind of XML document.

Since the conference organizers are familiar with editing XML but are not familiar with databases, it might be nice to provide them with an XML-based format to communicate the set of rules they need enforced to the system. This way, they just edit a simple XML file to make changes or add new rules, and the system can do the rest. Example 5-14 shows about the simplest possible XML document that will serve our purpose.

Example 5-14. Ruleset Document Describing a Set of XPath Validation Rules

```
<ruleset name="AbstractSubmission">
  <rule name="Submission must have an abstract">
    /Submission/Abstract
  </rule>
  <rule name="Author must supply First name, Last name, and Email">
     /Submission/Author[Name/First and Name/Last and Email]
  </rule>
```

Example 5-14. Ruleset Document Describing a Set of XPath Validation Rules (continued)

```
  <rule name="Title must be longer than 12 characters">
    string-length(/Submission/Title) > 12
  </rule>
  <rule name="You must have previous presentation experience.">
    //Author/PreviousExperience = "Yes"
  </rule>
</ruleset>
```

Notice that:

- The `<ruleset>` element has a `name` attribute and contains one or more `<rule>` elements.
- Each `<rule>` element has a `name` attribute as well, giving a user-readable description of the rule, and each `<rule>` element contains its corresponding XPath expression as text content.

The organizers can use their favorite text editor or XML editor to modify the `<ruleset>` document, adding new rules or changing the content of the existing ones. To assist them in testing their ruleset *outside* the production submission system, we could even provide a standalone command-line utility that applies the rules in their `<ruleset>` document to an example submission to make sure the rules are working correctly. In fact, in Chapter 6 we'll show how to build this utility.

But here, let's focus on the system that validates the submission documents inside the database using PL/SQL. Since we're going to be validating a lot of submissions, we want to avoid having to constantly reparse the `<ruleset>` document that contains the validation rules we need to verify. So inside the production system, let's keep the ruleset information in a couple of database tables to make querying and accessing the rules very fast, with no parsing needed. No rocket science needed—just the two simple tables:

```
CREATE TABLE ruleset(
  id  NUMBER PRIMARY KEY,
  name       VARCHAR2(30) UNIQUE
);
```

and:

```
CREATE TABLE rule(
  ruleset    NUMBER,
  name       VARCHAR2(200),
  xpath_test VARCHAR2(4000),
  CONSTRAINT rule_pk PRIMARY KEY (ruleset,name),
  CONSTRAINT rule_in_set FOREIGN KEY (ruleset)
    REFERENCES ruleset ON DELETE CASCADE
);
```

and a quick database sequence to generate a unique primary key for each ruleset:

```
CREATE SEQUENCE ruleset_seq;
```

We can create a PL/SQL package called `xpath_rules_admin` that allows us to easily:

- Add a ruleset by passing in the XML `<ruleset>` document as an argument
- Drop a ruleset from the system, given the name

The package specification for `xpath_rules_admin` looks like this:

```
CREATE OR REPLACE PACKAGE xpath_rules_admin AS

  -- Add (or replace) a ruleset based on an XML <ruleset> document
  PROCEDURE addRuleSet( doc xmldom.DOMDocument );

  -- Drop a ruleset by name
  PROCEDURE dropRuleSet( ruleset_name VARCHAR2 );

END;
```

The package body appears in Example 5-15. The code for `addRuleSet` does the following:

1. Declares handy record variables using `ruleset%ROWTYPE` and `rule%ROWTYPE` to work with variables that have the same structure as the ruleset and rule tables, respectively
2. Uses `xpath.valueOf(doc,'/ruleset/@name')` to get the name of the ruleset being added from the `name` attribute on the `<ruleset>` element
3. Inserts the new ruleset into the ruleset table, after getting a new primary key from the `ruleset_seq` sequence and dropping any existing ruleset by the same name
4. Uses `xpath.selectNodes(doc,'/ruleset/rule')` to get a list of all `<rule>` elements declared in the document
5. Loops over the list of rules by using `xmldom.getLength(theRules)` to determine how many `<rule>` elements we found in step 4
6. Uses `xmldom.item(theRules, j-1)` to get the `j`th item in the (zero-based) list of matching `<rule>` elements
7. Uses `xpath.valueOf(curRuleNode,'@name')` to get the name of the current rule
8. Uses `xpath.valueOf(curRuleNode,'.',normalize=>TRUE)` to get the value of the current rule node—the XPath expression—with any extra whitespace normalized out of the value
9. Finally, inserts the data into the ruleset table

Example 5-15. Routines to Administer XPath Validation Rules

```
CREATE OR REPLACE PACKAGE BODY xpath_rules_admin AS

  PROCEDURE addRuleSet( doc xmldom.DOMDocument ) IS
    -- (1) Declare handy record variables to work with
    theRuleSet  ruleset%ROWTYPE;
    theRule     rule%ROWTYPE;
    theRules    xmldom.DOMNodeList;
    curRuleNode xmldom.DOMNode;
  BEGIN
    -- (2) Get the name of the ruleset being added
    theRuleSet.name := xpath.valueOf(doc,'/ruleset/@name');
    DropRuleSet(theRuleSet.name);
    -- (3) Get a new ruleset id and insert the new ruleset
    SELECT ruleset_seq.nextval INTO theRuleSet.id FROM DUAL;
    INSERT INTO ruleset(id,name) VALUES (theRuleSet.id, theRuleSet.name);
    -- (4) Get a list of all <rule> elements under <ruleset>
    theRules := xpath.selectNodes(doc,'/ruleset/rule');
    -- (5) Loop over the list of <rule> elements we found
    FOR j IN 1..xmldom.getLength(theRules) LOOP
      -- (6) Get the j-th rule in the list (zero-based!)
      curRuleNode := xmldom.item(theRules,j-1);
      theRule.ruleset := theRuleSet.id;
      -- (7) Get the name of the current rule
      theRule.name := xpath.valueOf(curRuleNode,'@name');
      -- (8) Get the normalized value of the current rule element ('.')
      theRule.xpath_test := xpath.valueOf(curRuleNode,'.',normalize=>TRUE);
      -- (9) Insert the current rule into the rule table
      INSERT INTO rule(ruleset,name,xpath_test)
       VALUES (theRule.ruleset, theRule.name, theRule.xpath_test);
    END LOOP;
    COMMIT;
  END;

  PROCEDURE dropRuleSet( ruleset_name VARCHAR2 ) IS
  BEGIN
    DELETE FROM ruleset WHERE name = ruleset_name;
    COMMIT;
  END;
END;
```

To load the current version of the XPath ruleset for conference paper proposal submissions into our system, assume that the conference organizers have emailed us the ruleset document from Example 5-14 in a file named *AbstractSubmissionRules.xml*. We save the attachment into our *C:\XMLFILES* directory on our database server machine. Since we will be loading rulesets from XML `<ruleset>` files frequently, we can think ahead and create a stored procedure to automate the steps:

```
CREATE OR REPLACE PROCEDURE loadRulesetFromFile( dir      VARCHAR2,
                                                 filename VARCHAR2) IS
  rulesXMLFile BFILE;
  xmldoc xmldom.DOMDocument;
```

```
BEGIN
  -- Get a handle to the ruleset file
  rulesXMLFile := BFileName(dir,filename);
  -- Parse the file to get an XML Document
  xmldoc := xml.parse(rulesXMLFile);
  -- Add a new ruleset based on the document
  xpath_rules_admin.addRuleset(xmldoc);
  -- Free the memory used by the parsed XML Document
  xml.freeDocument(xmldoc);
EXCEPTION
  WHEN OTHERS THEN xml.freeDocument(xmldoc); RAISE;
END;
```

Then, to load our ruleset from the *AbstractSumbmissionRules.xml* files, we can just execute a one-liner at the SQL*Plus command prompt:

```
EXEC loadRulesetFromFile('XMLFILES','AbstractSubmissionRules.xml');
```

To verify that our rules were loaded correctly, we can try the SELECT statement:

```
SELECT r.name, xpath_test
  FROM rule r, ruleset rs
 WHERE rs.name = 'AbstractSubmission'
   AND r.ruleset = rs.id
```

and indeed we see that our rules have been loaded out of the *Abstract-SubmissionRules.xml* file and stored for safekeeping in the rule table:

```
NAME               XPATH_TEST
------------------ ------------------------------------------------------
Author must supply /Submission/Author[Name/First and Name/Last and Email]
First name, Last
name, and Email

Submission must    /Submission/Abstract
have an abstract

Title must be      string-length(/Submission/Title) > 12
longer than 12
characters

You must have      //Presenter/PreviousExperience = "Yes"
previous
presentation
experience.
```

The last step in implementing our solution is to write a routine to validate an XML document against a ruleset that we've loaded into the database. The `xpath_rules.validate` method below should do just fine:

```
CREATE OR REPLACE PACKAGE xpath_rules AS

  -- Validate an XML document based on a named ruleset
  -- Return any offending errors in the errors argument
```

```
    PROCEDURE validate( doc          IN xmldom.DOMDocument,
                        ruleset_name IN VARCHAR2,
                        valid       OUT BOOLEAN,
                        errors      OUT VARCHAR2
                      );
  END;
```

Since the hard part of enforcing the rules is done by simply using `xpath.test` to evaluate whether a given XPath rule is true or false, the code for the `validate` routine only needs to do the following:

1. Loop over all the rules in the rule table for the ruleset name passed in.
2. Call `xpath.test()` on the current rule's XPath expression.
3. Keep track of any rules that fail and report the failing rules in the `errors` variable that is returned to the caller.

The straightforward implementation for the `xpath_rules` package is in Example 5-16.

Example 5-16. Validating XML Document Against an XPath Ruleset

```
CREATE OR REPLACE PACKAGE BODY xpath_rules AS

  FUNCTION idForRuleset(ruleset_name VARCHAR2) RETURN NUMBER IS
    theId NUMBER;
  BEGIN
    SELECT id
      INTO theId
      FROM ruleset
     WHERE name = ruleset_name;
     RETURN theId;
  EXCEPTION
    WHEN NO_DATA_FOUND THEN RETURN NULL;
  END;

  PROCEDURE validate( doc          IN xmldom.DOMDocument,
                      ruleset_name IN VARCHAR2,
                      valid       OUT BOOLEAN,
                      errors      OUT VARCHAR2
                    ) IS
    errcount  NUMBER := 0;
    rulesetId NUMBER := idForRuleSet(ruleset_name);
  BEGIN
    IF xmldom.isNull(doc) THEN
      valid  := FALSE;
      errors := 'Cannot validate. Document is null';
    ELSIF rulesetId IS NULL THEN
      valid  := FALSE;
      errors := 'Cannot validate. Ruleset '||ruleset_name||' does not exist.';
    ELSE
      -- Assume the doc is valid until proven otherwise
      valid := TRUE;
```

Example 5-16. Validating XML Document Against an XPath Ruleset (continued)

```
      -- (1) Loop over all the rules for the ruleset whose name is passed in
      FOR curRule IN (SELECT name, xpath_test
                        FROM rule
                       WHERE ruleset = rulesetId) LOOP
        -- (2) Call xpath.test on the current rule's expression
        IF NOT xpath.test(doc,curRule.xpath_test) THEN
          -- (3) Keep track of rules that fail by bumping error count
          errcount := errcount + 1;
          -- Mark the doc invalid
          valid := FALSE;
          -- Put 2nd through Nth error on a new line.
          IF errcount > 1 THEN
            errors := errors ||CHR(10);
          END IF;
          errors := errors || '('||errcount||') '||curRule.name;
        END IF;
      END LOOP;
    END IF;
  END;
END;
```

Next, we need to write a **handleNewSubmission** routine to handle new abstract submissions. It needs to apply the general **xpath_rules** package—which can validate any XML document against any ruleset—to validate **<Submission>** documents against the particular **AbstractSubmission** ruleset. We need the routine to:

1. Call **xpath_rules.validate** using the **AbstractSubmission** ruleset to verify that all of the rules for abstract submissions are in order.
2. Insert the key information for the abstract into the database and assign the submission an ID number for tracking if the abstract being considered passes all the validation rules.
3. Send an email notification to the submitter indicating that we received the abstract. If there are any validation errors, the email should indicate what was wrong with the submission.

The new **utl_smtp** built-in package that ships with Oracle8*i* makes sending email over SMTP from within PL/SQL possible. The **sendEmail** procedure in Example 5-17 uses the routines in **utl_smtp** to send an email using the SMTP protocol directly from inside the database. Since the package is implemented in a generic way, you might find plenty of other uses for it in your work as well.

Example 5-17. Sending an Email from Inside Oracle8i Using PL/SQL

```
CREATE OR REPLACE PROCEDURE sendEmail(smtp_server  VARCHAR2,
                                      from_userid  VARCHAR2,
                                      to_userid    VARCHAR2,
                                      subject      VARCHAR2,
                                      body         VARCHAR2,
```

Example 5-17. Sending an Email from Inside Oracle8i Using PL/SQL (continued)

```
                                          from_name    VARCHAR2 := NULL,
                                          to_name      VARCHAR2 := NULL,
                                          content_type VARCHAR2 := NULL)
IS
  c utl_smtp.connection;
  from_domain VARCHAR2(200) := SUBSTR(from_userid,INSTR(from_userid,'@')+1);

  PROCEDURE header(name VARCHAR2, value VARCHAR2) IS
  BEGIN
    utl_smtp.write_data(c, name || ': ' || value || utl_tcp.CRLF);
  END;

BEGIN
  c := utl_smtp.open_connection( smtp_server );
  utl_smtp.helo(c, from_domain );
  utl_smtp.mail(c, from_userid );
  utl_smtp.rcpt(c, to_userid );
  utl_smtp.open_data(c);
  header('From','"'||NVL(from_name,from_userid)||'" <'||from_userid||'>');
  header('To','"'||NVL(to_name,to_userid)||'" <'||to_userid||'>');
  header('Subject', subject );
  header('Content-Type', NVL(content_type,'text/plain'));
  utl_smtp.write_data(c, utl_tcp.CRLF || body );
  utl_smtp.close_data(c);
  utl_smtp.quit(c);
EXCEPTION
  WHEN utl_smtp.transient_error OR utl_smtp.permanent_error THEN
    utl_smtp.quit(c);
    raise_application_error(-20199,'Error sending mail: ' || sqlerrm);

END;
```

We'll implement the `handleNewSubmission` procedure to accomplish the three required steps noted previously: calling `xpath.validate` to check the submission against the ruleset, inserting the information into the database if it's valid, and then sending an email notification with `sendEmail`. The table we'll need to store the submission information is:

```
CREATE TABLE accepted_submission (
  id          NUMBER PRIMARY KEY,
  title       VARCHAR2(80),
  presenter   VARCHAR2(80),
  email       VARCHAR2(80),
  abstract    VARCHAR(4000)
);
```

and the sequence we'll need for generating submission IDs is:

```
CREATE SEQUENCE accepted_submission_seq START WITH 600;
```

Example 5-18 shows the code for `handleNewSubmission`.

Example 5-18. Procedure to Coordinate New Paper Submission Handling

```
CREATE OR REPLACE PROCEDURE handleNewSubmission(theSubmission CLOB) IS
  isValid          BOOLEAN;
  EmailSubject     VARCHAR2(80);
  EmailBody        VARCHAR2(32767);
  doc              xmldom.DOMDocument;
  submission       accepted_submission%ROWTYPE;
BEGIN
  doc := xml.parse(theSubmission);
  xpath_rules.validate(doc,
                       ruleset_name => 'AbstractSubmission',
                       valid        => isValid,
                       errors       => EmailBody);

  submission.email := xpath.valueOf(doc,'/Submission/Author/Email');

  IF isValid THEN
    -- Assign a new submission id
    SELECT accepted_submission_seq.nextval INTO submission.id FROM DUAL;
    -- Collect the info we need from the XML Paper Submission
    submission.title     := xpath.valueOf(doc,'/Submission/Title',TRUE);
    submission.presenter := xpath.valueOf(doc,'/Submission/Author/Name/First')||
                            ' '||xpath.valueOf(doc,'/Submission/Author/Name/Last');
    submission.abstract  := xpath.valueOf(doc,'/Submission/Abstract',TRUE);
    -- Insert it into our accepted submissions table
    INSERT INTO accepted_submission
    VALUES(submission.id,submission.title,submission.presenter,
           submission.email,submission.abstract);
    EmailSubject := 'Your abstract was accepted. Reference# '||submission.id;
    EmailBody    := 'Thank you.';
  ELSE
    EmailSubject := 'Your abstract was rejected because...';
    -- EmailBody already contains errors flagged by XPath Validation
  END IF;

  IF submission.email IS NOT NULL THEN
    sendEmail(smtp_server => 'mailserver@you.com',
              from_userid => 'smuench@yahoo.com',
                to_userid => submission.email,
                  subject => EmailSubject,
                     body => EmailBody);
  END IF;
  xml.freeDocument(doc);
  COMMIT;
EXCEPTION
  WHEN OTHERS THEN xml.freeDocument(doc); ROLLBACK; RAISE;
END;
```

So we can call **handleNewSubmission** to handle a single new abstract submission, but what if we want to handle all of the abstracts that have been submitted today in batch? Since we're using PL/SQL, it's a simple matter of looping over the abstracts submitted today and calling **handleNewSubmission** for each one. The aptly named **handleTodaysSubmissions** procedure looks like this:

```
CREATE OR REPLACE PROCEDURE handleTodaysSubmissions IS
BEGIN

  -- Loop over any Submission in the xml_documents table submitted today.
  FOR currentSubmission IN (SELECT xmldoc
                              FROM xml_documents
                             WHERE timestamp > TRUNC(SYSDATE)
                               AND docname like 'Abstract%') LOOP

    -- Handle the current abstract
    handleNewSubmission( currentSubmission.xmldoc );

  END LOOP;
END;
```

We're done! To review, we've implemented the following code:

xpath_rules_admin
: A package to add XPath rulesets based on **<ruleset>** documents

xpath_rules
: A package to validate an XML document against any ruleset

sendEmail
: A procedure to send email from inside the database

handleNewSubmission
: A procedure to validate a **<Submisson>** document against the **AbstractSubmisson** ruleset and notify the submitter by email of their status

handleTodaysSubmissions
: A procedure to process all new submissions that arrived today in batch

Let's test out the system on a few sample paper submissions. We'll be working with the two submissions **Abstract_With_Error.xml** and **Abstract_Good.xml**, shown in Example 5-19.

Example 5-19. Two Sample Abstract Submissions to Process

```
<!-- Abstract_With_Error.xml -->
<Submission>
  <Title>Using XPath</Title>
  <Author>
    <Name>
      <First>Steve</First>
    </Name>
    <Email>smuench@yahoo.com</Email>
    <Company>Oracle</Company>
    <PreviousExperience>No</PreviousExperience>
  </Author>
</Submission>
```

Example 5-19. Two Sample Abstract Submissions to Process (continued)

```
<!-- Abstract_Good.xml -->
<Submission>
  <Title>Using XPath Expressions as Validation Rules</Title>
  <Author>
    <Name>
      <First>Steve</First>
      <Last>Muench</Last>
    </Name>
    <Email>smuench@yahoo.com</Email>
    <Company>Oracle</Company>
    <PreviousExperience>Yes</PreviousExperience>
  </Author>
  <Abstract>

     By storing XPath expressions in a database table, grouped
     into rulesets, data-driven validation rules can be
     applied to an XML document by iterating over the list of
     rules in a ruleset and testing whether each XPath expression
     is true or false.

  </Abstract>
</Submission>
```

First, we load the two sample submissions into our xml_documents table from the *XMLFILES* directory by using `xmldoc.save`. In the real system, the submissions will be inserted by a web server into the xml_documents table by a routine that calls `xmldoc.save` in response to the posting of the HTML form that authors will use to post their submissions from their browser:

```
BEGIN
  -- Load the two XML files from the file system into our xml_documents table
  xmldoc.save('AbstractOne',BFileName('XMLFILES','Abstract_With_Error.xml'));
  xmldoc.save('AbstractTwo',BFileName('XMLFILES','Abstract_Good.xml'));
END;
```

Then we run our batch process by executing the `handleTodaysSubmissions` routine from the SQL*Plus command line:

```
EXEC handleTodaysSubmissions;
```

If you are on a Unix platform running Oracle8*i* version 8.1.6, you might receive an error when trying to run this example, with the symptoms:

```
ORA-29540: class oracle/plsql/net/TCPConnection
           does not exist
ORA-06512: at "XMLBOOK.HANDLENEWSUBMISSION", line 45
```

To remedy the situation, connect as SYS and run:

```
?/rdbms/admin/initplsj.sql.
```

In a few minutes, the first email notification arrives, bringing the bad news about the first submission:

```
Return-Path: <smuench@yahoo.com>
Date: Mon, 3 Apr 2000 17:16:53 -0700 (PDT)
From: "smuench@yahoo.com" <smuench@yahoo.com>
To: "smuench@yahoo.com" <smuench@yahoo.com>
Subject: Your abstract was rejected because...
Content-Type: text/plain

 (1) Author must supply First name, Last name, and Email
 (2) Submission must have an abstract
 (3) Title must be longer than 12 characters
 (4) You must have previous presentation experience.
```

If you go back and review the contents of *Abstract_With_Error.xml* above, you'll see indeed that it fails all of the XPath validation rules, so the abstract was correctly handled and no data regarding the abstract was entered into the accepted_submission table.

Shortly thereafter, another email arrives with the joyous announcement that the second abstract was received and assigned the tracking number of 600:

```
Return-Path: <smuench@yahoo.com>
Date: Mon, 3 Apr 2000 17:47:28 -0700 (PDT)
From: "smuench@yahoo.com" <smuench@yahoo.com>
To: "smuench@yahoo.com" <smuench@yahoo.com>
Subject: Your abstract was accepted. Reference# 600
Content-Type: text/plain

Thank you.
```

So everything is working as designed. Next, we'll look at the basic processing required to post XML to another server and receive XML back in return. This would, for example, allow us to post our accepted paper submissions in XML format to a server at another company that is coordinating the paper selection process, or eventually send information on accepted presenters to a company that might be coordinating their hotel reservations and flight arrangements.

Working with XML Messages

In this section, we'll investigate examples of using XML as a structured data exchange mechanism between applications. First we'll look at synchronous approaches like posting and getting XML messages over HTTP; then we'll learn the basics of Oracle's Advanced Queuing (AQ) mechanism to support asynchronous XML message passing between applications using reliable queues.

Sending and Receiving XML Between Servers

Since XML can represent structured data in an open, standard way, it is quickly becoming the preferred method of data exchange over the Web. In a year or two, it will be the dominant method. Sites that serve up information in HTML—useful primarily to human eyeballs—will add the ability to retrieve the information in an XML-based format that will allow other servers to use that data more easily. Businesses whose current web-based applications only allow *human* interaction through web-based HTML forms are scrambling to add the ability to accept posted requests in XML formats to enable Business-to-Business automation.

In this way, the Web will rapidly evolve to offer a business application developer a sea of XML-based information services, where your application can check on the status of an order, cancel a reservation, or book a flight simply by sending and receiving appropriate XML datagrams. It goes without saying that the ability to write programs that post and receive XML is a core competence for any developer building the next generation of web applications. Here we'll explore how these key activities can be done with PL/SQL inside Oracle8*i*.

To be very precise, when we talk about "posting XML to another server over the Web," what we mean is sending an HTTP POST request to that server, containing an XML document in the request body with a MIME `Content-Type` of `text/xml`.

Therefore, a fundamental ingredient in posting XML over the Web is the ability to send an HTTP POST request. Since the HTTP protocol is a set of conventions layered on top of TCP/IP, we can make use of the Oracle8*i* built-in package called `utl_tcp` to build our HTTP POSTing solution.

The `utl_tcp` package exposes the low-level routines necessary to open a TCP/IP connection, write data into the connection, and read data back from the connection. By writing the appropriate HTTP commands and data to the connection, we can easily implement our PL/SQL-based XML posting functionality. For example, to post this XML document:

```
<moreovernews>
  <article>
    <url> http://www.xmlhack.com/read.php?item=400 </url>
    <headline_text> XSL Working Group to address extension concerns
    </headline_text>
    <source> XMLHack.com </source>
  </article>
</moreovernews>
```

to a web service located at the URL:

http://services.example.com:2775/add-news-story.xsql

we need to do the following:

1. Open a TCP/IP connection to the `services.example.com` machine on port 2775.
2. Write the header information to the connection:

   ```
   HTTP POST /add-news-story.xsql HTTP/1.0
   Content-Type: text/xml
   Content-Length: 240
   ```

3. Write a carriage return to the connection to separate the header from the body.
4. Write the XML document to the connection.

Then we read the response from the connection. In Appendix A you can check out the full source code of the package that implements this HTTP behavior on top of the lower-level facilities provided by the `utl_tcp` package. Here, we just need to see the API for our `http` package, which looks like this:

```
CREATE OR REPLACE PACKAGE http AS

  -- HTTP POST a document to url and return response

  PROCEDURE post(doc                   VARCHAR2,
                 content_type          VARCHAR2,
                 url                   VARCHAR2,
                 resp              OUT VARCHAR2,
                 resp_content_type OUT VARCHAR2,
                 proxyServer           VARCHAR2 := NULL,
                 proxyPort             NUMBER   := 80);

  -- HTTP GET resource at url and return response document

  PROCEDURE get(url                   VARCHAR2,
                resp              OUT VARCHAR2,
                resp_content_type OUT VARCHAR2,
                proxyServer           VARCHAR2 := NULL,
                proxyPort             NUMBER   := 80);

END;
```

This package lets us easily HTTP POST or HTTP GET any information over the Web.

Built on top of the `post` and `get` procedures in the `http` package, we can build another helper package called `xml_http` which makes posting and getting XML-based information a little easier. Example 5-20 shows the package specification for `xml_http`.

Example 5-20. The xml_http Helper Package Specification

```
CREATE OR REPLACE PACKAGE xml_http AS

  -- POST XML document in string buffer to URL, return response as XML Document

  PROCEDURE post(doc                VARCHAR2,
                 url                VARCHAR2,
                 resp           OUT xmldom.DOMDocument,
                 proxyServer        VARCHAR2 := NULL,
                 proxyPort          NUMBER   := 80);

  -- HTTP POST XML document to URL and return response as an XML document

  PROCEDURE post(doc                xmldom.DOMDocument,
                 url                VARCHAR2,
                 resp           OUT xmldom.DOMDocument,
                 proxyServer        VARCHAR2 := NULL,
                 proxyPort          NUMBER   := 80);

  -- HTTP GET resource at url and return response as an XML document

  PROCEDURE get(url                VARCHAR2,
                resp           OUT xmldom.DOMDocument,
                proxyServer        VARCHAR2 := NULL,
                proxyPort          NUMBER   := 80);

END;
```

You'll see in the implementation of `xml_http` in Example 5-21 that the procedures here simply add the convenience of being able to directly post an `xmldom.DOMDocument` object as well return the response of a POST or a GET directly as an `xmldom.DOMDocument` for further processing.

Example 5-21. Implementation of xml_http Helper Package

```
CREATE OR REPLACE PACKAGE BODY xml_http AS

  PROCEDURE xmlDocForResponse(response          VARCHAR2,
                              content_type      VARCHAR2,
                              xmldoc        OUT xmldom.DOMDocument) IS
  BEGIN
    IF response IS NOT NULL THEN
      IF content_type LIKE 'text/xml%' OR
         content_type LIKE 'application/xml%' THEN
        xmldoc := xml.parse(response);
      END IF;
    END IF;
  END;

  PROCEDURE post(doc                VARCHAR2,
                 url                VARCHAR2,
                 resp           OUT xmldom.DOMDocument,
```

Example 5-21. Implementation of xml_http Helper Package (continued)

```
                proxyServer      VARCHAR2 := NULL,
                proxyPort        NUMBER   := 80)
  IS
    response     VARCHAR2(32767);
    content_type VARCHAR2(400);
  BEGIN
    http.post(doc,'text/xml',
              url,response,content_type,proxyServer,proxyPort);
    xmlDocForResponse(response,content_type,resp);
  END;

  PROCEDURE post(doc xmldom.DOMDocument,
                 url VARCHAR2,
                 resp OUT xmldom.DOMDocument,
                 proxyServer VARCHAR2 := NULL,
                 proxyPort   NUMBER   := 80)
  IS
    response     VARCHAR2(32767);
    content_type VARCHAR2(400);
  BEGIN
    http.post(xpath.extract(doc),'text/xml',
              url,response,content_type,proxyServer,proxyPort);
    xmlDocForResponse(response,content_type,resp);
  END;

  PROCEDURE get(url               VARCHAR2,
                resp          OUT xmldom.DOMDocument,
                proxyServer       VARCHAR2 := NULL,
                proxyPort         NUMBER   := 80) IS
    response VARCHAR2(32767);
    content_type VARCHAR2(400);
  BEGIN
    http.get(url,response,content_type,proxyServer,proxyPort);
    xmlDocForResponse(response,content_type,resp);
  END;

END;
```

With all these routines in place, it's time to put them to work. First, we'll try posting a news story to a server that supports a "Post a New Newstory Service." Figure 5-2 illustrates the XML-over-HTTP exchange that takes place between our database server and the news story service.

The requester posts an XML-based news story in an expected XML format like the Moreover.com news format, and the service returns an XML-based message to indicate the status of the request. Here, the returning XML message only contains a status message, but the datagram sent back by the server could contain lots of additional useful information besides a status.

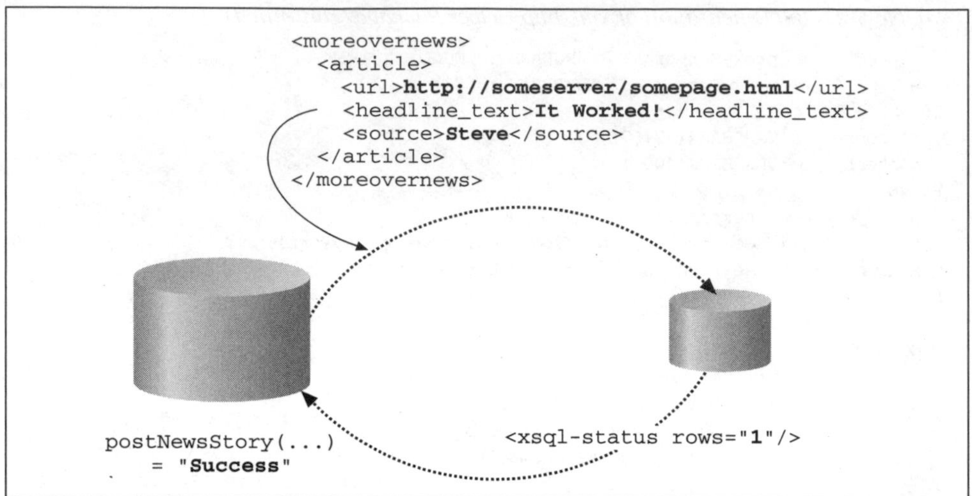

Figure 5-2. Posting an XML-based news story datagram to a web service

Example 5-22 shows a `postNewsStory` procedure that:

1. Concatenates the argument values passed to the function at the appropriate places in the `<moreovernews>` XML datagram
2. Posts the news story datagram to the web service URL using `xml_http.post`
3. Tests the content of the returned XML document using `xpath.test` to see if the POST request succeeded.

Example 5-22. Posting XML-based News Stories to Another Web Server

```
CREATE OR REPLACE FUNCTION postNewsStory( story_headline VARCHAR2,
                                          story_source   VARCHAR2,
                                          story_url      VARCHAR2
                                        ) RETURN VARCHAR2 IS
  msg          VARCHAR2(32767);
  service_url  VARCHAR2(80);
  xml_response xmldom.DOMDocument;
  retval       VARCHAR2(10);
BEGIN
  -- This is the URL for the Post-a-New-Newstory Web Service
  service_url := 'http://xml/xsql/demo/insertxml/insertnewsstory.xsql';

  -- Prepare the XML document to post by "gluing" the values of
  -- the headline, news source, and URL of the article into the
  -- XML message at the appropriate places.
  msg := '<moreovernews>
           <article>
            <url>'|| story_url ||'</url>
            <headline_text>'|| story_headline ||'</headline_text>
            <source>'||story_source||'</source>
           </article>
          </moreovernews>';
```

Example 5-22. Posting XML-based News Stories to Another Web Server (continued)

```
  -- Post the XML document to the web service URL and get the Response
  xml_http.post(msg,service_url,xml_response);

  -- Check the response to see if it was a success.
  -- This service returns <xsql-status rows="1"/> if it was a success.
  IF xpath.test(xml_response,'/xsql-status/@rows="1"') THEN
    retval := 'Success';
  ELSE
    retval := 'Failed';
  END IF;

  -- Free the XML document
  xml.freeDocument(xml_response);

  -- Return the status
  RETURN retval;

EXCEPTION
  WHEN OTHERS THEN xml.freeDocument(xml_response); RAISE;
END;
```

We can quickly test the function from SQL*Plus by creating a SQL*Plus variable named `status`, and executing the function like this:

```
SQL> variable status varchar2(10);
SQL> exec :status := postNewsStory('It Worked!','Steve','http://someserver/
somepage.html');

PL/SQL procedure successfully completed.

SQL> print status

STATUS
------------
Success
```

Printing the value of the `status` variable shows that the request was a `Success`.

Next, we'll try an HTTP GET example. Sometimes, web services simply take the information they need to carry out their task as parameters on a URL. In these cases, it is not required to post any XML document. Instead we just do an HTTP GET on the service's URL with appropriate parameter values tacked on to the end of the URL.

Figure 5-3 shows the exchange between our database and a web service that allows us to look up the name of an airport, given its three-letter description. The database running at the site offering this "Airport Lookup" service contains the three-letter codes and descriptions of more than 10,000 worldwide airports. We can look up the code for any airport code `XYZ` by doing an HTTP GET on the URL:

```
http://ws5.olab.com/xsql/demo/airport/airport.xsql?airport=XYZ
```

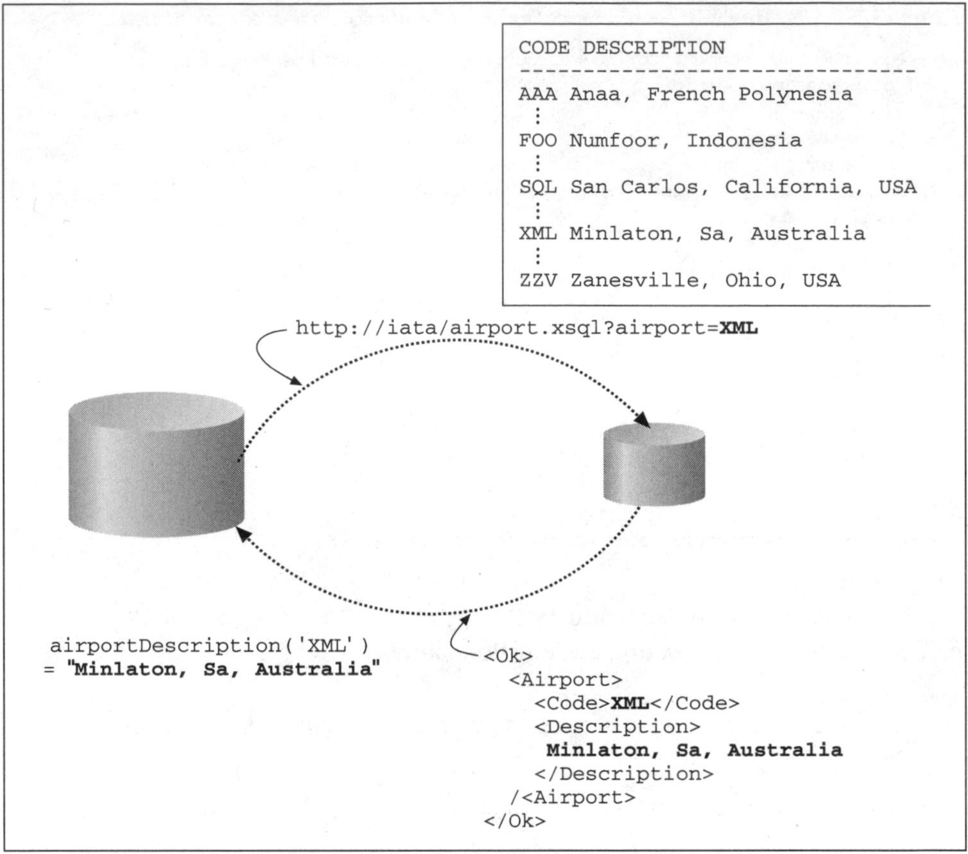
CODE DESCRIPTION
AAA Anaa, French Polynesia
FOO Numfoor, Indonesia
SQL San Carlos, California, USA
XML Minlaton, Sa, Australia
ZZV Zanesville, Ohio, USA
http://iata/airport.xsql?airport=XML
airportDescription('XML')
= "Minlaton, Sa, Australia"
<Ok>
<Airport>
<Code>XML</Code>
<Description>
Minlaton, Sa, Australia
</Description>
/<Airport>
</Ok>

Figure 5-3. Getting XML from a web service

To do this, we create a quick `airportDescription` function that:

1. Concatenates the argument value passed to the function at the end of the web service's URL
2. Gets the datagram from the web service using `xml_http.get`
3. Tests the content of the return XML document using `xpath.test` to see if the POST request succeeded.

Here is the code:

```
CREATE OR REPLACE FUNCTION airportDescription(code VARCHAR2) RETURN VARCHAR2 IS
  description  VARCHAR2(80);
  proxyServer  VARCHAR2(80) := 'www-proxy.us.oracle.com';
  service_url  VARCHAR2(80);
  xml_response xmldom.DOMDocument;
BEGIN
  -- This is the url of the XML web service to look up airports by code
  service_url := 'http://ws5.olab.com/xsql/demo/airport/airport.xsql';
```

```
  -- Do an HTTP GET of the service_url, tacking on the "airport" parameter
  xml_http.get(service_url||'?airport='||code,
               xml_response,
               proxyServer);

  -- If the Document Element is <Ok>, then return the description
  IF xpath.test(xml_response,'Ok') THEN
    RETURN xpath.valueOf(xml_response,'/Ok/Airport/Description');
  ELSE
    RETURN NULL;
  END IF;
END;
```

Again, we can quickly test our new `airportDescription` function from SQL*Plus like this to see what airport corresponds to the three-letter abbreviation `XML`:

```
SQL> VARIABLE descrip VARCHAR2(80);
SQL> EXEC :descrip := airportDescription('XML');

PL/SQL procedure successfully completed.

SQL> PRINT descrip

DESCRIP
-------------------------
Minlaton, Sa, Australia
```

So using this web service, we discover that to *really* travel to the heart of XML country, you'll need to fly Qantas.

Handling Asynchronous XML Messages in Queues

Whether you're processing bank customers at a teller window or customer orders on a web site, both theory and practice concur that queues are an optimal approach to handle the job. Queues allow work to pile up in an orderly fashion, and enable a flexible number of workers to be assigned to process the work as soon as is feasible. During rush hour, more workers can be assigned to the task. During off hours, a skeleton crew can hold down the fort. In our scenario, the queue of work is handled by an Oracle Advanced Queueing queue whose contents are managed in a queue table, and the "workers" are programs that dequeue messages and process them.

Since Oracle's AQ facility leverages the Oracle8*i* database extensively, the messages you place in the queues have the same reliability guarantees as all database data. In layman's terms, this means that messages are reliably delivered and never get lost. Oracle AQ even handles the automatic propagation of messages between queues on different machines and between different queuing systems. So it should be clear that it's worth our time to investigate how to tap into this powerful feature for exchanging XML messages asynchronously.

Figure 5-4 illustrates the basic idea of a queue in the database. One or more processes add work to be done into the queue by enqueuing a message, and other worker processes dequeue the messages for handling. The default is intuitively the "fairest" mechanism, first-in, first-out, but AQ supports many other dequeuing methods as well. A simple example might be to dequeue high-priority orders first, or orders from platinum customers.

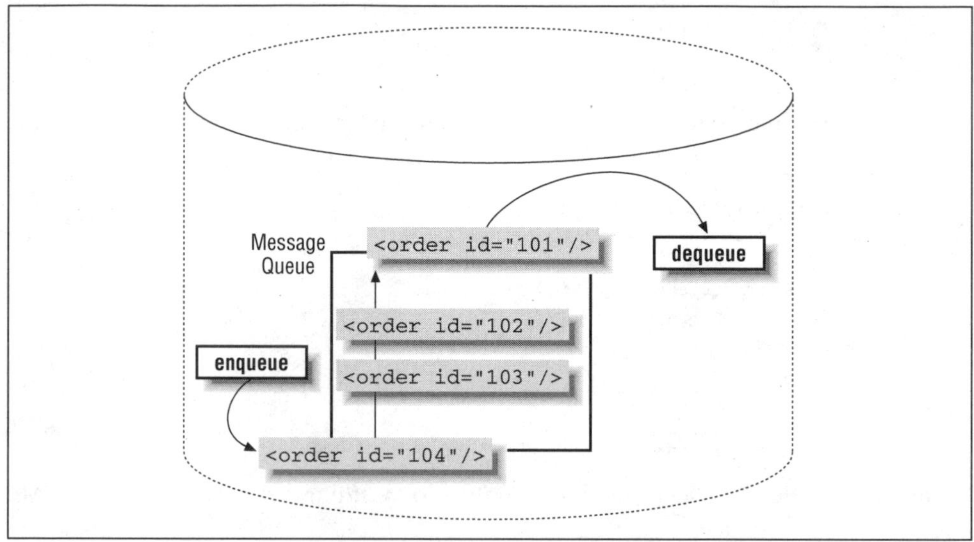

Figure 5-4. Enqueuing and dequeuing XML messages with Oracle AQ

Setting up a queue to use is easy to do. If you have been granted the AQ_ADMINISTRATOR_ROLE, you can do all the maintenance operations to create, alter, and drop queues and queue tables. If a DBA like SYS grants you the following permissions, you'll be in business:

```
connect sys/password
GRANT AQ_ADMINISTRATOR_ROLE TO xmlbook;
GRANT EXECUTE ON SYS.DBMS_AQADM TO xmlbook;
GRANT EXECUTE ON SYS.DBMS_AQ TO xmlbook;
GRANT EXECUTE ON SYS.DBMS_AQIN TO xmlbook;
```

We'll create an **xml_msg_queue** to store our XML messages while they await further processing. A queue is associated with a companion table used to store and enable querying of queued messages, so we first create a queue table, then a queue that lives in that table, by running an anonymous block of PL/SQL like this:

```
DECLARE
  queueTableName VARCHAR2(30) := 'xml_msg_queuetable';
  queueName      VARCHAR2(30) := 'xml_msg_queue';
BEGIN
  -- Drop the queue table, ignoring an error if it does not
```

```
  BEGIN
    dbms_aqadm.drop_queue_table(queueTableName);
  EXCEPTION WHEN OTHERS THEN NULL;
  END;

  -- Create the queue table
  dbms_aqadm.create_queue_table(queue_table => queueTableName,
                                queue_payload_type => 'RAW');

  -- Create the queue based on the queue table
  dbms_aqadm.create_queue(queueName,queueTableName);

  -- Start the queue (enabling enqueues and dequeues to occur)
  dbms_aqadm.start_queue(queueName);
END;
```

Note that we're using the simplest kind of queue, which supports a raw binary payload of up to 32K bytes, for learning about the mechanics. Once you have the basics under your belt for how to work with XML messages in these raw-payload queues, you'll find that experimenting with AQ's other facilities will become much easier. As we've done with other XML-related technologies that we plan to use over and over, let's build a helper package to work with XML messages and advanced queues. Example 5-23 shows the package specification of the `xmlq` package. It's very simple: it contains just two routines, an enqueue and a dequeue. The `enqueue` procedure takes an `xmldom.DOMDocument` and the name of the queue into which the XML message should be enqueued. The `dequeue` function takes a queue name and `wait` flag, and returns the dequeued message as an `xmldom.DOMDocument`.

Example 5-23. The xmlq Helper Package Specification

```
CREATE OR REPLACE PACKAGE xmlq AS

  -- Exception raised when queue is empty and dequeue with no wait is attempted

  queue_empty EXCEPTION;

  PRAGMA EXCEPTION_INIT(queue_empty,-25228);

  -- Enqueue an XML document to the (raw-payload) 'queueName' queue.

  PROCEDURE enqueue( xmldoc xmldom.DOMDocument, queueName VARCHAR2 );

  -- Dequeue an XML document from the (raw-payload) 'queueName' queue.

  FUNCTION  dequeue( queueName VARCHAR2, wait BOOLEAN := TRUE )
    RETURN xmldom.DOMDocument;

END;
```

The implementation of the `xmlq` package is nearly as simple as its specification. The only points worth noting are the use of the `utl_raw.cast_to_raw` function to cast the XML message passed in as a block of raw bytes, and the `utl_raw.cast_to_varchar2` to perform the reverse operation on the dequeue. If the caller passed in a `wait` flag value of TRUE, we set the corresponding option in the dequeue options record structure. This tells Oracle AQ that if no message is presently waiting for us in the queue, we intend on sleeping until a message arrives:

```
CREATE OR REPLACE PACKAGE BODY xmlq AS

  msgProp  dbms_aq.message_properties_t;

  ---------------------------------------------------------------------
  -- Enqueue an XML document to the (raw-payload) 'queueName' queue.
  -- Raw-payload queues have a message-size limit of 32767 bytes.
  ---------------------------------------------------------------------
  PROCEDURE enqueue( xmldoc xmldom.DOMDocument, queueName VARCHAR2 ) IS
   enqOpt dbms_aq.enqueue_options_t;
   msgHdl RAW(16);
  BEGIN
    dbms_aq.enqueue(queue_name => queueName,
               enqueue_options => enqOpt,
            message_properties => msgProp,
                       payload => utl_raw.cast_to_raw(xpath.extract(xmldoc)),
                         msgid => msgHdl);
    COMMIT;
  END;

  ---------------------------------------------------------------------
  -- Dequeue an XML document from the (raw-payload) 'queueName' queue.
  --
  -- If the 'wait' parameter is TRUE (the default) the function blocks
  -- until a message is available on the queue. If 'wait' is false,
  -- either an XML document is returned, or the 'empty_queue' exception
  -- is thrown.
  ---------------------------------------------------------------------
  FUNCTION  dequeue( queueName VARCHAR2, wait BOOLEAN := TRUE )
    RETURN  xmldom.DOMDocument IS
    deqOpt  dbms_aq.dequeue_options_t;
    retval  xmldom.DOMDocument;
    msgHdl  RAW(16);
    message RAW(32767);
  BEGIN
    IF NOT wait THEN
      deqOpt.wait := dbms_aq.NO_WAIT;
    END IF;
    dbms_aq.dequeue(queue_name => queueName,
               dequeue_options => deqOpt,
            message_properties => msgProp,
                       payload => message,
                         msgid => msgHdl);
  COMMIT;
```

```
    RETURN  xml.parse(utl_raw.cast_to_varchar2(message));
  END;

END;
```

Notice that in the **xmlq** package specification we use an EXCEPTION_INIT pragma to associate a meaningful exception name like **xmlq.queue_empty** with the error condition that occurs when we attempt to dequeue a message without waiting and there is no message there.

To illustrate a simple example of enqueuing a few XML orders, the following anonymous block of PL/SQL should suffice. It creates and enqueues five new XML-based order messages by calling **xmlq.enqueue**. Each order looks like <order id="101"/>:

```
set serveroutput on
DECLARE
  xmldoc xmldom.DOMDocument;
  xmlOrder VARCHAR2(200);
BEGIN
  dbms_output.put_line('XML Enqueue Test in Session '|| userenv('SESSIONID'));
  FOR ordId IN 101..105 LOOP
    -- Build a little XML order document like <order id="xxx"/>
    xmlOrder := '<order id="'||ordId||'"/>';
    -- Parse the current order document
    xmldoc := xml.parse(xmlOrder);
    -- Enqueue the current order to the 'xml_msg_queue' queue
    xmlq.enqueue(xmldoc,'xml_msg_queue');
    -- Free the current XML document
    xml.freeDocument(xmldoc);
    -- Print out a log message
    dbms_output.put_line('Placed order '||ordId||' in the queue.');
  END LOOP;
END;
```

Running this code shows that our first five orders are now on their way into the order processing "pipeline" of workflow steps, managed by the queue:

```
XML Enqueue Test in Session 1682
Placed order 101 in the queue.
Placed order 102 in the queue.
Placed order 103 in the queue.
Placed order 104 in the queue.
Placed order 105 in the queue.
```

Logging in from a different SQL*Plus session, we can illustrate dequeuing the orders. As shown in Example 5-24, we execute a loop that calls **xmlq.dequeue** with the **wait** flag set to **false**. By including an EXCEPTION block that includes a WHEN **xmlq.queue_empty** clause, we can trap and handle this condition sensibly.

Example 5-24. Dequeuing Messages Until a Queue Is Empty

```
set serveroutput on
DECLARE
  xmldoc xmldom.DOMDocument;
  ordId  NUMBER;
  c      NUMBER := 0;
BEGIN
  dbms_output.put_line('XML Dequeue Test in Session '|| userenv('SESSIONID'));
  WHILE (TRUE) LOOP

    -- Dequeue XML message from the 'xml_msg_queue' queue (Don't Wait)
    xmldoc := xmlq.dequeue('xml_msg_queue', wait=>false);

    -- Use xpath.valueOf to look in XML message content to find ordId
    ordId := xpath.valueOf(xmldoc,'/order/@id');

    -- Processing the current message (Here just print a message!)
    dbms_output.put_line('Processing Order #'||ordId);

    -- Free the current XML document
    xml.freeDocument(xmldoc);

  END LOOP;
EXCEPTION
  WHEN xmlq.queue_empty THEN
    dbms_output.put_line('No more orders to process.');
END;
```

Running this code shows the first-in, first-out nature of a queue that's been created with all default settings, like our **xml_msg_queue** was. One by one, the messages are dequeued until we empty the queue:

```
XML Dequeue Test in Session 1684
Processing Order #101
Processing Order #102
Processing Order #103
Processing Order #104
Processing Order #105
No more orders to process.
```

In Chapter 6 we will learn how to have Java programs enqueue and dequeue messages so Java and PL/SQL programs can cooperate asynchronously through queues by passing XML messages.

Producing and Transforming XML Query Results

In this section, we'll briefly cover the following mechanisms available to PL/SQL in Oracle8*i* for producing XML from SQL queries and for transforming XML using XSLT transformations:

- The XML SQL Utility provides capabilities to automatically deliver the results of any valid SELECT statement as an XML document.
- The Oracle XSLT processor implements a transformation engine for XML documents that is compliant with the W3C XSLT 1.0 Recommendation (see *http://www.w3.org/TR/1999/REC-xslt-19991116*), and that allows you to transform XML in one format into XML, HTML, or plain text of another format.

These topics are covered in detail in Chapter 7, *Transforming XML with XSLT*, and Chapter 9, *XSLT Beyond the Basics*, so here we will focus mostly on the basic PL/SQL syntax of working with the XML SQL Utility and the Oracle XSLT processor. First, we'll cover the steps required to verify that these facilities are properly installed in your database, then we'll cover simple examples of their use.

Installing the XML SQL Utility and XSLT Processor

First, check to see if the Oracle XML SQL Utility is already installed in your Oracle8*i* database by doing the following:

1. Connect to your Oracle8*i* database with SQL*Plus:

   ```
   sqlplus xmlbook/xmlbook
   ```

2. Check the status of the `oracle.xml.sql.query.OracleXMLQuery` class by running the following SQL statement:

   ```
   SELECT SUBSTR(dbms_java.longname(object_name),1,35) AS class, status
     FROM all_objects
    WHERE object_type = 'JAVA CLASS'
      AND object_name = dbms_java.shortname('oracle/xml/sql/query/OracleXMLQuery')
   ```

   You should see the result:

   ```
   CLASS                               STATUS
   ----------------------------------- -------
   oracle/xml/sql/query/OracleXMLQuery VALID
   ```

   If instead you see the SQL*Plus message `no rows selected`, skip the following verification step and proceed to the steps in the next list to install the Oracle XML SQL Utility in your Oracle8*i* database.

3. Try to describe the `xmlgen` package from the SQL*Plus command line:

   ```
   DESCRIBE xmlgen
   ```

If you see a description of the procedures and functions in the `xmlgen` package, then the Oracle XML SQL Utility is already installed and is ready to be used. You do *not* need to complete any further installation steps.

If instead you get an error like `ORA-04043: object xmlgen does not exist`, complete the following steps to install the Oracle XML SQL Utility in your Oracle8*i* database:

1. Make sure you've *already* loaded the Oracle XML Parser for Java into Oracle8*i*.

   The XML SQL Utility depends on it, but we did this earlier in this chapter, so you should be set.

2. Download the latest release of the Oracle XML SQL Utility from *http://technet.oracle.com/tech/xml*:

   — If your database is Oracle8*i* Release 2 (8.1.6) or later, download the *XSU12.tar.gz* or *XSU12.zip*

   — If your database is Oracle8*i* Release 1 (8.1.5), download the *XSU111.tar.gz* or *XSU111.zip*

3. Extract the *.zip* or the *.tar.gz* file into a convenient directory.

4. Change directory to the *./lib* subdirectory of the distribution.

5. Load the *xsu12.jar* file (or *xsu111.jar* for 8.1.5) into your schema:

   ```
   loadjava -verbose -resolve -user xmlbook/xmlbook xsu12.jar
   ```

6. Run the SQL script to create the XML SQL Utility PL/SQL package:

   ```
   sqlplus xmlbook/xmlbook @xmlgenpkg.sql
   ```

Repeat the previous test to confirm that you can now describe the `xmlgen` package, so the XML SQL Utility is ready to be used in the server.

Installation for the Oracle XSLT processor is very simple, since its implementation is an integrated part of the Oracle XML Parser for Java and its PL/SQL API is an integrated part of the Oracle XML Parser for PL/SQL packages.

We do not need to install the Oracle XSLT processor separately. It's already properly installed if the Oracle XML Parser for PL/SQL is working on your system.

Producing XML from SQL Queries

Let's assume that the conference abstract submission system we built earlier in this chapter needs to coordinate over the Web with another system that is managing the abstract selection process. We need to post the accepted submissions as we receive them to the other system's server using our `xml_http.post` routine.

Because of the processing and reporting that we want to do on the accepted submissions, we have chosen to save the information from the accepted submissions into an accepted_submission table in our database. In this way, we enable our existing tools and applications to easily make use of the data, instead of retrofitting them or rewriting them to understand how to work with the XML-based `<Submission>` documents that authors submit through our web site.

So, for an accepted submission that we've received and processed, we need to take the relevant data in our accepted_submission table and send it in XML format to the other server. Luckily, the XML SQL Utility's **xmlgen** package makes this SQL-to-XML job straightforward with its **getXML** function. In fact, the **submissionXML** function in Example 5-25 is all the code we need to select the appropriate data from accepted_submission for a particular submission ID and produce it as an XML document.

Example 5-25. Serving SQL Query Results for an Accepted Submission in XML

```
CREATE OR REPLACE FUNCTION submissionXML( id NUMBER ) RETURN CLOB IS
  query VARCHAR2(100);
BEGIN
  query := 'SELECT *
              FROM accepted_submission
             WHERE id = '||id;

  RETURN xmlgen.getXML(query);

END;
```

Here we've done a SELECT * query, but the XML SQL Utility can handle *any* query that is valid to execute against the Oracle database and produce the XML for its results. As with the PL/SQL functions earlier, we can use these queries inside other PL/SQL programs as well as directly inside SQL statements like this one:

```
SELECT submissionXML(600) FROM DUAL
```

which produces the following dynamic XML document:

```
SUBMISSIONXML(600)
-------------------------------------------------------------
<?xml version = '1.0'?>
<ROWSET>
   <ROW num="1">
      <ID>600</ID>
      <TITLE>Using XPath Expressions as Validation Rules</TITLE>
      <PRESENTER>Steve Muench</PRESENTER>
      <EMAIL>smuench@yahoo.com</EMAIL>
      <ABSTRACT>By storing XPath expressions in a database table,
grouped into &quot;rule sets&quot;, data-driven validation rules
can be applied to an XML document by iterating over the list of
rules in a rule set and testing whether each XPath expression is
true or false.</ABSTRACT>
   </ROW>
</ROWSET>
```

In Chapter 11, *Generating Datagrams with Java*, we cover all of the various options available with the XML SQL Utility that control how it converts SQL to XML—for example, whether the tags are generated in upper- or lowercase, what tag should be used for each row of the result, etc.—but for now, we'll just use the default settings.

The **xmlgen** package supports SQL statements with named bind variables, too, so we can rewrite Example 5-25 as follows to use a bind variable **:id** instead of concatenating the value of the **id** parameter as literal text into the SELECT statement:

```
CREATE OR REPLACE FUNCTION submissionXML( id NUMBER ) RETURN CLOB IS
  query VARCHAR2(100);
BEGIN
  query := 'SELECT *
              FROM accepted_submission
             WHERE id = :id';

  xmlgen.clearBindValues;
  xmlgen.setBindValue('id',id);

  RETURN xmlgen.getXML(query);

END;
```

Next we'll see how to use an XSLT transformation in combination with the XML SQL Utility to produce dynamic XML documents from SQL queries that comply with any needed XML format.

Transforming XML Using XSLT

Chapters 7 and 9 go into detail about using XSLT transformations to morph the original XML structure of a document into any other XML, HTML, or text format you need to deliver the information. Here we'll cover a simple example for the purpose of seeing how to tap into this XSLT transformation functionality from within PL/SQL.

The company with whom we are coordinating over the Web to handle the abstract selection process expects to receive information on the abstract submissions in their standard **<TechnicalPaper>** submission format, which looks like this:

```
<TechnicalPaper Id="101" Conference="XML Europe">
  <Subject>XSLT For Fun and Profit</Subject>
  <Presenter Email="smuench@yahoo.com">
    <Name>Steve Muench</Name>
  </Presenter>
  <Summary>

    This paper discusses the fun and profit
    that are yours for the taking by cleverly
    applying XSLT Transformations to database-driven
    XML information.

  </Summary>
</TechnicalPaper>
```

The selection company's servers are not configured to handle information in the default ROWSET/ROW format produced by the XML SQL Utility, so we'll need to transform the resulting XML to deliver it in the format the company requires.

To help us out, the selection company has provided us with *TechnicalPaper.dtd*, an XML document type description (DTD) that illustrates exactly the XML format they expect to receive from our system. Using a tool like XML Authority, we can view the expected document structure, as shown in Figure 5-5.

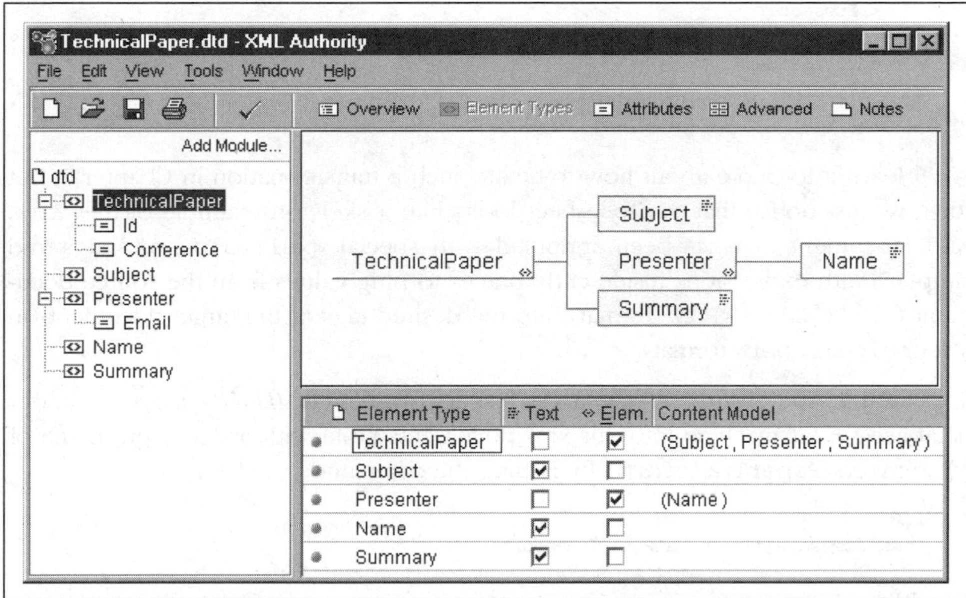

Figure 5-5. Viewing structure of TechnicalPaper DTD using XML Authority

We can even use XML Authority's *File → Export → Example XML Document...* to produce a skeleton XML file to work with in the expected format. Here is the example XML document produced by the tool for the *TechnicalPaper.dtd* file:

```
<?xml version ="1.0"?>
<!DOCTYPE TechnicalPaper SYSTEM "TechnicalPaper.dtd">
<!-- Generated by XML Authority -->
<TechnicalPaper Id = "string" Conference = "string">
  <Subject>only text</Subject>
  <Presenter Email = "string">
    <Name>only text</Name>
  </Presenter>
  <Summary>only text</Summary>
</TechnicalPaper>
```

We can easily edit this skeleton XML document to turn it into the *TechnicalPaper.xsl* stylesheet in Example 5-26. This XSLT stylesheet will transform the default XML SQL Utility output we saw earlier into the expected <TechnicalPaper> format that our business partner needs.

Example 5-26. Stylesheet to Transform ROWSET/ROW to TechnicalPaper

```
<!-- TechnicalPaper.xsl -->
<xsl:stylesheet xmlns:xsl="http://www.w3.org/1999/XSL/Transform" version="1.0">
  <xsl:output indent="yes" doctype-system="TechnicalPaper.dtd"/>
  <xsl:param name="Conference"/>
  <xsl:template match="/ROWSET/ROW">
    <TechnicalPaper Id="{ID}" Conference="{$Conference}">
      <Subject><xsl:value-of select="TITLE"/></Subject>
        <Presenter Email="{EMAIL}">
          <Name><xsl:value-of select="PRESENTER"/></Name>
        </Presenter>
      <Summary><xsl:value-of select="ABSTRACT"/></Summary>
    </TechnicalPaper>
  </xsl:template>
</xsl:stylesheet>
```

We'll learn a lot more about how to create such a transformation in Chapter 7, but for now just notice that the stylesheet looks like a skeleton example of the *target* XML document that has been sprinkled with special `<xsl:value-of>` tags and simple XPath expressions inside curly braces to plug values from the source document (in <ROWSET>/<ROW> format) into the desired tags of the target document (in `<TechnicalPaper>` format).

We can load the *TechnicalPaper.xsl* stylesheet from the *XMLFILES* directory on our database server machine into our xml_documents table with a document name of `'TechnicalPaperTransform'` by issuing the command:

```
BEGIN
  xmldoc.save('TechnicalPaperTransform',
              BFileName('XMLFILES','TechnicalPaper.xsl'));
END;
```

Now we're ready to show how to leverage the Oracle XSLT processor inside the database to perform the transformation using the stylesheet we just created and loaded into our xml_documents table. The raw ingredients are provided by the Oracle XML Parser for PL/SQL's `xslprocessor` package, but as we've done before, to put the most commonly used facilities right at our fingertips we can create a final `xslt` helper package, as shown in Example 5-27. It contains helper functions to do the following:

- Create an XSLT stylesheet object from its XML source in a VARCHAR2, CLOB, BFILE, `xmldom.DOMDocument`, or from a URL
- Transform an XML document using an XSLT stylesheet object, producing the result in plain text format
- Transform an XML document using an XSLT stylesheet object, returning the transformed XML document as an `xmldom.DOMDocument` for further processing

- Create a parameter list to pass to a transformation to support parameterized stylesheets
- Free the memory used by an XSLT stylesheet when you're done using it

Example 5-27. The xslt Helper Package Specification

```
CREATE OR REPLACE PACKAGE xslt AS
  TYPE name_value IS RECORD( NAME VARCHAR2(40), VALUE VARCHAR2(200));
  TYPE paramlist IS TABLE OF name_value INDEX BY BINARY_INTEGER;

  none paramlist;

  -- Return an XSLT stylesheet based on XML document of the stylesheet source

  FUNCTION stylesheet(doc xmldom.DOMDocument) RETURN xslprocessor.Stylesheet;
  FUNCTION stylesheet(doc VARCHAR2)           RETURN xslprocessor.Stylesheet;
  FUNCTION stylesheet(doc CLOB)               RETURN xslprocessor.Stylesheet;
  FUNCTION stylesheet(doc BFILE)              RETURN xslprocessor.Stylesheet;
  FUNCTION stylesheetFromURL(url VARCHAR2)    RETURN xslprocessor.Stylesheet;

  -- Transform an XML Document by an XSLT stylesheet, returning a String

  FUNCTION transform(source xmldom.DOMDocument,
                      style xslprocessor.Stylesheet,
                     params paramlist := none) RETURN VARCHAR2;
  FUNCTION transform(source VARCHAR2,
                      style  xslprocessor.Stylesheet,
                     params paramlist := none) RETURN VARCHAR2;
  FUNCTION transform(source CLOB,
                      style xslprocessor.Stylesheet,
                     params paramlist := none) RETURN VARCHAR2;

  -- Transform an XML Document by an XSLT stylesheet, returning an XML doc

  FUNCTION transformToDOM(source xmldom.DOMDocument,
                          style  xslprocessor.Stylesheet,
                          params paramlist := none)
                          RETURN xmldom.DOMDocument;
  FUNCTION transformToDOM(source VARCHAR2,
                          style  xslprocessor.Stylesheet,
                          params paramlist := none)
                          RETURN xmldom.DOMDocument;
  FUNCTION transformToDOM(source CLOB,
                          style  xslprocessor.Stylesheet,
                          params paramlist := none)
                          RETURN xmldom.DOMDocument;

  -- Return a paramlist to be used for a transformation.

  FUNCTION params( n1 VARCHAR2,        v1 VARCHAR2,
                   n2 VARCHAR2:=NULL,v2 VARCHAR2:=NULL,
                   n3 VARCHAR2:=NULL,v3 VARCHAR2:=NULL,
                   n4 VARCHAR2:=NULL,v4 VARCHAR2:=NULL,
                   n5 VARCHAR2:=NULL,v5 VARCHAR2:=NULL) RETURN paramlist;
```

Example 5-27. The xslt Helper Package Specification (continued)

```
  -- Release the memory used by a Stylesheet

  PROCEDURE freeStylesheet( style xslprocessor.Stylesheet);

END;
```

As before, you'll find the full source code for the **xslt** package body in Appendix A.

With these useful facilities of our **xslt** helper package in hand, we can modify our original **submissionXML** function that we created in the previous section to apply the *TechnicalPaper.xsl* transformation before returning the result to the requester. The modified version appears in Example 5-28.

Example 5-28. Modified submissionXML Function Uses the xslt Helper Package

```
CREATE OR REPLACE FUNCTION submissionXML( id NUMBER ) RETURN VARCHAR2 IS
  query      VARCHAR2(100);
  queryXML   xmldom.DOMDocument;
  stylesheet xslprocessor.Stylesheet;
  retval     VARCHAR2(32767);
BEGIN
  query := 'select *
             from accepted_submission
            where id = :id';
  xmlgen.clearBindValues;
  xmlgen.setBindValue('id',id);
  -- (1) Create the stylesheet from TechnicalPaper.xsl loaded by
  --     name from the xml_documents table.
  stylesheet := xslt.stylesheet(xmldoc.get('TechnicalPaperTransform'));
  -- (2) Transform the xmlgen.getXML(query) results by the stylesheet,
  --     passing the value of "XML Europe" for the top-level stylesheet
  --     parameter named 'Conference'
  retval := xslt.transform(xmlgen.getXML(query),
                           stylesheet,
                           xslt.params('Conference','XML Europe'));
  -- (3) Free the stylesheet
  xslt.freeStylesheet(stylesheet);
  -- Return the transformed result
  RETURN retval;
END;
```

Notice that we've added code to do the following:

1. Create an XSLT stylesheet object from the *TechnicalPaper.xsl* stylesheet, loaded by name from our xml_documents table using **xmldoc.get**:

   ```
   stylesheet := xslt.stylesheet(xmldoc.get('TechnicalPaperTransform'));
   ```

2. Transform the results returned from **xmlgen.getXML(query)** by the stylesheet, passing **'XML Europe'** as the value for the top-level stylesheet parameter named **Conference**:

   ```
   retval := xslt.transform(xmlgen.getXML(query),
                            stylesheet,
                            xslt.params('Conference','XML Europe'));
   ```

3. Free the stylesheet when we're done:

   ```
   xslt.freeStylesheet(stylesheet);
   ```

To exercise the new version of **submissionXML**, we can just try to select a submission by number from the dual table using the function:

```
SELECT submissionxml(600) FROM dual
```

which gives the resulting XML document in precisely the **<TechnicalPaper>** format needed by our business partner:

```
SUBMISSIONXML(600)
--------------------------------------------------------------------------------
<?xml version = '1.0' encoding = 'UTF-8'?>
<!DOCTYPE TechnicalPaper SYSTEM "TechnicalPaper.dtd">
<TechnicalPaper Id="600" Conference="XML Europe">
  <Subject>Using XPath Expressions as Validation Rules</Subject>
  <Presenter Email="smuench@yahoo.com">
    <Name>Steve Muench</Name>
  </Presenter>
  <Summary>By storing XPath expressions in a database table, grouped into
"rule sets", data-driven validation rules can be applied to an XML document by
iterating over the list of rules in a rule set and testing whether each XPath
expression is true or false.</Summary>
</TechnicalPaper>
```

At this point, we could easily combine functionality of our **xml_http** package and our **submissionXML** function to post abstract submissions over the Web as we submit them to our partner in the expected XML format.

6

Processing XML with Java

In this chapter:
- *Introduction to Oracle8i JServer*
- *Parsing and Programmatically Constructing XML*
- *Searching XML Documents with XPath*
- *Working with XML Messages*
- *Producing and Transforming XML Query Results*

In its relatively brief history, Java has become a dominant programming language for new software development projects and the main language taught to waves of new programmers in universities. Initially conceived as a portable language for *client-side* agents and user interfaces, Java's most rapid adoption has been for writing complex, *server-side* applications. Since nearly any interesting server-side application makes heavy use of a relational database, Oracle responded to the strong demand for server-side Java and database integration by introducing Oracle8*i*'s JServer product and has moved quickly to provide support for Java servlets and JavaServer Pages (JSPs) in its application server offerings. Starting with Oracle8*i* version 8.1.5, JServer has been provided with the database.

XML emerged in the age of Java and has been nearly inseparable from it. It is frequently said that, "Java is portable *code*, and XML is portable *data*"—a natural fit. In fact, from the beginning, the majority of software tools available for processing XML have been Java-based, and that tradition continues today. Vendors like Oracle and IBM—as well as organizations like the Apache Software Foundation—have done all of their XML innovation in Java first, with other language implementations—C, C++, PL/SQL, Perl, and others—being delivered in later phases. Given these dynamics, it's not hard to figure out why Oracle8*i*'s integration of rich server-side support for the industry's new standard for information exchange (XML) with the most popular server-side programming language (Java) and the existing standard for data access and manipulation (SQL) has caught a lot of developers' attention. The fact that Java and PL/SQL can be used together seamlessly inside Oracle8*i* means that existing Oracle developers and DBAs can learn Java at their own pace while new college grads dive headlong into Java.

By the end of this chapter, you'll understand how to combine Java, JDBC, SQL, and XML—both outside and inside Oracle8*i*—in order to:

- Load external XML files into the database
- Parse XML using the Oracle XML Parser for Java
- Search XML documents in memory using XPath expressions
- Post an XML message to another server and get an XML response back
- Enqueue and dequeue XML messages from Oracle AQ queues

In addition, we'll cover the basic mechanics of producing XML automatically from SQL queries and transforming the results into any desired XML structure using XSLT stylesheets. These two topics are also covered in full in their own chapters later in the book.

Introduction to Oracle8i JServer

Before jumping into XML-specific Java programming with Oracle, you need to understand exactly what Oracle8*i* JServer is and what options exist for the Java programmer regarding:

- Where Java code can be deployed
- How the deployed Java code talks to the database
- How the deployed Java code can be accessed by clients

Then we'll cover the basics of connecting to the Oracle8*i* database and the fundamentals of working with CLOBs—Oracle8*i*'s native datatype for large character data documents like XML documents.

What Is JServer?

JServer is Oracle's Java virtual machine (VM), the execution environment for Java code that runs in the same process space as the Oracle8*i* database server. While functionally compatible with any Java VM, JServer was completely written from scratch to exploit and tightly integrate with Oracle's scalable and reliable server infrastructure. This makes Java in Oracle8*i* a safe choice for server programming. Logging into Oracle8*i* Release 2 or later using the SQL*Plus command-line tool, we can see that JServer announces itself as a built-in part of the database server:

```
SQL*Plus: Release 8.1.6.0.0 - Production on Fri Apr 14 21:31:51 2000
(c) Copyright 1999 Oracle Corporation.  All rights reserved.
Connected to:
Oracle8i Enterprise Edition Release 8.1.6.0.0 - Production
With the Partitioning option
JServer Release 8.1.6.0.0 - Production
SQL>
```

Of course, Oracle has been a programmable database server since version 7.0, which introduced PL/SQL, but in Oracle8*i*, Java joins PL/SQL as a peer in this capacity. Any server contexts where PL/SQL can be used—stored procedures, functions, packages, triggers, and object types—can now be written using Java as well. Besides the obvious differences in language syntax, the key difference for programmers between PL/SQL and Java is that Java programs that access Oracle data and process XML can run unchanged both outside and inside the database.

Figure 6-1 shows where your Java code can run and what options are available for integrating Java with Oracle database data.

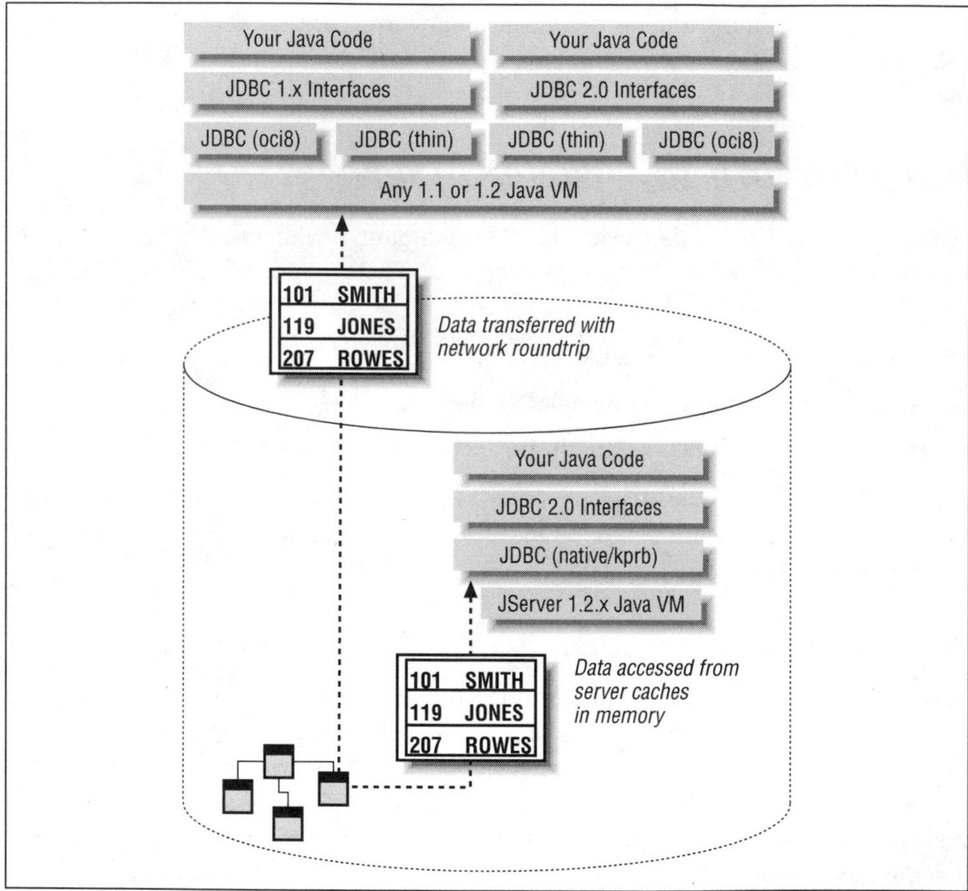

Figure 6-1. Understanding where Java runs and how it talks to Oracle

Your Java code can run outside the database or inside JServer. In either case, your code uses the standard JDBC (Java DataBase Connectivity) interfaces to access and manipulate Oracle data. These interfaces are exactly the same both outside the database and inside JServer, so your database-centric Java code can work unchanged in either place. The key differences lie in the implementation details:

- Outside the database, you can use a Java 1.1– or Java 1.2–based JDK. Inside JServer, your code runs on its Java 1.2–compliant virtual machine.
- Outside the database, you can use either JDBC 1.x or JDBC 2.0 drivers. Inside JServer, use the built-in JDBC 2.0–compliant driver.
- Outside the database, you can choose the pure-Java `thin` driver or the `oci8` JDBC driver implementation. Inside JServer, use the built-in native driver.

While the drivers support identical JDBC interfaces, a big difference in the implementation of the thin and oci8 drivers used outside the database and the native driver used inside the database is the mechanism for data transport. Your code running outside the database sends and receives data over a network connection, while the native driver in JServer accesses data from the Oracle8*i* server's in-memory caches. Data-intensive Java code can perform better when it is sitting right on top of the data being manipulated inside of JServer, instead of sending and receiving the data in packets over the network.

Developers using a version of Oracle prior to Oracle8*i* do not have the option of running Java inside the database. However, since almost everything we explore in this chapter works unchanged outside the database as well, you can run programs that way just fine.

Figure 6-2 illustrates the different deployment scenarios for Java code using Oracle8*i*. Your code can be deployed inside JServer as:

- Java stored procedures, accessed from SQL and PL/SQL through JDBC
- CORBA servers, accessed through a CORBA remote interface by a client
- Enterprise Java Beans, accessed through an EJB remote interface by a client
- Java servlets (in Oracle8*i* Release 3, version 8.1.7), accessed through HTTP

Your code can also be run outside JServer anywhere Java is supported and can connect to the database using JDBC, CORBA, or EJB.

While the details of JServer CORBA and EJB are beyond the scope of this book, Java stored procedures—due to their simplicity and wide-ranging uses—are the most interesting option here, and are an ideal choice for existing Oracle customers in any event.

Simply put, a Java stored procedure is a PL/SQL stored program *specification*, with a Java static method *implementation* for the body. Since it has a PL/SQL specification, it appears to SQL and PL/SQL as an indistinguishable twin of its pure-PL/SQL counterpart. Since it has a Java implementation, it can leverage the rich functionality in the JDK classes or any supporting Java classes that you load into the server.

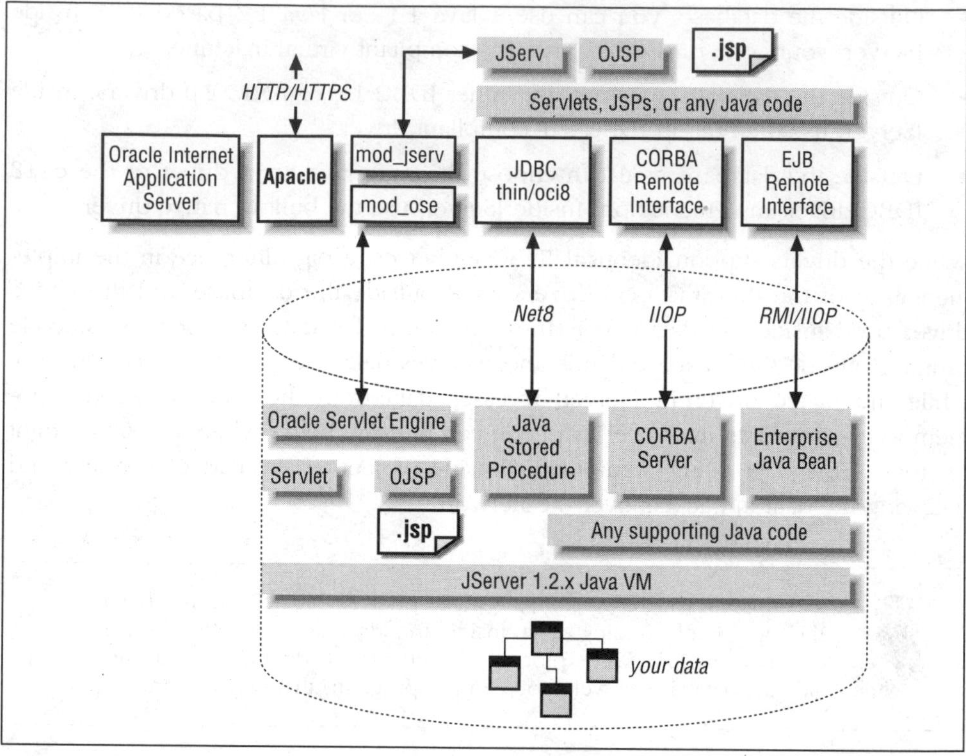

Figure 6-2. Available deployment scenarios for Java code with Oracle8i

Java stored procedures can be functions or procedures—either top-level or contained in packages—as well as triggers or object type bodies. Figure 6-3 shows how a Java stored procedure works. After loading the `SomeClass` Java class into JServer, you publish the Java stored procedure to the SQL and PL/SQL world as follows:

- Create a procedure as you normally would, but use the AS LANGUAGE JAVA syntax to associate the PL/SQL specification with the Java implementation.
- Use the AUTHID CURRENT_USER or AUTHID DEFINER clause to indicate whether the procedure should run with the privileges of the user invoking the routine (new in Oracle8*i*) or of the user who created the procedure.
- Supply the *NAME* '*Class.Method(Args)*' clause to indicate the static method in the class that provides the implementation. This also serves to indicate the desired datatype mapping between PL/SQL arguments (and function return values, if applicable) and Java object arguments.

Once you've published the `Do_Something` procedure, you can invoke it as you would any other stored procedure. As we'll see later, JDeveloper automates all of these steps for you to make the job as easy as a single menu selection.

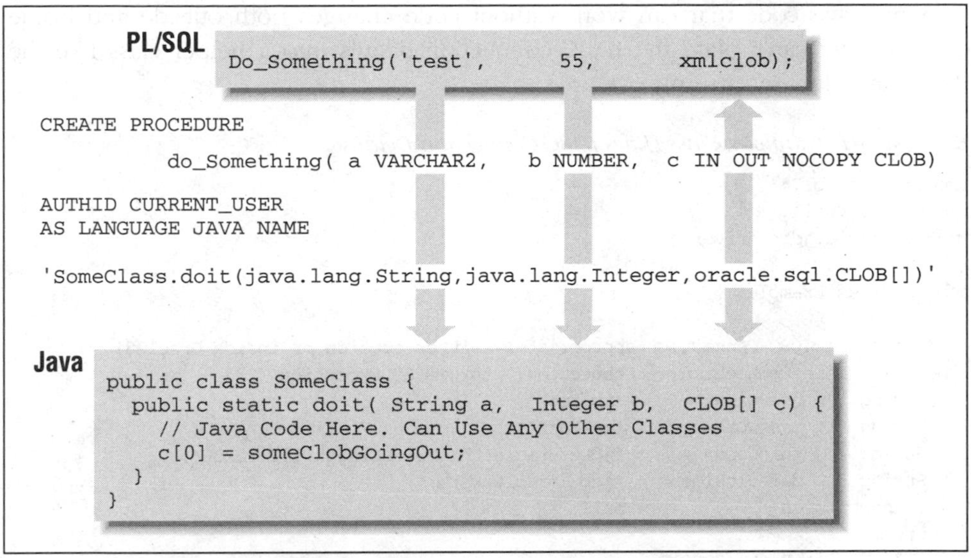

PL/SQL
```
Do_Something('test',        55,         xmlclob);
```

```
CREATE PROCEDURE
        do_Something( a VARCHAR2,   b NUMBER,  c IN OUT NOCOPY CLOB)
AUTHID CURRENT_USER
AS LANGUAGE JAVA NAME
'SomeClass.doit(java.lang.String,java.lang.Integer,oracle.sql.CLOB[])'
```

Java
```
public class SomeClass {
  public static doit( String a,  Integer b,  CLOB[] c) {
    // Java Code Here. Can Use Any Other Classes
    c[0] = someClobGoingOut;
  }
}
```

Figure 6-3. Publishing a Java static method as a Java stored procedure

Connecting to the Database in Java

In contrast to Chapter 5, *Processing XML with PL/SQL*, whose PL/SQL examples always run inside the database in the context of the currently connected database user, Java code can execute either outside or inside the Oracle8*i* database. When acquiring a database connection using the JDBC `DriverManager.getConnection` method, code running outside the database chooses either the Oracle `oci8` driver or the pure-Java `thin` driver by using an appropriate JDBC connection string:

- `jdbc:oracle:oci8:`
- `jdbc:oracle:thin:`

Code running inside the database uses a special, in-memory JDBC driver implementation called the JServer Native Driver whose driver string is `jdbc:oracle:kprb:`. Since code running inside the database is already running in the context of a currently connected database user, no username or password is required. Examples of complete JDBC connection strings using these three drivers are:

- `jdbc:oracle:oci8:scott/tiger`
- `jdbc:oracle:thin:scott/tiger@xmlapps:1521:ORCL`
- `jdbc:oracle:kprb:`

To write Java code that can work without code changes both outside and inside Oracle8*i*, we can isolate the JDBC connection details into a helper class like the `Examples` class in Example 6-1.

Example 6-1. Examples Class Hides JDBC Connection Details

```
import java.sql.*;
import java.util.*;
import oracle.jdbc.driver.*;

public class Examples {

  // Return a JDBC Connection appropriately either outside or inside Oracle8i
  public static Connection getConnection() throws SQLException {
    String     username       = "xmlbook";
    String     password       = "xmlbook";
    String     thinConn       = "jdbc:oracle:thin:@localhost:1521:ORCL";
    String     default8iConn = "jdbc:oracle:kprb:";
    Connection cn             = null;
    try {
      // Register the JDBC Driver
      Driver d = new oracle.jdbc.driver.OracleDriver();
      // Connect with the Native (kprb) Driver if inside Oracle8i
      if (insideOracle8i()) {
        cn = DriverManager.getConnection(default8iConn);
      }
      else { // Connect with the Thin Driver
        cn = DriverManager.getConnection(thinConn,username,password);
      }
      // Make sure JDBC Auto-Commit is off.
      cn.setAutoCommit(false);
      return cn;
    }
    catch (Exception e) {throw new SQLException("Error Loading JDBC Driver"); }
  }
  public static boolean insideOracle8i() {
    // If oracle.server.version is non-null, we're running in the database
    String ver = System.getProperty("oracle.server.version");
    return (ver != null && !ver.equals(""));
  }
}
```

You may be wondering, "Is the Java class in Example 6-1 missing a `package` declaration?" Yes and no. To keep Java class names short, all of the examples in the book use classes that are not declared to be part of a specific package. This is okay; it is still legal Java and saves some typing.

`Examples.getConnection` detects that it's running *inside* the Oracle8*i* server by checking whether the `oracle.server.version` system property is defined. This property provides the major and minor version number of the Oracle database we're connected to, (for example, 8.1.5, 8.1.6, etc.), and will only exist when we're running inside the database. `Examples.getConnection` uses the `insideOracle8i` method to decide which connection string to use. All of the Java examples in this chapter and others call `Examples.getConnection` to acquire their JDBC connection appropriately for the context in which they are running.

To run the examples, you may have to edit the `thinConn` JDBC database connection string in the *Examples.java* code. That string assumes that your database is on the current machine, `localhost`, has a SID of `ORCL`, and is listening for connections on port `1521`.

Reading XML from and Writing XML to CLOBs

The Oracle8*i* built-in Character Large Object (CLOB) datatype offers a way to store character data like XML documents of any size from one character to four gigabytes. Since CLOB is the principal datatype used for storing XML documents or document fragments in the server, here we'll explore the basics of reading and writing CLOBs in Java.

Oracle's JDBC driver provides built-in support for:

- Reading the contents of a CLOB as an `InputStream` or `Reader`
- Writing the contents of an `OutputStream` or `Writer` to a CLOB

To work with an existing CLOB column value, you select it into a variable of type `oracle.sql.CLOB` using a SELECT statement with an appropriate WHERE clause to identify the row(s) you want to work with. For example:

```
SELECT docname /* VARCHAR2 */, xmldoc /* CLOB */
  FROM xml_documents
 WHERE docname /* Primary Key Column */ = ?
```

What you select from the database is not immediately the entire *contents* of the CLOB, but just a handle to the actual contents, called the *locator*. You access the contents of the CLOB by calling one of the following methods on the instance of the CLOB locator:

`YourClob``.getCharacterStream()`
: To return a character-based `Reader`

`YourClob``.getAsciiStream()`
: To return a byte-based `InputStream`

Neither of these method names seems like a good name for what it *actually* returns, but that's what we have to work with. Example 6-2 shows the **ReadCLOB** class, whose **fromColumn** method allows you to pass the name of any table, CLOB column in the table, and primary key column name in the table. It returns a **Reader** on the value of the CLOB in the row whose primary key column matches the primary key value passed in. The companion **fromColumnAsInputStream** method does the real work of using a JDBC **PreparedStatement** to construct an appropriate SELECT statement and to select the CLOB value to return.

Example 6-2. Reading a Stream of Characters from a CLOB

```
import oracle.sql.*;
import java.sql.*;
import oracle.jdbc.driver.*;
import java.io.*;
import org.w3c.dom.Document;

public class ReadCLOB {
  // Read a Clob from any column in any table, returning a character Reader
  public static Reader fromColumn(Connection conn, String tableName,
                                  String colName,String idCol, String idVal)
                              throws FileNotFoundException {
    InputStream is = fromColumnAsInputStream(conn,tableName,colName,idCol,idVal);
    return is != null ? new InputStreamReader(is) : null;
  }
  // Read a Clob from any column in any table, returning an InputStream
  public static InputStream fromColumnAsInputStream(Connection conn,
                                                    String tableName,
                                                    String colName,
                                                    String idCol,
                                                    String idVal)
                                                throws FileNotFoundException {

    try {
      PreparedStatement p = conn.prepareStatement("SELECT " + colName   +
                                                "  FROM " + tableName +
                                                " WHERE " + idCol + "= ?");

      CLOB theClob = null;
      p.setString(1,idVal);
      ResultSet rs = p.executeQuery();
      boolean exists = false;
      if (rs.next()) {
        exists  = true;
        theClob = ((OracleResultSet)rs).getCLOB(1);
      }
      rs.close();
      p.close();
      if (!exists) {
        throw new FileNotFoundException(idVal);
      }
      else {
        return theClob.getAsciiStream();
```

Example 6-2. Reading a Stream of Characters from a CLOB (continued)

```
      }
    }
    catch (SQLException s) {
      return null;
    }
  }
}
```

Figure 6-4 shows the xml_documents table we created in Chapter 5.

xml_documents		
docname	**timestamp**	**xmldoc**
/book/Chapter1.xml	04/14/00 22:30	<?xml version="1.0"?> <!DOCTYPE chapter "Book.dtd"> <chapter> : </chapter>
/test/Book.dtd	04/14/00 22:30	<!ELEMENT chapter (section+)> :
/messages/order.xml	04/12/00 09:11	<order sym="ORCL" qty="3"/>
/style/ebiz.xsl	04/08/00 17:44	<xsl:stylesheet version="1.0"> : </xsl:stylesheet>

Figure 6-4. Simple table for storing XML documents in CLOBs

We can retrieve the value of a document named */messages/order.xml* by using our `ReadCLOB` class like this:

```
Reader r = ReadCLOB.fromColumn(myJDBCConnection,          // JDBC Connection
                               "xml_documents",           // Table Name
                               "xmldoc",                  // CLOB Column Name
                               "docname",                 // Key Column Name
                               "/messages/order.xml"); // Key Column Value
```

To *write* the contents of a document into a CLOB, you must first either:

- Insert a new row into the table containing the CLOB column, using the `empty_clob()` function to create a "blank" CLOB instance in the row
- Use a SELECT...FOR UPDATE statement to retrieve an existing CLOB and lock the row for modification

Then use one of these methods on `oracle.sql.CLOB` to retrieve an output stream:

- `getCharacterOutputStream()` to return a character-based `Writer`
- `getAsciiOutputStream()` to return a byte-based `OutputStream`

With a `Writer` or `OutputStream` in hand, you simply write the document's data into the CLOB's output stream. The changes become permanent when you commit the transaction. Example 6-3 shows a companion helper class to **ReadCLOB** called `WriteCLOB`. Its `fromReader` method takes the contents of any `Reader` and writes it into the CLOB's output stream.

Notice that the code uses the CLOB's `getChunkSize` method to determine the optimal buffer size for copying data into the output stream. The optimal size depends on your database's DB_BLOCK_SIZE parameter in the *INIT.ORA* file.

Example 6-3. Writing Data from a Character Reader into a CLOB

```
import java.sql.SQLException;
import oracle.sql.CLOB;
import java.io.*;

public class WriteCLOB {
  // Write the contents read from a Reader into a CLOB
  public static void fromReader( Reader in, CLOB theClob ) throws SQLException {
    // Open character output stream for writing to the CLOB
    Writer out = theClob.getCharacterOutputStream();
    // Read in chunks from the input and write to the output,
    // asking the CLOB for its optimal ChunkSize
    int chunk = theClob.getChunkSize();
    char[] buffer = new char[chunk];
    int length = -1;
    try {
      while ((length = in.read(buffer)) != -1) {
        out.write(buffer, 0, length);
      }
    // Close streams
    in.close();
    out.close();
    }
    catch (IOException iox) { }
  }
}
```

Since the CLOB's `getOutputStream` method returns a `Writer`, we can use any Java code that can write data to a `Writer` to set the contents of the CLOB. For example, the following code creates a `BufferedWriter` on a CLOB using its optimal chunk size and then calls the `print` method on the **XMLDocument** object passed in to "print" the serialized text representation of the XML document into the CLOB:

```
import oracle.sql.CLOB;
import java.io.*;
import oracle.xml.parser.v2.XMLDocument;

public class XMLDocumentToClob {
  public static void write( XMLDocument doc, CLOB theClob ) throws Exception {
    // Open a writer for writing into the CLOB, buffering the writes using
    // the CLOB's optimal chunk size.
    BufferedWriter out = new BufferedWriter(theClob.getCharacterOutputStream(),
                                            theClob.getChunkSize());
    // "print" the XML document into the clob
    doc.print(new PrintWriter(out));
    // Close the writer
    out.close();
  }
}
```

If you take another look at Figure 6-4 you'll see that, while the structure of the xml_documents table is simple, it provides all we need to store useful XML documents inside the database in a generic way. Although the table's **docname** column can be any String value, we could constrain our **docname** string values to look like fully qualified filenames. In this way, we can think of the value of the `xmldoc` CLOB column in the row of xml_documents with a **docname** equal to `/book/Chapter1.xml` as the contents of the *Chapter1.xml* file in the */book* directory.

We can build up a useful helper class called `XMLDocuments` to encapsulate the access to our xml_documents table in a way that makes it very easy to retrieve, delete, list, and save XML documents stored there. Building on the `ReadCLOB` and `WriteCLOB` helpers we wrote above, we can provide methods in our new class like the following:

`getReader()`

To return a `Reader` on a CLOB in xml_documents with a given **docname**:

```
public static Reader getReader(Connection conn, String docname)
                               throws FileNotFoundException {
  return ReadCLOB.fromColumn(conn,"xml_documents","xmldoc","docname",docname);
}
```

`delete()`

To delete a row with a given **docname** from the table:

```
public static void delete(Connection conn,String docname) throws SQLException{
  PreparedStatement stmt = conn.prepareStatement("DELETE FROM xml_documents"+
                                                 " WHERE docname = ?");
  stmt.setString(1,docname);
  stmt.execute();
  stmt.close();
  conn.commit();
}
```

list()

To provide a list of documents matching a given `docname`:

```
public static void list(Connection conn,String docname,PrintWriter out)
          throws SQLException {
  PreparedStatement ps =  conn.prepareStatement(
                          "SELECT docname,TO_CHAR(timestamp,'Mon DD HH24:MI')"
                         +"  FROM xml_documents"
                         +" WHERE docname LIKE REPLACE(?,'*','%')||'%'"
                         +" ORDER BY docname");
  ps.setString(1,docname);
  ResultSet rs = ps.executeQuery();
  while (rs.next()) {
    out.println(rs.getString(2)+" "+rs.getString(1));
  }
  ps.close();
}
```

save()

To save the contents of any `Reader` as a named document in xml_documents:

```
public static void save(Connection conn,String docname,Reader input)
                  throws SQLException, SAXException {
  // Delete existing row if present
  delete(conn,docname);
  // Insert a new row with empty_clob()
  CallableStatement stmt = conn.prepareCall(
      "BEGIN " +
      "  INSERT INTO xml_documents( docname, xmldoc) " +
      "  VALUES( ?, empty_clob()) "+
      "  RETURNING xmldoc INTO ?;" + // Use RETURNING...INTO to get CLOB
      "END;");
  stmt.setString(1,docname); // Bind var in VALUES()
  stmt.registerOutParameter(2,OracleTypes.CLOB); // RETURNING INTO
  stmt.execute(); // Do it
  // Retrieve the returned values of CLOB locator
  CLOB theXMLClob = ((OracleCallableStatement)stmt).getCLOB(2);
  stmt.close();
  // Write the input to the CLOB
  WriteCLOB.fromReader( input, theXMLClob );
  // Commit the changes and close the connection.
  conn.commit();
}
```

With these routines in our `XMLDocuments` class to encapsulate access to xml_documents, we can build a helpful command-line tool like `XMLDoc` in Example 6-4 to really make our lives easier. The `XMLDoc` utility will let us:

- Save a file into xml_documents:

  java XMLDoc save *filename docname*

- Retrieve a document:

  java XMLDoc get *docname*

- List documents matching a **docname**:

```
java XMLDoc list docname
```

- Delete a document:

```
java XMLDoc delete docname
```

Setting Up to Run Examples

To successfully run the **XMLDoc** example and other command-line Java programs in this chapter and the rest of the book, the following two things must be true:

1. You must have a Java runtime environment properly set up.
2. You must list the fully qualified names of any directories and Java archive (*.jar*) files containing classes you wish to run—as well as classes on which these classes depend—in your CLASSPATH environment variable.

If you have installed JDeveloper 3.1 from the CD-ROM accompanying this book, then one option is to run the examples from within the JDeveloper 3.1 IDE. In this scenario, everything is set up to work properly in the workspace of example files that you downloaded from the O'Reilly web site. If you want to run the examples from the command line, you can simply run the **.\bin\setvars.bat** script to set up your Java runtime environment correctly. If you have installed JDeveloper into the *C:\JDev* directory, then the syntax to run **setvars** looks like this:

```
C:\>  c:\jdev\bin\setvars   c:\jdev
```

The first argument to **setvars** gives the name of the directory where JDeveloper is installed. The script sets up your PATH and CLASSPATH to properly run Java programs. However, as noted in step 2, you still may need to add additional directories and/or *.jar* filenames to the CLASSPATH environment variable in order to run particular programs.

For example, if you have compiled the examples for this chapter into the *C:\xmlbook\ch06\classes* directory, and those examples depend on the Oracle XML Parser for Java, you should add two entries to the front of the CLASSPATH with the syntax (all on one line when you type it in):

```
C:\> set CLASSPATH=C:\xmlbook\ch06\classes;
                C:\JDev\lib\xmlparserv2_2027.jar;%CLASSPATH%
```

The syntax to do this on Unix platforms will differ slightly, as will the directory separator character, but follow the syntax you normally use on your platform for setting environment variable values.

Example 6-4. XMLDoc Lists, Loads, Saves, and Deletes XML Documents

```
import java.io.*;
import java.sql.*;
import java.net.URL;
import XMLDocuments;
import oracle.xml.parser.v2.*;

// Command-line utility to get, delete, list, and save XML documents
public class XMLDoc {
  public static void main(String[] args) throws Exception {
    Connection conn = Examples.getConnection();
    PrintWriter out = new PrintWriter(System.out);
    int argCount = args.length;
    if (argCount > 1) {
      String filename   = null;
      try {
        String cmd      = args[0];
        filename        = args[1];
        if (cmd.equals("get")) {
          writeReader(XMLDocuments.getReader(conn,filename),out);
        }
        else if (cmd.equals("list")) { XMLDocuments.list(conn,filename,out);}
        else if (cmd.equals("delete")) { XMLDocuments.delete(conn,filename);}
        else if (cmd.equals("save") && argCount > 2) {
          String docname = args[2];
          URL    u = URLUtils.newURL(filename);
          // From Example 6-5
          Reader r = new InputStreamReader(u.openStream());
          XMLDocuments.save(conn,docname,r);
        }
      }
      catch (FileNotFoundException fnf) {
        out.println("File '"+filename+"' not found.");
      }
    }
    else {
      out.println("usage: XMLDoc [get|delete|list|[save file]] docname");
    }
    out.close(); conn.close();
  }
  // Write a Reader to a Writer
  private static void writeReader(Reader r, Writer out)
  throws IOException {
    char[] buffer = new char[8192];
    int length = -1;
    while ((length = r.read(buffer)) != -1) {
      out.write(buffer, 0, length);
    }
    out.flush();
  }
}
```

So if we just happen to have Shakespeare's *A Midsummer Night's Dream* in XML lying around in the current directory (courtesy of Jon Bosak):

```
<?xml version="1.0"?>
<!DOCTYPE PLAY SYSTEM "play.dtd">
<PLAY>
<TITLE>A Midsummer Night's Dream</TITLE>

   <!-- ... etc ... -->

</PLAY>
```

we can load the files *dream.xml* and its accompanying DTD *play.dtd* into a "directory" named **/plays/shakespeare** in our xml_documents table with these two simple commands:

```
java XMLDoc save dream.xml /plays/shakespeare/dream.xml
java XMLDoc save play.dtd /plays/shakespeare/play.dtd
```

and list the contents of **/plays/shakespeare** with the command:

```
java XMLDoc list /plays/shakespeare
```

which shows us the XML documents stored in CLOBs in xml_documents as if they were files with timestamps.

```
Apr 14 18:39 /plays/shakespeare/dream.xml
Apr 14 18:39 /plays/shakespeare/play.dtd
```

So, in effect, we've built a little CLOB-based "filesystem" inside the Oracle8*i* database that is sure to come in handy. In Chapter 13, *Searching XML with interMedia*, we'll learn how to create an interMedia XML Search index on the **xmldoc** CLOB column of the xml_documents table to enable fast XML searches over the document content as well.

We'll see the full source code of the **XMLDocuments** class later in this chapter.

Parsing and Programmatically Constructing XML

The Oracle XML Parser for Java is an amazing little piece of software. It provides everything we need to:

- Parse XML documents and DTDs
- Validate XML documents against a DTD
- Programmatically construct and manipulate XML documents
- Search XML documents using XPath expressions
- Transform XML documents using XSLT stylesheets

By the end of this chapter, we'll have done all these tasks, but in the next few sections we focus on the first three. First, let's make sure we've got the latest version of the Oracle XML Parser for Java software and that it's properly installed in your Oracle8*i* database.

Installing Oracle XML Parser for Java

To verify that the Oracle XML Parser for Java is properly installed in your Oracle8*i* database, do the following:

1. Connect to your Oracle8*i* database with SQL*Plus:

   ```
   sqlplus xmlbook/xmlbook
   ```

2. Check the status of the `oracle.xml.parser.v2.DOMParser` class by running the following SQL statement:

   ```
   SELECT SUBSTR(dbms_java.longname(object_name),1,30) AS class, status
     FROM all_objects
    WHERE object_type = 'JAVA CLASS'
      AND object_name = dbms_java.shortname('oracle/xml/parser/v2/DOMParser')
   ```

If you see the result:

```
CLASS                          STATUS
------------------------------ -------
oracle/xml/parser/v2/DOMParser VALID
```

then the Oracle XML Parser for Java is already installed and ready to be used. You do *not* need to complete any further installation steps.

If instead you see the SQL*Plus `no rows selected` message, complete the following steps to install the Oracle XML Parser for Java in your Oracle8*i* database:

1. Locate the *xmlparserv2.jar* file that contains the executable code for the XML Parser for Java. You can do this in one of two ways:
   — Download the latest release of the Oracle XML Parser for Java version 2 from *http://technet.oracle.com/tech/xml.* You'll find the *xmlparserv2.jar* file in the *./lib* subdirectory of the *.zip* or *.tar.gz* file that you download.
   — Use the *xmlparserv2.jar* file in the *./jlib* subdirectory of your Oracle8*i* server installation home directory. Note, however, that this may *not* be the latest version available.
2. Change directory to the directory that contains the *xmlparserv2.jar* file you'll be installing.
3. Load the *xmlparserv2.jar* file into your schema using the `loadjava` command:

   ```
   loadjava -verbose -resolve -user xmlbook/xmlbook xmlparserv2.jar
   ```

If the `loadjava` command does not appear to work, make sure that the *./bin* subdirectory of your Oracle installation home is in your system path.

Repeat the test above to confirm that the status of the class is now `VALID`, so the XML Parser for Java is ready to be used in the server.

Parsing XML from Files, Streams, and Strings

Before we get started, it's good to get an overview of the Java packages we'll use most frequently for basic XML processing. Table 6-1 provides a list that you'll find comes in handy over and over again.

Table 6-1. Commonly Used Java Packages for Basic XML Processing

To do this	Import this package	And use these classes/interfaces
Parse and optionally validate XML documents	`oracle.xml.parser.v2.*`	`DOMParser` or `SAXParser`
Transform XML documents with XSLT	`oracle.xml.parser.v2.*`	`XSLStylesheet` and `XSLProcessor`
Work with the individual nodes in the "tree" of an XML document's "object model"	`org.w3c.dom.*`	`Document`, `Element`, `Attribute`, `Text`, etc.
Work with URLs	`java.net.*`	`URL`
Work with input and output streams of characters or bytes	`java.io.*`	`Reader`, `InputStream`, `Writer`, `OutputStream`, etc.
Handle generic parsing events and/or catch generic parsing exceptions	`org.xml.sax.*`	`InputSource` and `SAXParseException`

The Oracle XML Parser for Java supplies the `oracle.xml.parser.v2` package classes; the other most commonly used packages are not Oracle-specific:

- The `java.net` and `java.io` packages are part of the standard JDK.
- The `org.w3c.dom` package of Document Object Model (DOM) interfaces is available from the W3C web site at *http://www.w3.org/TR/REC-DOM-Level-1/java-binding.zip*.
- The `org.xml.sax` package of Simple API for XML interfaces is available from *http://www.megginson.com/SAX/saxjava-1.0.zip*.

You don't really have to download the `org.w3c.dom` and `org.xml.sax` packages, however; for your convenience, Oracle includes them in the Oracle XML Parser for Java's *xmlparserv2.jar* file archive. With this public service message out of the way, we're ready to start parsing.

Recall a slightly modified version of our *FAQWithMultipleEntities.xml* file from Chapter 2, *Working with XML*:

```
<?xml version="1.0"?>
<!DOCTYPE FAQ-List SYSTEM "FAQ-List.dtd"[
  <!ENTITY jdev "Oracle JDeveloper">
  <!ENTITY ver  "3.1">
  <!ENTITY lastyears SYSTEM "1999-Questions.xml">
  <!ENTITY webq_and_a SYSTEM "http://xml.us.oracle.com/webquestions.xml">
]>
<FAQ-List>
  <FAQ Submitter="smuench@oracle.com">
    <Question>Is it easy to get started with XML?</Question>
    <Answer>Yes!</Answer>
  </FAQ>
  <FAQ Submitter="smuench@oracle.com" Level="Neophyte">
    <Question>What is the current version of &jdev;?</Question>
    <Answer>The current version is &jdev; &ver;</Answer>
  </FAQ>
  &webq_and_a;
  &lastyears;
</FAQ-List>
```

Parsing the file requires three basic steps:

1. Construct an instance of the `DOMParser` class.
2. Create a `FileReader` to read the file we want to parse.
3. Parse the stream of XML in the `FileReader` by calling the `DOMParser`'s `parse` method:

```
import oracle.xml.parser.v2.*;
import org.xml.sax.SAXParseException;
import java.io.FileReader;

public class ParseFAQ {
  public static void main(String[] args) throws Exception {
    String filename = "FAQWithMultipleEntities.xml";
    // (1) Create a new XML Parser
    DOMParser dp = new DOMParser();
    // (2) Open a Reader on the file (assuming its in current directory)
    FileReader fileRdr = new FileReader(filename);
    try {
      // (3) Attempt to parse the stream
      dp.parse(fileRdr);
      System.out.println("Parsed ok.");
    }
    catch (SAXParseException spe) {
      System.out.println(spe.getMessage());
    }
  }
}
```

However, running this code fails with the error:

```
Error opening external DTD 'FAQ-List.dtd'.
```

Let's look again at the line:

```
<!DOCTYPE FAQ-List SYSTEM "FAQ-List.dtd"[
```

Since the `SYSTEM` Identifier for the `DOCTYPE` does not refer to an absolute URL, the relative reference to `"FAQ-List.dtd"` here means, intuitively, "Find *FAQ-List.dtd* in the same directory as the current file." If you double-check, you'll see that *FAQ-List.dtd* is indeed in the same directory as the file we're parsing. The problem is that since we fed the XML Parser a stream of characters by calling:

```
dp.parse(fileRdr); // Parse a stream of characters
```

it has no way of inferring the filename from the sequence of characters we fed it. Without understanding the filename it's currently parsing, it's logical that the parser also has no way of knowing what directory the source XML is coming from. Without knowing the name of the current directory, it is impossible for the parser to figure out what "find the DTD in the same directory as the current file" means, so it gives up by complaining that it cannot find the external DTD.

The solution to the problem is to call the `setBaseURL` method on the `DOMParser` we're currently using to help it find the filename that corresponds to the stream of characters we're asking it to parse:

```
// Help the parser know what file:// URL this stream represents
dp.setBaseURL(urlForFile(filename));
```

The `setBaseURL` method expects a `URL` object, which in the case of a file URL looks like `file:///somedir/somefile.ext`. We can use a method like `urlForFile` below to convert a name like `file.xml` into the proper file URL it represents (including the full absolute path to the directory it lives in) with a little code, like this:

```
private static URL urlForFile(String filename) throws MalformedURLException {
    // Get the absolute path of the file
    String path = (new File(filename)).getAbsolutePath();
    // If directory separator character is not a forward slash, make it so.
    if (File.separatorChar != '/') {
      path = path.replace(File.separatorChar,'/');
    }
    // Add a leading slash if path doesn't start with one (e.g. E:/foo/bar)
    if (!path.startsWith("/")) {
      path = "/"+path;
    }
    // Return the file URL
    return new URL("file://" + path);
  }
```

After we make these changes to our program, rerunning it to parse our file with an external DTD gives a successful result. Note that while these examples have focused on using a `FileReader`, the `DOMParser` cares only that the object you pass in is a `Reader` of some kind, so any valid `Reader` subclass is easy to pass in for parsing. In fact, either a Reader or an InputStream can be used. Just be sure to call setBaseURL to tell the parser what it's parsing in case the document has any external resources (DTD or external entities) to read in from locations relative to the current document's location.

Since we'll end up using this urlForFile logic over and over in our examples, it makes sense to create a URLUtils helper class with a newURL method that takes any URL in string form, and returns a valid URL object that it represents. In particular, for URLs with no protocol, the code in Example 6-5 assumes the reference is to a file, and it determines the appropriate file URL.

Example 6-5. Helper Class to Handle String-based URLs Intelligently

```
import java.io.*;
import java.net.*;
public class URLUtils {
   // Create a new URL from a string
   static URL newURL(String filename) throws MalformedURLException
   {
      URL url = null;
      try {
         // First try to see if filename is *already* a valid URL
         url = new URL(filename);
      }
      // If not, then assume it's a "naked" filename and make a URL
      catch (MalformedURLException ex) {
        // Get the absolute path of the file
        String path = (new File(filename)).getAbsolutePath();
        // If directory separator character is not a forward slash, make it so.
        if (File.separatorChar != '/') {
          path = path.replace(File.separatorChar,'/');
        }
        // Add a leading slash if path doesn't start with one (e.g. E:/foo/bar)
        if (!path.startsWith("/")) {
          path = "/"+path;
        }
        // Construct the file URL
        url = new URL("file://" + path);
     }
     return url;
   }
}
```

Now we can immediately put URLUtils to work in an example that shows another way to use the DOMParser. In this example, we'll parse a URL directly, rather than send it in a character stream. While we're at it, since it's just one extra line of code, let's ask the DOMParser to perform validation against the DTD as well. Example 6-6 shows the code required.

Example 6-6. Parsing and Validating an XML File from a URL

```
import org.xml.sax.SAXParseException;
import org.xml.sax.InputSource;
import org.w3c.dom.Document;
import oracle.xml.parser.v2.*;
import java.io.*;
import java.net.*;
import URLUtils;

public class ParseFAQWithValidation {
  public static void main(String[] args) throws Exception {
    String filename = "FAQWithMultipleEntities.xml";
    // Use a URL directly from the beginning. No need to set SystemId
    URL fileURL = URLUtils.newURL(filename);
    // Create a new XML Parser
    DOMParser dp = new DOMParser();
    // Validate the document against its DTD
    dp.setValidationMode(true);
    try {
      // Attempt to parse the URL
      dp.parse(fileURL);
      System.out.println("Parsed ok.");
      // Get the parsed document
      Document xmldoc = dp.getDocument();
      // Print the document
      ((XMLDocument)xmldoc).print(System.out);
    }
    catch (SAXParseException spe) {
      System.out.println(spe.getMessage());
    }
  }
}
```

As we saw when using the `oraxml` command-line tool with the `-v` flag in Chapter 2, the validation error against the DTD is shown:

```
Attribute value 'Neophyte' should be one of the declared enumerated values.
```

Because it is common to pass small XML documents as `String` arguments to methods for processing, developers frequently ask "How can I parse an XML document from a string?" Luckily, it's quite easy. Since we learned earlier that the `DOMParser` can parse any `Reader`, and since the `java.io` package conveniently has the class `StringReader` to read the contents of any `String`, we can put two and two together to parse the string-based XML document by:

1. Constructing a `StringReader` from our `String`:

   ```
   StringReader myStringRdr = new StringReader(myXmlStringVar);
   ```

2. Passing it to the `DOMParser` as input:

   ```
   dp.parse(myStringRdr);
   ```

A working sample is shown in Example 6-7.

Example 6-7. Parsing XML from a String Using a StringReader

```
import org.xml.sax.SAXParseException;
import java.io.StringReader;
import org.w3c.dom.Document;
import oracle.xml.parser.v2.*;

public class ParseFromString {
  public static void main(String[] args) throws Exception {
    String xmldocString = "<this>"+
                          "  <that/>"+
                          "  <!-- and the other -->"+
                          "</this>";
    // Open a character reader on the string
    StringReader sr = new StringReader(xmldocString);
    // Create a new XML Parser
    DOMParser dp = new DOMParser();
    try {
      // Attempt to parse the reader
      dp.parse(sr);
      // Get the parsed document
      Document xmldoc = dp.getDocument();
      // Print the document
      ((XMLDocument)xmldoc).print(System.out);
    }
    catch (SAXParseException spe) {
      System.out.println(spe.getMessage());
    }
  }
}
```

As expected, this example prints out:

```
<this>
   <that/>
   <!-- and the other -->
</this>
```

Parsing XML in all of its forms is such a common operation that it, too, is a great candidate for a quick helper class like `XMLHelper` in Example 6-8. In addition to helpful methods for quickly parsing `Readers`, `InputStreams`, `Strings`, and `URLs`, we've also included a handy method to format the `SAXParseException` for display, indicating the position and cause of the parsing error.

Example 6-8. XMLHelper Class to Simplify XML Parsing Tasks

```
import org.w3c.dom.*;
import oracle.xml.parser.v2.*;
import org.xml.sax.*;
import java.io.*;
import java.net.*;
```

Example 6-8. XMLHelper Class to Simplify XML Parsing Tasks (continued)

```
public class XMLHelper {
  // Parse an XML document from a character Reader
  public static XMLDocument parse( Reader r, URL baseUrl )
                       throws IOException, SAXParseException, SAXException  {
    // Construct an input source from the Reader
    InputSource input = new InputSource(r);
    // Set the base URL if provided
    if (baseUrl != null) input.setSystemId(baseUrl.toString());
    // Construct a new DOM Parser
    DOMParser xp = new DOMParser();
    // Parse in Non-Validating Mode
    xp.setValidationMode(false);
    // Preserve Whitespace
    xp.setPreserveWhitespace(true);
    // Attempt to parse XML coming in from the Reader
    xp.parse(input);
    // If the parse is successful, return the DOM Document
    return (XMLDocument) xp.getDocument();
  }
  // Parse XML from an InputStream
  public static XMLDocument parse( InputStream is, URL baseURL )
                       throws SAXParseException, SAXException, IOException {
    // Construct a Reader and call parse(Reader)
    return parse( new InputStreamReader(is), baseURL );
  }
  // Parse XML From a String
  public static XMLDocument parse( String xml, URL baseurl )
                          throws MalformedURLException, IOException,
                                 SAXParseException, SAXException {

    // Construct a reader and call parse(Reader)
    return parse(new StringReader(xml),baseurl);
  }
  // Parse XML from a URL
  public static XMLDocument parse( URL url ) throws IOException,
                                                    SAXParseException,
                                                    SAXException  {
    // Construct an InputStream and call parse(InputStream)
    // Use the url passed-in as the baseURL
    return parse( url.openStream(), url);
  }
  // Format information for a parse error
  public static String formatParseError(SAXParseException s) {
     int lineNum = s.getLineNumber();
     int  colNum = s.getColumnNumber();
     String file = s.getSystemId();
     String  err = s.getMessage();
     return "XML parse error " + (file != null ? "in file " + file + "\n" : "")+
            "at line " + lineNum + ", character " + colNum + "\n" + err;
  }
}
```

Because XMLHelper can help us parse any InputStream, it can, in particular, easily parse compressed XML contained in a *.zip* or *.gzip* file using built-in classes like GZIPInputStream in the JDK's *java.util.zip* package. This process is so simple that it doesn't even warrant a full example, just a few lines of code:

```
import java.util.zip.GZIPInputStream;
  :
// Create a URL for the GZip'd resource
URL u = URLUtils.newURL("test.xml.gz");
// Create a GZIPInputStream over the compressed stream of XML in the GZip file.
GZIPInputStream gz = new GZIPInputStream(u.openStream());
// Parse it with our XMLHelper like any other InputStream, passing base URL!
XMLDocument x = XMLHelper.parse(gz,u);
```

Next we'll look at some potential problems related to parsing XML documents from CLOB columns inside the database, and come up with a nifty solution.

Simplifying CLOB-based XML Parsing

Let's apply what we've already learned to parsing XML from database CLOB columns. Earlier, we used our **XMLDoc** utility to load the contents of Shakespeare's *A Midsummer Night's Dream* file, dream.xml, and its corresponding play.dtd into our xml_documents table. We can parse the XML contents of the CLOB with the help of three of our helper classes:

Examples.getConnection
: To connect to the database

XMLDocuments.getReader
: To get a Reader for the CLOB where *dream.xml* is stored

XMLHelper.parse
: To parse the Reader

We are stoked; this will be easy! We try the following example code that puts these three steps into action to read the document */plays/shakespeare/dream.xml*:

```
import XMLHelper;
import java.io.Reader;
import java.sql.Connection;

public class ReadDream {
  public static void main(String[] args) throws Exception {
    // Connect to the database
    Connection conn = Examples.getConnection();
    // Get a reader for the CLOB named '/plays/shakespeare/dream.xml'
    Reader r = XMLDocuments.getReader(conn,"/plays/shakespeare/dream.xml");
    try { // To parse it...
      XMLHelper.parse(r,null);
    }
    catch (Exception ex) {    // Doh!
      System.out.println(ex);
    }
```

```
        conn.close();                 // Disconnect
      }
    }
```

We get the following dreaded error because the parser cannot find the *play.dtd* in the same directory as the *dream.xml* document it's currently parsing:

```
Error opening external DTD 'play.dtd'.
```

Well, we know how to fix that, don't we? We just call `setBaseURL()` with the URL of the document we're parsing, right? Then the parser can properly find *play.dtd* in the same directory as the current document. But let's think a little. What is the URL of the current character stream of *dream.xml* coming from a CLOB? Not `file://`*`something`* because we're not reading it from a filesystem. Not `http://`*`something`* because we're not retrieving the document over the Web. Certainly not `ftp://`*`something`* or `gopher://`*`something`*. So what kind of URL is it? Aye, there's the rub.

You might be tempted to say:

- It's a database URL.
- It's a CLOB URL.
- It's an xml_documents table URL.

But none of these would be exactly right. The answer is that there *is* no URL that describes the resource identified by the row in the xml_documents table whose `docname` column value is `/play/shakespeare/dream.xml`. But since the "U" in URL stands for "uniform"—suggesting that it's been designed to handle any possible need—we're in luck. The URL system is designed to be extensible, so we can build the URL we need and slot it into the grand scheme of things. Since we're trying to describe resources that live in the xml_documents table, let's invent a new kind of URL protocol named `xmldoc:` so we can work with our CLOB-based document using the following single line of Java code:

```
URL u = new URL("xmldoc:/play/shakespeare/dream.xml");
```

to refer to the resource we were trying unsuccessfully to parse earlier.

It turns out that it is not very much work at all to implement a new URL protocol. Figure 6-5 illustrates the steps involved in building our `xmldoc:` handler.

The steps are as follows:

1. We need to create a class that implements the `java.net.URLStreamHandlerFactory` interface.

   This is required for any class that is intended to assist the URL mechanism in deciding how to handle opening a stream for a URL. The default implementation of `URLStreamHandlerFactory` can delegate responsibility to the correct

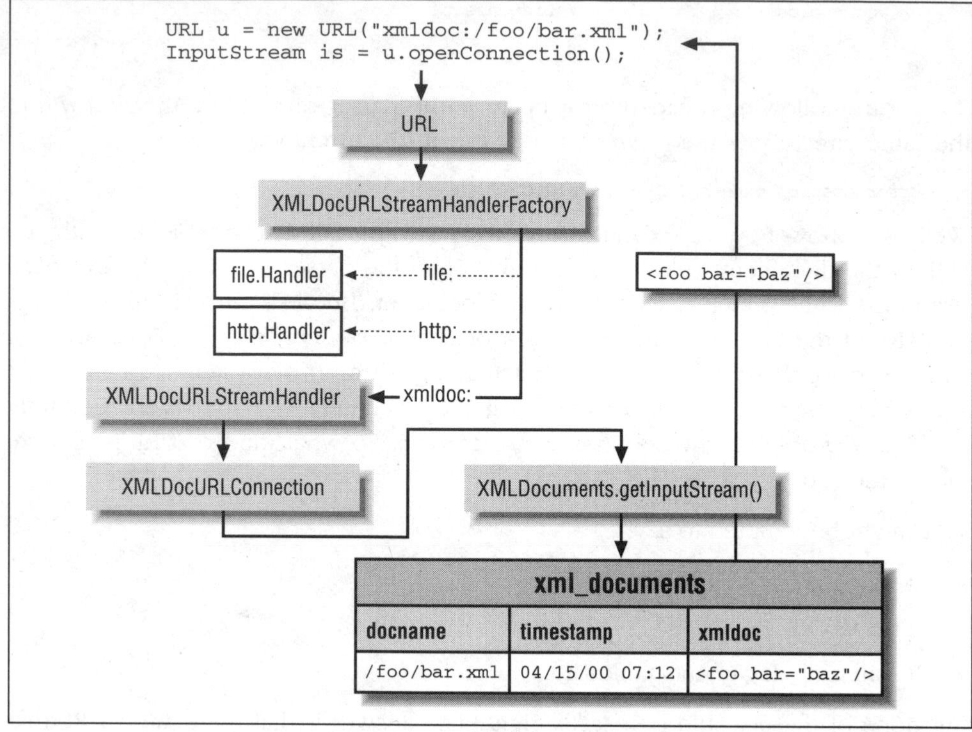

Figure 6-5. Implementing an xmldoc: URL protocol handler

`URLStreamHandler` based on the protocol. We need to implement our `XMLDocURLStreamHandlerFactory` so that it properly handles a request for our new `xmldoc` protocol, but hands control back to the default mechanism for any other protocol by returning `null`. Here's the code:

```
import java.net.*;
import XMLDocURLStreamHandler;

public class XMLDocURLStreamHandlerFactory implements URLStreamHandlerFactory {
  public URLStreamHandler createURLStreamHandler(String protocol) {
    // If the URL being constructed is an xmldoc:/foo/bar.xml Url, we do...
    if (protocol.equals("xmldoc")) return new XMLDocURLStreamHandler();
    // Otherwise, let the default URL mechanism handle it.
    else return null;
  }
}
```

2. We need to create a class that extends `URLStreamHandler` and defines what the `openConnection()` method means for one of our new `xmldoc:` URLs. In our case, we want it to return a new `XMLDocURLConnection` object to represent the connection to the resource that the URL represents:

```
import java.net.*;
import java.io.IOException;
import XMLDocURLConnection;

public class XMLDocURLStreamHandler extends URLStreamHandler {
  protected URLConnection openConnection(URL u) throws IOException {
    return new XMLDocURLConnection(u);
  }
}
```

3. Finally, we need our **XMLDocURLConnection** to extend **URLConnection** and override the **getInputStream()** method to return the input stream that we want for **xmldoc:** URLs. We want to return the **InputStream** for the CLOB in the xml_documents table whose **docname** equals the URL's filename. As shown in the code for **XMLDocURLConnection** in Example 6-9, we use our **XMLDocuments.getInputStream** to do the real work.

Example 6-9. Returning the Input Stream for an xmldoc: URL from a CLOB

```
import java.net.*;
import java.io.*;
import java.sql.*;
import oracle.jdbc.driver.*;
import XMLDocuments;
import Examples;

public class XMLDocURLConnection extends URLConnection {
  Connection conn = null;
  public XMLDocURLConnection (URL u) {
    super(u);
  }
  public void connect() {
    // Don't need to do anything here, but must implement this method
  }
  public InputStream getInputStream() throws IOException {
    Connection conn = null;
    try {
      // Get the default Oracle8i connection for the current user
      conn = Examples.getConnection();
    }
    catch (SQLException s) {
      throw new IOException("Fatal error getting database connection");
    }
    // Return InputStream for the requested "file" in xml_documents table
    return XMLDocuments.getInputStream(conn,url.getFile());
  }
  public void finalize() {
    // Close the database connection when object is garbage-collected
    try { if (conn != null) conn.close(); } catch (SQLException s) {}
  }
}
```

And with this, we're done. Well, almost done. We need to add a method to our `XMLDocuments` class that puts our `XMLDocURLStreamHandlerFactory` in charge instead of the default `URLStreamHandlerFactory`. That code for this method looks like this:

```
// Enable the use of xmldoc:/dir1/dir2/file.xml URLs in this session
public static void enableXMLDocURLs() {
  try {
    // Give *our* handler first chance to handle URL.openConnection() requests
    URL.setURLStreamHandlerFactory(new XMLDocURLStreamHandlerFactory());
  }
  catch(java.lang.Error alreadyDefined) { /* Ignore */ }
}
```

Now we're ready to test out our shiny new **xmldoc:** URLs. We already have our Shakespeare *dream.xml* and *play.dtd* in our xml_documents table, but just for good measure, let's load another document with external references of different kinds to make sure everything is working properly. The following *EntityText.xml* document contains a relative URL reference to its external *test.dtd* in a *dtd* subdirectory, an external entity using a relative URL **"external.xml"**, an external entity using an **http:** URL, and an external entity using a **file:** URL:

```
<?xml version="1.0" encoding="UTF-8"?>
<!-- DTD is in the "dtd" subdirectory -->
<!DOCTYPE test SYSTEM "dtd/test.dtd" [

 <!-- This external entity is in the "same" relative directory -->
 <!ENTITY e SYSTEM "external.xml">

 <!-- This external entity is retrieved by HTTP -->
 <!ENTITY f SYSTEM "http://xml.us.oracle.com/http-external.xml">

 <!-- This external entity is retrieved from the file system -->
 <!ENTITY g SYSTEM "file:///C:/xmlfiles/file-external.xml">
]>
<test>
  &e;
  &f;
  &g;
</test>
```

If our **xmldoc:** protocol is working properly, it should handle any references relative to the original document being parsed because a URL relative to an **xmldoc:** URL will also be an **xmldoc:** URL. The **file:** and **http:** URL entities should be retrieved correctly. So using **XMLDoc**, we can load these extra few test files into our xml_documents table:

```
java XMLDoc save EntityTest.xml /testdir/EntityTest.xml
java XMLDoc save external.xml   /testdir/external.xml
java XMLDoc save test.dtd       /testdir/dtd/test.dtd
```

and run the test program in Example 6-10.

Example 6-10. Testing Our New xmldoc: URL Handler

```
import java.net.URL;
import oracle.xml.parser.v2.*;
import java.io.*;
import XMLDocURLStreamHandlerFactory;
import XMLHelper;

public class TestXMLDocURL {
  // debug_main is Oracle8i Java stored procedure Debugging entry point
  public static void debug_main() throws Exception {
    main(null);
  }
  public static void main(String[] args) throws Exception {
    // Enable the use of xmldoc URLs in this session
    XMLDocuments.enableXMLDocURLs();
    // Create an xmldoc URL for the /plays/shakespeare/dream.xml file
    URL u = new URL("xmldoc:/plays/shakespeare/dream.xml");
    // Parse the shakespeare document
    XMLDocument xmldoc = XMLHelper.parse(u);
    // Create an xmldoc URL for the /testdir/EntityTest.xml'
    u = new URL("xmldoc:/testdir/EntityTest.xml");
    // Parse the test document
    xmldoc = XMLHelper.parse(u);
    // Print out the test document
    xmldoc.print(System.out);
  }
}
```

Eureka! The program successfully parses *dream.xml* without complaining about the *play.dtd* as before, and parses *EntityTest.xml* correctly to print out the document with all of its external entities properly retrieved:

```
<?xml version = '1.0' encoding = 'UTF-8'?>
<!-- DTD is in the "dtd" subdirectory -->
<!DOCTYPE test SYSTEM "xmldoc:/testdir/dtd/test.dtd" [
<!ENTITY e  SYSTEM "xmldoc:/testdir/external.xml">
<!ENTITY f  SYSTEM "http://xml.us.oracle.com/http-external.xml">
<!ENTITY g  SYSTEM "file:/C:/xmlfiles/file-external.xml">
]>
<test>
  <external>Local</external>
  <external>From HTTP</external>
  <external>From File</external>
</test>
```

Deploying and Debugging Stored Procedures

Now that we have demonstrated that our `xmldoc:` URL and its supporting classes work properly outside the database, let's deploy them into the Oracle8*i* JServer VM and make sure they work properly inside the database as well. The manual steps to deploy our `TestXMLDocUrl` class (and all the classes it depends on) to JServer are as follows:

1. Compile all Java classes related to `TestXMLDocUrl`.
2. Create a Java archive (e.g., *deploy.jar*) containing all the classes in Step 1.
3. Use the `loadjava` command-line tool to load the Java archive into JServer into the XMLBOOK schema:

   ```
   loadjava -verbose -resolve -user xmlbook/xmlbook deploy.jar
   ```

4. Determine the proper datatype mapping between PL/SQL types and Java types for the arguments in order to properly create a PL/SQL procedure specification.
5. Create a procedure specification using the AS LANGUAGE JAVA keywords that map to the `TestXMLDocUrl.debug_main` static method.

In JDeveloper 3.1, the process is completely wizard-driven. The first time you want to deploy, just select *Project → Deploy → New Deployment Profile...* from the menu to create a new Oracle8*i* stored procedure deployment profile, as shown in Figure 6-6.

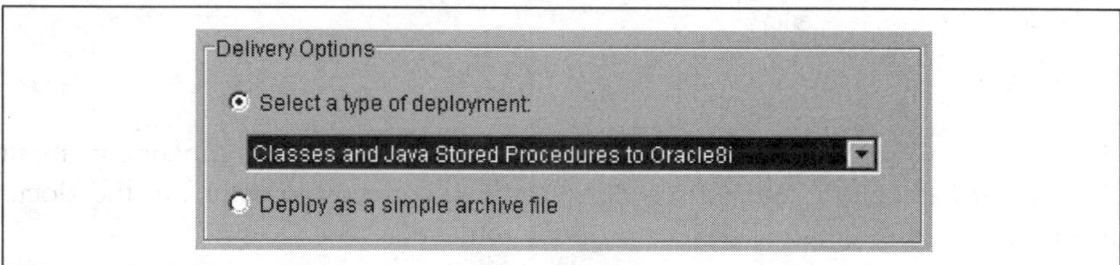

Figure 6-6. Selecting the type of deployment

Next, select the files from your project you want to deploy, as illustrated in Figure 6-7.

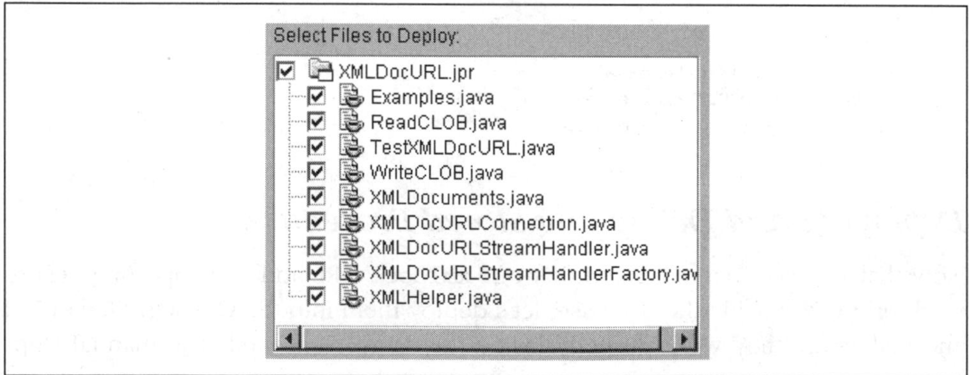

Figure 6-7. Selecting the files to deploy

JDeveloper analyzes class dependencies to make sure you don't forget any. Then select which of the available static methods in the classes you are deploying should be published as Java stored procedures as shown in Figure 6-8. You also select a "Database package" name and choose whether your new Java stored procedures should run with the privileges of the `CURRENT_USER` or the `DEFINER`.

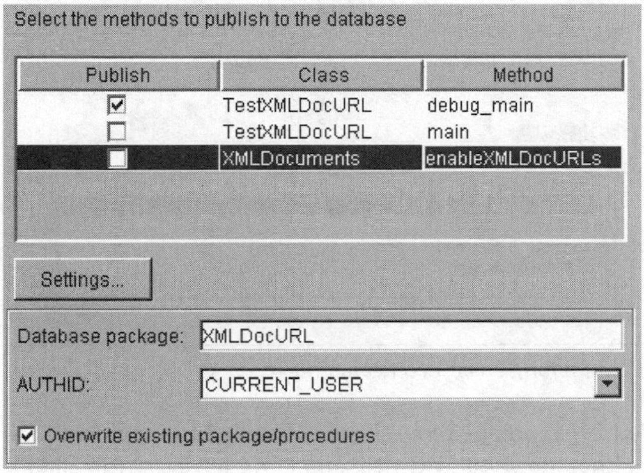

Figure 6-8. Selecting static methods to publish as stored procedures

Pick a database connection to use for the deployment from the list of preconfigured connections on the next panel, and then, finally, provide a name for the deployment profile so your project's files can be redeployed at any time with a single menu click. If you make changes to any of your code, just select *Deploy* from the context menu on your deployment profile, as shown in Figure 6-9, and your files are instantly redeployed to JServer, no questions asked.

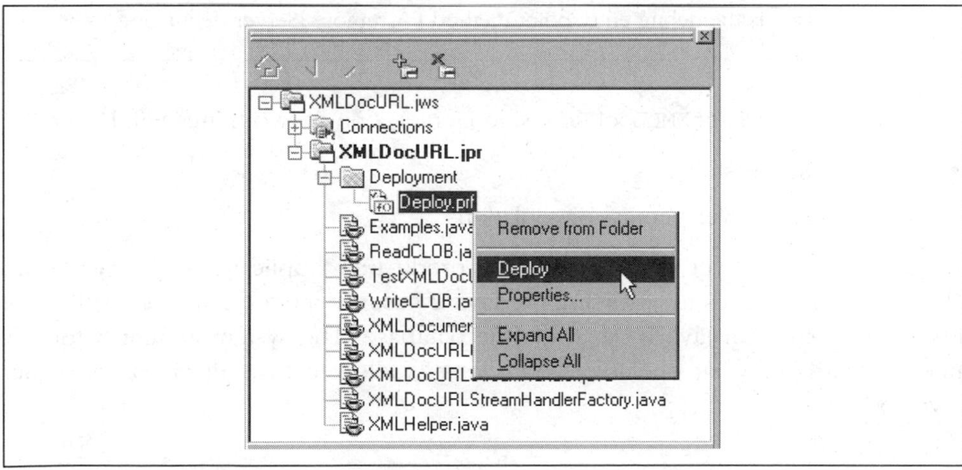

Figure 6-9. Redeploying a project with an existing profile

If something about your Java code running in JServer is not functioning as expected, you can easily do remote debugging against the JServer virtual machine by visiting your project's *Properties* dialog and setting the *Debug Files as:* pop-up list to "Oracle8i Stored Procedure", as shown in Figure 6-10.

Figure 6-10. Setting up for JServer Java debugging

Set your desired breakpoints, then click on the Debug icon in the toolbar to begin your remote debugging session with JServer. As illustrated in Figure 6-11, you can set breakpoints, examine the call stack and any variables, step through, into, and out of routines, and even see the JServer output conveniently in the JDeveloper message log instead of having to hunt through server trace files to find your debugging messages.

For Java stored procedure debugging, the program that you want to debug must have the following method defined:

```
public static void debug_main()
```

This is the debug entry point method for remote JServer debugging.

When we run the `TestXMLDocURL` inside JServer, one of two things will happen:

- It works successfully.
- It fails with JServer permission violations.

Being a secure server environment for production applications, JServer is no slouch when it comes to enforcing the Java 2 security model. This means that not just anyone can run Java code inside the database. The system administrator has fine control over what operations each user is allowed to perform in his or her Java code.

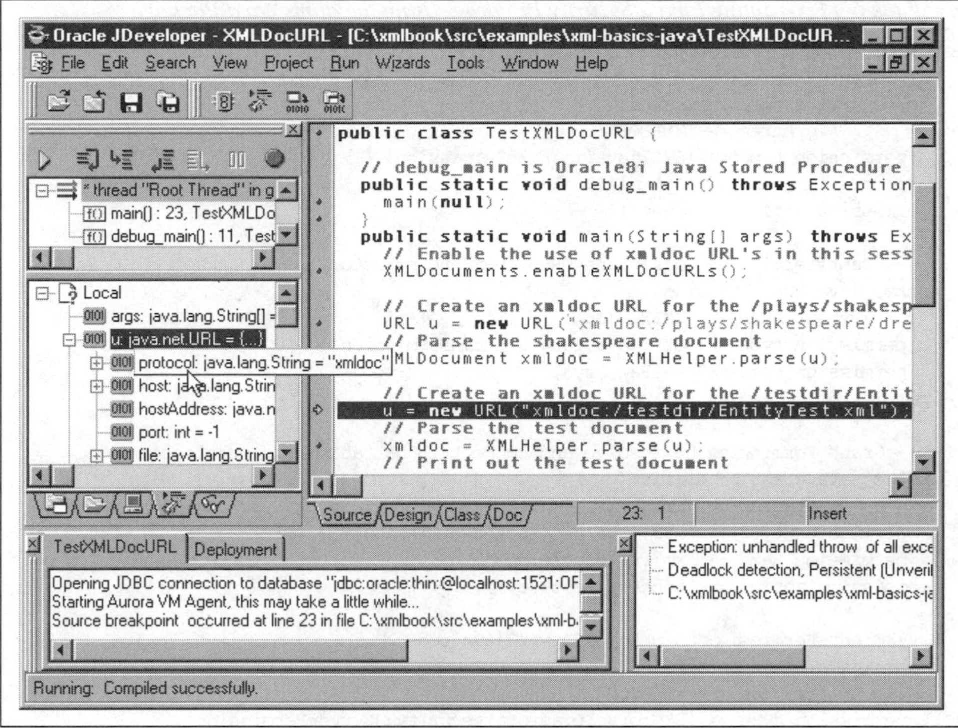

Figure 6-11. JDeveloper 3.1 debugging Java stored procedures

In order for `TestXMLDocURL` to work properly inside JServer, we need permissions to:

- *Set* the `URLStreamHandlerFactory` to enable `xmldoc:` URLs
- *Resolve* the machine name `xml.us.oracle.com` and *connect* to it to allow the XML Parser running inside JServer to retrieve the external entity from SYSTEM Identifier `http://xml.us.oracle.com/http-external.xml`
- *Read* the files in the *C:\xmlfiles* directory on the local (i.e., database server) machine to allow the XML Parser to retrieve the external entity from SYSTEM Identifier `file:///C:/xmlfiles/file-external.xml`
- *Debug* the code running in JServer

The system administrator manages Java 2 security policies and permissions using the `grant_permission`, `revoke_permission`, `enable_permission`, `disable_permission`, and `delete_permission` procedures in the `DBMS_JAVA` package. The script in Example 6-11, if run as SYS, grants the privileges necessary to successfully debug and test the `TestXMLDocURL` Java stored procedure.

Example 6-11. Granting Java 2 Security Privileges Using the dbms_java Package

```
BEGIN
    -- Grant Permission to read a file in the C:\xmlfiles directory
    dbms_java.grant_permission(
             grantee => 'XMLBOOK',
     permission_type => 'SYS:java.io.FilePermission',
     permission_name => 'C:\xmlfiles\*',
   permission_action => 'read');

    -- Grant Permission to set the URLStreamHandlerFactory
    dbms_java.grant_permission(
             grantee => 'XMLBOOK',
     permission_type => 'SYS:java.lang.RuntimePermission',
     permission_name => 'setFactory',
   permission_action => '');

    -- Grant Permission to resolve and connect to URL at xml.us.oracle.com
    dbms_java.grant_permission(
             grantee => 'XMLBOOK',
     permission_type => 'SYS:java.net.SocketPermission',
     permission_name => 'xml.us.oracle.com',
   permission_action => 'connect,resolve');

    -- Grant Permission to debug JServer java code
    dbms_java.grant_permission(
             grantee => 'XMLBOOK',
     permission_type => 'SYS:oracle.aurora.security.JServerPermission',
     permission_name => 'Debug',
   permission_action => '');
  COMMIT;
END;
```

You can verify what privileges you have by running the useful SELECT SQL statement against the data dictionary view `java_user_policy` in Example 6-12.

Example 6-12. Listing URL-Related Java Security Policies in Oracle8i

```
PROMPT +===========================================================+
PROMPT | Your URL, File, and Debug-Related Java Security Settings |
PROMPT +===========================================================+
set pages 999
column "Permission" format a30
column "Name" format a20
column "Action" format a15
column "Enab?"  format a5
column "Key"    format 99999
SELECT SUBSTR(type_name,INSTR(type_name,'.',-1)+1)||CHR(10)||
       '('||SUBSTR(type_name,1,INSTR(type_name,'.',-1)-1)||')'
        AS "Permission",
       name      AS "Name",
       action    AS "Action",
       DECODE(SUBSTR(enabled,1,1),'E','Y','N')   AS "Enab?",
       seq       AS "Key"
```

Example 6-12. Listing URL-Related Java Security Policies in Oracle8i (continued)

```
 FROM user_java_policy
WHERE GRANTEE_NAME IN (USER,'JAVADEBUGPRIV') /* Eliminate PUBLIC privs */
  AND (type_name = 'java.net.SocketPermission'
      OR type_name = 'java.io.FilePermission'
      OR type_name = 'java.lang.RuntimePermission'
      OR type_name = 'java.util.PropertyPermission'
      OR (     type_name = 'oracle.aurora.security.JServerPermission'
          AND       name = 'Debug')
      )
ORDER BY 1,3,2
/
```

After running the `grant` script in Example 6-11, Example 6-12 should produce results like this:

```
+==========================================================+
| Your URL, File, and Debug-Related Java Security Settings |
+==========================================================+

Permission                      Name                 Action          Enab?  Key
------------------------------- -------------------- --------------- ----- ------
FilePermission                  C:\xmlfiles\*        read            Y        249
(java.io)
JServerPermission               Debug                                Y         61
(oracle.aurora.security)
RuntimePermission               setFactory                           Y        246
(java.lang)
SocketPermission                xml.us.oracle.com    connect,resolve Y        266
(java.net)
```

Table 6-2 gives a summary of the most common JServer permissions for working with XML inside the database.

Table 6-2. Common JServer Permissions Used for Working with XML

If you want to	You need this permission	With this name	And these action(s)
Resolve a URL	`SYS:java.net.SocketPermission`	`machine.domain.com` or `*.domain.com`	`connect, resolve`
Open a file	`SYS:java.io.FilePermission`	`/dir/file.ext` or `/dir/*`	`read`
Debug Java in JServer	`SYS:oracle.aurora.security.JServerPermission`	`Debug`	
Use custom `URLStreamHandlerFactory`	`SYS:java.lang.RuntimePermission`	`setFactory`	
Set a system property	`SYS:java.util.PropertyPermission`	`propname`	`write`

Last, but not least, we end this section with Example 6-13, the full source code of the **XMLDocuments** class used previously to create a simple, CLOB-based filesystem on top of the xml_documents table. Recall that our **XMLDoc** utility was a simple command-line shell over the methods in the **XMLDocuments** class.

Example 6-13. Implementing a CLOB-based "Filesystem" Inside JServer

```
import java.sql.Connection;
import org.w3c.dom.Document;
import org.xml.sax.SAXException;
import oracle.jdbc.driver.*;
import java.sql.*;
import oracle.sql.*;
import java.net.URL;
import java.io.*;
import java.sql.*;
import XMLDocURLStreamHandlerFactory;
import XMLHelper;
import ReadCLOB;
import WriteCLOB;

public class XMLDocuments {
  // get: Read an XML document from the xml_documents table.
  public static Document get(Connection conn,String idVal)
                        throws FileNotFoundException, SAXException {
    Reader r = getReader(conn,idVal);
    try { return r != null ? XMLHelper.parse(r,null) : null; }
    catch (FileNotFoundException fnf) { throw fnf; }
    catch (IOException iox) { }
    return null;
  }
  // Return Reader on XML document named 'docname' from xml_documents table
  public static Reader getReader(Connection conn, String docname)
                               throws FileNotFoundException {
    return ReadCLOB.fromColumn(conn,"xml_documents","xmldoc","docname",docname);
  }
  // Return InputStream on XML document named 'docname' from xml_documents
  public static InputStream getInputStream(Connection conn, String docname)
                                  throws FileNotFoundException {
    return ReadCLOB.fromColumnAsInputStream(conn,"xml_documents","xmldoc",
                                            "docname",docname);
  }
  // Save contents of a Reader into xml_documents with doc name of 'docname'
  public static void save(Connection conn,String docname,Reader input)
                     throws SQLException, SAXException {
    // Delete existing row if present
    delete(conn,docname);
    // Insert a new row with empty_clob()
    CallableStatement stmt = conn.prepareCall(
          "BEGIN " +
          "  INSERT INTO xml_documents( docname, xmldoc) " +
          "  VALUES( ?, empty_clob()) "+
          "  RETURNING xmldoc INTO ?;" + // Use RETURNING...INTO to get CLOB
          "END;");
    stmt.setString(1,docname); // Bind var in VALUES()
```

Example 6-13. Implementing a CLOB-based "Filesystem" Inside JServer (continued)

```
    stmt.registerOutParameter(2,OracleTypes.CLOB); // RETURNING INTO
    stmt.execute(); // Do it
    // Retrieve the returned values of CLOB locator
    CLOB theXMLClob = ((OracleCallableStatement)stmt).getCLOB(2);
    stmt.close();
    // Write the input to the CLOB
    WriteCLOB.fromReader( input, theXMLClob );
    // Commit the changes and close the connection.
    conn.commit();
  }
  // Delete XML document named 'docname' from xml_documents
  public static void delete(Connection conn,String docname) throws SQLException{
    PreparedStatement stmt = conn.prepareStatement("DELETE FROM xml_documents"+
                                                   " WHERE docname = ?");
    stmt.setString(1,docname);
    stmt.execute();
    stmt.close();
    conn.commit();
  }
  // Print a list of documents in xml_documents matching 'docname'
  // Allow either % or * as wildcard character in the name.
  public static void list(Connection conn,String docname,PrintWriter out)
           throws SQLException {
    PreparedStatement ps =
      conn.prepareStatement("SELECT docname,TO_CHAR(timestamp,'Mon DD HH24:MI')"
                           +"  FROM xml_documents"
                           +" WHERE docname LIKE REPLACE(?,'*','%')||'%'"
                           +" ORDER BY docname");
    ps.setString(1,docname);
    ResultSet rs = ps.executeQuery();
    while (rs.next()) {
      out.println(rs.getString(2)+" "+rs.getString(1));
    }
    ps.close();
  }
  // Enable the use of xmldoc:/dir1/dir2/file.xml URLs in this session
  public static void enableXMLDocURLs() {
    try {
      // Give *our* handler first chance to handle URL.openConnection() requests
      URL.setURLStreamHandlerFactory(new XMLDocURLStreamHandlerFactory());
    }
    catch(java.lang.Error alreadyDefined) { /* Ignore */ }
  }
}
```

Constructing XML from Ill-Formed HTML Input

In this section, we'll study an example that illustrates how to use the Oracle XML Parser for Java to programmatically construct an XML document on the fly. To anyone excited about the power of separating data from presentation, it remains a sad fact of life that most of the interesting information on the Web today is still presented in HTML format. Book searches at Amazon.com, stock quotes from *http://quote.yahoo.com*, or the latest international currency exchange rates at *http://www.x-rates.com* are all available only as HTML pages. This is great for human eyeballs, but depressingly useless if you'd like to have a computer application make heads or tails of the valuable information contained in all those `<TD>` tags!

If HTML could be parsed as easily as XML, we might be able to attack the problem of scraping the interesting data *out* of the advertisement-laden presentations, but, alas, most web developers create their HTML without regard to its being well-formed. But a light at the end of this dim tunnel is a clean-sounding, clever utility named "Tidy," by Dave Raggett, the lead for the HTML working group at the World Wide Web Consortium (W3C). Tidy, which we introduced in Chapter 3, understands many of the most common mistakes made by HTML page designers and quickly corrects them to produce a well-formed XML document out of the messy HTML page you give it.*

Even more interesting for us at the moment is Andy Quick's Java port of Dave's Tidy utility, called "JTidy". If you download JTidy from *http://www3.sympatico.ca/ac.quick/jtidy.html*, you can be parsing HTML and turning it into XML in no time.

We're going to build a class called `JTidyConverter` that illustrates how to put JTidy to work to parse an arbitrary HTML page and produce a well-formed XML tree of nodes in memory. Then we'll use the Oracle XML Parser's implementation of the Document Object Model APIs to walk JTidy's in-memory tree structure and programmatically construct an instance of `XMLDocument` on which we can perform further processing, like data extraction.

Our goal is to start with an HTML page like the one shown in Figure 6-12 and end up with an `XMLDocument` containing only the data we're interested in, like the Ticker and Price information shown in Example 6-14.†

Example 6-14. Dynamically Scraping XML Data out of Existing HTML Pages

```
<?xml version = '1.0' encoding = 'UTF-8'?>
<QuoteStream time="Tue Jun 20 3:57pm ET - U.S. Markets Closed.">
  <Quote Ticker="ORCL" Price="86.188"/>
  <Quote Ticker="GE" Price="50.500"/>
  <Quote Ticker="MSFT" Price="74.688"/>
  <Quote Ticker="IBM" Price="118.188"/>
  <Quote Ticker="T" Price="34.125"/>
  <Quote Ticker="LU" Price="59.812"/>
  <Quote Ticker="CSCO" Price="67.938"/>
</QuoteStream>
```

* More information on the original C language version of Tidy is at *http://www.w3.org/People/Raggett/tidy/*.

† While our Yahoo Quotes! example demonstrates the basic techniques needed to acquire information published in HTML and transform it for further processing into a clean XML format, in practice, you must check the information supplier's policy on reuse of information before including it in an application you build.

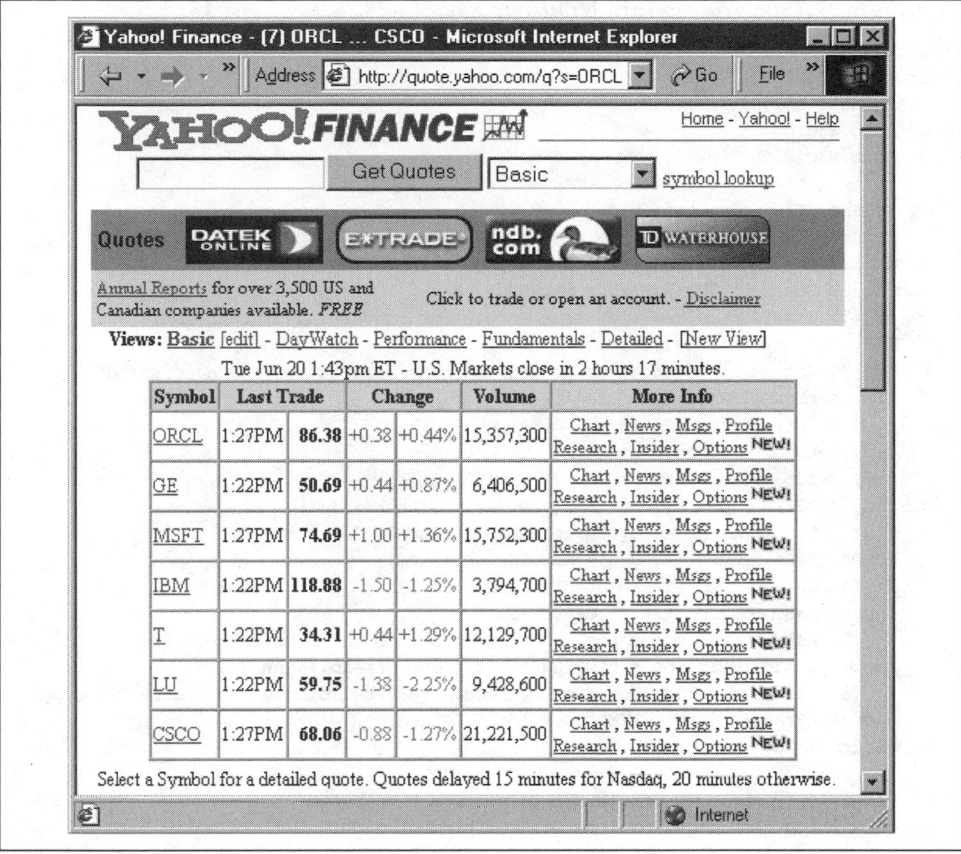

Figure 6-12. HTML stock quote information from Yahoo!

Since the JTidy bean does the "rocket science" part of the problem, we'll see that programmatically creating the XML document based on JTidy's results is actually very straightforward. Example 6-15 shows that to "XML-ify" HTML in our `XMLifyHTMLFrom` method, we must perform these steps:

1. Construct an instance of JTidy's `Tidy` bean.
2. Set some JTidy HTML conversion options for the best results.
3. Construct a new `XMLDocument` object to use as the root of the well-formed XML document our method will return.
4. Obtain an `InputStream` on the desired HTML page to tidy up by calling `openStream()` on its URL.
5. Call `tidy.parse()` to parse the HTML `InputStream` into JTidy's in-memory DOM representation.
6. Call `cloneXMLFragment()` on the root node of the JTidy DOM document to recursively construct an Oracle XML Parser DOM tree.

Example 6-15. Using JTidy to Turn HTML into XML

```
import java.io.*;
import java.net.URL;
import oracle.xml.parser.v2.*;
import org.w3c.dom.*;
import org.w3c.tidy.Tidy;

public class JTidyConverter {
  // Parse a URL returning for a possibly ill-formed HTML page and return
  // a "tidied" up XML document for the page using JTidy
  public XMLDocument XMLifyHTMLFrom(URL u) throws IOException {
    // (1) Construct a new Tidy bean to use for converting HTML to XML
    Tidy tidy = new Tidy();
    // (2) Set some Tidy options to get the best results for "data scraping"
    tidy.setMakeClean(true);
    tidy.setBreakBeforeBR(true);
    tidy.setShowWarnings(false);
    tidy.setOnlyErrors(true);
    tidy.setErrout(new PrintWriter(new StringWriter()));
    // (3) Construct an empty target Oracle XML DOM document
    XMLDocument xmldocToReturn = new XMLDocument();
    // (4) Get an InputStream of HTML from the URL
    InputStream HTMLInput = u.openStream();
    // (5) Ask Tidy to parse the incoming HTML into an in-memory DOM tree
    Document tidiedHTMLDoc = tidy.parseDOM(u.openStream(), null);
    // (6) Clone the JTidy DOM tree by recursively building up an Oracle DOM copy
    cloneXMLFragment(tidiedHTMLDoc,xmldocToReturn);
    return xmldocToReturn;
  }
  // Recursively build an Oracle XML Parser DOM tree based
  // on walking the JTidy DOM tree of the "tidied" page.
  private void cloneXMLFragment(Node node, Node curTarget) {
    if ( node == null ) return;
    Document d = curTarget instanceof Document ? (Document)curTarget :
                                     curTarget.getOwnerDocument();
    int type = node.getNodeType();
    switch ( type ) {
      // If we get the root node of the document, start the recursion
      // by calling build the Doc Element
      case Node.DOCUMENT_NODE:
        cloneXMLFragment(((Document)node).getDocumentElement(),d);
        break;

      // If we get an Element in the JTidy DOM, create Element in Oracle DOM
      // and append it to the current target node as a child. Also build
      // Oracle DOM attribute nodes for each attrib of the JTidy DOM Element
      case Node.ELEMENT_NODE:
        Element e = d.createElement(node.getNodeName());
        NamedNodeMap attrs = node.getAttributes();
        for ( int i = 0; i < attrs.getLength(); i++ ) {
          e.setAttribute(attrs.item(i).getNodeName(),
                         attrs.item(i).getNodeValue());
        }
```

Example 6-15. Using JTidy to Turn HTML into XML (continued)

```
            curTarget.appendChild(e);
            NodeList children = node.getChildNodes();

            // Recurse to build any children
            if ( children != null ) {
               int len = children.getLength();
               for ( int i = 0; i < len; i++ ) {
                  cloneXMLFragment(children.item(i),e);
               }
            }
            break;
         // If we get a Text Node in the JTidy DOM, create Text Node in Oracle
         // DOM and append it to the current target node as a child
         case Node.TEXT_NODE:
            curTarget.appendChild(d.createTextNode(node.getNodeValue()));
            break;
      }
   }
}
```

The **cloneXMLFragment** method is where the dynamic XML document creation is really happening. Observe that our routine behaves differently depending on what type of DOM tree node we're currently processing:

- If we see the root **DOCUMENT_NODE**, we start the recursive tree copy by calling **cloneXMLFragment** on the top-level document element in the JTidy document.
- Whenever we see an **ELEMENT_NODE**, we do the following:
  1. Create a new Element node in the Oracle XML DOM tree with the same name.
  2. Append it to the current target node in the Oracle XML DOM tree as a child.
  3. Copy all the Attribute name/value pairs from the JTidy DOM element to the Oracle DOM element.
  4. Recursively call **cloneXMLFragment** on each child node of the current element (if any).
- Whenever we see a **TEXT_NODE**, we create a new Text node in the Oracle XML DOM tree and append it to the current target node.

As a result, to retrieve any HTML page and convert it to an XML document for subsequent processing, we need just three lines of code:

```
// Construct a JTidyConverter
JTidyConverter j = new JTidyConverter();
// Pick a URL with some HTML to process
URL u = new URL("http://quote.yahoo.com q?d2=v1&o=d&s=ORCL+GE+MSFT+IBM+T+LU+CSCO");
// Get back an XML document for the HTML page to process further
XMLDocument voila = j.XMLifyHTMLFrom(u);
```

Since server-side programs querying information from relational databases produce most dynamically generated HTML pages, it's logical that these HTML pages will have some predictable, repeating HTML structure. Imagine the pseudo-code for the Yahoo! Quotes web page service:

```
// Server-side Pseudo-code for the Yahoo! Quotes HTML page
printYahooFinanceBanner();
printSymbolLookupForm();
printAdsForPartners();
// 's' is the parameter passed in the URL with list of quotes
printQuoteTableFor(s);
printFooter();
```

The `printQuoteTableFor(s)` routine loops over the 20-minute delayed quote prices in the database for the ticker symbols you've passed in and prints out a row of the HTML table for each one.

If we actually run the three lines of code to put our `JTidyConverter` class to work on the Yahoo! Quotes page, we get an `XMLDocument` containing the entire, well-formed content of the dynamically produced page. Even though there's a lot of random HTML stuff around the wee bit of data we're looking for, with XML in hand we're now in much better shape. The `XMLDocument` returned by `XMLifyHTMLFrom` (with a few comments added to highlight the parts we're interested in) looks like Example 6-16.

Example 6-16. Tidied Version of the Yahoo Quotes HTML Page

```
<?xml version = '1.0' encoding = 'UTF-8'?>
<html>
   <head>
      <meta content="HTML Tidy, see www.w3.org" name="generator"/>
      <title>Yahoo! Finance - (7) ORCL ... CSCO</title>
   </head>
   <body>
      <div style="text-align: center">
         <!-- Ads, Banner, and other preceding HTML removed for brevity -->
         <!-- Time of quotes is value of the <p> element preceding <table> -->
         <p>Tue Jun 20 3:57pm ET - U.S. Markets Closed.</p>
         <!--
          | Stock quotes start with the <table> whose first <th> header cell
          | in the first <tr> row has the value "Symbol"
          +-->
         <table cellspacing="0" cellpadding="1" border="1">
            <tr bgcolor="#dcdcdc">
               <th nowrap="">Symbol</th>
               <th colspan="2" nowrap="">Last Trade</th>
               <th colspan="2" nowrap="">Change</th>
               <th nowrap="">Volume</th>
               <th nowrap="">More Info</th>
            </tr>
            <!-- Stock Quote *data* starts in the 2nd <tr> row after headers -->
```

Example 6-16. Tidied Version of the Yahoo Quotes HTML Page (continued)

```
          <tr align="right">
             <!-- Ticker symbol is the value of the first <td> cell -->
             <td align="left" nowrap="">
                <a href="/q?s=ORCL&#38;d=t">ORCL</a>
             </td>
             <td align="center" nowrap="">Apr 14</td>
             <!-- Price is the value of third <td> cell -->
             <td nowrap="">
                <b>86.188</b>
             </td>
             <td style="color: #ff0020" nowrap="">+0.38</td>
             <td style="color: #ff0020" nowrap="">+0.44%</td>
             <td nowrap="">15,357,300</td>
             <td align="center" nowrap="">
             </td>
          </tr>
          <!-- Other identical "Stock Quote" <TR> rows removed for brevity -->
       </table>
       <!-- Other stuff removed -->
    </div>
  </body>
</html>
```

Since the HTML page is now well-formed XML, it's easier to recognize the repeating patterns we are interested in:

- Out of many `<table>`s in the returned document, the `<table>` containing the stock quotes is the one where the first `<th>` table header in the first `<tr>` table row has the value `Symbol`.
- The effective time of the quote information is the value of the first `<p>` element preceding this table.
- The actual stock quote data is in the individual `<tr>` rows of this `<table>`, starting with the second row, since the first row is just column headers.
- In each row of stock quotes, the Ticker symbol is the value of the first `<td>` table data cell, and the Price is the value of the third `<td>` cell.

By the *value* of the `<td>` cell we mean the text content inside the `<td>` element or any of its nested elements (disregarding attribute values). So the value of:

```
<td>
   <b>86.188</b>
</td>
```

is the text `86.188`.

We can use an XSLT transformation to encapsulate the patterns we discovered above into a simple stylesheet, like this:

```
<!-- YahooQuotes-to-QuoteStream.xsl -->
<xsl:stylesheet xmlns:xsl="http://www.w3.org/1999/XSL/Transform" version="1.0">
  <xsl:template match="/">
    <!-- Find the <table> whose first row's first table header has "Symbol" -->
    <xsl:for-each select="//table[tr[1]/th[1]='Symbol']">
      <!-- The time of the quotes is in the first <p> preceding this table -->
      <QuoteStream time="{preceding::p[1]}">
        <!-- For each row after the first row -->
        <xsl:for-each select="tr[position()>1]">
          <!-- Ticker is value of first <td> cell -->
          <!-- Price  is value of third <td> cell -->
          <Quote Ticker="{td[1]}"
                 Price="{format-number(number(td[3]),'###,###.000')}"/>
        </xsl:for-each>
      </QuoteStream>
    </xsl:for-each>
  </xsl:template>
</xsl:stylesheet>
```

We'll learn a lot more about how to create transformations like this in Chapters 7 and 9, but it's pretty straightforward. The *elements* that start with `<xsl:*something*>` are XSLT transformation actions. `<xsl:for-each>` lets us loop over elements in the source document that match a particular pattern, described using an XPath expression. The *attributes* whose values are surrounded by curly braces like `time="{preceding::p[1]}"` are created in the result with a value that also comes from evaluating an XPath expression relative to the current loop.

This transformation reads the source XML document (our well-formed HTML page of Yahoo! Quotes) and does the following:

1. For each `<table>` with `Symbol` in the first row's first header column, it creates a `<QuoteStream>` element in the result with a `time` attribute equal to the value of the `<p>` element preceding the table
2. Nested inside this `<QuoteStream>` element, it creates one `<Quote>` element for each `<tr>` row of stock quote data matched in the sources.
3. For each `<Quote>` element, it creates `Ticker` and `Price` attributes with the respective values pulled in from the first and third `<td>` elements in the current `<tr>` row

That's it. As we saw in Chapter 3, *Combining XML and Oracle*, we *could* use the `oraxsl` command-line utility to transform the single, tidied-up Yahoo! Quotes page above into a corresponding XML `<QuoteStream>` document with the command:

```
oraxsl TidiedUpYahooQuotesPage.xml YahooQuotes-to-QuoteStream.xsl
```

But this will just produce XML results for a single page. We want to serve this real-time data over the Web, so let's build a server-side Java program that leverages the cool machinery we've just built.

Implementing a Java servlet is the standard way to write applications that respond to client requests over the Web. While traditionally used to serve dynamic HTML pages in response to requests from web browsers, by design, servlets are more general-purpose in nature. Requests can come from *any* kind of client program, called a User Agent, and the servlet's response to those requests can be of *any* MIME type, including the basic type for XML documents, `text/xml`.

Technically, a servlet is any class that implements the `javax.servlet.Servlet` interface. In practice, most servlets *extend* the basic `javax.servlet.HttpServlet` class and override its methods as appropriate to handle HTTP requests for a particular application. To respond to an HTTP GET request, override the `doGet` method. To respond to an HTTP POST request, override `doPost`. While `doGet` and `doPost` are the most common methods, Table 6-3 gives a short list of servlet methods that developers typically override.

Table 6-3. Overview of HttpServlet Methods

Method Name	Description
`init`	Called when the servlet is initialized. Servlet-wide resources such as database connections can be acquired here and shared across multiple servlet threads (see the discussion following the table).
`doGet`	Called in response to a User Agent's request for a page using the HTTP GET method. A GET request is called when the User Agent wants to retrieve a page of information. It is not expected that a GET request will modify any persistent state in the server. This is the most frequent kind of HTTP request.
`doPost`	Called in response to a User Agent's request for a page using the HTTP POST method, typically used to post the contents of an HTML form to the server. A POST method typically implies that the server will modify some persistent data using the results of the request, then return a page indicating the status of the operation or presenting the next step in a sequence of tasks to the user.
`destroy`	Called when the servlet is destroyed. Typically used to free system resources like database connections that the servlet might have been using.

With this brief introduction to servlets in hand, let's take our Yahoo! Quotes example one last step and build a Java servlet that makes use of the `JTidyConverter` class and the Oracle XSLT processor to enable the data-scraping mechanism to be used dynamically over the Web. Example 6-17 shows the implementation of a `YahooXMLQuotesServlet` that does the job.

In the servlet's `init()` method, we construct an instance of a `JTidyConverter` and an `XSLStylesheet` to use for processing each request. To show off yet another technique for parsing XML from a stream, Example 6-17 uses the `getClass().getResourceAsStream("filename")` method to load the source of the XSLT stylesheet *YahooQuotes-to-QuoteStream.xsl* from the same location in the CLASSPATH as the current servlet class is found.

In the servlet's `doGet()` method, which runs each time a request for this servlet comes into the web server, we do the following:

1. Set the MIME type of the servlet response to be `text/xml`.
2. Get the value of the HTTP parameter named `symbols`.
3. Create a URL for the Yahoo! Quotes page, tacking on the list of ticker symbols after replacing commas with plus signs.
4. Call `jtc.XMLifyHTMLFrom` on the URL to get a tidied-up XML version of the returned Yahoo! Quotes HTML page.
5. Create an instance of `XSLProcessor` and call `processXSL()` on it to transform the XML results of our Yahoo! Quotes into a `<QuoteStream>`.

Example 6-17. Servlet to Convert Yahoo! Quotes to XML Quotes in Real Time

```
import javax.servlet.http.*;
import oracle.xml.parser.v2.*;
import java.net.URL;
import javax.servlet.*;
import java.io.*;
import JTidyConverter;

public class YahooXMLQuotesServlet extends HttpServlet {
  JTidyConverter jtc    = null;
  XSLStylesheet  sheet = null;

  protected void doGet(HttpServletRequest req, HttpServletResponse resp)
  throws ServletException, IOException {
    String YahooQuotesURL = "http://quote.yahoo.com/q?d2=v1&o=d&s=";
    String quotes = req.getParameter("symbols");
    // First, tell the requestor we're sending her XML data as the response.
    resp.setContentType("text/xml");
    // Then, get the Servlet's output Writer to write the response into.
    PrintWriter out = resp.getWriter();
    if (quotes != null) {
      URL yahooUrl  = new URL(YahooQuotesURL+quotes.replace(',','+'));
      try {
        // Convert the dynamically produced Yahoo! Quotes page to XML doc
        XMLDocument yahooquotes = jtc.XMLifyHTMLFrom(yahooUrl);
        // Transform the document using our stylesheet into <QuoteStream>
        // and let the XSLT processor write the result to our 'out' Writer
        XSLProcessor xslt        = new XSLProcessor();
        xslt.processXSL(sheet,yahooquotes,out);
      }
```

Example 6-17. Servlet to Convert Yahoo! Quotes to XML Quotes in Real Time (continued)

```
      catch (Exception ex) {out.println("<error>"+ex.getMessage()+"</error>");}
    }
    else { out.println("<error>No Symbols Provided</error>"); }
  }

  public void init(ServletConfig sc) throws ServletException {
    super.init(sc);
    // Make sure the Servlet can "see" through the corporate firewall...
    System.setProperty("proxySet","true");
    System.setProperty("proxyHost","yourproxyserver.you.com");
    System.setProperty("proxyPort","80");
    // Construct a JTidyConverter. We can use the same one over and over.
    jtc   = new JTidyConverter();
    try {
      // Read the Yahoo2Xml.xsl stylesheet from the CLASSPATH as a resource.
      InputStream styleSource =
         getClass().getResourceAsStream("YahooQuotes-to-QuoteStream.xsl");
      if (styleSource == null) {
        throw new ServletException("YahooQuotes-to-QuoteStream.xsl not found.");
      }
      // Cache a new stylesheet. Note: XSLStylesheet object is not threadsafe
      // in Oracle XSLT processor 2.0.2.7, but ok for this demo
      sheet = new XSLStylesheet(styleSource,null); // No base URL needed here!
    }
    catch (XSLException xslx) {
      throw new ServletException("Error preparing XSLT stylesheet.");
    }
  }
}
```

Now any user can browse our web server with a URL like this:

```
http://server/YahooXMLQuotesServlet?symbols=WBVN,YHOO,EBAY
```

and instantly receive an appropriate XML `<QuoteStream>` datagram over the Web containing just the quotes they care about right now:

```
<?xml version = '1.0' encoding = 'UTF-8'?>
<QuoteStream time="Sun Apr 16 2:55pm ET - U.S. Markets Closed.">
  <Quote Ticker="WBVN" Price="5.688"/>
  <Quote Ticker="YHOO" Price="116.000"/>
  <Quote Ticker="EBAY" Price="139.562"/>
</QuoteStream>
```

Later in the chapter, we'll build an "XML Quote Service" that runs inside the Oracle8*i* database as an example of how this kind of XML processing can be integrated into the server to periodically retrieve XML-based information from another site and store it in tables in your database for fast, local processing.

While we're talking about basic XML processing and servlets, it's worth mentioning here that in addition to allowing the kind of remote JServer debugging we saw earlier, Oracle's JDeveloper 3.1 product also supports both local and remote debugging of Java servlets. This means that you can quickly test and debug a servlet on your own machine, or attach the debugger to a live, remote Apache JServ server where you are load-testing your production servlet code. The debugging facilities are identical in every configuration, so this can really be a lifesaver for your web-based XML development with Oracle.

For local debugging of a servlet, no special settings are necessary. Just click the Debug icon and a single-user, local Java servlet engine is used to step through your code. To enable remote debugging of servlets—or, in fact, any remotely executing Java code—visit your JDeveloper *Project Properties* and set *Debug Files as:* to "Remote Debugging", as shown in Figure 6-13.

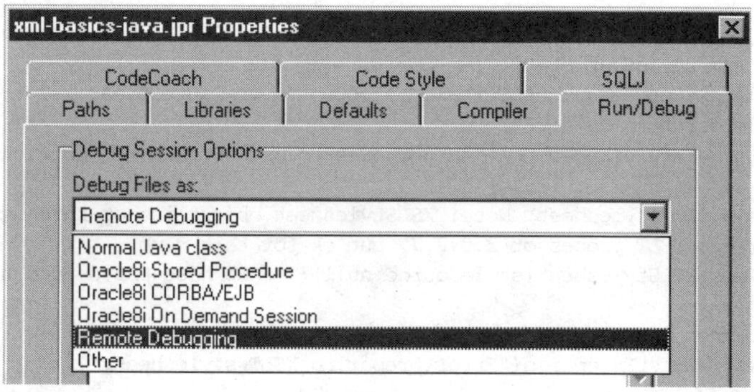

Figure 6-13. Setting up for remote Java debugging

Click on the Debug icon in JDeveloper and tell the debugger the machine name and debugging port it should connect to, as shown in Figure 6-14.

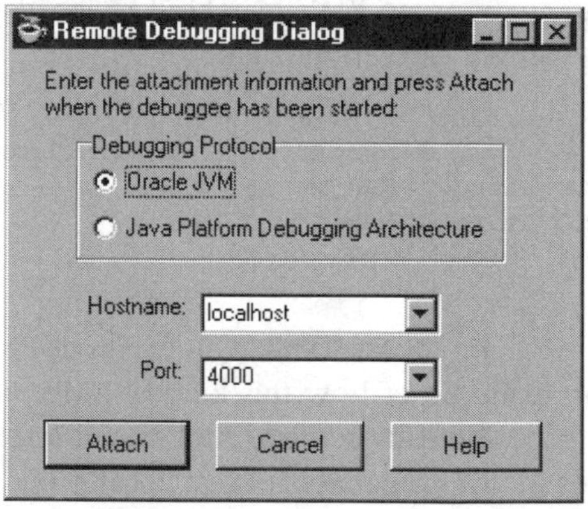

Figure 6-14. Remote debugger attach dialog

When you dismiss the remote debugging dialog, the debugger attempts to attach to the running process, and you're off to find the cause of the problem without resorting to `System.out.println()` messages in an external file.

Apache JServ here is just an example. JDeveloper remote debugging works with any remotely executing Java code running on a Java 1.2–compliant virtual machine. You can find details on setting up your own server for remote debugging in JDeveloper's online help system.

Handling Very Large XML Data Streams

In the last section, we walked the in-memory tree structure of an XML document to copy its nodes. A common question that developers ask is, "For a really big XML file, won't that in-memory tree of DOM objects get really big?" Great question: the answer is a resounding "yes!" However, the size of the tree of objects in memory is a function of how many elements, attributes, and text nodes the tree contains, not strictly of its file size. For a concrete example, consider the following two XML documents:

```
<!-- This document is 180 bytes long -->
<doc>
  Just one big text node here with
  lots of text in it. And some more
  and some more and some more and
  some more and...
</doc>
```

and:

```
<!-- This document is 180 bytes long -->
<doc>
 <a><b><c><d><e><f><g><h><i/></h></g></f></e></d></c></b></a>
 <a><b><c><d><e><f><g><h><i/></h></g></f></e></d></c></b></a>
</doc>
```

Both documents are exactly the same size—180 bytes—but parsing the first document produces the in-memory structure shown in Figure 6-15.

This structure has a root node representing the `Document`, an `Element` node child of the root representing the document element named <doc>, and a single `Text` node child of the document element. This makes a total of just three objects in memory. On the other hand, parsing the 180-byte file in the second example produces the in-memory tree of objects, shown in Figure 6-16.

That tree contains a root node representing the `Document`, an `Element` node child of the root representing the document element named <doc>, and then 18 additional `Element` nodes and three `Text` nodes representing the whitespace (*ws*)—carriage returns, line feeds, spaces, and tabs—in the file that makes the elements

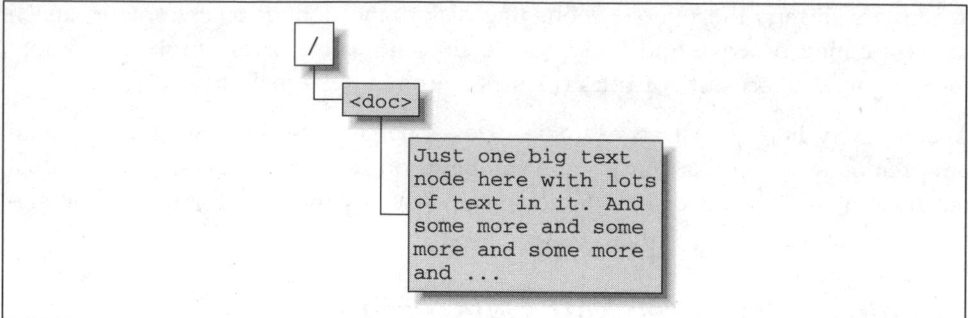

Figure 6-15. Node tree representation with a single text node

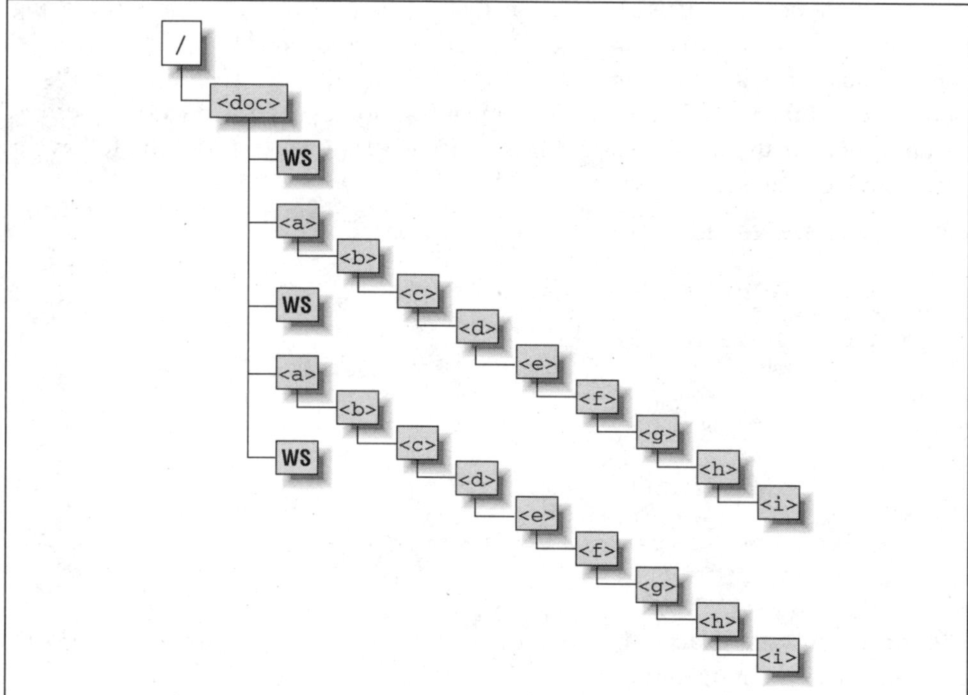

Figure 6-16. Node tree representation with nested elements

appear on different lines and look indented. So the 180-byte file in the first example requires just three objects in memory, while the second file needs 23 objects. Clearly, the amount of memory required to parse an XML document is a function both of its sheer size in bytes and of the number of elements, attributes, and text nodes it contains. This is not an argument against using lots of elements in your XML, just a sign that for large files we need a technique other than the straightforward parse-it-all-into-memory approach.

When an XML file is used to export a large *data set*—for example, one year's worth of detailed stock quote closing prices for all listed securities on the NASDAQ exchange—parsing the resulting XML file into a single, in-memory tree of nodes can be impractical due to the amount of memory required. However, it is often the case that these gigantic XML documents are composed of a single containing element like `<YearOfNasdaqCloses>` in Example 6-18, whose children are a series of a million repeating subdocuments like the contents of each `<ClosingQuote>` element in this example.

Example 6-18. A Year of Closing Price Information for NASDAQ Stocks

```
<!--
 | File size is approximately (137 bytes per entry) times (5207 securities)
 | times (5 days a week) times (52 weeks per year) = 176MB of XML
 +-->
<YearOfNasdaqCloses Year="1999" TotalSecurities="5207">
  <ClosingQuote Ticker="AAABB">
    <Date>01/01/1999</Date>
    <Price>6.25</Price>
    <Percent>0.5</Percent>
  </ClosingQuote>
  <ClosingQuote Ticker="AABC">
    <Date>01/01/1998</Date>
    <Price>7.05</Price>
    <Percent>1.25</Percent>
  </ClosingQuote>

  <!-- 1,353,817 Additional Entries Removed -->

  <ClosingQuote Ticker="ZVXI">
    <Date>12/31/1999</Date>
    <Price>16.10</Price>
    <Percent>-1.05</Percent>
  </ClosingQuote>
</YearOfNasdaqCloses>
```

An actual XML file containing closing quotes for each of the 5207 stocks on the NASDAQ for each of the 5 business days in each of 52 weeks during the year—at about 140 bytes per entry—works out to be approximately 176MB of XML! Since these huge XML data files are typically produced by looping over rows of data in a relational table and writing out each row as a subdocument, it's understandable that the subdocuments have a consistent, repeating structure. We will take advantage of this fact to come up with a new approach to processing these large files.

Using a time-honored divide and conquer strategy, we'll design and implement a mechanism here to split up the huge file into a sequence of subdocuments, processing each subdocument *separately* instead of loading the entire 176MB into memory before starting. For this task, instead of using the now-familiar

`DOMParser`, we'll make use of its companion `SAXParser` class in the `oracle.xml.parser.v2` package.

The acronym SAX* stands for the "Simple API for XML," an API that allows us to process an XML document as a stream of events instead of as a tree of nodes. When the `SAXParser` reads in the stream of characters comprising the XML document, it simply announces the arrival of each recognizable syntactic construct in the document. So the first of our earlier 180-byte example files would be announced, in sequence, by the `SAXParser` as:

1. "Starting to parse the document"
2. "Starting to parse an element named `doc` with no attributes"
3. "Starting to parse a text node with these characters: 'Just one big...' "
4. "Done parsing the element named `doc`"
5. "Done parsing the document"

In fact, announcing the syntactic constructs as it encounters them is the only thing a `SAXParser` does! It does not create any in-memory objects that represent these structures, as the `DOMParser` does. Given this fact, it's easy to understand why parsing a file with the `SAXParser` requires very little memory: it just does I/O and sends parsing event notifications. The tradeoff is that you have to write code to handle these events to actually do something interesting with the XML document streaming in. The `SAXParser` scans the incoming characters and announces each construct it encounters by calling an appropriate method of the SAX `DocumentHandler` interface:

```
public interface DocumentHandler {
  void setDocumentLocator(Locator p0);
  void startDocument() throws SAXException;
  void processingInstruction(String p0, String p1) throws SAXException;
  void startElement(String p0, AttributeList p1) throws SAXException;
  void characters(char[] p0, int p1, int p2) throws SAXException;
  void ignorableWhitespace(char[] p0, int p1, int p2) throws SAXException;
  void endElement(String p0) throws SAXException;
  void endDocument() throws SAXException;
}
```

Any class that implements the `DocumentHandler` interface above can be notified by the `SAXParser` of these parsing events after calling the parser's `setDocumentHandler()` method to register itself for notification. In addition to `DocumentHandler`, there are other `org.xml.sax` handler interfaces like `EntityResolver`, `DTDHandler`, and `ErrorHandler`, so if necessary, your class can have complete control over every aspect of the document being parsed.

* You can find more details on SAX at *http://www.megginson.com*.

To handle our task of splitting a large XML document into its many repeating subdocuments, we'll implement an appropriately named `XMLDocumentSplitter` class. Since the useful base class `org.xml.sax.HandlerBase` provides a default implementation for all of the SAX handling interfaces, our `XMLDocumentSplitter` will extend this and override *only* the handling methods that make sense for our task.

So what *is* the task, exactly? Given the name of the XML element representing the repeating subdocument—for instance, `<ClosingQuote>` in our `<YearOfNasdaqCloses>` example—it will be `XMLDocumentSplitter`'s job to handle the `startElement` and `endElement` SAX events to enable the separate handling of each subdocument.

Since working with SAX's event-based parsing can be confusing to developers who are not used to such a programming paradigm, we'll choose a path that blends the best of the SAX and the DOM approaches:

- We'll use a `SAXParser` in `XMLDocumentSplitter` to handle XML documents of arbitrary size.
- For each subdocument we encounter, we'll build a DOM document for it and call a method to handle that individual subdocument's processing.

This approach kills two birds with one stone: it alleviates the need to have all of the large XML document in memory at once without sacrificing the easier-to-use DOM model to handle each subdocument. Since we want `XMLDocumentSplitter` to be reusable, it makes sense to create an `XMLDocumentHandler` interface to define the contract between the component doing the splitting of the large XML file and the component that will handle the processing of each subdocument:

```
import java.net.URL;
import org.w3c.dom.Document;
public interface XMLDocumentHandler {
  void handleDocument( Document d , URL u ) throws Exception;
}
```

With this simple interface in place, we can see how the interaction between SAX and DOM will work in Figure 6-17.

`XMLDocumentSplitter` parses the entirety of the large file using a `SAXParser`. It registers itself to be the handler for all of the `startElement` and `endElement` parsing events. In the `startElement` handler, based on checking the name of the element being started, it does one of the following:

- Creates a new subdocument, if it's the start event for the splitter element
- Creates a new `Element` for the element being started and appends it to the current element in the current subdocument under construction

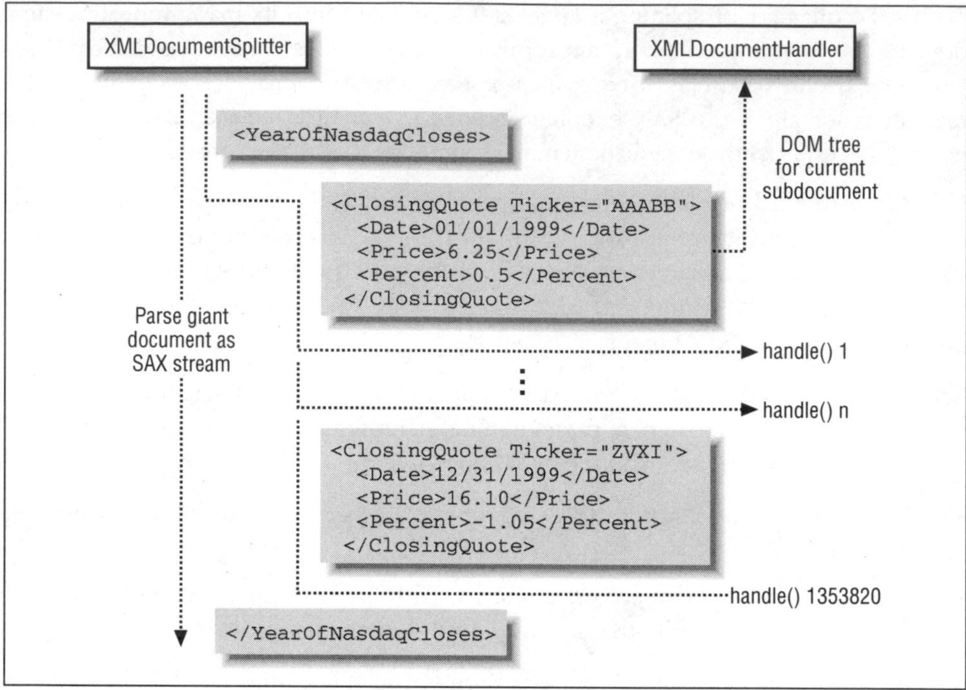

Figure 6-17. Combining the best of SAX and DOM for large, repetitive XML

- Ignores the element if it's *not* between the start and end element tags of the splitter element

In the `endElement` handler, again based on checking the name of the element being ended, `XMLDocumentSplitter` does one of the following:

- Calls the `XMLDocumentHandler` to handle the current subdocument, if we're seeing the closing tag for the splitter element
- Sets the current node in the subdocument under construction to the parent of the *current* current node, if we're "ending" any other element inside the subdocument
- Ignores the element if it's not between the start and end element tags of the splitter element

Example 6-19 shows the commented source code for `XMLDocumentSplitter`.

Example 6-19. Processing Large Streams of Repeating Subdocuments

```
import org.xml.sax.*;
import org.w3c.dom.*;
import java.io.*;
import java.net.*;
import oracle.xml.parser.v2.*;
```

Example 6-19. Processing Large Streams of Repeating Subdocuments (continued)

```
public class XMLDocumentSplitter extends HandlerBase {
  private Document curDoc;
  private Node     curNode;
  private Element  curElement;
  private URL      fileURL;
  private XMLDocumentHandler handler;
  private String splitOnElement = null;
  boolean seenDocElementYet = false;
  // Remember the XMLDocumentHandler we're being asked to use.
  public XMLDocumentSplitter(XMLDocumentHandler handler) {
   this.handler = handler;
  }
  // Split a large XML document into N subdocuments, each one identified
  // by the an opening 'splitElement' element. Invoke an XMLDocumentHandler
  // to process each subdocument encountered.
  public void split(URL fileURL, String splitElement)
   throws SAXParseException,SAXException,IOException {
   this.fileURL        = fileURL;
   this.splitOnElement = splitElement;
   // Create a new SAXParser
   Parser parser = new SAXParser();
   // Register the current instance of this class as the Document Handler
   parser.setDocumentHandler(this);
   // Create a SAX InputSource on the URL's InputStream
   InputSource is = new InputSource(fileURL.openStream());
   // Start parsing the stream of XML
   parser.parse(is);
  }
  // Handle the <Element> "start-element" parsing event
  public void startElement(String name,AttributeList atl) throws SAXException {
   // If we were given a null element name to split on, behave "normally"
   // by using the document element as the splitElement.
   if (splitOnElement == null && !seenDocElementYet) {
     splitOnElement = name;
     seenDocElementYet = true;
   }
   // Construct a DOM Element node for the current element being parsed
   curElement = new XMLElement(name);
   // Add DOM Attribute nodes to the element for each attribute parsed
   for (int i=0; i<atl.getLength(); i++) {
     curElement.setAttribute(atl.getName(i),atl.getValue(i));
   }
   // If we're NOT currently building a subdocument and the element name
   // is the split element, then create a new XMLDocument for new subdocument
   if (curDoc == null) {
     if (name.equals(splitOnElement)) {
       curDoc = new XMLDocument();
       curNode = curDoc;
     }
     else {
       // If we're NOT building a subdocument but this element
       // is not the splitterElement, then do nothing.
```

Example 6-19. Processing Large Streams of Repeating Subdocuments (continued)

```
        return;
      }
    }
    // Append the current DOM Element as a child of the current node in the
    // subdocument being constructured, and set it to be the new current node
    curNode.appendChild(curElement);
    curNode = curElement;
  }
  // Handle the </Element> "end-element" parsing event
  public void endElement(String name) throws SAXException {
    // If we're NOT building a subdocument, we don't care. Just return.
    if (curDoc == null) return;
    // If this is the endElement event for the subdocument splitElement
    // then we're done with the subdocument and are ready to call the
    // handler to handle it.
    if (name.equals(splitOnElement)) {
     if (curDoc != null) {
       try {
         // Call the XMLDocumentHandler.handle() method for current subdoc
         handler.handleDocument(curDoc,fileURL);
       }
       catch (Exception e) {
         System.err.println(e.getMessage());
       }
     }
     // Get ready for the next subdoc by nulling out our 'current' variables
     curDoc = null;
     curNode = null;
     curElement = null;
    }
    else {
     // If this is the endElement for any other element, make
     // its parent the new current node
     curNode = curNode.getParentNode();
    }
  }
  // Handle the "just got some text" parsing event
  public void characters(char[] cbuf, int start, int len) {
    // If we get text characters, create a new DOM Text node and
    // append it as a child of the current node.
    curElement.appendChild(new XMLText(new String(cbuf,start,len)));
  }
}
```

Now let's apply `XMLDocumentSplitter` to solve a problem with a large XML file. Imagine that you are trying use Oracle8*i*'s powerful data warehousing features to analyze your web site's weekly "click stream" information. Further, let's suppose that your web server outputs the raw information for each web page access in an XML file like the one shown in Example 6-20.

Example 6-20. Excerpt from XML-based Web Server Access Log File

```
<accesslog>
  <!--
      h="Host Making the Request"
      t="Time of Request"
      r="HTTP Request Header"
      s="Status of Request"
      b="Bytes Sent"
      f="Referred from URL"
      u="User Agent"/>
  -->
  <req h="146.74.93.17"
      t="13/Sep/1999:20:53:34 -0500"
      r="GET / HTTP/1.0"
      s="200"
      b="11058"
      f="http://www.yesyesyes.com/keylists/example.html"
      u="Mozilla/4.08 [en] (WinNT; I ;Nav)"/>
  <req h="146.74.93.17"
      t="13/Sep/1999:20:53:35 -0500"
      r="GET /sis_logo.jpg HTTP/1.0"
      s="200"
      b="26025"
      f="http://www.spunkyworld.com/"
      u="Mozilla/4.08 [en] (WinNT; I ;Nav)"/>
  <req h="146.74.93.17"
      t="13/Sep/1999:20:53:36 -0500"
      r="GET /services.gif HTTP/1.0"
      s="200"
      b="856"
      f="http://www.spunkyworld.com/"
      u="Mozilla/4.08 [en] (WinNT; I ;Nav)"/>

  <!-- Millions more page-views in the log where these came from! -->

</accesslog>
```

To quickly load this large XML file into an access_log table into your data warehouse, you need to perform just two steps:

1. Write a `LogEntryInsertHandler` class that implements `XMLDocumentHandler` and contains the code to handle a `<req>` subdocument by inserting its data into a row of the access_log table.
2. Write an `InsertAccessLog` command-line program that takes a given access log XML file, constructs an `XMLDocumentSplitter` to process the log in chunks, and uses the `LogEntryInsertHandler` as the `XMLDocumentHandler` for the job.

The code for LogEntryInsertHandler is straightforward because:

- It only needs to handle a single <req> subdocument.
- We don't have to learn a new paradigm for handling this simple document just because it happens to live in a huge file.
- We can use Oracle DOM methods like valueOf to simplify the job.

The code for LogEntryInsertHandler appears in Example 6-21.

Example 6-21. Handling the Insert for a Single Web Access Log Entry

```
import java.net.URL;
import java.sql.*;
import org.w3c.dom.Document;
import java.sql.Connection;
import oracle.xml.parser.v2.XMLDocument;
import java.sql.Date;

public class LogEntryInsertHandler implements XMLDocumentHandler{
  private Connection conn;
  private CallableStatement cs;
  private long rows = 0;
  private long commitBatch = 10;
  // Remember the commit-batch quantity and database connection
  public LogEntryInsertHandler(Connection conn, long commitBatch)
                                throws SQLException {
    this.commitBatch = commitBatch;
    this.conn = conn;
    setupCallableStatement();
  }
  // Return number of rows processed so far
  public long getRowsHandled() { return rows; }
  // Handle the processing of a single <req> document
  public void handleDocument( Document doc , URL u ) throws Exception {
    XMLDocument d = (XMLDocument)doc;
    // Bump the row counter
    rows++;
    // Bind the values for the insert from values of XPath over current doc
    cs.setString(1,d.valueOf("/req/@h")); // host
    cs.setString(2,d.valueOf("/req/@r")); // request made
    cs.setString(3,d.valueOf("/req/@t")); // time of request
    cs.setString(4,d.valueOf("/req/@f")); // referred from
    cs.setString(5,d.valueOf("/req/@u")); // user agent
    // Do the insert
    cs.execute();
    if (rows % commitBatch == 0) {
      // Commit every 'commitBatch' rows
      conn.commit();
    }
  }
  // Setup reusable statement for inserts
  private void setupCallableStatement() throws SQLException {
```

Example 6-21. Handling the Insert for a Single Web Access Log Entry (continued)

```
    if (cs != null) {
      try { cs.close(); }
      catch (SQLException s) {}
    }
    cs = conn.prepareCall("INSERT INTO access_log VALUES(?,?,?,?,?)");
  }
  // Commit any uncommitted rows, and close statement and connection.
  protected void finalize() throws Throwable {
    try { conn.commit(); } catch (SQLException s) {}
    try { cs.close();    } catch (SQLException s) {}
    try { conn.close();  } catch (SQLException s) {}
  }
}
```

Note that this class uses `valueOf()` with an XPath expression relative to the document being handled to retrieve the values of the <req> document content to be inserted. The `InsertAccessLog` command-line driver program appears in Example 6-22.

Example 6-22. Utility to Insert XML-based Web Server Access Log File

```
public class InsertAccessLog {
  public static void main(String[] args) throws Exception {
    // Take the access log filename from the first command-line argument
    String filename     = args[0];
    // Split up the giant AccessLog file treating
    // each <req> element as its own subdocument.
    String splitElement = "req";
    // Create an instance of the document handler. Commit every 100
    LogEntryInsertHandler dochandler =
           new LogEntryInsertHandler(Examples.getConnection(),100);
    // Create a XMLDocumentSplitter
    XMLDocumentSplitter xds = new XMLDocumentSplitter(dochandler);
    long start = System.currentTimeMillis();
    // Tell the splitter to split based on the splitElement 'req'
    xds.split(URLUtils.newURL(filename),splitElement);
    long end   = System.currentTimeMillis();
    long rows  = dochandler.getRowsHandled();
    System.out.println("Inserted "+dochandler.getRowsHandled()+" rows..."+
                       "in " + (end-start)+"ms." +
                       " (" + ((end-start)/rows)+" ms. per row)");
  }
}
```

This example creates an instance of `LogEntryInsertHandler` indicating that the handler should COMMIT every 100 records and passes it to the constructor of the `XMLDocumentSplitter`. Then it calls the `split()` method on the document splitter to split—and handle—the contents of the entire web server log file whose name is passed in as an argument. The result is that the contents of an arbitrarily large XML-based web log file will be loaded into the access_log table.

In Chapter 14, *Advanced XML Loading Techniques*, we'll expand on this example to show combining **XMLDocumentSplitter** with a handler that enables any size XML document to be inserted into any number of database tables.

Let's give our new utility a spin with the command:

```
java InsertAccessLog AccessLog.xml
```

For a 6MB *AccessLog.xml* log file containing 27625 **<req>** subdocuments, we can monitor the memory usage using Windows NT's Task Manager as shown in Figure 6-18 to observe that using this technique really does not require much memory at all to process very large files.

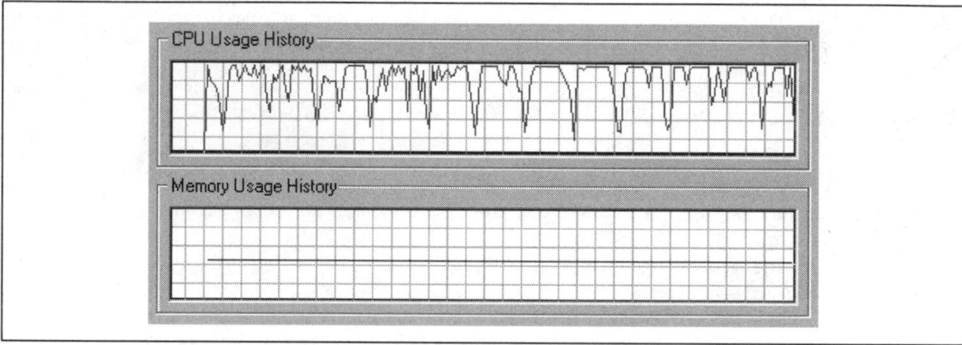

Figure 6-18. Low, flat memory usage on large XML files with SAX

The test works fine and prints out a status message of:

```
Inserted 27265 rows...in 173049ms. (6 ms. per row)
```

Searching XML Documents with XPath

In this section, we'll work through several examples that illustrate the power and productivity offered by the Oracle XML Parser's tightly integrated XPath support. Using these XPath capabilities, we'll see how easy searching, extracting, evaluating, and retrieving the value of the nodes in an XML document can be, avoiding tons of tedious DOM node manipulation code.

Basic Use of XPath in Java

Oracle's implementation of the Document Object Model extends the basic DOM APIs to provide some simple yet powerful additional methods that can save you lots of time when writing applications that process XML. These extensions come in the form of the following extra methods on the **XMLNode** object:

`selectNodes` *(XPathExpr)*
: Returns a DOM `NodeList` containing the nodes matching an XPath expression

`selectSingleNode` *(XPathExpr)*
: Returns the first DOM node matching an XPath expression

`valueOf` *(XPathExpr)*
: Returns a String with the text value of the nodes matching an XPath expression

`print` *(Writer | OutputStream)*
: Serializes the node and its children to an output stream as XML markup

These methods are all defined on the **XMLNode** class that implements the DOM **Node** interface in the Oracle XML Parser. Since **XMLDocument** extends from **XMLNode**, you can use any of these methods on an entire XML document, or just scope them to a particular node. Since the methods are not defined by the W3C's base DOM interfaces, in order to call the methods you have to cast a **Node** object into an **XMLNode** before you can call them, like this:

```
for (int z = 0; z < matches; z++) {
  // Retrieve current node in a NodeList and cast it to an XMLNode
  XMLNode curNode = (XMLNode)myNodeList.item(z);
  // Use a method that is on XMLNode but not on the Node interface...
  System.out.println(curNode.valueOf("connection/username"));
}
```

Since the **selectNodes** and **print** methods will do all the hard work, it's easy to write an XPath-enabled **ecgrep** utility to search the contents of an XML file for nodes matching an XPath expression passed on the command line and print out the matches. If you have not used Unix, where **grep** is a mainstay utility for searching through the contents of text files using regular expressions, you may instead be familiar with the Windows **findstr** utility, which does the same thing. To write our XPath-enabled **grep** utility requires three steps:

1. Use `selectNodes()` to get a `NodeList` of matches.
2. Loop over the nodes in the list.
3. Call `print()` on each node to serialize it as XML markup.

Example 6-23 shows the simple source code for such an **XPathGrep** utility.

Example 6-23. XPathGrep Searches XML Files with XPath Expressions

```
import java.net.URL;
import oracle.xml.parser.v2.*;
import org.w3c.dom.*;
import org.xml.sax.*;
import java.io.*;

public class XPathGrep {
  public static void main(String[] args) throws Exception {
```

Example 6-23. XPathGrep Searches XML Files with XPath Expressions (continued)

```
    if (args.length == 2) {
      XPathGrep xpg = new XPathGrep();
      xpg.run(args[0],args[1]);
    }
    else {
      System.err.println("usage: XPathGrep filename.xml XPathExpr");
      System.exit(1);
    }
  }
  void run(String filename, String XPath) throws Exception {
    URL xmlurl = URLUtils.newURL(filename);
    DOMParser d = new DOMParser();
    try {
      d.parse(xmlurl);
    }
    catch(SAXParseException spe) {
      System.out.println("XPathGrep: File "+ filename+" is not well-formed.");
      System.exit(1);
    }
    catch(FileNotFoundException f) {
      System.out.println("XPathGrep: File "+filename+" not found.");
      System.exit(1);
    }
    // Cast getDocument() to an XMLDocument to have selectNodes() Method
    XMLDocument xmldoc = (XMLDocument)d.getDocument();
    if (XPath.equals("/")) {
      // If the path is the root, print the entire document
      xmldoc.print(System.out);
    }
    else {
      NodeList nl = null;
      // Otherwise handle the matching nodes
      try {
        // Select nodes matching XPath
        nl = xmldoc.selectNodes(XPath);
      }
      catch (XSLException err) {
        System.out.println("XPathGrep: "+err.getMessage());
        System.exit(1);
      }
      int found = nl.getLength();
      if (found > 0) {
        // Loop over matches
        for (int z=0; z < found; z++) {
          XMLNode curNode = (XMLNode)nl.item(z);
          // Print the current node as XML Markup to the output
          curNode.print(System.out);
          // Print a new line after Text or Attribute nodes
          int curNodeType = curNode.getNodeType();
          if (curNodeType == Node.ATTRIBUTE_NODE ||
              curNodeType == Node.TEXT_NODE ||
              curNodeType == Node.CDATA_SECTION_NODE) {
```

Example 6-23. XPathGrep Searches XML Files with XPath Expressions (continued)

```
          System.out.print("\n");
        }
      }
    }
    else { System.out.println("XPathGrep: No matches for "+ XPath); }
  }
}
}
```

A lot of the code in **XPathGrep** is needed only to process the command-line arguments! The real XPath work is a piece of cake. We can quickly try it out on our *dream.xml* file to **grep** for all **<LINE>**s in the play containing the word **wood** in a **<SPEECH>** spoken by the **<SPEAKER>** named **HELENA**:

```
java XPathGrep dream.xml //SPEECH[SPEAKER='HELENA']/LINE[contains(.,'wood')]
```

This produces the output:

```
<LINE>Then to the wood will he to-morrow night</LINE>
<LINE>Nor doth this wood lack worlds of company,</LINE>
<LINE>We should be wood and were not made to woo.</LINE>
<LINE>I told him of your stealth unto this wood.</LINE>
```

If we turn our new utility loose on our *YahooQuotesinXML.xml* file to find all attributes in the file:

```
java XPathGrep YahooQuotesinXML.xml //@*
```

XPathGrep will produce:

```
time="Sun Apr 16 2:42am ET - U.S. Markets Closed."
Ticker="ORCL"
Price="86.188"
Ticker="GE"
Price="50.500"
Ticker="MSFT"
Price="74.688"
Ticker="IBM"
Price="118.188"
Ticker="T"
Price="34.125"
Ticker="LU"
Price="59.812"
Ticker="CSCO"
Price="67.938"
```

Besides being simple to implement, you'll find **XPathGrep** a handy sidekick in your daily work with XML.

Using XPath for Reading Configuration Files

With the latest releases of the specifications for Java servlets and Enterprise Java Beans, Sun has moved to an all-XML format for its configuration information. Here we show how simple it is to do the same for our own programs using XPath.

Let's say we have the following *Connections.xml* file, which stores named database connections and the appropriate connection information for each:

```
<!-- Connections.xml -->
<connections>
  <connection name="default">
    <username>xmlbook</username>
    <password>xmlbook</password>
    <dburl>jdbc:oracle:thin:@localhost:1521:ORCL</dburl>
  </connection>
  <connection name="demo">
    <username>scott</username>
    <password>tiger</password>
    <dburl>jdbc:oracle:thin:@xml.us.oracle.com:1521:xml</dburl>
  </connection>
  <connection name="test">
    <username>test</username>
    <password>test</password>
    <dburl>jdbc:oracle:thin:@linuxbox:1721:ORCL</dburl>
  </connection>
</connections>
```

We can create a `ConnectionFactory` class that reads the *Connections.xml* file as a resource from the CLASSPATH, and returns a JDBC connection for the connection name passed in. Example 6-24 shows the implementation, which leverages the following methods:

`selectSingleNode()`
: To find the named connection in the XML-based configuration file

`valueOf()`
: On the `<connection>` element we find, to quickly grab the values of the interesting child elements containing the JDBC connection information

Example 6-24. Using an XML File for Configuration Information

```
import java.sql.*;
import oracle.jdbc.driver.*;
import oracle.xml.parser.v2.*;
import java.io.*;

public class ConnectionFactory {
  private static XMLDocument root;
  public static Connection getConnection(String name) throws Exception {
    if (root == null) {
      // Read Connections.xml from the runtime CLASSPATH
      Class c = ConnectionFactory.class;
```

Example 6-24. Using an XML File for Configuration Information (continued)

```
      InputStream file = c.getResourceAsStream("Connections.xml");
      if (file == null) {
        throw new FileNotFoundException("Connections.xml not in CLASSPATH");
      }
      // Parse Connections.xml and cache the XMLDocument of config info
      root = XMLHelper.parse(file,null);
    }
    // Prepare an XPath expression to find the connection named 'name'
    String pattern = "/connections/connection[@name='"+name+"']";
    // Find the first connection matching the expression above
    XMLNode connNode      = (XMLNode) root.selectSingleNode(pattern);
    if (connNode != null) {
      String username     = connNode.valueOf("username");
      String password     = connNode.valueOf("password");
      String dburl        = connNode.valueOf("dburl");
      String driverClass  = "oracle.jdbc.driver.OracleDriver";
      Driver d = (Driver)Class.forName(driverClass).newInstance();
      System.out.println("Connecting as " + username + " at " + dburl);
      return  DriverManager.getConnection(dburl,username,password);
    }
    else return null;
  }
}
```

Then, in any program where you want to make use of this named database connection facility, just include the lines:

```
import java.sql.Connection;
import ConnectionFactory;
    :
Connection myConn = ConnectionFactory.getConnection("default");
```

With this, you'll be on your way. It's easy to edit the *Connections.xml* file at any time to make changes or add new named connections, and the code in `ConnectionFactory` doesn't need to change to accommodate it.

Using XPath Expressions as Validation Rules

In Chapter 5, we learned how the XPath expression language can be used to create a set of flexible validation rules for XML documents. By simply attempting to select the current node with any XPath expression applied to it as a predicate:

```
myNode.selectSingleNode("./self::node()[AnyXPathExpr]")
```

we can determine whether the predicate is true or false. If we successfully select the current node, then the predicate is true. If not, the predicate is false.

In Chapter 5, we built a system to load a XPath `<ruleset>` document like the following into the database.

```
<ruleset name="AbstractSubmission">
  <rule name="Submission must have an abstract">
    /Submission/Abstract
  </rule>
  <rule name="Author must supply First name, Last name, and Email">
     /Submission/Author[Name/First and Name/Last and Email]
  </rule>
  <rule name="Title must be longer than 12 characters">
    string-length(/Submission/Title) > 12
  </rule>
  <rule name="You must have previous presentation experience.">
    //Author/PreviousExperience = "Yes"
  </rule>
</ruleset>
```

However, we hinted there that it would be very useful to supply a command-line utility that allowed developers creating **ruleset** files to test their sets of rules against example XML documents *outside* the production database environment. Let's build that utility here.

The basic algorithm for validating a source XML document against a **ruleset** of XPath-based validation rules is as follows. For each **<rule>** in the **<ruleset>**:

1. Evaluate the current rule's XPath expression as a predicate applied to the root node of the XML document.
2. If the current rule's XPath expression tests false, then print out the current rule's name to indicate that the rule failed.

The code in Example 6-25 is all we need to accomplish the job.

Example 6-25. Command-line Tool Validates XML Against XPath Rulesets

```
import java.net.URL;
import oracle.xml.parser.v2.*;
import org.w3c.dom.*;

public class XPathValidator {
  public static void main(String[] args) throws Exception {
    if (args.length == 2) {
      XPathValidator xpv = new XPathValidator();
      xpv.validate(args[0],args[1]);
    }
    else errorExit("usage: XPathValidator xmlfile rulesfile");
  }
  // Validate an XML document against a set of XPath validation rules
  public void validate(String filename, String rulesfile) throws Exception {
    // Parse the file to be validated and the rules file
    XMLDocument source = XMLHelper.parse(URLUtils.newURL(filename));
    XMLDocument rules  = XMLHelper.parse(URLUtils.newURL(rulesfile));
    // Get the name of the Ruleset file with valueOf
    String ruleset = rules.valueOf("/ruleset/@name");
    if (ruleset.equals("")) errorExit("Not a valid ruleset file.");
    System.out.println("Validating "+filename+" against " +ruleset+" rules...");
```

Example 6-25. Command-line Tool Validates XML Against XPath Rulesets (continued)

```
    // Select all the <rule>s in the ruleset to evaluate
    NodeList ruleList = rules.selectNodes("/ruleset/rule");
    int rulesFound    = ruleList.getLength();
    if (rulesFound < 1) errorExit("No rules found in "+rulesfile);
    else {
      int errorCount = 0;
      for (int z = 0; z < rulesFound; z++) {
        XMLNode curRule = (XMLNode)ruleList.item(z);
        String  curXPath = curRule.valueOf(".").trim();
        // If XPath Predicate test fails, print out rule name as an err message
        if ( !test(source,curXPath) ) {
          String curRuleName = curRule.valueOf("@name");
          System.out.println("("+(++errorCount)+") "+curRuleName);
        }
      }
      if (errorCount == 0) System.out.println("No validation errors.");
    }
  }
  // Test whether an XPath predicate is true with respect to a current node
  public boolean test(XMLNode n, String xpath) {
    NodeList matches = null;
    try { return n.selectSingleNode("./self::node()["+xpath+"]") != null; }
    catch (XSLException xex) { /* Ignore */ }
    return false;
  }
  private static void errorExit(String m){System.err.println(m);System.exit(1);}
}
```

So we can validate an XML document like our conference abstract submission:

```
<!-- Abstract_With_Error.xml -->
<Submission>
  <Title>Using XPath</Title>
  <Author>
    <Name>
      <First>Steve</First>
    </Name>
    <Email>smuench@yahoo.com</Email>
    <Company>Oracle</Company>
    <PreviousExperience>No</PreviousExperience>
  </Author>
</Submission>
```

using the command-line utility:

```
java XPathValidator Abstract_With_Error.xml AbstractSubmissionRules.xml
```

and immediately see the validation errors:

```
Validating Abstract_With_Error.xml against AbstractSubmission rules...
(1) Submission must have an abstract
(2) Author must supply First name, Last name, and Email
(3) Title must be longer than 12 characters
(4) You must have previous presentation experience.
```

even before loading the <ruleset> into the database. This tool is sure to come in handy for more general kinds of XML document sanity checking as well. Just build a ruleset file describing the XPath assertions you'd like to validate, and use this generic command-line tool to report any errors.

Working with XML Messages

In this section, we'll learn the basic Java techniques required to exchange XML data:

- Over the Web in real time, by posting an XML message over HTTP to another server and immediately receiving an XML-based response
- Asynchronously between processes, by enqueuing XML messages into and dequeuing them out of Oracle AQ queues

These two important tasks are fundamental to the implementation of web services, the business-to-business interchange of information using XML message formats and the HTTP protocol.

Sending and Receiving XML Between Servers

As we saw in Chapter 1, *Introduction to XML*, the general approach for moving information of any kind around the Web involves the exchange via requests and responses of text or binary resources over the HTTP protocol. A requester requests information by using its Uniform Resource Locator (URL) and a server handling requests for that URL responds appropriately, delivering the requested information or returning an error. HTTP's request/response paradigm supports including a resource with the request as well as receiving a resource back in the response, so it's a two-way street for information exchange.

Any resources being exchanged between requester and server are earmarked by a distinguishing MIME type so the receiver can understand what kind of information it is getting. The registered MIME type for XML-based information resources is `text/xml`. Putting it all together, the phrase "posting XML to another server" means precisely this: sending an HTTP POST request to that server containing an XML document in the request body with a MIME `Content-Type` of `text/xml`.

Posting an XML datagram in the request is useful when you need to submit richly structured information to the server for it to provide its service correctly. At other times, simple parameters in the request are enough to get the answer you need. Here are two examples that make the difference clear.

Each year, more and more Americans are filing their income taxes electronically over the Web. An income tax return comprises a number of forms and schedules, each full of structured data that the Internal Revenue Service wants to collect from you. Imagine a simplified tax return in XML as shown in Example 6-26.

Example 6-26. Simplified XML Tax Form

```
<Form id="1040" xmlns="http://www.irs.gov">
  <Filer EFileECN="99454">
    <Name>Steven Muench</Name>
    <TaxpayerId>123-45-6789</TaxpayerId>
    <Occupation>XML Evangelist</Occupation>
  </Filer>
  <!-- etc. -->
  <Form id="8283">
    <Donation Amount="300" Property="yes">
      <ItemDonated>Working Refrigerator</ItemDonated>
      <Donee>Salvation Army</Donee>
    </Donation>
  </Form>
  <Schedule id="B">
    <Dividend Amount="-58.74">
      <Payer>Bank of America</Payer>
    </Dividend>
    <Dividend Amount="1234.56">
      <Payer>E*Trade Securities</Payer>
    </Dividend>
  </Schedule>
</Form>
```

Before filing your return electronically, you might first want to take advantage of a tax advice web service: you submit your tax return—over secure HTTP (`https:`) of course—and the service instantly returns information about errors in your return and suggestions on how to reduce your tax liability. To submit your tax return to the tax advice service, you need to post a structured XML datagram to the URL of the tax advice service:

```
https://www.goodtaxadvice.com/AdviceService
```

so the service can do its job analyzing all the information in your return. In response to posting the XML tax form above, the tax advice service might reply in kind with an XML datagram back to you that looks like this:

```
<TaxAdvice for="Steven Muench">
  <Reminder Form="8283">
    Make sure you include a documented receipt for
    your "Working Refrigerator" charitable property donation!
  </Reminder>
  <Error Schedule="B" Line="1">
    Negative dividends are not permitted. Check dividend amount of -58.74!
  </Error>
</TaxAdvice>
```

Once you've successfully filed your return electronically with the IRS, you may be interested in getting an updated filing status for your return. In this case, sending your entire tax return as an XML datagram is not required. You need only provide your Social Security number as a parameter on the URL request, like this:

```
https://www.irs.gov/EFile/FilingStatus?ssn=123-45-6789
```

and the service might respond with an XML datagram like this:

```
<Form DCN="12-34567-123-33" id="1040" xmlns="http://www.irs.gov">
  <Filer EFileECN="99454">
    <Name>Steven Muench</Name>
    <TaxpayerId>123-45-6789</TaxpayerId>
    <Occupation>XML Evangelist</Occupation>
  </Filer>
  <StatusHistory>
    <Status time="17 Apr 2000 23:59:59">
      Your tax return was received successfully.
    </Status>
    <Status time="18 Apr 2000 08:11:20">
      Your tax return was accepted. Your DCN is 12-34567-123-33
    </Status>
  </StatusHistory>
</Form>
```

indicating that your return has been assigned a Document Control Number. The "send-my-whole-tax-return-in-XML" scenario is an example of doing an HTTP POST request—when a structured XML datagram must accompany the request. The "check-the-status-of-my-return" scenario—where only URL parameters are needed—is an example of an HTTP GET request. In both cases, you get a structured XML response back from the server.

To simplify these XML POSTs and XML GETs over the Web, let's implement an `XMLHttp` helper class to handle the details. The class needs methods like these:

```
// POST an XML document to a Service's URL, returning XML document response
XMLDocument doPost(XMLDocument xmlToPost, URL target)
// GET an XML document response from a Service's URL request
XMLDocument doGet(URL target)
```

The `doPost` method needs to:

1. Open an `HttpUrlConnection` to the target URL
2. Indicate a request method of `POST`
3. Set the MIME type of the request body to `text/xml`
4. Indicate that we want to both write and read from the connection
5. Write the content of the XML datagram to be posted into the connection
6. Get an `InputStream` from the connection to read the server's response
7. Use `XMLHelper.parse` to parse and return the response as an `XMLDocument`

The `doGet` method is extremely simple. It only needs to use `XMLHelper.parse(url)` to parse and return the response from the URL request as an `XMLDocument`.

Example 6-27 provides a straightforward implementation of these two useful facilities.

Example 6-27. XMLHttp Class Simplifies Posting and Getting XML

```
import java.net.*;
import oracle.xml.parser.v2.*;
import java.io.*;
import org.xml.sax.*;
import java.util.Properties;

public class XMLHttp {
  // POST an XML document to a Service's URL, returning XML document response
  public static XMLDocument doPost(XMLDocument xmlToPost, URL target)
  throws IOException, ProtocolException {
    // (1) Open an HTTP connection to the target URL
    HttpURLConnection conn = (HttpURLConnection)target.openConnection();
    if (conn == null) return null;
    // (2) Use HTTP POST
    conn.setRequestMethod("POST");
    // (3) Indicate that the content type is XML with appropriate MIME type
    conn.setRequestProperty("Content-type","text/xml");
    // (4) We'll be writing and reading from the connection
    conn.setDoOutput(true);
    conn.setDoInput(true);
    conn.connect();
    // (5) Print the message XML document into the connection's output stream
    xmlToPost.print(new PrintWriter(conn.getOutputStream()));
    // (6) Get an InputStream to read the response from the server.
    InputStream responseStream = conn.getInputStream();
    try {
      // (7) Parse and return the XML document in the server's response
      //     Use the 'target' URL as the base URL for the parsing
      return XMLHelper.parse(responseStream,target);
    }
    catch (Exception e) { return null; }
  }
  // GET an XML document response from a Service's URL request
  public static XMLDocument doGet(URL target) throws IOException {
    try { return XMLHelper.parse(target); }
    catch (SAXException spx) { return null; }
  }
  // Set HTTP proxy server for current Java VM session
  public static void setProxy(String serverName, String port) {
    System.setProperty("proxySet","true");
    System.setProperty("proxyHost",serverName);
    System.setProperty("proxyPort",port);
  }
}
```

We can test out `XMLHttp` to post a new `<moreovernews>` XML newsgram to a web service that accepts news stories from roving web correspondents with a little program like `TestXmlHttp` in Example 6-28.

Example 6-28. Utility to Test Posting XML Newsgrams to a Web Server

```
import XMLHttp;
import oracle.xml.parser.v2.XMLDocument;
import java.net.URL;

public class TestXmlHttp {
  // Test posting a new News Story to our Web Site that accepts stories in XML
  public static void main(String args[]) throws Exception {
    // Make sure we can see through the firewall
    XMLHttp.setProxy("yourproxyserver.you.com","80");
    // Here's the XML 'datagram' to post a new news story in a String
    String xmlDoc =
    "<moreovernews>"+
    " <article>"+
    "  <url> http://technet.oracle.com/tech/xml </url>"+
    "  <headline_text> Posting from Java </headline_text>"+
    "  <source> you </source>"+
    " </article>"+
    "</moreovernews>";
    // Parse XML message in a string, no external references so null BaseURL OK
    XMLDocument docToPost = XMLHelper.parse(xmlDoc,null);
    // Here's the URL of the service that accepts posted XML news stories
    String url = "http://ws5.olab.com/xsql/demo/insertxml/insertnewsstory.xsql";
    // Construct the target service URL from the string above
    URL target = new URL(url);
    // Post the XML message.
    XMLDocument response = XMLHttp.doPost(docToPost,target);
    // Print the response.
    response.print(System.out);
  }
}
```

This parses the newsgram from a String, posts it to the appropriate service URL, and prints out the XML response from the server indicating that one story was received and accepted:

```
<?xml version = '1.0'?>
<xsql-status action="xsql:insert-request" rows="1"/>
```

Let's generalize Example 6-28 by building a useful utility called `PostXML` that allows us to post any XML file to any web service from the command line. Example 6-29 shows the `PostXML` utility that processes command-line arguments, then calls `XMLHelper.parse` and `XMLHttp.doPost`.

Example 6-29. PostXML Posts XML to Any URL from the Command Line

```
import oracle.xml.parser.v2.*;
import java.net.*;
import org.xml.sax.*;
import XMLHttp;

public class PostXML {
  public static void main(String[] args) throws Exception {
```

Example 6-29. PostXML Posts XML to Any URL from the Command Line (continued)

```
    String filename = null,targetURL = null, proxy = null;
    for (int z=0;z < args.length; z++) {
      if (args[z].equals("-x")) {
        if (args.length > z + 1) proxy = args[++z];
        else errorExit("No proxy specified after -x option");
      }
      else if (filename  == null) filename  = args[z];
      else if (targetURL == null) targetURL = args[z];
    }
    if (filename != null && targetURL != null) {
      // If user supplied a proxy, set it
      if (proxy != null) XMLHttp.setProxy(proxy,"80");
      // Post the xml!
      PostXML px = new PostXML();
      px.post(filename,targetURL);
    }
    else errorExit("usage: PostXML [-x proxy] xmlfile targetURL");
  }
  // Post XML document in 'filename' to 'targetURL'
  public void post(String filename, String targetURL) {
    try {
      // Parse the file to be posted to make sure it's well-formed
      XMLDocument message = XMLHelper.parse(URLUtils.newURL(filename));
      // Construct the URL to make sure it's a valid URL
      URL target = new URL(targetURL);
      // Post the XML document to the target URL using XMLHttp.doPost
      XMLDocument response = XMLHttp.doPost(message,target);
      if (response == null) errorExit("Null response from service.");
      // If successful, print out the XMLDocument response to standard out
      else response.print(System.out);
    }
    // If the XML to post is ill-formed use XMLHelper to print err
    catch (SAXParseException spx) {errorExit(XMLHelper.formatParseError(spx));}
    // Otherwise, print out appropriate error messages
    catch (SAXException sx) { errorExit("Error parsing "+filename); }
    catch (MalformedURLException m){ errorExit("Error: "+targetURL+" invalid");}
    catch (Exception ex) { errorExit("Error: "+ex.getMessage()); }
  }
  private static void errorExit(String m){System.err.println(m);System.exit(1);}
}
```

We can now accomplish what the previous sample code did in a generic way from the command line by using `PostXML` to post the XML newsgram from a file:

```
java PostXML -x yourproxyserver.you.com NewsStory.xml http://server/service
```

But we can use the `PostXML` utility for lots of other purposes. It will come in handy to test out any server-side code written to handle incoming, posted XML documents. In fact, let's look next at exactly what the server-side Java code looks like on the *receiving* end of a posted XML datagram. Since these messages are posted over HTTP, and since Java servlets are designed to enable you to easily write server-side programs that handle HTTP requests, it's natural to study a servlet example.

While the service it provides is arguably of little value, the **XMLUpperCaseStringServlet** in Example 6-30 serves as a complete example for:

1. Receiving an XML datagram in the HTTP POST request and parsing it
2. Processing the data by using XPath expressions and selectNodes
3. Changing the document in some interesting way
4. Writing back an XML document as a response

The service we're providing in Example 6-30 is to accept any posted XML document, search it for `<String>` elements, uppercase the value of each of these `<String>` elements, and write the modified document back as the response XML datagram.

In Chapters 8, 9, and 11, we'll see how to make these services *much* more interesting by interacting with your database information.

Example 6-30. Receiving, Parsing, Searching, and Manipulating Posted XML

```
import javax.servlet.http.*;
import oracle.xml.parser.v2.*;
import org.w3c.dom.*;
import org.xml.sax.SAXException;
import java.net.URL;
import javax.servlet.ServletException;
import java.io.*;

public class XMLUpperCaseStringServlet extends HttpServlet {
  // Handle the HTTP POST request
  protected void doPost(HttpServletRequest req, HttpServletResponse resp)
  throws ServletException, IOException {
    XMLDocument incomingXMLDoc = null;
    // Tell the requester she's getting XML in response
    resp.setContentType("text/xml");
    // Get the character writer to write the response into
    PrintWriter out = resp.getWriter();
    try {
      // If we're receiving posted XML
      if (req.getContentType().equals("text/xml")) {
        // Get the InputStream on the HTTP POST request's request body
        InputStream incomingXMLStream = req.getInputStream();
        // Parse it with our helper
        incomingXMLDoc = XMLHelper.parse(incomingXMLStream,null);
        // Find any <String> elements in the posted doc using selectNodes
        NodeList stringElts = incomingXMLDoc.selectNodes("//String");
        // Loop over any matching nodes and uppercase the string content
        int matches = stringElts.getLength();
        for (int z=0; z<matches; z++) {
          Text t = (Text)stringElts.item(z).getFirstChild();
```

Example 6-30. Receiving, Parsing, Searching, and Manipulating Posted XML (continued)

```
        // Uppercase the node value of the first text-node Child
        t.setNodeValue(t.getNodeValue().toUpperCase());
      }
      // Write posted XML doc (with <String>'s now uppercased) to response
      incomingXMLDoc.print(out);
    }
    else out.println("<error>You did not post an XML document</error>");
  }
  catch (SAXException s) {
    out.println("<error>You posted an ill-formed XML document</error>");
  }
  catch (XSLException x) {
    out.println("<error>Error processing selectNodes</error>");
  }
 }
}
```

You'll notice that the only new trick is the use of the **getContentType** method on the **HttpServletRequest** to sense if we're receiving posted XML, and the **getInputStream** method to retrieve the contents of the posted document. If we use **PostXML** to test out our new servlet on the following *Sample.xml* file:

```
<!-- Sample.xml -->
<Something>
   <Containing>
     <String>this is a string</String>
     <String>this is too</String>
   </Containing>
   <String>And a third...</String>
</Something>
```

with the command line:

```
java PostXML Sample.xml http://localhost/servlets/XMLUpperCaseStringServlet
```

We get back the XML response that includes the results of the service:

```
<!-- Sample.xml -->
<Something>
   <Containing>
     <String>THIS IS A STRING</String>
     <String>THIS IS TOO</String>
   </Containing>
   <String>AND A THIRD...</String>
</Something>
```

So we now we've seen how to both pitch and catch XML information over the Web.

Acquiring XML Data from Another Server

Next let's walk through an example of retrieving XML information from another web site from inside Oracle8*i*. Just to mix things up a little, we'll show how Java and PL/SQL can be used together to accomplish the job. We will do the following:

1. Build a class called `CaptureQuotes` that will:
   - Use our `JTidyConverter` and *YahooQuotes-to-QuoteStream.xsl* transformation to retrieve live XML `<QuoteStream>` data from Yahoo! Quotes over the Web
   - Insert the Ticker and Price information returned with each `<Quote>` into the database by invoking a stored procedure to do the handling
2. Create the latest_quotes table and an `insert_quote` stored procedure in PL/SQL that will make sure only a single latest quote per day per ticker symbol stays in our table
3. Test our `CaptureQuotes` outside the database, then deploy it as a Java stored procedure so it can be executed periodically by a `DBMS_JOB` database job
4. Deal with a few new JServer permissions that we'll need to make the whole thing work

So let's get started, taking the simple steps first. We can create the table to store our latest quotes with the following command:

```
CREATE TABLE latest_quotes (
  ticker VARCHAR2(7),
  price  NUMBER,
  day    DATE
);
```

And creating the PL/SQL stored procedure to handle inserting a quote is easy, too:

```
CREATE OR REPLACE PROCEDURE insert_quote(sym VARCHAR2,cost NUMBER,eff DATE) IS
BEGIN
  -- Remove any previous "latest" quote from today for this symbol.
  -- Make sure an Oracle8i Functional index on (TRUNC(day),ticker) exists!
  DELETE FROM latest_quotes
   WHERE ticker = sym
     AND TRUNC(day) = TRUNC(eff);
  INSERT INTO latest_quotes VALUES(sym,cost,eff);
END;
```

Note that `insert_quote` first deletes any existing "latest" quote for the current `ticker` symbol by searching the table for a row with the current `ticker` symbol and a `TRUNC(day)` equal to the `TRUNC(eff)` effective date of the current quote being handled. Since this latest_quotes table may contain millions of rows—as we might accumulate years of historical stock quotes—we need this DELETE statement to be fast. Normally a WHERE clause that uses a function like `TRUNC()` on a column immediately forfeits the use of the index, but Oracle8*i* sports a neat new feature called *functional indexes* that allows us to happily issue the CREATE INDEX statement:

```
CREATE INDEX latest_quotes_idx ON latest_quotes (TRUNC(day),ticker);
```

Your database user needs to be granted the QUERY REWRITE privilege—or be granted a role that has been granted the permission—in order to successfully create a functional index.

So any search on the combination of `ticker` symbol and `TRUNC(day)` will be lightning fast. Next we'll create `CaptureQuotes`. The guts of this class will borrow from our earlier `YahooXMLQuotesServlet`, but with a few interesting twists. First, we'll read the XSLT stylesheet to perform the transformation using the handy `xmldoc` URLs we created earlier. This means that we can store the *YahooQuotes-to-QuoteStream.xsl* stylesheet in our xml_documents table and easily retrieve it for use at any time without leaving the database. Second, rather than simply spitting back the XML `<QuoteStream>` as the servlet did earlier, we'll use the XPath searching facilities to loop over all of the matching quotes and insert each one in the database. Third, we'll use a JDBC `CallableStatement` to execute the `insert_quote` stored procedure after binding the values of the current quote information.

Note that after retrieving the Yahoo! Quotes as an XML `<QuoteStream>` we could simply call `XMLDocuments.save()` to save our `<QuoteStream>` XML document in a CLOB, but this is not our intention here. We want the historical data to be usable by existing report writing tools like Oracle Reports, and existing data warehousing tools like Oracle Discoverer. We want to use powerful SQL queries to sort and group and summarize the data to look for trends and quickly generate charts and graphs. So having the information in regular rows of a regular database table makes a whole lot of sense.

Example 6-31 shows the code for `CaptureQuotes`.

Example 6-31. Java Stored Procedure to Retrieve and Store Web Stock Quotes

```
import javax.servlet.http.*;
import oracle.xml.parser.v2.*;
import org.w3c.dom.*;
import java.net.URL;
import java.sql.*;
import java.io.*;
import JTidyConverter;
import XMLDocuments;
import Examples;
```

Example 6-31. Java Stored Procedure to Retrieve and Store Web Stock Quotes (continued)

```
public class CaptureQuotes {
  private static CaptureQuotes cq = null;
  private Connection          conn = null;
  private JTidyConverter       jtc = null;
  private XSLStylesheet      sheet = null;
  private CallableStatement  stmt = null;
  private static final String YQUOTES = "http://quote.yahoo.com/q?d2=v1&o=d&s=";
  public CaptureQuotes(Connection conn) {
    this.conn = conn;
  }
  // Oracle8i Java stored procedure debugging entry point for testing.
  public static void debug_main() throws Exception {
    storeLatestQuotesFor("ORCL,INTC,MSFT");
  }
  // Static method to expose as Java stored procedure
  public static void storeLatestQuotesFor(String symbolList) throws Exception {
    if (cq == null) {
      cq = new CaptureQuotes(Examples.getConnection());
      cq.initialize();
    }
    cq.retrieve(symbolList);
  }
  // Retrieve Yahoo Quotes and save quote data in a table
  private void retrieve(String symbolList) throws Exception {
    if (symbolList != null && !symbolList.equals("")) {
      URL yahooUrl  = new URL(YQUOTES+symbolList.replace(',','+'));
      // Convert the dynamically produced Yahoo! Quotes page to XML doc
      XMLDocument yahooquotes = jtc.XMLifyHTMLFrom(yahooUrl);
      // Transform the document using our stylesheet into <QuoteStream>
      // getting the transformed result in a DocumentFragment
      XSLProcessor xslt        = new XSLProcessor();
      DocumentFragment result = xslt.processXSL(sheet,yahooquotes);
      // Get the document element of the transformed document
      XMLElement e = (XMLElement)result.getFirstChild();
      // Search for all <Quotes> in the resulting <QuoteStream>
      NodeList quotes = e.selectNodes(".//Quote");
      int matches = quotes.getLength();
      // Loop over any quotes retrieved; insert each by calling stored proc
      for (int z = 0; z < matches; z++) {
        XMLNode curQuote = (XMLNode)quotes.item(z);
        // Bind the 1st stored procedure argument to valueOf Ticker attribute
        stmt.setString(1,curQuote.valueOf("@Ticker"));
        // Bind the 2ND stored procedure argument to valueOf Price attribute
        stmt.setString(2,curQuote.valueOf("@Price"));
        // Execute the stored procedure to process this quote
        stmt.executeUpdate();
      }
      conn.commit();
    }
  }
  // Setup proxy server, Cache XSL Transformation, and Callable Statement
  private void initialize() throws Exception {
```

Example 6-31. Java Stored Procedure to Retrieve and Store Web Stock Quotes (continued)

```
    if (jtc == null) {
      // Make sure the Servlet can "see" through the corporate firewall...
      System.setProperty("proxySet","true");
      System.setProperty("proxyHost","yourproxyserver.you.com");
      System.setProperty("proxyPort","80");
      // Construct a JTidyConverter. We can use the same one over and over.
      jtc   = new JTidyConverter();
      XMLDocuments.enableXMLDocURLs();
      // Read the Yahoo2Xml.xsl stylesheet from an xmldoc:// URL in the DB
      URL u = new URL("xmldoc:/transforms/YahooQuotes-to-QuoteStream.xsl");
      InputStream styleSource = u.openStream();
      // Cache a new stylesheet. Not threadsafe in 2.0.2.7 but OK for demo.
      sheet = new XSLStylesheet(styleSource,null); // No base URL needed here!
      // Cache a reusable CallableStatement for invoking the PL/SQL Stored Proc
      stmt = conn.prepareCall("BEGIN insert_quote(?,?,SYSDATE); END;");
    }
  }
}
```

Note that the `initialize()` routine:

- Sets Java System properties to allow the program to talk to URLs outside the firewall
- Constructs a `JTidyConverter` to use for the life of the session
- Reads the stylesheet from *xmldoc:/transforms/YahooQuotes-to-QuoteStream.xsl* and constructs a new `XSLStylesheet` object to use for the life of the session
- Creates a reusable `CallableStatement` object to execute over and over again with different bind variable values to invoke the stored procedure

Also note that we've added a `debug_main()` method so we can use JDeveloper's JServer debugging feature to find any problems that crop up. To test `CaptureQuotes` outside the database, we can put the following lines of code in a little tester class:

```
CaptureQuotes.storeLatestQuotesFor("ORCL,INTC");
CaptureQuotes.storeLatestQuotesFor("WBVN,MSFT,IBM,WEBM");
```

This will test to make sure we can make multiple calls to the `CaptureQuotes` class in the same session with no problem. After doing this, if we execute the SQL statement:

```
SELECT ticker, price, TO_CHAR(day,'MM/DD/YY HH24:MI') day
  FROM latest_quotes
 WHERE TRUNC(day) = TRUNC(SYSDATE)
ORDER BY 3,1
```

we'll see the latest quote data retrieved from over the Web sitting comfortably in our local database table:

```
TICKER          PRICE DAY
------- ---------- --------------
IBM        111.875 04/17/00 17:47
INTC           123 04/17/00 17:47
MSFT        75.875 04/17/00 17:47
ORCL        74.812 04/17/00 17:47
WBVN         4.531 04/17/00 17:47
WEBM         61.75 04/17/00 17:47
```

Finally, we'll deploy **CaptureQuotes** as a Java stored procedure into JServer. We went through the basic steps earlier in the chapter, so we'll just highlight what's unique this time.

We use JDeveloper to create a new Java stored procedure deployment profile and select the **debug_main** and **storeLatestQuotesFor** static methods of the **CaptureQuotes** class to be published. We choose a name like **YAHOOQUOTES** (it can be different from the class name) for the package in which JDeveloper will publish our two selected methods as package procedures.

Before deploying your Java stored procedure, you need to load the *.jar* file for the JTidy bean into the database. This is done with the one-line command:

```
loadjava -verbose -resolve -user xmlbook/xmlbook tidy.jar
```

Then you can select your Java stored procedure profile to deploy it and everything should go smoothly. JDeveloper's deployment wizard will automatically create the necessary Java stored procedure specification:

```
CREATE OR REPLACE PACKAGE YAHOOQUOTES AUTHID CURRENT_USER AS
PROCEDURE STORELATESTQUOTESFOR ("symbolList" IN VARCHAR2)
AS LANGUAGE JAVA
NAME 'CaptureQuotes.storeLatestQuotesFor(java.lang.String)';
END YAHOOQUOTES;
```

And after loading the XSLT stylesheet into our xml_documents table (arguments all go on one line):

```
java XMLDoc save YahooQuotes-to-QuoteStream.xsl
                 /transforms/YahooQuotes-to-QuoteStream.xsl
```

we're good to go!

You can connect to the database in SQL*Plus and give the new Java stored procedure a whirl by typing something like this to get the latest quotes for Apple Computer, Oracle, and Healtheon:

```
EXEC yahooquotes.storeLatestQuotesFor('AAPL,ORCL,HLTH')
```

At this point, it will either work correctly, or fail with a JServer security violation. The XMLBOOK user needs the appropriate **java.util.PropertyPermission** to be able to set the System variables to affect the proxy server name, as well as the familiar `java.net.SocketPermission` from an earlier example for the `*.yahoo.com` domain. The script in Example 6-32—run as SYS—grants XMLBOOK the appropriate privileges.

Example 6-32. Granting Privileges to Connect to an External Web Site

```
BEGIN
    -- Grant Permission to set the proxy* System properties
    dbms_java.grant_permission(
             grantee => 'XMLBOOK',
     permission_type => 'SYS:java.util.PropertyPermission',
     permission_name => 'proxySet',
   permission_action => 'write');
    dbms_java.grant_permission(
             grantee => 'XMLBOOK',
     permission_type => 'SYS:java.util.PropertyPermission',
     permission_name => 'proxyHost',
   permission_action => 'write');
    dbms_java.grant_permission(
             grantee => 'XMLBOOK',
     permission_type => 'SYS:java.util.PropertyPermission',
     permission_name => 'proxyPort',
   permission_action => 'write');
    -- Grant Permission to resolve and connect to URL at *.yahoo.com
    dbms_java.grant_permission(
             grantee => 'XMLBOOK',
     permission_type => 'SYS:java.net.SocketPermission',
     permission_name => '*.yahoo.com',
   permission_action => 'connect,resolve');

  COMMIT;
END;
```

Retry the stored procedure and rerun the query from before:

```
TICKER       PRICE DAY
------- ---------- --------------
IBM        111.875 04/17/00 17:47
INTC           123 04/17/00 17:47
MSFT        75.875 04/17/00 17:47
WBVN         4.531 04/17/00 17:47
WEBM         61.75 04/17/00 17:47
AAPL       123.875 04/17/00 18:27
HLTH        19.375 04/17/00 18:27
ORCL        74.812 04/17/00 18:27
```

to see that the new quotes for AAPL and HLTH have been added and the latest quote for ORCL for today has been properly revised by the `insert_quote` procedure. We'll leave it as an exercise to investigate setting up a periodic execution of `yahooquotes.storeLatestQuotesFor` in a database *cron* job. The steps are the same as in the "Move bad XML documents to another table in batch" exercise in Chapter 5 that used the `DBMS_JOB.SUBMIT` procedure.

Handling Asynchronous XML Messages in Queues

The examples in the previous few sections dealt with posting and getting XML in real time over the Web. This meant making a request and waiting for the response. Sometimes the requester may be interested in getting the process started, but may not be prepared to sit around waiting for a response. This is typically the case when delivering the ultimate response—like receiving a book in the mail that you ordered online—involves multiple, potentially time-consuming steps. This is a perfect scenario for exploiting Oracle8*i*'s Advanced Queuing (AQ) feature.

In Chapter 5, we created an AQ queue called **xml_msg_queue** and used a PL/SQL helper package called **xmlq** to easily enqueue and dequeue XML-based messages. Here we'll uncover the analogous facilities in Oracle AQ's Java API and get the PL/SQL and Java programs talking XML through the queue. An Oracle AQ can have one of two kinds of message payloads: a "Raw" payload of up to 32K bytes, or a structured Oracle8 object type. We'll study the simplest of the two—the Raw payload—in order to learn the ropes.

The *.jar* file for Oracle's AQ Java API is in *./rdbms/jlib/aqapi.jar* under your Oracle installation home. AQ also offers a Java Messaging Service (JMS)-compliant API. Our examples use the AQ native Java API.

To use an AQ queue, you need to do the following:

1. Be in the context of a JDBC database connection
2. Create a session with the queuing system
3. Ask the session to give you a handle to the queue you want to work with, given the schema and name of the queue

We handle these administrative steps in the **XMLQueue** constructor in Example 6-33. So to work with an queue like XMLBOOK's **xml_msg_queue**, we'll use code like this:

```
XMLQueue q = new XMLQueue(conn, "xmlbook","xml_msg_queue");
```

to get started. Since our **XMLQueue** class encapsulates access to an AQ queue, we need it to model the two key operations we want to do with XML documents over a queue: enqueue an XML message and dequeue an XML message. Appropriately, we'll add **enqueue** and **dequeue** methods to our **XMLQueue** class. The steps involved in *enqueuing* an XML message are as follows:

1. Serialize the in-memory XML document as a byte array of XML markup.
2. Ask the queue to create a new, empty message.

3. Get a handle to the message's RawPayload "bay."
4. Write the byte array into the payload.
5. Enqueue the message.
6. Commit.

The steps required to dequeue a message are as follows:

1. Optionally set a flag to indicate whether we want to wait for a message.
2. Attempt to dequeue the message, raising an error if the queue is empty and we chose not to wait.
3. Get a handle to the message's RawPayload "bay."
4. Create an `InputStream` on the byte array in the message.
5. Parse the `InputStream` of bytes into an `XMLDocument`.
6. Commit, and return the `XMLDocument`.

The full implementation is shown in Example 6-33.

Example 6-33. XMLQueue Class Simplifies Enqueuing and Dequeuing XML

```
import oracle.xml.parser.v2.*;
import java.sql.*;
import oracle.AQ.*;
import java.io.*;
import org.xml.sax.SAXException;
import XMLQueueEmptyException;

public class XMLQueue {
  private Connection conn = null;
  private AQSession  sess = null;
  private AQQueue   queue = null;
  // Constructing an XMLQueue "binds" it to a particular AQ Queue
  public XMLQueue(Connection conn, String schema,String queueName)
                 throws AQException,SQLException {
    this.conn = conn;
    conn.setAutoCommit(false);
    // Create the AQ Driver
    AQOracleDriver driver = new AQOracleDriver();
    // Create a new session to work in
    sess = AQDriverManager.createAQSession(conn);
    // Get a handle to the requested queue
    queue = sess.getQueue (schema,queueName);
  }
  // Enqueue an XMLDocument to the queue
  public void enqueue( XMLDocument xmldoc ) throws AQException,IOException,
                                                  SQLException {
    ByteArrayOutputStream baos = new ByteArrayOutputStream();
    // Print the XML document to serialize it as XML Markup
    xmldoc.print(baos);
    // Get the bytes to enqueue into the "Raw" message
```

Example 6-33. XMLQueue Class Simplifies Enqueuing and Dequeuing XML (continued)

```
    byte[] messageBytes = baos.toByteArray();
    // Ask the queue to create an empty message
    AQMessage message = queue.createMessage();
    // Get the Raw Payload "bay" to write the message into
    AQRawPayload payload = message.getRawPayload();
    // Set the contents of the payload to be the bytes of our XML Message
    payload.setStream(messageBytes,messageBytes.length);
    // Send the new message on its way into the queue
    queue.enqueue(new AQEnqueueOption(),message);
    // Sign, seal, and deliver
    conn.commit();
  }
  // Dequeue and return an XMLDocument from the queue
  public XMLDocument dequeue(boolean wait) throws AQException,
                                                  SQLException,
                                                  XMLQueueEmptyException {
    AQDequeueOption dqOpt = new AQDequeueOption();
    // If user asked NOT to wait, then set this flag in the Dequeue Options
    if (!wait) {
      dqOpt.setWaitTime(AQDequeueOption.WAIT_NONE);
    }
    AQMessage message = null;
    try {
      // Try to dequeue the message
      message = queue.dequeue(dqOpt);
    }
    catch (oracle.AQ.AQOracleSQLException aqx) {
     // If we get an error 25228 then queue was empty and we didn't want to wait
     if (java.lang.Math.abs(aqx.getErrorCode()) == 25228) {
       throw new XMLQueueEmptyException();
     }
    }
    // Retrieve the Raw Payload "bay" from the message
    AQRawPayload payload = message.getRawPayload();
    // Create an InputStream on the bytes in the message
    ByteArrayInputStream bais = new ByteArrayInputStream(payload.getBytes());
    XMLDocument dequeuedDoc = null;
    try {
      // Parse the XML message
      dequeuedDoc = XMLHelper.parse(bais,null);
    }
    catch (Exception spe) { /* Ignore, doc will be null */ }
    // Finalize the transactional dequeue operation by committing
    conn.commit();
    // Return the XMLDocument
    return dequeuedDoc;
  }
}
```

We can write a quick command-line test program called `AQ` to experiment with enqueuing and dequeuing XML orders. Here we'll exercise the **`XMLQueue`** class to enqueue and dequeue orders that are very simple—albeit perfectly valid—XML documents like:

```
<order id="101"/>
```

but the mechanics are identical for enqueuing and dequeuing any XML message up to 32K bytes with the Raw payload technique. The implementation is shown in Example 6-34.

By using an Oracle AQ queue with an object type payload—instead of the Raw payload we're experimenting with here—and basing it on an object type with a CLOB attribute like:

```
CREATE TYPE xml_message AS OBJECT(xml CLOB [, other-attrs]);
```

you can easily enqueue and dequeue XML messages of essentially any size by storing the XML message in the CLOB attribute of the object type message.

Example 6-34. Utility to Test Enqueuing and Dequeuing Messages

```
import java.sql.*;
import oracle.AQ.*;
import Examples;
import java.io.*;
import oracle.xml.parser.v2.*;
import XMLQueue;
import XMLQueueEmptyException;

public class AQ {
  // Fun little utility to test enqueuing and dequeing XML "Orders"
  public static void main(String[] args) throws Exception {
    Connection conn = Examples.getConnection();
    if (args.length > 0) {
      // Bind to the queue we want to work with
      XMLQueue xmlq = new XMLQueue(conn,"xmlbook","xml_msg_queue");
      // If user wants to enqueue a message
      if (args[0].startsWith("nq")) {
        int msgs = 0;
        for (int argpos=1; argpos < args.length; argpos++) {
          msgs++;
          String id = args[argpos];
          // Create a little <order> XML datagram (very little!)
          String xml ="<order id='"+id+"'></order>";
          // Parse the message into an XMLDocument
          XMLDocument xmldoc = XMLHelper.parse(xml,null);
          // Enqueue the XML message
          xmlq.enqueue(xmldoc);
          System.out.println("Successfully enqueued order# "+id);
        }
        System.out.println("Enqueued "+msgs+" new messages");
      }
```

Example 6-34. Utility to Test Enqueuing and Dequeuing Messages (continued)

```
      // If user wants to dequeue a message
      else if (args[0].startsWith("dq")) {
        // If they passed "dqw" then the "w" is for WAIT
        boolean wait = args[0].endsWith("w");
        XMLDocument dqDoc = null;
        try {
          // Dequeue the XML message
          dqDoc = xmlq.dequeue(wait);
          // Print it out
          dqDoc.print(System.out);
        }
        catch (XMLQueueEmptyException qee) {
          System.out.println("xml_msg_queue is empty.");
        }
      }
      else usage();
    }
    else usage();
  }
  private static void usage() {
    System.out.println("usage: AQ [nq ordid|dq[w]]");
    System.exit(1);
  }
}
```

The syntax for playing with our `AQ` command-line utility is:

`java AQ nq` *`xxx`* `[` *`yyy zzz`* `...]`
: To enqueue orders with order IDs *xxx*, *yyy*, *zzz*, etc.

`java AQ dq`
: To dequeue an order if one is available without waiting.

`java AQ dqw`
: To dequeue an order, waiting for one to arrive if none is presently in the queue.

We see the AQ utility in action in two separate command windows in Figure 6-19. The action unfolds like this:

1. Top window enqueues three orders with IDs `123`, `456`, and `789`.
2. Bottom window dequeues an order and gets `<order id="123"/>`.
3. Bottom window dequeues an order and gets `<order id="456"/>`.
4. Bottom window dequeues an order and gets `<order id="789"/>`.
5. Bottom window dequeues an order and gets "queue is empty" message.
6. Bottom window dequeues—and elects to wait for—an order. Since none is there, his window sleeps until one comes in.

7. Top window enqueues an order with id `1011`.
8. A moment later, bottom window wakes up and dequeues `<order id="1011"/>`.

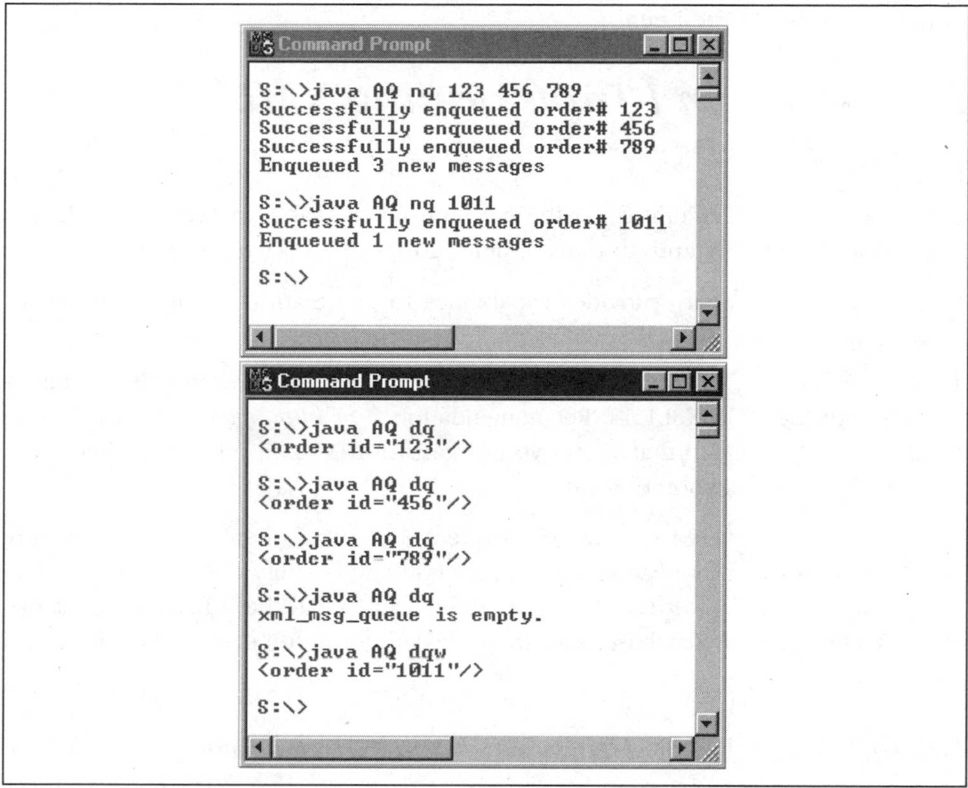

Figure 6-19. Experimenting with enqueuing and dequeuing XML orders

Since queues, like database tables, are technology- and language-agnostic, you can quite easily experiment using the examples from Chapter 5 to enqueue orders and our Java-based AQ command-line utility to dequeue them, or vice versa.

In your applications, you can use `XMLQueue` or similar Java code to post orders in a servlet to a queue and have multiple database-resident agent programs listening on the queues to process them. If the workflow of your orders involves multiple, logical phases, or perhaps involves interacting with partners' systems to accomplish some of the phases, you can use multiple queues to manage this assembly line of work. Since the queues are stored in tables, you can easily use familiar SQL to look at your work loads and study your message traffic.

We are really just scraping the surface of the power of Oracle Advanced Queuing here. We've built up some practical experience with using AQ together with XML messages, but we've taken all the default options and not explored many of AQ's more sophisticated features. But even when you leverage multiple-subscriber, SQL-predicate-based message subscription, and automatic, distributed queue propagation, the basic model of enqueuing and dequeuing XML messages doesn't change from what we've learned here.

Producing and Transforming XML Query Results

In this section, we'll briefly cover the mechanisms available in Java for producing XML from SQL queries and for transforming XML using XSLT transformations:

- The XML SQL Utility provides capabilities to automatically deliver the results of any valid SELECT statement as an XML document.
- The Oracle XSLT processor implements an XML transformation engine compliant with the W3C XSLT 1.0 Recommendation (see *http://www.w3.org/TR/1999/REC-xslt-19991116*) that allows you to transform XML in one format into XML, HTML, or text of another format.

These topics are covered in detail in Chapters 7 and 9, so here we'll focus mostly on the basic mechanics of working with the XML SQL Utility and the Oracle XSLT processor. First, we cover the steps required to verify that these facilities are properly installed in your database, and then we'll present some simple examples of their use.

Installing XML SQL Utility and XSLT Processor

First, check to see if the Oracle XML SQL Utility is already installed in your Oracle8*i* database by doing the following:

1. Connect to your Oracle8*i* database with SQL*Plus:

   ```
   sqlplus xmlbook/xmlbook
   ```

2. Check the status of the `oracle.xml.sql.query.OracleXMLQuery` class by running the following SQL statement:

   ```
   SELECT SUBSTR(dbms_java.longname(object_name),1,35) AS class, status
     FROM all_objects
    WHERE object_type = 'JAVA CLASS'
      AND object_name = dbms_java.shortname('oracle/xml/sql/query/OracleXMLQuery')
   ```

   You should see the result:

   ```
   CLASS                               STATUS
   ----------------------------------- -------
   oracle/xml/sql/query/OracleXMLQuery VALID
   ```

If, instead, you see the SQL*Plus `no rows selected` message, complete the following steps to install the Oracle XML SQL Utility in your Oracle8*i* database:

1. Make sure you've already loaded the Oracle XML Parser for Java into Oracle8*i*. The XML SQL Utility depends on it, but we did this earlier in this chapter, so you should be all set.
2. Download the latest release of the Oracle XML SQL Utility from *http://technet.oracle.com/tech/xml*. Use the following table to decide which version(s) of the utility to download:

If you are using XML SQL utility	Download this version
Inside Oracle8*i* Release 2 (8.1.6) or later	*XSU12.zip*
Inside Oracle8*i* Release 1 (8.1.5)	*XSU111.zip*
Outside the database with Oracle 8.1.5 JDBC Driver in *classes111.zip*	*XSU111.zip*
Outside the database with Oracle 8.1.6 JDBC Driver for JDBC 1.x in *classes111.zip*	*XSU111.zip*
Outside the database with Oracle 8.1.6 JDBC Driver for JDBC 2.0 in *classes12.zip*	*XSU12.zip*
Outside the database with any other JDBC 1.x–based driver	*XSU111.zip*
Outside the database with any other JDBC 2.0–based driver	*XSU12.zip*

3. Extract the *.zip* or the *.tar.gz* file into a convenient directory.
4. Change directory to the *./lib* subdirectory of the distribution.
5. Load the *xsu12.jar* file into your schema (or *xsu111.jar* for 8.1.5):

```
loadjava -verbose -resolve -user xmlbook/xmlbook xsu12.jar
```

Repeat the test above to verify that the `oracle.xml.sql.query.OracleXMLQuery` class is now loaded and `VALID`.

Because the implementation of the Oracle XSLT processor is an integrated part of the Oracle XML Parser for Java, we do not need to install the Oracle XSLT processor separately.

Producing XML from SQL Queries

The XML SQL Utility automates the task of returning an XML document representing the result set of any valid SQL query. It can handle any SQL language feature or datatype that Oracle8*i* supports, so we can immediately put it to the test on one of the most clever, little-known Oracle SQL tricks: the CURSOR expression. Consider the following table:

```
CREATE TABLE course_assignments(
  school_id NUMBER,
  name      VARCHAR2(80),
  age       NUMBER,
  course    VARCHAR2(80)
);
```

This is a "flat" table:

```
 SCHOOL_ID NAME      AGE COURSE
---------- -------- ---- ----------
     12332 matt       23 psych-399
     12332 joe        22 psych-399
     12332 steve      23 math-202
     12332 brenda     19 eecs-101
```

The CURSOR expression allows us to create nested grouping of information from an otherwise flat table, or easily nest master/detail table information instead of flattening it into a join query. For example, based on this flat list of course assignments, we can summon forth a list of distinct courses and students who are assigned to each course using the query:

```
SELECT course, CURSOR(SELECT name,age
                        FROM course_assignments b
                       WHERE b.course = a.course
                     ) AS students
 FROM course_assignments a
GROUP BY course
ORDER BY course
```

Example 6-35 shows a sample program that uses this query together with the XML SQL Utility's `OracleXMLQuery` class to instantly produce nested XML query results for the data in question. We create an instance of `OracleXMLQuery`, set some of its XML-generation options, and then call its `getXMLString()` method to retrieve the "XML-ified" query results.

Example 6-35. Producing Nested XML from a SQL Query with XML SQL Utility

```
import java.sql.*;
import oracle.xml.sql.query.*;

public class CourseAssignments {
  public static void main (String arg[]) throws Exception {
    // Get the database connection to our XMLBOOK user
    Connection cn = Examples.getConnection();
    String query = "SELECT course, CURSOR(SELECT name,age "+
                   "                        FROM course_assignments b"+
                   "                       WHERE b.course = a.course"+
                   "                     ) AS students"+
```

Example 6-35. Producing Nested XML from a SQL Query with XML SQL Utility (continued)

```
                    "  FROM course_assignments a"+
                    " GROUP BY course"+
                    " ORDER BY course";
    // Create an instance of the OracleXMLQuery object
    OracleXMLQuery q = new OracleXMLQuery(cn,query);
    // Set some of its XML Generation options
    q.useLowerCaseTagNames();
    q.setRowsetTag("courses");
    // Print it out and close the connection
    System.out.println(q.getXMLString());
    cn.close();
  }
}
```

Running `CourseAssignments` produces the XML document in Example 6-36.

Example 6-36. Output from OracleXMLQuery Class

```
<?xml version = '1.0'?>
<courses>
   <row num="1">
      <course>eecs-101</course>
      <students>
         <students_row num="1">
            <name>brenda</name>
            <age>19</age>
         </students_row>
      </students>
   </row>
   <row num="2">
      <course>math-202</course>
      <students>
         <students_row num="1">
            <name>steve</name>
            <age>23</age>
         </students_row>
      </students>
   </row>
   <row num="3">
      <course>psych-399</course>
      <students>
         <students_row num="1">
            <name>matt</name>
            <age>23</age>
         </students_row>
         <students_row num="2">
            <name>joe</name>
            <age>22</age>
         </students_row>
      </students>
   </row>
</courses>
```

Notice that nested rowsets created by the CURSOR expression are naturally reflected as nested XML information in the document. In the next section, we'll see how to combine `OracleXMLQuery` with an XSLT transformation to produce XML query results in an arbitrary XML format—for example, in a business partner's specific DTD format.

Appetite whetted? Good. We explore the full functionality of the XML SQL Utility in Chapters 11, 12, and 14, and it's quite a gem, as we'll discover.

Transforming XML Using XSLT

One of the most common questions on the Oracle Technology Network's XML Support forum is "How do I serve my database data into the format of a *particular* DTD?" Here we go, step by step, though the answer. The high-level steps involved in the process are:

1. Use the XML SQL Utility to produce an XML document for your database query results. You can do this with a Java program that leverages `OracleXMLQuery` or simply use the `OracleXML getXML` command-line utility we'll learn more about in Chapters 11 and 12. This is your *source* XML document.
2. Start with an example XML document that complies with your target DTD. You may have such an example on hand, or if you use a DTD or schema editing tool, it may support creating an example XML instance document from a DTD to jump-start this process. This is an example of your *target* XML document format.
3. Evolve that example document into an XSLT stylesheet by replacing literal data with special `<xsl:value-of>` tags to plug your database query results into the template in the right places.
4. Use the `oraxsl` command-line utility to test transforming your source XML query results into your target DTD format until you're satisfied with the result.
5. Finally, automate the transformation of live XML SQL query results into your desired DTD's target format using the Oracle XSLT processor in your own program.

Let's take the process one step at a time. We performed Step 1 in the previous section, producing an example of the XML SQL query results. Step 2 involves producing an example document in our desired DTD format. Our business partner has supplied us with an *Enrollment.dtd* file that describes the format in which they need to receive our enrollment information. Figure 6-20 shows what this *Enrollment.dtd* looks like, using the XML Authority tool from Extensibility.

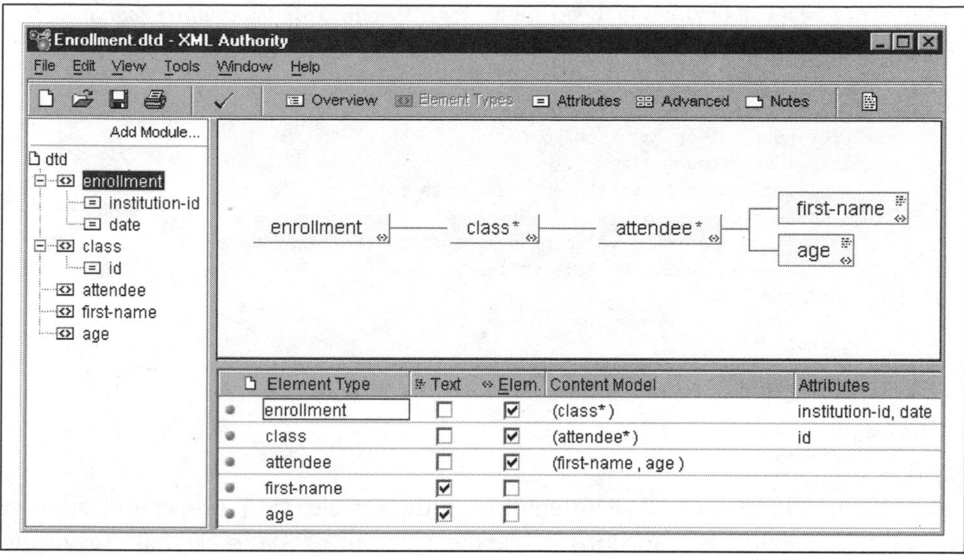

Figure 6-20. Studying the target DTD using XML Authority

Using XML Authority's *File → Export → Example XML Document...* feature, we can produce a skeleton XML document to work with in our desired DTD format:

```
<?xml version ="1.0"?>
<!DOCTYPE SYSTEM "Enrollment.dtd">
<!--Generated by XML Authority.-->
<enrollment institution-id = "string" date = "string">
 <class id = "string">
  <attendee>
   <first-name>only text</first-name>
   <age>only text</age>
  </attendee>
 </class>
</enrollment>
```

For Step 3, we can turn the example document into an XSLT stylesheet like the one shown in Example 6-37. We do this by wrapping it in an `<xsl:stylesheet>` element and using `<xsl:for-each>`, `<xsl:value-of>`, and XSLT attribute value templates (`attr="{`*`expr`*`}"`) to plug data, parameters, or even Java function values into the target document as part of the transformation. We cover a cookbook approach to creating this kind of stylesheet in Chapter 8, *Publishing Data with XSQL Pages.*

Example 6-37. Stylesheet Turns ROWSET/ROW into a Specific XML Vocabulary

```
<!-- Enrollment.xsl -->
<xsl:stylesheet version="1.0" exclude-result-prefixes="date"
  xmlns:xsl="http://www.w3.org/1999/XSL/Transform"
  xmlns:date="http://www.oracle.com/XSL/Transform/java/java.util.Date">
  <xsl:output indent="yes" doctype-system="Enrollment.dtd"/>
```

Example 6-37. Stylesheet Turns ROWSET/ROW into a Specific XML Vocabulary (continued)

```
  <xsl:param name="School"/>
  <xsl:template match="/">
    <enrollment institution-id="{$School}" date = "{date:toString(date:new())}">
      <xsl:for-each select="courses/row">
        <class id = "{course}">
          <xsl:for-each select="students/students_row">
            <attendee>
              <first-name><xsl:value-of select="name"/></first-name>
              <age><xsl:value-of select="age"/></age>
            </attendee>
          </xsl:for-each>
        </class>
      </xsl:for-each>
    </enrollment>
  </xsl:template>
</xsl:stylesheet>
```

Note that in *Enrollment.xsl* we're employing the Oracle XSLT processor's support for XSLT Java extension functions to use the **java.util.Date** class as part of the transformation definition in order to generate today's date. We'll see full details on this Java extension capability in Chapter 16, *Extending XSQL and XSLT with Java*, but this will suffice for now. For Step 4, we use the **oraxsl** command-line tool to test out our transformation, passing the value of the stylesheet's top-level **School** parameter on the command line:

```
oraxsl -p School='12332' CourseAssignments.xml Enrollment.xsl
```

This produces the resulting XML document in the correct *Enrollment.dtd* format shown in Example 6-38.

Example 6-38. Course Assignments Datagram in <enrollment> Format

```
<?xml version = '1.0' encoding = 'UTF-8'?>
<!DOCTYPE enrollment SYSTEM "Enrollment.dtd">
<enrollment institution-id="12332" date="Mon Apr 10 11:16:49 PDT 2000">
   <class id="eecs-101">
      <attendee>
         <first-name>brenda</first-name>
         <age>19</age>
      </attendee>
   </class>
   <class id="math-202">
      <attendee>
         <first-name>steve</first-name>
         <age>23</age>
      </attendee>
   </class>
   <class id="psych-399">
      <attendee>
         <first-name>matt</first-name>
         <age>23</age>
```

Example 6-38. Course Assignments Datagram in <enrollment> Format (continued)

```
      </attendee>
      <attendee>
         <first-name>joe</first-name>
         <age>22</age>
      </attendee>
   </class>
</enrollment>
```

This looks pretty good. We'll dedicate the rest of this section to implementing Step 5 to automate the combination of XML SQL query results and XSLT transformation to allow any queried information to be returned in *Enrollment.dtd* format. The first class we'll create is `EnrollmentWriter`. This takes the basic code from Example 6-35 and adds the following extras:

1. Calls `getXMLDOM()` on `OracleXMLQuery` instead of `getXMLString()` to return an in-memory DOM tree for the XML SQL query results. This is more efficient because getting the results as a string would force us to reparse the string into an `XMLDocument` to transform it.
2. Creates and caches an `XSLStylesheet` object to use for the transformation. Depending on whether we're running inside or outside the database, this either opens an *xmldoc:/transforms/Enrollment.xsl* URL, or reads the *Enrollment.xsl* file from the current directory on the filesystem.
3. Creates an `XSLProcessor` object to carry out the transformation, based on the transformation instructions that are described in the `XSLStylesheet` object.
4. Calls `processXSL` on the `XSLProcessor` to effect the transformation and write out the result to a `PrintWriter`, all in one step.

Example 6-39 shows the full implementation.

A very common mistake developers make is using the `XSLTProcessor` class's `processXSL` method incorrectly. If your stylesheet contains an `<xsl:output>` element, which provides hints governing how the results should be serialized, you must use:

```
public void processXSL(XSLStylesheet style,
                       XMLDocument source,
                       PrintWrinter out);
```

to see the effects of your `<xsl:output>` instruction. If instead you accidentally use the method:

```
public DocumentFragment processXSL(XSLStylesheet style,
                                   XMLDocument source);
```

then the XSLT processor produces the transformed tree of nodes but is never given the opportunity to serialize the results according to the `<xsl:output>` hints. We will learn about all the specifics of `<xsl:output>` in Chapter 7, *Transforming XML with XSLT*.

Example 6-39. Programmatically Transforming ROWSET/ROW Query Results

```
import java.sql.*;
import oracle.xml.sql.query.*;
import oracle.xml.parser.v2.*;
import java.net.URL;
import java.io.*;
import XMLDocuments;
import URLUtils;
import Examples;

public class EnrollmentWriter {
  // Cache the stylesheet for the duration of the session
  private static XSLStylesheet sheet = null;
  private Connection conn = null;
  String  schoolId = null;
  public EnrollmentWriter(String schoolId,Connection conn) {
    this.schoolId = schoolId;
    this.conn     = conn;
  }
  // Print out the XML for an Enrollment by schoolid
  public void printXML(PrintWriter output) throws Exception {
    // Use a CURSOR() expression to get master/detail, nested results
    // of distinct courses and the students in each course
    String query = "SELECT course, CURSOR(SELECT name,age "+
                   "                        FROM course_assignments b"+
                   "                       WHERE b.course = a.course"+
                   "                     ) AS students"+
                   "  FROM course_assignments a"+
                   " WHERE school_id = "+ schoolId +
                   " GROUP BY course"+
                   " ORDER BY course";
    // Create an instance of the OracleXMLQuery object
    OracleXMLQuery q = new OracleXMLQuery(conn,query);
    // Set some of its XML Generation options
    q.useLowerCaseTagNames();
    q.setRowsetTag("courses");
    // Retrieve the results as an in-memory XMLDocument
    XMLDocument xmldoc = (XMLDocument)q.getXMLDOM();
    // If the stylesheet is null, go set it up the first time
    if (sheet == null) setupStylesheet();
    // Set the top-level stylesheet parameter named "School"
    // Note that the value needs to be quoted!
    sheet.setParam("School","'"+schoolId+"'");
    // Transform the XML document using the stylesheet
    // Writing the output to System.out, then close the connection
    XSLProcessor xslt = new XSLProcessor();
    xslt.processXSL(sheet,xmldoc,output);
  }
  // Setup and cache XSLT stylesheet
  private void setupStylesheet() throws Exception {
    URL stylesheetURL = null;
    // If we're inside Oracle8i, read Enrollment.xsl from xml_documents table
    if (Examples.insideOracle8i()) {
      XMLDocuments.enableXMLDocURLs();
```

Example 6-39. Programmatically Transforming ROWSET/ROW Query Results (continued)

```
        stylesheetURL = new URL("xmldoc:/transforms/Enrollment.xsl");
      }
      // If we're outside Oracle8i, read Enrollment.xsl from current directory
      else stylesheetURL = URLUtils.newURL("Enrollment.xsl");
      try {
        // Construct the stylesheet from the XML coming in from the reader
        sheet = new XSLStylesheet(stylesheetURL,stylesheetURL);
      }
      catch (Exception e) {
        throw new RuntimeException("Failed to read Enrollment.xsl");
      }
    }
}
```

Now we need a program to drive **EnrollmentWriter**. We'll write an **Enrollment** class that acts as a command-line driver, as well as a Java stored procedure driver, allowing a user in either scenario to supply a school ID. We'll construct an instance of **EnrollmentWriter**—passing the school ID—and call its **printXML()** method to write out the XML results. In the code for **Enrollment** in Example 6-40, we've implemented a **debug_main** method to enable JServer debugging, a standard **main** method for command-line access, and a **getAsCLOB** method to wrap as a Java stored procedure.

Example 6-40. Class with Static Methods to Publish as Stored Procedures

```
import java.sql.*;
import oracle.sql.CLOB;
import oracle.xml.sql.query.*;
import oracle.xml.parser.v2.*;
import java.net.URL;
import java.io.*;
import EnrollmentWriter;

public class Enrollment {
  // For debugging this inside JServer
  public static void debug_main() throws Exception {
    CLOB[] clob = new CLOB[1];
    getAsCLOB("12332",clob);
    TemporaryCLOB.free(Examples.getConnection(),(Clob)clob[0]);
  }
  // For running on the command line.
  public static void main (String args[]) throws Exception {
    if (args.length < 1) {
      System.err.println("usage: Enrollment schoolid");
      System.exit(1);
    }
    Connection conn = Examples.getConnection();
    EnrollmentWriter ew = new EnrollmentWriter(args[0],conn);
    ew.printXML(new PrintWriter(System.out));
    conn.close();
  }
```

Example 6-40. Class with Static Methods to Publish as Stored Procedures (continued)

```
  // For running inside a SQL Statement
  public static void getAsCLOB(String schoolId, CLOB[] clob ) throws Exception {
    Connection conn = Examples.getConnection();
    EnrollmentWriter ew = new EnrollmentWriter(schoolId,conn);
    clob[0] = (CLOB)TemporaryCLOB.create(Examples.getConnection());
    ew.printXML(new PrintWriter(clob[0].getCharacterOutputStream()));
    conn.close();
  }
}
```

Study the argument list for the **getAsCLOB** method. It accepts a **CLOB[]**—an array of type CLOB—as an argument. Why? Because the PL/SQL stored procedure we want to map to **getAsCLOB** needs to have the signature:

```
PROCEDURE GETASCLOB ("schoolId" IN VARCHAR2, "clob" IN OUT NOCOPY CLOB)
```

using the IN OUT NOCOPY modifier on the CLOB attribute. It's a rule that any PL/SQL argument with an OUT mode must map Java into an array of one element of the appropriate object type. This allows the called program to set the value of the *zero*th array element and have the calling program see the changes.

We're targeting a stored procedure specification with an IN OUT NOCOPY CLOB argument instead of a function that returns a CLOB because:

- The NOCOPY modifier avoids a potentially expensive memory copy of the CLOB's contents, so we want to use it.
- Currently, the NOCOPY modifier is not supported on function return values, just on OUT arguments.

Because the results of the transformed **Enrollment** datagram are being created on the fly, they do not exist as a CLOB column in any table. We need to leverage Oracle8*i*'s temporary CLOB feature to create transient character values to return to SQL values that can be very large. The **TemporaryCLOB** helper in Example 6-41 shows the code to create a temporary CLOB and to free it when we've finished using it.

Example 6-41. Helper Class to Create and Free Temporary CLOB

```
import java.sql.*;
import oracle.jdbc.driver.*;

public class TemporaryCLOB {
  // Return a new temporary CLOB
  public static Clob create(Connection conn) {
    CallableStatement cs = null;
    Clob clob = null;
    try {
      cs = conn.prepareCall("begin dbms_lob.createtemporary(?,false);end;");
      cs.registerOutParameter(1,Types.CLOB);
      cs.execute();
```

Example 6-41. Helper Class to Create and Free Temporary CLOB (continued)

```
      clob = CS.getClob(1);
      CS.close();
      return clob;
    }
    catch (SQLException s) {
      try { CS.close(); } catch (SQLException s2) { }
    }
    return null;
  }
  // Free a temporary CLOB
  public static void free(Connection conn, Clob clob) {
    PreparedStatement PS = null;
    try {
      PS = conn.prepareStatement("begin dbms_lob.freetemporary(?);end;");
      PS.setClob(1,clob);
      int rows = PS.executeUpdate();
      PS.close();
    }
    catch (SQLException s) {
      try { PS.close(); } catch (SQLException s2) { }
    }
  }
}
```

After following the steps in JDeveloper (now quite familiar to us) to create a stored procedure deployment profile and automatically deploy our `Enrollment` class to the database, we can use JDeveloper's database browser to inspect the `ENROLLMENT` specification package it created for us to publish `Enrollment` as a Java stored procedure, as shown in Figure 6-21.

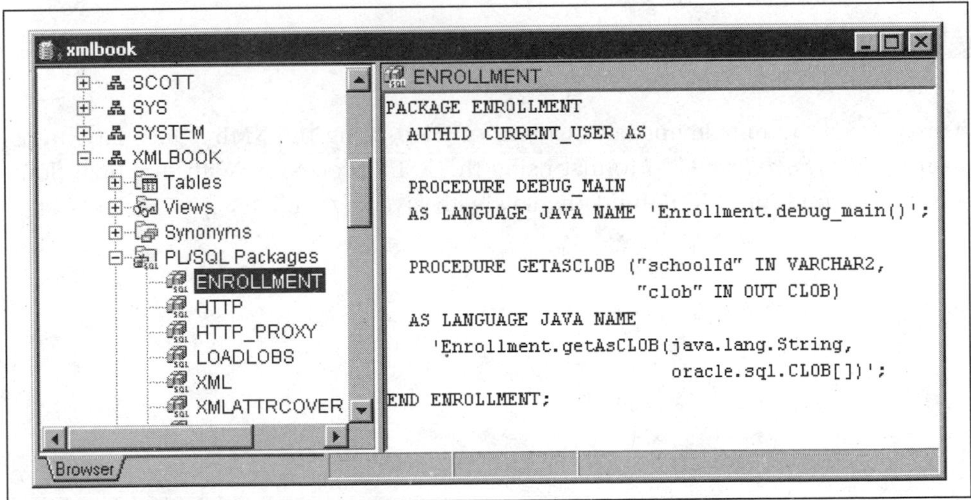

Figure 6-21. Browsing a stored procedure specification

Notice that JDeveloper was not able to infer that we wanted the NOCOPY option, so we can copy and paste the source code for the default package and add NOCOPY ourselves, like this:

```
CREATE OR REPLACE PACKAGE ENROLLMENT
  AUTHID CURRENT_USER AS

  PROCEDURE DEBUG_MAIN
  AS LANGUAGE JAVA NAME 'Enrollment.debug_main()';

  PROCEDURE GETASCLOB ("schoolId" IN VARCHAR2,
                       "clob" IN OUT NOCOPY CLOB)
  AS LANGUAGE JAVA NAME
    'Enrollment.getAsCLOB(java.lang.String,
                          oracle.sql.CLOB[])';
END ENROLLMENT;
```

After rerunning this script to create the package, we're ready to try it out. We can use `ENROLLMENT.getAsCLOB()` immediately in any PL/SQL program, but to include it directly inside a SELECT statement, it must be a function. We can create the `enrollmentxml` wrapper function to achieve this:

```
CREATE OR REPLACE FUNCTION enrollmentxml(schoolid VARCHAR2) RETURN VARCHAR2
IS
 c CLOB;
 retval VARCHAR2(32767);
BEGIN
    enrollment.getAsCLOB(schoolid,c);
    retval := dbms_lob.substr(c);
    dbms_lob.freetemporary(c);
    RETURN retval;
END;
```

And give it a quick spin in a handy SELECT FROM dual statement:

```
SELECT enrollmentxml('12332') FROM dual
```

This returns the enrollment information, queried using the XML SQL Utility, transformed into *Enrollment.dtd* format using the XSLT processor. With that final flourish, our grand tour of XML fundamentals with Java is complete.

In this chapter:

- XSLT Processing Mechanics
- Single-Template Stylesheets
- Understanding Input and Output Options
- Improving Flexibility with Multiple Templates

7 Transforming XML with XSLT

We've used XSLT stylesheets in previous chapters to transform database-driven XML into HTML pages, XML datagrams of a particular vocabulary, SQL scripts, emails, and so on. If you're a developer trying to harness your database information to maximum advantage on the Web, you'll find that XSLT is the Swiss Army knife you want permanently attached to your belt. In a world where the exchange of structured information is core to your success, and where the ability to rapidly evolve and repurpose information is paramount, Oracle XML developers who fully understand how to exploit XSLT are way ahead of the pack.

XSLT 1.0 is the W3C standard language for describing transformations between XML documents. It is closely aligned with the companion XPath 1.0 standard and works in concert with it. As we'll see in this chapter, XPath let's you say what to transform, and XSLT provides the complementary language describing how to carry out the transformation. An XSLT stylesheet describes a set of rules for transforming a source XML document into a result XML document. An XSLT processor is the software that carries out the transformation based on these rules.

In the simple examples in previous chapters, we have seen three primary ways to use the Oracle XSLT processor. We've used the `oraxsl` command-line utility, the XSLT processor's programmatic API, and the `<?xml-stylesheet?>` instruction to associate a stylesheet with an XSQL page. In this chapter, we begin exploring the full power of the XSLT language to understand how best to use it in our applications.

XSLT Processing Mechanics

An XSLT stylesheet describes a transformation that operates on the tree-structured infoset of a source XML document and produces a tree of nodes as its output.

Consider a simple XML document like this:

```
<!-- Emp.xml -->
<ROWSET>
  <ROW num="1">
    <EMPNO>7839</EMPNO>
    <ENAME>KING</ENAME>
  </ROW>
  <ROW num="2">
    <EMPNO>7788</EMPNO>
    <ENAME>SCOTT</ENAME>
  </ROW>
</ROWSET>
```

A transformation of this document operates on the document's corresponding node tree (shown in Figure 7-1). The tree of nodes for an XML document always starts with a root node that represents the document itself. Child nodes of the root can be the single document element node—**<ROWSET>**, in our example—as well as comments and processing instructions. Child nodes of the document element can be any combination of text nodes and element nodes, each of which may, in turn, have similar child nodes. This nesting of nodes forms a tree.

Remember that an XML document can look like this:

```
<ROWSET>
  <ROW num="1">
    <X>Y</X>
  </ROW>
</ROWSET>
```

or it can look like this:

```
<ROWSET><ROW num="1"><X>Y</X></ROW></ROWSET>
```

While both expressions contain a logically equivalent element structure, the former example contains additional whitespace (denoted by `WS` nodes in Figure 7-1) to give it that indented look. Specifically, it contains a carriage return at the end of every line followed by a series of spaces at the start of the next line. When considering an XML document as a tree of nodes, don't forget that the text nodes containing whitespace also count as nodes the same as text like `7788` or **SCOTT**. Since you can't see it, whitespace is easy to forget about.

To carry out a transformation, an XSLT processor requires two ingredients:

- The source tree of nodes
- An XSLT stylesheet containing a set of transformation rules

An XSLT stylesheet is an XML document that uses elements from the XSLT vocabulary to describe a transformation. The document element of every stylesheet is an

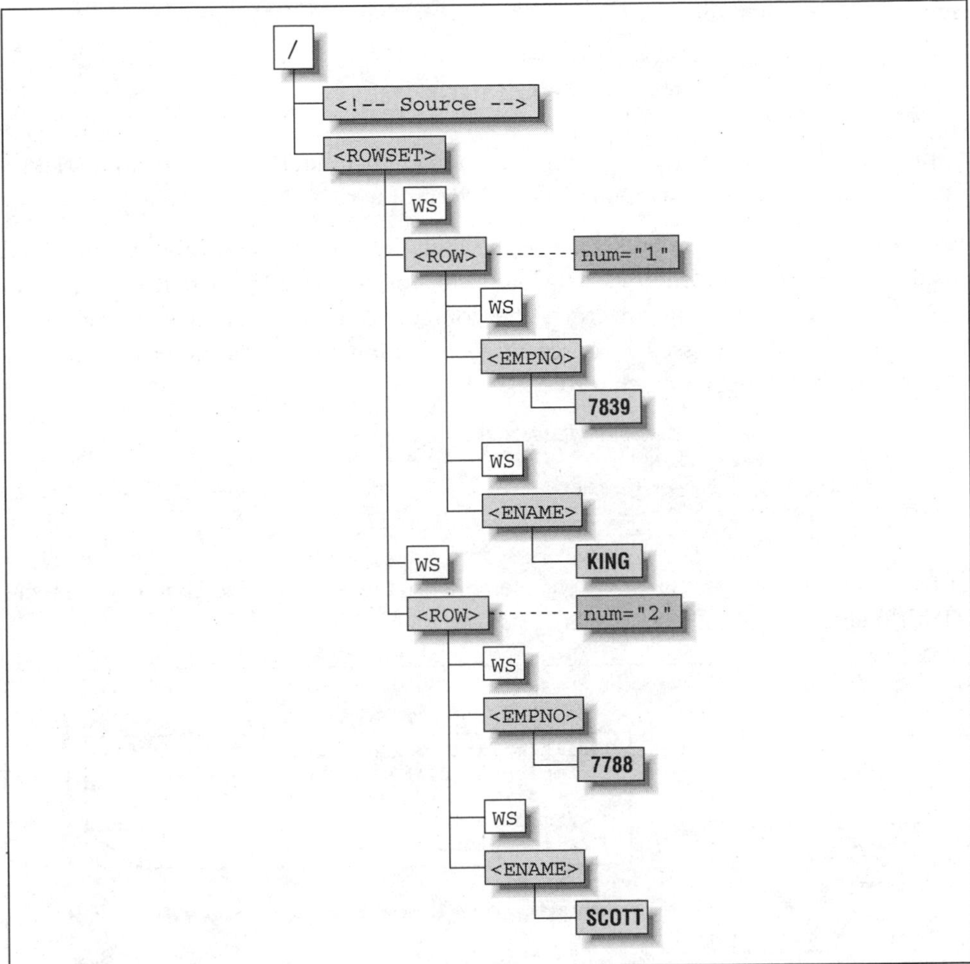

Figure 7-1. Node tree for a simple ROWSET document

`<xsl:stylesheet>` element whose content is a set of rules describing the transformation to be performed. Each rule in the stylesheet contains an associated XPath pattern that matches the nodes in the source document to which that rule should apply. Each rule is called a *template* and is represented by an `<xsl:template>` element with a `match="pattern"` attribute for its associated XPath match pattern. For example, a rule like this:

```
<xsl:template match="/">
  <!-- Some Result Content: Elements, Attributes, Text, etc. -->
</xsl:template>
```

applies to the root node of the document, matching the XPath pattern "/".

Similarly, a rule like this:

```
<xsl:template match="ROWSET/ROW[ENAME]">
  <!-- Some Result Content: Elements, Attributes, Text, etc. -->
</xsl:template>
```

applies only to <ROW> elements in the source document that have an <ENAME> child element and occur as immediate children of a <ROWSET> element.

Each rule is called a template because the literal elements and attributes contained inside the body of the rule act as a blueprint for constructing a part of the result tree. The XSLT processor constructs the content of a rule's template in the result tree whenever it processes a source node matching the rule's pattern. Figure 7-2 illustrates what happens when a rule like this:

```
<xsl:template match="ROWSET/ROW[ENAME]">
  <Employee id="NX-{EMPNO}">
    <xsl:value-of select="ENAME"/>
  </Employee>
</xsl:template>
```

is triggered by processing a <ROW> element in the source tree that matches the XPath pattern ROWSET/ROW[ENAME].

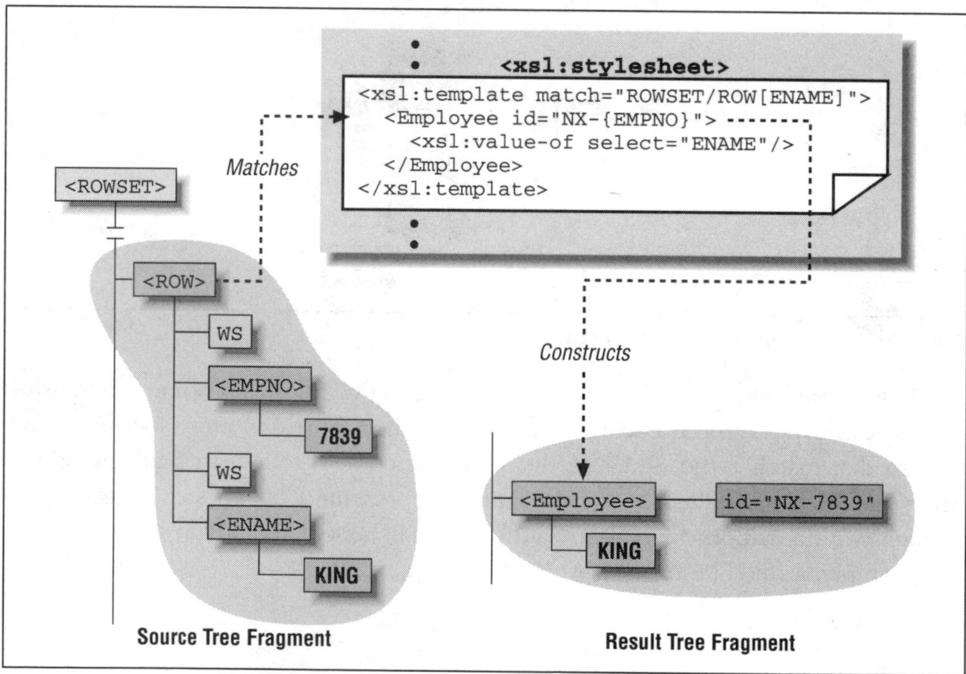

Figure 7-2. Matching source tree node and constructing result fragment

As the matching template is instantiated, the following three things occur:

1. Literal result elements and attributes in the template are created in the result tree. Result elements and attributes that are *not* from the XSLT namespace are considered "literal" since they are constructed as is in the result tree. In the example just given, the `<Employee>` element and its `id` attribute are created.
2. Any *attribute value* templates of the form `{XPathExpr}` contained within literal attribute values are replaced by the value of their XPath expression. In the example, the `{EMPNO}` inside the literal attribute value `NX-{EMPNO}` is replaced by the value of the `EMPNO` XPath expression. This evaluates to `7839`, so the final value for the `id` attribute in the result tree is `NX-7839`.
3. Any elements in the XSLT namespace are processed in document order. The `<xsl:value-of>` element is processed and is replaced by a text node containing the string value of the XPath expression in its `select` attribute—in this case, `KING`.

The basic operation can be summarized as follows: when a node in the source matches a rule's pattern, the content of that rule is created in the result tree. Once you grasp this basic operation, the overall XSLT processing model is easy to understand. Given a source tree and a stylesheet, the XSLT processor carries out the transformation described by rules in the stylesheet by following a sequence of steps, just like the ones we have described.

A list of nodes in the source tree is processed to create a portion, or "fragment," of the result tree. The result tree fragment for the list of nodes is created by processing the nodes in order and concatenating each of their respective result tree fragments together in the same order. The node in the current node list being processed is known, not surprisingly, as the *current node*. The current node is processed by considering the set of all possible rules that match it and then selecting the single rule that matches it best. Only a single rule is ever used to process the current node in the current node list.

To start the process, the XSLT processor begins with a node list containing only the document root. It finds the template matching this root node—typically the rule with `match="/"`—and instantiates the contents of the template in the result tree, following the three basic processing steps to complete the job. If the template contains elements from the XSLT namespace that select other nodes to process, the sequence of matching and template content instantiation continues recursively until there are no nodes left to process. When processing is completed, the result tree represents the target document produced by the transformation.

Single-Template Stylesheets

Many useful transformations can be expressed with just a single-root template. We'll examine the single-template stylesheet here, but we'll spend the rest of this chapter learning why there's a world beyond the root template and why it's worth learning about.

All of the stylesheets we've seen so far for transforming XML into HTML either have looked like this:

```
<xsl:stylesheet version="1.0" xmlns:xsl="http://www.w3.org/1999/XSL/Transform">
  <!-- The "root" or "main" template -->
  <xsl:template match="/">
    <html>
      <body>
        <!--
         | Literal result elements and attributes, intermingled with
         | <xsl:for-each>, <xsl:value-of>, attribute value templates, etc.
         +-->
      </body>
    </html>
  <xsl:template>
</xsl:stylesheet>
```

or have used the simple form of the single-root template stylesheet, which looks like this:

```
<!-- In the "simple form" of a stylesheet, the root template is implied -->
<html xsl:version="1.0" xmlns:xsl="http://www.w3.org/1999/XSL/Transform">
  <body>
    <!--
     | Literal result elements and attributes, intermingled with
     | <xsl:for-each>, <xsl:value-of>, attribute value templates, etc.
     +-->
  </body>
</html>
```

When you see the **xsl** namespace declaration:

```
xmlns:xsl="http://www.w3.org/1999/XSL/Transform"
```

it is natural to think that the XSLT processor will try to access that URL when your stylesheet is processed. However, the declaration is only used as a unique string to identify the namespace for XSLT. If you do not provide this *exact* string as the namespace URI for the **xsl** namespace prefix, the XSLT processor will simply ignore **<xsl:template>**, **<xsl:for-each>**, **<xsl:value-of>**, and other elements with the **xsl** prefix since it will not recognize them as XSLT actions.

Consider the stylesheet in Example 7-1.

Example 7-1. Single-Root Template Stylesheet to Transform Emp.xml to HTML

```
<xsl:stylesheet version="1.0" xmlns:xsl="http://www.w3.org/1999/XSL/Transform">
  <xsl:template match="/">
    <html>
      <body>
        <xsl:for-each select="ROWSET">
          <table border="1" cellspacing="0">
            <xsl:for-each select="ROW">
              <tr>
                <td><xsl:value-of select="EMPNO"/></td>
                <td><xsl:value-of select="ENAME"/></td>
              </tr>
            </xsl:for-each>
          </table>
        </xsl:for-each>
      </body>
    </html>
  </xsl:template>
</xsl:stylesheet>
```

This transforms our simple *Emp.xml* `<ROWSET>` document into an HTML document with the employee data in a table, as shown in Figure 7-3.

7839	KING
7788	SCOTT

Figure 7-3. Employee data in an HTML table

The content of the root template is a mixture of the familiar literal HTML elements `<html>`, `<body>`, `<table>`, `<tr>`, and `<td>`, strategically sprinkled with `<xsl:for-each>` and `<xsl:value-of>` elements. When the XSLT processor instantiates the root template, the document root node is the current node. The `<xsl:for-each>` element:

1. Selects a list of source tree nodes to process
2. Makes this list of selected nodes the current node list
3. Begins processing the nodes in the current node list in order

The content of the `<xsl:for-each>` element is instantiated in the result tree for each node in the current node list. The content of this instantiated result tree fragment is processed (with respect to the current node) for additional XSLT elements, if any.

Any `<xsl:value-of>` elements encountered in the instantiated result tree fragments are replaced by the string value of the XPath expression in their `select` attribute. Figure 7-4 illustrates the process.

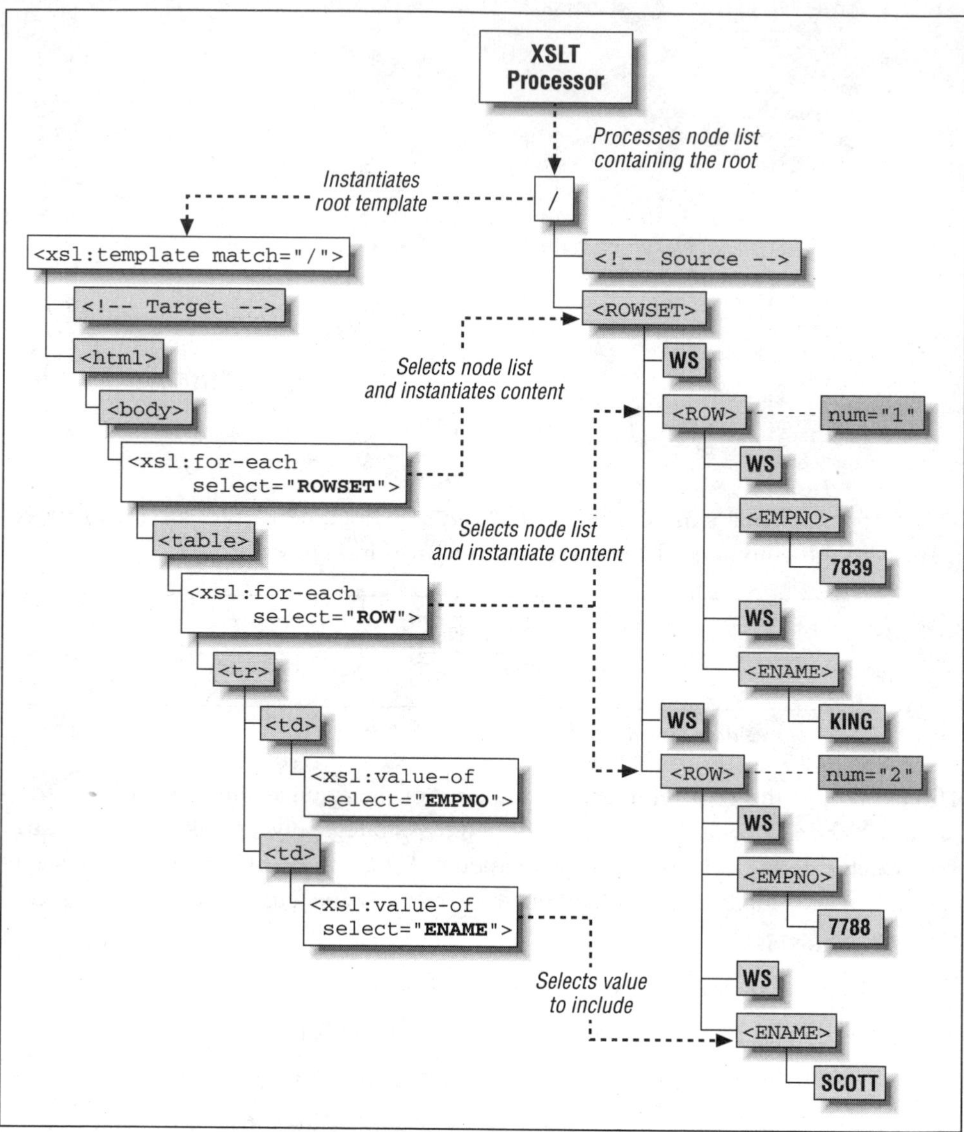

Figure 7-4. Understanding a single-template stylesheet

The resulting HTML document is shown in Example 7-2.

Example 7-2. Output of Emp.xml Using Single-Root Template Stylesheet

```
<html>
   <body>
      <table border="1" cellspacing="0">
         <tr>
            <td>7839</td>
            <td>KING</td>
         </tr>
         <tr>
            <td>7788</td>
            <td>SCOTT</td>
         </tr>
      </table>
   </body>
</html>
```

In this example, the XSLT processor only performs template matching for the root node. All subsequent nodes selected for processing are the result of processing the **<xsl:for-each>** action's **select** patterns and iterating over the node-sets they return.

If a stylesheet uses only the root template, then it can optionally use the simple-form stylesheet syntax that allows **<xsl:stylesheet>** and **<xsl:template match="/">** to be left out. In this case, the literal element that would have been the first element in the *root* template is instead the first element of the entire stylesheet. You must include the namespace declaration for the XSLT namespace on the literal result element that is now the document element of the stylesheet document, as well as add the namespace-qualified **xsl:version="1.0"** attribute to the element:

```
<html xsl:version="1.0" xmlns:xsl="http://www.w3.org/1999/XSL/Transform">
  <body>
    <xsl:for-each select="ROWSET">
      <table border="1" cellspacing="0">
        <xsl:for-each select="ROW">
          <tr>
            <td><xsl:value-of select="EMPNO"/></td>
            <td><xsl:value-of select="ENAME"/></td>
          </tr>
        </xsl:for-each>
      </table>
    </xsl:for-each>
  </body>
</html>
```

This produces the same results as the stylesheet with normal syntax we saw earlier.

Understanding Input and Output Options

The XSLT transformation process described earlier was explained in terms of node trees. These trees of nodes are the logical form that both the source and result of a transformation can take on the "inside" of a transformation being performed by an XSLT processor. However, this is what happens on the outside:

- The source document typically begins as a stream of human-readable characters.
- The result of the transformation typically needs to be written out as another stream of human-readable characters—for example, to send the result back to a requesting browser or to save the result in a file for later.

The input to an XSLT transformation must be a tree of source nodes produced by either parsing a well-formed XML document or creating the tree programmatically (for example, via DOM or SAX APIs).

All XSLT transformations process the source node tree to produce a tree of result nodes. If multiple transformations are being applied in sequence by your application, the result tree of one transformation becomes the source tree of the next transformation in sequence. When no more transformations need to be done, the final tree of result nodes needs to be written out as a stream of characters again. This process is called *serializing* the result tree.

Simple-form stylesheets take advantage of default serialization rules described by the XSLT 1.0 specification to make common cases simple. They serialize transformed output in the default UTF-8 character set and support either of the following output formats:

- Indented, properly formatted HTML output, with a media type of `text/html`
- Non-indented XML output with no `DOCTYPE` and a media type of `text/xml`

Going beyond these defaults requires using the more verbose, standard XSLT stylesheet syntax that begins with an `<xsl:stylesheet>` element that includes as a direct child an `<xsl:output>` element, which offers control over the serialization process.

The most important serialization control to understand is the *output method*. This governs the basic rules that the XSLT processor will use when serializing the result tree nodes to an output stream. XSLT 1.0 supports three different output methods:

`<xsl:output method="xml"/>`
: This method is the default and outputs the nodes as well-formed XML.

`<xsl:output method="html"/>`
: This method is the default for result trees whose document element is `<html>`, `<HTML>`, or any case-variation in between. It serializes elements and attributes

in an HTML 4.0–friendly way that ensures existing browsers will recognize it. In particular, it does *not* write out well-formed XML.

`<xsl:output method="text"/>`
: This method outputs only the text nodes in the result tree in document order. It is used for transforming XML into programming language source files, emails, or other plain text output.

Consider the following example source document:

```
<!-- King.xml -->
<ROWSET>
  <ROW>
    <EMPNO>7839</EMPNO>
    <ENAME>KING</ENAME>
  </ROW>
</ROWSET>
```

The following stylesheet uses the `xml` output method to transform this *King.xml* `<ROWSET>` document into an `<Invitation>` document:

```
<xsl:stylesheet version="1.0" xmlns:xsl="http://www.w3.org/1999/XSL/Transform">
  <xsl:output method="xml" indent="yes"/>
  <xsl:template match="/">
    <Invitation>
      <To>
        <xsl:value-of select="ROWSET/ROW/ENAME"/>
        <xsl:text> &amp; Family</xsl:text>
      </To>
    </Invitation>
  </xsl:template>
</xsl:stylesheet>
```

Transforming *King.xml* using this stylesheet produces the following result:

```
<?xml version="1.0"?>
<Invitation>
  <To>KING &#38; Family</To>
</Invitation>
```

Remember that XSLT stylesheets are well-formed XML documents, so characters that need to be escaped (like & and <) must be escaped with `&` and `<` in your stylesheets, too. While the `>` entity exists to escape the > character, its use is optional. Finally, note that a numerical character entity like `&` can be used as an alternative to represent the character whose Unicode number in decimal is 38, which is the ampersand, and some processors choose to emit all reserved characters using this numerical approach. In your own stylesheets, if you are more comfortable with hexadecimal, you can use a hexadecimal numerical entity as well. For example, a carriage return, Unicode number 10 or 0A in hex, can be represented alternatively as `
` using decimal or `
` using hex.

The following stylesheet uses the **html** output method and transforms the **<ROWSET>** document into a simple HTML page with a paragraph tag and an image:

```
<xsl:stylesheet version="1.0" xmlns:xsl="http://www.w3.org/1999/XSL/Transform">
  <xsl:output method="html"/>
  <xsl:template match="/">
    <html>
      <body>
        <p>
          <xsl:value-of select="ROWSET/ROW/ENAME"/>
          <xsl:text> &amp; Family</xsl:text>
        </p>
        <img src="images/{ROWSET/ROW/EMPNO}.gif"/>
      </body>
    </html>
  </xsl:template>
</xsl:stylesheet>
```

Transforming *King.xml* using this stylesheet produces the following result:

```
<html>
  <body>
    <p>KING &#38; Family</p>
    <img src="images/7839.gif">
  </body>
</html>
```

Finally, this third example stylesheet uses the **text** output method to transform the **<ROWSET>** document into plain text output with no markup tags:

```
<xsl:stylesheet version="1.0" xmlns:xsl="http://www.w3.org/1999/XSL/Transform">
  <xsl:output method="text"/>
  <xsl:template match="/">
    <xsl:text>Hello </xsl:text>
    <xsl:value-of select="ROWSET/ROW/ENAME"/>
      <xsl:text> &amp; Family,&#x0A;</xsl:text>
      <xsl:text>Your id is </xsl:text>
      <xsl:value-of select="ROWSET/ROW/EMPNO"/>
  </xsl:template>
</xsl:stylesheet>
```

This produces the result:

```
Hello King & Family,
Your id is 7839
```

Note that we're using **<xsl:text>** elements to include literal text in the result of the transformation. In general, whitespace is ignored in the stylesheet document, so tags can be nicely indented for readability. However, the whitespace inside of **<xsl:text>** elements is respected, so we use **<xsl:text>** when we want precise control over the whitespace that gets created in the resulting document. Literal spaces, tabs, and carriage returns included in **<xsl:text>** elements are included verbatim in the result. Note the use of `
` to represent the literal carriage return in the result.

Figure 7-5 illustrates the source document, source node tree, result node trees, and final serialization of the previous three transformations, abiding by each transformation's specified output method.

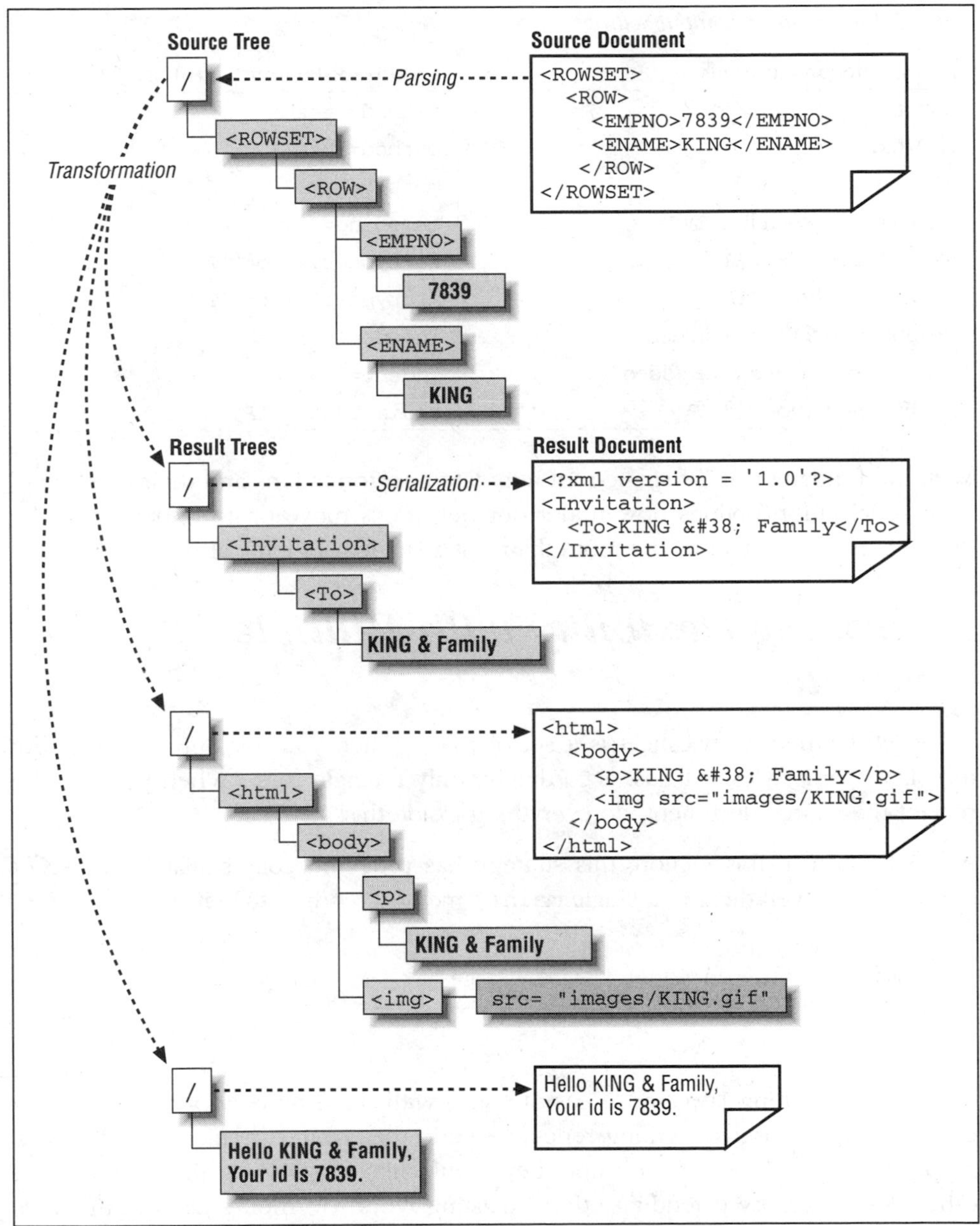

Figure 7-5. Understanding how XSLT output methods affect serialization

In addition to the output method, several other interesting serialization hints can be specified on the `<xsl:output>` element in a stylesheet. Table 7-1 summarizes the `<xsl:output>` settings that come in handy most frequently.

Table 7-1. Common xsl:output Settings

If target document needs	Set this <xsl:output> attribute
Raw text output	`method="text"`
HTML output	`method="html"`
XML output	`method="xml"`
Character set encoding *ENC*	`encoding="`*ENC*`"`
SYSTEM Identifier *URI*	`doctype-system="`*URI*`"`
PUBLIC Identifier *URI*	`doctype-public="`*URI*`"`
Beautifying whitespace added	`indent="yes"`
No additional whitespace added	`indent="no"`
MIME/Media Type of *TYP*	`media-type="`*TYP*`"`

With the fundamentals of single-root template transformations and their most common serialization options now under our belts, let's move on to understand why developers ever bother to use more than just a single-root template.

Improving Flexibility with Multiple Templates

As we've learned, a stylesheet is a set of rules. When you use only a single-root template, your stylesheet has, accordingly, only a single rule: "When you see the root of the source document, do everything inside this!"

As we'll learn in this section, this strategy has pros and cons similar to those of adopting an "everything in a single `main()` method" coding style in Java:

```
public class doit {
  public static void main() (String[] args) {
    // When this program runs, do everything inside this!
  }
}
```

Developers learning Java find it easy to start with this simple approach, but they quickly find themselves writing repetitive code that would be nice to factor into helper methods. When this occurs, they would like to stand on the shoulders of other developers by extending others' existing work, overriding just the methods that need to behave differently.

We'll see that there is a nice conceptual analogy between methods in Java classes and templates in XSLT stylesheets. In Java, methods are both the unit of behavior and the unit of overriding. If you write a class with all of the programming logic in a single `main()` method, then someone extending your class can only override that single `main()` method. This means they have to rewrite all the logic just to change one small behavioral aspect. The more effectively a class's methods are logically factored to represent the set of subtasks the class must perform, the easier it is to reuse a single useful method when appropriate, and the easier it is to override just a part of the existing behavior, if necessary.

In XSLT, *templates* are the unit of behavior as well as the unit of overriding. Similar to the Java analogy above, if you write a stylesheet with all of the transformation logic in a single-root template, then someone extending your stylesheet can only override that entire template to change the way your transformation behaves. The more effectively a stylesheet's templates are logically factored to reflect the individual transformation tasks to be performed, the easier it is to reuse a single useful template when appropriate, and the easier it is to override just a part of the existing transformation behavior, if necessary.

Using Multiple Templates

Example 7-3 shows what our single-root template stylesheet from the previous section looks like if we factored it into multiple templates. We've created a template for each element in the source document that we will encounter and we have made each template responsible for a small part of the transformation job. Each template uses the **<xsl:apply-templates>** action to tell the XSLT processor to "carry on processing my children nodes" so recursive processing of the tree can continue.

Example 7-3. Simple Stylesheet to Produce HTML Using Multiple Templates

```
<xsl:stylesheet xmlns:xsl="http://www.w3.org/1999/XSL/Transform" version="1.0">
  <xsl:output indent="no"/>
  <xsl:template match="/">
    <html>
      <body><xsl:apply-templates/></body>
    </html>
  </xsl:template>
  <xsl:template match="ROWSET">
    <table border="1" cellspacing="0"><xsl:apply-templates/></table>
  </xsl:template>
  <xsl:template match="ROW">
    <tr><xsl:apply-templates/></tr>
  </xsl:template>
  <xsl:template match="EMPNO">
    <td><xsl:apply-templates/></td>
  </xsl:template>
  <xsl:template match="ENAME">
    <td><xsl:apply-templates/></td>
  </xsl:template>
</xsl:stylesheet>
```

The way to read a template that looks like this:

```
<xsl:template match="ROWSET">
  <table border="1" cellspacing="0"><xsl:apply-templates/></table>
</xsl:template>
```

is as follows:

> Whenever we match a <ROWSET> element in the source tree, construct a <table> element in the result tree to contain the results of processing the *children* of the current <ROWSET>, and go process those children now!

When the XSLT processor encounters an <xsl:apply-templates> action, it processes the current node's children and includes any result tree fragments constructed by that processing at the location in the result tree where the <xsl:apply-templates> appears. Accordingly, since here <xsl:apply-templates> is nested inside the literal <table> result element, the result of processing the children of the current <ROWSET> element will be nested inside the <table> element in the result tree.

You can read the entire stylesheet in Example 7-3 as shown in the following table:

When we match	Construct
The source document's root "/"	<html> element and nested <body> element in the result tree to contain the results of processing the document—that is, the children of the root
<ROWSET> element	<table> to contain the results of processing the current <ROWSET>'s child nodes
<ROW> element	<tr> to contain the results of processing the current <ROW>'s child nodes
<EMPNO> element	<td> to contain the results of processing the current <EMPNO>'s child nodes
<ENAME> element	<td> to contain the results of processing the current <ENAME>'s child nodes

Figure 7-6 illustrates the process that takes place during the transformation.

As usual, the processor begins by processing the root node in the source tree and finding a rule that matches it. Our stylesheet has a match="/" template, so it is instantiated with the root node as the current node. The root template constructs the <html> and <body> elements, and then the <xsl:apply-templates> is executed to process the list of children of the document root. The list of children of the root includes one comment node and one element node, the <ROWSET>. To construct the result tree fragment for this list of nodes, the processor processes each one in order. The comment node is ignored (we'll learn why in a minute) and then the <ROWSET> element is processed by finding a rule that matches it. Our match="ROWSET" template matches, so the processor instantiates it in the result

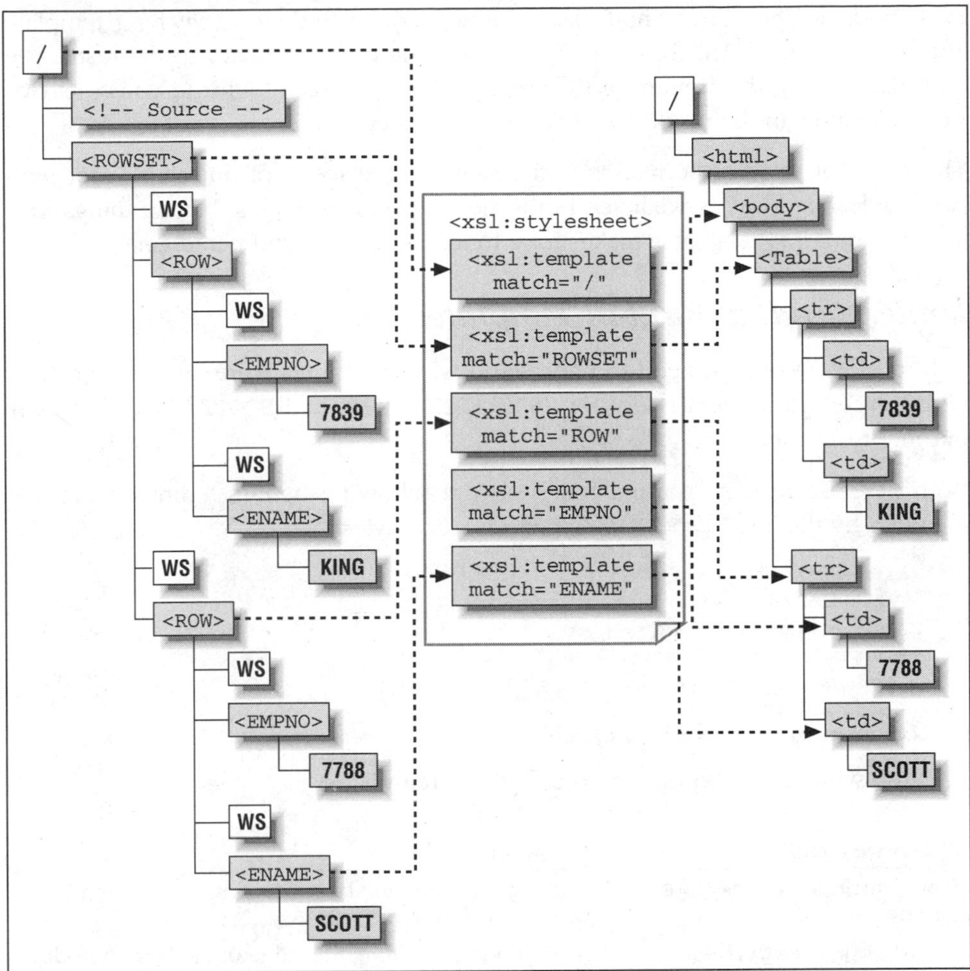

Figure 7-6. Transforming a source document using multiple templates

tree. This creates a literal `<table>` element in the result tree nested inside the previously instantiated `<html>` and `<body>` elements; then `<xsl:apply-templates>` is executed to process the list of children of the current `<ROWSET>` element. The children of the current `<ROWSET>` element are the following four nodes, listed here in order:

1. Text node containing whitespace
2. `<ROW>` element
3. Text node containing whitespace
4. `<ROW>` element

Each node in the current node list is processed by finding a matching template and instantiating it. This has the effect of copying the whitespace to the result tree and instantiating the content of the `match="ROW"` template twice to construct two `<tr>` elements in the result tree. And the process continues.

The result of this transformation is the same as the result of our single-root template stylesheet, but as we'll see in the next several examples, having things broken into multiple templates makes for a much more powerful paradigm.

Understanding Built-in Templates

Before moving on, we need to understand why comments were ignored and how whitespace and the text nodes for `7839`, `KING`, `7788`, and `SCOTT` found their way into the result tree.

Both of these results occurred based on the following built-in templates that are included by the XSLT processor as part of every stylesheet:

```
<xsl:template match="/|*">
  <xsl:apply-templates/>
</xsl:template>
<xsl:template match="text()|@*">
  <xsl:value-of select="."/>
</xsl:template>
<xsl:template match="processing-instruction()|comment()"/>
```

The following table shows how to read these templates:

When we match	Construct
The source document's root "/" or any element "*"	Nothing, but continue by processing the children nodes of the current node
A text node "`text()`" or an attribute "`@*`"	A text node containing the value of the current node, effectively copying the text or attribute value to the result tree
A processing instruction or a comment	Nothing

These built-in rules serve as fallbacks to keep the recursive processing going in case the current node is not explicitly matched by any other template in the stylesheet. Their definitions reveal a couple of interesting points:

- A rule can match any one of several patterns by using the XPath union operator "`|`" between the patterns in its `match` attribute.
- To create a rule that matches a pattern and explicitly does nothing—that is, creates no result tree nodes and does not continue processing to its children—just define an empty `<xsl:template>` node.

To better understand the built-in rules, let's try to transform our simple *Emp.xml* document using the following stylesheet that contains no **<xsl:template>** rules:

```
<xsl:stylesheet xmlns:xsl="http://www.w3.org/1999/XSL/Transform" version="1.0">
  <!-- This stylesheet contains no rules -->
</xsl:stylesheet>
```

We can use the **oraxsl** command-line tool with the command:

```
oraxsl Emp.xml OnlyBuiltinRules.xsl
```

to get the following result:

```
<?xml version = '1.0' encoding = 'UTF-8'?>

    7839
    KING

    7788
    SCOTT
```

The built-in rule for matching elements and the document root keeps the recursion going without constructing any elements in the result tree. Each element that is encountered matches this rule, which immediately says "process the children of the current node." When those children nodes are the text nodes containing whitespace, or the text nodes containing 7839, KING, 7788, and SCOTT, the built-in rule for text() is matched, and its default action is to do **<xsl:value-of select="."/>**, which copies the string value of the current node—the text node, in this case—to the result tree. Accordingly, the result tree is just a pile of all the text nodes in the document at any level, in document order. Although this is interesting, and helpful to remember for debugging, we won't likely be putting our empty stylesheet into production use any time soon.

Wildcard Matching and Whitespace Handling

Let's turn our attention back to the multiple-template stylesheet from Example 7-3. One of the things that should bother you about it is that both of the following templates:

```
<xsl:template match="EMPNO">
  <td><xsl:apply-templates/></td>
</xsl:template>
<xsl:template match="ENAME">
 <td><xsl:apply-templates/></td>
</xsl:template>
```

are doing the same thing. They each match an element that we expect to be a child element of the <ROW> and create a table cell <td> element to contain the result of processing the children. The following query produced the simple *Emp.xml* document:

```
SELECT empno, ename
  FROM emp
  WHERE ename in ('KING','SCOTT')
  ORDER BY SAL
```

But what if we included all of the columns in the emp table? Would we have to perpetuate these repetitive templates to cover each new element, like `<SAL>`, `<COMM>`, `<DEPTNO>`, and so on? We could, but we should start getting the feeling that there must be a better way. Since we want to do the same thing for every element that occurs as a child of the `<ROW>`, namely, construct a `<td>` table cell to contain the result of processing its children, we can simply use XPath to say exactly what we want. The pattern to match any element that is a child of a `<ROW>` element is `ROW/*`. So we can eliminate all of the templates for each individual `<ROW>` child element and create a more generic template to the job:

```
<!-- Match any element child of a ROW -->
<xsl:template match="ROW/*">
  <td><xsl:apply-templates/></td>
</xsl:template>
```

This leaves us the with the stylesheet in Example 7-4, which is ready to accommodate future expansion in the number of columns by processing any child elements of a `<ROW>` in a generic way.

Example 7-4. Stylesheet Using Multiple Templates for ROWSET/ROW Data

```
<xsl:stylesheet version="1.0" xmlns:xsl="http://www.w3.org/1999/XSL/Transform">
  <!--
   | EmpUsingRowStar.xsl:
   | Transform Emp.xml Into <table> using ROW/* to handle any column
   +-->
  <xsl:template match="/">
    <html>
      <body><xsl:apply-templates/></body>
    </html>
  </xsl:template>
  <xsl:template match="ROWSET">
    <table border="1" cellspacing="0"><xsl:apply-templates/></table>
  </xsl:template>
  <xsl:template match="ROW">
    <tr><xsl:apply-templates/></tr>
  </xsl:template>
  <!-- Match any element child of a ROW -->
  <xsl:template match="ROW/*">
    <td><xsl:apply-templates/></td>
  </xsl:template>
</xsl:stylesheet>
```

This should produce the same result as before, so let's try it. Using the command-line **oraxsl** tool to transform our *Emp.xml* document using *EmpUsingRowStar.xsl* with the command:

```
oraxsl Emp.xml EmpUsingRowStar.xsl
```

We get the output:

```
<html>
   <body>
      <table border="1" cellspacing="0">
  <tr>
    <td>7839</td>
    <td>KING</td>
  </tr>
  <tr>
    <td>7788</td>
    <td>SCOTT</td>
  </tr>
</table>
   </body>
</html>
```

But wait. This does not look exactly the same as the nicely indented output we saw in Example 7-2 using the single-root template stylesheet from Example 7-1. The indenting of the **<tr>** elements and closing **</table>** tag is wrong, for some reason. It's important to understand why, since it relates to how XSLT handles whitespace in the source document. Recall that what makes the *Emp.xml* document look indented is whitespace characters, like carriage returns and spaces. Figure 7-7 illustrates what the document would look like if we could see these whitespace characters.

```
<!-- Emp.xml -->↵
<ROWSET>↵
▯▯<ROW num="1">↵
▯▯▯▯<EMPNO>7839</EMPNO>↵
▯▯▯▯<ENAME>KING</ENAME>↵
▯▯</ROW>↵
▯▯<ROW num="2">↵
▯▯▯▯<EMPNO>7788</EMPNO>↵
▯▯▯▯<ENAME>SCOTT</ENAME>↵
▯▯</ROW>↵
</ROWSET>
```

▯ Space
↵ Carriage Return

Figure 7-7. Emp.xml document with whitespace highlighted

When the template matching <ROWSET> is processed in *EmpUsingRowStar.xsl*, it constructs the **<table>** tag and continues recursive processing of <ROWSET>'s child nodes with `<xsl:apply-templates>`. Recall from Figure 7-1 that the first-level child nodes of `<ROWSET>` are the following, listed here in order:

1. A text node containing the whitespace characters to indent the line: carriage return, space, space
2. A `<ROW>` element
3. A text node containing the indentation whitespace characters: carriage return, space, space
4. A `<ROW>` element

Using the multiple-template approach, the XSLT processor processes these child nodes of `<ROWSET>`, in order and tries to find templates that match. When processing the first text node child, no explicit templates in *EmpUsingRowStar.xsl* match this text node, so the built-in template matching `"text()|@*"` matches as a fallback and performs its built-in action of copying the text to the result tree. There is nothing special about how whitespace-only text nodes are handled by the built-in rule: the characters are simply copied verbatim to the result like any text node. These extra carriage returns copied as is into the result by the built-in template explain why the indenting behavior of the output was slightly disturbed.

It's equally important to understand why our stylesheet in Example 7-1 did *not* run into this problem. Using that single-root template stylesheet, the XSLT processor does template matching only for the root node. After this, the only nodes that are processed are the ones explicitly selected by actions like `<xsl:for-each>`. Since that stylesheet never explicitly selected any text nodes for processing, the problem of copying their contents to the result never materialized.

To remedy the situation for *EmpUsingRowStar.xsl*, we can instruct the XSLT processor to strip, and hence ignore for transformation, any text nodes in the source tree that consist entirely of whitespace characters. We can accomplish this by adding an `<xsl:strip-space>` element to the top level of our stylesheet:

```
<xsl:stylesheet version="1.0" xmlns:xsl="http://www.w3.org/1999/XSL/Transform">
  <!--
   | Strip text node children consisting entirely of whitespace for
   | all elements in the source document.
   +-->
  <xsl:strip-space elements="*"/>
```

The value of the `elements` attribute of `<xsl:strip-space>` is a whitespace-separated list of element names whose text node children consist entirely of whitespace you would like to strip. Using an asterisk (*) strips space from all elements. To strip space from all but one or all but a few elements, you can use `<xsl:strip-space>` in combination with the companion `<xsl:preserve-space>` element which takes an analogous `elements` attribute, listing elements for which you want to preserve whitespace. By default, an XSLT processor preserves whitespace child nodes from all elements in the source document.

With this issue sorted out, let's build the following simple XSQL page to test *EmpUsingRowStar.xsl* on live database data:

```
<?xml version="1.0"?>
<!-- Emp.xsql -->
<xsql:query connection="xmlbook" xmlns:xsql="urn:oracle-xsql">
  SELECT empno, ename, sal, deptno
    FROM emp
   ORDER BY ename DESC
</xsql:query>
```

The query in this page includes a couple of extra columns and, instead of just returning the rows for 'KING' and 'SCOTT', will return all the rows in the emp table. As we saw in Chapter 3, *Combining XML and Oracle*, we can reuse the data from the *Emp.xsql* page by including it in other XSQL pages with the `<xsql:include-xsql>` action. In this way, we can apply different stylesheets to the same data page produced. This will come in handy to test the various stylesheets we develop in the rest of this chapter.

For example, we can create an *EmpUsingRowStar.xsql* page that includes *Emp.xsql* and associates the *EmpUsingRowStar.xsl* stylesheet to it. The page looks like this:

```
<?xml version="1.0"?>
<!-- EmpUsingRowStar.xsql -->
<?xml-stylesheet type="text/xsl" href="EmpUsingRowStar.xsl"?>
<!-- Include Emp.xsql and style it with EmpUsingRowStar.xsl -->
<xsql:include-xsql href="Emp.xsql" xmlns:xsql="urn:oracle-xsql"/>
```

Running *EmpUsingRowStar.xsql* from JDeveloper 3.1 we can see the results shown in Figure 7-8.

So our `ROW/*` template is correctly working not only for the `<EMPNO>` and `<ENAME>` elements, but also for the additional `<SAL>` and `<DEPTNO>` elements in the result. However, the results look pretty plain and are missing column headers. Let's fix that.

Processing Source Nodes in Different Modes

Today, many developers creating HTML pages use Cascading Style Sheets (CSS) to separate the presentation style information for many pages into a single, external stylesheet file, then reference the CSS stylesheet from the HTML pages to control font and color information globally. We can leverage this same tried and true technique in the HTML pages we create simply by placing the correct `<link>` tag inside the `<head>` section of our HTML page. If our CSS stylesheet is called *Table.css* then the `<head>` and `<link>` elements we need look like this:

```
<head><link rel="stylesheet" type="text/css" href="Table.css"/></head>
```

7521	WARD	1250	30
7844	TURNER	1500	30
7369	SMITH	800	20
7788	SCOTT	3000	20
7934	MILLER	1300	10
7654	MARTIN	1250	30
7839	KING	5000	10
7566	JONES	2975	20
7900	JAMES	950	30
7902	FORD	3000	20
7782	CLARK	2450	10
7698	BLAKE	2850	30
7499	ALLEN	1600	30
7876	ADAMS	1100	20

Figure 7-8. Transformed HTML output of EmpUsingRowStar.xsql

To create table column headers in a generic way, we need to process all child elements of a <ROW> and then use the *names* of the elements—as opposed to their values—as the content of the table header cells. However, we already have a template with a `ROW/*` match pattern to process the children of a <ROW>; we're using it to create the table cells for each row generically.Specifically, we need a way to process the same source tree elements multiple different ways to generate the column headers. We need to process the children of a <ROW> as follows:

- Once in a special "Column Headers" mode, to transform the children of a <ROW> into the appropriate column headers
- Once in a regular way to format the query results

Luckily, XSLT has just the functionality we need. When you create a template, in addition to the match pattern, it can also have a `mode` attribute that assigns a name to the special mode in which you want to invoke the template. Since we need a special mode to format column headers, we can create a template with `match="ROW/*"` and `mode="ColumnHeaders"`. The name of the mode needs to be meaningful only to us; the processor never interprets the name in any way. The template looks like this:

```
<!-- Match any element child of a ROW when in "ColumnHeaders" Mode -->
  <xsl:template match="ROW/*" mode="ColumnHeaders">
    <th>
      <!-- Put the value of the *name* of the current element -->
      <xsl:value-of select="name(.)"/>
    </th>
  </xsl:template>
```

Now, when we're processing a `<ROW>` element child in `ColumnHeaders` mode, we create `<th>` table header elements instead of `<td>` table cell elements, and we use the XPath `name()` function to refer to the name of the current element instead of to its value. Remember that in XPath, the dot represents the current node, so *`name(.)`* is the name of the current node.

When you create templates with an associated mode, you have to *explicitly* request that the engine process a list of nodes using that mode. You accomplish this by going beyond the default use of `<xsl:apply-templates>` (which, by default, processes the children of the current node without using any special mode) to include a `mode="CurrentHeaders"` attribute, like this:

```
<!-- Apply templates to children of the current node in "ColumnHeader" mode -->
<xsl:apply-templates mode="ColumnHeaders"/>
```

We need the column headers to be created before all of the `<ROW>` elements are processed to produce the table rows, so we add the above `<xsl:apply-templates>` inside our `ROWSET` template, like this:

```
<xsl:template match="ROWSET">
  <table border="1" cellspacing="0">
    <!-- Apply templates in "ColumnHeader" mode first -->
    <xsl:apply-templates mode="ColumnHeaders"/>
    <!-- Then apply templates to all child nodes normally -->
    <xsl:apply-templates/>
  </table>
</xsl:template>
```

However, if we attempt to use this template as is, the `<xsl:apply-templates>` for the `ColumnHeader` mode will process all of the child nodes of the `<ROWSET>`, since that's what `<xsl:apply-templates>` does. This will produce a set of column headers across the top for each `<ROW>` in the `<ROWSET>`, which will give us many repeated column headers. We need to process just a single child `<ROW>` of the `<ROWSET>` to pick up the column header names.

We can handle this easily by modifying the default behavior of `<xsl:apply-templates>` by adding an optional `select` attribute that specifies an XPath expression, identifying the list of nodes to process. We accomplish this by changing:

```
<xsl:apply-templates mode="ColumnHeaders"/>
```

to:

```
<xsl:apply-templates select="ROW[1]/*" mode="ColumnHeaders"/>
```

Now we can select the list of child elements under only the first `<ROW>` child of `<ROWSET>`. This will give us just a single set of column headers.

There is no longer anything specific to the *Emp.xml* document left in this stylesheet. It can handle the task of transforming any `<ROWSET>` into an HTML table with column headers, so we'll name it appropriately. The final *TableBaseWithCSS.xsl* stylesheet, incorporating CSS and column headers, produced using modes, appears in Example 7-5.

Example 7-5. Transforming Any ROWSET into a Table with Headers

```
<xsl:stylesheet version="1.0" xmlns:xsl="http://www.w3.org/1999/XSL/Transform">
  <!--
   | TableBaseWithCSS:
   | Basic stylesheet to format any ROWSET of ROWS into a table
   | with column headings in a generic way. Leverages Table.css
   | CSS stylesheet to control font/color information for the page.
   +-->
  <xsl:template match="/">
    <html>
      <!-- Generated HTML result will be linked to Table.css CSS stylesheet -->
      <head><link rel="stylesheet" type="text/css" href="Table.css"/></head>
      <body><xsl:apply-templates/></body>
    </html>
  </xsl:template>
  <xsl:template match="ROWSET">
    <table border="1" cellspacing="0">
      <!-- Apply templates in "ColumnHeader" mode to just *first* ROW child -->
      <xsl:apply-templates select="ROW[1]/*" mode="ColumnHeaders"/>
      <!-- Then apply templates to all child nodes normally -->
      <xsl:apply-templates/>
    </table>
  </xsl:template>
  <xsl:template match="ROW">
    <tr><xsl:apply-templates/></tr>
  </xsl:template>
  <!-- Match any element child of a ROW -->
  <xsl:template match="ROW/*">
    <td><xsl:apply-templates/></td>
  </xsl:template>
  <!-- Match any element child of a ROW when in "ColumnHeaders" Mode-->
  <xsl:template match="ROW/*" mode="ColumnHeaders">
    <th>
      <!-- Put the value of the *name* of the current element -->
      <xsl:value-of select="name(.)"/>
    </th>
  </xsl:template>
</xsl:stylesheet>
```

If we create an XSQL page to test the stylesheet above, we see that the result looks like Figure 7-9.

We've seen that by using multiple templates, it's possible to build stylesheets that process source nodes in a more generic way, and that we can use modes to process the same source tree nodes in different ways. Next, we'll start to see how templates can be overridden to build on base libraries of existing templates to create custom templates for new tasks.

EMPNO	ENAME	SAL	DEPTNO
7521	WARD	1250	30
7844	TURNER	1500	30
7369	SMITH	800	20
7788	SCOTT	3000	20
7934	MILLER	1300	10
7654	MARTIN	1250	30
7839	KING	5000	10
7566	JONES	2975	20
7900	JAMES	950	30
7902	FORD	3000	20
7782	CLARK	2450	10
7698	BLAKE	2850	30
7499	ALLEN	1600	30
7876	ADAMS	1100	20

Figure 7-9. HTML table with column headers

Reusing and Customizing Existing Stylesheets

Let's say we need to produce a table displaying employee information where employees who earn more than $2000 are highlighted. This task differs from our previous work in only one small detail: `ROW`s with a `SAL > 2000` need to be highlighted differently from other `ROW`s. We hope it's possible to focus just on this new requirement. It most definitely is possible with XSLT.

We can create a new *EmpOver2000.xsl* stylesheet that builds on our *TableBaseWithCSS.xsl* stylesheet and adds one new template to handle the new highlighting task. We can leverage our previous work by using the `<xsl:import>` action at the top level of our stylesheet to import all of the templates we've already created for doing the basic job of formatting a `<ROWSET>` as a table. Example 7-6 shows the minimal syntax we need.

Example 7-6. Importing a Base Stylesheet and Adding New Templates

```
<xsl:stylesheet version="1.0" xmlns:xsl="http://www.w3.org/1999/XSL/Transform">
  <!-- Import all the templates from "TableBaseWithCSS.xsl" as a base -->
  <xsl:import href="TableBaseWithCSS.xsl"/>
  <!-- Override imported template for ROW to match ROWs with a SAL > 2000 -->
  <xsl:template match="ROW[ SAL > 2000 ]">
    <tr class="Highlight"><xsl:apply-templates/></tr>
  </xsl:template>
</xsl:stylesheet>
```

We've imported the *TableBaseWithCSS.xsl* stylesheet and added a template with the match pattern of `ROW[SAL>2000]` to match nodes with a `<SAL>` child element whose value is greater than 2000. Rather than hard-coding font and color information directly into the template, notice that we're using a CSS `class` attribute to refer to the name of a CSS class called **Highlight** that will externally specify the fonts and colors to use for highlighted rows. If we enhance our previous *Table.css* to include the new **Highlight** CSS class like this:

```
body { font-family: Verdana      }
  th { background-color: yellow }
.Highlight { background-color: #e7e7e7 }
```

then all that's left to do is to build an XSQL page to include our original *Emp.xsql* information and transform it using *EmpOver2000.xsl* like this:

```
<?xml version="1.0"?>
<?xml-stylesheet type="text/xsl" href="EmpOver2000.xsl"?>
<xsql:include-xsql href="Emp.xsql" xmlns:xsql="urn:oracle-xsql"/>
```

Now, when we request this new *EmpOver2000.xsql* page, we see what's shown in Figure 7-10.

EMPNO	ENAME	SAL	DEPTNO
7521	WARD	1250	30
7844	TURNER	1500	30
7369	SMITH	800	20
7788	SCOTT	3000	20
7934	MILLER	1300	10
7654	MARTIN	1250	30
7839	KING	5000	10
7566	JONES	2975	20
7900	JAMES	950	30
7902	FORD	3000	20
7782	CLARK	2450	10
7698	BLAKE	2850	30
7499	ALLEN	1600	30
7876	ADAMS	1100	20

Figure 7-10. HTML table with high-paid employees highlighted

When processing the source tree using this stylesheet, for each child `<ROW>` in the list of children of the `<ROWSET>` element, the XSLT processor looks for templates that match `<ROW>`. Earlier, there was only a single template with a match pattern of `"ROW"`, so there was only one template to choose from. However, in *EmpOver2000.xsl* the `match="ROW"` template is imported from the *TableBaseWithCSS.xsl* stylesheet, and we've also added a new `match="ROW[SAL>2000]"` template. This means that when processing a `<ROW>` element in the current node list for rows that have a `<SAL>` over 2000, the processor finds two matching templates. Since the current node is a `<ROW>` element, it matches the `match="ROW"` template, but since it's a `<ROW>` with a SAL greater than 2000, it also matches the `match="ROW[SAL>2000]"` template.

Remember from the basic transformation rules we learned earlier in this chapter that the processor considers all matching templates and then selects the one that matches best. In this case, the `ROW[SAL>2000]` is a more specific pattern than the basic `ROW` pattern, so `ROW[SAL>2000]` qualifies as a better match.

Let's try another example that imports *TableBaseWithCSS.xsl* and:

- Formats even-numbered rows in one color
- Formats odd-numbered rows in a different color
- Formats rows in the "Top-Secret" department to say "Classified"

The stylesheet that accomplishes these tasks appears in Example 7-7.

Example 7-7. Formatting Alternating Rows and Conditionally Hiding Data

```
<xsl:stylesheet xmlns:xsl="http://www.w3.org/1999/XSL/Transform" version="1.0">
  <!-- Import all the templates from "TableBaseWithCSS.xsl" as a base -->
  <xsl:import href="TableBaseWithCSS.xsl"/>
  <!-- Match all ROWS in Top-Secret Department 20 -->
  <xsl:template match="ROW[ DEPTNO = 20 ]">
    <tr>
      <td align="center" colspan="{count(*)}">
        <table border="0">
          <tr>
            <td>Classified</td>
          </tr>
        </table>
      </td>
    </tr>
  </xsl:template>
  <!-- Match all even ROWS -->
  <xsl:template match="ROW[ position() mod 2 = 0 ]">
    <tr class="Even"><xsl:apply-templates/></tr>
  </xsl:template>
  <!-- Match all odd ROWS -->
  <xsl:template match="ROW[ position() mod 2 = 1 ]">
    <tr class="Odd"><xsl:apply-templates/></tr>
  </xsl:template>
</xsl:stylesheet>
```

The stylesheet contains three additional templates that match:

- Even rows with `ROW[ position() mod 2 = 0 ]`
- Odd rows with `ROW[ position() mod 2 = 1 ]`
- Top-Secret rows with `ROW[ DEPTNO=20 ]`

The stylesheet leverages the XPath `position()` function and `mod` operator to calculate the remainder by integer division by two of the current position in the current node list. Rows in even-numbered positions will be divisible by two so they have a zero remainder. Rows in odd-numbered positions have a remainder of one.

Applying this stylesheet produces the results shown in Figure 7-11. This does format the even and odd rows but—oops!—we've just revealed our Top-Secret Department 20 information to users browsing the page.

EMPNO	ENAME	SAL	DEPTNO
7521	WARD	1250	30
7844	TURNER	1500	30
7369	SMITH	800	20
7788	SCOTT	3000	20
7934	MILLER	1300	10
7654	MARTIN	1250	30
7839	KING	5000	10
7566	JONES	2975	20
7900	JAMES	950	30
7902	FORD	3000	20
7782	CLARK	2450	10
7698	BLAKE	2850	30
7499	ALLEN	1600	30
7876	ADAMS	1100	20

Figure 7-11. HTML table with alternating employee rows highlighted

This unexpected result occurs because of the way XSLT resolves conflicts among multiple matching XPath expressions. For rows in Department 20, the XSLT processor considers all the templates that match the <ROW> element in question. If the row is in an even position in the list, it will match both `ROW[position() mod 2 = 0]` and `ROW[DEPTNO=20]`. Similarly, if it's in an odd position in the list, it will match the `ROW[position() mod 2 =0]` template and the `ROW[DEPTNO=20]` template. Unlike the previous example we worked with (when it was clear to the processor that one template was more specific than another), in this case, both templates match a specific <ROW> element name and both templates have a qualifying predicate. Based on the XSLT template conflict resolution rules, neither one is better. In this situation, the processor picks the template that occurs last in the stylesheet. `ROW[DEPTNO=20]` was never selected because it was at the top of the stylesheet, above both the "even row" and "odd row" templates.

Avoiding Template Conflicts with Priorities

The basic scheme for determining which templates are more specific than others is as follows: the generic pattern `*` is less specific than a pattern like *SOMETHING* or *xyz:SOMETHING*, which is less specific than *SOMETHING[predicate]* or *SOMETHING/SOMETHINGELSE*.

But when multiple patterns exist at the same level of specificity, you have to help the XSLT processor by telling it explicitly which templates are higher priority than others. You can assist the processor in this tie-breaking task by assigning a `priority="realnumber"` attribute on your template. The priority can be any positive or negative real number. When no "best" template can be selected automatically by the processor, the template with the highest assigned priority wins. A priority greater than `0.5` makes your template more important than any of the built-in priorities.

So, if we add a `priority="2"` attribute to our `ROW[DEPTNO=20]` template, we make it more important than the even row and odd row templates. When a row with `DEPTNO` equal to `20` is processed, the `ROW[DEPTNO=20]` template will be chosen by the processor. Example 7-8 shows the stylesheet with the priority properly indicated.

Example 7-8. Getting the Right Template to Fire by Indicating Priorities

```
<xsl:stylesheet xmlns:xsl="http://www.w3.org/1999/XSL/Transform" version="1.0">
  <!-- Import all the templates from "TableBaseWithCSS.xsl" as a base -->
  <xsl:import href="TableBaseWithCSS.xsl"/>
  <!-- Match all ROWS in Top-Secret Department 20 -->
  <xsl:template match="ROW[ DEPTNO = 20 ]" priority="2">
    <tr>
      <td align="center" colspan="{count(*)}">
        <table border="0">
          <tr>
            <td>Classified</td>
          </tr>
        </table>
      </td>
    </tr>
  </xsl:template>
  <!-- Match all even ROWS -->
  <xsl:template match="ROW[ position() mod 2 = 0 ]">
    <tr class="Even"><xsl:apply-templates/></tr>
  </xsl:template>
  <!-- Match all odd ROWS -->
  <xsl:template match="ROW[ position() mod 2 = 1 ]">
    <tr class="Odd"><xsl:apply-templates/></tr>
  </xsl:template>
</xsl:stylesheet>
```

Rerunning the example with this modified stylesheet shows us that the result is now what we are expecting, as illustrated in Figure 7-12.

Creating Reusable Named Templates

Next, we'll look at a simple example of formatting numbers to make salaries appear as dollars and cents and we'll refine our strategy for coloring the alternating rows. XSLT includes the `format-number()` function, which allows any element whose value can be converted to a number to be formatted using the

EMPNO	ENAME	SAL	DEPTNO
7521	WARD	1250	30
7844	TURNER	1500	30
Classified			
Classified			
7934	MILLER	1300	10
7654	MARTIN	1250	30
7839	KING	5000	10
Classified			
7900	JAMES	950	30
Classified			
7782	CLARK	2450	10
7698	BLAKE	2850	30
7499	ALLEN	1600	30
Classified			

Figure 7-12. Template priorities at work to produce correct output

number format masks specified by the `java.text.DecimalFormat` class in the Java JDK. We see this function in action in the following stylesheet:

```
<xsl:stylesheet version="1.0" xmlns:xsl="http://www.w3.org/1999/XSL/Transform">
  <!-- Import all the templates from "TableBaseWithCSS.xsl" as a base -->
  <xsl:import href="TableBaseWithCSS.xsl"/>
  <!-- Another technique for alternating row colors -->
  <xsl:template match="ROW">
    <!-- value of class attribute will alternate between "tr0" and "tr1" -->
    <tr class="tr{position() mod 2}"><xsl:apply-templates/></tr>
  </xsl:template>
  <xsl:template match="ROW/SAL">
    <td align="right">
      <xsl:value-of select="format-number(.,'$0.00')"/>
    </td>
  </xsl:template>
</xsl:stylesheet>
```

Here we're again importing the *TableBaseWithCSS.xsl* and including a template to accomplish alternating row coloring, as well as a template matching `ROW/SAL` to override the formatting of `<SAL>` elements that occur as children of `<ROW>` elements. Note that we're employing a different technique to handle the alternating rows in this example. Rather than using separate even row and odd row templates, we use a single `<ROW>` template but alternate the name of the CSS class in use on the row by using an attribute value template:

```
<tr class="tr{position() mod 2}"><xsl:apply-templates/></tr>
```

This constructs `<tr>` elements in the result that will have a class attribute whose value will alternate between `tr0` and `tr1`, depending on whether we're in an even or odd row, respectively. We can add CSS classes in our *Table.css* CSS stylesheet to define the colors we want, like this:

```
body { font-family: Verdana; font-size: 8pt }
  th { background-color: yellow }
.Highlight { background-color: #e7e7e7 }

.tr1  {background-color: #f7f7e7; color: black}
.tr0  {background-color: #f9f9f9; color: black}
```

By building a quickie XSQL page to include *Emp.xsql* and format it with this new stylesheet, as follows:

```
<?xml version="1.0"?>
<?xml-stylesheet type="text/xsl" href="FormatSal.xsl"?>
<xsql:include-xsql href="Emp.xsql" xmlns:xsql="urn:oracle-xsql"/>
```

we can request the page and see the results shown in Figure 7-13.

EMPNO	ENAME	SAL	DEPTNO
7521	WARD	$1250.00	30
7844	TURNER	$1500.00	30
7369	SMITH	$800.00	20
7788	SCOTT	$3000.00	20
7934	MILLER	$1300.00	10
7654	MARTIN	$1250.00	30
7839	KING	$5000.00	10
7566	JONES	$2975.00	20
7900	JAMES	$950.00	30
7902	FORD	$3000.00	20
7782	CLARK	$2450.00	10
7698	BLAKE	$2850.00	30
7499	ALLEN	$1600.00	30
7876	ADAMS	$1100.00	20

Figure 7-13. HTML table showing employees with formatted salaries

If we anticipate frequently needing to format table cells with numeric values, we can further factor our templates for reuse by creating a named template to handle the formatting. We can replace the `match` attribute on the `<xsl:template>` element with a `name` attribute to turn the template into a callable subroutine to be used in any situation requiring a table cell to be formatted as dollars and cents, like this:

```
<!-- "Utility" template to format money is a common way -->
<xsl:template name="moneyCell">
  <td align="right"><xsl:value-of select="format-number(.,'$0.00')"/></td>
</xsl:template>
```

Then, wherever we need to invoke the template, we can use `<xsl:call-template>` to invoke the subroutine by name with the syntax:

```
<xsl:call-template name="moneyCell"/>
```

Named templates are never automatically triggered by the processor; they must be explicitly invoked. When a calling template invokes a named template using `<xsl:call-template>`, the literal elements and `xsl` actions in the named template are instantiated as if they had been included at the current position in the invoking template. This means that the called template sees the same current node as the template that invoked it, in contrast to `<xsl:apply-templates select="`*`pattern`*`"/>`, which changes the current node list.

Like other templates, named templates can be included in a "library" stylesheet that is destined to be imported when their functionality is needed; for example:

```
<xsl:stylesheet version="1.0" xmlns:xsl="http://www.w3.org/1999/XSL/Transform">
  <!-- Handle even/odd formatting of rows using CSS classes "tr0" and "tr1" -->
  <xsl:template match="ROW">
    <tr class="tr{position() mod 2}"><xsl:apply-templates/></tr>
  </xsl:template>
  <!-- "Utility" template to format money is a common way -->
  <xsl:template name="moneyCell">
    <td align="right"><xsl:value-of select="format-number(.,'$0.00')"/></td>
  </xsl:template>
</xsl:stylesheet>
```

We can include both our alternating row coloring and our named `moneyCell` template in this *CommonLibrary.xsl* stylesheet and then import it into the following *FormatSalUsingLibrary.xsl* stylesheet:

```
<xsl:stylesheet version="1.0" xmlns:xsl="http://www.w3.org/1999/XSL/Transform">
  <xsl:import href="TableBaseWithCSS.xsl"/>
  <xsl:import href="CommonLibrary.xsl"/>
  <xsl:template match="ROW/SAL">
    <xsl:call-template name="moneyCell"/>
  </xsl:template>
</xsl:stylesheet>
```

Notice that the `ROW/SAL` template here uses an `<xsl:call-template>` to invoke the common `moneyCell` template's services by name. The result is the same as that produced by our earlier stylesheet, but now we're reusing common templates from two different libraries, including both normal pattern-matching templates and named templates.

At this point, we've got our XSLT feet firmly planted on the ground and we're ready to delve deeper into using the Oracle XSQL Pages facility in the next chapter. We'll see in the many examples throughout the rest of this book that by using XSQL pages together with stylesheets, we can publish any data in any format we need for the Web.

At this point, we've got our XSLT feet firmly planted on the ground and we're ready to delve deeper into using XSLT in combination with Oracle XSQL Pages in the next chapter. Then in Chapter 9, *XSLT Beyond the Basics*, we cover a number

Common Template Errors

As you begin using match-pattern-based templates and named templates together in your XSLT work, a very common mistake is to accidentally type:

```
<!-- My template to match ROWSET/ROW incorrectly -->
<xsl:template name="ROWSET/ROW">
```

when you mean:

```
<!-- My template to match ROWSET/ROW -->
<xsl:template match="ROWSET/ROW">
```

Another related mistake is to accidentally type:

```
<!-- Apply templates matching ROWSET/ROW incorrectly-->
<xsl:apply-templates match="ROWSET/ROW">
```

when you mean:

```
<!-- Apply templates matching ROWSET/ROW -->
<xsl:apply-templates select="ROWSET/ROW">
```

If it seems that your templates are not being triggered properly, these common errors are typically the first thing you should check. To help further diagnose the problem, you can add an `<xsl:message>` element at any point in a template to emit a helpful debugging message. Anything that is legal in a template can be used as the content of `<xsl:message>`.

By placing a strategic `<xsl:message>` element in your template and using the `oraxsl` command-line utility to perform thc transformation, you will see all messages on the console. If you use the optional `-debug` flag when invoking `oraxsl`, you will see helpful line number information for each message as well.

You can use `<xsl:message>` to emit a simple string argument like this:

```
<xsl:message>Got Here!</xsl:message>
```

or the value of any XPath expression, including any variable values:

```
<xsl:message>
  <xsl:value-of select="XPathExpression"/>
<xsl:message>
```

For example, to print out the value of the `<EMPNO>` element, you can do this:

```
<xsl:message>
  <xsl:value-of select="EMPNO"/>
</xsl:message>
```

of important XSLT topics beyond the basics we've learned here, including using XSLT variables, efficient sorting and grouping of information, and a number of basic transformation techniques for XML datagrams. We'll see in the many examples throughout the rest of this book that by using XSQL Pages together with stylesheets, we can publish any data in any format we need for the Web.

8

In this chapter:
- *Introduction to XSQL Pages*
- *Transforming XSQL Page Results with XSLT*
- *Troubleshooting Your XSQL Pages*

Publishing Data with XSQL Pages

Once you discover the advantages of working with database information in XML, you'll find yourself building XML datagrams from SQL statements for many common tasks. In addition to providing XML components that simplify this job for developers, Oracle has anticipated a much broader interest in serving database-driven XML, and has provided an easier route for non-programmers. Using Oracle's XSQL Pages facility, anyone who is familiar with SQL can quickly and easily build XML data pages from easy-to-author templates.

Introduction to XSQL Pages

XSQL pages are templates in **.xsql* files that allow *anyone* familiar with SQL to declaratively:

- Assemble dynamic XML "data pages" based on one or more parametrized SQL queries
- Transform a data page to produce a final result in any desired XML, HTML, or text-based format using an associated XSLT stylesheet

These templates are processed by a common XSQL page processor engine shared by the XSQL Servlet, the XSQL command-line utility, and the programmatic API for processing XSQL pages called the `XSQLRequest` class, as shown in Figure 8-1.

As this chapter will illustrate, you can accomplish surprising things in a declarative way by combining SQL, XML, and XSLT.

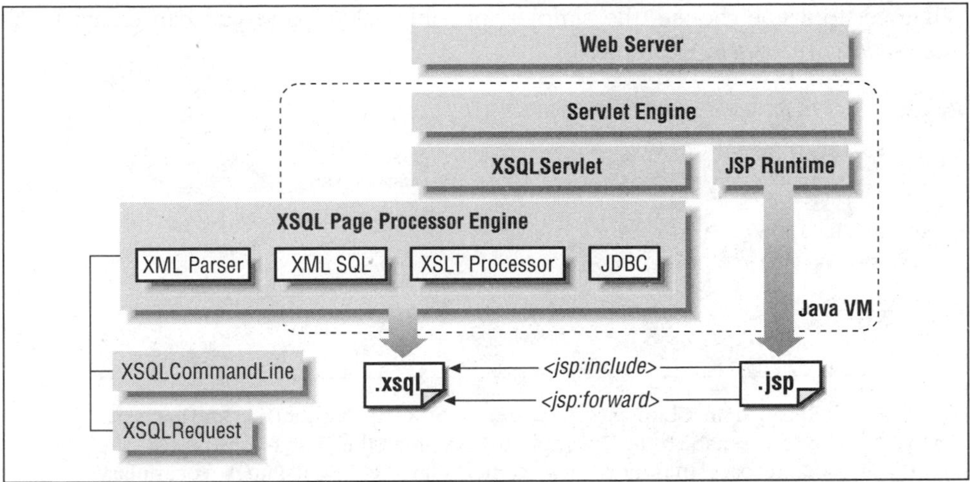

Figure 8-1. Overview of XSQL Pages architecture

As part of the Oracle XML Developer's Kit, Oracle XSQL Pages is included in Oracle JDeveloper 3.1 and is pre-installed and ready to use with Oracle Internet Application Server and Oracle8*i* Release 3. In addition, the technology is designed to work with *any* servlet engine (Apache JServ, Tomcat, JRun, ServletExec, etc.) and can be downloaded from the Oracle Technology Network web site at *http://technet.oracle.com/tech/xml.* You'll find complete installation instructions for using XSQL Pages with several popular servlet engines in Appendix B, *Installing the Oracle XSQL Servlet.*

Your First XSQL Page

An XSQL page template is an XML document that uses `<xsql:query>` tags anywhere you want dynamic XML query results to be included. By convention, the template lives in a file with an *.xsql* extension. To serve new kinds of XML datagrams as new needs arise, you simply build new XSQL pages rather than writing, compiling, debugging, and deploying custom programs or servlets every time. The Oracle XSQL Servlet does the dirty work of handling requests for any of your XSQL pages automatically.

Since XSQL pages are themselves XML documents, you can build them in your favorite text editor or XML editing tool. As we learned in Chapter 4, *Using JDeveloper for XML Development*, Oracle JDeveloper 3.1 is a great choice since it provides color-coded XML syntax highlighting, integrated XML syntax checking, and built-in support for testing your XSQL pages.

Whatever tool you choose, the simplest possible XSQL page you can create looks like *HelloWorld.xsql* in Example 8-1.

Example 8-1. HelloWorld.xsql, the Simplest XSQL Page

```
<?xml version="1.0"?>
<xsql:query connection="xmlbook" xmlns:xsql="urn:oracle-xsql">

   SELECT 'Hello, World!' AS text
     FROM DUAL

</xsql:query>
```

Recall from Chapter 2, *Working with XML*, that **xmlns:xsql="urn:oracle-xsql"** in Example 8-1 defines the **xsql** prefix for the namespace that identifies elements in the XSQL Pages vocabulary whose unique namespace identifier is the string **urn:oracle-xsql**. This allows us to freely and unambiguously mix elements in the XSQL vocabulary with any other XML element in a document. You must include this declaration in your document or it won't be recognized as an XSQL page.

This simple example uses a single **<xsql:query>** tag as the document element of the template. The **connection="xmlbook"** attribute on the document element (not just in any child element) of the XSQL page determines which named database connection to use. The SQL statement inside the **<xsql:query>** tag defines the query to be executed, which in this case will return a single row with a single column containing the literal text **Hello, World!** in a column aliased to the name **TEXT** (assuming that your servlet engine is configured to serve XSQL).

Immediately after saving *HelloWorld.xsql* to disk, you can request the page through a browser using a URL such as:

```
http://xmlapps/examples/HelloWorld.xsql
```

and you will receive the following XML datagram in your browser:

```
<?xml version = '1.0'?>
<ROWSET>
   <ROW num="1">
      <TEXT>Hello, World!</TEXT>
   </ROW>
</ROWSET>
```

If you want to run these examples on your own machine, replace `xmlapps` in the `http://xmlapps/examples/HelloWorld.xsql` URL with `localhost`. If you're working in JDeveloper 3.1, you can save your XSQL page and test it immediately by selecting *Run* from the right mouse button menu in the project navigator. Your local host machine will be used to serve the content from the XSQL Servlet.

If, instead, you're trying this on your own web server, substitute `xmlapps` in the `http://xmlapps/examples/HelloWorld.xsql` URL with the name of your server.

For testing and debugging purposes, or to use your XSQL pages from within command scripts for offline XML data publishing, Oracle provides the companion XSQL command-line utility. Both the XSQL Servlet and the XSQL command-line utility use the same XSQL page processor engine internally, so the command:

```
xsql examples/HelloWorld.xsql
```

produces the same results as requesting that page by URL, making it easy to save the results in a file for inspection or further processing.

Here we returned the raw data page as a datagram in response to the request, but the page can also include a reference to an XSLT stylesheet, like this:

```
<?xml version="1.0"?>
<?xml-stylesheet type="text/xsl" href="HelloWorld.xsl"?>
<xsql:query connection="xmlbook" xmlns:xsql="urn:oracle-xsql">

   SELECT 'Hello, World!' AS text
     FROM DUAL

</xsql:query>
```

This indicates your intention to transform the data page in the server using the following *HelloWorld.xsl* stylesheet:

```
<html xsl:version="1.0" xmlns:xsl="http://www.w3.org/1999/XSL/Transform">
 <body>
  <h2>Server Says</h2>
  <font size="+2" color="blue">
   <xsl:value-of select="ROWSET/ROW/TEXT"/>
  </font>
 </body>
</html>
```

before returning the final, transformed result to the requester. As we learned in Chapter 7, *Transforming XML with XSLT*, the special element `<xsl:value-of>` from the `xsl` namespace makes it easy to plug information from your data page into the stylesheet that acts as a template for your desired output document. So, in this simple example, rather than seeing the <ROWSET> and <ROW> tags from the raw data page, the requester's browser receives a document like this:

```
<html>
   <body>
      <h2>Server Says</h2>
      <font size="+2" color="blue">Hello, World!</font>
   </body>
</html>
```

To the requester's browser, this is just a regular HTML page, so it will be displayed as such. The requester has no way of knowing that you produced this dynamic result by plugging information from your XSQL data page into an XSLT stylesheet. As we'll explore in more detail later, XSLT stylesheets can be used to easily transform the structure of your XSQL page into any other structure you might be looking to deliver: XML of another shape, HTML, or just plain text.

HelloWorld.xsql is the simplest possible example. Your XSQL pages can:

- Contain SQL statements of arbitrary complexity in their `<xsql:query>` tags
- Use the values of requester-supplied parameters in any query
- Include multiple queries in a page
- Control XML generation options on each query
- Transform the output differently depending on the requesting program or browser

We cover all of this and much more in this chapter and even more features of XSQL in Chapter 15, *Using XSQL Pages as a Publishing Framework.* As this simple example shows, the XSQL Pages facility lets you easily serve any data in XML, and easily transform that data into any format required by the requester, cleanly separating the data *content* from the data *presentation.*

Defining Your Database Connections Settings

When you include a `connection="`*`connname`*`"` attribute on the document element of an XSQL page, the Oracle XSQL page processor consults its configuration file, *XSQLConfig.xml,* to determine the actual username, password, driver, and dburl values to use for the database connection. *XSQLConfig.xml* is an XML-based configuration file that is read from the CLASSPATH of the environment in which the XSQL page processor is running. The file contains a connection definition section like the following:

```
<?xml version="1.0"?>
<connectiondefs dumpallowed="no">
  <connection name="xmlbook">
    <username>xmlbook</username>
```

```
    <password>xmlbook</password>
    <dburl>jdbc:oracle:thin:@localhost:1521:ORCL</dburl>
    <driver>oracle.jdbc.driver.OracleDriver</driver>
  </connection>
  <connection name="demo">
    <username>scott</username>
    <password>tiger</password>
    <dburl>jdbc:oracle:thin:@demo-machine:1521:demo</dburl>
    <driver>oracle.jdbc.driver.OracleDriver</driver>
  </connection>
  <connection name="lite">
    <username>system</username>
    <password>manager</password>
    <dburl>jdbc:Polite:POlite</dburl>
    <driver>oracle.lite.poljdbc.POLJDBCDriver</driver>
  </connection>
</connectiondefs>
```

Each connection you want to use with your XSQL pages should be defined in this file with an appropriate `<connection>` element, which should have a unique value for its `name` attribute. Each `<connection>` element should have the four child elements `<username>`, `<password>`, `<dburl>`, and `<driver>`, which provide the information necessary to properly establish a JDBC connection using the indicated JDBC driver class name. If the `<driver>` is omitted, its value defaults to `oracle.jdbc.driver.OracleDriver`, but any JDBC driver is okay to use.

By default, the *XSQLConfig.xml* file is found in the */lib* subdirectory of the XSQL Pages installation directory. If you use JDeveloper 3.1 to edit and test your XSQL pages, you'll also want to edit the *XSQLConfig.xml* file found in the */lib* subdirectory of the JDeveloper 3.1 installation.

It is important that you keep the *XSQLConfig.xml* file in a directory that is *not* browsable by URL from your web server. This means you do not want it in a subdirectory or any directory mapped to a virtual path in your web server configuration file. Failure to check this may allow users to browse your database configuration information, which is definitely undesirable.

Using Parameters in Your Queries

An XSQL page is even more versatile when its results can change based on the values of one or more parameters supplied by the requester. To accommodate this, you can reference the values of any number of substitution parameters in your `<xsql:query>` tag's SELECT statement using the notation `{@paramname}`. Use this notation wherever you want the value of parameter ***`paramname`*** to be substituted in the query. The value of the parameter *paramname* is derived from the first of the following criteria to be met:

1. The value of the URL parameter named *paramname*, if supplied
2. The value of the HTTP session object named *paramname*, if present
3. The value of the XML attribute named *paramname* on the current `<xsql:query>` element, if present
4. The value of the first XML attribute named *paramname* found on any ancestor element of the current query element, if found
5. An empty string

So, as Example 8-2 illustrates, the `msg` parameter can be referenced in the query with `{@msg}` and a default value can be specified by providing a value for the `msg` attribute on the `<xsql:query>` element. If the requester does not provide a value for the `msg` parameter in the request, the default value of `Hello, World!` is used.

Example 8-2. Using Parameters in a Query

```
<?xml version="1.0"?>
<xsql:query connection="xmlbook" msg="Hello, World!"
            xmlns:xsql="urn:oracle-xsql">

   SELECT '{@msg}' AS text,
          TO_CHAR(sysdate,'DD-MON-YYYY HH24:MI:SS')  AS sent
     FROM dual

</xsql:query>
```

If the requester provides a value for the `msg` parameter; for example, using the URL:

```
http://xmlapps/examples/HelloWorld.xsql?msg=Welcome
```

the XSQL page processor produces the result:

```
<?xml version = '1.0'?>
<ROWSET>
   <ROW num="1">
      <TEXT>Welcome</TEXT>
      <SENT>05-SEP-1999 15:11:45</SENT>
   </ROW>
</ROWSET>
```

An identical result is produced if a value for the `msg` parameter is provided on the command line of the XSQL command-line processor using the syntax:

```
xsql HelloWorld.xsql msg=Welcome
```

In Example 8-2, we used the parameter in the SELECT list. You can also use a parameter in a WHERE clause to match a column like the `id` of a doctor:

```
<?xml version="1.0"?>
<xsql:query connection="xmlbook" xmlns:xsql="urn:oracle-xsql">
```

```
    SELECT *
      FROM doctor
     WHERE id = '{@id}'

</xsql:query>
```

This parameterized XSQL page can be used to retrieve information about doctors, given the value of their email `id` in the requesting URL like this:

```
http://xmlapps/examples/DoctorInfo.xsql?id=bproto
```

which returns the datagram:

```
<?xml version = '1.0'?>
<ROWSET>
   <ROW num="1">
      <ID>bproto</ID>
      <FIRSTNAME>Bryan</FIRSTNAME>
      <LASTNAME>Proto</LASTNAME>
      <HOMEOFFICE>French44</HOMEOFFICE>
   </ROW>
</ROWSET>
```

Parameter references like `{@`*`paramname`*`}` in an XSQL page's **`<xsql:query>`** are substituted with their appropriate parameter values from the query string whenever the page is requested. This means you can build a page that uses parameters to provide parts of the query statement, like this:

```
<?xml version="1.0"?>
<xsql:query connection="xmlbook" select="*" where="1=1" order="1"
            xmlns:xsql="urn:oracle-xsql">

    SELECT {@select}
      FROM {@from}
     WHERE {@where}
  ORDER BY {@order}

</xsql:query>
```

This XSQL page allows the requester to control all the parts of the syntax of the SELECT statement. You can use XML attributes with the same names as the parameters to provide defaults in case the requester does not provide a specific value.

Taking the last example a step further, you can build a page that uses a parameter to represent the entire SQL statement:

```
<?xml version="1.0"?>
<xsql:query connection="xmlbook" xmlns:xsql="urn:oracle-xsql">

  SELECT *
    FROM ( {@sql} )

</xsql:query>
```

Such a page allows any requester with the authorization to access the page the ability to return XML datagrams for any SQL statement on your server. This obviously is not something you would want to use on a production system without appropriate authentication. Since XSQL pages can be secured using standard web page security mechanisms, this access can be set up so it is not abused.

Customizing the XSQL Results

The most basic way to get XML results from queries into your XSQL page is to include the text of the desired SQL query between the `<xsql:query>` and `</xsql:query>` tags. Using this technique, each query in the page will produce the following structure by default:

- A <ROWSET> element containing the query's results
- A <ROW> element and a row identifier, for each row in the result set
- A child element for each *non-NULL* column in each <ROW>

The element names for each column in the result set are derived from the column names or column aliases if provided.

Changing element names by aliasing columns

You can use the standard SQL *columnname AS alias* syntax to rename a column included in the SELECT list or to specifically provide a column alias for a SQL expression like this:

```
<?xml version="1.0"?>
<xsql:query connection="scott" xmlns:xsql="urn:oracle-xsql">

  SELECT dept.deptno AS department,
         SUM(sal) AS "TOTAL-SALARIES"
    FROM emp,dept
   WHERE dept.deptno = emp.deptno
   GROUP BY dept.deptno
   ORDER BY 1

</xsql:query>
```

If you include the column alias in double quotes, the alias will be used verbatim; otherwise, names are converted to uppercase. In this case, the double quotes are required, since a name with a dash in it, like `TOTAL-SALARIES` in the following example, is not a valid SQL column name:

```
<?xml version = '1.0'?>
<ROWSET>
   <ROW num="1">
      <DEPARTMENT>10</DEPARTMENT>
      <TOTAL-SALARIES>8750</TOTAL-SALARIES>
   </ROW>
```

```
    <ROW num="2">
      <DEPARTMENT>20</DEPARTMENT>
      <TOTAL-SALARIES>10875</TOTAL-SALARIES>
    </ROW>
    <ROW num="3">
      <DEPARTMENT>30</DEPARTMENT>
      <TOTAL-SALARIES>9400</TOTAL-SALARIES>
    </ROW>
  </ROWSET>
```

Tailoring XML query results

In addition to using column aliasing and parameter values to control the query's XML output, you can also specify values for any combination of the **<xsql:query>** tag attributes in Table 8-1. This allows you to further refine each query's XML results.

Table 8-1. xsql:query Attributes to Control XML Output

Attribute Name	Description
`rowset-element`	Element name to use as a parent for the rowset of query results. The default name is <ROWSET>. Set equal to the empty string to suppress printing an element for the rowset.
`row-element`	Element name to use as a parent element for each row in the query results. The default name is <ROW>. Set equal to the empty string to suppress printing a row element.
`max-rows`	Maximum number of rows to fetch from the query. Useful in combination with an ORDER BY in your query for fetching the top-*N* rows. When used in combination with `skip-rows`, it's easy to implement getting the next-*N* rows from a query result to page through a set of query results. The default is to fetch all rows.
`skip-rows`	Number of rows to skip over before returning the query results. The default is not to skip any rows.
`id-attribute`	Attribute name for the row identifier attribute for each row in the query result. The default is `num`.
`id-attribute-column`	Column name to use to supply the value of the row identifier attribute for each row in the query result. The default is to use the row count as the value.
`null-indicator`	If set to `y` or `yes`, causes a `null-indicator` attribute to be used on the element for any column whose value is NULL. The default is to omit the element in the result for any column with a NULL value.
`tag-case`	If set to `upper`, causes the element names for columns in the query result to be in uppercase. If set to `lower`, causes the element names for columns in the query result to be in lowercase. The default is to use the case of the column name (or column aliases if provided) from the query.
`fetch-size`	Explicitly sets the number of records retrieved in each round-trip to the database for this query. This overrides the default fetch size set in the XSQL configuration file.

For example, using `rowset-element` and `row-element` you can serve a datagram for a list of department numbers and a sum of all the salaries in each department as a `<DEPARTMENT-LIST>` document with nested `<DEPARTMENT>` elements. The XSQL page for this looks like the following:

```
<?xml version="1.0"?>
<xsql:query connection="xmlbook" xmlns:xsql="urn:oracle-xsql"
            rowset-element="DEPARTMENT-LIST" row-element="DEPARTMENT">

  SELECT dept.deptno AS "NUMBER",
         sum(sal) AS "TOTAL-SALARIES"
    FROM emp,dept
   WHERE dept.deptno = emp.deptno
   GROUP BY dept.deptno
   ORDER BY 1

</xsql:query>
```

Requesting this page produces the result:

```
<?xml version = '1.0'?>
<DEPARTMENT-LIST>
   <DEPARTMENT num="1">
      <NUMBER>10</NUMBER>
      <TOTAL-SALARIES>8750</TOTAL-SALARIES>
   </DEPARTMENT>
   <DEPARTMENT num="2">
      <NUMBER>20</NUMBER>
      <TOTAL-SALARIES>10875</TOTAL-SALARIES>
   </DEPARTMENT>
   <DEPARTMENT num="3">
      <NUMBER>30</NUMBER>
      <TOTAL-SALARIES>9400</TOTAL-SALARIES>
   </DEPARTMENT>
</DEPARTMENT-LIST>
```

To suppress the row identifier attribute, and force all of the XML element names to lowercase, we can add the `id-attribute=""` and `tag-case="lower"` attributes:

```
<?xml version="1.0"?>
<xsql:query connection="xmlbook" id-attribute="" tag-case="lower"
       rowset-element="DEPARTMENT-LIST" row-element="DEPARTMENT"
       xmlns:xsql="urn:oracle-xsql">

  SELECT dept.deptno AS "NUMBER",
         sum(sal) AS "TOTAL-SALARIES"
    FROM emp,dept
   WHERE dept.deptno = emp.deptno
   GROUP BY dept.deptno
   ORDER BY 1

</xsql:query>
```

This produces the expected changes in the resulting datagram:

```
<?xml version = '1.0'?>
<department-list>
   <department>
      <number>10</number>
      <total-salaries>8750</total-salaries>
   </department>
   <department>
      <number>20</number>
      <total-salaries>10875</total-salaries>
   </department>
   <department>
      <number>30</number>
      <total-salaries>9400</total-salaries>
   </department>
</department-list>
```

You may set either or both `rowset-element` and `row-element` to the empty string to suppress their output. Doing so can be useful when you know that the results of the query will produce a single row or a single column and you don't need the extra levels of `<rowset>` and `<row>` elements in the resulting document. As an example, the following XSQL page:

```
<?xml version="1.0"?>
<xsql:query connection="xmlbook" id-attribute="" xmlns:xsql="urn:oracle-xsql"
            rowset-element="" row-element="">

  SELECT sum(sal) AS "TOTAL"
    FROM emp,dept
   WHERE dept.deptno = emp.deptno
     AND dept.deptno = {@dept}
   GROUP BY dept.deptno
   ORDER BY 1

</xsql:query>
```

produces this one-element document containing only the `<TOTAL>` tag generated for the `TOTAL` column in the results:

```
<?xml version = '1.0'?>
<TOTAL>10875</TOTAL>
```

When suppressing `rowset-element` or `row-element` in an XSQL page comprised of only a single query tag, you must ensure that your results still generate a well-formed XML document. For example, this XSQL page, which specifies both `rowset-element=""` and `row-element=""`:

```
<?xml version="1.0"?>
<xsql:query connection="xmlbook" rowset-element="" row-element=""
            xmlns:xsql="urn:oracle-xsql">

  /* This query returns one row, two columns */

  SELECT 1 AS VALUE1, 2 AS VALUE2 FROM DUAL

</xsql:query>
```

would generate the following result:

```
<?xml version = '1.0'?>
<VALUE1>1</VALUE1>
<VALUE2>2</VALUE2>
```

This is not a well-formed XML document, since it has two top-level elements instead of the single document element required by the XML specification. Similarly, an example like this:

```
<?xml version="1.0"?>
<xsql:query connection="xmlbook" rowset-element="" row-element="PERSON"
            xmlns:xsql="urn:oracle-xsql">

  /* This query returns two rows of one column each */

  SELECT 'Emma'  AS NAME FROM DUAL
  UNION
  SELECT 'Amina' AS NAME FROM DUAL

</xsql:query>
```

returns two rows but suppresses the `rowset-element`:

```
<?xml version = '1.0'?>
<PERSON>
  <NAME>Emma</NAME>
</PERSON>
<PERSON>
  <NAME>Amina</NAME>
</PERSON>
```

This again, is not well-formed XML. In both cases, rather than returning an invalid page, the XSQL page processor will return an error:

```
Oracle XSQL Command Line page processor
XSQL-014: Resulting page is an empty document or had multiple document elements.
```

If you are building a page with a query that you think should return a single row, you can guarantee that only a single row will be returned by using the `max-rows="1"` attribute on your query tag to avoid this situation.

Using parameters in <xsql:query> tag attributes

In addition to using parameters in the SQL statement for an `<xsql:query>` tag, the values of `<xsql:query>` tag attributes can also reference parameters. This makes it easy for the requester to pass in values for the attributes that control the query's XML output. For example, a page like this:

```
<?xml version="1.0"?>
<xsql:query connection="xmlbook" cat="news" skip="0"
             max-rows="2" skip-rows="{@skip}" xmlns:xsql="urn:oracle-xsql">

       SELECT title,url
         FROM site_entry
```

```
        WHERE categories like '%'||UPPER('{@cat}')||'%'
      ORDER BY id desc

</xsql:query>
```

uses the following `<xsql:query>` tag attributes:

`cat="news"`
: Specifies `news` as the default category for requested headlines

`skip="0"`
: Defaults the value of the `skip` parameter to zero

`max-rows="2"`
: Shows at most two rows of results

`skip-rows="{@skip}"`
: Skips the number of rows specified in the `skip` parameter before returning data

So the following URL:

```
http://xmlapps/examples/BrowseHeadlines.xsql
```

produces an XML datagram showing the first two stories from the `news` category:

```
<?xml version = '1.0'?>
<ROWSET>
   <ROW num="1">
      <TITLE>New XML Content on Oracle TechNet</TITLE>
      <URL>http://technet.oracle.com/tech/xml</URL>
   </ROW>
   <ROW num="2">
      <TITLE>XML.org Premieres As Repository For Schemas</TITLE>
      <URL>http://www.infoworld.com/cgi-bin/displayStory.pl?990526.ice.htm</URL>
   </ROW>
</ROWSET>
```

If we add the URL parameter `skip=2`, then the `skip-rows="{@skip}"` attribute on the query tag will evaluate to 2, overriding the default value of zero. So the result of requesting:

```
http://xmlapps/examples/BrowseHeadlines.xsql?skip=2
```

is the XML datagram showing just the third and fourth rows of the results:

```
<?xml version = '1.0'?>
<ROWSET>
   <ROW num="3">
      <TITLE>Microsoft's Maritz at TechEd on XML</TITLE>
      <URL>http://www.infoworld.com/cgi-bin/displayStory.pl?990524.icmaritz.htm</URL>
   </ROW>
   <ROW num="4">
      <TITLE>IBM XML Translator Generator</TITLE>
      <URL>http://www.alphaworks.ibm.com/tech/xmltranslatorgenerator</URL>
   </ROW>
</ROWSET>
```

Providing a value for the `cat` parameter in the URL allows the requester to request a different category of stories. The following request:

```
http://xmlapps/examples/BrowseHeadlines.xsql?cat=software&skip=4
```

shows the fifth and sixth news stories in the `software` category:

```
<?xml version = '1.0'?>
<ROWSET>
   <ROW num="5">
      <TITLE>Beta 1.5 of Microsoft XML Notepad</TITLE>
      <URL>http://msdn.microsoft.com/xml/notepad/intro.asp</URL>
   </ROW>
   <ROW num="6">
      <TITLE>SAXON 4.2 Released</TITLE>
      <URL>http://home.iclweb.com/icl2/mhkay/saxon.html</URL>
   </ROW>
</ROWSET>
```

Here we've seen parameters in use for attribute values to control the behavior of individual `<xsql:query>` tags, but as a final note to this section, we recall that it's also possible to use a parameter to control the page-level connection. By simply including a parameter in the `connection` attribute on the document element, you can build a page that allows the requester to provide the name of the named connection as a parameter to the request. So, with a page that begins like this:

```
<page xmlns:xsql="urn:oracle-xsql" connection="{@conn}">
```

the requester can provide a parameter like `conn="prod"` or `conn="test"` to select between the production database whose named definition is `prod` and the test database instance whose named definition is `test`. Using the techniques we learned earlier, a default value for the `conn` attribute can be supplied using an attribute of that name on the document element, like this:

```
<page xmlns:xsql="urn:oracle-xsql" conn="prod" connection="{@conn}">
```

This causes the page to default to the connection named `prod`, but allows the `conn="test"` parameter to be supplied to override the default value and use the `test` database connection for a particular request.

Using Multiple Queries on a Page

Our examples so far have all used a single `<xsql:query>` tag as the only element in the XSQL page. However, there is no limit to the number of queries that can appear in a page or to where the `<xsql:query>` tags can appear in the page. The only overriding rule is that the XSQL page itself must be a well-formed XML document: an `<xsql:query>` tag can appear anywhere an element can appear in a document:

```
<?xml version="1.0"?>
<a-query connection="xmlbook" xmlns:xsql="urn:oracle-xsql">
  <can-go-here/>
  <xsql:query> SELECT * FROM table1 </xsql:query>
  <or-here>
    <xsql:query> SELECT * FROM table2 </xsql:query>
  </or-here>
  Or even <xsql:query> SELECT * FROM table3 </xsql:query> here.
</a-query>
```

Conversely, anywhere it would be illegal to put an XML element in a well-formed document is an illegal place for an `<xsql:query>` tag. The following page shows three illegal places for an `<xsql:query>` tag to appear:

```
<?xml version="1.0"?>
<a-query connection="xmlbook" xmlns:xsql="urn:oracle-xsql">
  <cannot go-here="<xsql:query> SELECT * FROM table1 </xsql:query>"/>
  <or-here<xsql:query> SELECT * FROM table2</xsql:query>/>
  <!--
       Ok here, but has no effect in a comment
       <xsql:query> SELECT * FROM table3 </xsql:query>
   -->
</a-query>
<but-not-here>
  <xsql:query> SELECT * FROM table4 </xsql:query>
</but-not-here>
```

An `<xsql:query>` tag cannot appear:

- Inside the value of an XML attribute
- As part of an element or attribute name.
- Outside the document element

Of course it's legal, even useful sometimes, to include an `<xsql:query>` tag inside a comment between `<!--` and `-->` in the page, but when it's inside a comment it won't be executed by the XSQL page processor.

Example 8-3 shows an XSQL page for returning a client's stock portfolio information; it includes `<xsql:query>` tags wherever we need dynamic output inserted.

Example 8-3. Portfolio of Quotes Using Multiple Queries

```
<?xml version="1.0"?>
<client-portfolio connection="xmlbook" xmlns:xsql="urn:oracle-xsql">
  <xsql:query rowset-element="" row-element="">

    select to_char(sysdate,'DD-MON-YYYY') as "effective-date" from dual

  </xsql:query>
  <client>
    <info>
      <xsql:query rowset-element="" row-element="" id-attribute="" tag-case="lower">
```

Example 8-3. Portfolio of Quotes Using Multiple Queries (continued)

```
        SELECT id, name, homeaddress, workaddress
          FROM clients
         WHERE id = {@id}

      </xsql:query>
    </info>
  </client>
  <xsql:query rowset-element="portfolio" row-element="quote" tag-case="lower" >

    SELECT q.symbol,
           q.price,
           q.change
      FROM quotes q, portfolio_stocks ps
     WHERE q.symbol = ps.symbol
    AND ps.owner = {@id}

 </xsql:query>
</client-portfolio>
```

Let's examine a few things that make this XSQL page different from those we've seen previously:

- The page starts with the `<client-portfolio>` element instead of an `<xsql:query>` tag.
- Since it must appear on the *document element* of the page, the `connection="xmlbook"` appears on the `<client-portfolio>` element instead of on any individual `<xsql:query>` element.
- The page uses three `<xsql:query>` tags instead of just a single one.
- The second `<xsql:query>` tag appears nested inside the static elements `<client>` and `<info>`.
- Two different queries in the page both refer to the `{@id}` parameter.

Requesting this page with the URL:

```
http://xmlapps/examples/ ClientPortfolio.xsql?id=101
```

produces the output shown in Example 8-4.

Example 8-4. Results of an XSQL Page with Multiple Queries

```
<?xml version = '1.0'?>
<client-portfolio>
   <effective-date>26-SEP-1999</effective-date>
   <client>
      <info>
         <id>101</id>
         <name>
            <givenname>Tim</givenname>
            <familyname>Jones</familyname>
         </name>
```

Example 8-4. Results of an XSQL Page with Multiple Queries (continued)

```
        <homeaddress>
          <street>301 Ruxpin Road</street>
          <city>Palo Alto</city>
          <state>CA</state>
          <postcode>94301</postcode>
          <country>USA</country>
        </homeaddress>
        <workaddress>
          <street>12 Infinite Loop</street>
          <city>Cupertino</city>
          <state>CA</state>
          <postcode>95014</postcode>
          <country>USA</country>
        </workaddress>
      </info>
    </client>
    <portfolio>
      <quote num="1">
        <symbol>GE</symbol>
        <price>103.50</price>
        <change>0.80</change>
      </quote>
      <quote num="2">
        <symbol>ORCL</symbol>
        <price>27.33</price>
        <change>3.40</change>
      </quote>
    </portfolio>
</client-portfolio>
```

This example is worth examining a little more closely. The first query uses `rowset-element=""` and `row-element=""` to produce a single `<effective-date>` element in the result as a child element of the `<client-portfolio>` element. This technique can be used anywhere a single, dynamic element is useful.

The second query in the page produces an additional, nested element structure for the `<name>`, `<homeaddress>`, and `<workaddress>` elements in the result. This is an example of what automatically occurs when the datatype for a column is a user-defined object type, rather than one of the simple scalar datatypes like VARCHAR2, DATE, or NUMBER.

In this case, since we define the clients table as:

```
CREATE TABLE clients (
  id          NUMBER PRIMARY KEY,
  name        PERSON_NAME,
  homeaddress ADDRESS,
  workaddress ADDRESS
);
```

the user-defined **PERSON_NAME** and **ADDRESS** datatypes are being used and the results automatically reflect the nested structure of their attributes.

If we come up with a simple query over the Oracle Data Dictionary views USER_TAB_COLUMNS and USER_TYPE_ATTRS, we can quickly build an XSQL page like the one in Example 8-5 to examine the structure of any table or type in our schema interactively.

Example 8-5. Describe.xsql Explores the Oracle Data Dictionary

```
<?xml version="1.0"?>
<xsql:query connection="xmlbook" rowset-element="COLUMNS" row-element="COLUMN"
       tag-case="lower" id-attribute="" xmlns:xsql="urn:oracle-xsql">

  SELECT column_id as id, column_name as name, data_type as "TYPE"
    FROM user_tab_columns
   WHERE table_name = UPPER('{@obj}')
  UNION
  SELECT attr_no as id, attr_name as name, attr_type_name as "TYPE"
    FROM user_type_attrs
   WHERE type_name = UPPER('{@obj}')
   ORDER BY id

</xsql:query>
```

We can use this page to confirm our theory about why the extra nested structure appeared in the query over the clients table. By requesting the page with the URL parameter of `obj=clients`, like this:

```
http://xmlapps/examples/Describe.xsql?obj=clients
```

as shown in Example 8-6, we'll immediately see a list of the columns and datatypes for the clients table.

Example 8-6. Column Information for Table with Object-Type Columns

```
<?xml version = '1.0'?>
<columns>
   <column>
      <id>1</id>
      <name>ID</name>
      <type>NUMBER</type>
   </column>
   <column>
      <id>2</id>
      <name>NAME</name>
      <type>PERSON_NAME</type>
   </column>
   <column>
      <id>3</id>
      <name>HOMEADDRESS</name>
      <type>ADDRESS</type>
   </column>
```

Example 8-6. Column Information for Table with Object-Type Columns (continued)

```
  <column>
     <id>4</id>
     <name>WORKADDRESS</name>
     <type>ADDRESS</type>
  </column>
</columns>
```

We can see that the results are as we expected them to be: the user-defined type names appear as the datatypes for the columns NAME, HOMEADDRESS, and WORKADDRESS. Repeating the request to examine the structure of the ADDRESS type:

```
http://xmlapps/examples/Describe.xsql?obj=address
```

produces the results shown in Example 8-7.

Example 8-7. Querying the Data Dictionary for Column-Type Information

```
<?xml version = '1.0'?>
<columns>
   <column>
      <id>1</id>
      <name>STREET</name>
      <type>VARCHAR2</type>
   </column>
   <column>
      <id>2</id>
      <name>CITY</name>
      <type>VARCHAR2</type>
   </column>
   <column>
      <id>3</id>
      <name>STATE</name>
      <type>VARCHAR2</type>
   </column>
   <column>
      <id>4</id>
      <name>POSTCODE</name>
      <type>VARCHAR2</type>
   </column>
   <column>
      <id>5</id>
      <name>COUNTRY</name>
      <type>VARCHAR2</type>
   </column>
</columns>
```

Here we see that the ADDRESS type has been defined to have attributes STREET, CITY, STATE, POSTCODE, and COUNTRY, all of type VARCHAR2. Note that the query in the *Describe.xsql* page used the SQL UNION operator to select information from a combination of the USER_TAB_COLUMNS and USER_TYPE_ATTRS tables. Since a table and a type cannot both have the same name, for any given value of the `obj` parameter passed our page, the query will return either table information or type information, but not both.

Producing XML from SQL with Nested Structure

Let's look more closely at the different ways to produce XML with nested structure. Structured columns can be one of three types:

- Strongly typed, user-defined object
- Strongly typed, user-defined collection
- Untyped collection based on a SQL statement

The underlying Oracle XML SQL Utility for Java natively supports producing richly structured XML from SQL statements that make use of these types, so your Oracle XSQL Pages has this capability. We'll look at two simple examples.

Using user-defined object types

Suppose that you have used the object/relational capabilities of Oracle8*i* to create a user-defined object type called `POINT` using the command:

```
CREATE TYPE POINT AS OBJECT (X NUMBER, Y NUMBER);
```

and have used your new `POINT` type as the datatype of the `ORIGIN` column in your LOCATION table with the following DDL statement:

```
CREATE TABLE LOCATION (
  NAME   VARCHAR2(80),
  ORIGIN POINT
);
```

Suppose further that you have inserted a row into this LOCATION table using an INSERT statement with the `POINT()` constructor, like this:

```
INSERT INTO LOCATION VALUES ( 'Someplace', POINT(11,17) );
COMMIT;
```

Then you can construct an XSQL page like *point.xsql* that does a query over the LOCATION table like this:

```
<xsql:query connection="xmlbook" xmlns:xsql="urn:oracle-xsql">
  SELECT name, origin
    FROM location loc
   WHERE loc.origin.x = {@x-coord}
</xsql:query>
```

When requested using a URL like:

```
http://yourmachine.com/xsql/demo/point.xsql?x-coord=11
```

this page produces the following output:

```
<ROWSET>
   <ROW num="1">
      <NAME>Someplace</NAME>
      <ORIGIN>
         <X>11</X>
         <Y>17</Y>
      </ORIGIN>
   </ROW>
</ROWSET>
```

This demonstrates how the nested X and Y attributes in the POINT datatype structure of the ORIGIN column appear automatically as nested <X> and <Y> elements in the XML output. It is about the simplest example of using a user-defined type to get more richly structured XML output from your object/relational database. In Chapter 12, *Storing XML Datagrams*, we cover Oracle8 object types more extensively as we explore how to use them to model the structure of XML documents to be inserted into the database, and in Chapter 17, *XSLT-Powered Portals and Applications*, we illustrate how to use object views with nested collection types to group master/detail information for a news portal we build in that chapter.

Using the CURSOR operator for nested rowsets

If you have not created object types that contain a predefined structure, you can still introduce nested structure into your SQL queries using the CURSOR operator, which allows you to select a nested rowset as a column in the SELECT list of a query. While almost *any* nested query is legal to include inside the CURSOR operator in the SELECT list, the most useful query selects a nested set of detail rows for the current master row.

Taking the familiar dept and emp tables as an example, the following XSQL page contains a query that selects the DNAME column from the dept table and, for each row returns a nested rowset of the EMPLOYEES from the emp table who work in that department:

```
<xsql:query connection="demo" xmlns:xsql="urn:oracle-xsql">
  SELECT dname,
         CURSOR( SELECT ename,sal
                   FROM emp
                  WHERE emp.deptno = dept.deptno) as employees /* Column Alias */
    FROM dept
   WHERE deptno = {@department}
</xsql:query>
```

Requesting this page:

```
http://yourserver.com/xsql/demo/empdept.xsql?department=10
```

produces the resulting XML data page:

```
<ROWSET>
   <ROW num="1">
      <DNAME>ACCOUNTING</DNAME>
      <EMPLOYEES>
         <EMPLOYEES_ROW num="1">
            <ENAME>CLARK</ENAME>
            <SAL>2450</SAL>
         </EMPLOYEES_ROW>
         <EMPLOYEES_ROW num="2">
            <ENAME>KING</ENAME>
            <SAL>5000</SAL>
         </EMPLOYEES_ROW>
         <EMPLOYEES_ROW num="3">
            <ENAME>MILLER</ENAME>
            <SAL>1300</SAL>
         </EMPLOYEES_ROW>
      </EMPLOYEES>
   </ROW>
</ROWSET>
```

Note that the second column in the SELECT statement is the CURSOR() expression used to select the details. Since it is a column like any other, it can be aliased to the column name **EMPLOYEES** by using the AS COLUMNALIAS syntax as shown above. Since the **EMPLOYEES** column is a nested rowset, it appears as a set of **<EMPLOYEES_ROW>** elements nested within its parent **<ROW>**.

Given the following facts, you can quickly see how structured information can be created on the fly in almost any structure you are looking for:

- One or more CURSOR operators can be used in the SELECT list of any SQL statement.
- One or more CURSOR operators can be used in the SELECT list of SQL statements that appear inside any CURSOR operator (to any level of nesting).
- Virtually any valid SQL statement (including GROUP BY and ORDER BY, etc.) may appear with the CURSOR operator.
- Any SQL statement can be included in an **<xsql:query>** tag in an XSQL page.

This allows you to exploit the processing speed of the database for sorting and grouping instead of having to rely on slower techniques that would attempt these operations on flat data from within the XSLT stylesheet.

By using these query techniques in the **<xsql:query>** tags of an XSQL page, you can combine master/detail XML data pages with the database sorting and grouping. These database operations are applied to the data pages by the SQL engine before *subsequently* applying an XSLT stylesheet to the resulting data page (as we learned earlier). In this way, we can transform the resulting data page into any presentation format you need.

Providing a Fallback Query

Under normal circumstances, if an `<xsql:query>` tag in your XSQL page contains a SELECT statement that returns no rows when the page is processed, the `<xsql:query>` tag is simply replaced by an empty `<ROWSET/>` element with no `<ROW>` elements as children. However, sometimes it is useful to attempt an alternate query as a fallback when the original query produces no rows.

This most often comes in handy when you want to look up some information by an exact match on a parameter value in the original query, and then retry a different query which searches for a fuzzy match using the LIKE operator if no exact match is found. Employing a fallback query in your XSQL page is easy. For any `<xsql:query>` tag in your XSQL page, the XSQL page processor recognizes a nested `<xsql:no-rows-query>` tag as the fallback query to try in case the parent query retrieves no rows. All of the attributes available to control the output of the `<xsql:query>` tag are equally functional on the nested `<xsql:no-rows-query>`.

Consider the *ValidateAirport.xsql* page in Example 8-8. It implements an HTTP-based airport validation service against a database table named AIRPORT containing the more than 9000 airports on the planet and their International Air Transport Association (IATA) three-letter abbreviations. The page includes a single `<xsql:query>` tag that searches case-insensitively for an airport whose three-letter code exactly matches the value of the `{@code}` parameter. Nested inside the outer `<xsql:query>` is a `<xsql:no-rows-query>` that searches for any airports whose description contains the value of the `{@code}` parameter, case-insensitively using SQL's UPPER function.

Example 8-8. XSQL Page to Validate Airport Codes

```
<?xml version="1.0"?>
<xsql:query connection="xmlbook" max-rows="1" rowset-element="Ok"
            row-element="Airport" xmlns:xsql="urn:oracle-xsql">

 SELECT tla "Code", description "Description"
  FROM AIRPORT
 WHERE tla = UPPER('{@code}')

  <xsql:no-rows-query max-rows="4" rowset-element="Error" row-element="Airport">

    SELECT tla "Code", description "Description"
     FROM AIRPORT
     WHERE UPPER(description) LIKE UPPER('%{@code}%')
     ORDER BY 2

  </xsql:no-rows-query>
</xsql:query>
```

Note these highlights in the example page:

- The <xsql:query> sets rowset-element="Ok" while the <xsql:no-rows-query> sets rowset-element="Error". This allows the returned page to signal the success or failure of the exact match while also providing additional information on matching airports in either case.
- The <xsql:query> expects an exact match and specifies max-rows="1" while the <xsql:no-rows-query> uses a max-rows="4" to return the first four fuzzy matches.

Any software that wants to validate the existence of an airport by code can do so over the Web by requesting a URL like:

```
http://xmlapps/examples/ValidateAirport.xsql?code=xml
```

This attempts to validate the existence of an airport with XML as its three-letter code. Surprisingly, this request produces an exact match with the result:

```
<?xml version = '1.0'?>
<Ok>
   <Airport num="1">
      <Code>XML</Code>
      <Description>Minlaton, Sa, Australia</Description>
   </Airport>
</Ok>
```

The 900 residents of this small South Australian town must be quite proud of all the attention their fine airport is now receiving! An attempt to validate an airport code of good using the same page:

```
http://xmlapps/examples/ValidateAirport.xsql?code=good
```

fails the exact match and falls back to the <xsql:no-rows-query> to produce the result:

```
<?xml version = '1.0'?>
<Error>
   <Airport num="1">
      <Code>YGH</Code>
      <Description>Ft. Good Hope, Nwt, Canada</Description>
   </Airport>
   <Airport num="2">
      <Code>GNG</Code>
      <Description>Gooding, Idaho, Usa</Description>
   </Airport>
   <Airport num="3">
      <Code>GLD</Code>
      <Description>Goodland, Kansas, Usa</Description>
   </Airport>
   <Airport num="4">
      <Code>GNU</Code>
      <Description>Goodnews Bay, Alaska, Usa</Description>
   </Airport>
</Error>
```

The requesting agent, which may be a Java program using the Oracle XML Parser or a dynamic HTML page in Internet Explorer 5.0 with its integrated client-side XML parser, can notice that the document element of the returned XML datagram is `<Error>` and can proceed to collect the list of suggested matches for subsequent processing or display to the user. It is worth noting that while any `<xsql:query>` can have at most one nested `<xsql:no-rows-query>`, a `<xsql:no-rows-query>` itself can have a nested `<xsql:no-rows-query>` with no limit on the depth.

Transforming XSQL Page Results with XSLT

Since the data page that results from executing the queries in your XSQL page template is an XML document, and since XSLT offers a robust, declarative mechanism for transforming XML documents into anything else, we can put the two together to achieve a highly effective one-two punch:

1. The XSQL page assembles XML information relevant to the task at hand.
2. The XSLT stylesheet transforms it into an appropriate format for delivery.

We'll look at a few examples in this section that illustrate this approach.

Associating a Stylesheet with an XSQL Page

To associate an XSLT stylesheet with an XSQL page, we use the standard technique prescribed by the W3C (see *http://www.w3.org/TR/xml-stylesheet*), the `<?xml-stylesheet?>` processing instruction. It goes after the `<?xml version="1.0"?>` declaration and before the document element in your XSQL page. It must include as attributes two key pieces of information required to identify the stylesheet:

- An `href` attribute that describes the absolute or relative location of the desired stylesheet
- A `type="text/xsl"` attribute that indicates the type of stylesheet in use

Including an `<?xml-stylesheet?>` instruction of type `"text/xsl"` in your XSQL page causes the XML document obtained by expanding the XSQL page's `<xsql:query>` tags to be transformed by the indicated stylesheet in the server before returning the results to the requester. Only an `<?xml-stylesheet?>` instruction with an attribute of `type="text/xsl"` will be considered for use, since the XSQL page processor supports only this type of stylesheet.

Using a Stylesheet to Produce HTML

A simple example of an XSQL page that includes a reference to an XSLT stylesheet is the following:

```
<?xml version="1.0"?>
<?xml-stylesheet type="text/xsl" href="Bookmark.xsl"?>
<xsql:query connection="xmlbook" xmlns:xsql="urn:oracle-xsql">

  SELECT title, url
    FROM bookmark
   ORDER BY title

</xsql:query>
```

This page queries information about web browser bookmarks from the bookmark table, and uses the following *Bookmark.xsl* stylesheet to format the results:

```
<html xsl:version="1.0" xmlns:xsl="http://www.w3.org/1999/XSL/Transform">
  <head>
    <title>My Bookmarks</title>
  </head>
  <body>
    <h2>My Bookmarks</h2>
    <ul>
      <xsl:for-each select="ROWSET/ROW">
      <li><a href="{URL}"><xsl:value-of select="TITLE"/></a></li>
      </xsl:for-each>
    </ul>
  </body>
</html>
```

This means that in response to the web request:

```
http://xmlapps/examples/Bookmark.xsql
```

The requester won't get the basic raw data page delivered as an XML datagram:

```
<?xml version = '1.0'?>
<ROWSET>
   <ROW num="1">
      <TITLE>Free XML Software</TITLE>
      <URL>http://www.stud.ifi.uio.no/~larsga/linker/XMLtools.html</URL>
   </ROW>
   <ROW num="2">
      <TITLE>Oracle Technet XML Page</TITLE>
      <URL>http://technet.oracle.com/tech/xml</URL>
   </ROW>
</ROWSET>
```

Instead, the requester will receive the following, which the browser will display as shown in Figure 8-2:

```
<html>
   <head>
      <title>My Bookmarks</title>
   </head>
   <body>
      <h2>My Bookmarks</h2>
      <ul>
         <li>
           <a href="http://www.stud.ifi.uio.no/~larsga/linker/
                      XMLtools.html">Free XML Software</a>
         </li>
         <li>
     <a href="http://technet.oracle.com/tech/xml">Oracle
                                        Technet XMLPage< a>
         </li>
      </ul>
   </body>
</html>
```

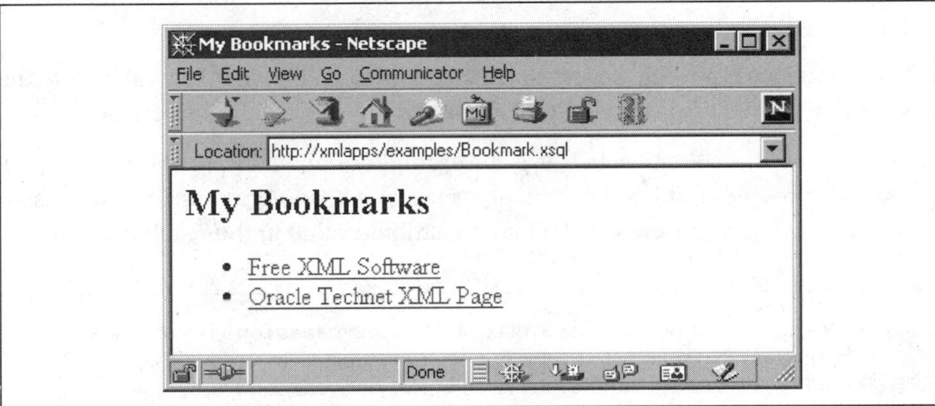

Figure 8-2. HTML list of bookmarks produced using a stylesheet

It's easy to change the name of the stylesheet being referenced in the XSQL page to change the look of the page. If you change the stylesheet being referenced, by modifying the value of the **href** attribute in your **<?xml-stylesheet?>** instruction to refer to a different stylesheet, you can format the same web bookmark data formatted differently in no time at all. Suppose, for instance, that you use this stylesheet instead:

```
<html xsl:version="1.0" xmlns:xsl="http://www.w3.org/1999/XSL/Transform">
  <head>
    <link rel="stylesheet" type="text/css" href="Bookmark.css" />
    <title>My Bookmarks</title>
  </head>
  <body>
    <h2>My Bookmarks</h2>
    <table border="1" cellspacing="0">
      <xsl:for-each select="ROWSET/ROW">
```

```
        <tr>
        <td><a href="{URL}"><xsl:value-of select="TITLE"/></a></td>
        </tr>
        </xsl:for-each>
      </table>
    </body>
</html>
```

Using an example of the desired HTML page as a template, this XSLT stylesheet:

1. Declares the `xsl` namespace on the root `<html>` tag so we can use XSL elements in the stylesheet to loop over data and plug values into the result page
2. Uses `<xsl:for-each select="ROWSET/ROW">` to loop through all the `<ROW>` elements that appear as children of the `<ROWSET>` element, creating an HTML table row and table data tag for each `<ROW>` encountered
3. Specifies the attribute value template `href="{URL}"` on the `<a>` element to plug the value of the `<URL>` element from the current `<ROW>` into the `<xsl:for-each>` loop
4. Uses `<xsl:value-of select="TITLE"/>` to plug in the value of the `<TITLE>` element from the current `<ROW>` as the text for the hyperlink

Note the use of the `{URL}` syntax. It is an example of an XSLT *attribute value template*, which provides the handy shortcut syntax of `{`*`XPathExpression`*`}` for inserting the value of an XPath expression into an attribute value in the result document.

The XSLT attribute value syntax of `{`*`XPathExpression`*`}` is very similar to the syntax for referring to a parameter in an XSQL page `{@`*`paramname`*`}`, but they are used in two different contexts.

The XSLT stylesheet transforms the XSQL data page into an HTML page that uses tables and has a linked CSS stylesheet *Bookmark.css* to be used by the browser:

```
body { font-family: Garamond }
h2 { color: red }
td { font-size: 12pt ; background: yellow }
```

Requesting the page now produces the list of bookmarks with a different look.

We'll learn even more of what you can do with XSLT stylesheets in Chapter 9, *XSLT Beyond the Basics*, but from this simple example you should be able to see that the clean separation of powers between the XSQL page for data and the XSL stylesheet for transformation is going to be big. Really big!

Using a Stylesheet to Produce a Datagram

Besides serving your web bookmarks in HTML for convenient browser access and navigation, it makes sense to serve the data in the XML Bookmark Exchange Language (XBEL) (see *http://www.python.org/topics/xml/xbel/*). XBEL is an XML DTD created by the Python XML Special Interest Group (see *http://www.python.org/sigs/xml-sig/*) to support the automated exchange of web links over the Web.

We can copy the *Bookmark.xsql* page to a new filename like *XBEL-Bookmark.xsql*, replacing the `href` attribute in the `<?xml-stylesheet?>` instruction with the name of an XSLT stylesheet that transforms the XSQL data page into a valid XBEL document:

```
<?xml version="1.0"?>
<?xml-stylesheet type="text/xsl" href="XBEL.xsl" ?>
<xsql:query connection="xmlbook" xmlns:xsql="urn:oracle-xsql">

  SELECT title, url
    FROM bookmark
   ORDER BY title

</xsql:query>
```

We happen to have the *XBEL.xsl* stylesheet, which does just this, lying around:

```
<xbel xsl:version="1.0" xmlns:xsl="http://www.w3.org/1999/XSL/Transform">
  <info>
    <metadata owner="Steve Muench"/>
  </info>
  <folder id="myfolder">
    <title>My Bookmarks</title>
    <xsl:for-each select="ROWSET/ROW">
    <bookmark href="{URL}">
      <title><xsl:value-of select="TITLE"/></title>
    </bookmark>
    </xsl:for-each>
  </folder>
</xbel>
```

Using an example of an XBEL document as a template, the XSLT stylesheet:

1. Declares the `xsl` namespace on the root `<xbel>` tag so we can use XSL elements in the stylesheet to loop over data and plug values into the result document
2. Uses `<xsl:for-each select="ROWSET/ROW">` to loop through all the rows of data in the XSQL data page, creating one `<bookmark>` element for each `<ROW>` encountered
3. Specifies the attribute value template `href="{URL}"` on the `<bookmark>` element to plug the value of the `<URL>` element from the current `<ROW>` of the `<xsl:for-each>` loop

4. Uses `<xsl:value-of select="TITLE"/>` to plug in the value of the `<TITLE>` element from the current `<ROW>` as the value of the XBEL document's `<title>` element

Now, if we request:

```
http://xmlapps/examples/XBEL-Bookmark.xsql
```

it uses the *XBEL.xsl* stylesheet in the server to return the following XBEL document to the requester:

```
<xbel>
   <info>
      <metadata owner="Steve Muench"></metadata>
   </info>
   <folder id="myfolder">
      <title>My Bookmarks</title>
      <bookmark href="http://www.stud.ifi.uio.no/~larsga/linker/XMLtools.html">
         <title>Free XML Software</title>
      </bookmark>
      <bookmark href="http://technet.oracle.com/tech/xml">
         <title>Oracle Technet XML Page</title>
      </bookmark>
   </folder>
</xbel>
```

Using XSQL and XSLT, any tool or program that understands bookmarks in the XBEL format could import any bookmarks from your database using the dynamically produced XBEL document as the exchange medium.

Using a Stylesheet on Static XML Documents

You can use the XSQL Servlet to do server-side XSLT transformation on any XML document. While all of the examples we've seen so far have contained at least one `<xsql:query>` tag and a `connection` attribute indicating what database connection to use, neither of these characteristics is a strict requirement. If the XSQL page processor doesn't notice any `<xsql:query>` tags to process, it moves on to perform its normal server-side XSLT transformation based on the `<?xml-stylesheet?>` processing instruction in your document.

The simplest way to feed a static XML document to the XSQL page processor is to rename it to have an *.xsql* file extension. For example, take Jon Bosak's *dream.xml*, an XML version of Shakespeare's *A Midsummer Night's Dream*, shown in Example 8-9.

Example 8-9. Excerpt from XML Version of A Midsummer Night's Dream

```
<?xml version="1.0"?>
<?xml-stylesheet type="text/xsl" href="shakespeare.xsl" ?>

<!DOCTYPE PLAY SYSTEM "play.dtd">
<PLAY>
<TITLE>A Midsummer Night's Dream</TITLE>

<FM>
<P>Text placed in the public domain by Moby Lexical Tools, 1992.</P>
<P>SGML markup by Jon Bosak, 1992-1994.</P>
<P>XML version by Jon Bosak, 1996-1998.</P>
<P>This work may be freely copied and distributed worldwide.</P>
</FM>

<PERSONAE>
<TITLE>Dramatis Personae</TITLE>

<PERSONA>THESEUS, Duke of Athens.</PERSONA>
<PERSONA>EGEUS, father to Hermia.</PERSONA>

<!-- etc. -->

</PLAY>
```

If you rename the file to *dream.xsql*, then requesting:

```
http://xmlapps/examples/dream.xsql
```

causes the XSQL page processor to transform *dream.xsql* using the associated *shakespeare.xsl* stylesheet and return the formatted results to the requester. Technically speaking, it would be fine if *dream.xsql* had no `<?xml-stylesheet?>` instruction. The net effect would be to serve the XML document for *A Midsummer Night's Dream* to the requester verbatim. Serving a raw XML document using the XSQL page processor with no `<xsql:query>` tags and no `<?xml-stylesheet?>` instruction would only make sense if you intended to introduce either of these instructions into the document later. If no dynamic data and no server-side XSLT transformation are necessary, letting your web server serve the static *dream.xml* page off the filesystem will be faster.

A more mundane use for an XSQL page with purely static XML elements might be as a prototyping technique to put some static XML elements in place—representing information you will eventually query from a database—while you work on the XSLT stylesheets to present those elements. For example, say we start by keeping the menu structure of our web site in a static XML document like the one shown in Example 8-10.

Example 8-10. Static XML Datagram Describing Web Site Structure

```
<?xml version="1.0"?>
<?xml-stylesheet type="text/xsl" href="SiteMenu.xsl"?>
<website>
  <categories>
    <category>
      <name>News</name>
      <icon>news.gif</icon>
      <url>newshome.html</url>
    </category>
    <category>
      <name>Software</name>
      <icon>software.gif</icon>
      <url>software.html</url>
    </category>
    <category>
      <name>Standards</name>
      <icon>stds.gif</icon>
      <url>standard.html</url>
    </category>
    <category>
      <name>Resources</name>
      <icon>resources.gif</icon>
      <url>helpfullinks.html</url>
    </category>
  </categories>
</website>
```

By associating the *SiteMenu.xsl* stylesheet from Example 8-11 to the XSQL page containing the site structure elements, the HTML page for the web site's navigation bar is produced.

Example 8-11. Simple XSLT Stylesheet for an HTML Menu Bar

```
<html xsl:version="1.0" xmlns:xsl="http://www.w3.org/1999/XSL/Transform">
 <head><title>XML Central</title></head>
 <body>
  <center>
   <table border="0" cellpadding="10">
    <tr>
     <xsl:for-each select="website/categories/category">
      <td>
       <img border="0" align="absmiddle" src="{icon}"/>
       <a href="{url}"><b><xsl:value-of select="name"/></b></a>
      </td>
     </xsl:for-each>
    </tr>
   </table>
  </center>
 </body>
</html>
```

Using an example of the desired HTML page as a template, this XSLT stylesheet does the following:

1. Declares the `xsl` namespace on the root `<html>` tag so we can use XSL elements in the stylesheet to loop over data and plug values into the result page
2. Uses `<xsl:for-each select="website/categories/category">` to loop through all the `<category>` elements that appear as children of the `<categories>` element within the `<website>` element, creating an HTML table data tag for each `<category>` encountered
3. Specifies the attribute value template `src="{icon}"` on the `<img>` element to plug the value of the `<icon>` element from the current `<category>` into the loop
4. Specifies the attribute value template `href="{url}"` on the `<a>` element to plug in the value of the `<url>` element from the current `<category>`
5. Uses `<xsl:value-of select="name"/>` to plug in the value of the `<name>` element from the current `<category>` as the text for the hyperlink

Now if we request the URL:

```
http://xmlapps/examples/SiteMenu.xsql
```

the XSQL page processor produces the HTML results shown in Figure 8-3.

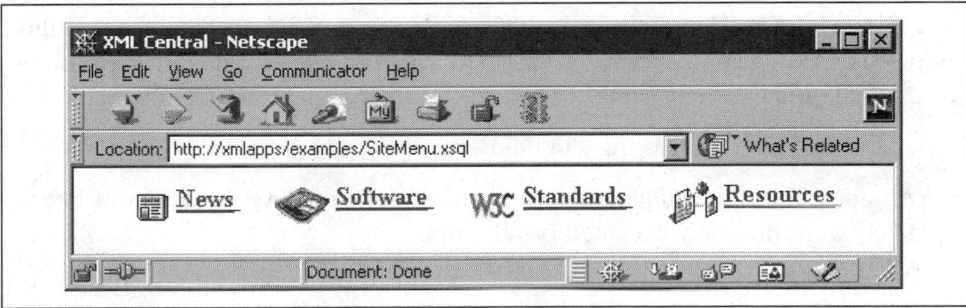

Figure 8-3. Web site menu bar rendered with a stylesheet

If the structure of the site becomes more dynamic later on, you can substitute the static XML tags in the XSQL page with dynamic XML results using the now familiar `<xsql:query>` tag as shown in Example 8-12.

Example 8-12. Querying Web Site Categories from a Table

```
<?xml version="1.0"?>
<?xml-stylesheet type="text/xsl" hret="SiteMenu.xsl"?>
<website connection="xmlbook" xmlns:xsql="urn:oracle-xsql">
    <xsql:query rowset-element="categories" row-element="category"
                tag-case="lower">
```

Example 8-12. Querying Web Site Categories from a Table (continued)

```
      SELECT name, icon, url
        FROM site_category
       ORDER BY pos

    </xsql:query>
</website>
```

By setting the `<xsql:query>` tag's attributes appropriately:

- `rowset-element="categories"`
- `row-element="category"`
- `tag-case="lower"`

the element names in the dynamic results stay the same as they were in the static case, so no changes are required in your XSLT stylesheet.

Offline Publishing of XSQL Pages

We've seen how to use the XSQL Pages facility to materialize data and apply XSLT transformations. If the data used in a page is not changing frequently, you can improve performance by processing the XSQL page offline and serving the static results instead of dynamically transforming the same content on each request. We can use the XSQL command-line utility to process any XSQL page offline to support this style of working where it makes sense. To process an XSQL page offline, simply use the `oracle.xml.xsql.XSQLCommandLine` class and send the output to standard out or to a filename we provide as an argument on the command line.

Command-line page processing can be useful as:

- An automation technique to produce the results of XSQL pages from interactively or periodically executed batch scripts
- A data page "snapshot" technique to deliver an example XML document to a web designer who has no access to a database connection
- An optimization technique to avoid requerying database information that does not change frequently by capturing it as static XML elements

The full syntax of running the XSQL command-line utility is:

```
java oracle.xml.xsql.XSQLCommandLine xsqlURI [outputFile]
```

If you take advantage of the *.\bin\xsql.bat* DOS batch file and *.\bin\xsql* shell script that are provided as a convenience with the XSQL Pages distribution, you can use the shorter command:

```
xsql xsqlURI [outputFile]
```

Both the batch file and the shell script set up the CLASSPATH to contain all of the required *.jar* files, then call Java to run the `oracle.xml.xsql.XSQLCommandLine` class. Note that you may need to edit the path values in the script for the **xsql** script to work in your environment.

You can set the value of parameters your page uses by providing them on the command line in the following way:

```
xsql StatusReport.xsql week=27-SEP-99 title="My Status"
```

If you want to send the output to an output file instead of standard out, the output file comes before the parameters, like this:

```
xsql StatusReport.xsql MyReport.html week=27-SEP-99 title="My Status"
```

Troubleshooting Your XSQL Pages

While you're developing your XSQL pages, if for any reason you receive an unexpected result, the following techniques may help diagnose the problem.

Common Problems for XSQL Pages with No Stylesheet

If your page does *not* include any **<?xml-stylesheet?>** instructions, there are only a few problems that can affect the page:

- If you request the page and receive a result that still has your **<xsql:query>** tags in it, the problem is one of the following:
  - You are running an XSQL page from within the JDeveloper 3.1 environment and have not properly included the "XSQL Runtime" library in your current project's library list. To remedy this, select *Project* → *Project Properties...* from the main JDeveloper 3.1 menu, and select the *Libraries* tab of the *Project Properties* dialog. Click the *Add* button and select the "XSQL Runtime" library from the list to add it to your project.
  - You are running the XSQL Servlet using a servlet engine that has not been correctly configured to associate the **oracle.xml.xsql.XSQLServlet** class to the file extension **.xsql*. To remedy, see Appendix B for instructions on setting this up correctly for your servlet engine.
  - You have used an incorrect namespace URI to define the **xsql** namespace prefix for use on your **<xsql:query>** elements. To remedy, double-check that your namespace declaration is exactly as follows:

    ```
    xmlns:xsql="urn:oracle-xsql"
    ```

- If your returned "data page" contains **<xsql-error>** elements like:

```
<xsql-error action="xsql:query">
  <message>No connection attribute specified on document element.</message>
</xsql-error>
```

you have forgotten to put a connection="*connname*" attribute on the document element of your page. The document element is the outermost enclosing element of the template. XSQL pages do not strictly require a connection attribute; however, if any of the action elements used on the page (<xsql:query>, for example) require a database connection to do their job, you'll get this error message as part of the resulting data page.

- If your returned data page contains <xsql-error> elements like:

```
<xsql-error action="xsql:query">
  <statement>select ename, sal where sal > 50</statement>
  <message>ORA-00923: FROM keyword not found where expected</message>
</xsql-error>
```

  your query has a syntax error that needs to be resolved.

- If your page contains <ERROR> tags like:

```
<ERROR>
  oracle.xml.sql.OracleXMLSQLException:
  invalid character xx in tag yyxx
</ERROR>
```

  your <xsql:query> likely contains a SQL statement with expressions in the SELECT list that have not been aliased to names that qualify as valid XML element names. For example, the following query would produce this error:

```
SELECT 10+20, SYSDATE+2 FROM dual
```

  because the first column's unaliased column name would be the string "10+20" and the second column's unaliased column name would be "SYSDATE+2", neither of which is a valid XML element name. Use column aliases like:

```
SELECT 10+20 AS thirty, SYSDATE+2 AS futuredate FROM dual
```

  to make sure that the column names are legal XML element names.

Common Problems for Pages with a Stylesheet

If your page includes one or more <?xml-stylesheet?> instructions, errors in your data page like the ones mentioned in the previous section can cause the transformation to behave incorrectly. If you request a page and receive an unexpected result or blank screen in your browser, chances are your stylesheet is not correctly matching the structure of the elements in your data page. This can happen because:

- The underlying data page had errors, so the elements your stylesheet was expecting weren't actually in the data page it tried to process.
- The select patterns or {attribute value templates} in your stylesheet contained typographical errors or incorrect path expression.

In either case, you need to take a look at what data page the XSLT engine is seeing when it performs the transformation. If your page does not disallow it with an `allow-client-style="no"` attribute on its document element, temporarily disable the transformation your page is attempting to perform by adding the parameter `xml-stylesheet=none` to the URL requesting the page. For example if you are receiving strange or blank transformation results from a page called *SomePage.xsl*, you can request the page again with the URL:

```
http://xmlapps/SomePage.xsql?xml-stylesheet=none
```

to view the raw data page underneath. After your page is working correctly, you may wish to prevent further client overrides of your stylesheet (including the ability to disable the stylesheet with `xml-stylesheet=none`) by adding the `allow-client-style="no"` attribute to your XSQL page's document element.

Summary of Basic Error Messages

If you receive an XSQL error message, the following information may help you determine what the problem is and what action to take to resolve it:

XSQL-001: Cannot locate requested XSQL file. Check the name.

Cause: You requested a page that the XSQL page processor cannot find.

Action: Make sure the path to the file is correct. As a test, put an HTML file in the same directory and try to request it from your browser.

XSQL-002: Cannot acquire database connection from pool: connname.

Cause: A database error prevented the XSQL page processor from acquiring a connection from the pool of connections it maintains for the connection named *connname*.

Action: This could be caused by a database shutdown or a database resource's being exceeded. Check the connection using SQL*Plus (or some JDBC program, if available, if the problem is specific to JDBC). Contact the database administrator to find out if there are problems with the server.

XSQL-003: Failed to find 'XSQLConfig.xml' file in server CLASSPATH.

Cause: The directory containing the file *XSQLConfig.xml* is not listed in CLASSPATH.

Action: Make sure you have included the name of the directory where the *XSQLConfig.xml* file is located in the Java CLASSPATH of your servlet engine. The way to set the CLASSPATH of the servlet engine is different for each engine, but typically involves changing configuration files or setting the CLASSPATH environment variable before starting your web server. Detailed instructions for setting up the XSQL Servlet properly are included in Appendix B.

XSQL-004: Could not acquire a database connection named: connname

Cause: Your page specifies a value for the `connection` attribute on its document element that does not correspond to a named connection defined in the `<connectiondefs>` section of the *XSQLConfig.xml* file.

Action: Check the value of your connection attribute for typographical errors. If it's correct, make sure that there is a matching `<connection>` entry in the `<connectiondefs>` section of the *XSQLConfig.xml* file. If it's there, make sure that your servlet engine's CLASSPATH is not pointing at some archive or directory containing another *XSQLConfig.xml* file that might be found *before* the one you're looking at.

XSQL-005: XSQL page is not well-formed.

Cause: Your XSQL page does not parse properly because it is not well-formed XML.

Action: This error is accompanied by the specific XML Parser error, including line and character position information, to help correct the error. After correcting the syntax error in your page, request the page again to see the results. You can use the *Check XML Syntax . . .* feature in Oracle JDeveloper 3.1 to check the well-formedness of your XSQL page before attempting to request it.

XSQL-006: XSLT stylesheet is not well-formed: stylesheet.xsl.

Cause: Your XSLT stylesheet does not parse properly because it is not well-formed XML.

Action: This error is accompanied by the specific XML Parser error, including line and character position information to help correct the error. After correcting the syntax error in your stylesheet, request the XSQL page that references it again to see the results. You can use the *Check XML Syntax...* feature in Oracle JDeveloper 3.1 to check the well-formedness of your XSLT stylesheet before attempting to request an XSQL page that uses it.

XSQL-007: Cannot acquire a database connection to process page.

Cause: The named connection referenced in the XSQL page's `connection` attribute was valid, but the attempt to connect to the database using the information for this connection in *XSQLConnections.xml* produced an error.

Action: The specific error should be given in the error message. Check the values of the `<username>`, `<password>`, `<dburl>`, and `<driver>` elements for this connection name nested inside your `<connection>` definition in the `<connectiondefs>` section of *XSQLConfig.xml.*

XSQL-008: Cannot find XSLT Stylesheet: stylesheet.xsl.

Cause: You specified an `href` attribute on an `<?xml-stylesheet?>` instruction whose value references an XSLT stylesheet the XSQL page processor cannot find. Alternatively, if your `href` attribute indicates a stylesheet using an HTTP-based URL, the attempt to retrieve the stylesheet over the Web failed.

Action: Make sure that the path to the file is correct. The stylesheet URI is relative to the location of the requested XSQL page, unless specified as an absolute URL. If you are trying to use an HTTP-based URL, make sure that the address is correct and that you've defined the proxy server settings appropriately in the *XSQLConfig.xml* file if your server sits behind a firewall.

XSQL-009: Missing arguments on command line.

Cause: You failed to provide the minimum number of arguments to the XSQL command-line utility.

Action: Provide at least the name of the XSQL page to process, and optionally the name of an output file.

XSQL-010: Error creating: outfilename.

Cause: The XSQL command-line utility encountered an error opening the *outfilename* file for writing the results of the page processing request.

Action: Check that the directory exists, that you have permission to write in it, that the file doesn't already exist and is read-only, and that your disk has space left on it.

XSQL-011: Error processing XSLT stylesheet: stylesheet.xsl.

Cause: The XSQL page processor encountered a runtime error while processing your stylesheet.

Action: This error could be caused by the use of an undefined function or unrecognized element in the `xsl` namespace in the stylesheet. It is accompanied by the specific error raised by the XSLT Engine to assist in tracking down the problem.

XSQL-012: Cannot read XSQL page.

Cause: The XSQL page exists but an I/O error was encountered trying to open it.

Action: Make sure that the contents of the file are not corrupt and verify the file permissions on your page. Specifically, the page must be readable by the user under which the servlet engine is running.

XSQL-013: XSQL page URI is null or has an invalid format.

Cause: This error only occurs if the XSQL Servlet is used by a servlet engine which incorrectly implements the Servlet API.

Action: Try another servlet engine. The list of supported servlet engines appears in Appendix B.

XSQL-014: Resulting page is an empty document or had multiple document elements.

Cause: You suppressed the default `rowset-element` and/or `row-element` attributes on an `<xsql:query>` tag at the root of your XSQL page such that the resulting XML representation of your query results is not a well-formed XML document.

Action: Use `max-rows="1"` to limit the number of rows or don't suppress the `row-element` and the `rowset-element` attributes if your query returns more than one column.

XSQL-017: Unexpected error occurred.

Cause: An unexpected Java exception was thrown by a user-written action handler or by the XSQL page processor itself. A complete stack trace of the offending statement accompanies the error page.

Action: If the unexpected error is caused by your own action handler, debug the problem using Oracle JDeveloper 3.1's remote debugging feature, as described in Chapter 16, to find out why the exception is being thrown. If the error is thrown by the XSQL page processor itself, report the problem to Oracle Support with a test case that reproduces the problem.

XSQL-018: Unexpected error occurred processing stylesheet: stylesheet.xsl.

Cause: An unexpected Java exception was thrown by a user-written XSLT extension function or by the Oracle XSLT processor itself. A complete stack trace of the offending statement accompanies the error page.

Action: If the unexpected error is caused by your own XSLT Java extension function, debug the problem using Oracle JDeveloper 3.1's remote debugging feature to find out why the exception is being thrown. If it was thrown by the Oracle XSLT processor itself, report the problem to Oracle Support with a test case that reproduces the problem.

In this chapter:

- *Using XSLT Variables*
- *The Talented Identity Transformation*
- *Grouping Repeating Data Using SQL*
- *Sorting and Grouping Repeating Data with XSLT*

XSLT Beyond the Basics

In this chapter, I delve into some of the most common kinds of transformations you will want to do on datagrams. In the process, we'll explore several XSLT features and techniques you can use to perform these transformations.

Using XSLT Variables

This section explains how to use XSLT variables and how to steer clear of some common traps that first-time XSLT developers run into when trying to use them.

What Are XSLT Variables?

XSLT variables allow you to assign a meaningful name to the value of an XPath expression or result tree fragment and to refer to that value by name later. The value assigned to a variable can be any of the four basic XPath data types (`string`, `number`, `boolean`, and `node-set`) or a literal tree of XML nodes.

Defining a variable is easy. You just use:

```
<xsl:variable name="varname" select="XPathExpression"/>
```

to assign the value of the *`XPathExpression`* to the variable named *`varname`*, or the alternative syntax:

```
<xsl:variable name="varname">
  <some>
    <nodes val="xx">
      <here/>
    </nodes>
  </some>
</xsl:variable>
```

If you use the latter syntax, and if the tree of nodes you include between `<xsl:variable>` and `</xsl:variable>` is a single text node like this:

```
<xsl:variable name="varname">Some Value</xsl:variable>
```

then this is equivalent to setting the variable to a string value containing the value of that text node.

A common mistake developers make when assigning a string value to a variable is to use:

```
<xsl:variable name="var" select="MyString"/>
```

This is not syntactically wrong, but it does not do what you think. Recall that the value of the `select` attribute on `<xsl:variable>` is an XPath expression, and that the XPath expression `MyString` selects the set of `<MyString>` elements that are children of the current node. So assuming that your source document does not have any `<MyString>` elements that are children of the current node, the variable `var` will be assigned a value that is an empty node-set. To assign the string `'MyString'` to the variable `var`, you need to include the value in quotes to be treated as a literal string and not as a pattern matching an element name:

```
<!-- Extra enclosing quotes around 'MyString' -->
<xsl:variable name="var" select="'MyString'"/>
```

or you can use the following less error-prone alternative:

```
<xsl:variable name="var">MyString</xsl:variable>
```

Variables can be defined inside a template or at the top level of the stylesheet. If you define a variable at the top level of the stylesheet outside any template, as a direct child of the `<xsl:stylesheet>` element, you can reference the variable in *any* template in the stylesheet. If defined inside a particular template, the value of a variable may be referenced on any sibling elements following the `<xsl:variable>` element that assigned the value, as well as on any descendent elements of those siblings. To refer to the value of a variable when it is in scope, use the `$varname` notation. This example illustrates the variable scoping rules:

```
<xsl:template match="something">
  <a>
    <!--
     | Count number of ROW elements have a SAL greater than 2000
     | and assign to a variable named 'var'.
     +-->
    <xsl:variable name="var" select="count(ROW[SAL > 2000])"/>
    <b><xsl:value-of select="$var"/></b><!-- $var is visible here -->
    <c abc="{$var}"><!-- and here in an attribute value template -->
      <d><xsl:value-of select="$var * 10"/></d><!-- And here -->
    </c>
  </a>
```

```
  <!-- Outside here $var is undefined and will produce an error. -->
  <xsl:value-of select="$var"/>
</xsl:template>
```

As with any language, variables are useful for storing values so you can reference them later one or more times without having to recalculate the values. If the `select` expression used in the `<xsl:variable>` assignment produces a set of nodes as its result, as would an example like this:

```
<!--
 | Select all <error> elements at any level below the current node
 | and assign this list of error nodes to the variable named 'var'.
 +-->
<xsl:variable name="errors" select=".//error"/>
```

then you can use the variable as the first step in a subsequent XPath expression:

```
<!--
 | Select all <code> child elements of <error> elements in
 | the node-set assigned to the 'errors' variable
 +-->
<xsl:for-each select="$errors/code">
```

Before moving on to some more advanced ways to assign a variable its value, we need to understand one final fundamental trait of XSLT variables that can cause confusion for Java and PL/SQL developers. Once an `<xsl:variable>` element assigns a value to a variable, that variable behaves like a constant. Its value cannot be reassigned in the same scope inside a template in which the existing variable is visible. This is similar to how local final variables behave in Java:

```
final String var = "Some Value";
```

or CONSTANT variables in PL/SQL:

```
var CONSTANT VARCHAR2(10) := 'Some Value';
```

The constant nature of variables allows the XSLT processor to perform optimizations at runtime that would not be possible if variable values could be arbitrarily reassigned.

Assigning a Variable a Computed Value

When you assign a tree of nodes to a variable using the syntax:

```
<xsl:variable name="var">
  <!-- Something here -->
</xsl:variable>
```

it is not immediately obvious that you can make use of *nested* XSLT elements inside the variable assignment. At first, this concept may strike you as odd, but the idea has a lot of potential. Using this technique, you can assign an arbitrarily complex computed value to a variable by using any elements that are valid content for an `<xsl:template>` inside an `<xsl:variable>` to construct its value. Inside an `<xsl:variable>` element, literal elements and other XSLT elements instantiate a tree of nodes in much the same way they would when used inside `<xsl:template>`. The differences are as follows:

- Inside `<xsl:template>`, the instantiated nodes are created in the result tree.
- Inside `<xsl:variable>`, the instantiated nodes are created in a node tree fragment that is simply assigned to the variable.

If the constructed tree of nodes consists entirely of text nodes, then the variable is assigned the string value of all the text nodes concatenated together. The following example illustrates this technique. It makes use of the `<xsl:for-each>`, `<xsl:sort>`, `<xsl:value-of>`, `<xsl:if>`, and `<xsl:text>` elements to assign a comma-separated list of employee names to a variable in ascending alphabetical order:

```
<!-- Assign sorted, comma-separated list of employee names to a variable -->
<xsl:variable name="empNameList">
  <!-- Select all ROW children of ROWSET for processing -->
  <xsl:for-each select="/ROWSET/ROW">
    <!-- Sort ascending by ENAME -->
    <xsl:sort select="ENAME"/>
    <!-- Select the text of ENAME into the fragment being constructed -->
    <xsl:value-of select="ENAME"/>
    <!-- If not the last one, add a literal comma and a space -->
    <xsl:if test="position() != last()"><xsl:text>, </xsl:text></xsl:if>
  </xsl:for-each>
</xsl:variable>
```

This assigns a string value like:

```
BLAKE, CLARK, FORD, JONES, KING, SCOTT
```

to the `empNameList` variable.

We haven't seen the `<xsl:sort>` element yet in our XSLT travels, so we'll defer an explanation to later in this chapter, where we cover it in detail. Here we'll just note that it allows you to sort nodes selected by an `<xsl:for-each>`. We also haven't seen the `<xsl:if>` element before, but it shouldn't present any surprises. If the boolean XPath expression in its `test` attribute evaluates to true, then its content is instantiated; otherwise, it is not.

As another illustration of a computed variable assignment, consider the following example; this one assigns `maxSalary` to have the maximum value of `SAL` elements in a `/ROWSET/ROW` node-set:

```
<!-- Select max value of salaries being formatted -->
<xsl:variable name="maxSalary">
  <xsl:for-each select="/ROWSET/ROW">
    <xsl:sort data-type="number" select="SAL" order="descending"/>
```

```
    <xsl:if test="position()=1">
      <xsl:value-of select="SAL"/>
    </xsl:if>
  </xsl:for-each>
</xsl:variable>
```

This example achieves its effect by using a combination of:

`<xsl:for-each>`
: To select a list of `/ROWSET/ROW` elements

`<xsl:sort>`
: To sort the list numerically in descending order based on the value of the `<SAL>` child element in the `<ROW>`s

`<xsl:if>`
: To select only the *first* item in the ordered list

Since the list of `<ROW>` elements is sorted in descending order by `<SAL>`, selecting the value of the first `<SAL>` in the list results in assigning the maximum `SAL` value to the `maxSalary` variable.

We've directly embedded XSL elements inside `<xsl:variable>` to construct a computed value to assign to the variable. It is worth noting that it is also totally legal to invoke a named template like a subroutine to calculate the value. The syntax for assigning the content constructed by a named template `myUsefulTemplate` as the value of a variable `var` looks like this:

```
<xsl:variable name="var">
  <!-- Invoke a named template to construct the value -->
  <xsl:call-template name="myUsefulTemplate">
    <xsl:with-param name="arg1" select="value-1"/>
      <!-- any number of args can be passed
        to the template -->
    <xsl:with-param name="argn" select="value-n"/>
  </xsl:call-template>
</xsl:variable>
```

Conditionally Assigning Variable Values

The conditional assignment of a variable is a fundamental task in any programming language. For example, in PL/SQL:

```
/* Conditionally setting a variable in PL/SQL */
IF b > 45 THEN
  n := 15;
ELSE
  n := 20;
END IF;
```

or in Java:

```
/* Conditionally setting a variable in Java */
if (b > 45) {
  n = 15;
}
else {
  n = 20;
}
```

XSLT provides the <xsl:choose> element, which you can use to perform if-then-else kinds of decisions in a stylesheet, so this is a natural element to investigate for conditional variable assignment. The basic syntax of <xsl:choose> is:

```
<xsl:choose>
  <xsl:when test="BooleanXPathExpression-1">
    <!-- Something here if first expression is true -->
  </xsl:when>
    <!-- Any number of <xsl:when> elements -->
  <xsl:when test="BooleanXPathExpression-N">
    <!-- Something here if Nth expression is true -->
  </xsl:when>
  <xsl:otherwise>
    <!-- Something here if no <xsl:when>'s test expression is true -->
  </xsl:otherwise>
</xsl:choose>
```

Using <xsl:choose> to conditionally assign a variable, as a Java or PL/SQL developer your first instinct would likely compel you to do the following:

```
<!-- Variable n does not exist here since it's not been set yet -->
<xsl:choose>
  <xsl:when test="b > 45">
    <xsl:variable name="n" select="15"/>
    <!-- Variable n has value "15" inside this <xsl:when> -->
  </xsl:when>
  <xsl:otherwise>
    <xsl:variable name="n" select="20"/>
    <!-- Variable n has value "20" inside this <xsl:otherwise> -->
  </xsl:otherwise>
</xsl:choose>
<!-- Variable n does not exist here since it's out of scope -->
```

While this is completely legal XSLT, it is probably not what you intended. It creates a variable n with value 15 that is scoped to the part of the stylesheet tree nested inside the <xsl:when> element where the variable is set. So the variable n comes into existence, but no other element nested within the <xsl:when> element makes use of its value. It dies a silent death, unnoticed. Then within the <xsl:otherwise> a new variable—coincidentally, also named n—is bound to the value 20; however, it meets a similar fate. If the developer tries to reference the value of n outside of this <xsl:choose>, it will be undefined because of the scoping rules we learned earlier.

Rather than thinking of conditionally assigning a variable, in XSLT you need to think instead of assigning a variable a conditional value. An example will make things clear. Here is the right way to assign the variable **n** to the conditional value 15 or 20:

```
<xsl:variable name="n">
  <!-- Conditionally instantiate a value to be assigned to the variable -->
  <xsl:choose>
    <xsl:when test="b > 45">
      <xsl:value-of select="15"/><!-- We either instantiate a "15" -->
    </xsl:when>
    <xsl:otherwise>
      <xsl:value-of select="20"/><!-- ... or a "20" -->
    </xsl:otherwise>
  </xsl:choose>
</xsl:variable>
<!-- Value of n is visible here and will be either 15 or 20 -->
```

Copying Variables to the Result Tree

Before I close this section, I'll point out a common pitfall that developers encounter when using XSLT variables. Once you have assigned a value to a variable, you may want to copy the variable value to the result tree. There are two ways to do this: **<xsl:value-of>** and **<xsl:copy-of>**. Both of these XSLT elements take a **select** attribute whose value is an XPath expression, so both of the following are legal:

```
<xsl:value-of select="$var"/>
<xsl:copy-of select="$var"/>
```

If the XPath expression in the **select** attribute (including the simple **$var** variable reference) identifies a string, number, or boolean value, then these two elements behave identically: they create a text node in the result tree with the value of the expression as its text. The key difference between them occurs when the type of the expression being evaluated is a node-set or result tree fragment, the two XSLT data types that have an inherent structure. In this case, **<xsl:copy-of>** copies the value of the expression to the result tree with its structure intact, that is, *without* first converting it to a string. So to select a list of all XYZ elements into a variable named **var**, and then copy the entire list of XYZ elements to the result tree, you would do this:

```
<!-- Select node-set of XYZ elements into 'var' variable -->
<xsl:variable name="var" select="XYZ"/>
<!-- Then later, copy the list of XYZ elements intact into the result -->
<xsl:copy-of select="$var"/>
```

With these variables now under our belt, let's venture on to meet the identity transformation and learn how many common transformation tasks can be accomplished by extending its basic functionality.

The Talented Identity Transformation

The XSLT identity transformation is a stylesheet that transforms a document into itself. It does this using a single template that matches any node or any attribute (`"node()|@*"`) and whose content is the single `<xsl:copy>` action that copies the current node. Example 9-1 shows what the identity transformation looks like:

Example 9-1. The XSLT Identity Transformation

```
<!-- The Identity Transformation -->
<xsl:stylesheet version="1.0" xmlns:xsl="http://www.w3.org/1999/XSL/Transform">
  <!-- Whenever you match any node or any attribute -->
  <xsl:template match="node()|@*">
    <!-- Copy the current node -->
    <xsl:copy>
      <!-- Including any attributes it has and any child nodes -->
      <xsl:apply-templates select="@*|node()"/>
    </xsl:copy>
  </xsl:template>
</xsl:stylesheet>
```

The `<xsl:copy>` action copies the current node and its namespaces; however, by default it doesn't copy any of the current node's attributes or child nodes. You indicate which attributes and child nodes should be copied by instantiating them in the body of the `<xsl:copy>` element. In the case of the identity transformation, the template selects all attributes and all child nodes to be included recursively.

Renaming and Suppressing Elements

Whenever you want to make global changes to a document but leave its fundamental structure intact, the identity transformation is a great place to start. By importing the *Identity.xsl* stylesheet into your new transformation, you can provide additional templates that effect the changes you want, while the identity transformation's `match="node()|@*"` template copies the rest of the structure intact.

For example, consider the following simple *ItemList.xml* document:

```
<ItemList>
  <Item Id="1234" Color="Red">
    <Description>Singular Red Hat</Description>
    <Price>15.00</Price>
  </Item>
  <Item Id="9876" Color="Blue">
    <Description>Blue Jeans</Description>
    <Price>25.00</Price>
  </Item>
</ItemList>
```

If you want to rename all elements named `<Description>` to `<Name>`, you can build a stylesheet like this:

```
<!-- Rename.xsl: Rename <Description> to <Name> -->
<xsl:stylesheet version="1.0" xmlns:xsl="http://www.w3.org/1999/XSL/Transform">
  <!-- Import the identity transformation. -->
  <xsl:import href="Identity.xsl"/>
  <!-- Whenever you match a Description, construct a Name -->
  <xsl:template match="Description">
    <Name><xsl:apply-templates select="@*|node()"/></Name>
  </xsl:template>
</xsl:stylesheet>
```

Given *ItemList.xml* above as the source, this transformation produces:

```
<ItemList>
  <Item Id="1234" Color="Red">
    <Name>Singular Red Hat</Name>
    <Price>15.00</Price>
  </Item>
  <Item Id="9876" Color="Blue">
    <Name>Blue Jeans</Name>
    <Price>25.00</Price>
  </Item>
</ItemList>
```

To rename many elements, just include more templates. The stylesheet in Example 9-2, for example, renames all of the elements and attributes into Italian.

Example 9-2. Renaming Multiple Elements into Another Language

```
<!-- RenameIntoItalian.xsl: Rename elements and attributes into Italian -->
<xsl:stylesheet version="1.0" xmlns:xsl="http://www.w3.org/1999/XSL/Transform">
  <!-- Import the identity transformation. -->
  <xsl:import href="Identity.xsl"/>
  <!-- Translate all elements into their Italian equivalents -->
  <xsl:template match="ItemList">
    <ListaArticoli><xsl:apply-templates select="@*|node()"/></ListaArticoli>
  </xsl:template>
  <xsl:template match="Item">
    <Articolo><xsl:apply-templates select="@*|node()"/></Articolo>
  </xsl:template>
  <xsl:template match="Description">
    <Descrizione><xsl:apply-templates select="@*|node()"/></Descrizione>
  </xsl:template>
  <xsl:template match="Price">
    <Prezzo><xsl:apply-templates select="@*|node()"/></Prezzo>
  </xsl:template>
  <xsl:template match="@Color">
    <xsl:attribute name="Colore">
      <xsl:value-of select="."/>
    </xsl:attribute>
  </xsl:template>
</xsl:stylesheet>
```

When applied to *ItemList.xml*, this stylesheet produces the following:

```
<ListaArticoli>
  <Articolo Id="1234" Colore="Red">
    <Descrizione>Singular Red Hat</Descrizione>
    <Prezzo>15.00</Prezzo>
  </Articolo>
  <Articolo Id="9876" Colore="Blue">
    <Descrizione>Blue Jeans</Descrizione>
    <Prezzo>25.00</Prezzo>
  </Articolo>
</ListaArticoli>
```

You can build a stylesheet to suppress certain elements and attributes as well. The next stylesheet suppresses the `Color` attribute and the `<Price>` element by including a template that matches these, but with no template body:

```
<!-- NoPriceColor.xsl: Suppress Color attribute and Price Element -->
<xsl:stylesheet version="1.0" xmlns:xsl="http://www.w3.org/1999/XSL/Transform">
  <!-- Import the identity transformation. -->
  <xsl:import href="Identity.xsl"/>
  <!-- Strip text nodes that are all whitespace -->
  <xsl:strip-space elements="*"/>
  <!-- Indent the result -->
  <xsl:output indent="yes"/>
  <!-- Whenever you match a Color attribute or Price element, do nothing -->
  <xsl:template match="@Color|Price"/>
</xsl:stylesheet>
```

To avoid having blank slots in the result where whitespace was copied to the result tree but an element like `<Price>` was removed, we can use `<xsl:strip-space>` to disregard all extraneous whitespace in the source tree. We can still get nicely indented output by adding an `<xsl:output>` with `indent="yes"`. This produces:

```
<ItemList>
   <Item Id="1234">
      <Description>Singular Red Hat</Description>
   </Item>
   <Item Id="9876">
      <Description>Blue Jeans</Description>
   </Item>
</ItemList>
```

Adding and Stripping Whitespace

While on the subject of indenting, let me mention that you can build a stylesheet that will indent any existing XML document that might be missing whitespace with the stylesheet:

```
<!-- Indent.xsl: Indents the source datagram -->
<xsl:stylesheet version="1.0" xmlns:xsl="http://www.w3.org/1999/XSL/Transform">
  <!-- Import the identity transformation. -->
  <xsl:import href="Identity.xsl"/>
```

```
  <!-- Strip text nodes that are all whitespace -->
  <xsl:strip-space elements="*"/>
  <!-- Indent the result -->
  <xsl:output indent="yes"/>
</xsl:stylesheet>
```

This would transform a document like:

```
<a><b><c/></b></a>
```

into:

```
<a>
  <b>
    <c/>
  </b>
</a>
```

With the reverse strategy, we have a stylesheet that removes whitespace:

```
<!-- RemoveWhitespace.xsl: Removes extraneous whitespace from source doc -->
<xsl:stylesheet version="1.0" xmlns:xsl="http://www.w3.org/1999/XSL/Transform">
  <!-- Import the identity transformation. -->
  <xsl:import href="Identity.xsl"/>
  <!-- Strip text nodes that are all whitespace -->
  <xsl:strip-space elements="*"/>
  <!-- Indent the result -->
  <xsl:output indent="no"/>
</xsl:stylesheet>
```

This transforms our *ItemList.xml* document into:

```
<ItemList><Item Id="1234" Color="Red"><Description>Singular Red Hat</Description>
<Price>15.00</Price></Item><Item Id="9876" Color="Blue"><Description>Blue Jeans</
Description><Price>25.00</Price></Item></ItemList>
```

Converting Between Elements and Attributes

We could write a stylesheet to transform all subelements of `<Item>` into attributes on `<Item>` instead:

```
<!-- ItemChildrenToAttributes.xsl: Turn subelements of Item into attributes -->
<xsl:stylesheet version="1.0" xmlns:xsl="http://www.w3.org/1999/XSL/Transform">
  <!-- Import the identity transformation. -->
  <xsl:import href="Identity.xsl"/>
  <xsl:template match="Item">
    <xsl:copy>
      <xsl:apply-templates select="@*|*"/>
    </xsl:copy>
  </xsl:template>
  <xsl:template match="Item/*">
    <xsl:attribute name="{name(.)}">
      <xsl:value-of select="."/>
    </xsl:attribute>
  </xsl:template>
</xsl:stylesheet>
```

One template matches `<Item>` and copies it, selecting attributes and children elements as the content to include. The other template matches an element under `<Item>` and uses `<xsl:attribute>` to construct an attribute whose name is dynamically assigned. `name="{name(.)}"` uses an attribute value template to set the attribute's `name` being created to the name of the current node. This turns *ItemList.xml* into:

```
<ItemList>
  <Item Id="1234" Color="Red" Description="Singular Red Hat" Price="15.00"/>
  <Item Id="9876" Color="Blue" Description="Blue Jeans" Price="25.00"/>
</ItemList>
```

To do the reverse, here's the *AttrToElement.xsl* stylesheet, which turns attributes into elements:

```
<!-- AttrToElement.xsl: Turn all attributes into subelements -->
<xsl:stylesheet xmlns:xsl="http://www.w3.org/1999/XSL/Transform" version="1.0">
  <!-- Import the identity transformation. -->
  <xsl:import href="Identity.xsl"/>
  <xsl:strip-space elements="*"/>
  <xsl:output indent="yes"/>
  <!-- Match any Attribute and turn it into an element -->
  <xsl:template match="@*">
    <xsl:element name="{name(.)}"><xsl:value-of select="."/></xsl:element>
  </xsl:template>
</xsl:stylesheet>
```

Its template matches any attribute `@*` and uses `<xsl:element>` to construct an element with a dynamically assigned name. The `name="{name(.)}"` on `<xsl:element>` uses an attribute value template to set the `name` of the element being created to the `name(.)` of the current node. This transforms *ItemList.xml* into:

```
<ItemList>
   <Item>
      <Id>1234</Id>
      <Color>Red</Color>
      <Description>Singular Red Hat</Description>
      <Price>15.00</Price>
   </Item>
   <Item>
      <Id>9876</Id>
      <Color>Blue</Color>
      <Description>Blue Jeans</Description>
      <Price>25.00</Price>
   </Item>
</ItemList>
```

Annotating Elements in the Source Tree

So far, we've employed very simple XPath expressions in our templates that augment the identity transformation. Your templates can use more specific XPath expressions containing predicates to affect only certain elements in the source. For example, the following stylesheet adds an **<OnSale>** element to any **<Item>** whose **Color** is **Red** and whose **Price** is under $20.00:

```
<!-- MarkcheapRedItemsOnSale.xsl: Adds <OnSale> to Red items under $20.00 -->
<xsl:stylesheet version="1.0" xmlns:xsl="http://www.w3.org/1999/XSL/Transform">
  <!-- Import the identity transformation. -->
  <xsl:import href="Identity.xsl"/>
  <!-- Strip text nodes that are all whitespace -->
  <xsl:strip-space elements="*"/>
  <!-- Indent the result -->
  <xsl:output indent="yes"/>
  <xsl:template match="Item[@Color='Red' and 20 > Price]">
    <xsl:copy>
      <!-- First copy Item's attributes -->
      <xsl:apply-templates select="@*"/>
      <!-- Then add a literal <OnSale> element -->
      <OnSale/>
      <!-- Then copy the rest of any children nodes -->
      <xsl:apply-templates select="node()"/>
    </xsl:copy>
  </xsl:template>
</xsl:stylesheet>
```

This transforms *ItemList.xml* into:

```
<ItemList>
   <Item Id="1234" Color="Red">
      <OnSale/>
      <Description>Singular Red Hat</Description>
      <Price>15.00</Price>
   </Item>
   <Item Id="9876" Color="Blue">
      <Description>Blue Jeans</Description>
      <Price>25.00</Price>
   </Item>
</ItemList>
```

Note that in **match="Item[@Color='Red' and 20 > Price]"** above we use **20 > Price** instead of **Price < 20**. They are equivalent, but using **Price < 20** would mean having to escape the less-than sign as **<** in the attribute value.

Performing Value Lookups

Sometimes you need to transform a source document and translate data within it using some form of a lookup table. These kinds of transformations are easy to do using the XSLT **document()** function that gives you access to the node tree of another XML source tree during the transformation. Using `document()`, it is possible to select additional source nodes from:

- An external XML file
- A URL returning an XML document
- The stylesheet source tree itself

`document()` takes a string argument that is a URI of another XML resource. The XSLT processor reads that resource and parses it as an XML document into its source tree, then returns a node-set containing the root node of that new, external source tree. Typically, the string value passed to the `document()` function will either be a relative URL—interpreted as relative to the stylesheet containing the node where the `document()` function appears in an expression—or an absolute URL. The external resource is retrieved only once per transformation.

Consider a simple `<TripReports>` document like this:

```
<TripReports>
  <Report>
    <Purpose>102</Purpose>
    <Comment>Flight was late. Peanuts were ok.</Comment>
  </Report>
  <Report>
    <Purpose>101</Purpose>
    <Comment>Food was actually good. Coffee was piping hot</Comment>
  </Report>
</TripReports>
```

Imagine that we need to transform the numerical value of the `<Purpose>` code in this source document into a textual equivalent via a lookup table contained in an external XML document, like this *TripReportLookup.xml* document:

```
<!-- TripReportLookup.xml -->
<Lookup>
   <Msg id="101">
      <Text lang="it">Vacanze</Text>
      <Text lang="en">Vacation</Text>
   </Msg>
   <Msg id="102">
      <Text lang="it">Affari</Text>
      <Text lang="en">Work</Text>
   </Msg>
</Lookup>
```

The lookup document contains text messages keyed by their message ID. Multiple languages are included so that a transformation can request the text version of a particular purpose code in either English or Italian. The *TranslateTripCode.xsl* stylesheet in Example 9-3 provides a top-level stylesheet parameter to indicate the language into which the purpose codes should be translated, defaulting to the value `en` for English. As a convenience, it selects the root node of the external lookup document into the `codes` variable.

Example 9-3. Looking Up External Information During a Transformation

```
<!-- TranslateTripCode.xsl: Lookup Codes from external file -->
<xsl:stylesheet version="1.0" xmlns:xsl="http://www.w3.org/1999/XSL/Transform">
  <!-- Import the identity transformation. -->
  <xsl:import href="Identity.xsl"/>
  <!-- Parameterize language for lookup code translation, default to "en" -->
  <xsl:param name="lang" select="'en'"/>
  <!-- Select root node of external document into "codes" variable -->
  <xsl:variable name="codes" select="document('TripReportLookup.xml')"/>
  <!--
   | Whenever you match a Purpose element, replace numeric value by
   | lookup up codes from external file.
   +-->
  <xsl:template match="Purpose">
    <xsl:copy>
      <xsl:value-of select="$codes/Lookup/Msg[@id=current()]/Text[@lang=$lang]"/>
    </xsl:copy>
  </xsl:template>
</xsl:stylesheet>
```

The template that matches `<Purpose>` uses `<xsl:copy>` to copy the `<Purpose>` element, and the content of the `<xsl:copy>` includes an `<xsl:value-of>` to select the text child node of `<Purpose>` in the result. The `select` expression used by this `<xsl:value-of>` illustrates two concepts we have not seen yet:

- If you select a node-set into a variable, then you can use the node-set variable directly as the root of an XPath expression.
- You can use the XSLT `current()` function to refer to the node that is the current node.

The expression here:

```
$codes/Lookup/Msg[@id=current()]/Text[@lang=$lang]
```

selects the `<Msg>` element having an `id` attribute equal to the value of the current node—that is, the current `<Purpose>` element—then selects the `<Text>` child of the `<Msg>` identified in the previous step whose `lang` attribute is equal to the value of the `$lang` parameter. The result is that the `<Text>` element for the `<Msg>` corresponding to the current `<Purpose>` element's numerical code value is returned in the proper language.

We find the `current()` function handy here because using the `.` inside square brackets to represent the current node does not do what we want. For example, suppose the previous expression were written like this:

```
$codes/Lookup/Msg[@id=.]/Text[@lang=$lang]
```

This would look for the `<Msg>` element whose `id` attribute was equal to the value of the `<Msg>` element. Within the square brackets, the node being qualified is the current node *inside the predicate*. The `current()` function, on the other hand, always returns a node-set containing the current node as it was at the *start* of the current expression.

Note the use of a top-level `<xsl:param>` element, which defines a top-level stylesheet parameter. As we'll see in many examples in Chapter 17, *XSLT-Powered Portals and Applications*, parameters—like variables—can be defined inside individual templates or as top-level items. The key difference between XSLT variables and parameters is that the value assigned to a parameter acts as the default value, which can be overridden by the caller. If the `<xsl:param>` appears in a template, then by invoking the template with `<xsl:call-template>` or `<xsl:apply-templates>`, you can use the optional `<xsl:with-param>` element to pass a specific value for the parameter. If the `<xsl:param>` appears at the top level, the XSLT 1.0 specification provides a processor-specific way to assign these stylesheet-level parameters. The `oraxsl` command-line utility supports a `-p` flag that allows one or more command-line arguments to be passed to assign values to stylesheet parameters. The `XSLStylesheet` object supports similar APIs to allow the same thing to be done programmatically.

We can try out the transformation with `oraxsl`:

```
oraxsl TripReports.xml TranslateTripCode.xsl
```

which produces the result:

```
<TripReports>
  <Report>
    <Purpose>Work</Purpose>
    <Comment>Flight was late. Peanuts were ok.</Comment>
  </Report>
  <Report>
    <Purpose>Vacation</Purpose>
    <Comment>Food was actually good. Coffee was piping hot</Comment>
  </Report>
</TripReports>
```

If we pass a different value for the top-level stylesheet parameter as follows:

```
oraxsl -p lang='it' TripReports.xml TranslateTripCode.xsl
```

the result document has the lookup code translate values into Italian instead of English:

```
<TripReports>
  <Report>
    <Purpose>Affari</Purpose>
    <Comment>Flight was late. Peanuts were ok.</Comment>
  </Report>
```

```
    <Report>
      <Purpose>Vacanze</Purpose>
      <Comment>Food was actually good. Coffee was piping hot</Comment>
    </Report>
  </TripReports>
```

As an alternative, you can store lookup information in the stylesheet itself, and use the `document('')` function with an empty string argument to refer to the root of the stylesheet document. This technique can avoid rereading the external "lookup" document on each run of the stylesheet if your applications cache stylesheets—as the XSQL Servlet does for you. You can use the XPath expression:

```
document('')/xsl:stylesheet/m:Lookup
```

Refer to the `<m:Lookup>` element embedded in the stylesheet as a child of the `<xsl:stylesheet>` document element. Elements appearing at the top level of a stylesheet must be qualified with a namespace other than the XSLT namespace. The stylesheet in Example 9-4 performs the same lookup functionality as the *TranslateTripCode.xsl* stylesheet in Example 9-3.

Example 9-4. Embedding Lookup Information Inside the Stylesheet Itself

```
<!-- TranslateTripCodeInternal.xsl: Lookup Codes from inside stylesheet -->
<xsl:stylesheet version="1.0" xmlns:xsl="http://www.w3.org/1999/XSL/Transform"
                              xmlns:m="temp">
  <!-- Import the identity transformation. -->
  <xsl:import href="Identity.xsl"/>
  <!-- Parameterize language for lookup code translation, default to "en" -->
  <xsl:param name="lang" select="'en'"/>
  <!-- Select root node of stylesheet lookup codes  -->
  <xsl:variable name="codes" select="document('')/xsl:stylesheet/m:Lookup"/>
  <!--
   | Whenever you match a Purpose element, replace numeric value by
   | lookup up codes from external file.
   +-->
  <xsl:template match="Purpose">
    <xsl:copy>
      <xsl:value-of
         select="$codes/m:Msg[@id=current()]/m:Text[@lang=$lang]"/>
    </xsl:copy>
  </xsl:template>

  <!-- Lookup Codes inside the stylesheet must be qualified by a namespace -->
  <m:Lookup>
     <m:Msg id="101">
        <m:Text lang="it">Vacanze</m:Text>
        <m:Text lang="en">Vacation</m:Text>
     </m:Msg>
     <m:Msg id="102">
        <m:Text lang="it">Affari</m:Text>
        <m:Text lang="en">Work</m:Text>
     </m:Msg>
  </m:Lookup>
</xsl:stylesheet>
```

So we've seen that by using simple templates to augment the identity transformation, we can do lots of very interesting kinds of transformations.

Grouping Repeating Data Using SQL

One of the most common questions developers learning XSLT ask is, "How can I use XSLT to group repeating information?" In this section, we'll learn how to exploit the database to do the bulk of the grouping and sorting for us, and then use XSLT to format the information. In situations where you don't have the luxury of formulating the database query yourself—for example, if you receive the XML document from a business partner—you still need to perform grouping and sorting. In the following section, we outline techniques for performing the grouping in your stylesheet, including a state-of-the-art approach that uses XSLT "keys" like database indexes to increase by an order of magnitude the speed of traditional pure XSLT grouping techniques. Either way, by the end of this chapter, you'll be aware of all the grouping approaches available and which is best for the task at hand.

Multilevel Grouping with CURSOR Expressions

If we are producing XML documents from SQL query results, we can leverage the native grouping functionality provided by Oracle to deliver the results straight from the database grouped the way we want. Let's start with a simple XSQL page that queries information about software bugs and the developer who is assigned to fix them:

```
<xsql:query connection="xmlbook" rowset-element="open-bugs" row-element="bug"
            id-attribute="" tag-case="lower" xmlns:xsql="urn:oracle-xsql" >

  SELECT ID,ABSTRACT,OWNER,PRIORITY FROM BUG
  ORDER BY PRIORITY

</xsql:query>
```

Requesting this XSQL page produces a result like the one shown in Example 9-5.

Example 9-5. Result from XSQL Bug Query Page

```
<open-bugs>
   <bug>
      <id>10677</id>
      <abstract>NullPointerException Entering Blank Name Value</abstract>
      <owner>rjust</owner>
      <priority>1</priority>
   </bug>
   <bug>
      <id>11601</id>
      <abstract>Expanding Node Makes Project Tree Flicker</abstract>
      <owner>echan</owner>
```

Example 9-5. Result from XSQL Bug Query Page (continued)

```
      <priority>2</priority>
   </bug>

   <!-- etc. -->

   <bug>
      <id>10445</id>
      <abstract>Resizing Methods Panel Doesn't Resize Control</abstract>
      <owner>rjust</owner>
      <priority>3</priority>
   </bug>
</open-bugs>
```

Suppose that instead of this flat list of <bug>s and assigned <owner>s we would like the output to be grouped by developer, showing each distinct owner and a nested list of the bugs assigned to that developer. Assuming that you've created appropriate indexes on your tables—for example, an index on the OWNER column in the Bug table—grouping the data inside the database engine will be very efficient.

We can change our query to use the nested CURSOR expression we learned about in the last chapter to group the data by the owner and, while we're at it, include a count of the bugs assigned to each developer. As one of the columns in the query, we can use a CURSOR expression to select, for each unique developer, the appropriate list of assigned bugs:

```
<xsql:query connection="xmlbook" rowset-element="open-bugs" row-element="bug"
          id-attribute="" tag-case="lower" xmlns:xsql="urn:oracle-xsql" >

  SELECT OWNER,COUNT(ID) as "count",
         CURSOR( SELECT ID,ABSTRACT,PRIORITY
                   FROM BUG b
                   WHERE b.OWNER = BUG.OWNER
                 ORDER BY PRIORITY
         ) AS buglist
    FROM BUG
    GROUP BY OWNER
    ORDER BY OWNER

</xsql:query>
```

Queries containing ORDER BY clauses in nested subqueries or in view definitions will not work in versions of Oracle prior to Oracle8*i*.

In Oracle8*i* we can even include an ORDER BY in the nested SELECT statement in the CURSOR expression, which is quite handy. With our rewritten query, our XSQL page now produces the results shown in Example 9-6.

Example 9-6. Two-Level Query Results Using a CURSOR Expression

```
<open-bugs>
   <bug>
      <owner>echan</owner>
      <count>1</count>
      <buglist>
         <buglist_row num="1">
            <id>11601</id>
            <abstract>Expanding Node Makes Project Tree Flicker</abstract>
            <priority>2</priority>
         </buglist_row>
      </buglist>
   </bug>

   <!-- etc. -->

   <bug>
      <owner>rjust</owner>
      <count>2</count>
      <buglist>
         <buglist_row num="1">
            <id>10677</id>
            <abstract>NullPointerException Entering Blank Name Value</abstract>
            <priority>1</priority>
         </buglist_row>
         <buglist_row num="2">
            <id>10445</id>
            <abstract>Resizing Methods Panel Doesn't Resize Control</abstract>
            <priority>3</priority>
         </buglist_row>
      </buglist>
   </bug>
</open-bugs>
```

We can take the CURSOR grouping to as many levels as needed. Consider the following tables:

BUG
: All bugs reported against a software product

PERSON
: Developers assigned to fixing the bugs

TEAM
: Groups of developers working together

The page in Example 9-7 consists of a single query with two levels of nested details:

- Select the list of teams that have developers with open bugs to fix, calculate the total bug count for the team, and order by the bug count so the team with the most bugs is listed first.

- For each team in the list, include the set of developers on the team who have open bugs to fix along with their *individual* bug count, and order the list to show which developers on the team have the most open bugs assigned to them.
- In each row of these particular developers, include the set of open bugs assigned to them.

The XSQL page in Example 9-7 produces the data page for the Developer's Bug List. Note that we've already included a reference to the *DevBugList.xsl* stylesheet we'll write in the next section to format this multilevel data into HTML.

Example 9-7. Multilevel Query Using Nested CURSOR Expressions

```
<?xml version="1.0"?>
<?xml-stylesheet type="text/xsl" href="DevBugList.xsl"?>
<xsql:query connection="xmlbook" row-element="team" xmlns:xsql="urn:oracle-xsql"
            tag-case="lower" fixby="3.0">

  SELECT t.name,
         COUNT(b.id) TEAMBUGS,
         /* Detail Set of Team Members With Open Bugs for Current Team */
         CURSOR( SELECT b1.owner,
                        COUNT(b1.id) AS bugs,
                        /* Detail Set of Open Bugs for Current Developer */
                        CURSOR( SELECT b2.id bug,
                                       b2.priority,
                                       InitCap(b2.abstract) abstract
                                  FROM bug b2
                                 WHERE b2.owner = b1.owner
                                   AND b2.status = 11
                                   AND b2.fixby = '{@fixby}'
                                 ORDER BY b2.priority, b2.id DESC
                              ) as BUGLIST
                    FROM team t1, person p1, bug b1
                   WHERE p1.teamid = t1.id
                     AND t1.name = t.name
                     AND b1.owner  = p1.name
                     AND status = 11
                     AND fixby = '{@fixby}'
                   GROUP BY b1.owner, p1.teamid
                   ORDER BY 2 DESC
                ) AS members
    FROM team t, person p, bug b
   WHERE p.teamid = t.id
     AND b.owner  = p.name
     AND b.status = 11
     AND b.fixby = '{@fixby}'
   GROUP BY t.name
   ORDER BY 2 DESC

</xsql:query>
```

As we learned in the last chapter, by requesting the page with the `xml-stylesheet=none` parameter like this:

```
http://server/DevBugList.xsql?xml-stylesheet=none
```

we can temporarily suppress the processing of the transformation indicated in the `<?xml-stylesheet?>` instruction to inspect the page's raw XML output. This reveals the three levels of nested information, grouped in the way we need it, as shown in Example 9-8.

Example 9-8. Three-level Query Results Using Nested CURSOR Expressions

```
<?xml version = '1.0'?>
<rowset>
  <team num="1">
   <name>Design Time</name>
   <teambugs>3</teambugs>
   <members>
     <members_row num="1">
      <owner>rjust</owner>
      <bugs>2</bugs>
      <buglist>
        <buglist_row num="1">
         <bug>10677</bug>
         <priority>1</priority>
         <abstract>Nullpointerexception Entering Blank Name Value</abstract>
        </buglist_row>
        <buglist_row num="2">
         <bug>10445</bug>
         <priority>3</priority>
         <abstract>Resizing Methods Panel Doesn't Resize Control</abstract>
        </buglist_row>
      </buglist>
     </members_row>
     <members_row num="2">
      <owner>echan</owner>
      <bugs>1</bugs>
      <buglist>
        <buglist_row num="1">
         <bug>11601</bug>
         <priority>2</priority>
         <abstract>Expanding Node Makes Project Tree Flicker</abstract>
        </buglist_row>
      </buglist>
     </members_row>
   </members>
  </team>
  <!-- etc. -->
</rowset>
```

The CURSOR expression is very powerful for shaping data, but you need to understand how it works to avoid using it irresponsibly. Including a CURSOR expression in your SELECT list asks the database to open a cursor for the SQL statement inside the CURSOR expression and return a "handle" to that open cursor in the result set. In order to access the data in the result set represented by the returned cursor handle, the client application—the XML SQL Utility, or SQL*Plus, for example—must fetch the rows from that nested cursor using its handle. This equates to a network round-trip per nested cursor if the client application is running outside the database. This shouldn't be a shocking revelation, since this behavior is the same as would be required for a database client program doing nested loops over cursor results, but you should keep this in mind when using CURSOR expressions

Formatting Grouped Data into HTML

We can create a stylesheet to format our three-level nested datagram from the previous section by:

1. Using an HTML editor to design a mockup like the one shown in Figure 9-1
2. Using the `tidy -indent -asxml` command to turn the HTML into well-formed XML
3. Adding the `xsl:version="1.0"` and `xmlns:xsl` namespace declaration to the `<HTML>` element to turn it into an XSLT stylesheet

TeamTeamTeam (3 Open)				
DevDevDev	Abstract Abstract Abstract Abstract Abstract Abstract Abstract Abstract	1 3	10677 10445	2
DevDevDev	Abstract Abstract Abstract Abstract	2	11601	1

Figure 9-1. HTML mockup for bug summary display

Then we can introduce three nested `<xsl:for-each>` loops to iterate over:

- Each team in the rowset with `select="rowset/team"`
- Each member of the current team with `select="members/member_row"`
- Each bug in current members' buglist with `select="buglist/buglist_row"`

This produces the *DevBugList.xsl* stylesheet in Example 9-9.

Example 9-9. Simple-Form Stylesheet to Format Multilevel Bug Information

```
<html xsl:version="1.0" xmlns:xsl="http://www.w3.org/1999/XSL/Transform">
 <head>
  <title>Open Bugs By Team By Developer</title>
 </head>
 <body style="font-family:verdana; font-size: 8pt">
  <table border="0" cellspacing="0" cellpadding="4" width="100%">
   <!-- v-[ Team ]-v --><xsl:for-each select="rowset/team">
    <tr>
     <td bgcolor="#DADADA" width="*">
      <b><xsl:value-of select="name"/></b>
      (<xsl:value-of select="teambugs"/> Open)
     </td>
    </tr>
    <tr>
     <td width="100%">
      <table width="100%" border="1" cellspacing="0" cellpadding="4">
       <!-- v-[ Team Member ]-v --><xsl:for-each select="members/members_row">
        <tr>
         <td width="50" align="center" bgcolor="#EAEAEA">
          <xsl:value-of select="owner"/>
         </td>
         <td width="*">
          <table width="100%" border="0" cellpadding="2" cellspacing="2">
           <!-- v-[ Bug ]-v --><xsl:for-each select="buglist/buglist_row">
            <tr>
             <td width="*"><xsl:value-of select="abstract"/></td>
             <td width="20" align="center"><xsl:value-of select="priority"/></td>
             <td width="20" align="center"><xsl:value-of select="bug"/></td>
            </tr>
           <!-- ^-[ Bug ]-^ --></xsl:for-each>
          </table>
         </td>
         <td width="10" align="center" bgcolor="#EAEAEA">
          <xsl:value-of select="bugs"/>
         </td>
        </tr>
       <!-- ^-[ Team Member ]-^ --></xsl:for-each>
      </table>
     </td>
    </tr>
   <!-- ^-[ Team ]-^ --></xsl:for-each>
  </table>
 </body>
</html>
```

Requesting the *DevBugList.xsql* page with this stylesheet produces an executive summary of the teams with open bugs and shows which teams have the most open bugs and which developers on each team have the biggest open bug count. The results are illustrated in Figure 9-2.

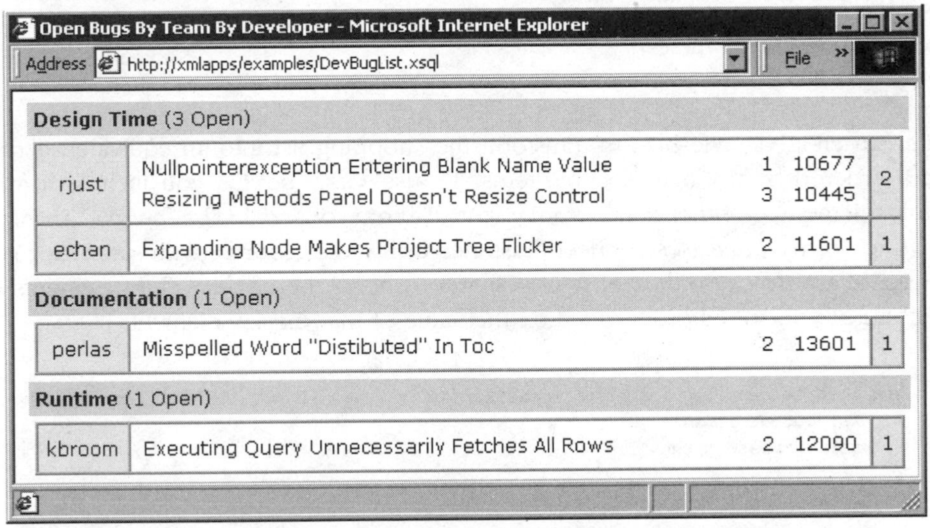

Open Bugs By Team By Developer - Microsoft Internet Explorer

Address http://xmlapps/examples/DevBugList.xsql

Design Time (3 Open)

rjust	Nullpointerexception Entering Blank Name Value	1	10677	2
	Resizing Methods Panel Doesn't Resize Control	3	10445	
echan	Expanding Node Makes Project Tree Flicker	2	11601	1

Documentation (1 Open)

perlas	Misspelled Word "Distibuted" In Toc	2	13601	1

Runtime (1 Open)

kbroom	Executing Query Unnecessarily Fetches All Rows	2	12090	1

Figure 9-2. HTML bug summary grouped by team and by developer

Sorting and Grouping Repeating Data with XSLT

If you do not have the luxury of controlling the SQL statement producing the XML information you are working with, XSLT 1.0 can be used to sort and group any information in an XML document. The `<xsl:sort>` action allows you to sort your node lists—either selected by `<xsl:for-each>` or matched through `<xsl:apply-templates>`—based on any string or number values that they contain. However, such a claim cannot be made for grouping repeating information. In short, there is no `<xsl:group>` action that provides this capacity.

Sorting on Element or Attribute Values

The `<xsl:sort>` action allows you to sort by string or number values as a part of your transformation. Let's look at some examples of how you can put this action to use. Suppose we have a simple shopping list document like this:

```
<!-- ShoppingList.xml -->
<list>
  <item maker="Friendly Foods">
    <name>Granola Crust Pizza</name>
    <price>11.99</price>
  </item>
  <item maker="Ammondale Farms">
    <name>Yogurt</name>
    <price>1.00</price>
  </item>
```

```
  <item maker="Ammondale Farms">
    <name>ChocoFlakes</name>
    <price>3.49</price>
  </item>
</list>
```

We can create a stylesheet to transform the shopping list into an equivalent structure ordered by the name of the items. To use **<xsl:sort>**, you include it as a child element of either **<xsl:apply-templates>** or **<xsl:for-each>**. The following *SortByName.xsl* stylesheet illustrates using **<xsl:sort>** with **<xsl:apply-templates>** to cause the XSLT processor to process the **<item>** child elements of the **<list>** in sorted order based on the value of the **<name>** element:

```
<!-- SortByName.xsl: Sort shopping-list items by name -->
<xsl:stylesheet version="1.0" xmlns:xsl="http://www.w3.org/1999/XSL/Transform">
  <xsl:output indent="yes"/>
  <xsl:template match="list">
    <xsl:copy>
      <xsl:apply-templates select="item">
        <xsl:sort select="name"/>
      </xsl:apply-templates>
    </xsl:copy>
  </xsl:template>
  <xsl:template match="item">
    <xsl:copy-of select="."/>
  </xsl:template>
</xsl:stylesheet>
```

The **select** attribute of the **<xsl:sort>** element selects the expression that identifies the value to be sorted. The **select** expression is relative to the current node list of matching **<item>** elements in this case, so **select="name"** on **<xsl:sort>** indicates that you want to sort on the value of the **<name>** element child of **<item>** elements.

If we transform *ShoppingList.xml* using *SortByName.xsl* like this:

```
oraxsl ShoppingList.xml SortByName.xsl
```

we see the result document with **<item>** elements now sorted by item name:

```
<?xml version = '1.0' encoding = 'UTF-8'?>
<list>
   <item maker="Ammondale Farms">
    <name>ChocoFlakes</name>
    <price>3.49</price>
  </item>
   <item maker="Friendly Foods">
    <name>Granola Crust Pizza</name>
    <price>11.99</price>
  </item>
   <item maker="Ammondale Farms">
    <name>Yogurt</name>
```

```
    <price>1.00</price>
  </item>
</list>
```

We can sort information either as strings or as numbers. The default is to sort values as strings. To indicate that you want to sort values numerically, add the optional `data-type="number"` attribute to your `<xsl:sort>` element. The following *SortByPrice.xsl* stylesheet transforms our shopping list into a plain text document that lists the name and price of each item, sorted numerically by item price:

```
<!-- SortByPrice.xsl: Sort shopping-list items by price -->
<xsl:stylesheet version="1.0" xmlns:xsl="http://www.w3.org/1999/XSL/Transform">
  <xsl:output method="text" />
  <xsl:template match="/">
    <xsl:for-each select="list/item">
      <xsl:sort select="price" data-type="number"/>
      <xsl:value-of select="name"/>
      <xsl:text>, $</xsl:text>
      <xsl:value-of select="price"/>
      <xsl:text>&#x0A;</xsl:text>
    </xsl:for-each>
  </xsl:template>
</xsl:stylesheet>
```

Note that in this example we're using `<xsl:sort>` as a child of `<xsl:for-each>`. The result of transforming *ShoppingList.xml* using *SortByPrice.xsl* looks like this:

```
Yogurt, $1.00
ChocoFlakes, $3.49
Granola Crust Pizza, $11.99
```

If we had forgotten to put `data-type="number"` on `<xsl:sort>`, then the value of the price element would have been sorted lexically instead of numerically, so that the prices starting with the character `1` would sort before those starting with the character `3`, like this:

```
Yogurt, $1.00
Granola Crust Pizza, $11.99
ChocoFlakes, $3.49
```

The value of the `select` attribute on `<xsl:sort>` can be any XPath expression, so it's easy to sort on attribute values by simply selecting the desired attribute with the `@`*`attrname`* syntax. Besides being able to sort on any expression, you can also sort on any number of keys by listing multiple `<xsl:sort>` elements. The first `<xsl:sort>` defines the primary key for sorting, the second one defines the secondary sort key, and so on.

The following *SortByMakerByPriceDesc.xsl* stylesheet illustrates a multi-key sort. First it sorts by the value of the `maker` attribute, and then by the value of the `<price>` element. By adding the additional `order="descending"` attribute on the second <xsl:sort>, we can indicate that we want the prices sorted numerically in descending order:

```
<!-- SortByMakerByPriceDesc.xsl: Sort shopping-list items by maker by price -->
<xsl:stylesheet version="1.0" xmlns:xsl="http://www.w3.org/1999/XSL/Transform">
  <xsl:output method="text"/>
  <xsl:template match="/">
    <xsl:for-each select="list/item">
      <!-- Can sort on anything you can select, so attributes work fine -->
      <xsl:sort select="@maker"/>
      <!-- Can sort on multiple keys, and control ascending/descending -->
      <xsl:sort select="price" data-type="number" order="descending"/>
      <xsl:value-of select="@maker"/>
      <xsl:text>: </xsl:text>
      <xsl:value-of select="name"/>
      <xsl:text>, $</xsl:text>
      <xsl:value-of select="price"/>
      <xsl:text>&#x0A;</xsl:text>
    </xsl:for-each>
  </xsl:template>
</xsl:stylesheet>
```

The result of transforming *ShoppingList.xml* using *SortByMakerByPrice.xsl* is:

```
Ammondale Farms: ChocoFlakes, $3.49
Ammondale Farms: Yogurt, $1.00
Friendly Foods: Granola Crust Pizza, $11.99
```

We've seen that sorting in XSLT is quite straightforward. Grouping is another story. Since there is no analogous <xsl:group> element to make grouping easy, we're forced to invent a mechanism to achieve grouping functionality by using other built-in XSLT facilities. As we'll see in the following sections, there are two basic techniques, one that is slow but a little easier to understand, and one that is fast but a little more obscure.

Grouping by Scanning Preceding Elements

Grouping is the process of converting flat data with repeating values into a nested set of data that factors out the unique values of the repeating information. For example, suppose we start with an XML document that looks like this:

```
<staff>
  <employee><deptno>20</deptno><name>Angel</name></employee>
  <employee><deptno>10</deptno><name>Collins</name></employee>
  <employee><deptno>20</deptno><name>Roger</name></employee>
  <employee><deptno>10</deptno><name>Mark</name></employee>
</staff>
```

We frequently will want to perform transformations that group flat information like the employees in the list above into a nested set of data that factors out a repeating value like <deptno> and groups the employees into their respective departments to produce a result document like this one:

```
<staff>
  <department id="10">
    <employee><name>Collins</name></employee>
    <employee><name>Mark</name></employee>
  </department>
  <department id="20">
    <employee><name>Angel</name></employee>
    <employee><name>Roger</name></employee>
  </department>
</staff>
```

To simulate a grouping facility, it is common practice among XSLT developers to scan all elements that precede the current one to determine whether the current element's value is occurring for the first time in the document. By selecting only the first occurrences of values for a given element, you can produce the unique list of values that particular element takes on in the document. For example, consider the XML document of open bugs assigned to developers in Example 9-10.

Example 9-10. Open Bug List, Sorted by Priority

```
<open-bugs>
   <bug>
      <id>6708</id>
      <abstract>Error Occured for Table with Chinese Character</abstract>
      <dev>Juan</dev>
      <priority>2</priority>
   </bug>
   <bug>
      <id>7468</id>
      <abstract>Tester Tool Flickers When View Selected</abstract>
      <dev>Charles</dev>
      <priority>2</priority>
   </bug>
   <bug>
      <id>6714</id>
      <abstract>Xml Data Generator Ignores Attribute Selection</abstract>
      <dev>Steve</dev>
      <priority>3</priority>
   </bug>
   <bug>
      <id>2085</id>
      <abstract>Upgrade XML SQL Utility To Latest</abstract>
      <dev>Steve</dev>
      <priority>3</priority>
   </bug>
   <bug>
      <id>11675</id>
      <abstract>After Insert New Master Row, Icon Disappears</abstract>
      <dev>Juan</dev>
      <priority>3</priority>
   </bug>
   <bug>
      <id>600</id>
      <abstract>View Criteria Needs "Smarts" About LIKE Queries</abstract>
```

Example 9-10. Open Bug List, Sorted by Priority (continued)

```
    <dev>Steve</dev>
    <priority>4</priority>
  </bug>
</open-bugs>
```

It appears that whoever produced this XML document performed a query that sorted the bugs by priority. However, let's assume that we need to produce a list of bugs grouped by unique developer. The "scan all preceding" technique works like this:

- If the current element does not appear among preceding elements having the value of the current element, then you have just found the first occurrence.
- If the current node does appear among nodes preceding it, then it is not the first occurrence.

We can write an XSLT stylesheet to produce the list of bugs grouped by developer using this technique by simply using a clever XPath expression to select each `open-bugs/bug/dev` element having a value that does not occur in any of the preceding <dev> elements. The XPath pattern for this is:

```
/open-bugs/bug/dev[not(preceding::dev=.)]
```

This selects the `/open-bugs/bug/dev` elements that do not have any preceding <dev> elements with the value of the *current* <dev> element.

Using the syntax `preceding::`*`elementName`* instead of just *`elementName`* in one of the steps of an XPath pattern indicates that you want to find *`elementName`* elements that occur in the set of preceding nodes—that is, nodes that come earlier in the document order than the current node, excluding nodes that are your parent nodes. The `preceding::` qualifier changes the default behavior of finding *`elementName`* elements that occur as *children* of the current node for a step of the path expression. Similarly, you can use `following::`*`elementName`* to find *`elementName`* elements that follow the current node in document order.

A stylesheet that exploits the XPath expression above to select unique developers and construct a list of the bugs assigned to them appears in Example 9-11.

Example 9-11. Grouping Repeating Data in XSLT the Slow Way

```
<!-- SlowerGrouping.xsl: The slow way to group repeating info by scanning -->
<xsl:stylesheet xmlns:xsl="http://www.w3.org/1999/XSL/Transform" version="1.0">
  <xsl:output indent="yes"/>
  <xsl:template match="/">
    <BugsByDeveloper>
      <!--
       | Select all unique developer names by selecting the
       | unique "open-bugs/bug/dev" elements. A unique "dev" is one
       | having no preceding dev element with the same value as it has.
       +-->
```

Example 9-11. Grouping Repeating Data in XSLT the Slow Way (continued)

```
      <xsl:for-each select="/open-bugs/bug/dev[not(preceding::dev=.)]">
        <!-- Sort by the value of dev, the current node "." -->
        <xsl:sort select="."/>
        <BugList for="{.}">
          <!-- Select and copy all bugs for the current developer -->
          <xsl:for-each select="/open-bugs/bug[dev = current()]">
            <!-- Copy the current <bug> node -->
            <xsl:copy>
              <!-- Including children <id>,<abstract>,<priority> -->
              <xsl:copy-of select="id|abstract|priority"/>
            </xsl:copy>
          </xsl:for-each>
        </BugList>
      </xsl:for-each>
    </BugsByDeveloper>
  </xsl:template>
</xsl:stylesheet>
```

The **preceding::** and **following::** modifiers are known as *search axes*. Other axes available to explicitly override the default for searching among children nodes are:

- **ancestor::**, which searches among the parent node of the current node and its parent node, and so on, up to the document root
- **preceding-sibling::**, which searches among sibling nodes that come earlier in the document than the current node
- **following-sibling::**, which searches among sibling nodes that come after the current node in the document

This is not the complete list of axes, but these are the most commonly used ones.

Using the command-line **oraxsl** utility to perform the transformation:

```
oraxsl OpenBugs.xml SlowerGrouping.xsl
```

produces the result shown in Example 9-12.

Example 9-12. Results of Grouping Bug List by Developer

```
<?xml version = '1.0' encoding = 'UTF-8'?>
<BugsByDeveloper>
   <BugList for="Charles">
      <bug>
         <id>7468</id>
         <abstract>Tester Tool Flickers When View Selected</abstract>
         <priority>2</priority>
      </bug>
   </BugList>
```

Example 9-12. Results of Grouping Bug List by Developer (continued)

```
  <BugList for="Juan">
     <bug>
        <id>6708</id>
        <abstract>Error Occured for Table with Chinese Character</abstract>
        <priority>2</priority>
     </bug>
     <bug>
        <id>11675</id>
        <abstract>After Insert New Master Row, Icon Disappears</abstract>
        <priority>3</priority>
     </bug>
  </BugList>
  <BugList for="Steve">
     <bug>
        <id>6714</id>
        <abstract>Xml Data Generator Ignores Attribute Selection</abstract>
        <priority>3</priority>
     </bug>
     <bug>
        <id>2085</id>
        <abstract>Upgrade XML SQL Utility To Latest</abstract>
        <priority>3</priority>
     </bug>
     <bug>
        <id>600</id>
        <abstract>View Criteria Needs "Smarts" About LIKE Queries</abstract>
        <priority>4</priority>
     </bug>
  </BugList>
</BugsByDeveloper>
```

Since this technique involves scanning and rescanning the nodes in the document, you can imagine that it is far from efficient. For example, if we increase the number of <bug> elements in the <open bugs> document to a number like 642, then the above transformation takes about nine seconds to perform on a Pentium II 450MHz laptop.

Before learning the better performing technique, let's build a quick-and-dirty benchmark program to perform the transformation programmatically five times and print out the average. The code for this utility appears in Example 9-13.

Example 9-13. Simple Utility to Measure Stylesheet Performance

```
import oracle.xml.parser.v2.*;
import java.io.*;
// Quick-and-Dirty XSLT processor benchmarking test
public class BenchmarkXSLT {
  // Assume 1st arg is name of XML file, 2nd arg is name of XSLT stylesheet
  public static void main(String[] arg) throws Exception {
    // Open FileReaders on the XML source and XSLT stylesheet
    FileReader    xmlfile      = new FileReader(arg[0]);
```

Example 9-13. Simple Utility to Measure Stylesheet Performance (continued)

```
    FileReader    xslfile      = new FileReader(arg[1]);
    // Create an XML Parser to parse both documents
    DOMParser     parser       = new DOMParser();
    // Parse and get the XML source for the transformation
    parser.parse(xmlfile);
    XMLDocument   xmlSource    = (XMLDocument) parser.getDocument();
    // Parse and get the XSL stylesheet source for the transformation
    parser.parse(xslfile);
    XMLDocument   xslSource    = (XMLDocument) parser.getDocument();
    // Construct an XSLStylesheet object from the XSL source
    XSLStylesheet xslTransform = new XSLStylesheet(xslSource, /*baseurl*/null);
    // Create an XSLT processor
    XSLProcessor  processor    = new XSLProcessor();
    long sumOfFiveTries = 0;
    for (int z = 1; z <= 5; z++) {
      long start = System.currentTimeMillis();
      // Do the transformation, ignoring the DocumentFragment return
      processor.processXSL(xslTransform,xmlSource);
      long time  = System.currentTimeMillis() - start;
      System.out.println("Run " + z + " = " + time + " msecs.");
      sumOfFiveTries += time;
    }
    long avg = sumOfFiveTries / 5;
    System.out.println("Five Run average time: " + avg + " msecs.");
  }
}
```

We'll use this program in a minute to demonstrate the dramatic difference in performance of the new technique for grouping described in the next section.

Faster Grouping Using XSL Keys

To improve on the performance of grouping, it should be clear that we need to avoid all the scanning and rescanning of document nodes to determine uniqueness. If we think a moment about database queries, we'll recall this familiar maxim: "To make sure your query performance is optimized, avoid full table scans by creating indexes on the frequently accessed columns."

XSLT 1.0 supports a feature called `<xsl:key>` that allows you to effectively create *functional indexes* on any frequently accessed expression in any node-set. The syntax for `<xsl:key>` is:

```
<xsl:key name="index-name"
         match="XPathPattern"
           use="RelativeExpressionToIndex"/>
```

You assign a meaningful name to the index using the `name` attribute, provide an XPath pattern in the `match` attribute to describe the particular node-set you are interested in creating an index on, and indicate with the `use` attribute the relative expression you would like indexed.

To create an index named **dev-index** on the value of <dev> in the node-set identified by the pattern **/open-bugs/bug**, use the syntax:

```
<xsl:key name="dev-index"
        match="/open-bugs/bug"
          use="dev"/>
```

If you stretch your imagination a little, you'll realize that this is conceptually similar to creating functional indexes over a database view. Imagine a pseudo-SQL syntax like:

```
CREATE INDEX dev-index ON NodeSet{/open-bugs/bug}( dev )
```

to index the **dev** expression in the **/open-bugs/bug** node-set.

Once this index is defined—by including the <xsl:key> element as a top-level element in your stylesheet—you can easily exploit the named **dev-index** by using the built-in XSLT **key()** function. The syntax of the **key()** function looks like this:

```
key('index-name', valueToLookup)
```

This returns the set of all nodes in the indexed node-set having ***valueToLookup*** as the value of their indexed expression. As a concrete example, if our stylesheet has used <xsl:key> to declare **dev-index**, then we can *very* efficiently return a list of all <bug> elements having the value "Steve" as their <dev> by using the expression **key('dev-index','Steve')**. Just as creating an index can make a night-and-day difference with SQL GROUP BY performance, using an <xsl:key> index in place dramatically speeds up grouping in XSLT.

When you define a *database index*, you are requesting the Oracle database engine to use a little extra storage space to keep track of a lookup table that organizes the list of ROWIDs that match each unique value of the indexed expression for fast retrieval. It is an additional structure whose only purpose in life is to avoid full table scans for searches involving the indexed column in the indexed table.

Exactly the same concept applies to an XSLT *key-based index*. When you define an <xsl:key> index, you are requesting the XSLT processor to use a little extra memory to manage a lookup table that organizes the list of internal node IDs that match each unique value of the indexed expression. It is an additional memory structure whose only purpose in life is to avoid full document tree scans for searches involving the indexed expression in the indexed node-set. Figure 9-3 illustrates the in-memory lookup table that an <xsl:key>-based index maintains.

In order to select a list of the unique <dev> elements in the **/open-bugs/bug** node-set, we need only figure out a way to select the *first* <bug> element in the index's list of <bug> elements that match each unique **dev** value. Once we find the first <bug> element for a given value of <dev>, we can select its <dev> child

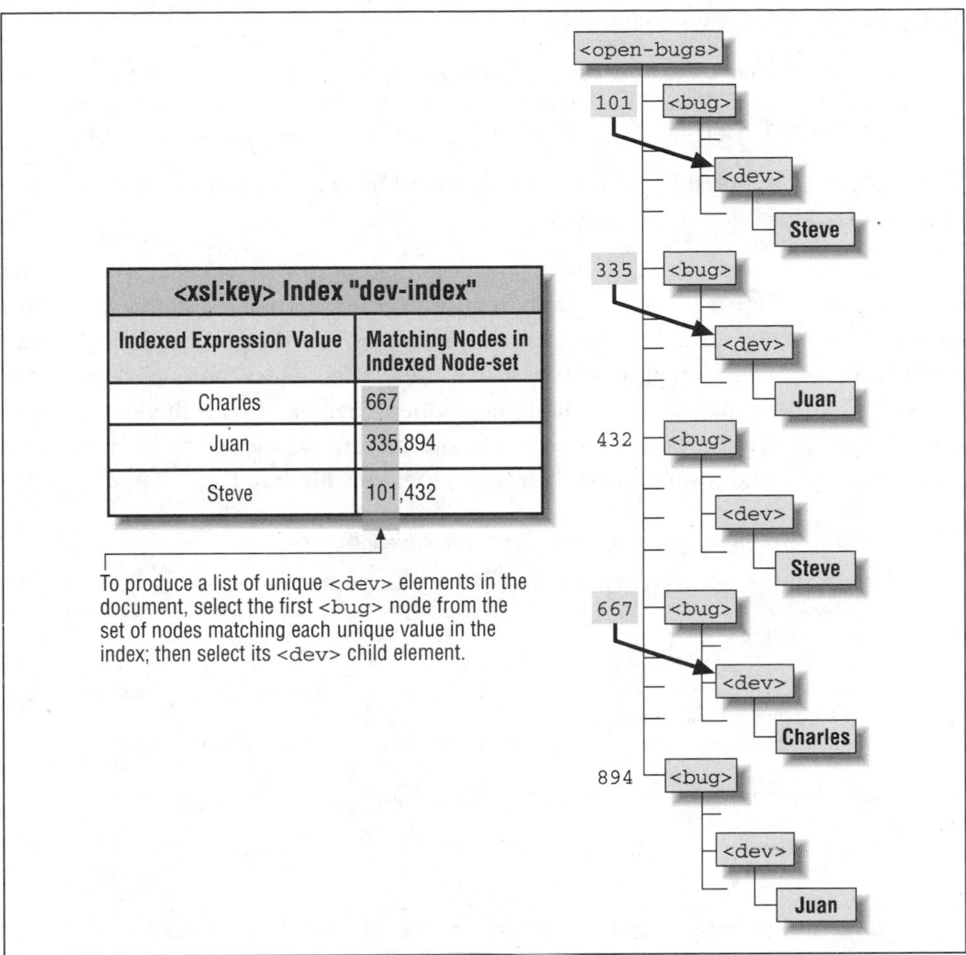

Figure 9-3. Understanding why xsl:key accelerates grouping

to get a <dev> element representing the unique value we seek. The XPath expression that accomplishes this is:

```
/open-bugs/bug/dev[generate-id(.) =
                   generate-id( key('dev-index',.)[1]/dev )]
```

The XSLT built-in `generate-id()` function allows you to access the internal node ID of any node in the source tree. This is *not* the value of the `id` attribute on any element. It is a machine-generated unique ID that the XSLT processor has assigned to the source node. During a transformation, the internal node IDs are guaranteed to be unique; however, the values of these internal IDs are not guaranteed to be the same in different runs of the same stylesheet. Consequently, they are useful only for determining if two nodes are exactly the same node within the context of a single transformation.

The previous XPath expression says:

> Select the /open-bugs/bug/dev elements having an internal node ID equal to the internal node ID of the <dev> child element of the *first* node in the dev index's lookup table of nodes that has a dev with the current <dev> node's value.

That's a mouthful you'll find easier to understand after looking at the vertical stripe of node IDs illustrated in Figure 9-3.

Example 9-14 shows an XSLT transformation that performs effectively the same grouping task done earlier using the "scan preceding elements" strategy, but this example leverages <xsl:key> to create an index on the dev value of the /open-bugs/bug node-set. Then it exploits that index to select unique developers' names. While looping over the unique developers' names, it uses the key again to quickly retrieve the list of bugs assigned to the current developer and copies these bug elements to the result tree as their developer-specific bug list.

Example 9-14. Grouping Repeating Data Using an xsl:key Index

```
<!-- FasterGrouping.xsl: Leverage XSLT key's like database indexes -->
<xsl:stylesheet xmlns:xsl="http://www.w3.org/1999/XSL/Transform" version="1.0">
  <xsl:output indent="yes"/>
  <!--
   | Use xsl:key to create index on the "dev" value in /open-bugs/bug node-set
   | This is conceptually similar to:
   |    CREATE INDEX dev-index ON /open-bugs/bug ( dev ) in a SQL-like Syntax
   +-->
  <xsl:key name="dev-index" match="/open-bugs/bug" use="dev"/>
  <xsl:template match="/">
    <BugsByDeveloper>
      <!--
       | Select all unique developer names by selecting the
       | first node indexed by the XSLT key for the current value of <dev>
       +-->
      <xsl:for-each select="/open-bugs/bug/dev[generate-id(.)=
                                  generate-id(key('dev-index',.)[1]/dev)]">
        <!-- Sort by the value of dev, the current node "." -->
        <xsl:sort select="."/>
        <BugList for="{.}">
          <!--
           | Select and copy all bugs for the current developer.
           | Given the dev name, the key('dev-index',.) returns
           | the node-set of all that developer's bugs.
           +-->
          <xsl:for-each select="key('dev-index',.)">
            <!-- Copy the current <bug> node -->
            <xsl:copy>
              <!-- Including children <id>,<abstract>,<priority> -->
              <xsl:copy-of select="id|abstract|priority"/>
            </xsl:copy>
          </xsl:for-each>
        </BugList>
```

Example 9-14. Grouping Repeating Data Using an xsl:key Index (continued)

```
      </xsl:for-each>
    </BugsByDeveloper>
  </xsl:template>
</xsl:stylesheet>
```

Within the `<xsl:for-each>` loop that efficiently selects a list of unique `<dev>` elements, we need to select the list of `<bug>` elements assigned to that developer. We could certainly use the pattern:

```
/open-bugs/bug[dev=current()]
```

to select the list of bugs for the current developer; however, we can do better. Remember that the `<xsl:key>` index already *has* a fast-access list of the `<bug>` elements matching each unique value of `dev`. So we can use the `key('dev-index',.)` expression to select the list of all `<bug>` elements matching the value of the current node—the current developer's name—and then copy each of the `<bug>` elements found to the result tree with `<xsl:copy>`.

Using the `BenchmarkXSLT` program we showed earlier in the expanded "open bugs" document containing 642 `<bug>` elements, we find the following:

```
C:\> java BenchmarkXSLT C:\temp\bugs642.xml SlowerGrouping.xsl
Run 1 = 8312 msecs.
Run 2 = 8011 msecs.
Run 3 = 7401 msecs.
Run 4 = 7030 msecs.
Run 5 = 7220 msecs.
Five Run average time: 7594 msecs.

C:\> java BenchmarkXSLT C:\temp\bugs642.xml FasterGrouping.xsl
Run 1 = 1643 msecs.
Run 2 = 490 msecs.
Run 3 = 491 msecs.
Run 4 = 411 msecs.
Run 5 = 410 msecs.
Five Run average time: 689 msecs.
```

This shows that the `<xsl:key>`-based technique is more than ten times faster than the "scan preceding nodes" technique for grouping. Nice!

10

In this chapter:

- *Programmatically Generating XML Using PL/SQL*
- *Automatic XML Generation with DBXML*

Generating Datagrams with PL/SQL

Developers using the Oracle database, the Oracle Developer toolset, or any of Oracle's family of packaged applications are likely to be familiar with Oracle's built-in procedural language, PL/SQL. Conceived as a language for data processing, PL/SQL features seamless integration with SQL and makes quick work of virtually any task that involves programmatically querying or modifying database data. This chapter covers the basic techniques available in PL/SQL for delivering XML datagrams as part of your Oracle XML applications. Even Java developers may find PL/SQL comes in handy for some database stored procedures and triggers, so we start with a quick overview of PL/SQL.

Programmatically Generating XML Using PL/SQL

In releases of the Oracle database prior to Oracle8*i*, PL/SQL is the language for server-side application code. In Oracle8*i*, where Java and PL/SQL may be used interchangeably for server-side development, even Java developers may find PL/SQL easier to use for certain data-intensive tasks.

Here we take a rapid tour of the bare necessities required to understand the structure of PL/SQL programs and to put the basic PL/SQL language constructs to work for XML data publishing.

For more detailed information on PL/SQL, see the O'Reilly Oracle Center online at *http://oracle.oreilly.com/* for numerous authoritative titles on the subject, including *Oracle PL/SQL Programming*, second edition, by Steven Feuerstein and Bill Pribyl.

Organization of PL/SQL Code

PL/SQL programs are organized into code blocks that define the scope in which declared variables are visible and in which exceptions can be handled. A block of PL/SQL code is delimited with the BEGIN and END keywords. Any code block may include a declaration section where locally scoped variables are declared, as well as an exception section where exceptions are handled. Blocks of PL/SQL code can be nested to any level.

Example 10-1 shows a simple block of PL/SQL code with both a declaration section and an exception section.

Example 10-1. Sample PL/SQL Code Block

```
DECLARE
  symbol    VARCHAR2(40);
  price     NUMBER;
  lastTrade DATE;
BEGIN
  SELECT ticker_symbol, selling_price, trade_date
    INTO symbol, price, lastTrade
    FROM stock_trades
   WHERE transaction_id = 12345;
EXCEPTION
  WHEN NO_DATA_FOUND THEN
    MyErrorHandlingProcedure(12345);
END;
```

The database server can parse, compile, and execute a block of PL/SQL code on the fly, typed in by hand, or run from a script file. You can also create stored procedures and functions in PL/SQL that allow a block of PL/SQL code to easily accept any number of parameters and to be easily reused by name by other database programs. For improved modularity, groups of one or more PL/SQL procedures and functions can be grouped into packages, allowing a clean separation of the programming interface of the reusable routines from their implementation.

Your own PL/SQL packages can take advantage of the functionality provided in the built-in packages Oracle supplies with the database server. The built-in packages offer easy access to many, many useful database capabilities through simple APIs. *Oracle Built-in Packages*, by Steven Feuerstein, Charles Dye, and John

Beresniewicz (O'Reilly & Associates) offers a complete rundown of all of the built-in packages, their interfaces, and techniques for using them effectively in your programs.

We'll immediately put a few of these built-in packages to work in the next section as we see how to generate text output for the Web from database queries.

Formatting Data for Output Using PL/SQL

Because code that runs inside the database is not associated with a particular terminal or web browser, outputting text-based information of any kind requires printing the desired text to an intermediate buffer during the execution of your PL/SQL code. Upon completion of your operation, the "page buffer" can then be flushed to the terminal or web browser originating the request. Oracle provides a built-in `DBMS_OUTPUT` package that you can use to generate text-based output, including information from database query results, to the console for debugging. We'll look at this basic text-output technique, then shift our focus to web-based output.

Hello World example in PL/SQL

Example 10-2 illustrates the simplest possible PL/SQL code for outputting text from the database.

Example 10-2. PL/SQL Hello World

```
BEGIN
  DBMS_OUTPUT.PUT_LINE('Hello World');
END;
```

The most common routines in the `DBMS_OUTPUT` package are the `PUT` and `PUT_LINE` procedures that print a string to the output buffer and print an entire line (with carriage return) to the output buffer, respectively. Developers routinely use the routines in the `DBMS_OUTPUT` package to help debug their PL/SQL programs, but you can use the same facility to output text of any kind based on database query results.

Processing database query results in PL/SQL

In order to output information from the result set of a SQL query, we need to loop over the rows in the result. Fortunately, looping over data in PL/SQL is one of the language's strong points. The FOR...IN...LOOP construct lets us easily iterate the results of any SQL statement, as shown in Example 10-3.

Example 10-3. PL/SQL FOR Loop

```
BEGIN
  FOR curQuote IN ( SELECT symbol, price, change
                     FROM quotes
                    WHERE change > 3.00 )
  LOOP
    DBMS_OUTPUT.PUT_LINE(' Symbol: '||curQuote.symbol||
                         '  Price: '||curQuote.price ||
                         ' Change: '||curQuote.change);
  END LOOP;
END;
```

Notice that we provide **curQuote** as the name of the *cursor loop variable*, which is then referenced inside the loop to access the column values of the current row. To access a ***columnName*** column in the current row, use the ***loopVariable.columnName*** syntax. The cursor loop variable is a *record variable* that is dynamically declared to match the structure of the result set of the SQL query used in the loop.

If you plan to use several queries, your code may be more manageable and easier to read if you assign meaningful names to your queries using a cursor via the CURSOR statement. A cursor lets you define the queries you need in the declaration section of your program, then loop through the results of those queries as needed in the body, referring to the queries by their cursor name. In Example 10-4, we see that instead of supplying a SQL query in-line in the FOR... IN...LOOP, we can use the name of a cursor, like **c_BigMovers**.

Example 10-4. PL/SQL FOR Loop with a Cursor

```
DECLARE
  CURSOR c_BigMovers
    IS SELECT symbol, price, change
         FROM quotes
        WHERE change > 3.00;
BEGIN
  FOR curQuote IN c_BigMovers
  LOOP
    DBMS_OUTPUT.PUT_LINE(' Symbol: '||curQuote.symbol||
                         '  Price: '||curQuote.price ||
                         ' Change: '||curQuote.change);
  END LOOP;
END;
```

In practice, most interesting queries will depend on some kind of bind variable value being provided. Examples include a customer ID, a shipping reference code, a purchase order number, a beginning and ending date range, and so on. Cursors can optionally define a list of bind variables that can be referenced in the cursor's SQL statement anywhere bind variables are allowed.

Any time such a cursor is used, specific values can be assigned to the bind variables by passing them as arguments to the cursor. The declared cursor bind variables can have associated default values, as shown in Example 10-5, to be used if the caller does not provide a specific value.

Example 10-5. PL/SQL FOR Loop with a Cursor and Bind Variables

```
DECLARE
  CURSOR c_BigMovers (cp_Symbol VARCHAR2 DEFAULT '%')
      IS SELECT symbol, price, change
           FROM quotes
          WHERE change > 3.00
            AND symbol LIKE '%'||cp_Symbol||'%';
BEGIN
  FOR curQuote IN c_BigMovers('ORCL')
  LOOP
    DBMS_OUTPUT.PUT_LINE(' Symbol: '||curQuote.symbol||
                         '  Price: '||curQuote.price ||
                         ' Change: '||curQuote.change);
  END LOOP;
END;
```

To complete the basic overview of PL/SQL for outputting database query information, we show that the PL/SQL block in Example 10-5 can easily be turned into a stored procedure using the CREATE PROCEDURE command, taking any number of arguments required by the caller. In Example 10-6, the **ShowBigMovers** procedure takes a single VARCHAR2 argument named **theSymbol** that is passed internally as the parameter to the **c_BigMovers** cursor to appropriately restrict its query results.

Example 10-6. PL/SQL Procedure Taking a Parameter

```
CREATE PROCEDURE ShowBigMovers( theSymbol VARCHAR2 ) IS
  CURSOR c_BigMovers (cp_Symbol VARCHAR2 DEFAULT '%')
      IS SELECT symbol, price, change
           FROM quotes
          WHERE change > 3.00
            AND symbol LIKE '%'||cp_Symbol||'%';
BEGIN
  FOR curQuote IN c_BigMovers( theSymbol )
  LOOP
    DBMS_OUTPUT.PUT_LINE(' Symbol: '||curQuote.symbol||
                         '  Price: '||curQuote.price ||
                         ' Change: '||curQuote.change);
  END LOOP;
END ShowBigMovers;
```

Formatting Database Data for the Web

The process of generating dynamic web pages based on database query results is nearly identical to the process used in the previous examples, which made use of the `DBMS_OUTPUT` package. The only difference is that instead of using `DBMS_OUTPUT`, you use the Oracle Web Agent's `HTP` package to print the lines of text you want to return.

The Oracle Web Agent PL/SQL packages

Oracle provides a set of PL/SQL packages with the Oracle Internet Application Server that makes returning dynamic web pages based on database query results much easier. Originally provided as part of the Oracle Web Agent utility, these packages have retained that heritage in their names. In fact, most people refer to them as the *OWA packages.*

These packages help you print data from database query results along with the HTML tags needed to format the information. Similar in function to the `DBMS_OUTPUT` package, the OWA routines populate a temporary page buffer whose contents are returned to the web server upon successful completion of your stored procedure.

Web servers that support serving pages directly from the Oracle database using the OWA packages are:

- Oracle Internet Application Server 1.0 (via `modplsql`)
- Oracle WebDB Lightweight Listener
- Oracle Application Server 4.0
- Oracle Web Application Server 3.0
- Oracle Web Server 2.1

`modplsql` is the name of the Apache web listener module from Oracle that enables PL/SQL procedures using the OWA packages to serve database-driven content over the Web. The Oracle HTTP Server, an integral part of the Oracle Internet Application Server, which Oracle released in the summer of 2000, is powered by Apache and uses `modplsql` to deliver the functionality we discuss in this chapter.

Table 10-1 lists the packages most commonly used by web developers working in PL/SQL.

Table 10-1. Oracle Web Agent Packages

Package Name	Description
HTP	Procedures to print HTML markup to the current page buffer.
HTF	Functions to print HTML markup to the current page buffer. They offer the same functionality as the HTP package, but the function versions are used within string expressions.
OWA_UTIL	Procedures and functions to work with the information in the HTTP request and response.
OWA_COOKIE	Procedures and functions to read and write HTTP cookies.
OWA_SEC	Procedures and functions to work with security information of the requesting user.

We'll use these packages in the next section to format a web page containing database query results.

Returning an HTML page of stock quotes

By creating a PL/SQL procedure that uses the OWA packages to print dynamic content to the PL/SQL agent's page buffer, we can create web pages that format the results of database queries. The two main differences between Examples 10-6 and 10-7 are:

- We're using `HTP.P` instead of `DBMS_OUTPUT.PUT_LINE` to print the formatted data to the output buffer.
- We're printing extra HTML tags around the data values.

That's it! The net effect is that the dynamic output of HTML tags and query results goes to the Oracle Web Agent's page buffer instead of to `DBMS_OUTPUT`'s output buffer. When invoked through a web server (which we'll see how to do soon) the page produced by the stored procedure is automatically returned to the user agent requesting the page; no additional work is necessary.

Example 10-7. Procedure to Return HTML Page of Stock Quotes

```
CREATE PROCEDURE QuotesForStocksInPortfolio( id NUMBER ) IS
  -- Select all stocks for the user with id passed in
  CURSOR c_QuotesForUserid( cp_Userid NUMBER )
      IS SELECT q.symbol, q.price, q.change
           FROM quotes q, portfolio_stocks ps
          WHERE q.symbol = ps.symbol
            AND ps.owner = cp_Userid;
BEGIN
  HTP.P('<HTML><BODY><TABLE>');
      HTP.P('<TR>');
        HTP.P('<TH>Symbol</TH>');
        HTP.P('<TH>Price</TH>');
        HTP.P('<TH>Change</TH>');
        HTP.P('</TR>');
```

Example 10-7. Procedure to Return HTML Page of Stock Quotes (continued)

```
    FOR curQuote IN c_QuotesForUserid( id )
    LOOP
    HTP.P('<TR>');
      HTP.P('<TD>' || curQuote.symbol || '</TD>');
      HTP.P('<TD>' || curQuote.price  || '</TD>');
      HTP.P('<TD>' || curQuote.change || '</TD>');
      HTP.P('</TR>');
    END LOOP;
    HTP.P('</TABLE></BODY></HTML>');
END QuotesForStocksInPortfolio;
```

Once you've created a procedure to format query results for the Web, you can test it one of two ways:

- You can execute the procedure from the SQL*Plus command line using the EXEC command as follows:

  ```
  EXEC QuotesForStocksInPortfolio(101)
  ```

  After successful execution, you can see the resulting contents of the web page buffer by issuing:

  ```
  EXEC OWA_UTIL.SHOWPAGE
  ```

  If you have previously issued SET SERVEROUTPUT ON from SQL*Plus, you will see the contents of the page buffer in your SQL*Plus command console. After requesting the page buffer, the OWA routines flush the buffer.

- If you are using one of the web servers listed earlier on a computer named *yourserver*, and you have properly registered a virtual path location named *yourpath* to point to the database schema where you created the previous PL/SQL procedure, you can request the page through a web browser (or any program capable of making an HTTP request) using the URL:

  ```
  http://yourserver/yourpath/QuotesForStocksInPortfolio?id=101
  ```

Formatting Database Data in XML Using PL/SQL

The process of generating dynamic XML documents in PL/SQL based on query results is identical to the procedure used for generating HTML:

1. Identify the set of data to publish in XML by executing one or more SQL queries.
2. Loop over the resulting data.
3. Output the data, surrounded by appropriate XML tags.

Returning an XML stock quote datagram

When you want to format database query results in XML instead of HTML, the programming techniques remain the same; only the tags around the data change. By making slight modifications to Example 10-7, we can generate dynamic XML datagrams filled with stock quotes in no time.

Studying Example 10-8, you'll notice a few obvious changes:

- We're explicitly setting the MIME type of the returned document to `text/xml` using the `MIME_HEADER` routine in the built-in `OWA_UTIL` package.
- We're outputting an XML declaration instead of an `<HTML>` tag as the very first text in the page.
- The tags used to mark up the data have meaningful element names that reflect the structure of the query result's information, unlike the fixed set of HTML tags, like `<TD>`, which signify visual presentation of the data.

Example 10-8. Procedure to Return XML Stock Quote Datagram

```
CREATE PROCEDURE XMLQuotesForStocksInPortfolio( id NUMBER ) IS
  -- Select all stocks for the user with id passed in
  CURSOR c_QuotesForUserid( cp_Userid NUMBER )
      IS SELECT q.symbol, q.price, q.change
           FROM quotes q, portfolio_stocks ps
          WHERE q.symbol = ps.symbol
            AND ps.owner = cp_Userid;
BEGIN
  OWA_UTIL.MIME_HEADER('text/xml');
  HTP.P('<?xml version="1.0"?>');
  HTP.P('<Quotes>');
  FOR curQuote IN c_QuotesForUserid( id )
  LOOP
    HTP.P('<Quote>');
    HTP.P('<Symbol>' ||curQuote.symbol||'</Symbol>');
    HTP.P('<Price>'  ||curQuote.price ||'</Price>');
    HTP.P('<Change>' ||curQuote.change||'</Change>');
    HTP.P('</Quote>');
  END LOOP;
  HTP.P('</Quotes>');
END XMLQuotesForStocksInPortfolio;
```

We have to set the MIME type of the result to `text/xml` so that a requesting user agent can make an informed decision about how it wants to handle the XML document we're returning. Depending on the web server you're using, you may also have to register `text/xml` as one of the valid MIME types the server recognizes.

Web developers producing static pages with graphics and text never need to think about MIME types, since most modern web servers automatically set the MIME type of requested web resources like *.html* and *.gif* files based on their file extension.

In addition, many developers producing dynamic HTML pages don't have to think about MIME types, since most web servers default the MIME type of dynamically generated pages to `text/html`. With dynamically generated XML, however, we must take care to set the MIME type manually; otherwise, your data pages will most likely be handled like HTML when they get to their destination.

If you begin to write lots of PL/SQL stored procedures that format XML, you'll quickly get tired of printing out the tags manually. Just as the **HTP** and **HTF** packages offer routines for more reliably creating common HTML tags, we can write a quick helper routine to assist with the formatting of opening and closing tags for our XML.

Example 10-9 creates a PL/SQL package named **xmlhelper** by providing its PACKAGE specification and companion PACKAGE BODY, defining the implementation of the routines in the package.

Example 10-9. Helper Package to Simplify XML Creation

```
CREATE OR REPLACE PACKAGE xmlhelper IS
   PROCEDURE   prolog;
   PROCEDURE startTag( elementName VARCHAR2 );
   PROCEDURE       tag( elementName VARCHAR2,
                        content VARCHAR2 := NULL);
   PROCEDURE   endTag( elementName VARCHAR2 );
 END xmlhelper;

CREATE OR REPLACE PACKAGE BODY xmlhelper IS
  PROCEDURE prolog IS
  BEGIN
    OWA_UTIL.MIME_HEADER('text/xml');
    HTP.P('<?xml version="1.0"?>');
  END prolog;

  PROCEDURE startTag( elementName VARCHAR2 ) IS
  BEGIN
    HTP.P('<'||elementName||'>');
  END startTag;

  PROCEDURE tag( elementName VARCHAR2,
                 content VARCHAR2 := NULL) IS
  BEGIN
    HTP.P(   '<'||elementName||'>'
               ||content    ||
          '</'||elementName||'>');
  END tag;

  PROCEDURE endTag( elementName VARCHAR2 ) IS
  BEGIN
    HTP.P('</'||elementName||'>');
  END endTag;
END xmlhelper;
```

The `prolog` routine encapsulates the setting of the `text/xml` MIME type as well as the printing of the XML declaration. `prolog` should always be called *before* calling any of the other routines to generate tags for the content of the page. The `startTag` and `endTag` routines do what their names imply, while the `tag` routines combine these to print the start tag, some text content, and the end tag in one command.

If we were to rewrite Example 10-8 using our new `xmlhelper` package, our code would look like Example 10-10.

Example 10-10. Improved Procedure Returning XML Stock Quotes

```
CREATE PROCEDURE XMLQuotesForStocksInPortfolio( id NUMBER ) IS
  -- Select all stocks for the user with id passed in
  CURSOR c_QuotesForUserid( cp_Userid NUMBER )
      IS SELECT q.symbol, q.price, q.change
           FROM quotes q, portfolio_stocks ps
          WHERE q.symbol = ps.symbol
            AND ps.owner = cp_Userid;
BEGIN
  xmlhelper.prolog;
  xmlhelper.startTag('Quotes');
  FOR curQuote IN c_QuotesForUserid( id )
  LOOP
    xmlhelper.startTag('Quote');
    xmlhelper.tag('Symbol', curQuote.symbol);
    xmlhelper.tag('Price',  curQuote.price);
    xmlhelper.tag('Change', curQuote.change);
    xmlhelper.endTag('Quote');
  END LOOP;
  xmlhelper.endTag('Quotes');
END XMLQuotesForStocksInPortfolio;
```

As before with the HTML-producing stored procedure, we can test the output of our XML-producing stored procedure using:

```
EXEC XmlQuotesForStocksInPortfolio(101)
```

followed by:

```
EXEC OWA_UTIL.SHOWPAGE
```

from the SQL*Plus command line, or by browsing the URL:

http://*yourserver*/*yourpath*/XmlQuotesForStocksInPortfolio?id=101

Automatic XML Generation with DBXML

We could certainly continue with PL/SQL examples, demonstrating how to write stored procedures to:

- Format the query results from multiple SQL statements into a single resulting XML page
- Generically process any SQL query, using the built-in `DBMS_SQL` package, generating appropriate XML tags for their column names
- Automatically search for additional information in related tables by checking the database dictionary views for metadata about foreign key and primary key constraints

But luckily, we don't have to write this code ourselves, since Oracle provides all this functionality in the freely downloadable set of XML Utilities for PL/SQL called PLSXML which includes lots of demos and source code (see *http://technet.oracle.com/tech/xml/info/plsxml/xml4plsql.htm*). The *readme.html* file in the *readme* directory in the PLSXML distribution provides setup instructions.

Letting DBXML Do the Work for You

The heart of the PLSXML suite of utilities is a PL/SQL package called `DBXML`. The package offers a key procedure named `Query` that accepts a SQL query to be processed and automatically produces the XML output in the OWA page buffer. As Example 10-11 illustrates, it is practically no work at all to use `Dbxml.Query`. Passing any query to it as a string causes the appropriately formatted XML document representing its query results to be sent to the `HTP` page buffer.

Example 10-11. Automatically Producing Stock Quote XML with DBXML

```
CREATE PROCEDURE StockQuotesDbxmlBasic( id NUMBER ) IS
BEGIN
  Dbxml.Query('SELECT q.symbol as Symbol,
                      q.price  as Price,
                      q.change as Change
                 FROM quotes q, portfolio_stocks ps
                WHERE q.symbol = ps.symbol
                  AND ps.owner = ' || id);
END;
```

With a single line of PLSQL, any query can be published in XML over the Web! By default, for a query whose leading table name is *`TABLENAME`* in the FROM clause, `Dbxml.Query` creates:

- A *`<TABLENAMELIST>`* element to wrap the entire set of rows
- A *`<TABLENAME>`* element to wrap each row of data
- The database column names as element names for each column's data

The default output from **Dbxml.Query** for a simple query like Example 10-11 looks like this:

```
<?xml version="1.0" ?>
<!-- Oracle DBXML Version 1.1.10 Query Results at 20-JUN-2000 22:10:57 -->
<!--
SELECT SYMBOL,PRICE,CHANGE
FROM quotes q, portfolio_stocks ps
WHERE q.symbol = ps.symbol
   AND ps.owner = 101
-->
<QLIST>
  <Q>
    <SYMBOL>GE</SYMBOL>
    <PRICE>103.5</PRICE>
    <CHANGE>.8</CHANGE>
  </Q>
  <Q>
    <SYMBOL>ORCL</SYMBOL>
    <PRICE>27.33</PRICE>
    <CHANGE>3.4</CHANGE>
  </Q>
</QLIST>
```

By providing values for some of **Dbxml.Query**'s optional parameters, you can control certain aspects of its automatic XML generation. A simple example of this is to substitute the default tags with custom values, as in Example 10-12.

Example 10-12. XML Stock Portfolio Using DBXML

```
CREATE PROCEDURE StockQuotesDbxml( id NUMBER ) IS
BEGIN
  Dbxml.Query('SELECT q.symbol as Symbol,
                      q.price  as Price,
                      q.change as Change
                 FROM quotes q, portfolio_stocks ps
                WHERE q.symbol = ps.symbol
                  AND ps.owner = ' || id,
   theDocElement => 'PORTFOLIO',
   tableElement  => 'QUOTE' );
END;
```

This produces the requested effect on the output:

```
<?xml version="1.0" ?>
<!-- Oracle DBXML Version 1.1.11 Query Results at 05-JUL-1999 18:58:12 -->
<!--
SELECT SYMBOL,PRICE,CHANGE
  FROM quotes q, portfolio_stocks ps
 WHERE q.symbol = ps.symbol
   AND ps.owner = 101
-->
<PORTFOLIO>
  <QUOTE>
    <SYMBOL>GE</SYMBOL>
```

```
    <PRICE>103.5</PRICE>
    <CHANGE>.8</CHANGE>
  </QUOTE>
  <QUOTE>
    <SYMBOL>ORCL</SYMBOL>
    <PRICE>27.33</PRICE>
    <CHANGE>3.4</CHANGE>
  </QUOTE>
</PORTFOLIO>
```

After looking in the next section at using `Dbxml.Query` to work with information for multiple tables in a single request, we'll cover all of the options available to control `Dbxml.Query`'s output.

Returning XML Information for Multiple Tables

One of the key values of XML is its ability to elegantly represent *trees* of related information. For example, if you imagine an XML document representing a patient's medical history, you would assume such a document should include information about the patient, the patient's medical visits with various doctors at one or more medical facilities, as well as other details. In a relational database like Oracle, the information for each of these different kinds of business entities is stored in separate tables, and relationships between the entities are captured by *referential constraints* between tables. As an example, Figure 10-1 shows a simple schema for a Medical Visit Tracking application.

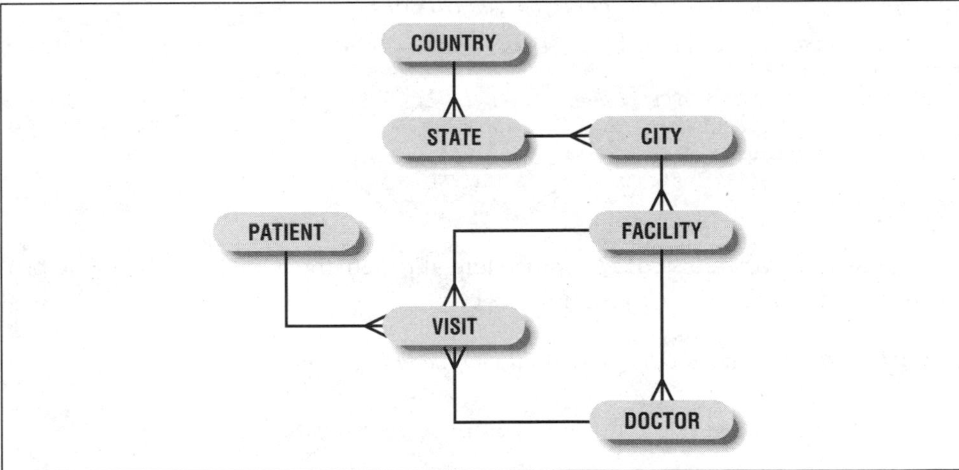

Figure 10-1. Sample schema to track medical visits

Depending on the information needs of the moment, the tables in Figure 10-1 provide the foundation for many different XML documents:

- A `<PATIENT>` profile, with related information about the patient's `<VISIT>`s and which `<DOCTOR>`s the patient saw at what `<FACILITY>`s

- A <DOCTOR> profile, with related information about the list of the doctor's <VISIT>s and <PATIENT>s visited
- A <STATE> profile, with related information about the list of <CITY>s in the state, and what medical <FACILITY>s exist in each city

The list could clearly go on. The key point is that the tables in a relational database, together with the referential constraints among them, have the potential to represent many different XML documents, depending on your desired point of view.

`Dbxml.Query` offers a built-in capability to "walk" relationships and include data tables that are related to the table you provide as the starting point. By providing `Dbxml.Query` an initial query based on the PATIENT table, for example, it will include information about related medical visits from the VISIT table. The process is recursive, so information from the VISIT table will be supplemented by related details from the FACILITY table where the visit took place as well as information from the DOCTOR table about the doctor who saw the patient. You can provide a parameter upon invoking `Dbxml.Query` to indicate which tables you wish to exclude from the set of details to control how far the "walking" goes.

Let's look at a couple of simple examples using this feature of `Dbxml.Query` and the tables from Figure 10-1. Example 10-13 shows an example of a patient profile datagram.

Example 10-13. Multi-Table Patient Profile with DBXML

```
CREATE PROCEDURE PatientProfile( id NUMBER ) IS
BEGIN
  Dbxml.Query('SELECT * FROM patient
               WHERE id = '|| id ,
              includeDetails       => 'Y',
              detailExclusionList => 'FACILITY');
END;
```

Executing the `PatientProfile` procedure through the Oracle Web Agent produces the XML document in Example 10-14.

Example 10-14. Nested DBXML Query Results for the Patient Table

```
<?xml version="1.0" ?>
<!-- Oracle DBXML Version 1.1.10 Query Results at 20-JUN-2000 22:27:22 -->
<!--
SELECT *
FROM patient
WHERE id = 2099344
-->
<PATIENTLIST>
  <PATIENT>
    <ID>2099344</ID>
```

Example 10-14. Nested DBXML Query Results for the Patient Table (continued)

```
    <FIRSTNAME>Laurel</FIRSTNAME>
    <LASTNAME>Birch</LASTNAME>
    <VISITLIST>
      <VISIT>
        <ID>198554</ID>
        <VISITDATE>05-JUL-99</VISITDATE>
        <PATIENTID>2099344</PATIENTID>
        <FACILITYID>Bay03</FACILITYID>
        <DOCTORID>bproto</DOCTORID>
        <DOCTOR>
          <ID>bproto</ID>
          <FIRSTNAME>Bryan</FIRSTNAME>
          <LASTNAME>Proto</LASTNAME>
          <HOMEOFFICE>French44</HOMEOFFICE>
        </DOCTOR>
      </VISIT>
      <VISIT>
        <ID>197111</ID>
        <VISITDATE>24-JUN-99</VISITDATE>
        <PATIENTID>2099344</PATIENTID>
        <FACILITYID>French44</FACILITYID>
        <DOCTORID>bproto</DOCTORID>
        <DOCTOR>
          <ID>bproto</ID>
          <FIRSTNAME>Bryan</FIRSTNAME>
          <LASTNAME>Proto</LASTNAME>
          <HOMEOFFICE>French44</HOMEOFFICE>
        </DOCTOR>
      </VISIT>
      <VISIT>
        <ID>196223</ID>
        <VISITDATE>11-JUN-99</VISITDATE>
        <PATIENTID>2099344</PATIENTID>
        <FACILITYID>Bay03</FACILITYID>
        <DOCTORID>krhymes</DOCTORID>
        <DOCTOR>
          <ID>krhymes</ID>
          <FIRSTNAME>Kathryn</FIRSTNAME>
          <LASTNAME>Rhymes</LASTNAME>
          <HOMEOFFICE>Bay03</HOMEOFFICE>
        </DOCTOR>
      </VISIT>
    </VISITLIST>
  </PATIENT>
</PATIENTLIST>
```

Passing a `'Y'` for the `includeDetails` parameter tells `Dbxml.Query` to "walk" to find related information in the initial table, PATIENT. The `detailExclusionList` parameter is a list of table names to exclude from the set of related details. By setting this value equal to `'FACILITY'` we're asking that no additional details from the related FACILITY table be included in the resulting XML document. This effectively eliminates not only information from the FACILITY table, but also any of its details.

Again using the tables from Figure 10-1, the stored procedure in Example 10-15 produces results by starting with the identified row in the STATE table, and by proceeding to format related information from CITY and FACILITY, but excluding the details that would have been included by default from COUNTRY, DOCTOR, and VISIT.

Example 10-15. Multi-Table State Profile with DBXML

```
CREATE PROCEDURE StateProfile( abbrev VARCHAR2 ) IS
BEGIN
  Dbxml.Query('SELECT * FROM state
                WHERE name = '''|| abbrev ||'''' ,
               includeDetails       => 'Y',
               detailExclusionList => 'COUNTRY,DOCTOR,VISIT');
END;
```

The results of this stored procedure appear in Example 10-16.

Example 10-16. Nested DBXML Query Results for the State Table

```
<?xml version="1.0" ?>
<!-- Oracle DBXML Version 1.1.10 Query Results at 20-JUN-2000 22:29:23 -->
<!--
SELECT *
  FROM state
 WHERE name = 'CA'
-->
<STATELIST>
  <STATE>
    <NAME>CA</NAME>
    <COUNTRYNAME>USA</COUNTRYNAME>
    <CITYLIST>
      <CITY>
        <NAME>San Francisco</NAME>
        <STATENAME>CA</STATENAME>
        <FACILITYLIST>
          <FACILITY>
            <CODE>Bay03</CODE>
            <NAME>Bayside Medical</NAME>
            <ADDRESS>201 Oceanview Rd.</ADDRESS>
            <CITY>San Francisco</CITY>
          </FACILITY>
          <FACILITY>
            <CODE>French44</CODE>
            <NAME>Downtown French Campus</NAME>
            <ADDRESS>11 Battery Street</ADDRESS>
            <CITY>San Francisco</CITY>
          </FACILITY>
        </FACILITYLIST>
      </CITY>
```

Example 10-16. Nested DBXML Query Results for the State Table (continued)

```
      <CITY>
        <NAME>Oakland</NAME>
        <STATENAME>CA</STATENAME>
        <FACILITYLIST>
        </FACILITYLIST>
      </CITY>
      <CITY>
        <NAME>Los Angeles</NAME>
        <STATENAME>CA</STATENAME>
        <FACILITYLIST>
        </FACILITYLIST>
      </CITY>
    </CITYLIST>
  </STATE>
</STATELIST>
```

Controlling How the XML Is Generated

Table 10-2 provides the full list of optional parameters to `Dbxml.Query` that control how it generates XML documents.

Table 10-2. Dbxml.Query Parameters to Control Output

Parameter Name	Description
`theQuery`	The SQL statement to execute. This is the only required parameter.
`theDocElement`	Name of the element to use for the entire set of rows in the query result. (Default is `'ROWSET'`, which produces the `<ROWSET>` tag we've seen in the example output.)
`tableElement`	Name of the element to use for each row of the query result. (Default is `'ROW'`, which produces the `<ROW>` tag we've seen in the example output.)
`maximumRows`	Maximum number of rows to fetch from the query. If combined with an `ORDER BY` in the query statement, can be useful for retrieving the top *N* rows from a query. (Default is to fetch up to 200 rows.)
`includeDetails`	If set to `'Y'`, causes DBXML to attempt its "relationship walking" for including detail data. (Default is `'N'`.)
`detailExclusionList`	Comma-separated list of table names to exclude from the detail table traversal. If a table appears in the list, neither it nor any of its details will appear in the result. Useful for defining the boundaries of what related information to include from a complex schema with many related tables. (Default is NULL, which includes all details.)
`stylesheet`	Provides the relative or absolute URL of the stylesheet to be included by reference using an `<?xml-stylesheet?>` processing instruction at the top of the resulting XML document. (Default is NULL, which omits any stylesheet reference.)

Table 10-2. Dbxml.Query Parameters to Control Output (continued)

Parameter Name	Description
`NoRowsException`	If set to `'Y'`, causes a PL/SQL `NO_DATA_FOUND` exception to be raised if no rows are found by the query. (Default is `'N'` which raises no exception when no rows are found, and returns just an XML document with an empty `<ROWSET>` document element.)
`theMainTable`	If the query is a join, or DBXML has trouble identifying the main table by parsing the query statement, use this to indicate the name of the table to use for the purpose of traversing to find related details. (Default is PL/SQL NULL.)
`singleRow`	If set to `'Y'`, causes DBXML to fetch only a single row and causes it not to use the top-level `<ROWSET>` element as the document element. (Default is `'N'`.)

In your code, use PL/SQL's *named parameter* calling syntax to provide values for any of the optional **`Dbxml.Query`** parameters you want to use. After specifying a SQL query string as the first argument to **`Dbxml.Query`**, the optional named parameters can appear in any order in your procedure call.

We've seen that writing PL/SQL to loop over database query results and produce XML datagrams is quite straightforward, and the techniques presented in this section work in virtually any version of the Oracle database server with any release of the Oracle Internet Application Server or previous application server products from Oracle. For many typical cases, **`Dbxml.Query`** can completely automate the rendering of SQL query results as an XML document, optionally including a set of detail information from related tables.

In this chapter:
- *Generating XML Using Java*
- *Serving XML Datagrams over the Web*
- *Automatic XML from SQL Queries*

11

Generating Datagrams with Java

Java programmers using Oracle8*i* have a myriad of options for outputting database information as XML. This chapter covers all of the available approaches, proceeding in order from the most manual to the most automatic, with examples every step of the way.

Generating XML Using Java

In this section, we'll learn the basics of using Java to generate XML datagrams containing database query results. The two basic programmatic techniques for accessing SQL query results from Java are the JDBC API and SQLJ.

Generating XML with JDBC

The most basic way in Java to produce XML from database information is to use a JDBC `ResultSet` to execute a SQL statement and loop over its results. Developers familiar with database programming using the JDBC interface will find this technique to be second nature. Example 11-1 issues a query to retrieve current stock quotes for all the positions in a particular customer's portfolio. Most interesting queries in an application depend on some kind of context information being supplied. Example 11-1 shows how to use a bind variable in the SQL statement, setting the value of the bind variable to the customer `id` passed in as a command-line argument. This allows the same SQL statement to be used for retrieving the appropriate stock quotes in *any* customer's portfolio.

Example 11-1. Using a JDBC Result Set to Produce XML

```
import java.sql.*;

class StockQuotesXmlJdbc
{
  public static void main (String arg[]) throws Exception
  {
    // Connect to the database
    Connection cn = Examples.getConnection();
    // Prepare the query statement containing a bind variable "?"
    PreparedStatement ps =
      cn.prepareStatement("SELECT q.symbol, q.price, q.change" +
                          "  FROM quotes q, portfolio_stocks ps" +
                          " WHERE q.symbol = ps.symbol" +
                          "   AND ps.owner = ?");
    // Use first command line arg as customer id
    int id = Integer.parseInt( arg[0] );
    // Bind value of customer id to first (and only) bind variable
    ps.setInt( 1, id );
    // Execute the query
    ResultSet rs = ps.executeQuery();
    // Generate the XML document
    System.out.println("<?xml version=\"1.0\"?>");
    System.out.println("<Quotes>");
    // Loop over the rows in the query result
    while (rs.next ()) {
    System.out.println("<Quote>");
      System.out.println("<Symbol>" + rs.getString(1) + "</Symbol>");
      System.out.println( "<Price>" + rs.getString(2) + "</Price>") ;
      System.out.println("<Change>" + rs.getString(3) + "</Change>");
    System.out.println("</Quote>");
    }
    System.out.println("</Quotes>");
    rs.close(); ps.close(); cn.close();
  }
}
```

For each row of stock quote information retrieved, we generate an appropriate `<Quote>` element with nested elements wrapping the stock quote data. All of this data is nested inside the top-level `<Quotes>` element. Note from the following example output that Example 11-1 does not go out of its way to nicely indent the XML tags that structure the data:

```
<?xml version="1.0"?>
<Quotes>
<Quote>
<Symbol>GE</Symbol>
<Price>103.5</Price>
<Change>0.8</Change>
</Quote>
<Quote>
<Symbol>ORCL</Symbol>
<Price>27.33</Price>
```

```
<Change>3.4</Change>
</Quote>
</Quotes>
```

Of course, an XML parser is happy to read a document without the extra beautifying whitespace, but having it in there can make your dynamically generated documents easier for humans to understand. For now, we won't worry about the indenting in our examples. We'll see later in the chapter that some of the more automated techniques of producing XML from database information handle the "pretty-printing" for us.

With a technique similar to the one used in Example 11-1, we can create Java code to generate XML for any query we like. While this technique provides full control over the resulting XML document, writing code by hand to create the appropriate tags for many different SQL statements will soon have you looking for a more automated approach. By exploiting the fact that any `ResultSet` can provide information about its columns and their datatypes at runtime, we can certainly improve on this basic example.

Example 11-2 shows the `XMLForResultSet` class, whose `print()` method produces a valid XML document for the query results of any `ResultSet`. By calling the `getResultSetMetaData()` method on the `ResultSet` passed in, we can reference a companion `ResultSetMetaData` interface. We then can use it to determine interesting structural information about that `ResultSet`. Specifically, here we make use of:

- `getColumnCount()` to find the number of columns in the `ResultSet`'s SELECT list
- `getColumnName(` *n* `)` to retrieve the name of the *n*th column

Example 11-2. Generating XML for Any ResultSet Using ResultSetMetaData

```
import java.sql.*;
import java.io.*;

public class XMLForResultSet {
  public static void print(ResultSet rs, String resultElt, String rowElt,
                           PrintWriter out) throws SQLException {
    ResultSetMetaData rsMeta = rs.getMetaData();
    int colCount = rsMeta.getColumnCount();
    out.println("<?xml version=\"1.0\"?>");
    // Document element for the result
    out.println("<"+resultElt+">");
    // Loop over the rows in the query result
    while (rs.next ()) {
      // Element for each row
      out.println("<"+rowElt+">");
      // For each column in the result set
      for (int curCol = 1; curCol <= colCount; curCol++) {
```

Example 11-2. Generating XML for Any ResultSet Using ResultSetMetaData (continued)

```
        String curName = rsMeta.getColumnName(curCol);
        out.println("<"+curName+">"+rs.getString(curCol)+"</"+curName+">");
      }
      out.println("</"+rowElt+">");
    }
    out.println("</"+resultElt+">");
  }
}
```

`XMLForResultSet.print()` lets the caller pass in:

- The `ResultSet` providing the data
- The document element name to use for the query results
- The element name to generate for each row in the result
- The `java.io.PrintWriter` to use for output

With these four ingredients in hand, plus the information obtained from `ResultSetMetaData`, the job of producing an XML document from the `ResultSet`'s data is a straightforward task of looping over the rows, and for each row, looping over the columns in the row.

Example 11-3 demonstrates how to use `XMLForResultSet` in a simple program. We've rewritten Example 11-1 to call the `XMLForResultSet.print()` method in place of all the hand-coded XML tag generation. When XML utilities are driven off runtime metadata, one line of code can be very effective.

Example 11-3. Using XMLForResultSet.print() to Produce XML

```
import java.sql.*;
import java.io.*;

public class StockQuotesXml {
  public static void main (String arg[]) throws Exception
  {
    // Use first command line arg as customer id
    int id = Integer.parseInt( arg[0] );
    print(id, System.out);
  }
  public static void print(int customerId, OutputStream out) throws Exception {
    // Connect to the database
    Connection cn = Examples.getConnection();
    // Prepare the query statement (Note column aliases!)
    PreparedStatement ps =
      cn.prepareStatement("SELECT q.symbol as \"Symbol\", " +
                          "       q.price  as \"Price\", " +
                          "       q.change as \"Change\" " +
                          "  FROM quotes q, portfolio_stocks ps" +
                          " WHERE q.symbol = ps.symbol" +
                          "   AND ps.owner = ?");
```

Example 11-3. Using XMLForResultSet.print() to Produce XML (continued)

```
    // Bind value of the customerId parameter
    ps.setInt( 1, customerId );
    // Execute the Query
    ResultSet rs = ps.executeQuery();
    PrintWriter pw = new PrintWriter(out);
    // Generate the XML document for this ResultSet
    XMLForResultSet.print(rs,"Quotes","Quote", pw);
    pw.close(); rs.close(); ps.close(); cn.close();
  }
}
```

Besides removing a lot of code, we've also slightly changed the SQL query statement in this example. Example 11-3 introduces *column aliases* for each column in the SELECT list, which provide precise control over the case of the column names. If we left the query as it was in Example 11-1, our generic **XMLForResultSet** routine would have generated an XML document like this:

```
<?xml version="1.0"?>
<Quotes>
<Quote>
<SYMBOL>GE</SYMBOL>
<PRICE>103.50</PRICE>
<CHANGE>0.80</CHANGE>
</Quote>
<Quote>
<SYMBOL>ORCL</SYMBOL>
<PRICE>27.33</PRICE>
<CHANGE>3.40</CHANGE>
</Quote>
</Quotes>
```

The element names for **<SYMBOL>**, **<PRICE>**, and **<CHANGE>** are in uppercase, while the document element **<Quotes>** and the **<Quote>** row elements are in mixed case. By default, tables created in Oracle have uppercase column names, and column names in SQL statements are treated case-insensitively. By default, column aliases are treated case-insensitively and returned in uppercase as well, so we must use double quotes around the column alias if we want a mixed-case name. The query statement in Example 11-3 adopts this technique to create column aliases of **Symbol**, **Price**, and **Change** for the selected data. This causes the output to look like this instead:

```
<?xml version="1.0"?>
<Quotes>
<Quote>
<Symbol>GE</Symbol>
<Price>103.5</Price>
<Change>0.8</Change>
</Quote>
<Quote>
<Symbol>ORCL</Symbol>
```

```
<Price>27.33</Price>
<Change>3.4</Change>
</Quote>
</Quotes>
```

Generating XML with SQLJ

Real-world database applications in Java typically require a significant amount of SQL to SELECT, INSERT, UPDATE, and DELETE data to meet business processing needs. Even the few examples above, which only perform SELECT statements to retrieve data, illustrate that working with SQL in Java using JDBC can be quite tedious. Java developers using JDBC SQL in their code have to:

- Split long SQL statements into many line-sized chunks, making the SQL hard to read and even harder to edit
- Invoke several APIs, typically, to accomplish each SQL operation
- Set each bind variable value by position through code, making SQL statements with many bind variables hard to understand and more prone to editing errors
- Wait until runtime to discover SQL syntax errors
- Retrieve column values by passing the string name or position of the column and calling an appropriate `get` method, according to the datatype of the column value

While JDBC is really the only game in town for working with *dynamic* SQL in Java programs, for cases when SQL operations are known in advance, SQLJ offers an industry-standard syntax that enables developers to work with *static* SQL inside Java much more productively. SQLJ allows Java developers to include `#sql` directives in their Java source code to seamlessly embed, execute, and process the results of any SQL operation. A SQLJ source file is precompiled using the Oracle SQLJ command-line compiler. The compiler translates the preprocessor directives into Java source code, which invokes the JDBC APIs corresponding to the indicated operations. This gives the developer using SQL and Java a number of valuable benefits:

- SQL statements can be embedded verbatim in Java source code, spanning any number of lines
- SQL SELECT, INSERT, UPDATE, DELETE, and EXEC (stored procedure) operations are carried out without developer-written JDBC API calls
- SQL statements can reference Java variables by name as bind variables
- SQL syntax can be validated during precompilation for early error detection instead of waiting until runtime
- Type-safe iterators can be defined to access query results more conveniently than using native JDBC

As an added benefit, developers using the Oracle JDeveloper Integrated Development Environment (IDE) can work with SQLJ files as easily as with Java source code. The IDE handles invoking the Oracle SQL precompiler when necessary.

Example 11-4 illustrates the stock quotes example implemented using SQLJ. At the top, we use the **#sql iterator** directive to define a named, type-safe iterator class for iterating the results of the query. The line:

```
#sql iterator QuotesIter(String symbol, float price, float change);
```

declares an iterator class named **QuotesIter**, establishing the names and expected Java types of each column in a row of query results. The iterator column names *must* match the names of the columns in the SQL statement that you assign to the iterator later in the program. Note that neither the case of the column names nor their position needs to match exactly.

Example 11-4. Generating XML Using SQLJ

```
import java.sql.*;
import sqlj.runtime.ref.DefaultContext;

#sql iterator QuotesIter(String symbol, float price, float change);

class StockQuotesSqlj
{
  public static void main (String arg[]) throws Exception
  {
    QuotesIter quotes;
    // Connect to the Database
    DefaultContext.setDefaultContext(new DefaultContext(Examples.getConnection()));

    // Use first command line arg as customer id
    int id = Integer.parseInt( arg[0] );

    #sql quotes = { SELECT q.symbol as "Symbol",
                           q.price  as "Price",
                           q.change as "Change"
                      FROM quotes q, portfolio_stocks ps
                     WHERE q.symbol = ps.symbol
                       AND ps.owner = :id };

    System.out.println("<?xml version=\"1.0\"?>");
    System.out.println("<Quotes>");
    while (quotes.next()) {
      System.out.println("<Symbol>" + quotes.symbol() + "</Symbol>");
      System.out.println( "<Price>" + quotes.price()  + "</Price>") ;
      System.out.println("<Change>" + quotes.change() + "</Change>");
    }
    System.out.println("</Quotes>");
    quotes.close();
  }
}
```

SQLJ also simplifies sharing of the same database connection across many SQL operations in a program by hiding the details in the SQLJ default connection context. All the programmer has to do is construct a new **DefaultContext** instance, passing in the connection, and set it as the default. Then all subsequent **#sql** statements share the same connection without having to complicate their syntax.

Once the iterator is defined, we declare the Java program variable **quotes** to be of type **QuotesIter** and then use the following syntax:

```
#sql  quotes   = { SQL Statement  };
```

to assign the query to the iterator. Notice that the SQL statement appears intact in the code, without any distracting string concatenation, and that the Java program variable **id** can be directly referenced in the SQL statement using **:id**, prefixing the name of the variable with a colon to indicate its use as a bind variable. To loop over and reference the resulting data, we use the iterator's default **next** method and type-safe column-accessor methods. For example, the call to **quotes.price()** returns the **price** column of the current row as a **float** as defined in the iterator declaration.

Since SQLJ interoperates easily with JDBC, you can mix and match the two in the same program. A JDBC **ResultSet** can be cast to a SQLJ iterator, and any SQLJ iterator exposes its underlying **ResultSet** through the iterator's **getResultSet** method. Example 11-5 shows how the SQLJ-based stock quotes example can make use of our **XMLForResultSet** class to avoid handwritten XML tag generation code.

Example 11-5. Generating XML Using SQLJ with XMLForResultSet

```
import java.sql.*;
import java.io.*;
import sqlj.runtime.ref.DefaultContext;

#sql iterator QuotesIter2(String symbol, float price, float change);

class StockQuotesSqljRsetMeta
{
  public static void main (String arg[]) throws Exception
  {
    QuotesIter2 quotes;
    // Connect to the Database
    DefaultContext.setDefaultContext(new DefaultContext(Examples.getConnection()));
    // Use first command line arg as customer id
    int id = Integer.parseInt( arg[0] );
    #sql quotes = { SELECT q.symbol as "Symbol",
                           q.price  as "Price",
                           q.change as "Change"
                      FROM quotes q, portfolio_stocks ps
                     WHERE q.symbol = ps.symbol
                       AND ps.owner = :id };
```

Example 11-5. Generating XML Using SQLJ with XMLForResultSet (continued)

```
    PrintWriter out = new PrintWriter(System.out);
    XMLForResultSet.print( quotes.getResultSet(),"Quotes","Quote",out);
    out.close();
    quotes.close();
  }
}
```

Serving XML Datagrams over the Web

The examples we've encountered so far in this chapter show that using Java to produce XML for database query results is straightforward. However, all of the examples we've seen so far print the XML datagram to the standard "console" output stream `System.out`. While this makes sense for use on the command line and in scripts, it is one step short of what we need for real Oracle XML applications. For these to be effective, we need to serve application information in XML over the Web.

Serving Datagrams Using Java Servlets

Leveraging the work we've already done in the `StockQuotesXml` class from Example 11-3, we can produce dynamic stock quote datagrams for web delivery by extending `HttpServlet` in a class called `StockQuotesXmlServlet` and performing these simple steps inside its overridden `doGet` method:

- Set the MIME type of the servlet's response to `text/xml`
- Retrieve the customer `id` from a URL parameter instead of a command-line argument
- Call `StockQuotesXml.print()` to produce the XML for the stocks in the customer's portfolio
- Pass the output stream to the Servlet's `HttpServletResponse` object instead of `System.out`

The `StockQuotesXmlServlet` class in Example 11-6 shows the code that gets the job done.

To run a Java servlet from JDeveloper 3.1, just select *Run* from the right mouse button menu in the project navigator. JDeveloper will launch a single-user web server on port 7070 and start your default browser to exercise the running servlet code. You can also debug servlet code by clicking on the *Debug* menu option instead of *Run*.

Example 11-6. Returning XML Stock Quotes Using a Servlet

```
import javax.servlet.*;
import javax.servlet.http.*;

public class StockQuotesXmlServlet extends HttpServlet {

  public void doGet(HttpServletRequest request, HttpServletResponse response)
                   throws ServletException, java.io.IOException {

    // Set MIME type of Response to indicate XML
    response.setContentType("text/xml");

    // Use HTTP request parameter 'id' as customer id
    int id = Integer.parseInt(request.getParameter("id"));

    try {
      // Use StockQuotesXml.print to generate the XML Stock Quotes,
      // passing the Servlet's HTTP Response OutputStream.
      StockQuotesXml.print(id, response.getOutputStream());
    }
    catch (Exception e) {
      throw new ServletException("Error processing query");
    }
  }
}
```

To generalize this servlet to handle requests for XML datagrams that may contain the results of any SQL statement, we start by creating another helper class called `XMLForQuery`. This class encapsulates the XML generation for a SQL statement provided as a string. Example 11-7 shows that we just need to:

1. Create a `ResultSet` from the SQL statement passed in
2. Pass the `ResultSet` to the `XMLForResultSet.print()` method
3. Handle any SQL errors that might come back from the query

Example 11-7. Generating XML for Any SQL Query

```
import java.sql.*;
import java.io.*;

public class XMLForQuery {
  public static void print(String sql, String resultElt, String rowElt,
                           PrintWriter out) throws SQLException {
    Connection cn = null;
    ResultSet  rs = null;
    try {
      cn = Examples.getConnection();
      // Execute the sql statement to produce a ResultSet
      rs = cn.createStatement().executeQuery(sql);
      XMLForResultSet.print(rs,resultElt,rowElt,out);
    }
```

Example 11-7. Generating XML for Any SQL Query (continued)

```
    catch (Exception e) {
      out.println("<?xml version=\"1.0\"?>"+
                  "<ERROR>"+
                    "<SQL>" +     sql          + "</SQL>"+
                    "<MSG>" + e.getMessage() + "</MSG>"+
                  "</ERROR>");
    }
    finally {
      // Clean up
      try {rs.close();cn.close();}
      catch (Exception e2) { /* Ignore */ }
    }
  }
}
```

We include the error handling block to make sure that an XML datagram is printed to the output even if the SQL statement passed in contains syntax errors or attempts to access tables that do not exist. As a useful extra touch, we generate an "errorgram" with the statement attempted and the SQL error message as XML element content.

By calling the `XMLForQuery.print()` method in Example 11-7, instead of `StockQuotesXml.print()` as we did in Example 11-6, we can quickly create a `XMLForQueryServlet`, as shown in Example 11-8, which can return the results of any SQL statement passed as a parameter in an HTTP request. In this example, we retrieve the SQL statement from the HTTP request parameter `sql`. This parameter can be specified as a parameter in a URL or as the value of an HTML `<FORM>` field.

Example 11-8. Returning XML for Any SQL Query Using a Servlet

```
import javax.servlet.*;
import javax.servlet.http.*;

public class XmlForQueryServlet extends HttpServlet {

  public void doGet(HttpServletRequest request, HttpServletResponse response)
                    throws ServletException, java.io.IOException {

    // Set MIME type of Response to indicate XML
    response.setContentType("text/xml");

    // Use value of URL parameter 'sql' as SQL statement to execute
    String query = request.getParameter("sql");

    try {
      // Use XMLForQuery.print to generate the XML Results,
      // passing the Servlet's HTTP Response PrintWriter.
      // Use "ROWSET" and "ROW" as top-level and per-row tags, respectively
      XMLForQuery.print(query, "ROWSET", "ROW", response.getWriter());
    }
```

Example 11-8. Returning XML for Any SQL Query Using a Servlet (continued)

```
    catch (Exception e) {
      throw new ServletException("Error processing query");
    }
  }
}
```

Since we are focusing on getting data *out* of the database in XML in this chapter, the examples here have only needed to override the `HttpServlet`'s `doGet` method. We have also consciously kept things simple by opening and closing the connection to the database with each request.

It is important to note, however, that servlets typically run inside multi-threaded web servers. These servers can handle multiple service requests simultaneously, so the onus of synchronizing access to any shared resources, such as database connections, network connections, or the servlet's own class and instance variables falls squarely on the servlet developer.

Serving Datagrams with JavaServer Pages

It's easy to use JavaServer Pages (JSPs) to produce dynamic XML documents. Just provide a skeleton XML page and use JavaBeans™ or Java scriptlets to fill in the dynamic content. Example 11-9 shows dynamic information plugged into an XML-based JSP page.

Example 11-9. JSP Page Using a Scriptlet Expression and a JavaBean

```
<?xml version="1.0"?>
<jsp:useBean id="ad" class="AdvertisementBean"/>
<timegram>
  <time><%= new Date() %></time>
  <sponsor>
    <name><jsp:getProperty name="ad" property="Sponsor"/></name>
    <url><jsp:getProperty name="ad" property="AdvertURL"/></url>
  </sponsor>
</timegram>
```

We see in Figure 11-1 that the `<%= new Date() %>` scriptlet expression has been evaluated and the `<jsp:getProperty>` tags have been replaced with the `AdvertisementBean`'s property values plugged in as the content of the XML tags in a `<timegram>` document. Using a browser like Internet Explorer 5.0 to test the *CurrentDateXML.jsp* page shows the default rendering of the XML `<timegram>` information, as seen in Figure 11-1.

Using *CurrentDateXML.jsp*, we can provide a useful service to *any* program on the network that wants to know what time it is on our server. Any program can request a `<timegram>` using the URL *http://xmlapps/CurrentDateXML.jsp* and process its contents to discover the time and the sponsor's name by using XPath to

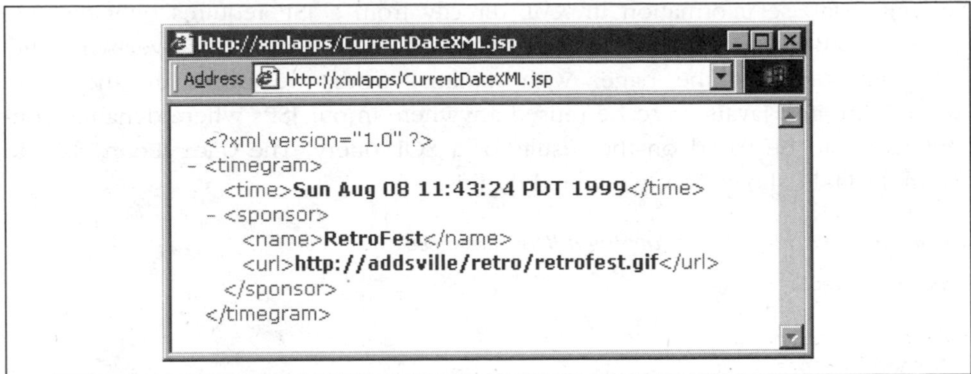

Figure 11-1. Viewing CurrentDateXML.jsp in Internet Explorer 5.0

search for the `timegram/time` and `timegram/sponsor/name` elements in the `<timegram>` it receives. Example 11-10 illustrates a simple Java client program that requests and processes a `<timegram>`.

Example 11-10. Retrieving a Timegram from CurrentDateXML.jsp

```
import oracle.xml.parser.v2.*;
import org.w3c.dom.NodeList;
public class TestTimegram{
  static XMLDocument theTimegram = null;
  public static void main(String arg[]) throws Exception {
    // Construct a parser
    DOMParser dp = new DOMParser();
    // Parse the XML document returned by CurrentDateXML.jsp
    dp.parse("http://xmlapps/ch11/CurrentDateXML.jsp");
    // Get the XML Document
    theTimegram = dp.getDocument();
    // Use XPath expression /timegram/time to fetch the time
    System.out.println("Current time: " +
       theTimegram.valueOf("/timegram/time"));
    // Use XPath expression /timegram/sponsor/name to fetch the time
    System.out.println(" Courtesy of: " +
       theTimegram.valueOf("/timegram/sponsor/name"));
  }
}
```

`TestTimegram` uses the Oracle XML Parser's `DOMParser` to parse the `<timegram>` document returned by the JSP page, and calls the the `valueOf` method on the root node to search the `<timegram>` in memory for the value of the desired elements. Notice that the searching is performed using XPath expressions that describe the elements we're looking for: `/timegram/time` and `/timegram/sponsor/name`. Obviously, serving up requests for the current time is probably not a winning business plan for the next great Silicon Valley startup, but this simple example demonstrates the same principles that would be used to serve and request any dynamic XML document built with a JSP page.

Serving database information in XML directly from a JSP requires only that we have a JavaBean handy to turn a SQL statement into a **ResultSet** over which we can then iterate in the page. With minimal work, we can wrap the JDBC **ResultSet** in a JavaBean to be reused anywhere in our JSPs where dynamic content needs to be based on the results of a SQL query. The **QueryBean** class in Example 11-11 shows how we would do this.

Example 11-11. JavaBean Wrapping a JDBC ResultSet

```
import java.sql.*;

public class QueryBean {
  Connection cn = null;
  ResultSet  rs = null;
  boolean    ownConnection = true;
  public void setConnection(Connection conn) {
    cn = conn; ownConnection = false;
  }
  public void setQuery(String sql) {
    try {
      if (cn == null) cn = Examples.getConnection();
      rs = cn.createStatement().executeQuery(sql);
    }
    catch (SQLException s) { /* Ignore */ }
  }
  public boolean next() {
    try { return (rs != null) ? rs.next() : false; }
    catch (SQLException s) { return false; }
  }
  public String column(int colNumber) {
    try { return (rs != null) ? rs.getString(colNumber) : ""; }
    catch (SQLException s) { return ""; };
  }
  public void close() {
    try { rs.close(); if (ownConnection) cn.close();}
    catch (Exception e) { /* Ignore */ }
  }
}
```

Our **QueryBean** automatically acquires itself a database connection without extra work on the JSP developer's part, making it easy to use **QueryBean** by itself on a JSP. Example 11-12 shows **QueryBean** used in a JSP page to render the results of our familiar stock portfolio query with the **<jsp:useBean>** tag.

Example 11-12. ShowQuotes.jsp Returning XML Using a QueryBean

```
<?xml version="1.0"?>
<Quotes>
<jsp:useBean id="qb" class="QueryBean"/>
<%@ page contentType="text/xml" %>
<% qb.setQuery("SELECT q.symbol, q.price, q.change"+
               "  FROM quotes q, portfolio_stocks ps"+
```

Example 11-12. ShowQuotes.jsp Returning XML Using a QueryBean (continued)

```
                " WHERE q.symbol = ps.symbol "+
                "   AND ps.owner = " + request.getParameter("id")); %>
<% while (qb.next ()) { %>
  <Quote>
    <Symbol><%= qb.column(1) %></Symbol>
    <Price><%=  qb.column(2) %></Price>
    <Change><%= qb.column(3) %></Change>
  </Quote>
<% } qb.close(); %>
</Quotes>
```

Once the `<jsp:useBean>` tag has been introduced, any subsequent part of the page can reference the instance of the bean in a scriptlet using the name you provide in the `<jsp:useBean>`'s `id` attribute. We take advantage of this fact in the three scriptlets this page uses.

The first scriptlet sets the `QueryBean`'s SQL statement, retrieving the desired customer ID from the URL parameter named `id`:

```
<% qb.setQuery("SELECT q.symbol, q.price, q.change"+
               "  FROM quotes q, portfolio_stocks ps"+
               " WHERE q.symbol = ps.symbol "+
               "   AND ps.owner = " + request.getParameter("id")); %>
```

This next scriptlet opens the `while` loop around the group of tags we want to repeat for each row in the `QueryBean`'s results:

```
<% while (qb.next ()) { %>
```

Finally, this scriptlet closes the `while` loop (note the matching, closing curly brace) and calls `close` on the `QueryBean` to close the query:

```
<% } qb.close(); %>
```

Inside the `while` loop, we use scriptlet expressions like `<%= qb.column(n) %>` to insert the value of the *n*th column in the query result. The net effect is that for each row returned in the query, a `<Quote>` element and its children appear in the resulting document. Figure 11-2 shows the results of requesting the *ShowQuotes.jsp* page for customer number 101.

Since a more complicated example may require pulling data from many different SQL queries on a single JSP page, let's introduce a JavaBean that wraps a JDBC `Connection`, and show how we can combine one `ConnectionBean` and several `QueryBeans` on the same page. This allows multiple `QueryBeans` to share the same database connection. The task of wrapping the `Connection` is even simpler than wrapping the `ResultSet`, requiring just one constructor and one `getConnection()` method, as shown in Example 11-13.

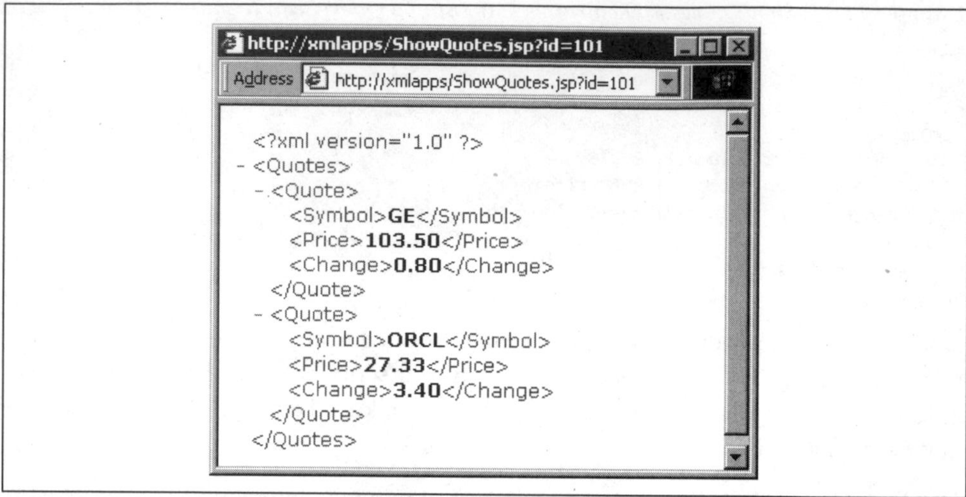

Figure 11-2. Viewing XML results of ShowQuotes.jsp in IE5

Example 11-13. Simple JavaBean Wrapping a JDBC Connection

```
import java.sql.*;

public class ConnectionBean {
  Connection cn = null;
  public ConnectionBean() {
    try { cn = Examples.getConnection();  }
    catch (SQLException s) { /* Ignore */ }
  }
  public Connection getConnection() { return cn; }
  public void close() {
    try {cn.close();}
    catch (Exception e) { /* Ignore */ }
  }
}
```

Using exactly the same techniques as for *ShowQuery.jsp*, we can build the *ShowPortfolio.jsp* page shown in Example 11-14, which:

1. Uses `ConnectionBean` with `<jsp:useBean>` to establish a connection object named `conn` for the page
2. Uses *two* instances of `QueryBean`, named `client` and `quotes`
3. Calls `setConnection()` and `setQuery()` on both `client` and `quotes` to set their connection and query respectively, using a scriptlet
4. Calls `close` on `conn` to close the connection

Example 11-14. Multiple QueryBeans in a Page Returning XML

```
<?xml version="1.0"?>
<Portfolio>
  <Date><%= new Date() %></Date>
<jsp:useBean id="dbConn" class="ConnectionBean"/>
<jsp:useBean id="client" class="QueryBean"/>
<jsp:useBean id="quotes" class="QueryBean"/>
<% client.setConnection(dbConn.getConnection());
   quotes.setConnection(dbConn.getConnection());
   client.setQuery("SELECT givenname, surname"+
                   "  FROM client_table"+
                   " WHERE id = " + request.getParameter("id"));
   quotes.setQuery("SELECT q.symbol, q.price, q.change"+
                   "  FROM quotes q, portfolio_stocks ps"+
                   " WHERE q.symbol = ps.symbol "+
                   "   AND ps.owner = " + request.getParameter("id")); %>
<% while (client.next()) { %>
 <Customer>
   <Name>
     <First><%= client.column(1) %></First>
     <Last><%=  client.column(2) %></Last>
   </Name>
 </Customer>
<% } client.close(); %>
<Quotes>
<% while (quotes.next()) { %>
  <Quote>
    <Symbol><%= quotes.column(1) %></Symbol>
    <Price><%=  quotes.column(2) %></Price>
    <Change><%= quotes.column(3) %></Change>
  </Quote>
<% } quotes.close(); dbConn.close(); %>
</Quotes>
</Portfolio>
```

The XML results of browsing this page are shown in Figure 11-3.

Although we have not explicitly said it so far, it is worth mentioning that the Java-Server Pages facility builds on the foundation of Java servlets, cleverly hiding the complexities of servlets with a simplifying layer on top. JSP's simpler packaging makes a large set of common dynamic pages easier to build, allowing a wider audience of developers to benefit. Here's a brief description of what's going on under the covers.

The first time a JavaServer page is accessed by your web server, you'll notice that it takes a little longer than subsequent requests do. That's because your web server's JSP Runtime environment first translates the page into the equivalent source code for a Java servlet that implements the page. Once translated, the servlet code for the JSP page is compiled, and finally executed to respond to the request. All subsequent requests are immediately executed by the compiled version of the page, so they do not suffer from the delay of the initial request. If you

Figure 11-3. Viewing XML results of ShowPortfolio.jsp in IE5

edit the JSP source code and save the changes, the JSP Runtime notices the change in time stamp on the JSP source code, and proceeds automatically to retranslate and recompile the page.

Automatic XML from SQL Queries

In Example 11-2, we wrote a class that produces the XML output of any SQL query using the JDBC `ResultSetMetaData` class. This example takes a straightforward approach, producing the XML representation for all of the rows of a `ResultSet` with columns of type NUMBER, DATE, and VARCHAR2. In practice, developers need a more robust solution that supports the full range of Oracle8*i* object-relational SQL features, including the ability to query user-defined datatypes. They need better control over the number of rows retrieved and the format of the output tags. Extending our `XMLForResultSet` class to offer generic support for these additional requirements would be a non-trivial task. Luckily, we don't have to build this code ourselves since Oracle provides the XML SQL Utility for Java, which includes the `OracleXMLQuery` component that automates the entire job.

Using OracleXMLQuery to Do the Work for You

`OracleXMLQuery` is a utility class that automates the task of producing XML from SQL query results. It gracefully handles all SQL queries, returning XML for result sets containing both scalar datatypes and user-defined object types in their row values. It offers numerous handy options to control the XML output and is equally adept at producing query results as XML text for web delivery, and in-memory Document Object Model (DOM) tree structures.

To exploit the facilities of the XML SQL Utility, you can use the `OracleXML` command-line program or you can use the `OracleXMLQuery` class in your own custom programs. To use the command-line program, ensure that the Java archive files for the XML SQL Utility, the Oracle XML Parser version 2, and the Oracle JDBC driver are in your CLASSPATH, and invoke the command:

```
java OracleXML
```

to see the command-line options. The first argument can either be the keyword `getXML` to exercise the functionality of retrieving XML from SQL, or `putXML` to store an XML file into a table or view. We'll see more of the `OracleXML` utility in Chapter 12, *Storing XML Datagrams.*

To use the XML SQL Utility's functionality in your own programs, you simply:

1. Create an instance of `OracleXMLQuery`, passing a `Connection` and either a SQL query `String` or an existing `ResultSet`
2. Call `set` methods to override any default XML-generation settings
3. Retrieve the XML results by calling either of the following methods:
   — `getXMLString()` to read the query results as an XML document in a string
   — `getXMLDOM()` to return the query results as a DOM Document

When using `getXMLString()` you can optionally include a document type definition reflecting the structure of the query results by calling `getXMLString(true)` instead of just `getXMLString()` as shown in Example 11-15. This shows a simple JavaServer Page using `OracleXMLQuery` to produce XML datagrams for any SQL statement passed in, optionally including a dynamically generated DTD.

Example 11-15. ShowQuery.jsp Returns XML for Any Query

```
<%@ page import="java.sql.*, Examples, oracle.xml.sql.query.*" contentType="text/xml"%>
<%
    // Get a connection
    Connection cn = Examples.getConnection();
    // SQL Statement from URL Parameters
    String sql = request.getParameter("sql");
    // Create SQL-to-XML Handler
```

Example 11-15. ShowQuery.jsp Returns XML for Any Query (continued)

```
    OracleXMLQuery q = new OracleXMLQuery(cn, sql);
    // Generate XML results and write to output
    out.println(q.getXMLString());
    cn.close();
%>
```

Requesting the URL:

```
http://xmlapps/ShowQuery.jsp?dtd=y&sql=select+*+from+doctor+where+id='bblatt'
```

produces the results:

```
<?xml version="1.0"?>
<!DOCTYPE ROWSET [
<!ELEMENT ROWSET (ROW)*>
<!ELEMENT ROW (ID, FIRSTNAME?, LASTNAME?, HOMEOFFICE?)>
<!ATTLIST ROW num CDATA #REQUIRED>
<!ELEMENT ID (#PCDATA)>
<!ELEMENT FIRSTNAME (#PCDATA)>
<!ELEMENT LASTNAME (#PCDATA)>
<!ELEMENT HOMEOFFICE (#PCDATA)>
]>
<ROWSET>
 <ROW num="1">
  <ID>bblatt</ID>
  <FIRSTNAME>Bruce</FIRSTNAME>
  <LASTNAME>Blatt</LASTNAME>
  <HOMEOFFICE>Bay03</HOMEOFFICE>
 </ROW>
</ROWSET>
```

By setting a few of `OracleXMLQuery`'s many XML-generation options, it is easy to limit the number of rows returned and to change the default element names used for the document element or for each row in the query result. For example, given an AIRPORT table, we can write a JSP page to return an `<AirportList>` of as many as four `<Airport>`s matching a `name` search string passed as a parameter in this URL. Example 11-16 shows the code for the page.

Example 11-16. AirportList.jsp List of Matching Airports

```
<%@page contentType="text/xml"
        import="Examples, java.sql.*, oracle.xml.sql.query.*"
%><%
    Connection cn = Examples.getConnection();
    // Retrieve airport code to be found from the "find" URL parameter
    String code = request.getParameter("find");
    // SQL statement to search table of all known airports
    // Uses an Oracle8i functional index on UPPER(Description)
    String qry = "SELECT tla as \"Code\", description as \"Name\""+
                 "  FROM airport "+
                 " WHERE tla = UPPER('" + code + "')"+
                 "    OR UPPER(description) LIKE UPPER('%"+ code + "%')"+
                 " ORDER BY UPPER(description)";
```

Example 11-16. AirportList.jsp List of Matching Airports (continued)

```
    // Create an OracleXMLQuery object
    OracleXMLQuery oxq = new OracleXMLQuery(cn, qry);
    // Retrieve only the first four matches
    oxq.setMaxRows(4);
    // Use <AirportList> as document element for Rowset
    oxq.setRowsetTag("AirportList");
    // Use <Airport> for each row in the result
    oxq.setRowTag("Airport");
    // Get the XML results as a String and write to the output stream
    out.println(oxq.getXMLString());
    cn.close();
%>
```

Here are a few key things to note in the example:

- `setMaxRows(4)` limits the number of rows returned to 4.
- `setRowsetTag("AirportList")` overrides the default <ROWSET> document element name.
- `setRowTag("Airport")` overrides the default <ROW> element name for each row.

It's also interesting to observe that the query's WHERE clause searches for a match against the three-letter abbreviation (`tla`) of the airport as well as against its description in a case-insensitive fashion using the `UPPER` function. Testing this page in Internet Explorer 5.0 to search for airports matching `sfo` produces the result shown in Figure 11-4.

The document returned includes both an exact match on the three-letter code `SFO` as well as three fuzzy matches on airports whose name includes the three consecutive letters `s`, `f`, and `o`. In many cases, when requesting an XML datagram like our `<AirportList>` above, it is desirable to *first* check for an exact match and return that immediately if found. If no exact match exists, then instead of returning an empty document, it can be more helpful to the requestor to receive a document which indicates that the exact match was not found and provides alternative information to assist in refining the original request

The XML document returned by such a web request can be thought of as an XML *validationgram*, since it validates whether or not a particular thing exists in the database, and it can provide useful information about that thing in the return document. Example 11-17 illustrates a JSP example of this technique. *ValidateAirport.jsp* uses an initial SQL query that attempts an exact match on the airport code provided in the `find` URL parameter. It calls the `setRaiseNoRowsException()` method to request that `OracleXMLQuery` raise a runtime exception in case the query returns no rows—that is, if no exact match exists on the airport code. When

Figure 11-4. List of airports matching sfo

handling this exception, the **catch** block attempts a different query, checking for any potential matches on the description.

Example 11-17. ValidateAirport.jsp Produces an Airport Validationgram

```
<%@page import="java.sql.*, Examples, oracle.xml.sql.query.*" %>
<%
    Connection cn = Examples.getConnection();
    String code = request.getParameter("find");

    // First try an exact match on the airport 3-letter code
    String qry = "SELECT tla as \"Code\", description as \"Name\""+
                 "  FROM airport "+
                 " WHERE tla = UPPER('" + code + "')";
    OracleXMLQuery oxq = new OracleXMLQuery( cn, qry);

    // Signal a catchable exception when no data found
    oxq.setRaiseNoRowsException(true);

    // Setting RowsetTag to "" omits it from the result.
    oxq.setRowsetTag("");
    oxq.setRowTag("Airport");

    try {
      out.println(oxq.getXMLString());
    }
    catch (oracle.xml.sql.OracleXMLSQLNoRowsException e) {
```

Example 11-17. ValidateAirport.jsp Produces an Airport Validationgram (continued)

```
      // If no rows found, try a "fuzzy" match on the airport description
      qry = "SELECT tla as \"Code\", description as \"Name\""+
            "  FROM airport "+
            " WHERE UPPER(description) LIKE UPPER('%"+ code + "%')"+
            " ORDER BY UPPER(description)";
      OracleXMLQuery oxq2 = new OracleXMLQuery(cn,qry);
      oxq2.setRowsetTag("Error");
      oxq2.setRowTag("Airport");
      out.println(oxq2.getXMLString());
    }
    cn.close();
%>
```

An attempt to retrieve information about the airport `sfo` produces an exact match, returning an XML document containing a single `<Airport>` element, as shown in Figure 11-5.

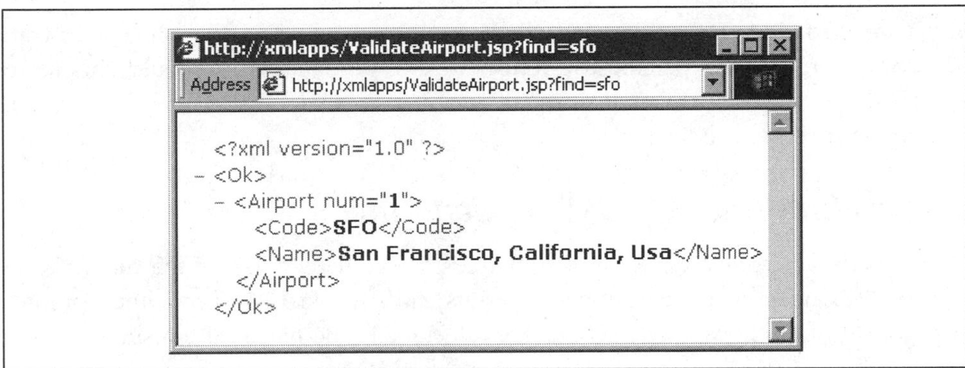

Figure 11-5. Validationgram indicating success from ValidateAirport.jsp

For the exact match case, we know there will be exactly one row matching, so we opt to use the `<Airport>` as the document element. By calling `setRowsetTag()` with an empty string, we indicate that we don't want a rowset-level tag to be generated. This only works when there is exactly one row in the query result. If you try to turn off the rowset-level tag when two or more rows are returned, an error will result, since the resulting document would not be valid XML.

An attempt to retrieve information about the airport `turin` fails the initial query attempt for the exact match, but succeeds in returning a list of two airports whose description matches the value of the `find` parameter passed in: Maturin, Venezuela, and Turin, Italy, as shown in Figure 11-6.

The second instance of `OracleXMLQuery` performs a case-insensitive fuzzy match using the `LIKE` operator, and uses `setRowsetTag()` to force the document element to be `<Error>`, sending a signal back to the requester that the search for an

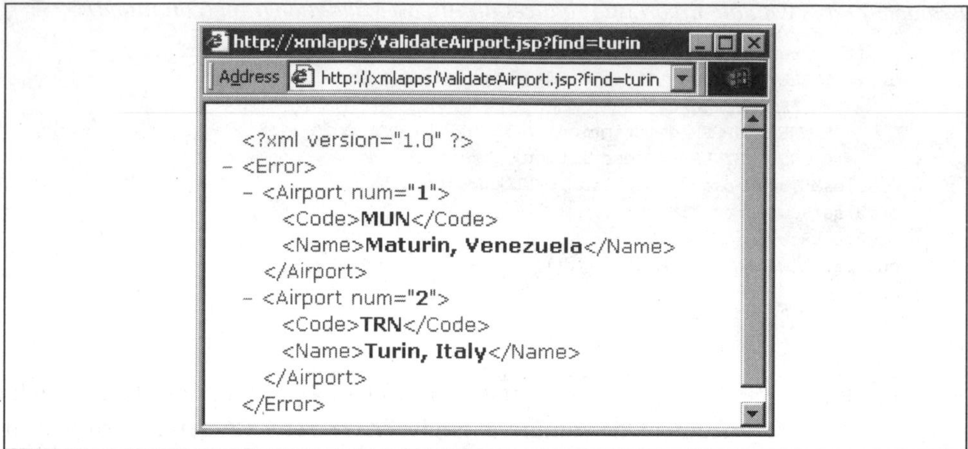

Figure 11-6. Validationgram indicating failure from ValidateAirport.jsp

exact match failed. The requesting client application, sensing the presence of an `<Error>` element after parsing the returned XML validationgram, could choose to search the in-memory document for all `<Airport>` elements to present a list of possible airports to the user.

Controlling How the XML Is Generated

In the examples shown earlier in this chapter, we've used a few of the methods on `OracleXMLQuery` to control how it outputs XML. Table 11-1 shows the comprehensive set of methods and describes the effect each one has on the resulting XML.

Table 11-1. OracleXMLQuery Methods to Control XML Output

Method Name	Description
`setRowsetTag( String )`	Element name to use for the query results. Set equal to the empty string to suppress printing a document element. (Default is `<ROWSET>`.)
`setRowTag( String )`	Element name to use for each row in the query results. Set equal to the empty string to suppress printing a row element. (Default is `<ROW>`.)
`setMaxRows( int )`	Maximum number of rows to fetch from the query. If the SQL query contains an ORDER BY clause, this is useful for fetching the top *N* or bottom *N* records. Use in combination with the `setSkipRows` method, to retrieve the next *N* rows from a query result. (Default is to fetch all rows.)

Table 11-1. OracleXMLQuery Methods to Control XML Output (continued)

Method Name	Description
`setSkipRows( int )`	Number of rows to skip over before returning the query results. Stateless applications can use this method to page through sets of rows in a query result. Use `setSkipRows(n)` in combination with `setMaxRows(m)` to retrieve the set of *m* rows from *n*+1 to *n*+1+*m*. (Default is to not skip any rows.)
`setRowIdAttrName ( String )`	Attribute name for the row identification attribute on each row in the query result. (Default is `num`.)
`setRowIdColumn ( String )`	Column name whose value should be used as the value of the row identifier attribute for each row in the query result. (Default is to use the running row count as the value of the row identification attribute.)
`useNullAttribute Indicator( boolean )`	If set to `true`, causes a null-indicator attribute to be used on the element for any column whose value is `NULL`. (Default is to omit the element in the result for any column with a `NULL` value.)
`useLowerCaseTagNames ( boolean )`	If set to `true`, causes the element names for columns in the query result to be in lowercase.
`useUpperCaseTagNames ( boolean )`	If set to `true`, causes the element names for columns in the query result to be in UPPERCASE.
`keepCursorState ( boolean )`	By default, the `ResultSet` is closed after returning the requested number of rows (or all rows, whichever comes first). Passing `true` to this method leaves the `ResultSet` open and subsequent requests will pick up where they left off, so to speak. Useful in combination with `setMaxRows` for *stateful* applications returning *N* rows at a time to the client.
`setErrorTag( String )`	Element name to use when reporting SQL errors. (Default is `<ERROR>`.)
`setRaiseException ( boolean )`	If set to `true`, causes an `OracleXMLSQLException` exception to be thrown if a SQL error is encountered while processing the query. (Default is to return an `<ERROR>` document showing the error.)
`setRaiseNoRowsException ( boolean )`	If set to `true`, causes an `OracleXMLSQLNoRowsException` to be thrown if the query returns no rows. Use this to catch the case when no rows are returned, typically to be able to attempt a different query instead of the original one. (Default is to return a document with no row elements).
`setStylesheet ( String )`	If a value is set, it is used as the URI in the `href` attribute of an `<?xml-stylesheet?>` processing instruction added to the top of the generated XML document.

By combining these settings appropriately, you'll find you can programmatically produce a wide range of XML datagrams, presenting virtually any information in your entire database in a useful XML format over the Web.

In this chapter, I've delved into the details of producing the XML for any database information that can be summoned by a SQL query. We've demonstrated how to serve that information over the Web in a *raw* XML format. As we saw in Chapter 6, *Processing XML with Java*, by combining this with a programmatically applied XSLT transformation, XML-based query results can be transformed into alternative XML formats or directly into HTML for web-based presentation.

In this chapter:
- *Overview of XML Storage Approaches*
- *Loading Datagrams with the XML SQL Utility*
- *Storing Posted XML Using XSQL Servlet*
- *Inserting Datagrams Using Java*

12

Storing XML Datagrams

As we'll see in this chapter, XML datagrams of any shape and size can be stored in the database via straightforward techniques using Oracle's XML SQL Utility. Once stored, any or all of the data can be retrieved and delivered on request using XSQL pages and XSLT transformations. This means that XML can be the lingua franca for data exchange outside the database without sacrificing any flexibility, scalability, or performance for data retrieval, processing and management inside the database.

As we've seen in previous chapters, XML datagrams are documents with a rigid, predictable structure, typically comprised of nested elements and attributes, as Example 12-1 shows.

Example 12-1. Credit Card Authorization Datagram

```
<?xml version="1.0"?>
<!DOCTYPE AuthorizationRequest SYSTEM "creditcardauth.dtd">
<AuthorizationRequest>
  <CardNumber>4678223355451001</CardNumber>
  <Expiration>10/2001</Expiration>
  <Amount Currency="ITL">118000</Amount>
  <MerchantId>84592342</MerchantId>
  <Date>27-12-1999 11:27:04</Date>
</AuthorizationRequest>
```

In contrast to the rigid structure of XML datagrams, XML documents that represent the written word in some form—technical manuals, contracts, legal proceedings, screenplays, news articles, and others—often contain text mixed with embedded markup tags. Often, a datagram will contain a fragment of this mixed text and markup as an embedded structure, like the `<Description>` of the `<Book>` in Example 12-2.

Example 12-2. Datagram with a Mixed Markup Document Fragment

```
<?xml version="1.0"?>
<Book>
   <ISBN>0395415012</ISBN>
   <Title>Sunrise With Seamonsters</Title>
   <Price>12.75 </Price>
   <Author>
      <First>Paul</First>
      <Last>Theroux</Last>
   </Author>
   <Description>
     Published by <Pub>Houghton Mifflin Co</Pub> in
     <Year>1985</Year>, this <Ed>First</Ed> Edition,
     has a blue and grey <Cov>Hard</Cov> cover.
     <Damage>Light wear to top of spine</Damage>.
     <DJ>Very good</DJ> dust jacket.
   </Description>
</Book>
```

In this chapter, we'll study approaches to storing small to medium-sized datagrams of these two types.

What if you need to store XML documents that are multiple megabytes in size—typically because they contain thousands of nested records with the same, repeating structure? Chapter 14, *Advanced XML Loading Techniques*, provides a more advanced technique that builds on what we learn here and on techniques developed in Chapter 6, *Processing XML with Java*, to handle the job efficiently.

Overview of XML Storage Approaches

There are three basic approaches to storing XML information in an Oracle database:

- You can store an XML document's information content broken down into the columns of one or more databases tables.
- You can store the entire XML document intact in a single column in the database, with an ID value (like the ISBN number in the book example) that plays the role of the document ID.
- You can blend the two approaches to:
  - — Store information from elements containing pure data in their own database columns while storing elements containing "document chunks" intact as document fragments

— Store the entire XML document intact but save some metadata about the document in separate, individual columns

Figure 12-1 illustrates an example of the first approach. The <Book> datagram is stored into a combination of the BOOK and AUTHOR tables in the database. Since the data is in relational tables, it can be queried using SQL. If a <Book> datagram needs to be retrieved from the server, a join query over BOOK and AUTHOR produces the necessary data, which you can transform into a <Book> datagram using an XSLT stylesheet.

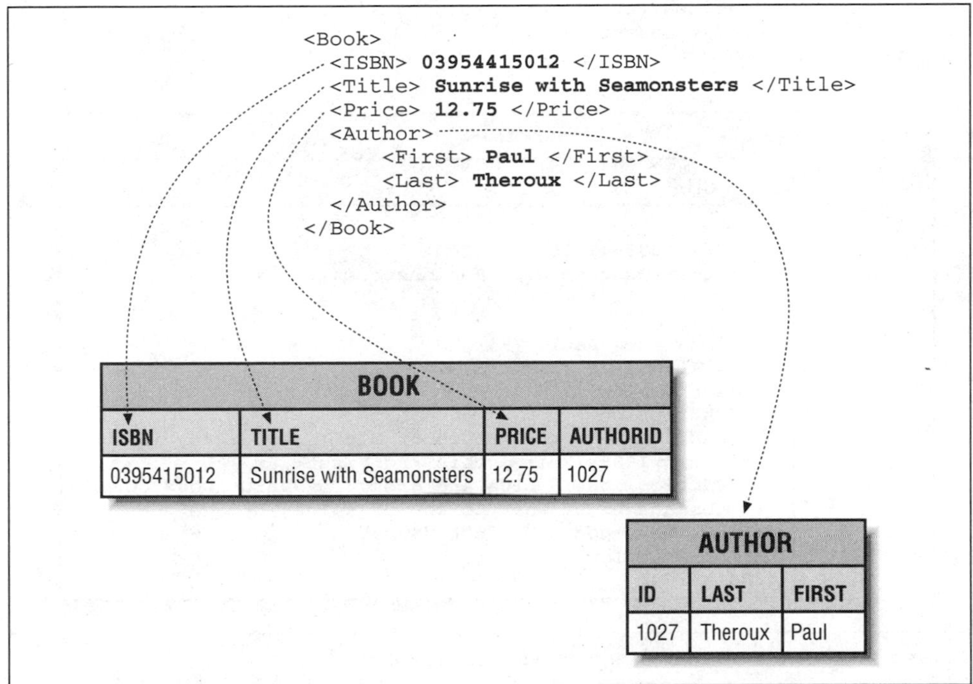

Figure 12-1. Storing datagram into one or more relational tables

Figure 12-2 shows an example of the second approach. The <Book> datagram is stored in a single Character Large Object (CLOB) column, and the <ISBN> number functions as the primary key for the document "row" in the table. As we'll see in Chapter 13, *Searching XML with interMedia,* the document column can be indexed using the Text component of interMedia to enable precise textual searches on the XML document, leveraging its XML element structure, attributes, and nested element hierarchy. Using the integrated InterMedia search operators in SQL, you can locate any books by Paul Theroux that have "Light wear" cited in the <Damage> element of their <Description>. If a <Book> datagram needs to be retrieved from the server, you simply return the contents of the CLOB column.

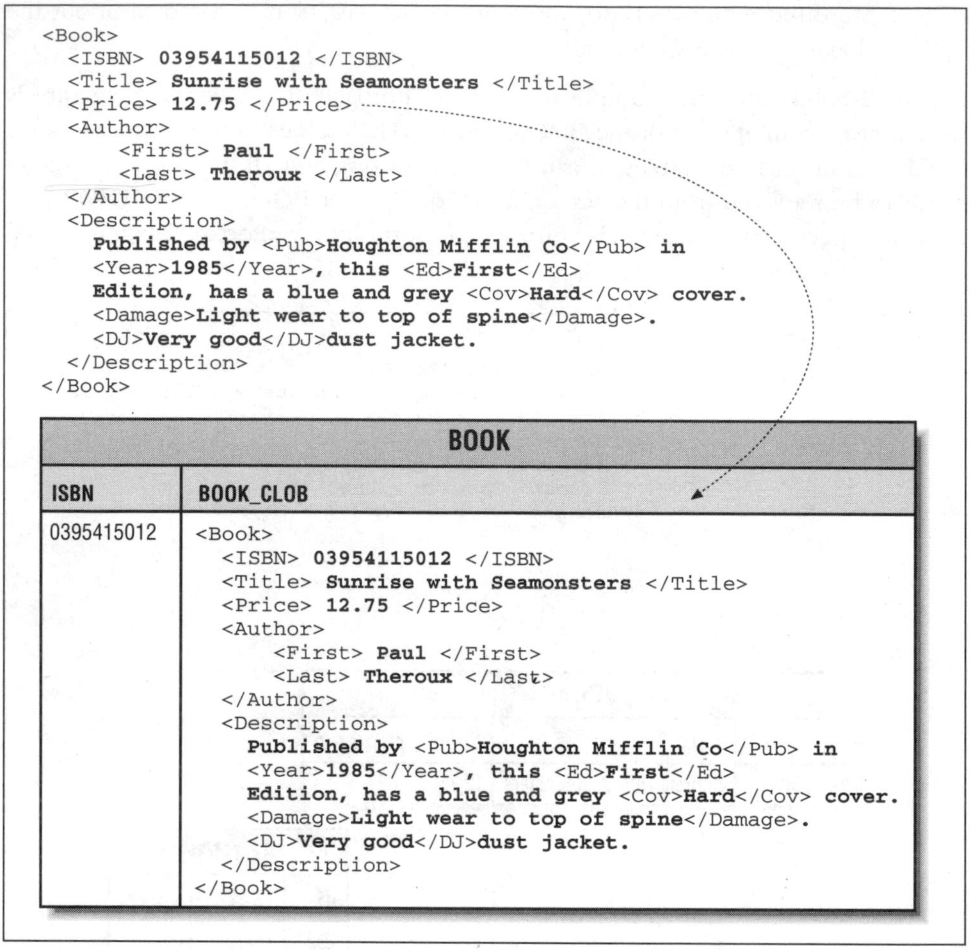

```
<Book>
  <ISBN> 03954115012 </ISBN>
  <Title> Sunrise with Seamonsters </Title>
  <Price> 12.75 </Price>
  <Author>
      <First> Paul </First>
      <Last> Theroux </Last>
  </Author>
  <Description>
    Published by <Pub>Houghton Mifflin Co</Pub> in
    <Year>1985</Year>, this <Ed>First</Ed>
    Edition, has a blue and grey <Cov>Hard</Cov> cover.
    <Damage>Light wear to top of spine</Damage>.
    <DJ>Very good</DJ>dust jacket.
  </Description>
</Book>
```

BOOK	
ISBN	**BOOK_CLOB**
0395415012	<Book> <ISBN> 03954115012 </ISBN> <Title> Sunrise with Seamonsters </Title> <Price> 12.75 </Price> <Author> <First> Paul </First> <Last> Theroux </Last> </Author> <Description> Published by <Pub>Houghton Mifflin Co</Pub> in <Year>1985</Year>, this <Ed>First</Ed> Edition, has a blue and grey <Cov>Hard</Cov> cover. <Damage>Light wear to top of spine</Damage>. <DJ>Very good</DJ>dust jacket. </Description> </Book>

Figure 12-2. Saving an entire document into a single column

Figure 12-3 demonstrates the third, hybrid approach. Pure data like the title, price, and author information goes into its own columns, while the `<Description>` document fragment is stored intact in a table column. Again, using a query over the BOOK and AUTHOR tables together with an appropriate XSLT stylesheet, you can retrieve information on demand in its original XML format.

We'll cover all these techniques for storing datagrams in this chapter.

Loading Datagrams with the XML SQL Utility

The Oracle XML SQL Utility is a command-line utility and a set of Java classes used to automate getting XML out of your database and putting XML into your database.

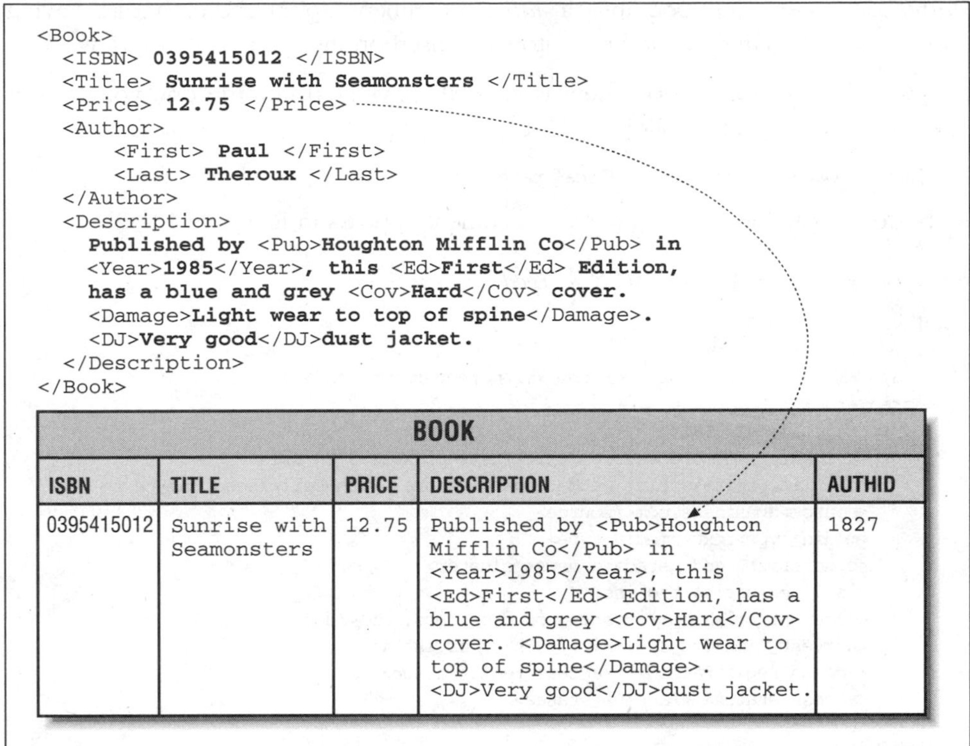
<Book>
<ISBN> 0395415012 </ISBN>
<Title> Sunrise with Seamonsters </Title>
<Price> 12.75 </Price>
<Author>
<First> Paul </First>
<Last> Theroux </Last>
</Author>
<Description>
Published by <Pub>Houghton Mifflin Co</Pub> in
<Year>1985</Year>, this <Ed>First</Ed> Edition,
has a blue and grey <Cov>Hard</Cov> cover.
<Damage>Light wear to top of spine</Damage>.
<DJ>Very good</DJ>dust jacket.
</Description>
</Book>
BOOK
ISBN
TITLE
PRICE
DESCRIPTION
AUTHID
0395415012
Sunrise with Seamonsters
12.75
Published by <Pub>Houghton Mifflin Co</Pub> in <Year>1985</Year>, this <Ed>First</Ed> Edition, has a blue and grey <Cov>Hard</Cov> cover. <Damage>Light wear to top of spine</Damage>. <DJ>Very good</DJ>dust jacket.
1827

Figure 12-3. Saving both data and document fragments in columns

We have seen that the `OracleXMLQuery` class handles all the details of getting SQL query results out of the database in a canonical XML format. The XML SQL Utility also contains a companion class called `OracleXMLSave` that performs the opposite job of putting XML information back into Oracle tables or views.

The `OracleXMLSave` class understands how to insert any information that `OracleXMLQuery` knows how to produce. In other words, the canonical structure of the *output* from `OracleXMLQuery` defines the kinds of structures for *input* that `OracleXMLSave` can automatically insert for us.

Transforming Datagrams for Insertion

The fact that `OracleXMLSave` can only insert XML documents that look like they were produced by `OracleXMLQuery` may at first sound like a drastic limitation. However, this is not the case by any stretch of the imagination. By taking advantage of an appropriate XSLT transformation, virtually any XML document can be transformed to the canonical format required by `OracleXMLSave`. Given an arbitrary XML document `YourDoc` and a database table or view into which you want to insert the document, you can create an XSLT transformation that transforms the *source* document `YourDoc` into a *target* document `YourDocCanonical` having precisely the structure needed for automatic insertion into your table or view.

Let's say that the source document is an XML news feed like the one you'd see if you were to browse the following URL:

```
http://www.moreover.com/cgi-local/page?index_xml+xml
```

A shortened version of such an XML document appears in Example 12-3.

Example 12-3. Moreover.com XML News Feed

```
<?xml version="1.0"?>
   <!DOCTYPE moreovernews
      SYSTEM "http://www.moreover.com/xml/moreovernews.dtd">
   <moreovernews>
      <article id="4227581">
         <url>http://d.moreover.com/click/here.pl?x4227575</url>
         <headline_text>Austin: webMethods gets deal with Dell</headline_text>
         <source>dbusiness.com</source>
         <media_type>text</media_type>
         <cluster>XML and metadata news</cluster>
         <tagline>Austin</tagline>
         <document_url>http://washington.dbusiness.com/</document_url>
         <harvest_time>Oct 30 1999  7:08AM</harvest_time>
         <access_registration> </access_registration>
         <access_status> </access_status>
      </article>
      <article id="4202251">
         <url>http://d.moreover.com/click/here.pl?x4202247</url>
         <headline_text>IBM Brings XML To MQSeries</headline_text>
         <source>Internet Week</source>
         <media_type>text</media_type>
         <cluster>XML and metadata news</cluster>
         <tagline></tagline>
         <document_url>http://www.internetwk.com/</document_url>
         <harvest_time>Oct 28 1999  4:28PM</harvest_time>
         <access_registration> </access_registration>
         <access_status> </access_status>
      </article>
   </moreovernews>
```

Next, let's say that you have a table called newsstory that you created with the following DDL statement:

```
CREATE TABLE newsstory(
 id     NUMBER PRIMARY KEY,
 title  VARCHAR2(200),
 url    VARCHAR2(200),
 source VARCHAR2(200)
);
```

And further, let's suppose you want to insert information from the Moreover.com XML news feed into this table. We need to produce an XSL transformation that transforms the information in the XML news feed from Moreover.com into the canonical format that `OracleXMLSave` knows how to insert into the newsstory table.

After inserting a sample news story, we start by using an XSQL page to quickly produce one row of canonical query results from the newsstory table. We can produce this with the XSQL page shown in Example 12-4.

Example 12-4. XSQL Page to Produce Canonical ROWSET/ROW Format

```
<?xml version="1.0"?>
<!-- newsstory-canonical.xsql -->
<xsql:query connection="xmlbook" max-rows="1" xmlns:xsql="urn:oracle-xsql">
 SELECT * FROM newsstory
</xsql:query>
```

We can either request this page through the web server, or more conveniently for this job, we can use the XSQL command-line utility to quickly put the XSQL page's output into a file:

```
xsql newstory-canonical.xsql newsstory.xml
```

This command processes the *newsstory.xsql* page and writes the output to the *newsstory.xml* file. The contents of the *newsstory.xml* file will look like this:

```
<?xml version = '1.0'?>
<ROWSET>
   <ROW num="1">
      <ID>1911</ID>
      <TITLE>Some Title</TITLE>
      <URL>http://somemachine/somepage.html</URL>
      <SOURCE>SomeSource</SOURCE>
   </ROW>
</ROWSET>
```

We can take this one row of canonical output from a SELECT * query over the newsstory table and immediately turn it into our "insert transformation" by following these steps:

1. Add an `xsl` namespace declaration to the document element and the required `xsl:version="1.0"` attribute to signal that this document will be used as an XSLT transformation.
2. Remove the `num="1"` attribute from the `<ROW>` element since it serves no purpose to the XML SQL Utility for inserts.
3. Remove any elements corresponding to columns whose values will be assigned by database triggers (for this example, we'll remove the `<ID>` element).
4. Surround the `<ROW>` element with an `<xsl:for-each>` that loops over the `<article>` elements in the source document from Moreover.com.

5. Replace the literal text between the `<TITLE>`, `<URL>`, and `<SOURCE>` elements with an appropriate `<xsl:value-of>` element to plug in the appropriate information from the *current* `<article>` we're looping over to the enclosing `<xsl:for-each>` loop.

Applying these changes to the *newsstory.xml* file produces the XSL transformation in Example 12-5.

Example 12-5. Transforming Moreover.com News to ROWSET/ROW Format

```
<!-- moreover-to-newsstory.xsl -->
<ROWSET xmlns:xsl="http://www.w3.org/1999/XSL/Transform" xsl:version="1.0">
  <xsl:for-each select="moreovernews/article">
    <ROW>
       <TITLE><xsl:value-of select="headline_text"/></TITLE>
       <URL><xsl:value-of select="url"/></URL>
       <SOURCE>
          <xsl:choose>
            <xsl:when test="source != ''">
              <xsl:value-of select="source"/>
            </xsl:when>
            <xsl:otherwise>Moreover.com</xsl:otherwise>
          </xsl:choose>
       </SOURCE>
    </ROW>
  </xsl:for-each>
</ROWSET>
```

Recall that this is the simple form of an XSLT transformation that looks like a literal example of the result.

This example illustrates:

- Adding the `xsl` namespace declaration to the `<ROWSET>` element and adding the required `xsl:version="1.0"` attribute:

  ```
  <ROWSET xmlns:xsl="http://www.w3.org/1999/XSL/Transform" xsl:version="1.0">
  ```

- Adding the `<xsl:for-each>` element to loop over each `<article>` element that occurs as a child of the `<moreovernews>` element in the source document:

  ```
  <xsl:for-each select="moreovernews/article">
  ```

  so that for each `<article>` we find in the source, we create a `<ROW>` in the target.

- Removing the `<ID>` element, since its value will be assigned by our database trigger that assigns new story IDs from a database sequence.

- Changing the following tags:

  ```
  <TITLE>Some Title</TITLE>
  <URL>http://somemachine/somepage.html</URL>
  ```

  to:

  ```
  <TITLE><xsl:value-of select="headline_text"/></TITLE>
  <URL><xsl:value-of select="url"/></URL>
  ```

  to plug in the value of the current `<headline_text>` and `<url>` elements for the current `<article>`.

- Using an `<xsl:choose>` element to conditionally provide the value of the <SOURCE> element indicating where this news story came from:

  ```
  <SOURCE>
    <xsl:choose>
      <xsl:when test="source != ''">
        <xsl:value-of select="source"/>
      </xsl:when>
      <xsl:otherwise>Moreover.com</xsl:otherwise>
    </xsl:choose>
  </SOURCE>
  ```

  This construct selects the value of the `<source>` element from the current article if its value is a non-empty string; otherwise, it assigns the hard-coded value of `Moreover.com` as the content of the <SOURCE> element in the target document.

If we rename the now-edited *newsstory.xml* file to *moreover-to-newsstory.xsl* to reflect its new role as an XSLT transformation, we can use the command-line **oraxsl** utility to test our transformation:

```
oraxsl moreover.xml moreover-to-newsstory.xsl out.xml
```

The *moreover.xml* file includes a doctype declaration with an `http://` reference to the MoreoverNews DTD:

```
<!DOCTYPE moreovernews
   SYSTEM "http://www.moreover.com/xml/MoreoverNews.dtd">
```

If you are working on a machine that accesses the Internet through a firewall, you need to provide the following three extra Java virtual machine parameters to allow the Oracle XML Parser to properly find and parse the DTD through your proxy server:

```
java -DproxySet=true
     -DproxyHost=yourproxyserver
     -DproxyPort=80
     oracle.xml.parser.v2.oraxsl moreover.xml moreover-to-
newsstory.xsl out.xml
```

Failure to do this when required will result in a long pause while the XML Parser times out waiting for a network connection to resolve the DTD location outside your firewall.

If we use Internet Explorer to browse the resulting *out.xml* file, we can see the results of the transformation in Figure 12-4.

```
<?xml version="1.0" encoding="UTF-8" ?>
- <ROWSET>
  - <ROW>
      <TITLE>Austin: webMethods gets deal with Dell</TITLE>
      <URL>http://d.moreover.com/click/here.pl?x4227575</URL>
      <SOURCE>dbusiness.com</SOURCE>
    </ROW>
  - <ROW>
      <TITLE>IBM Brings XML To MQSeries</TITLE>
      <URL>http://d.moreover.com/click/here.pl?x4202247</URL>
      <SOURCE>Internet Week</SOURCE>
    </ROW>
  </ROWSET>
```

Figure 12-4. Moreover news results transformed into ROWSET/ROW format

If we pass this resulting target document to the `OracleXML` utility using the `putXML` option, it will effortlessly insert all of the Moreover.com data into our newsstory table:

```
java OracleXML putXML -user xmlbook/xmlbok -fileName out.xml newsstory
```

However, if we try to execute this command now, we'll get the following error:

```
ORA-01400: cannot insert NULL into ("XMLBOOK"."NEWSSTORY"."ID")
```

This occurs because the transformed *out.xml* document (on purpose!) does not include any `<ID>` element for each NEWSSTORY `<ROW>`. Therefore, the `OracleXML` utility tries to insert a NULL for the `ID` column in the newsstory table that fails, since ID is the primary key for the table and therefore cannot be NULL.

To have the database automatically assign the `ID` column a unique NEWSSTORY ID value from a database sequence, we can use the standard trick of creating a BEFORE INSERT trigger on the newsstory table to select the new ID number from a sequence. Assuming that we have a sequence named **`newsstory_id_seq`** lying around, the code looks like Example 12-6.

Example 12-6. BEFORE INSERT Trigger Assigns Unique NEWSSTORY ID

```
CREATE TRIGGER newsstory_autoid
BEFORE INSERT ON newsstory FOR EACH ROW
BEGIN
  SELECT newsstory_id_seq.nextval
    INTO :new.id
    FROM dual;
END;
```

In the body of a database trigger, the values of the columns being inserted can be accessed as fields of the special, record-structured `new` bind variable. So by using `:new.id` in Example 12-6 as an INTO target variable for the SELECT statement, we're effectively setting the value of the `ID` column that's about to be inserted (remember, the example is a BEFORE INSERT trigger) to the next value from the database sequence.

When we try the command again:

```
java OracleXML putXML -user xmlbook/xmlbook -fileName out.xml newsstory
```

we get a successful outcome:

```
successfully inserted 2 rows into newsstory
```

So we've shown that given a news feed of stories from Moreover.com in their published XML news format, we can store the parts of the news stories we care about internally in a database table of our own choosing. To further underscore the fact that the *internal* storage of the news stories is a detail that external clients need not care about, let's see how we can serve the information in our newsstory table in the appropriate Moreover.com news format.

To retrieve the information back from the database in the Moreover.com news format, we again can use an XSLT transformation to transform the results of a standard <ROWSET>/<ROW> XML query over the newsstory table into the exact Moreover.com XML news format.

To create the *newsstory-to-moreover.xsl* transformation, we can follow a cookbook approach similar to what we did earlier to create the *moreover-to-newsstory.xsl* transformation in Figure 12-4:

1. Start with an XML document that is a literal example of your desired target format. In this case, we'll start with a minimal example of one article in a Moreover.com XML news feed, containing a single `<article>`:

```
<?xml version="1.0"?>
   <!DOCTYPE moreovernews
      SYSTEM "http://www.moreover.com/xml/moreovernews.dtd">
   <moreovernews>
      <article id="4227581">
         <url>http://d.moreover.com/click/here.pl?x4227575</url>
         <headline_text>Austin: webMethods gets deal with Dell</headline_text>
         <source>dbusiness.com</source>
         <media_type>text</media_type>
         <cluster>XML and metadata news</cluster>
         <tagline>Austin</tagline>
         <document_url>http://washington.dbusiness.com/</document_url>
         <harvest_time>Oct 30 1999  7:08AM</harvest_time>
```

```
        <access_registration> </access_registration>
        <access_status> </access_status>
    </article>
  </moreovernews>
```

2. Decide whether you can use the simple form of an XSLT transformation or whether you need to begin the transformation with an initial `<xsl:stylesheet>` element.

   In this case, since we want to include a `<!DOCTYPE>` in our transformed result, we need to use the `<xsl:output>` element to indicate the desired URI for the DTD in its `doctype-system` attribute. Since `<xsl:output>` is only legal if it appears at the top level of a transformation enclosed by an `<xsl:stylesheet>` element, we cannot use the simple form of the transformation.

3. Add the bits of necessary information to turn the literal example into a legal XSLT transformation. Given the simple form of a transformation, this means adding the XSLT namespace declaration and `xsl:version="1.0"` attribute to the document element of your transformation, like this:

   ```
   <DocElementName xsl:version="1.0"
     xmlns:xsl="http://www.w3.org/1999/XSL/Transform">
   ```

   For the more general case, this means adding:

   ```
   <xsl:stylesheet xmlns:xsl="http://www.w3.org/1999/XSL/Transform">
     <xsl:template match="/">
   ```

   before your opening document element name tag, and:

   ```
   </xsl:template>
   </xsl:stylesheet>
   ```

   after the closing document element name tag.

   So in this case we'll have:

   ```
   <?xml version="1.0"?>
   <xsl:stylesheet xmlns:xsl="http://www.w3.org/1999/XSL/Transform">
     <xsl:template match="/">
       <moreovernews>
          <!-- etc -->
       </moreovernews>
     </xsl:template>
   </xsl:stylesheet>
   ```

4. Wrap the literal elements that must repeat for each `<ROW>` of query results with an `<xsl:for-each select="ROWSET/ROW">` element. Since we want one `<article>` element in the Moreover.com format for each `<ROW>` in the query results from our newsstory table, we'll have:

   ```
   <?xml version="1.0"?>
   <xsl:stylesheet xmlns:xsl="http://www.w3.org/1999/XSL/Transform" version="1.0">
     <xsl:template match="/">
      <moreovernews>
        <xsl:for-each select="ROWSET/ROW">
   ```

```
        <article id="4227581">
           <url>http://d.moreover.com/click/here.pl?x4227575</url>
           <headline_text>Austin: webMethods gets deal with Dell</headline_text>
           <source>dbusiness.com</source>
           <media_type>text</media_type>
           <cluster>XML and metadata news</cluster>
           <tagline>Austin</tagline>
           <document_url>http://washington.dbusiness.com/</document_url>
           <harvest_time>Oct 30 1999  7:08AM</harvest_time>
           <access_registration> </access_registration>
           <access_status> </access_status>
        </article>
       </xsl:for-each>
     </moreovernews>
  </xsl:template>
</xsl:stylesheet>
```

5. Remove any literal elements and attributes that you don't want in the transformed output and:

   — Replace literal examples of *element text content* needing a dynamic value by an appropriate `<xsl:value-of select="*pattern*"/>` element.

   — Replace literal examples of *attribute value content* needing a dynamic value by an appropriate `{*pattern*}` attribute value template.

   Our transformation will look like this:

```
<?xml version="1.0"?>
<xsl:stylesheet xmlns:xsl="http://www.w3.org/1999/XSL/Transform">
  <xsl:template match="/">
   <moreovernews>
     <xsl:for-each select="ROWSET/ROW">
       <article id="{ID}">
          <url><xsl:value-of select="URL"/></url>
          <headline_text><xsl:value-of select="TITLE"/></headline_text>
          <source><xsl:value-of select="SOURCE"/></source>
       </article>
     </xsl:for-each>
    </moreovernews>
  </xsl:template>
</xsl:stylesheet>
```

   Here, `{ID}` is used to plug the value of the `<ID>` of the current `<ROW>` into the value of the `<article>` element's `id` attribute, and appropriate `<xsl:value-of>` elements are used to plug in the appropriate dynamic element values.

6. If you need to associate a DTD with the transformed result or wish to change the default for other output hints like indentation, add an `<xsl:output>` element. In this case, we need:

```
<xsl:output indent="yes"
    doctype-system="http://www.moreover.com/xml/moreovernews.dtd"/>
```

The final *newsstory-to-moreover.xsl* transformation is shown in Example 12-7.

Example 12-7. Transforming ROWSET/ROW to Moreover.com News Format

```
<!-- newsstory-to-moreover.xsl -->
<xsl:stylesheet version="1.0" xmlns:xsl="http://www.w3.org/1999/XSL/Transform">
  <xsl:output indent="yes"
             doctype-system="http://www.moreover.com/xml/moreovernews.dtd"/>
  <xsl:template match="/">
    <moreovernews>
      <xsl:for-each select="ROWSET/ROW">
        <article id="{ID}">
          <url><xsl:value-of select="URL"/></url>
          <headline_text><xsl:value-of select="TITLE"/></headline_text>
          <source><xsl:value-of select="SOURCE"/></source>
        </article>
      </xsl:for-each>
    </moreovernews>
  </xsl:template>
</xsl:stylesheet>
```

After learning some more advanced XSLT concepts in Chapter 14, we will create a stylesheet and an XSQL page that automate the creation of these insert transformations for any table or view.

If we build an XSQL page like *latest-news.xsql* in Example 12-8 to query a set of news stories from our newsstory table and associate our new *newsstory-to-moreover.xsl* transformation with it, we'll be in business.

Example 12-8. XSQL Page Displaying Two Most Recent Stories

```
<?xml version="1.0"?>
<!-- latest-news.xsql -->
<?xml-stylesheet type="text/xsl" href="newsstory-to-moreover.xsl"?>
<xsql:query connection="xmlbook" max-rows="2" xmlns:xsql="urn:oracle-xsql">
 SELECT *
   FROM newsstory
  ORDER BY ID DESC
</xsql:query>
```

Here we present the two most recent stories using an ORDER BY ID DESC (assuming that the greater the sequence-generated ID value, the more recently the story was added) and a `max-rows="2"` on the `<xsql:query>` element. Now anyone who wants to request the latest news stories in Moreover.com XML news format can request the URL:

```
http://yourserver/latest-news.xsql
```

and receive the following XML document:

```
<?xml version = '1.0' encoding = 'UTF-8'?>
<!DOCTYPE moreovernews
   SYSTEM "http://www.moreover.com/xml/moreovernews.dtd">
<moreovernews>
   <article id="2">
      <url>http://d.moreover.com/click/here.pl?x4202247</url>
      <headline_text>IBM Brings XML To MQSeries</headline_text>
      <source>Moreover.com</source>
   </article>
   <article id="1">
      <url>http://d.moreover.com/click/here.pl?x4227575</url>
      <headline_text>Austin: webMethods gets deal with Dell</headline_text>
      <source>Moreover.com</source>
   </article>
</moreovernews>
```

So we've walked through the complete loop of getting an XML datagram in and out of relational tables. The information arrives in Moreover.com XML news format and it goes out in Moreover.com news format, but internally we can work with it from existing or new applications using familiar SQL against the newsstory table.

A Slightly More Complicated Storage Example

Let's look at another example. Recall the credit card authorization from the beginning of the chapter:

```
<?xml version="1.0"?>
<!DOCTYPE AuthorizationRequest SYSTEM "creditcardauth.dtd">
<AuthorizationRequest>
  <CardNumber>4678223355451001</CardNumber>
  <Expiration>10/2001</Expiration>
  <Amount Currency="ITL">118000</Amount>
  <MerchantId>84592342</MerchantId>
  <Date>27-12-1999 11:27:04</Date>
</AuthorizationRequest>
```

Here are a few things that make this example different from the Moreover.com example we saw earlier:

- The `Currency` is an attribute on the `<Amount>` element.
- The `<Expiration>` element contains embedded month and year information in a `MM/YYYY` string format.
- The `<Date>` element uses a format that is not the standard Java date format.

We'll see that the same approach we took earlier still works here, but we need to make a few changes to accommodate these little twists.

Assume that our credit card authorization_request table looks like this:

```
CREATE TABLE authorization_request (
 request_id          NUMBER PRIMARY KEY,
 request_date        DATE,
 card_number         NUMBER(16,0),
 exp_month           NUMBER,
 exp_year            NUMBER,
 amount              NUMBER,
 currency            VARCHAR2(3),
 merchant_id         NUMBER,
 approved            VARCHAR2(1),
 authorization       NUMBER
);
```

As we did in Example 12-4, assuming there is at least one row of data in the table, we can obtain the canonical XML format of a row in this table by doing a SELECT * query from the table in an XSQL page with `max-rows="1"`:

```
<?xml version="1.0"?>
<xsql:query connection="xmlbook"  max-rows="1" xmlns:xsql="urn:oracle-xsql">
  SELECT * FROM authorization_request
</xsql:query>
```

If we save this XSQL page in a file called *creditcardauthcanonical.xsql*, we can quickly produce the canonical XML output into a temporary file like *out.xml* by using the XSQL command-line utility:

```
xsql creditcardauthcanonical.xsql out.xml
```

This produces the following output; the *out.xml* file can now be used as the basis for our insert transformation to transform the `<AuthorizationRequest>` into a `<ROWSET>` document that can be inserted:

```
<?xml version = '1.0'?>
<ROWSET>
   <ROW num="1">
      <REQUEST_ID>43</REQUEST_ID>
      <REQUEST_DATE>1999-12-27 11:27:04.0</REQUEST_DATE>
      <CARD_NUMBER>4678223355451001</CARD_NUMBER>
      <EXP_MONTH>10</EXP_MONTH>
      <EXP_YEAR>2001</EXP_YEAR>
      <AMOUNT>118000</AMOUNT>
      <CURRENCY>ITL</CURRENCY>
      <MERCHANT_ID>84592342</MERCHANT_ID>
   </ROW>
</ROWSET>
```

To morph this sample file of canonical XML query output from the authorization_request table into our insert transformation for credit card authorizations, we can follow a similar approach to the one we took in the previous section:

1. Add an xsl namespace declaration to the document element and the required xsl:version="1.0" attribute to signal that this document will be used as an XSLT transformation.
2. Remove the num="1" attribute from the <ROW> element.
3. Remove any elements corresponding to columns whose values will be assigned by database triggers (for this example, we'll remove <REQUEST_ID>).
4. Surround the <ROW> element with an <xsl:for-each> to make the transformation loop over any <AuthorizationRequest> elements in the source document, producing one <ROW> in the target for each <AuthorizationRequest> in the source.
5. Replace the literal text between the <REQUEST_DATE>, <CARD_NUMBER>, <EXP_MONTH>, <EXP_YEAR>, <AMOUNT>, <CURRENCY>, and <MERCHANT_ID> elements with an appropriate <xsl:value-of> element to plug in the appropriate information from the current <AuthorizationRequest>.

Applying these changes to the *out.xml* file and renaming it to a more meaningful name produces the *creditcardauth-to-rowset.xsl* transformation in Example 12-9.

Example 12-9. Transform AuthorizationRequest to ROWSET/ROW Format

```
<!-- creditcardauth-to-rowset.xsl -->
<ROWSET xmlns:xsl="http://www.w3.org/1999/XSL/Transform" xsl:version="1.0">
  <xsl:for-each select="AuthorizationRequest">
    <ROW>
      <REQUEST_DATE><xsl:value-of select="Date"/></REQUEST_DATE>
      <CARD_NUMBER><xsl:value-of select="CardNumber"/></CARD_NUMBER>
      <EXP_MONTH><xsl:value-of select="substring(Expiration,1,2)"/></EXP_MONTH>
      <EXP_YEAR><xsl:value-of select="substring(Expiration,4)"/></EXP_YEAR>
      <AMOUNT><xsl:value-of select="Amount"/></AMOUNT>
      <CURRENCY><xsl:value-of select="Amount/@Currency"/></CURRENCY>
      <MERCHANT_ID><xsl:value-of select="MerchantId"/></MERCHANT_ID>
    </ROW>
  </xsl:for-each>
</ROWSET>
```

Here we have done the following:

- Added the xsl namespace declaration to the <ROWSET> element:

  ```
  <ROWSET xmlns:xsl="http://www.w3.org/1999/XSL/Transform">
  ```

- Added the <xsl:for-each> element to loop over the (one) <AuthorizationRequest> element in the source document:

  ```
  <xsl:for-each select="AuthorizationRequest">
  ```

- Removed the <REQUEST_ID> element since its value will be assigned by a database trigger from a sequence.

- Changed the following tags:

```
<REQUEST_DATE>1999-12-27 11:27:04.0</REQUEST_DATE>
<CARD_NUMBER>4678223355451001</CARD_NUMBER>
<EXP_MONTH>10</EXP_MONTH>
<EXP_YEAR>2001</EXP_YEAR>
<AMOUNT>118000</AMOUNT>
<CURRENCY>ITL</CURRENCY>
<MERCHANT_ID>84592342</MERCHANT_ID>
```

  to:

```
<REQUEST_DATE><xsl:value-of select="Date"/></REQUEST_DATE>
<CARD_NUMBER><xsl:value-of select="CardNumber"/></CARD_NUMBER>
<EXP_MONTH><xsl:value-of select="substring(Expiration,1,2)"/></EXP_MONTH>
<EXP_YEAR><xsl:value-of select="substring(Expiration,4)"/></EXP_YEAR>
<AMOUNT><xsl:value-of select="Amount"/></AMOUNT>
<CURRENCY><xsl:value-of select="Amount/@Currency"/></CURRENCY>
<MERCHANT_ID><xsl:value-of select="MerchantId"/></MERCHANT_ID>
```

  to plug the values from the appropriate `<AuthorizationRequest>` child elements and attributes (using patterns that are relative to the current `<AuthorizationRequest>`) into the `<xsl:for-each>` loop.

  To plug the value of the `Currency` attribute of the `<Amount>` element in the source into the value of `<AMOUNT>` element in the target, we use the pattern `Amount/@Currency`. To pick out the two digits of the month and the four digits of the year from the `<Expiration>` element's MM/YYYY value, we make use of the XPath `substring()` function in the patterns for the values of `<EXP_MONTH>` and `<EXP_YEAR>`, respectively.

Although our example has only a single `<AuthorizationRequest>` element, it still makes sense to use `<xsl:for-each>` to loop over that element. This allows the `select` expressions in any nested `<xsl:value-of>` or XSL attribute value templates to be given as patterns relative to the current `<AuthorizationRequest>` in the loop, so it keeps the patterns shorter, requires less typing, and makes the transformation source easier to understand.

We can use the Oracle XSLT Processor's command-line utility `oraxsl` to transform the `<AuthorizationRequest>` in *creditcardauth.xml* using the *creditcardauth-to-rowset.xsl* transformation; we'll save the output into a temporary file called *out.xml*, which will have the canonical `<ROWSET>/<ROW>` structure the Oracle XML SQL Utility understands:

```
oraxsl creditcardauth.xml creditcardauth-to-rowset.xsl out.xml
```

The resulting *out.xml* file looks like this:

```
<?xml version = '1.0' encoding = 'UTF-8'?>
<ROWSET>
  <ROW>
    <REQUEST_DATE>27-12-1999 11:27:04</REQUEST_DATE>
    <CARD_NUMBER>4678223355451001</CARD_NUMBER>
    <EXP_MONTH>10</EXP_MONTH>
    <EXP_YEAR>2001</EXP_YEAR>
    <AMOUNT>118000</AMOUNT>
    <CURRENCY>ITL</CURRENCY>
    <MERCHANT_ID>84592342</MERCHANT_ID>
  </ROW>
</ROWSET>
```

which is ready for automatic insertion into the authorization_request table using the `OracleXML` command-line utility with this command (all arguments should be on one line):

```
java OracleXML putXML -user xmlbook/xmlbook
                      -dateFormat "d-M-y H:m:s"
                      -fileName out.xml
                      authorization_request
```

This time, we need to provide the **`-dateFormat`** flag, with a time pattern mask of `d-M-y H:m:s` corresponding to the format of the date value `27-12-1999 11:27:04` in our <REQUEST_DATE> element. We need this flag because our date format differs from the default Java string format, which would be `1999-12-27 11:27:04.0`.

The list of valid date formats the `OracleXML` utility accepts is documented in the JavaDoc for the `java.text.SimpleDateFormat` class, available at *http://java.sun.com/products/jdk/1.1/docs/api/java.text.SimpleDateFormat.html.*

To avoid the ORA-01400 error we got last time, we'll use a database sequence to create unique values:

```
CREATE SEQUENCE authorization_request_seq;
```

and a BEFORE INSERT trigger on the authorization_request table to make the assignment of the new `request_id` automatic:

```
CREATE TRIGGER authorization_request_befins
BEFORE INSERT ON authorization_request
FOR EACH ROW
BEGIN
  -- Only assign a new id number if one is not supplied
  IF :new.request_id IS NULL THEN
    SELECT authorization_request_seq.nextval
     INTO :new.request_id
     FROM dual;
  END IF;
END;
```

The code for this trigger is a slight variation on the trigger from Example 12-6. This trigger shows how to conditionally assign the `request_id` only in the case that it was not already provided.

Now, repeating the `OracleXML putXML` command from before:

```
java OracleXML putXML -user xmlbook/xmlbook
                      -dateFormat "d-M-y H:m:s"
                      -fileName out.xml
                      authorization_request
```

produces the success message:

```
successfully inserted 1 rows into authorization_request
```

Once the data has made its way successfully into our authorization_request table, we should be prepared to serve the data back on request in the appropriate `<AuthorizationRequest>` format. We can build an XSQL page like *creditcardauth.xsql* in Example 12-10 to create a datagram for the row of the authorization_request table with `request_id` matching the `id` passed in the request.

Example 12-10. Serving <AuthorizationRequest> Datagrams

```
<?xml version="1.0"?>
<!-- creditcardauth.xsql -->
<?xml-stylesheet type="text/xsl" href="rowset-to-creditcardauth.xsl"?>
<xsql:query xmlns:xsql="urn:oracle-xsql" connection="xmlbook"  max-rows="1" >

  SELECT card_number, exp_month, exp_year, amount, currency, merchant_id,
         /* Use TO_CHAR to format date as we want it in resulting XML */
         TO_CHAR(request_date,'DD-MM-YYYY HH24:MI:SS') as request_date
    FROM authorization_request
   WHERE request_id = {@id}

</xsql:query>
```

By associating an appropriate XSLT transformation to this XSQL page, we can ensure that the requester sees a perfectly valid `<AuthorizationRequest>` document instead of the default `<ROWSET>` document that an `<xsql:query>` would return by default. To create the appropriate stylesheet, we follow the same steps that we did earlier:

1. Start with an XML document that is a literal example of your desired target format. In this case, we'll start with an example of an `<AuthorizationRequest>`:

   ```
   <?xml version="1.0"?>
   <!DOCTYPE AuthorizationRequest SYSTEM "creditcardauth.dtd">
   <AuthorizationRequest>
     <CardNumber>4678223355451001</CardNumber>
   ```

```
  <Expiration>10/2001</Expiration>
  <Amount Currency="ITL">118000</Amount>
  <MerchantId>84592342</MerchantId>
  <Date>27-12-1999 11:27:04</Date>
</AuthorizationRequest>
```

2. Decide whether you can use the simple form of an XSLT transformation, or whether you need to begin the transformation with an initial **`<xsl:stylesheet>`** element. Since we want to include a `<!DOCTYPE>` in our transformed result, we need to use the **`<xsl:output>`** element to indicate the desired URI for the DTD in its `doctype-system` attribute.

3. Add the bits of necessary information to turn the literal example into a legal XSLT transformation. Here, we add:

   ```
   <xsl:stylesheet xmlns:xsl="http://www.w3.org/1999/XSL/Transform">
     <xsl:template match="/">
   ```

   before the `<AuthorizationRequest>` element, and:

   ```
     </xsl:template>
     </xsl:stylesheet>
   ```

   after the closing `</AuthorizationRequest>` tag.

   In this case, we'll have:

   ```
   <?xml version="1.0"?>
   <!DOCTYPE AuthorizationRequest SYSTEM "creditcardauth.dtd">
   <xsl:stylesheet xmlns:xsl="http://www.w3.org/1999/XSL/Transform">
     <xsl:template match="/">
       <AuthorizationRequest>
          <!-- etc -->
       </AuthorizationRequest>
     </xsl:template>
   </xsl:stylesheet>
   ```

4. Wrap the literal elements that must repeat for each `<ROW>` of query results with an **`<xsl:for-each select="ROWSET/ROW">`** element. Since we want one `<AuthorizationRequest>` for each `<ROW>` in the query results from our authorization_request table, we don't have to do anything in this step:

   ```
   <?xml version="1.0"?>
   <!DOCTYPE AuthorizationRequest SYSTEM "creditcardauth.dtd">
   <xsl:stylesheet xmlns:xsl="http://www.w3.org/1999/XSL/Transform">
     <xsl:template match="/">
       <xsl:for-each select="ROWSET/ROW">
         <AuthorizationRequest>
           <CardNumber>4678223355451001</CardNumber>
           <Expiration>10/2001</Expiration>
           <Amount Currency="ITL">118000</Amount>
           <MerchantId>84592342</MerchantId>
           <Date>27-12-1999 11:27:04</Date>
         </AuthorizationRequest>
       </xsl:for-each>
     </xsl:template>
   </xsl:stylesheet>
   ```

5. Remove any literal elements and attributes you don't want in the transformed output and:
   - Replace literal examples of *element text content* needing a dynamic value with an appropriate `<xsl:value-of select="pattern">` element.
   - Replace literal examples of *attribute value content* needing a dynamic value with an appropriate `{pattern}` attribute value template.

   For this case, our transformation will look like this:

```
<?xml version="1.0?">
<!DOCTYPE AuthorizationRequest SYSTEM "creditcardauth.dtd">
<xsl:stylesheet xmlns:xsl="http://www.w3.org/1999/XSL/
  Transform" xsl:version="1.0">
  <xsl:template match="/">
    <xsl:for-each select="ROWSET/ROW">
      <AuthorizationRequest>
        <CardNumber><xsl:value-of select="CARD_NUMBER"/></CardNumber>
        <Expiration>
          <xsl:value-of select="EXP_MONTH"/>
          <xsl:text>/</xsl:text>
          <xsl:value-of select="EXP_YEAR"/>
        </Expiration>
        <Amount Currency="{CURRENCY}"><xsl:value-of select="AMOUNT"/></Amount>
        <MerchantId><xsl:value-of select="MERCHANT_ID"/></MerchantId>
        <Date><xsl:value-of select="substring-before(REQUEST_DATE,'.')"/></Date>
      </AuthorizationRequest>
    </xsl:for-each>
  </xsl:template>
</xsl:stylesheet>
```

   Here we have appropriate `<xsl:value-of>` elements to plug in the appropriate dynamic values and `{CURRENCY}` to plug the value of `<CURRENCY>` in the current `<ROW>` into the value of the `<Amount>` element's `Currency` attribute.

6. If present, replace the `<!DOCTYPE>` with an `<xsl:output>` element to create the correct `DOCTYPE` in the transformed result by specifying a value for the `doctype-system` attribute.

   In this case, we need:

```
<xsl:output doctype-system="creditcardauth.dtd"/>
```

Example 12-11 shows the results of following the earlier steps.

Example 12-11. Transforming ROWSET/ROW to AuthorizationRequest Format

```
<!-- rowset-to-creditcardauth.xsl -->
<xsl:stylesheet xmlns:xsl="http://www.w3.org/1999/XSL/Transform" version="1.0">
  <xsl:output doctype-system="creditcardauth.dtd" indent="yes"/>
  <xsl:template match="/">
    <xsl:for-each select="ROWSET/ROW">
      <AuthorizationRequest>
        <CardNumber><xsl:value-of select="CARD_NUMBER"/></CardNumber>
```

Example 12-11. Transforming ROWSET/ROW to AuthorizationRequest Format (continued)

```
        <Expiration>
          <xsl:value-of select="EXP_MONTH"/>
          <xsl:text>/</xsl:text>
          <xsl:value-of select="EXP_YEAR"/>
        </Expiration>
        <Amount Currency="{CURRENCY}"><xsl:value-of select="AMOUNT"/></Amount>
        <MerchantId><xsl:value-of select="MERCHANT_ID"/></MerchantId>
        <Date><xsl:value-of select="REQUEST_DATE"/></Date>
      </AuthorizationRequest>
    </xsl:for-each>
  </xsl:template>
</xsl:stylesheet>
```

Now, if someone needs to retrieve information about an authorization request with an `id` of `2002322`, they simply request the URL:

```
http://yourserver/creditcardauth.xsql?id=2002322
```

and they will receive:

```
<?xml version = '1.0' encoding = 'UTF-8'?>
<!DOCTYPE AuthorizationRequest SYSTEM "creditcardauth.dtd">
<AuthorizationRequest>
   <CardNumber>4678223355451001</CardNumber>
   <Expiration>10/2001</Expiration>
   <Amount Currency="ITL">118000</Amount>
   <MerchantId>84592342</MerchantId>
   <Date>27-12-1999 11:27:04</Date>
</AuthorizationRequest>
```

This is the result of doing the query from authorization_request matching the `id` passed in, and applying the *rowset-to-creditcardauth.xsl* transformation from Example 12-11 before returning the result.

Using Object Types and Object Views for XML

The Morcover.com news stories and the authorization request were both fairly simple XML datagrams with a single level of child elements. Next, we'll look at a datagram that contains some nested structure. Since we don't need a complicated example to explain the concepts, we'll stick with a datagram that contains just a single example of nested structure. Once the basics are clear, we'll dig into a meatier example.

Relational databases support only the basic structure of rows of *scalar-valued* columns in a table. Object-relational databases such as Oracle8*i* extend the primitive set of scalar types like NUMBER, VARCHAR, and DATE with the ability to create your own user-defined types to model frequently occurring structures in your applications. In Oracle8*i*, user-defined structures, or *types*, are defined with the CREATE TYPE command:

```
CREATE TYPE Point AS OBJECT (
  Degrees    NUMBER(3),
  Minutes    NUMBER(2),
  Seconds    NUMBER(2,2),
  Hemisphere VARCHAR2(1)
);
```

A type is comprised of a list of attributes that can be all scalar-valued, as in the simple `Point` type above, or any mix of scalar values and user-defined types. So you can define a type called `Map_Location` that has `Longitude` and `Latitude` attributes of type `Point`:

```
CREATE TYPE Map_Location AS OBJECT (
  Latitude  Point,
  Longitude Point,
  Elevation NUMBER
);
```

and a type called `Airport` that comprises a `Name`, `Code`, and `Location` of type `Map_Location`:

```
CREATE TYPE Airport AS OBJECT (
  Name      VARCHAR2(30),
  Code      VARCHAR2(3),
  Location  Map_Location
);
```

and finally, a `Flight` type that has, among other attributes, an `Origin` and `Destination` airport of type `Airport`:

```
CREATE TYPE Flight AS OBJECT (
   Carrier       VARCHAR2(2),
   Flight_Number NUMBER,
   Origin        Airport,
   Destination   Airport
);
```

Although these examples are trivial, you can see that user-defined types allow you to build up complicated, user-defined objects to match the structure of the items in your problem domain.

Once user-defined types are created, they can be used virtually anywhere scalar types are allowed. For example, they can appear as the column types in a table. So our flight_schedule table can include a column named `flight` of type `Flight` along with the flight's scheduled departure date:

```
CREATE TABLE flight_schedule (
  flight     Flight,
  departs_at DATE
);
```

The SQL language in Oracle8*i* offers enhanced support for working with these user-defined structures, and the extended SQL can be used in combination with any other features of the SQL language. Example 12-12 demonstrates a query over the flight_schedule table to find the earliest departing flight on 26 April 2000 originating at an airport whose location is at zero degrees longitude.

Example 12-12. SQL Query Using Extended Dot Notation

```
SELECT *
  FROM ( SELECT *
           FROM flight_schedule fs
          WHERE fs.Flight.Origin.Location.Longitude.Degrees = 0
            AND TRUNC(departs_at) = '26-APR-2000'
       ORDER BY departs_at )
WHERE ROWNUM <= 1
```

The syntax of the query in Example 12-12:

```
SELECT * FROM ( SELECT ... ORDER BY ... )
```

is not a typo, but rather an example of a new SELECT feature of Oracle8*i* SQL called a *top N query*. The "inner" statement includes an ORDER BY that orders the data by some criteria you care about, and the "outer" SELECT uses the WHERE ROWNUM <= N clause to pick just the top N rows from the inner query based on your ordering. Here we're querying the single top `Flight` ordered by departure time, but the same trick can be used, for example, to show the top five salespeople ordered by quarterly sales. This type of query could not be done in a single SQL statement before Oracle8*i*.

Example 12-12 uses *extended dot notation* in the WHERE clause to navigate the nested structures of the user-defined types involved in the query:

```
WHERE fs.Flight.Origin.Location.Longitude.Degrees = 0
```

If this information were stored in several different tables, writing a similar WHERE clause would take numerous joins and complicated join-clause predicates. So besides helping to model real-world structure, types also benefit developers by simplifying queries, allowing them to be phrased more directly.

The XML SQL Utility offers bidirectional support for working with these user-defined structured data sources and XML documents. When retrieved through the XML SQL Utility or an XSQL page, the results of the query in Example 12-12 look like Example 12-13.

Example 12-13. Datagram from Query Using Object Types

```
<ROWSET>
   <ROW num="1">
      <FLIGHT>
         <CARRIER>BA</CARRIER>
         <FLIGHT_NUMBER>586</FLIGHT_NUMBER>
         <ORIGIN>
            <NAME>London Heathrow</NAME>
            <CODE>LHR</CODE>
            <LOCATION>
               <LATITUDE>
                  <DEGREES>51</DEGREES>
                  <MINUTES>28</MINUTES>
                  <SECONDS>34.02</SECONDS>
                  <HEMISPHERE>N</HEMISPHERE>
               </LATITUDE>
               <LONGITUDE>
                  <DEGREES>0</DEGREES>
                  <MINUTES>37</MINUTES>
                  <SECONDS>56.08</SECONDS>
                  <HEMISPHERE>W</HEMISPHERE>
               </LONGITUDE>
               <ELEVATION>119</ELEVATION>
            </LOCATION>
         </ORIGIN>
         <DESTINATION>
            <NAME>Venice Italy</NAME>
            <CODE>VCE</CODE>
            <LOCATION>
               <LATITUDE>
                  <DEGREES>45</DEGREES>
                  <MINUTES>26</MINUTES>
                  <SECONDS>0</SECONDS>
                  <HEMISPHERE>N</HEMISPHERE>
               </LATITUDE>
               <LONGITUDE>
                  <DEGREES>12</DEGREES>
                  <MINUTES>20</MINUTES>
                  <SECONDS>0</SECONDS>
                  <HEMISPHERE>E</HEMISPHERE>
               </LONGITUDE>
               <ELEVATION>10</ELEVATION>
            </LOCATION>
         </DESTINATION>
      </FLIGHT>
      <DEPARTS_AT>2000-04-26 08:40:00.0</DEPARTS_AT>
   </ROW>
</ROWSET>
```

Of course, extended dot notation can be used in the SELECT list as well, to return only a certain substructure from the complex object. For example, if we changed the query from Example 12-12 to be:

```
SELECT *
  FROM ( SELECT fs.Flight.Carrier||' '||fs.Flight.Flight_Number
     AS flight,
       fs.Flight.Origin.Name||' ('||fs.Flight.Origin.Code||')'
          AS "FROM",
       fs.Flight.Destination.Name||' ('||fs.Flight.Destination.Code||')'
          AS "TO",
       TO_CHAR(fs.departs_at,'HH24:MI')
          AS departs
       FROM flight_schedule fs
       ORDER BY departs_at )
WHERE ROWNUM <= 1
```

then our XML query results would look like this:

```
<ROWSET>
   <ROW num="1">
      <FLIGHT>BA 586</FLIGHT>
      <FROM>London Heathrow (LHR)</FROM>
      <TO>Venice Italy (VCE)</TO>
      <DEPARTS>08:40</DEPARTS>
   </ROW>
</ROWSET>
```

Besides supporting the creation of tables with object types as structured column values, Oracle8*i* also supports the creation of database views that can deliver structured rows of data.

We're familiar with the idea that database views can be used to join, project, and filter information to create new logical views based on one or more other tables (or views). In the same spirit, you can use database views in combination with user-defined object types to create structured logical views on the fly based on one or more other tables or views. Creating structured object views on top of relational tables allows you to have the best of all worlds:

- You can preserve investments in existing applications, tools, and training by keeping the fundamental storage model the same.
- You can create one or more logical views of your physical table data, allowing you to serve and store complex XML datagrams into the same underlying tables with less work.
- You can query the logical views of the structured data using extended dot notation with the same query performance as the more cumbersome join queries against the underlying flat tables.

This means that if we have a set of existing tables like these:

```
CREATE TABLE airport_table (
  Name            VARCHAR2(30),
  Code            VARCHAR2(3),
  Lat_Degrees     NUMBER(3),
  Lat_Minutes     NUMBER(2),
  Lat_Seconds     NUMBER(4,2),
  Lat_Hemisphere  VARCHAR2(1),
  Long_Degrees    NUMBER(3),
  Long_Minutes    NUMBER(2),
  Long_Seconds    NUMBER(4,2),
  Long_Hemisphere VARCHAR2(1),
  Elevation       NUMBER
);

CREATE TABLE flight_schedule_table (
   carrier             VARCHAR2(2),
   flight_number       NUMBER,
   departing           VARCHAR2(3),
   arriving            VARCHAR2(3),
   departs_at          DATE
);
```

we can create a view like `flight_schedule_view` in Example 12-14 to, in effect, superimpose a user-defined logical structure over the join of information from the two flat tables, airport_table and flight_schedule_table.

Example 12-14. Object View Imposes Rich Structure over Flat Tables

```
CREATE VIEW flight_schedule_view AS
SELECT Flight(ft.carrier,
              ft.flight_number,
              airport(ao.Name,
                      ao.Code,
                      Map_location(
                        Point(
                          ao.Lat_Degrees,
                          ao.Lat_Minutes,
                          ao.Lat_Seconds,
                          ao.Lat_Hemisphere),
                        Point(
                          ao.Long_Degrees,
                          ao.Long_Minutes,
                          ao.Long_Seconds,
                          ao.Long_Hemisphere),
                        ao.Elevation)),
              Airport(ad.Name,
                      ad.Code,
                      Map_location(
                        Point(
                          ad.Lat_Degrees,
                          ad.Lat_Minutes,
                          ad.Lat_Seconds,
```

Example 12-14. Object View Imposes Rich Structure over Flat Tables (continued)

```
                         ad.Lat_Hemisphere),
                       Point(
                         ad.Long_Degrees,
                         ad.Long_Minutes,
                         ad.Long_Seconds,
                         ad.Long_Hemisphere),
                       ad.Elevation))) as flight,
       ft.departs_at
  FROM flight_schedule_table ft,
       airport_table         ao, /* Origin Airport      */
       airport_table         ad  /* Destination Airport */
 WHERE ft.departing = ao.Code
   AND ft.arriving  = ad.Code;
```

Notice how in the SELECT list we use the `Flight()` constructor to create an instance of our user-defined `Flight` object. Nested inside the arguments passed to the `Flight()` constructor are other constructors to create nested instances of `Map_Locations` and `Points` where required. Viewing just the nesting of the constructors, without the extra detail, the SELECT statement looks like this:

```
SELECT Flight(...,
         Airport(...,
           Map_Location(
             Point(...),
             Point(...),...)),
         Airport(...,
           Map_Location(
             Point(...),
             Point(...),...))) as flight
```

This reflects the on-the-fly `Flight` structure we're imposing over the rows of data in the join between flight_schedule_table and airport_table.

A query over the `flight_schedule_view` using the XML SQL Utility or an XSQL page produces the exact same XML we saw from Example 12-13, but there is one big difference. Before, we had to create a single new table whose columns had the appropriate user-defined datatypes. Here, we've taken a set of existing tables and imposed the same object structure on top of them through the constructors in the object view definition. Object types can be used both for physical storage and for virtual, logical views, depending on your needs.

As we'll see in the next section, in addition to supporting structured querying of data, object views support inserts, updates, and deletes whose behavior can be customized using special database triggers designed for views called INSTEAD OF triggers. When combined with the XML SQL Utility, this facility gives us a nice approach to working with more complex XML datagrams.

Using Object Types and Object Views for Insert

Let's get started by recalling a simplified version of the <Book> datagram from Example 12-2:

```
<Book>
   <ISBN>0395415012</ISBN>
   <Title>Sunrise With Seamonsters</Title>
   <Price>12.75</Price>
   <Author>
      <First>Paul</First>
      <Last>Theroux</Last>
   </Author>
</Book>
```

Let's say we create two tables, author_table and book_table, where we store author and book information:

```
CREATE TABLE author_table (
          id NUMBER PRIMARY KEY,
  first_name VARCHAR2(80),
   last_name VARCHAR2(80)
);
```

and:

```
CREATE TABLE book_table (
  isbn      NUMBER PRIMARY KEY,
  title     VARCHAR2(80),
  price     NUMBER,
  author_id NUMBER,
  CONSTRAINT authored_by FOREIGN KEY (author_id)
                         REFERENCES author_table
);
```

We can create an object view as a query based on author_table and book_table to present a single, structured view to handle the <Book> datagram. We'll then use this object view to produce <Book> datagrams as well as insert new <Book> datagrams into the author_table and book_table tables.

We start by analyzing the <Book> datagram and thinking of its structure as a composition of objects. This is a pretty simple example, so it shouldn't surprise you that the two real-world items represented in the <Book> datagram are a Book and a Person, who is the author of the book. Figure 12-5 shows a UML object model of our two simple objects.

Since we want to work with <Book>-structured rows that have the same structure as the <Book> datagram, we'll create an object view to superimpose the correct logical structure on top of a join of the two physical tables.

We start by creating user-defined types for `Book_T` and `Person_T` for the `Book` and `Person` objects in our object model. These define the structure and the appropriate attribute names that we want to produce as our object view materializes

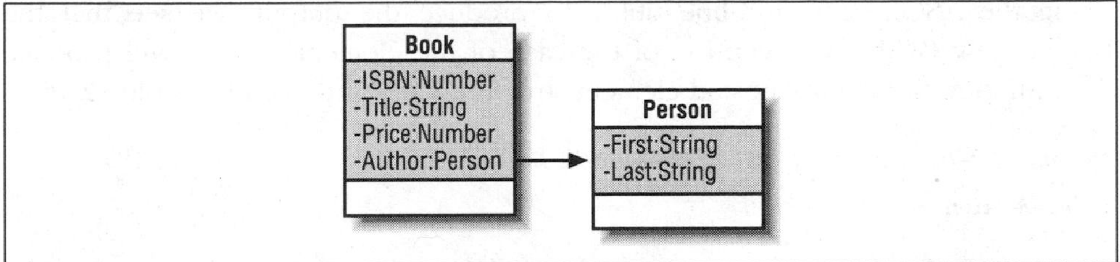

Figure 12-5. Modeling the <Book> datagram in objects

<Book>-structured rows. In other words, each row in our view will be an instance of the `Book_T` type.

The following syntax creates the two types we need:

```
CREATE TYPE Person_T AS OBJECT (
  first VARCHAR2(80),
  last  VARCHAR2(80)
);

CREATE TYPE Book_T AS OBJECT (
  isbn   NUMBER,
  title  VARCHAR2(80),
  price  NUMBER,
  author Person_T
);
```

Next, we create a **books** object view like the one in Example 12-15 that joins information from the book_table and author_table tables. It uses the `Book_T()` constructor to create instances of `Book_T` objects on the fly. Nested as an attribute to the `Book_T()` constructor is the `Person_T()` constructor used to create an instance of a `Person_T` as the <Book>'s `author`.

Example 12-15. Object View for the Book Datagram

```
CREATE VIEW books AS
SELECT Book_T( b.ISBN,
             b.Title,
             b.Price,
             Person_T( a.First_Name, a.Last_Name )
           ) as Book
  FROM book_table b,
       author_table a
 WHERE b.author_id = a.id;
```

With the **books** view in place, we can verify that it's producing the structure we want by building a quick XSQL page with a SELECT * FROM books query like:

```
<?xml version="1.0"?>
<xsql:query connection="xmlbook" max-rows="1" xmlns:xsql="urn:oracle-xsql">
  SELECT * FROM books
</xsql:query>
```

Using the XSQL command-line utility to produce the output, we see that the **books** view (with the exception of the case of the element names) will produce the XML output with the nested element structure we want, as in Example 12-16.

Example 12-16. Canonical XML Output for the Books View

```
<?xml version = '1.0'?>
<ROWSET>
   <ROW num="1">
      <BOOK>
         <ISBN>395415012</ISBN>
         <TITLE>Sunrise with Seamonsters</TITLE>
         <PRICE>12.75</PRICE>
         <AUTHOR>
            <FIRST>Paul</FIRST>
            <LAST>Theroux</LAST>
         </AUTHOR>
      </BOOK>
   </ROW>
</ROWSET>
```

In addition to allowing us to produce correctly-structured XML in each row, the new **books** view can be used as an insert target for the `OracleXML` utility's `putXML` option to automatically insert **<Book>** datagrams into the database.

As with most database views that involve multiple underlying database tables, we need to help the database understand our intended behavior for an insert into this join view by using an INSTEAD OF INSERT database trigger.

You can create INSTEAD OF triggers for INSERT, UPDATE, and/or DELETE operations on any database view in order to provide the appropriate implementation of that operation. As with any stored procedure or trigger in Oracle8*i*, INSTEAD OF triggers can be implemented in PL/SQL or Java.

Since the XML SQL Utility effectively does INSERT statements into the target table or view, we will focus our attention on the implementation of an INSTEAD OF INSERT trigger for the books view, which will properly insert into the underlying book_table and author_table tables.

To illustrate how an INSTEAD OF trigger can effectively handle both inserts and updates, Example 12-17 shows the PL/SQL code required to accomplish the following desired behavior:

1. If the inserted `<Book>` datagram has an `<Author>` with `<First>` and `<Last>` names matching an author we already have on file in the author_table, insert the value of the existing author's `id` into the book_table's `author_id` column.

2. If the author name does not match an existing author in the author_table, insert a row in author_table for this new author and insert the value of the author's (newly assigned) **id** for the insert into book_table for the **author_id** column.
3. If the ISBN number for the book being inserted is already on file in the book_ table, rather than doing an INSERT into the book table, do an UPDATE instead to reflect new information in the document about the existing book.

Example 12-17. INSTEAD OF Trigger Handles Book Datagram Inserts

```
CREATE TRIGGER instead_of_insert_on_books
INSTEAD OF INSERT ON books
FOR EACH ROW
DECLARE
  theAuthorId  NUMBER;
  theISBN      NUMBER;
BEGIN
  -- Check if the author being inserted already exists in the AUTHOR table.
  BEGIN
    SELECT id
      INTO theAuthorId
      FROM author_table
     WHERE first_name = :new.Book.Author.First
       AND last_name  = :new.Book.Author.Last;
  EXCEPTION
    -- If author not found, create a new row in the author table
    WHEN NO_DATA_FOUND THEN
      INSERT INTO author_table ( id, first_name, last_name )
             VALUES ( authorseq.nextval,
                      :new.Book.Author.First,
                      :new.Book.Author.Last )
        RETURNING id INTO theAuthorId;
  END;
  -- Check if a book already exists in the BOOK table with this ISBN
  SELECT isbn
    INTO theISBN
    FROM book_table
   WHERE isbn = :new.Book.ISBN;
  -- We found an existing book, so *update* BOOK instead of inserting.
  UPDATE book_table
     SET title     = :new.Book.Title,
         price     = :new.Book.Price,
         author_id = theAuthorId
   WHERE isbn      = :new.Book.ISBN;
EXCEPTION
  -- If no existing book found with the new ISBN, then
  -- insert the new book into the BOOK table.
  WHEN NO_DATA_FOUND THEN
  -- Insert the new book into the underlying BOOK table
  INSERT INTO book_table (isbn,title,price,author_id)
         VALUES (:new.Book.ISBN,:new.Book.Title,:new.Book.Price, theAuthorId );
END;
```

Since the books view has a column named Book, our intuition tells us that `:new.Book` refers to the value of the Book column in the row being inserted. In turn, since the Book column is of a user-defined Book type, you can use extended dot notation in PL/SQL to refer to any part of the nested attributes and structure of the Book column value. This allows us to use `:new.Book.Author.Last` to refer to the author's last name for the book being inserted.

Now let's put the books view to work on our <Book> XML datagram. If we assume a <Book> document like the following is in a file named *theroux.xml*:

```
<Book>
   <ISBN>0395415012</ISBN>
   <Title>Sunrise With Seamonsters</Title>
   <Price>12</Price>
   <Author>
      <First>Paul</First>
      <Last>Theroux</Last>
   </Author>
</Book>
```

Then we have just two steps to follow:

1. Transform *theroux.xml* into a <ROWSET>/<ROW> document that matches the canonical format we saw in Example 12-16.
2. Use `OracleXML putXML` to insert the transformed document into the books view.

Since the books view already has a structure that exactly matches the <Book> datagram, we only need to wrap a <ROWSET> and <ROW> tag around it to put it into canonical form for insert. This is done with a simple XSLT transformation like Example 12-18.

Example 12-18. Transforming Book Datagram for Insert

```
<!-- book-to-rowset.xsl -->
<ROWSET xmlns:xsl="http://www.w3.org/1999/XSL/Transform" xsl:version="1.0">
  <xsl:for-each select="//Book">
    <ROW><xsl:copy-of select="."/></ROW>
  </xsl:for-each>
</ROWSET>
```

This selects all the <Book> elements in the source document, and wraps each one verbatim in a <ROW> element using `<xsl:copy-of>`. Applying this transformation using:

```
oraxsl theroux.xml book-to-rowset.xsl out.xml
```

produces the following *out.xml* result document:

```
<?xml version = '1.0' encoding = 'UTF-8'?>
<ROWSET>
  <ROW>
    <Book>
      <ISBN>0395415012</ISBN>
      <Title>Sunrise With Seamonsters</Title>
      <Price>12</Price>
      <Author>
         <First>Paul</First>
         <Last>Theroux</Last>
      </Author>
    </Book>
  </ROW>
</ROWSET>
```

We can insert this document into the **books** view using:

```
java OracleXML putXML -user xmlbook/xmlbook
                      -fileName out.xml
                      -ignoreCase
                      books
```

The elements in *theroux.xml* (and consequently, in the transformed *out.xml*) have mixed-case names like `<Title>` and `<Author>`, so we need to specify the following flag:

```
-ignoreCase
```

since the corresponding columns in the **books** view have uppercase names like `TITLE` and `AUTHOR`.

Assuming that Paul Theroux is already an author in our author_table and has been assigned an `author_id` of `1027`, running `OracleXML putXML` does the following:

1. The `<Book>` datagram is inserted into the **books** view, causing the INSTEAD OF INSERT trigger to fire.
2. The trigger finds an existing author with first name "Paul" and last name "Theroux", so it uses his `author_id`.
3. The trigger also inserts a new row into the book_table for the new book with the existing author's `author_id`.

This was an example of a single book, but in addition suppose we had a file like *list-of-books.xml* in Example 12-19.

Example 12-19. Datagram Representing Multiple Books

```
<BookList>
  <Book>
     <ISBN>0449908585</ISBN>
     <Title>The Happy Isles of Oceania : Paddling the Pacific</Title>
     <Price>13</Price>
```

Example 12-19. Datagram Representing Multiple Books (continued)

```
      <Author>
         <First>Paul</First>
         <Last>Theroux</Last>
      </Author>
   </Book>
   <Book>
      <ISBN>0804104549</ISBN>
      <Title>Riding the Iron Rooster : By Train Through China</Title>
      <Price>11</Price>
      <Author>
         <First>Paul</First>
         <Last>Theroux</Last>
      </Author>
   </Book>
   <Book>
      <ISBN>0804104549</ISBN>
      <Title>Oracle: Forms Developer's Companion</Title>
      <Price>44</Price>
      <Author>
         <First>Steve</First>
         <Last>Muench</Last>
      </Author>
   </Book>
   <Book>
     <ISBN>0395415012</ISBN>
     <Title>Sunrise With Seamonsters</Title>
     <Price>19</Price>
     <Author>
       <First>Paul</First>
       <Last>Theroux</Last>
     </Author>
   </Book>
</BookList>
```

Since we've taken care of matching the structure of each **<Book>** with a row of our **books** view, we can use the same transformation from Example 12-18 to transform *list-of-books.xml* into **<ROWSET>**/**<ROW>** format:

```
oraxsl list-o-books.xml book-to-rowset.xsl out.xml
```

and insert the whole lot with:

```
java OracleXML putXML -user xmlbook/xmlbook
                      -fileName out.xml
                      -ignoreCase
                      books
```

This will successfully insert all four books in the *list-of-books.xml* file, resulting in several new rows and one updated row. If we go to SQL*Plus and look at the raw underlying data in book_table and author_table, we'll see that:

Using Mixed-Case Column Names

We could have created the books view with column names in mixed case to exactly match the element names in the <Book> document by aliasing each column in the view with a quoted name:

```
CREATE VIEW books AS
SELECT b.isbn,
       b.title as "Title",
       b.price as "Price",
       PERSON_NAME_TYPE(a.first_name, a.last_name) as "Author"
  FROM book b,
       author a
 WHERE b.author_id = a.id;
```

We did not do this because working in SQL with mixed-case column names requires that names *always* be quoted, which quickly becomes frustrating for developers, who cannot understand why:

```
SELECT title FROM books
```

gives them the confusing error:

```
ORA-00904: invalid column name
```

because the developer forgot to say:

```
SELECT "Title" FROM books
```

Since column aliases (including, of course, quoted, mixed-case column aliases) can be used on any SQL query in your XSQL pages or Java programs to specify exact names, using mixed-case column names in tables and views turns out to be more trouble than it's worth.

- The two new rows in book_table corresponding to the new <Book>s that had an <Author> of Paul Theroux were properly assigned the AUTHOR_ID for the existing row for Paul Theroux in author_table.
- A new row has been added to author_table for Steve Muench and to book_table for the *Forms Developer's Companion.*
- The price of the existing Paul Theroux book, *Sunrise with Seamonsters,* has been updated to 19.

We've seen that by using object views and object types to match the structure of a datagram, and by providing an appropriate INSTEAD OF trigger to implement any custom insert logic you desire, you can get more complex XML datagrams into the database.

Inserting Nested, Repeating Information

You'll often encounter a datagram like Example 12-20, which contains nested repeating information. This `<DepartmentList>` datagram contains a list of `<Department>` elements, each of which has a set of one or more `<Employee>` elements as nested, repeating information.

Example 12-20. Sample Datagram with Nested, Repeating Entries

```
<DepartmentList>
  <Department>
    <Id>98</Id>
    <Name>Research</Name>
    <Employees>
      <Employee>
        <Id>101</Id>
        <Name>Paul</Name>
        <Salary>2000</Salary>
      </Employee>
      <Employee>
        <Id>198</Id>
        <Name>Humphrey</Name>
        <Salary>3200</Salary>
      </Employee>
    </Employees>
  </Department>
  <Department>
    <Id>99</Id>
    <Name>Research</Name>
    <Employees>
      <Employee>
        <Id>167</Id>
        <Name>Amina</Name>
        <Salary>4350</Salary>
      </Employee>
    </Employees>
  </Department>
</DepartmentList>
```

Assuming that we have already created the dept and emp tables, our challenge will be to build an object view on top of the dept and emp tables that mimics the structure of the `<DepartmentList>` datagram. Once we accomplish this, we can use the XML SQL Utility to insert the `<DepartmentList>` datagram into the database through the object view, putting the department information in the dept table and the nested, repeating employee information into the emp table.

We saw in the previous section how we can use user-defined object types and object views on top of existing relational tables to create user-defined *virtual* structures that map directly to the structure we want in XML datagrams. However, we did not deal with nested, repeating information. To work with this kind of data, we can use collection types.

Once a user-defined object type is created, we can define a *collection type* to model a list or array of that type. So if we define an emp_t type to capture the logical structure of an <Employee> in our XML datagram like this:

```
CREATE TYPE emp_t AS OBJECT (
  empno NUMBER,
  ename VARCHAR2(80),
  sal   NUMBER
);
```

we can very easily create a type to represent a *list* of <Employee>s with the command:

```
CREATE TYPE emp_list AS TABLE OF emp_t;
```

We can use the emp_list type in an object view to model a repeating (unbounded) set of elements with the emp_t structure, like the repeating <Employee> elements in a <Department> in the datagram above.

Taking a closer look at the structure of the <DepartmentList> datagram, we see that it is just a set of <Department> elements. Trying to think of this as a set of rows, we can easily identify <DepartmentList> as a set of <Department> elements that repeat like rows in a rowset. If we can create an object view in which each row returned has the exact structure of a <Department> element, then we can transform the <DepartmentList> datagram into the canonical ROWSET/ROW format and have the XML SQL Utility insert it for us.

Each <Department> element contains the following:

- <DeptNo>
- <DName>
- <Employees>, a repeating collection of <Employee> elements

To mimic this row structure we create a view that selects the following columns:

- deptno column
- dname column from the dept table
- employees column of type emp_list with corresponding rows from the emp table for the current department

The appropriate view definition appears in Example 12-21.

Example 12-21. Department View with Nested Employees Collection

```
CREATE VIEW department
AS SELECT deptno, dname,
          CAST(MULTISET(SELECT empno, ename, sal
                        FROM emp
                        WHERE emp.deptno = dept.deptno
                        ) AS emp_list ) employees
     FROM dept;
```

Notice the use of the following syntax:

```
CAST(MULTISET(query) AS collection_type_name) column_alias
```

to cast the results of the query:

```
SELECT empno, ename, sal
FROM emp
WHERE emp.deptno = dept.deptno
```

into a collection-valued column of type emp_list with the name `employees`. The canonical output of the XML SQL Utility for a query against this new `department` view using the XML SQL Utility is shown in Example 12-22.

Example 12-22. Canonical Output for Object View with Nested Collection

```
<?xml version="1.0"?>
<ROWSET>
  <ROW  num="1">
    <DEPTNO>10</DEPTNO>
    <DNAME>ACCOUNTING</DNAME>
    <EMPLOYEES>
      <EMPLOYEES_ITEM>
        <EMPNO>7782</EMPNO>
        <ENAME>CLARK</ENAME>
        <SAL>2450</SAL>
      </EMPLOYEES_ITEM>
      <EMPLOYEES_ITEM>
        <EMPNO>7839</EMPNO>
        <ENAME>KING</ENAME>
        <SAL>5000</SAL>
      </EMPLOYEES_ITEM>
      <EMPLOYEES_ITEM>
        <EMPNO>7934</EMPNO>
        <ENAME>MILLER</ENAME>
        <SAL>1300</SAL>
      </EMPLOYEES_ITEM>
    </EMPLOYEES>
  </ROW>
</ROWSET>
```

which we can produce from the command line by issuing the command:

```
java OracleXML getXML
               -user xmlbook/xmlbook
               "select * from department where deptno = 10"
```

As we can see, the structure perfectly matches the structure of a <Department> row in the <DepartmentList> datagram. All we need to do now is to create an XSLT stylesheet that transforms a <DepartmentList> datagram into the canonical output of the department view.

Following the same cookbook approach we've taken previously, we create the transformation in Example 12-23.

Example 12-23. Transforming Master/Detail Information for Insert

```
<!-- deptemp.xsl -->
<ROWSET xmlns:xsl="http://www.w3.org/1999/XSL/Transform" xsl:version="1.0">
  <xsl:for-each select="DepartmentList/Department">
   <ROW>
     <DEPTNO><xsl:value-of select="Id"/></DEPTNO>
     <DNAME><xsl:value-of select="Name"/></DNAME>
     <EMPLOYEES>
       <xsl:for-each select="Employees/Employee">
         <EMPLOYEES_ITEM>
           <EMPNO><xsl:value-of select="Id"/></EMPNO>
           <ENAME><xsl:value-of select="Name"/></ENAME>
           <SAL><xsl:value-of select="Salary"/></SAL>
         </EMPLOYEES_ITEM>
       </xsl:for-each> <!-- Employees -->
     </EMPLOYEES>
   </ROW>
  </xsl:for-each> <!-- Departments -->
</ROWSET>
```

Notice that in this transformation we have two <xsl:for-each> loops:

<xsl:for-each select="DepartmentList/Department">
This loops over the <Department> element children of <DepartmentList>.

<xsl:for-each select="Employees/Employee">
This loops over each nested <Employee> element in the <Department>.

By applying the *deptemp.xsl* stylesheet to the original <DepartmentList> datagram with the command:

```
oraxsl deptemp.xml deptemp.xsl deptemp-transformed.xml
```

we can produce the *deptemp-transformed.xml* file in canonical XML format, shown in Example 12-24, that is ready to be inserted into the department view.

Example 12-24. Result of Transforming deptemp.xml for Insert

```
<?xml version = '1.0' encoding = 'UTF-8'?>
<ROWSET>
  <ROW>
    <DEPTNO>98</DEPTNO>
    <DNAME>Research</DNAME>
```

Example 12-24. Result of Transforming deptemp.xml for Insert (continued)

```
    <EMPLOYEES>
      <EMPLOYEES_ITEM>
        <EMPNO>101</EMPNO>
        <ENAME>Paul</ENAME>
        <SAL>2000</SAL>
      </EMPLOYEES_ITEM>
      <EMPLOYEES_ITEM>
        <EMPNO>198</EMPNO>
        <ENAME>Humphrey</ENAME>
        <SAL>3200</SAL>
      </EMPLOYEES_ITEM>
    </EMPLOYEES>
  </ROW>
  <ROW>
    <DEPTNO>99</DEPTNO>
    <DNAME>Research</DNAME>
    <EMPLOYEES>
      <EMPLOYEES_ITEM>
        <EMPNO>167</EMPNO>
        <ENAME>Amina</ENAME>
        <SAL>4350</SAL>
      </EMPLOYEES_ITEM>
    </EMPLOYEES>
  </ROW>
</ROWSET>
```

However, since we are working here with a *virtual* view with a collection structure based on multiple underlying tables, the database engine cannot infer the appropriate treatment of an insert into this view. We need to create an INSTEAD OF INSERT trigger to instruct the server with a little code of our own how we intend to handle an INSERT into this view:

```
CREATE TRIGGER department_ins
INSTEAD OF INSERT ON department
FOR EACH ROW
DECLARE
  emps emp_list; -- Holds a list of Employees
  emp  emp_t;    -- Holds a single Employee
BEGIN
  -- Insert the master
  INSERT INTO dept( deptno, dname )
  VALUES (:new.deptno, :new.dname );

  -- Insert the details, using value of :new.deptno as the DEPTNO
  emps := :new.employees;
  FOR i IN 1..emps.COUNT LOOP
    emp := emps(i);
    INSERT INTO emp(deptno, empno, ename, sal)
    VALUES (:new.deptno, emp.empno, emp.ename, emp.sal);
  END LOOP;
END;
```

This trigger inserts the `:new.deptno` and `:new.dname` values into the dept table, then loops over the collection of `<Employees>` being inserted and inserts the values of each one as a new row in the emp table, using the value of `:new.deptno` as the `DEPTNO` foreign key value in the emp table.

With the `department` view in place, and the `<DepartmentList>` datagram transformed into canonical format in the *deptemp-transformed.xml* file, we can insert the transformed document using `OracleXML` like this:

```
java OracleXML putXML
               -user xmlbook/xmlbook
               -fileName deptemp-transformed.xml
               department
```

This successfully inserts two rows into the `department` object view, with each row inserted in the object view translating into one row in the dept table and one or more rows added to the emp table.

Inserting Datagrams with Document Fragments

The `<product-list>` datagram in Example 12-25 contains the nested structure for `<weight>`, `<image>`, and `<dimensions>`, as well as an embedded document fragment of well-formed HTML in its `<features>` element.

Example 12-25. Product List Datagram with Nested Structure

```
<product-list>
  <product>
    <sku>1234567</sku>
    <class>CD Player</class>
    <manufacturer>Sony</manufacturer>
    <model>D-F411</model>
    <weight>
      <units>g</units>
      <amount>260</amount>
    </weight>
    <image>
      <small>df-411.gif</small>
      <large>df-411-large.gif</large>
    </image>
    <dimensions>
      <units>mm</units>
      <width>133</width>
      <length>152</length>
      <height>33</height>
    </dimensions>
    <price>159.95</price>
    <features>
      <ul>
        <li>
          <b>SteadySound</b>, The Next Generation Of Skip Protection, surpasses
          Sony's current 20-second Buffer Memory system.
        </li>
```

Example 12-25. Product List Datagram with Nested Structure (continued)

```
        <li>
          <b>Synthesized Digital AM/FM Stereo Tuner</b> precisely locks in the
          most powerful signal for accurate, drift-free reception.
        </li>
        <li>
          New <b>Compact Design</b> has attractive yet functional styling
        </li>
      </ul>
    </features>
  </product>
</product-list>
```

Since we've dealt with some of these situations in previous examples, we'll move a little faster through this example to get to the new nuance—the handling of the nested document fragment.

To capture the nested structure of **<weight>**, **<image>**, and **<dimensions>**, we create three appropriate user-defined types:

```
CREATE TYPE weight_type as object(
  units  VARCHAR2(5),
  amount NUMBER
);

CREATE TYPE dimension_type as object(
  units  VARCHAR2(5),
  width  NUMBER,
  length NUMBER,
  height NUMBER
);

CREATE TYPE imagegroup_type as object(
  small  VARCHAR2(200),
  large  VARCHAR2(200)
);
```

Then we make use of these types in appropriate column names of a table to store the product datagrams we receive:

```
CREATE TABLE product(
  sku          NUMBER PRIMARY KEY,
  class        VARCHAR2(80),
  manufacturer VARCHAR2(80),
  model        VARCHAR2(80),
  weight       weight_type,
  image        imagegroup_type,
  dimensions   dimension_type,
  price        NUMBER,
  features     VARCHAR2(4000) /* Could be a CLOB if you need > 4K */
);
```

If we can make the assumption that the **features** blurb of well-formed HTML will not exceed 4096 characters (4K), then we can use a VARCHAR2(4000) column to store these. If this is not a safe assumption, then it would be better to use a CLOB column that can store up to two gigabytes of document fragment. For this example, we'll stick with the VARCHAR2(4000) column for **features**.

Since we want to store the **<features>** element's nested well-formed HTML content as a textual document fragment, we must transform the resulting element tree:

```
<ul>
  <li>
    <b>SteadySound</b>, The Next Generation Of Skip Protection, surpasses
    Sony's current 20-second Buffer Memory system.
  </li>
  <li>
    <b>Synthesized Digital AM/FM Stereo Tuner</b> precisely locks in the
    most powerful signal for accurate, drift-free reception.
  </li>
  <li>
    New <b>Compact Design</b> has attractive yet functional styling
  </li>
</ul>
```

by parsing the **<product-list>** datagram into a single text string. We can do that by leveraging the **xmlMarkup** XSLT extension function that we will build in Chapter 16, *Extending XSQL and XSLT with Java*, as part of an identity transformation on the original **<product-list>** datagram. For now, suffice it to say that an XSLT transformation can invoke methods on user-defined Java objects when some functionality is more easily implemented in Java than in pure XSLT.

Example 12-26 shows the *insert-product.xsl* XSLT transformation we need.

Example 12-26. Transforming Document Fragment to Literal XML Markup

```
<!-- insert-product.xsl -->
<xsl:stylesheet version="1.0"
  xmlns:xsl="http://www.w3.org/1999/XSL/Transform"
  xmlns:ext="http://www.oracle.com/XSL/Transform/java/MarkupExtensions"
  exclude-result-prefixes="ext">
  <!-- Start with the identity Transformation -->
  <xsl:include href="identity.xsl"/>
  <!--
   | Use our xmlMarkup() extension function to write
   | out the features nested XML content as literal
   | XML text markup.
   +-->
  <xsl:template match="features">
    <features>
      <xsl:value-of select="ext:xmlMarkup(*)"/>
    </features>
  </xsl:template>
</xsl:stylesheet>
```

This example uses **<xsl:include>** to include the template for the identity transformation and augments this with an **<xsl:template>** that matches the **<features>** element:

```
<xsl:template match="features">
  <features>
    <xsl:value-of select="ext:xmlMarkup(*)"/>
  </features>
</xsl:template>
```

This template outputs the **<features>** element of each **<product>** as a textual "printout" of the nested elements within it. So, the result of transforming the **<product-list>** datagram using the *insert-product.xsl* stylesheet:

```
oraxsl product-list.xml insert-product.xsl product-to-insert.xml
```

is a *product-to-insert.xml* file that looks like Example 12-27.

Example 12-27. Results of Quoting the XML Markup for Product Features

```
<?xml version = '1.0' encoding = 'UTF-8'?>
<product-list>
  <product>
    <sku>1234567</sku>
    <class>CD Player</class>
    <manufacturer>Sony</manufacturer>
    <model>D-F411</model>
    <weight>
      <units>g</units>
      <amount>260</amount>
    </weight>
    <image>
      <small>df-411.gif</small>
      <large>df-411-large.gif</large>
    </image>
    <dimensions>
      <units>mm</units>
      <width>133</width>
      <length>152</length>
      <height>33</height>
    </dimensions>
    <price>159.95</price>
    <features>&#60;ul>
        &#60;li>
          &#60;b>SteadySound&#60;/b>, The Next Generation Of Skip Protection surpasses
          Sony's current 20-second Buffer Memory system.
        &#60;/li>
        &#60;li>
          &#60;b>Synthesized Digital AM/FM Stereo Tuner&#60;/b> precisely locks in the
          most powerful signal for accurate, drift-free reception.
        &#60;/li>
        &#60;li>
          New &#60;b>Compact Design&#60;/b> has attractive yet functional styling
        &#60;/li>
```

Example 12-27. Results of Quoting the XML Markup for Product Features (continued)

```
      &#60;/ul>
    </features>
  </product>
</product-list>
```

In this example, all the opening angle bracket characters in the content of the `<features>` element have been replaced by the numerical character entity `<` to represent a literal less-than sign, which is synonymous with the *named* character entity `<`.

Now we can use the following command to insert the transformed document into the product table:

```
java OracleXML putXML
                    -user xmlbook/xmlbook
                    -fileName product-to-insert.xml
                    -rowTag product
                    -ignoreCase
                    product
```

To complete the round-trip into the database and back out, let's look at how we would dynamically serve a `<product-list>` datagram out of our product table for a product with a particular SKU number on request over the Web.

Just as we used an XSLT transformation to convert the nested content of the `<features>` element to a text fragment of XML markup on the way into the database, we'll use XSLT again on the way out to turn the text fragment back into nested elements of the datagram we serve. We'll use a similar transformation that performs the identity transformation on all elements of the document except `<features>`, which we'll handle in a special way. Example 12-28 shows the required transformation.

Example 12-28. Transforming Document Fragment Text into Elements

```
<!-- features-frag-to-elts.xsl -->
<xsl:stylesheet xmlns:xsl="http://www.w3.org/1999/XSL/Transform" version="1.0">
  <xsl:output method="xml" omit-xml-declaration="yes"/>
  <xsl:include href="identity.xsl"/>
  <!--
   | <features> is a column with embedded XML markup in its
   | corresponding column in the database. By disabling
   | the output escaping it will be included verbatim
   | (i.e. angle-brackets intact instead of &lt; and &gt;)
   | in the resulting document
   +-->
  <xsl:template match="features">
    <features>
      <xsl:value-of select="." disable-output-escaping="yes"/>
    </features>
  </xsl:template>
</xsl:stylesheet>
```

Example 12-28 uses the disable-output-escaping="yes" attribute on <xsl:value-of> to request that the XSLT Processor include the text of the features document fragment *verbatim* in the transformed output instead of "escaping" the less-than signs in the text with a character entity like lt; or #60;.

To serve the <product-list> datagram, we just create a simple XSQL page with a SELECT * FROM PRODUCT query, and associate it with the *features-frag-to-elts.xsl* transformation in its <?xml-stylesheet?> instruction:

```
<?xml version="1.0"?>
<?xml-stylesheet type="text/xsl" href="features-frag-to-elts.xsl"?>
<xsql:query xmlns:xsql="urn:oracle-xsql" connection="xmlbook"
  rowset-element="product-list" row-element="product" id-attribute=""
    tag-case="lower">

  SELECT *
    FROM product
   WHERE sku = {@sku}

</xsql:query>
```

When a request comes in for this XSQL page with an appropriate sku parameter like:

```
http://yourserver/product.xsql?sku=1234567
```

this delivers a <product-list> datagram that looks exactly like what we started with at the beginning of this section.

You can use the output of one XSQL page as the input of another to format a dynamic XML datagram including document fragments as an attractive web page. Assuming that *show-product.xsl* is an XSLT stylesheet that transforms a <product-list> datagram into eye-catching HTML, you can use the <xsql:include-xsql> tag to include the output of the *product.xsql* page as part of the input data for another XSQL page called *show-product.xsql*. Simply create a *show-product.xsql* page that looks like:

```
<?xml version="1.0"?>
<?xml-stylesheet type="text/xsl" href="show-product.xsl"?>
<xsql:include-xsql href="product.xsql?sku={@sku}"
                   xmlns:xsql="urn:oracle-xsql" />
```

This associates the *show-product.xsl* stylesheet to the page. Now a web request for:

```
http://yourserver/show-product.xsql?sku=1234567
```

uses the *show-product.xsl* stylesheet to transform the output of the *product.xsql* page, a <product-list> datagram, into a lovely web page.

Storing Posted XML Using XSQL Servlet

We've seen that the general steps for inserting XML into the database are as follows:

1. Choose the table or view you want to use for inserting the XML information.
2. Create an XSL transformation that transforms the inbound document into the canonical format for this table or view.
3. Transform the inbound document into the canonical format for the table or view into which it will be inserted.
4. Insert the transformed document into your table or view with the `OracleXML` utility.

The Oracle XML SQL Utility works well for inserting XML documents you have in front of you in operating system files. However, if you need to have other computers post live XML information to your web site for insertion into your database, you'll need to use a slight twist on this approach.

Storing Posted XML Using XSQL Pages

The Oracle XSQL Servlet supports the `<xsql:insert-request>` action element, which you can include in any XSQL page to automate these steps:

1. Read a posted XML document from the HTTP request.
2. Transform it into the canonical format for insertion using any XSLT transformation you provide.
3. Insert the transformed document into the table or view of your choice.
4. Indicate the status of the operation by replacing the `<xsql:insert-request>` action element with an `<xsql-status>` element to show how many rows were inserted or to report an error.

Behind the scenes, the `insert_request` action handler makes programmatic use of the Oracle XSLT Processor to do the transformation and the Oracle XML SQL Utility to do the insert, so everything we've learned earlier applies here.

Given the name of the table or view to use as the insert target and the name of the XSLT transformation to use, you add the following tag anywhere in your XSQL page:

```
<xsql:insert-request table="table_or_view_name"
                     transform="transformname.xsl"/>
```

to transform and insert the posted XML document.

For example, recall the Moreover.com news feed from Example 12-3 and the *moreover-to-newsstory.xsl* transformation we created in Example 12-5. The XSQL page in Example 12-29 is all you need to insert posted XML news stories instead over the Web into your newsstory table.

Example 12-29. XSQL Page to Insert Posted XML News Stories

```
<?xml version="1.0"?>
<!-- SimpleNewsInsert.xsql -->
<xsql:insert-request connection="xmlbook" xmlns:xsql="urn:oracle-xsql"
                     table="newsstory"
                 transform="moreover-to-newsstory.xsl"/>
```

One tag, that's it! No custom servlet to write, no XML to parse, and no transformation to do manually. Deploying a new XSQL page to insert posted XML is as easy as copying the *.xsql* file to a directory on your web server.

We can test the *SimpleNewsInsert.xsql* page by using the XSQL command-line utility with the command:

```
xsql SimpleNewsInsert.xsql posted-xml=SomeFileToPost.xml
```

or, if the source of XML is coming directly from a URL, we can do this:

```
xsql SimpleNewsInsert.xsql posted-xml=http://example.com/someurl
```

Setting the `posted-xml` command-line parameter to the name of an XML file or URL returning XML causes the XSQL page processor to treat that XML source as the posted XML source for insert.

We can also test *SimpleNewsInsert.xsql* using any client program that can post an XML document full of news stories. One approach is to use JavaScript in an HTML page to post some XML to the server. In our example, we'll post XML the user types into a `<TEXTAREA>` so you can see what's going on, but the technique used in the example applies to any XML.

The Internet Explorer 5.0 browser includes support for an `XMLHttpRequest` object that makes quick work of the task from the browser client. Example 12-30 shows the JavaScript code of the `PostXMLDocument()` function, which does the job of posting any XML document you pass in to the URL you pass as a parameter.

Example 12-30. Function to Post XML Document to a Web Server from IE5

```
// PostXMLDocument.js
// Uses HTTP POST to send XML Document "xmldoc" to URL "toURL"
function PostXMLDocument (xmldoc, toURL)
{
   // Create a new XMLHttpRequest Object (IE 5.0 or Higher)
   var xmlhttp = new ActiveXObject ("Microsoft.XMLHTTP");
   // Open a synchronous HTTP Request for a POST to URL "toUrl"
   xmlhttp.open("POST", toURL ,  /* async = */ false );
   // Could set HTTP Headers Here (We don't need to in this example)
   // xmlhttp.setRequestHeader("some-header-param","some value");
   // Send the request with in-memory XML Document "xmldoc" as body
```

Example 12-30. Function to Post XML Document to a Web Server from IE5 (continued)

```
  xmlhttp.send(xmldoc);
  // Return the response from the request (assumes it is an XML Doc)
  return xmlhttp.responseXML;
}
```

The function does the following:

1. Creates an `XMLHttpRequest` Object
2. Opens the request, indicating a method of `POST`
3. Sends the request, passing the XML document as the request body
4. Returns the XML document sent back by the server as a response

---

If the XSQL Servlet encounters an `<xsql:insert-request>` action element and there is no posted XML document in the current request, it will replace the action element in the data page with the following innocuous `<xsql-status>` element:

```
<xsql-status action="xsql:insert-request"
   result="No Posted Document to Process" />
```

This will also be the case if any of the following is true:

- The XSQL page was requested as an HTTP GET.
- The MIME type of the HTTP POSTed document was not `text/xml`, or the request didn't contain a valid XML document.
- The request contained XML that was not well-formed.

We can use the `PostXMLDocument()` function in an HTML page by including the *PostXMLDocument.js* JavaScript file in a `<SCRIPT>` tag like this:

```
<SCRIPT src="PostXMLDocument.js"></SCRIPT>
```

This is just what we've done in the *newsstory.html* page in Example 12-31. It includes a `<TEXTAREA>` containing some sample XML that you can edit, a submit button that invokes the `parseXMLinTextAreaAndPostIt()` in its `onclick` event, and a `<DIV>` named `StatusArea` where the results returned from the server will be displayed.

Example 12-31. NewsStory.html Page Posts XML to SimpleNewsInsert.xsql

```
<HTML>
  <HEAD>
    <SCRIPT src="PostXMLDocument.js"></SCRIPT>
    <SCRIPT>
      function parseXMLinTextAreaAndPostIt(){
        // Create a new XML Parser Object
        var xmldoc  = new ActiveXObject ("Microsoft.XMLDOM");
```

Example 12-31. NewsStory.html Page Posts XML to SimpleNewsInsert.xsql (continued)

```
        // Do the parsing synchronously
        xmldoc.async = false;
        // Parse the text in the TEXTAREA as XML
        xmldoc.loadXML(xmldocText.value);
        // Post the parsed XML document to the SimpleNewsInsert.xsql Page
        var response = PostXMLDocument(xmldoc, "SimpleNewsInsert.xsql");
        // Display the XML text of the response in the "StatusArea" DIV
        StatusArea.innerText = response.documentElement.xml;
      }
    </SCRIPT>
  </HEAD>
  <BODY>
    <b>Type in an XML Document in Moreover.com News Format to Post:<b><br>
    <TEXTAREA rows="7" style="width:100%" cols="70" name="xmldocText">
<moreovernews>
  <article>
    <url> http://technet.oracle.com/tech/xml </url>
    <headline_text> Oracle Releases XML Parser </headline_text>
    <source> Oracle </source>
  </article>
</moreovernews></TEXTAREA>
    <INPUT TYPE="button" Value="Post XML Document"
           onclick=" parseXMLinTextAreaAndPostIt()">
    <br>Response:<hr>
    <DIV id="StatusArea" style="font-family:monospace"></DIV>
  </BODY>
</HTML>
```

Figure 12-6 shows the *newsstory.html* page in action. It allows the user to type in an XML document in Moreover.com news format and post it to the *SimpleNewsInsert.xsql* page for processing.

We can see that clicking on the button has posted the `<moreovernews>` datagram to the *SimpleNewsInsert.xsql* page. The text of the XML response datagram returned from the server is displayed in the status area of the web page, confirming the successful insertion of one news article.

In a real application, your client code could search the XML response using XPath expressions. The returned XML datagram might include elements or attributes to signal whether the request was successful or not, as well as other useful information.

In Internet Explorer 5.0, the `selectNodes()` function on any node of the document can assist with this task. For example, we can add this code:

```
// Try to find the rows attribute on <xsql-status rows="xx"/>
var result = response.selectSingleNode("//xsql-status/@rows");
if ( result != null ) {
  alert("Successfully posted " + result.text + " Stories ");
}
```

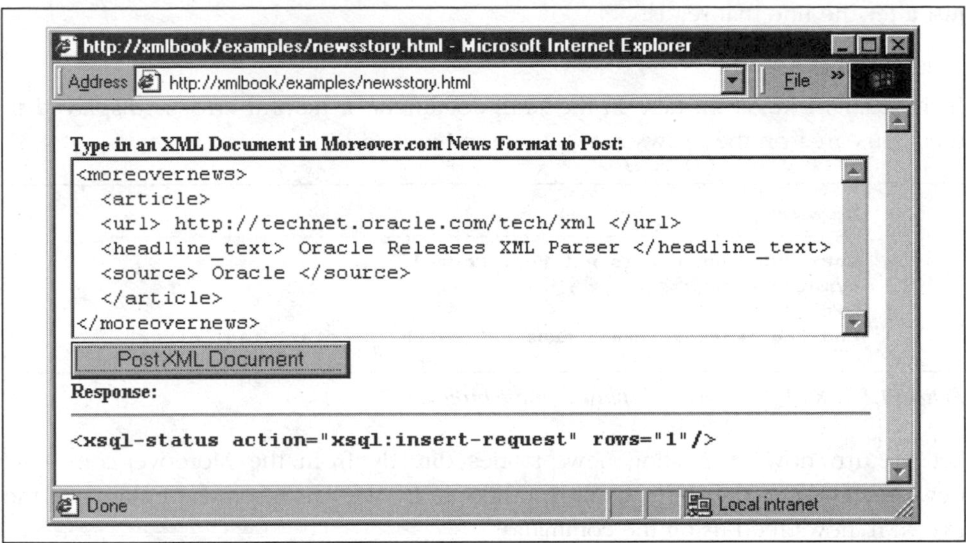

Figure 12-6. Posting XML to an XSQL page from IE5

```
else {
  // Try to message element child of an <xsql-error>
  result = response.selectSingleNode("//xsql-error/message");
  alert(result.text);
}
```

to the *newsstory.html* page just after the line that reads:

```
StatusArea.innerText = response.documentElement.xml;
```

you can see how easy it is to search the response for information and to do something with the data sent back in the XML response from the server.

You may be wondering what happens if the user makes a mistake in typing the XML. The answer: you get an error. On the client side, in this case, since the `xmldoc.loadXML()` method is attempting to parse the text in the <TEXTAREA> into an XML document. However, if you used another method to post an XML document to the server that is not well-formed, the server will likely just ignore it; this is what the XSQL Servlet will do if you post ill-formed XML.

We can prevent this from happening by adding a little code to check for parse errors and showing the user any errors it finds. Add the following code to the *newsstory.html* page:

```
err = xmldoc.parseError;
// Stop and show any parse error to the user
if (err != 0) {
  StatusArea.innerText = "Your XML document is not well-formed.\n" +
  err.srcText + "\n" + "Line " + err.line + ", Pos " + err.linepos +
  "\n" + err.reason;
  return;
}
```

just after the line that reads:

```
xmldoc.loadXML(xmldocText.value);
```

If the user makes a mistake in the XML document, a helpful error is displayed in the status area on the browser, as shown in Figure 12-7.

```
Response:

Your XML Document is not Well Formed.
</moreovernews>
Line 7, Pos 3
End tag 'moreovernews' does not match the start tag 'error'.
```

Figure 12-7. XML parse error displayed in the browser

Let's return now to posting news stories directly from the Moreover.com XML news feed. Using the XSQL command-line utility we can insert the entirety of the live XML news feed using the command:

```
xsql SimpleNewsInsert.xsql posted-xml=http://www.moreover.com/cgi-local/
                                              page?index_xml+xml
```

This will treat the XML document retrieved from the provided URL as the posted XML to the *SimpleNewsInsert.xsql* page, transform the results for insert, then perform the insert into the newsstory table, returning the resulting data page that indicates the successful insert of 30 news stories:

```
<?xml version = '1.0'?>
<!-- SimpleNewsInsert.xsql -->
<xsql-status action="xsql:insert-request" rows="30"/>
```

However, let's say that due to the nature of this news feed, news stories stay in the feed for a few days. If we want to avoid inserting the same story over and over again, we can easily do that by making sure we don't insert a story unless its title and URL are a unique combination in our newsstory table.

As we've done in previous examples, let's implement this behavior using a database INSTEAD OF INSERT trigger. In the code of the trigger, we can check for the uniqueness of the news story and only insert it if it is unique; otherwise, we'll just ignore it.

Since INSTEAD OF triggers can only be defined on database views in Oracle8*i*, we need to create the `newsstoryview` as follows:

```
CREATE VIEW newsstoryview AS
SELECT *
  FROM newsstory
```

Then we can create the INSTEAD OF INSERT trigger on the new `newsstoryview` with this code:

```
CREATE OR REPLACE TRIGGER insteadOfIns_newsstoryview
INSTEAD OF INSERT ON newsstoryview FOR EACH ROW
DECLARE
  notThere BOOLEAN := TRUE;
  tmp      VARCHAR2(1);
  CURSOR chk IS SELECT 'x'
                  FROM newsstory
                 WHERE title = :new.title
                   AND url   = :new.url;
BEGIN
  OPEN chk;
  FETCH chk INTO tmp;
  notThere := chk%NOTFOUND;
  CLOSE chk;
  IF notThere THEN
    INSERT INTO newsstory(title,url,source)
         VALUES (:new.title,:new.url,:new.source);
  END IF;
END;
```

Here we are assuming that the uniqueness of a story is defined by the combination of its `TITLE` and its `URL` columns.

To check for existing news stories quickly, we can create a unique index on the `(TITLE,URL)` combination with the command:

```
CREATE UNIQUE INDEX newsstory_unique_title_url
                 ON newsstory(title,url);
```

Finally, the only thing left to do is to change the `<xsql:insert-request>` action element in *SimpleNewsInsert.xsql* above to use the `newsstoryview` instead of the newsstory table by changing the line to read `table="newsstoryview"` instead of `table="newsstory"`:

```
<xsql:insert-request table="newsstoryview"
                 transform="moreover-to-newsstory.xsl"/>
```

Now, only unique news stories from the Moreover.com XML news feed will be inserted. Duplicate entries will be ignored when they are posted.

Our *SimpleNewsInsert.xsql* is a page with just a single `<xsql:insert-request>` action element. Of course, the `<xsql:insert-request>` tag can be combined with other XSQL action elements in a page like `<xsql:query>` to first insert any posted XML document and then return some data from queries. For example, the following XSQL page inserts any news stories from the posted XML document (if any) and then returns an XML datagram showing the two most recently added (`max-rows="2"`) news stories from the newsstory table:

```
<?xml version="1.0"?>
<page connection="xmlbook" xmlns:xsql="urn:oracle-xsql">
  <xsql:insert-request table="newsstoryview"
                 transform="moreover-to-newsstory.xsl"/>
  <lateststories>
    <xsql:query tag-case="lower" max-rows="2"
              rowset-element="" row-element="story" >
      select *
        from newsstoryview
      order by id desc
    </xsql:query>
  </lateststories>
</page>
```

If this XSQL page is saved in a file called *submitNewsStories.xsql*, then browsing the URL:

```
http://yourserver/submitNewsStories.xsql
```

from Internet Explorer 5.0 produces the results shown in Figure 12-8.

```
  <?xml version="1.0" ?>
- <page>
    <xsql-status action="xsql:insert-request" result="No Posted Document to Process" />
  - <lateststories>
    - <story num="1">
        <id>2</id>
        <title>IBM Brings XML To MQSeries</title>
        <url>http://d.moreover.com/click/here.pl?x4202247</url>
        <source>Moreover.com</source>
      </story>
    - <story num="2">
        <id>1</id>
        <title>Austin: webMethods gets deal with Dell</title>
        <url>http://d.moreover.com/click/here.pl?x4227575</url>
        <source>Moreover.com</source>
      </story>
    </lateststories>
  </page>
```

Figure 12-8. Browsing the raw data page for submitNewsStories.xsql

In this case, there was "No Posted Document to Process" since a browser uses the HTTP GET method to retrieve a page whose address you type into the "Address" field, and a GET method has no request body, just URL parameters. However, if this new *submitNewsStories.xsql* page were the target of an HTTP POST with an XML message body as in the *newsstory.html* page in Example 12-31, the raw XML message you see in the browser would be returned as the XML response datagram to the requester. The requester could use XPath expressions to programmatically process the two latest news stories.

As a final observation in this section, we see above that the raw XML datagram is returned to the browser because our XSQL page has no `<?xml-stylesheet?>` processing instruction to associate an XSL stylesheet with it. However, with the addition of one extra line in the XSQL page:

```
<?xml version="1.0"?>
<?xml-stylesheet type="text/xsl" href="latest-news-stories.xsl"?>
<page connection="xmlbook" xmlns:xsql="urn:oracle-xsql">
  <!-- etc -->
</page>
```

we could have an XSLT transformation called *latest-news-stories.xsl* format the `<story>` elements in the data page on the server and return a nicely formatted HTML page to present the results.

Posting and Inserting HTML Form Parameters

Sometimes, it's convenient to accept posted information as a set of HTML `<FORM>` parameters since this is the native way browsers use to post information to a server. Consider the following simple HTML page, which allows users to submit new news stories interactively from their browser, as shown in Figure 12-9.

Figure 12-9. HTML form collecting data to be inserted

Every HTML form specifies a URL to use as the "submit action" for the form. Typically, this action URL refers to some kind of server-side program that processes the set of HTML `<FORM>` parameters sent by the browser in the HTTP POST request:

```
<FORM METHOD="post" ACTION="/cgi-bin/somescript">
```

We can also use an XSQL page as the action URL for an HTML form:

```
<FORM METHOD="post" ACTION="/mydir/somepage.xsql">
```

This way, when the form is submitted by the user, the XSQL Servlet receives an HTTP POST request for the XSQL page with a message body containing all the HTML `<FORM>` parameters. This is not technically the same as receiving a posted XML document in the message body as we did in the previous section, but the XSQL Servlet allows the `<xsql:insert-request>` action element to work equally well in both cases.

In the case of an HTML form submission, if the XSQL Servlet encounters an `<xsql:insert-request>` action in your page, it synthesizes an XML document representing the HTTP request. This request document contains all of the HTTP request parameters, session variables, and cookies for the current request, and has the general form:

```
<request>
  <parameters>
    <param1>value1</param1>
    <param2>value2</param2>
       :
  </parameters>
  <session>
    <name1>val1</name1>
    <name2>val2</name2>
       :
  </session>
  <cookies>
    <cookiename1>value1</cookiename1>
       :
  </cookies>
</parameters>
```

Once this `<request>` document has been created, the processing of the `<xsql:insert-request>` tag behaves just as if an actual XML document had been posted. The value of the `transform` attribute can be the name of an XSLT transformation to be used for transforming the synthesized `<request>` document into the canonical format required for insertion into the table or view you specify in the `table` attribute.

So to get the HTML `<FORM>` parameters inserted into the `newsstoryview`, we need to create an XSLT stylesheet to transform the `<request>` document into the canonical format for the `newsstoryview`. It helps to have an example of an actual `<request>` document our HTML form produces when it is submitted. The easiest way to achieve this is to temporarily change the action URL of our HTML form to point to an XSQL page that will echo back the request document to the browser. The XSQL Servlet supports an `<xsql:include-request-params>` tag that does exactly this:

```
<?xml version="1.0"?>
<xsql:include-request-params xmlns:xsql="urn:oracle-xsql"/>
```

The `<xsql:include-request-params>` includes the synthesized `<request>` document for your posted form and returns it verbatim to the browser for inspection. If we name this file *echoPostedParams.xsql*, we can modify the source code of our earlier *NewsForm.html* page to have *echoPostedParams.xsql* as the action URL of the HTML form, like this:

Multiple Parameters with the Same Name

If multiple parameters are posted with the same name, they will automatically be "rowified" to make subsequent processing easier. For example, a request that posts or includes the following parameters:

- `id=101`
- `name=Steve`
- `id=102`
- `name=Sita`
- `operation=update`

will create a "rowified" set of parameters:

```
<request>
  <parameters>
    <row>
      <id>101</id>
      <name>Steve</name>
    </row>
    <row>
      <id>102</id>
      <name>Sita</name>
    </row>
    <operation>update</operation>
  </parameters>
        :
</request>
```

```
<html>
<body>
  Insert a new news story...
    <form action="echoPostedParams.xsql" method="post">
    <b>Title</b><input type="text" name="title_field" size="30"><br>
    <b>URL</b><input type="text" name="url_field" size="30"><br>
    <br>
    <input type="submit">
  </form>
<body>
</html>
```

If we browse the form, enter in some values into the `Title` and `URL` form fields, and submit the form, the *echoPostedParams.xsql* page includes the **`<request>`** XML document for the current form posting and returns the page back to your browser. From there, you can *View Source...* and save the source file to disk to work with as you build your XSLT transformation. In this case, we get back a **<request>** document that looks like this:

```
<request>
  <parameters>
    <title_field>Test Story</title_field>
    <url_field>http://foo.bar</url_field>
  </parameters>
  <session/>
  <cookies/>
</parameters>
```

This reflects the two input fields in the HTML form, **title_field** and **url_field**. We need to transform this request document into the following document:

```
<ROWSET>
   <ROW>
      <TITLE>Test Story</TITLE>
      <URL>http://foo.bar</URL>
      <SOURCE>Some Source</SOURCE>
   </ROW>
</ROWSET>
```

The simple stylesheet in Example 12-32 will perform this transformation.

Example 12-32. Transforming Request Datagram to ROWSET/ROW Format

```
<?xml version = '1.0'?>
<!-- request-to-newsstory.xsl -->
<ROWSET xsl:version="1.0" xmlns:xsl="http://www.w3.org/1999/XSL/Transform">
   <xsl:for-each select="request/parameters">
   <ROW>
      <TITLE><xsl:value-of select="title_field"/></TITLE>
      <URL><xsl:value-of select="url_field"/></URL>
      <SOURCE>User-Submitted</SOURCE>
   </ROW>
   </xsl:for-each>
</ROWSET>
```

Note that this stylesheet is nearly identical to Example 12-5. The only difference is that we're looping over **request/parameters** instead of over **moreovernews/article** elements.

Now we just need an XSQL page—let's call it *insertnewsform.xsql*—with an **<xsql:insert-request>** tag that refers to *request-to-newsstory.xsl* and provides a table name of **newsstoryview**:

```
<xsql:insert-request
      table="newsstoryview"
      transform="request-to-newsstory.xsl"/>
```

This, again, is just a slight variation on what we used for inserting XML posted in the Moreover.com news format into the newsstory table. By modifying our

NewsForm.html source to put the *insertnewsform.xsql* as the action URL as shown in Example 12-33, we'll finish the process.

Example 12-33. Inserting Posted HTML Form Parameters with XSQL

```
<html>
<body>
  Insert a new news story...
    <form action="insertnewsform.xsql" method="post">
    <b>Title</b><input type="text" name="title_field" size="30"><br>
    <b>URL</b><input type="text" name="url_field" size="30"><br>
    <br>
    <input type="submit">
  </form>
<body>
</html>
```

If we let a user fill out and post the form as is, the user will get the following raw XML as a response from the *insertnewform.xsql* page:

```
<xsql-status action="xsql:insert-request" rows="1"/>
```

This is surely not going to win awards for user-friendliness. However, we can use two familiar techniques to improve on this:

- Enhance *insertnewsform.xsql* to return the five latest news stories from the `newsstoryview` as part of the response by adding an `<xsql:query>` tag to the page as follows:

```
<?xml version="1.0"?>
<?xml-stylesheet type="text/xsl" href="lateststories.xsl"?>
<page connection="xmlbook" xmlns:xsql="urn:oracle-xsql">
  <xsql:insert-request table="newsstoryview"
                   transform="request-to-newsstory.xsl"/>
  <xsql:query tag-case="lower" max-rows="5"
              rowset-element="" row-element="story" >
    SELECT *
      FROM newsstoryview
      ORDER BY ID DESC
  </xsql:query>
</page>
```

- Associate a *lateststories.xsl* stylesheet to the *insertnewsform.xsql* page to transform the five latest news stories in the XSQL data page into an HTML document before returning it to the user:

```
<html xmlns:xsl="http://www.w3.org/1999/XSL/Transform" xsl:version="1.0">
  <head>
    <title>Latest Stories</title>
  </head>
  <body>
  <h2>Thanks for your Story!</h2>
  Here's a list of the latest stories we've received...
    <table border="0" cellspacing="0">
```

```
          <xsl:for-each select="page/story">
            <tr>
             <td><a href="{url}"><xsl:value-of select="title"/></a></td>
            </tr>
          </xsl:for-each>
        </table>
      </body>
    </html>
```

Now, when the user posts a new news story, the raw XML datagram returned by the *insertnewsform.xsql* page will be replaced by the HTML page, as shown in Figure 12-10.

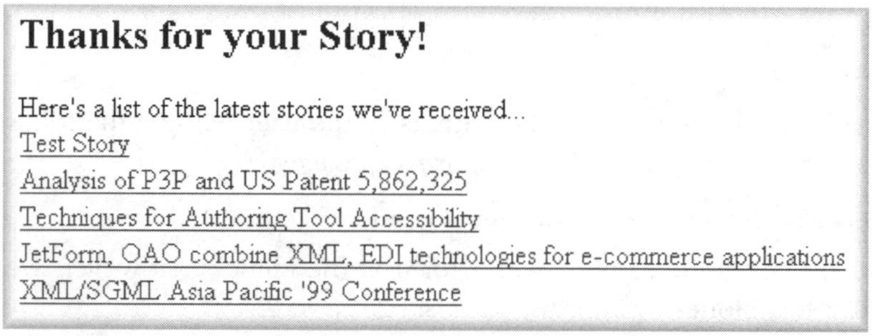

Thanks for your Story!

Here's a list of the latest stories we've received...

Test Story

Analysis of P3P and US Patent 5,862,325

Techniques for Authoring Tool Accessibility

JetForm, OAO combine XML, EDI technologies for e-commerce applications

XML/SGML Asia Pacific '99 Conference

Figure 12-10. Transformed results of posting a new news story

Inserting Datagrams Using Java

In this section, we'll study how the previous techniques can be applied from within your own Java programs.

Inserting Arbitrary XML Using Java

We've learned so far that the Oracle XML SQL Utility can be used to insert XML datagrams into database tables and views. We used the command-line `oraxsl` utility to transform the XML datagram into canonical <ROWSET>/<ROW> format before feeding it to the `OracleXML` utility for insertion into the database. Later, we saw how a simple `<xsql:insert-request>` action element could be used in an XSQL page to accomplish the same thing. The XSQL Servlet is able to automate these steps since both the Oracle XSLT Processor (`oraxsl`) and the Oracle XML SQL Utility (`OracleXML`) can be used programmatically by any Java program.

The API for the Oracle XSLT Processor comprises two simple-to-use objects, `XSLStylesheet` and `XSLProcessor`, and the API for the Oracle XML SQL Utility is even simpler. The `OracleXMLSave` object takes care of inserting XML into the database for us. Here we'll look at an example of using these three objects in a simple Java program to insert the contents of a live Moreover.com news story datagram fetched directly over the Web into our `newsstoryview`.

Example 12-34 does the following to accomplish this feat:

1. Parses the live XML news feed from Moreover.com by calling the **parse()** method of a **DOMParser** object, passing it a string URL to the live news feed:

```
// Create a DOM Parser to Parse the News Document
DOMParser dp = new DOMParser();
dp.parse( theNews );
// Parse the document at the URL specified in theURLString
XMLDocument moreoverNewsDoc = dp.getDocument();
```

2. Searches the XML datagram retrieved to count how many articles were received by using the **selectNodes()** method on the XML **Document** object, passing the XPath expression of **moreover/article**:

```
// Search for a list of all the matching articles and print the count
NodeList nl = moreoverNewsDoc.selectNodes("moreovernews/article");
int articleCount = nl.getLength();
System.out.println("Received " + articleCount + " articles...");
```

3. Constructs a new **XSLStylesheet** object by finding the *moreover-to-newsstory.xsl* transformation source file in the CLASSPATH using **getResourceAsStream()**:

```
// Load the XSL Stylesheet from the top-level directory on CLASSPATH
InputStream xslstream = Object.class.getResourceAsStream("/"+theXSL);
XSLStylesheet transform = new XSLStylesheet(xslstream,null);
```

4. Constructs an **XSLProcessor** object and calls **processXSL** on it to transform the incoming XML news feed document into the canonical format that **OracleXMLSave** understands using the XSL transformation:

```
// Create an instance of XSLProcessor to perform the transformation
XSLProcessor  processor = new XSLProcessor();
// Transform moreoverNewsDoc by theXSL and get result as a DOM Document Fragment
DocumentFragment df = processor.processXSL(transform, moreoverNewsDoc);
// Create a new XML Document and append the fragment to it
Document result = new XMLDocument();
result.appendChild(df);
```

5. Constructs an **OracleXMLSave** object, passing it a JDBC connection and the name of the **newsstoryview** we want to use for the insert operation:

```
// Pass the transformed document (now in canonical format) to OracleXMLSave
Connection   conn = Examples.getConnection();
OracleXMLSave oxs = new OracleXMLSave(conn,"newsstoryview");
```

6. Calls **insertXML** on the **OracleXMLSave** object, passing the transformed XML document in canonical format:

```
int rowsInserted = oxs.insertXML( result );
```

7. Commits the transaction and closes the connection:

```
conn.commit();
conn.close();
```

The result is the **MoreoverIntoNewsStory.java** program, which could be used to periodically pick up news feeds over the Web and dump them into your database. The full source is shown in Example 12-34.

Example 12-34. Programmatically Inserting News Stories

```
import oracle.xml.parser.v2.*;
import java.io.InputStream;
import org.w3c.dom.*;
import java.net.URL;
import java.sql.Connection;
import oracle.xml.sql.dml.OracleXMLSave;
import Examples;

public class MoreoverIntoNewsstory {

  public static void main( String[] arg ) throws Exception {

    String theNews = "http://www.moreover.com/cgi-local/page?index_xml+xml",
           theXSL  = "moreover-to-newsstory.xsl";

      // Create a DOM Parser to parse the news document
      DOMParser dp = new DOMParser();
      dp.parse( theNews );
      // Parse the document at the URL specified in theURLString
      XMLDocument moreoverNewsDoc = dp.getDocument();
      // Search for a list of all the matching articles and print the count
      NodeList nl = moreoverNewsDoc.selectNodes("moreovernews/article");
      int articleCount = nl.getLength();
      System.out.println("Received " + articleCount + " articles...");
      // Load the XSL Stylesheet from the top-level directory on CLASSPATH
      InputStream xslstream = Object.class.getResourceAsStream("/"+theXSL);
      XSLStylesheet transform = new XSLStylesheet(xslstream,null);
      // Create an instance of XSLProcessor to perform the transformation
      XSLProcessor  processor = new XSLProcessor();
      // Transform moreoverNewsDoc by theXSL and get result as a DOM Document Fragment
      DocumentFragment df = processor.processXSL(transform, moreoverNewsDoc);
      // Create a new XML Document and append the fragment to it
      Document result = new XMLDocument();
      result.appendChild(df);
      // Pass the transformed document (now in canonical format) to OracleXMLSave
      Connection    conn = Examples.getConnection();
      OracleXMLSave oxs = new OracleXMLSave(conn,"newsstoryview");
      int rowsInserted = oxs.insertXML( result );
      conn.commit();
      conn.close();
      System.out.println("Inserted " + rowsInserted + " articles...");
  }
}
```

Using XPath Expressions to Insert Data

When a truly custom storage mapping is required, XPath expressions can be used programmatically to select any necessary pieces of information from the incoming XML datagram that need to be stored in the database. You can then use standard Java or PL/SQL code to insert this information into one or more tables.

Recall that the Oracle XML Parser supports the programmatic use of XPath expressions using the following functions on any node of an XML document:

`selectNodes(`*`XPathExpression`*`)`
: Selects the set of nodes matching the arbitrary *`XPathExpression`* you supply.

`selectSingleNode(`*`XPathExpression`*`)`
: Selects the first node matching the *`XPathExpression`* you supply.

`valueOf(`*`XPathExpression`*`)`
: Selects the value of the *`XPathExpression`* you supply using the same semantics as the `<xsl:value-of select="`*`XPathExpression`*`"/>` you supply.

Recall our credit card `<AuthorizationRequest>` datagram from Example 12-1:

```
<?xml version="1.0"?>
<!DOCTYPE AuthorizationRequest SYSTEM "creditcardauth.dtd">
<AuthorizationRequest>
  <CardNumber>4678223355451001</CardNumber>
  <Expiration>10/2001</Expiration>
  <Amount Currency="ITL">118000</Amount>
  <MerchantId>84592342</MerchantId>
  <Date>27-12-1999 11:27:04</Date>
</AuthorizationRequest>
```

If `req` is a variable holding the `<AuthorizationRequest>` element as a result of calling `getDocumentElement()` on the parsed authorization request XML datagram, then this code:

```
String currency = req.valueOf("Amount/@Currency");
```

retrieves the value of the `Currency` attribute of the `<Amount>` element in the `<AuthorizationRequest>`, and the code:

```
NodeList nl = req.selectNodes("Amount[@Currency='GBP']");
```

retrieves a list of `<Amount>` elements (perhaps none!) that have a `Currency` attribute with the value `GBP` for British pounds sterling.

Observe in Example 12-35 how the `valueOf()` method is used on the document element of the incoming `<AuthorizationRequest>` XML datagram to extract all of the interesting data from it into program variables. Once we've extracted the data we want to insert into these variables, we can use a JDBC `PreparedStatement` or a SQLJ statement to do the database INSERT into the authorization_request table.

Example 12-35. Inserting AuthorizationRequest with XPath and SQLJ

```
import java.sql.*;
import oracle.xml.parser.v2.XMLElement;
import org.w3c.dom.Document;
import sqlj.runtime.ref.DefaultContext;
import Examples;

public class CreditAuthorization {

  public static long newRequest(Document authDoc)
  throws Exception {

    // Connect to the database
    DefaultContext.setDefaultContext(new DefaultContext(Examples.getConnection()));

    XMLElement req = (XMLElement)authDoc.getDocumentElement();

    // Get String values of important elements in XML Document
    // in preparation for insert
    String cardNumber  = req.valueOf("CardNumber");
    String expiration  = req.valueOf("Expiration");
    String amount      = req.valueOf("Amount");
    String currency    = req.valueOf("Amount/@Currency");
    String merchantId  = req.valueOf("MerchantId");
    String requestDate = req.valueOf("Date");

    // Split up the MM/YYYY expiration value for insert
    String expMonth     = expiration.substring(0,2);
    String expYear      = expiration.substring(3);

    // Request Id assigned to this request during the insert
    String requestId;

    // Insert the information content into appropriate
    // database columns, using a Sequence for generating
    // a unique request Id.

    #sql{BEGIN
          INSERT INTO authorization_request ( request_id,
                                              request_date,
                                              card_number,
                                              exp_month,
                                              exp_year,
                                              amount,
                                              currency,
                                              merchant_id )
          VALUES(authorization_request_seq.nextval,
                 TO_DATE(:requestDate,'DD-MM-YYYY HH24:MI:SS'),
                 :cardNumber,
                 :expMonth,
                 :expYear,
                 :amount,
                 :currency,
```

Example 12-35. Inserting AuthorizationRequest with XPath and SQLJ (continued)

```
            :merchantId )
        RETURNING request_id INTO :OUT requestId;
        COMMIT;
      END;
      };
    return Long.parseLong(requestId);
  }
}
```

This example is simple, but you can see that by applying the techniques demonstrated here to extract relevant information from the datagram using XPath expressions and to insert the information collected into one or more database tables, you can achieve an arbitrarily complicated storage mapping for any XML datagram that does not lend itself to the techniques discussed earlier.

13

Searching XML with interMedia

In this chapter:

- *Why Use interMedia?*
- *What Is interMedia?*
- *The interMedia Query Language*
- *Handling Heterogeneous Doctypes*
- *Handling Doctype Evolution*
- *Advanced interMedia*

In previous chapters, we've seen a variety of ways that XML datagrams can be broken up and stored relationally. Applications can then use XML for universal data exchange and SQL for sophisticated data management and speedy queries. However, not all XML documents are pure datagrams. When applied to pure documents and datagrams with embedded document fragments, the combined XML/SQL method stores at least some XML in its original form as marked-up text. In order to utilize stored marked-up text in a query, you'll need interMedia's Text component, which adds XML document search and full-text search capabilities to SQL.

Why Use interMedia?

To illustrate why interMedia is needed to fully leverage XML stored in Oracle, let's work through an example, using the simple insurance claim document shown in Example 13-1.

Example 13-1. Insurance Claim Document #77804

```
<!-- claim77804.xml -->
<Claim>
  <Payment>1000</Payment>
  <DamageReport>
    The insured's <Vehicle Make="Volks">Beetle</Vehicle>
    broke through the guard rail and plummeted into a ravine.
    The cause was determined to be <Cause>faulty brakes</Cause>.
    Amazingly there were no casualties.
  </DamageReport>
</Claim>
```

This document can be broken up and stored in a table as follows:

```
CREATE TABLE claim (
  claimid  NUMBER PRIMARY KEY,
```

```
    payment  NUMBER,
    damagereport  CLOB
  );
```

where the `<DamageReport>` fragment is stored in the **damagereport** column. Because it's a CLOB (Character Large Object) datatype, the **damagereport** column can store large text values, including entire XML documents or document fragments. We use a CLOB in this case instead of a VARCHAR2 column because a VARCHAR2 cannot exceed 4000 bytes, while a CLOB can hold up to 4 gigabytes of text.

Stored in the table, our example document would look like the sample shown in Figure 13-1.

CLAIM		
CLAIMID	**PAYMENT**	**DAMAGE REPORT**
77804	1000	The insured's <Vehicle Make="Volks">Beetle</Vehicle> broke through the guard rail and plummeted into a ravine. The cause was determined to be <Cause>faulty brakes</Cause>. Amazingly there were no casualties.

Figure 13-1. Insurance claim damage report stored in a CLOB column

The claim IDs and payment amounts are stored in NUMBER columns, for which Oracle provides a very rich feature set: you can index them, reference them in WHERE and ORDER BY clauses, and use them in calculations and functions. In contrast, the **damagereport** column is just a chunk of stored text. Oracle8*i* doesn't provide many native features to leverage this data other than simple pattern matching and extracting substrings by offset. How can we utilize the information that's now locked up in the **damagereport** column?

If the document were an XML file *outside* the database, you might think of using an XSLT stylesheet with templates that uses the XPath **contains()** function to search the document's **<DamageReport>** text. For example, the following stylesheet returns a message if the word "brakes" is found within a **<Cause>** element nested inside a **<DamageReport>** element:

```
<!-- search-cause.xsl -->
<xsl:stylesheet xmlns:xsl="http://www.w3.org/1999/XSL/Transform" version="1.0">
  <xsl:output method="text"/>
  <xsl:template match="/">
    <!-- XPath to find 'brakes' within <Cause> within <DamamgeReport> -->
    <xsl:if test=" //DamageReport//Cause[contains(.,'brakes')] ">
      Document Contains "brakes" inside the Cause
    </xsl:if>
  </xsl:template>
</xsl:stylesheet>
```

If we use the command-line **oraxsl** utility to apply this stylesheet to the *claim77804.xml* document in Example 13-1 like this:

```
oraxsl claim77804.xml search-cause.xsl
```

we'll get the result:

```
Document Contains "brakes" inside the Cause
```

On the other hand, applying the stylesheet to the following claim document, *claim77085.xml*, produces no output, because "brakes" is not found within the <Cause> element nested inside the <DamageReport>.

```
<!-- claim77805.xml -->
<Claim>
  <ClaimId>77805</ClaimId>
  <Payment>1200</Payment>
  <DamageReport>
    The insured's <Vehicle Make="Audi">TT</Vehicle>
    hit a tree. The cause was determined to be
    a <Cause>missing bolt</Cause> in the wheel assembly.
  </DamageReport>
</Claim>
```

Technically, this approach provides the document searching functionality we need, but it clearly doesn't scale. This brute force approach runs very slowly if the document is large or if you have hundreds of thousands of documents to plough through.

We want Oracle's proven scalability and its sophisticated query and data manipulation capabilities without sacrificing the functionality of the XPath `contains()` function for finding text within our XML documents and document fragments. We need the XPath `contains()` functionality *inside* Oracle—a way to search stored XML for specific words within specific XML elements.

The answer is interMedia, which provides exactly what we need. In fact, not only does interMedia provide XPath `contains()`–type XML text-searching functionality, it's also faster, scalable to data warehouses or content repositories of millions of XML documents, and supports searches that can be much more sophisticated than XPath substring pattern matching, as we'll see in this chapter.

What Is interMedia?

interMedia is a family of database extensions that allows Oracle8*i* to more effectively manage multimedia types such as images, movies, sound clips, and documents. interMedia Text is the component of interMedia that enables searching XML documents, document fragments, and other document content. While the interMedia extensions are technically a separate product, they are included on the Oracle8*i* CD and can be installed and used at no additional cost. The examples in this chapter require and assume that interMedia Text has been installed in your Oracle8*i* Release 2 (8.1.6) database.

The main feature of interMedia Text is scalable full-text search—that is, the ability to quickly search through a huge number of documents and find those that contain a certain word or phrase, like a web search engine. Let's walk through an example, returning to our claim table. We want to do XPath `contains()`-like full-text searches on the `damagereport` column. The first step is to build a specialized index on the column:

```
CREATE INDEX damagereportx ON claim(damagereport) INDEXTYPE IS ctxsys.context;
```

interMedia Text versions 8.1.5 and 8.1.6 use PL/SQL external procedures for indexing. This means that in order for a CREATE INDEX to work, you need to have a Net8 listener running and configured to invoke external procedures. If the listener is not running or is not properly configured, the CREATE INDEX statement will fail with the error message:

```
DRG-50704: Net8 listener is not running or cannot start
external procedures
```

Details on how to configure the *listener.ora* and *tnsnames.ora* files can be found in the *Oracle8i Administrator's Guide* (see the section "Managing Process for External Procedures") or in the interMedia 8.1.5 Technical Overview; both are available online at the Oracle Technology Network web site, *http://technet.oracle.com.*

The INDEXTYPE clause tells the database to build a special type of index called a *context index*, instead of the regular index used for other types of data. A regular index allows efficient equality and range searches. The context index, on the other hand, allows full-text searching, using the SQL CONTAINS() function:

```
SELECT claimid
  FROM claim
 WHERE CONTAINS(damagereport, 'brakes') > 0;
```

The first argument to CONTAINS is the column being searched. The second argument is the text search string. The CONTAINS function returns a number for each row indicating how closely the document matches the query. The number `0` (zero) means that the document does not match at all, so the `> 0` part of the query predicate is needed to eliminate rows that do not contain `brakes` from the result set. This does not mean that CONTAINS blindly marches down the table searching each row and returning `0` or non-zero for each one. On the contrary, CONTAINS uses the context index to go directly to matching ROWIDs in a way that's conceptually similar to how a range search uses a regular index.

Putting it all together, the example query will return the IDs of those claims where the word "brakes" appears anywhere in the text content of the XML fragment stored in **damagereport**. This will find our previous example claim 77804 row, and any other claims in the table that have "brakes" in **damagereport**. Furthermore, because it uses the context index, this query can be applied to tables containing millions of claims and return matching results in seconds or better.

So now we know how to do efficient full-text searches on our XML fragments. However, if we are only looking for claims where the *cause* involves brakes, we may get more claims than we want using this query. For instance, a damage report like this in a claim:

```
<DamageReport>
  The insured's <Vehicle Make="Toyota">Camry</Vehicle>
  <Cause>ran through a red light</Cause> and collided
  with another vehicle.  An inspection of the brakes found no defects.
</DamageReport>
```

also contains the word "brakes," although they're not the cause of the accident. Our earlier example XPath query:

```
//DamageReport//Cause[contains(.,'brakes')]
```

is more precise than the interMedia XML query expression we used:

```
WHERE CONTAINS(damagereport, 'brakes') > 0
```

because the former narrows the scope of the **contains()** function to the text content of the **<Cause>** element within the **DamageReport**. The latter finds the word "brakes" anywhere inside the damage report, not just inside the **<Cause>** tag. We need this more precise searching functionality in our interMedia query, too.

In order to reference XML elements in our SQL CONTAINS query, we need to modify the context index to use a component called a *sectioner*. The sectioner knows about structured formats like XML, and adds information about each document's structure to the index. The specific sectioner we'll use here is called the *autosectioner*.

Using the Autosectioner

To use the autosectioner in the index, first drop the existing index:

```
DROP INDEX damagereportx;
```

then recreate the index, specifying the autosectioner in the CREATE INDEX statement's PARAMETERS clause like this:

```
CREATE INDEX damagereportx ON claim(damagereport)
INDEXTYPE IS ctxsys.context
PARAMETERS ('section group ctxsys.auto_section_group');
```

We can use this same technique to create an XML document search index over the **xmldoc** column in our xml_documents table from Chapter 5, *Processing XML with PL/SQL*, and Chapter 6, *Processing XML with Java*. This enables fast XML searches over the XML documents stored there using the techniques in this chapter. The syntax is:

```
CREATE INDEX xmldoc_idx ON xml_documents(xmldoc)
INDEXTYPE IS ctxsys.context
PARAMETERS ('section group ctxsys.auto_section_group');
```

Once the index is built with the autosectioner, we can narrow the text search scope to particular XML tags using the WITHIN keyword:

```
SELECT claimid
  FROM claim
 WHERE CONTAINS(damagereport, 'brakes WITHIN cause') > 0;
```

This query looks for the word "brakes" in the **damagereport** text, but only when it occurs in between **<Cause>** and **</Cause>**. This would match claim 77804 but would not match a document with the previous Toyota Camry **<DamageReport>** since "brakes" was not within the **<Cause>** element there. Our goal was to achieve the functionality of matching documents where the following XPath expression was true:

```
//DamageReport//Cause[contains(.,'brakes')]
```

Modifying the previous query to include:

```
CONTAINS(damagereport, 'brakes WITHIN cause') > 0
```

delivers results that are semantically similar to the XPath example. However, the two queries are not exactly the same. There are some important differences between XPath and CONTAINS queries:

- An XPath query is designed to apply to a *single* document. The SQL CONTAINS, on the other hand, is designed to be applied to a whole table of documents, returning those that match the criteria. In order to apply the XPath query to a set of files, we would need to parse the entire set of documents into memory each time, or iterate over each file in the set, one at a time. Yikes!
- An XPath predicate can return parts of an XML document or fragment.

  The following XPath query uses the XSLT **document()** function to apply our earlier expression as a predicate on the *claim77804.xml* document, then continues to select only the **<Vehicle>** subelements:

```
document("claim77804.xml")[//DamageReport
                            //Cause[contains(.,'brakes')]
                           ]//Vehicle
```

This returns the <Vehicle> element if the text content of the <Cause> element, nested within the <DamageReport> element, contains the text "brakes."

The SQL query, on the other hand, returns what's in the SELECT list of your query, that is, full column values. So, in our example, you can get just the `claimid` of matching claims, or the sum of the payments with `SUM(payment)`, or the full text content of the <DamageReport> element, because these are column values. You cannot, however, get just the <Vehicle> part of the <DamageReport> element, as the above XPath query does, without parsing the content of each returned `damagereport` using a stored function like `xpath.extract()` from Chapter 5.

The hard part of the problem, finding only those documents in a large set that contain the word "brakes" within their damage report's <Cause> tag, is done very efficiently. If the number of documents in the result set will be reasonably small, parsing the document fragment of matching rows in the result set to extract child elements is very feasible.

- An XPath query can match documents based purely on the existence of elements. For instance:

  ```
  document("claim77804.xml")[//Cause]
  ```

  matches if the document has a <Cause> element. SQL CONTAINS, on the other hand, is built for text searching, so while you can find all documents where the <Cause> element contains a word or phrase, you cannot search just for the existence of the <Cause> element.

- Although it depends on the XPath query engine, most likely an XPath `contains()` is done through a brute force search of the element content, like a `grep` or a Search and Replace in a word processor. The SQL CONTAINS, on the other hand, uses the context index, which allows it to go directly to the matching documents. It's more like a fast web search engine.

- XPath `contains()` does substring matching like the SQL function INSTR. The SQL CONTAINS, on the other hand, does *word* matching.

  This means that an XPath `contains()` like:

  ```
  contains(., 'amount')
  ```

  would match any of these strings:

  ```
  amount
  amounting
  tantamount
  ```

  because they all have "amount" as a substring. However, only the first is the word "amount" and so a SQL CONTAINS like:

  ```
  CONTAINS(text, 'amount')
  ```

  would match only the first string. interMedia Text can do substring matching, but it is not the default behavior.

- Another difference resulting from substring matching versus word matching is phrase searching. When searching for phrases, interMedia looks for two words in a specific order; intervening whitespace and punctuation are ignored. The SQL CONTAINS:

  ```
  CONTAINS(text, 'faulty brakes')
  ```

  would match any of these strings:

  ```
  faulty brakes
  faulty(tab)brakes
  faulty(newline)brakes
  faulty: brakes
  ```

  but the XPath `contains()`:

  ```
  contains(.,'faulty brakes')
  ```

  would match only the first string, as it is doing strict substring matching. Even with the XPath `normalize-space()` function:

  ```
  contains(normalize-space(.,'faulty brakes'))
  ```

  XPath can match only the first three strings.

- By default, interMedia does *case-insensitive* word matching. For example, searching for "brakes" would find "brakes," "Brakes," or "BRAKES" in the indexed text. XPath, which does strict substring matching, will do case-sensitive matching. interMedia is capable of doing case-sensitive searching, but it is not the default behavior.

A future version of the Oracle8*i* database may offer native XPath element extraction in the core searching engine. But until then, the best strategy is to combine an interMedia search with the CONTAINS function to find the "needle in a haystack," so to speak, and then use the `xpath.extract()` function we built in Chapter 5 to dig into the document fragments so we can extract just the subelements we are looking for. A simple example of this would be:

```
SELECT claimid, xpath.extract(damagereport,'//Vehicle') as
VehicleFrag
  FROM claim
 WHERE CONTAINS(damagereport, 'brakes WITHIN cause') > 0;
```

This would return a result like:

```
CLAIMID VEHICLEFRAG
------- ----------------------------------------
77804   <Vehicle Make="Volks">Beetle</Vehicle>
```

Keep these differences in mind for the remainder of the chapter. When we see a SQL CONTAINS query and an XPath `contains()` query together, remember that they are only analogues, and not *direct* equivalents of each other.

From this point on in the chapter, when we discuss a CONTAINS query, we'll show only the text query string. However, we now understand that this string needs to be placed inside a CONTAINS function, and that the CONTAINS must be part of a whole, valid SQL statement, as in most of the previous examples. Similarly, for the rest of the chapter, when we see the syntax of an XPath predicate to compare it with the interMedia query syntax, it's understood that the predicate is being used to qualify a document root node, as in:

```
document("somedoc.xml")[ example-predicate ]
```

So far, we've seen basic text searching with interMedia: how to index and search text columns, and how to reference XML elements to increase precision. Now we'll take a closer look at the interMedia query language to see how we can perform more sophisticated XML searches.

The interMedia Query Language

As we've learned, interMedia by default performs case-insensitive word matching, ignoring punctuation. So the CONTAINS query:

```
snow
```

matches all the following:

```
snow man
Snow Day
Let it snow!
```

A multiple-word query is treated as a phrase search. The words must come in the specified order, with no intervening words. For instance, the query:

```
snow tires
```

matches:

```
Snow tires are required.
Very deep snow -- tires require chains.
```

but not:

```
Bob quickly tires -- snow shoveling is hard work.  (incorrect order)
Snow man tires are the best you can buy!           (intervening words)
```

The query language also offers familiar Boolean operators. The query:

```
snow AND tires
```

finds any document with the word "snow" as well as the word "tires," while:

```
snow OR tires
```

finds any document with the word "snow" or the word "tires," or both. Parentheses can be used for grouping:

```
(rain OR snow) AND tires
```

Keep in mind that this whole expression is a single argument to the SQL CONTAINS function, so a real query would look like this:

```
SELECT claimid
  FROM claim
 WHERE CONTAINS(damagereport, '(rain OR now) AND tires') > 0
```

The WITHIN Operator

The syntax of the WITHIN operator is fairly simple:

```
text_subquery WITHIN elementname
```

`text_subquery` can involve words, phrases, Boolean operators—pretty much anything and everything we've seen so far. `element` can be any XML tag. Although XML tags and XPath queries are case-sensitive, the interMedia query language is not, so all case variations of the tag are matched. In most search applications, this is actually a benefit, but if your queries must distinguish tag case, the index can use the XML sectioner—covered later in this chapter—instead of the autosectioner.

Like an XPath `contains()`, a WITHIN search searches the *entire* text content of the named tag, including the text content of all descendants of the tag. For instance, the query:

```
XML WITHIN title
```

would match this fragment:

```
<Title>
  Structured Documents
  <Subtitle>
    An introduction to HTML, XML, and SGML
  </Subtitle>
</Title>
```

even though the word "XML" is in the text content of `<Subtitle>`, and not in the direct text children of `<Title>`.

WITHIN has higher precedence than the AND and OR operators, so you need to use parentheses when using these in the text subquery. For example, if you were looking for claims caused by bad weather, you might try:

```
rain OR snow WITHIN cause
```

However, because of the tight binding, WITHIN will apply only to "snow," so this query will find documents where the word "snow" appears in between the `<Cause>` tags, and documents where the word "rain" appears anywhere in the text. This would be like the XPath `contains()` predicate:

```
contains(.,'rain') or .//Cause[contains(.,'snow')]
```

This isn't what we want. The correct syntax for our SQL CONTAINS query includes parentheses:

```
(rain OR snow) WITHIN cause
```

which is like the XPath:

```
.//Cause[contains(.,'rain') or contains(.,'snow')]
```

The parentheses force the WITHIN to apply to the whole subquery.

If you're using a text subquery, it must match a specific occurrence of the element. For instance, taking a fragment of the Shakespearean play example used in a previous chapter:

```
<LINE>Now, fair Hippolyta, our nuptial hour</LINE>
<LINE>Draws on apace; four happy days bring in</LINE>
```

we have two occurrences of the <LINE> element. The query:

```
(fair and days) WITHIN line
```

is similar to the XPath:

```
.//LINE[contains(.,'fair') and contains(.,'days')]
```

Neither matches this document fragment. Although the fragment contains the word "fair" and the word "days", and both are within <LINE> elements, they are in *different* <LINE> elements. The word "fair" is in the first occurrence, and "days" is in the second. We can rewrite the query as:

```
(fair WITHIN line) AND (days WITHIN line)
```

which is like the XPath:

```
.//LINE[contains(.,'fair')] and .//LINE[contains(.,'days')]
```

We now have two independent WITHIN clauses, and this query would match the fragment. To complete the example, the query:

```
(fair and hour) WITHIN line
```

also finds the fragment, because the words "fair" and "hour" appear within the same instance of the <LINE> element.

Combined WITHIN Clauses

An interMedia query can have multiple WITHIN clauses, allowing you to perform more sophisticated XML searches. Combining multiple WITHIN clauses with the AND operator searches different parts of the document at the same time, which is useful for finding data based on the intersection of criteria. As an example, let's take a database of movie description fragments:

```
<Movie>
  <Title>The Man Who Knew Too Much</Title>
  <Actors>
    <Actor>James Stewart</Actor>
    <Actor>Doris Day</Actor>
  </Actors>
  <Director>Alfred Hitchcock</Director>
</Movie>
```

with AND-combined WITHIN clauses, we can find Hitchcock movies with Jimmy Stewart:

```
(James Stewart WITHIN actor) AND (Alfred Hitchcock WITHIN director)
```

Combining WITHIN clauses with OR is useful when dealing with heterogeneous document sets—in which not all documents use the same doctype. In such cases, different DTDs might choose different tags to represent the same information. Consider a table with these two rows:

```
Row 1        <LastName>Chan</LastName>
Row 2        <Surname>Chan</Surname>
```

The first row's fragment uses `<LastName>` tags for the last name, while the second uses `<Surname>` tags. In order to search the whole table for Chan, you'll need to use OR-combined WITHIN clauses:

```
(chan WITHIN lastname) OR (chan WITHIN surname)
```

Later in this chapter we'll see an alternative method of handling heterogeneous doctypes using logical tags.

Nested WITHIN Clauses

The *element* part of a WITHIN query applies to any occurrence of the element in the XML at any level of the document—no matter where it is, how deeply it is nested, or what the ancestor elements are. In other words, the CONTAINS query:

```
brakes WITHIN cause
```

is similar to the XPath:

```
.//Cause[contains(.,'brakes')]
```

The `//` applies no constraints on the ancestry or level of `<Cause>`. Sometimes, however, parentage is very significant. Consider these three fragments from a multimedia catalog:

```
<Book>
  <Title>Oracle Design</Title>
  <Description>
    This book looks thoroughly at the field of Oracle
    relational database design
  </Description>
</Book>
```

```
<CD>
  <Title>Oracle: The Soundtrack</Title>
  <Description>
    Music inspired by the flexibility and speed of
    Everyone's favorite RDBMS
  </Description>
</CD>
<Book>
  <Title>Ancient Prophecies</Title>
  <Description>
    The history of Greece's Oracle at Delphi
  </Description>
</Book>
```

If you're looking for books on Oracle programming (and who wouldn't be?), you might try:

```
oracle WITHIN title
```

This is imprecise because it will also return the Oracle Soundtrack CD, which is not a book. You might then try:

```
oracle WITHIN book
```

This would filter out the CD, but now you'd get a history text because the word "Oracle" is mentioned in the `<Description>`, which is part of the `<Book>` element text content.

To perform this query, you need to nest WITHIN clauses:

```
(oracle WITHIN title) WITHIN book
```

This will search for the word "oracle" within the `<Title>` tags, but only where the `<Title>` tags are within a `<Book>` tag—in other words, this will find books whose titles include "oracle". This is analogous to the XPath:

```
.//Book//Title[contains(.,'oracle')]
```

There are several important things to keep in mind when you're using nested WITHIN searches:

- You must use parentheses around the inner WITHIN expression. The query:

  ```
  oracle WITHIN title WITHIN book
  ```

  is not legal syntax.

- The left-hand operand of WITHIN must be a text query and cannot be an element. The query:

  ```
  oracle WITHIN (title WITHIN book)
  ```

  is illegal.

- Like any WITHIN search, *direct* parentage is not guaranteed. The XPath analogue of the example nested WITHIN query is:

  ```
  .//Book//Title[contains(.,'oracle')]
  ```

  and not:

  ```
  .//Book/Title[contains(.,'oracle')]
  ```

- Because of the internal details of how XML element indexing is implemented, equal elements, which bracket the same text content, cannot be distinguished. For instance, the query:

  ```
  (important WITHIN italic) WITHIN bold
  ```

  would match:

  ```
  <Bold><Italic>Really Important</Italic></Bold>
  ```

  but it would also match:

  ```
  <Italic><Bold>Really Important</Bold></Italic>
  ```

Continuing with our multimedia catalog example, say that we're now looking for a general book on databases that discusses Oracle. The criteria are:

- It must be a book.
- Its title must contain the word "database".
- Its description must contain the word "oracle".

For this search, we need to use both nested WITHIN clauses and AND-combined WITHIN clauses:

```
((database WITHIN title) AND (oracle WITHIN description)) WITHIN book
```

This is similar to the XPath:

```
.//Book[.//Title[contains(.,'database') and
            .//Description[contains(.,'oracle')]]
```

Although relatively complex, this query leverages the entire XML element structure for a very precise and sophisticated text query.

We've seen how combined WITHIN clauses and nested WITHIN clauses can be used to improve search precision. AND-combined WITHIN clauses can narrow searches by the intersection of criteria, while nested WITHIN clauses can help filter out ambiguous uses of a tag. Nested AND-combined WITHIN clauses can perform more precise searches.

Namespaces

interMedia currently supports indexing based on the core XML 1.0 standard and is not currently aware of XML namespaces. For example, it does not know that the tag is composed of an arbitrary namespace prefix and tag name. In these two documents:

```
<x xmlns:edi='http://ecommerce.org/schema'>
  <edi:transid>12345</edi:transid>
</x>

<x xmlns:ecomm='http://ecommerce.org/schema'>
  <ecomm:transid>12345</ecomm:transid>
</x>
```

`<edi:transid>` and `<ecomm:transid>` are really the same element, because the namespace URIs (Uniform Resource Identifiers) are the same. However, interMedia treats these as *different* tags. To search both of them, you'll need to use OR-combined multiple WITHIN clauses:

```
(12345 WITHIN edi:transid) OR (12345 WITHIN ecomm:transid)
```

This is not a problem if your documents standardize on the namespace prefixes. Also, if there are only a few variants of namespace prefixes in your document set, you can use the XML sectioner, covered later in this chapter, to map them to the same logical tag name.

Attribute Value Searching

So far, we've covered the use of XML element names in the WITHIN clause. The autosectioner and WITHIN are also capable of text searching within attribute values. For instance, let's return to our original insurance fragment:

```
<DamageReport>
  The insured's <Vehicle Make="Volks">Beetle</Vehicle>
  broke through the guard rail and plummeted into a ravine.
  The cause was determined to be <Cause>faulty brakes</Cause>.
  Amazingly there were no casualties.
</DamageReport>
```

We might want to find all damage reports which involve Volkswagen cars. However, attribute text is not ordinarily searchable in interMedia. The query:

```
Volks WITHIN vehicle
```

will not find the fragment, nor will the simple query:

```
Volks
```

Why? Because, as in XPath, the text value of an element's attributes (or any nested element's attributes) is not considered part of the text content of an element. To search attribute text, you need to specify an attribute in the ***element*** operand of WITHIN:

```
text_subquery WITHIN elementname@attributename
```

Our query for **Volks** appearing within the **Make** attribute of the **<Vehicle>** element can be properly phrased as:

```
Volks WITHIN vehicle@make
```

which finds the example fragment. Note that this syntax is designed to be close to the analogous XPath:

```
.//Vehicle/@Make[contains(.,'Volks')]
```

Attribute searching in interMedia has some important limitations, however. The first limitation is that you cannot nest attribute searches. For instance, if you were looking for damage reports for Volkswagen Beetles, you might try to simulate the XPath:

```
.//Vehicle[@Make = "Volks" and contains(.,'Beetle')]
```

with the CONTAINS query:

```
((Volks WITHIN vehicle@make) AND Beetle) WITHIN vehicle
```

But this is not syntactically valid. This kind of query—an attribute value–sensitive WITHIN search—cannot be performed in the current version of interMedia Text. You can approximate the effect in this case with:

```
(Volks WITHIN vehicle@make) AND (Beetle WITHIN vehicle)
```

However, this approach breaks down when there is more than one **<Vehicle>** element.

The second limitation is that interMedia is a text-searching engine, so attribute values are searched as text. This has several implications:

- As with element text, there is no way to limit an attribute value search to exact equality. The query:

  ```
  John Doe WITHIN book@author
  ```

  would find the fragment:

  ```
  <Book Author="John Doe">Yes, That's My Real Name</Book>
  ```

  as well as cases where the **Author** attribute contains more than the search term:

  ```
  <Book Author="John Doe, Jr.">Yes, That's My Real Name</Book>
  ```

  In other words, the query is *not* equivalent to the XPath:

  ```
  .//Book[@Author = "John Doe"]
  ```

- Numeric and date values are not type-converted. This prevents some rows from being matched when searching attribute values. For instance:

  ```
  3 WITHIN review@rating
  ```

  would find the fragment:

  ```
  <Review Rating="3" Movie="The Big Sleep">A three-star movie</Review>
  ```

but would not find the fragment:

```
<Review Rating="3.0" Movie="The Big Sleep">A three-star movie</Review>
```

In the world of numbers, "3" is equal to "3.0"; however, in the world of text these are totally different.

- interMedia provides no way to do range searches on attribute values. You cannot do queries like finding books in a certain price range or news articles published this week.

The third limitation—again, as with text content—is that interMedia can search within attribute values, but cannot search for the existence of attributes. For instance, an XPath like:

```
//Vehicle[/@Make]
```

tests for the existence of a **Make** attribute of a **<Vehicle>** element. Because the product is primarily for text searching, there is no analogue in interMedia.

The attribute value searching functionality of interMedia is a subset of what is possible in XPath; on the other hand, interMedia has more sophisticated word search functionality combined with better performance and scalability. Moreover, interMedia is sufficient in many circumstances and will usually meet your needs if your XML data doesn't rely heavily on attributes.

For those cases where you find yourself needing to use numeric comparison or exact equality tests on attribute values, it's usually a better idea to factor out those values and store them redundantly in relational columns. You can then use Oracle's full feature set for those values in combination with interMedia for the text search, a technique we'll take a closer look at in the next section.

Mixing CONTAINS and SQL Predicates

So far we've seen that WITHIN clauses in a CONTAINS query can utilize data stored in XML fragments for precise searches. However, other columns may include equally important information. As Figure 13-2 illustrates, a datagram with embedded document fragments can be broken up and stored in a combination of atomic and unstructured text columns.

Since the fragment does not have the full XML document, a CONTAINS query alone is limited in the criteria it can use to find matching rows. To leverage all the data contained in the original XML document, you must combine the CONTAINS clause with other SQL predicates. Using our example, we can find books published in 1985 by Houghton Mifflin using CONTAINS alone:

```
SELECT ISBN, title
  FROM book
 WHERE CONTAINS(description,
                '(1985 WITHIN year) AND (Houghton Mifflin WITHIN pub)') > 0
```

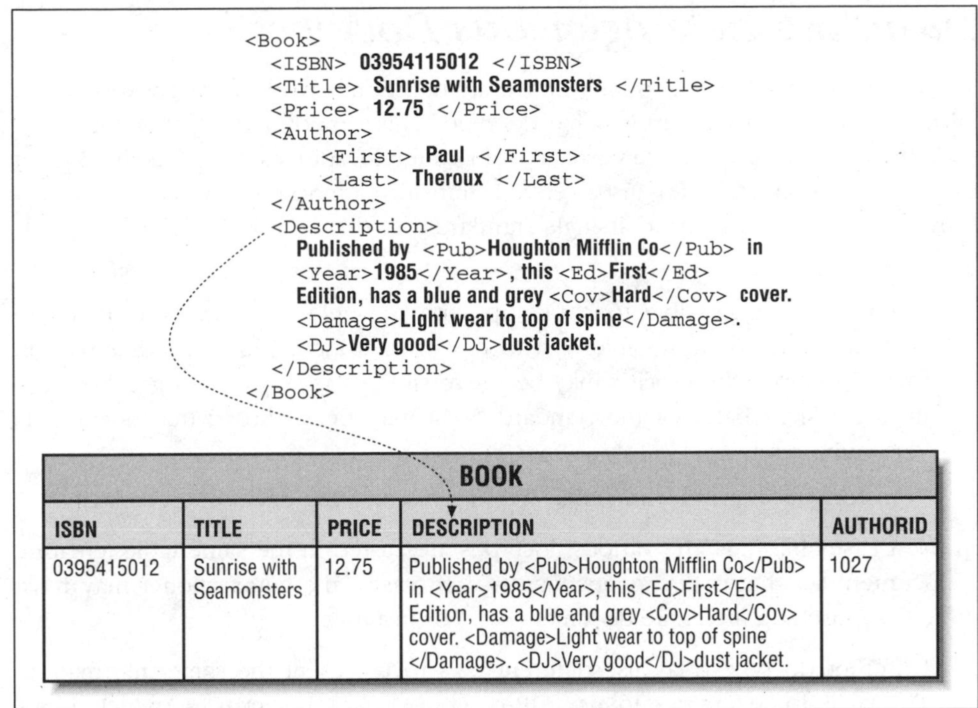

<Book>
<ISBN> 03954115012 </ISBN>
<Title> Sunrise with Seamonsters </Title>
<Price> 12.75 </Price>
<Author>
<First> Paul </First>
<Last> Theroux </Last>
</Author>
<Description>
Published by <Pub>Houghton Mifflin Co</Pub> in
<Year>1985</Year>, this <Ed>First</Ed>
Edition, has a blue and grey <Cov>Hard</Cov> cover.
<Damage>Light wear to top of spine</Damage>.
<DJ>Very good</DJ>dust jacket.
</Description>
</Book>
BOOK
ISBN
TITLE
PRICE
DESCRIPTION
AUTHORID
0395415012
Sunrise with Seamonsters
12.75
Published by <Pub>Houghton Mifflin Co</Pub> in <Year>1985</Year>, this <Ed>First</Ed> Edition, has a blue and grey <Cov>Hard</Cov> cover. <Damage>Light wear to top of spine </Damage>. <DJ>Very good</DJ>dust jacket.
1027

Figure 13-2. Storing a Book datagram into multiple columns

But what if we now wish to add a price range criteria? Price is not contained in the XML fragment, and interMedia doesn't provide range searching (even if it *did* contain the price). The solution is quite simple. Because interMedia searching is integrated with SQL, you merely add a SQL BETWEEN clause to the statement's WHERE clause:

```
SELECT ISBN, title
  FROM book
 WHERE price BETWEEN 10 and 20
   AND CONTAINS(description,
               '(1985 WITHIN year) AND (Houghton Mifflin WITHIN pub)') > 0
```

This relatively simple statement finds the ISBNs and titles of all books published by Houghton Mifflin in 1985 whose price is between $10.00 and $20.00. By combining SQL predicates and CONTAINS searches on relationally decomposed XML documents in this way, you can perform sophisticated and precise searches very quickly, often exceeding the capabilities and performance of what would be possible with intact XML documents stored in the filesystem or a document repository.

Handling Heterogeneous Doctypes

The examples we've seen so far with the autosectioner work relatively well when all of the documents have the same doctype. This cannot always be guaranteed. Information aggregators receive data from multiple sources that usually do not share a common DTD, for instance. XSL transformation could be used to transform incoming documents to a single standard, but this approach suffers from two limitations:

- It may not be possible to come up with a single standard DTD that can accommodate all expressible data in the various incoming DTDs. Even when this is possible, the process may be irreversible so that you can't get the original document back, or the standard DTD may be so broad that documents vary quite a bit.
- Transformation may be an expensive process, limiting data import capacity.

In most cases like this, the various doctypes are stored in the same table, creating a document set that is heterogeneous. In such cases, the autosectioner may have difficulty searching the entire document set. For instance:

- Different doctypes may use different tags to represent the same information. This will force queries to use OR-combined WITHIN clauses, which looks messy and is less efficient than single WITHIN clauses.
- Different doctypes may use the same tags to represent different information, or the autosectioner's inability to distinguish tag case may lead to a tag collision. These situations will make queries less precise because the WITHIN clause will be unable to distinguish between the two different uses of the same tag.

What's needed to handle these situations in heterogeneous document collections is a more abstract concept of document structure, independent of the lexical representation of tags—essentially, a "logical tag." These logical tags are called *sections* in interMedia, and interMedia Text provides the XML sectioner to index them and enable searching on them.

Using the XML Sectioner

Unlike the autosectioner, which automatically indexes every XML tag, the *XML sectioner* indexes only those tags specified by the user at the time the index is created. All other XML elements are disregarded. To illustrate this, let's index our first example using the XML sectioner instead of the autosectioner.

In our autosectioner example, we used the keywords `section group CTXSYS.AUTO_SECTION_GROUP` in the parameters string to employ the autosectioner. This tells the index to use the section group owned by CTXSYS named `AUTO_SECTION_GROUP`.

A *section group* is an object consisting of a section type specification and a collection of tags that should be indexed. The type specification tells the section group two things:

- The format of the documents being indexed. Different types exist to handle XML, HTML, and mail/news formats.
- How to parse the format.

Two types exist for XML: XML_SECTION_GROUP and AUTO_SECTION_GROUP. The difference between the two is that AUTO_SECTION_GROUP indexes every XML tag by default, while XML_SECTION_GROUP indexes only the tags in its tag collection.

For the AUTO_SECTION_GROUP type, a predefined section group exists—the referenced CTXSYS.AUTO_SECTION_GROUP, created at install time. No such predefined section group exists for the XML sectioner, so we need to create one using PL/SQL:

```
EXEC ctx_ddl.create_section_group('MYGRP','XML_SECTION_GROUP');
```

Users will need to execute the following statement to have the CTXAPP role in order to successfully run the command above. You or your DBA will need to:

```
GRANT CTXAPP TO YourUserName
```

This example creates an XML section group named MYGRP. Remember that unlike the AUTO_SECTION_GROUP, the XML_SECTION_GROUP type does not automatically index every tag. So, if we create the index on the table using this section group:

```
CREATE INDEX damagereportx ON claim(damagereport)
INDEXTYPE IS ctxsys.context
PARAMETERS ('section group mygrp');
```

we can do full text searches but not WITHIN searches. If we use a query like this:

```
SELECT claimid
  FROM claim
 WHERE CONTAINS(damagereport, 'faulty brakes WITHIN cause') > 0;
```

it produces the error:

```
ORA-20000: interMedia Text error: DRG-10837: section cause does not exist
```

This is because we did not declare <Cause> to be an indexed tag. The XML sectioner disregarded the <Cause> tag information, so it cannot perform the WITHIN search. To be able to perform this search, we have to drop the index, add <Cause> to the section group tag collection, and re-index:

```
DROP INDEX damagereportx;

EXEC ctx_ddl.add_zone_section('MYGRP','cause', 'Cause');
```

The first argument to **add_zone_section** is the section group name. The second is the section name, which we will call the *tag* in WITHIN searches. The third argument is the tag itself. This statement adds the **<Cause>** tag to the indexing list, naming it as the **cause** section. Don't worry too much about what a "zone" section is at this point. Suffice it to say that interMedia has several different types of sections; a zone section is bracketed by tags and indexed as a range of words.

Now that we have a **cause** section in our section group's tag collection, we can recreate the index by executing:

```
CREATE INDEX damagereportx ON claim(damagereport)
INDEXTYPE IS ctxsys.context
PARAMETERS ('section group mygrp');
```

With that, our WITHIN query works and finds our example document.

Although declaring all tags to index before creating the index is more work than using the autosectioner, it offers several advantages. The first is that this declaration process enables the XML sectioner to handle heterogeneous doctype collections. For instance, the third argument to **add_zone_section**, the tag, is case-sensitive. So, if instead we had done this:

```
EXEC ctx_ddl.add_zone_section('MYGRP','cause', 'cause');
```

our WITHIN query would not match our example document since the example XML document uses the tag **<Cause>**, not the tag **<cause>**. This means that, unlike the autosectioner, the XML sectioner can distinguish tag case.

A second advantage is that multiple tags can be mapped to the same section name. This separates logical structure from lexical expression, and allows a single WITHIN search to find content in multiple doctypes. For instance, let's take our last name fragments from earlier in the chapter:

```
Row 1       <LastName>Chan</LastName>
Row 2       <Surname>Chan</Surname>
```

We can map both the **<LastName>** and **<Surname>** tags to the section name **lname**:

```
EXEC ctx_ddl.add_zone_section('mygrp','lname','LastName');
EXEC ctx_ddl.add_zone_section('mygrp','lname','Surname');
```

Thus, we can find both documents with the query:

```
chan WITHIN lname
```

In contrast, the autosectioner, tied to the lexical expression of the tags, must use multiple OR-combined WITHIN clauses, which is less efficient and a more complicated and messier query.

The autosectioner also cannot effectively handle cases where different doctypes the same tag for different purposes. Take, for example, these two fragments:

```
<Book>
  <Title>Windsor Castle</Title>
</Book>

<Person>
  <Name>Prince Charles</Name>
  <Title>Duke of Windsor</Title>
</Person>
```

A simple WITHIN search on `title` cannot distinguish between these two different uses of the tag. Nested WITHIN clauses must be used to narrow the focus to books or people.

Using a special syntax for the tag in our section, you can specify a doctype limiter to address this. For instance:

```
EXEC ctx_ddl.add_zone_section('mygrp', 'booktitle', '(Book)Title');
EXEC ctx_ddl.add_zone_section('mygrp', 'persontitle', '(Person)Title');
```

Here we are mapping the tag `<Title>` of doctype `Book` to the section name `booktitle`, and the tag `<Title>` of doctype `Person` to the section name `persontitle`. Because these two different uses of the tag are indexed as different section names, WITHIN clauses can precisely specify which title to search:

```
windsor WITHIN persontitle
```

Attribute Value Searching

The XML sectioner is also able to index attribute values, as the autosectioner does. To declare an attribute value to index, you must add an attribute section, using the `add_attr_section` procedure. Use the *`tag@attribute`* syntax to specify the tag and attribute; for example:

```
EXEC ctx_ddl.add_attr_section('mygrp', 'make', 'Vehicle@Make');
```

To search an attribute value, simply use the section name. For instance, to find damage reports involving Volkswagen cars, specify:

```
Volks WITHIN make
```

Using the XML sectioner instead of the autosectioner clearly involves more work and planning. However, the abstraction of sections—*logical* tags can lead to more elegant and efficient queries on heterogeneous document sets, and is sometimes the only way to achieve precise queries when different doctypes use the same tags.

Handling Doctype Evolution

As time goes on, the DTD of your document collection may change, going through several versions as it evolves. A heterogeneous collection faces that challenge, as well as the challenge of new, unanticipated doctypes entering the system. How can interMedia cope with these changes?

The autosectioner indexes *every* XML tag, so as soon as a new XML tag appears in your collection, you can use it in WITHIN searches. The only trouble spot to watch out for is tag collision.

The XML sectioner has a harder time handling new tags. With the XML sectioner, the user must define which tags to keep before creating the index. Every undefined tag is thrown away. As new tags appear in the document collection, they are simply thrown away as well.

When this happens, the index owner must modify the index to add the new tags to the index's list of tags to keep. This is done using an ALTER INDEX command. If our `<DamageReport>` fragments start to include a `<Lawsuit>` tag, for instance, the following command:

```
ALTER INDEX damagereportx REBUILD
PARAMETERS ('add zone section lawsuit tag Lawsuit')
```

will modify the index metadata and add the tag `<Lawsuit>` as the section `lawsuit`. Don't be scared by the ALTER INDEX . . . REBUILD syntax—the index is not really going to be dropped and recreated. This is a quick metadata change only. In fact, because the index is not dropped and recreated, this will not affect documents already in the system, although documents added after this call with the `<Lawsuit>` tag will be searchable. Existing documents with the `<Lawsuit>` tag must be manually reindexed. The easiest way to do this is to update the row's value to itself, as shown here:

```
UPDATE claim
   SET damagereport = damagereport
 WHERE claimid = 12345;
```

In general, to force an XML searching index to be brought up to date with changes made to your document table, you can issue the command:

```
EXEC ctx_ddl.sync_index('indexname');
```

You'll need the CTXSYS user to grant you the CTXAPP role in order to perform the `sync_index()` operation. Since it's just a PL/SQL stored procedure, `sync_index()` can be easily included in a scheduled database job (e.g., with the `DBMS_JOB` package) to perform a sync on the index as frequently as makes sense for your application. For example, here's a command script that causes a database job to be created to sync the index named `xmldoc_idx` every 30 minutes:

```
SET SERVEROUTPUT ON
DECLARE
  jobId            NUMBER;
  resync_interval NUMBER        := 30;          -- In Minutes!
  index_name       VARCHAR2(30) := 'xmldoc_idx';
BEGIN
  dbms_job.submit(jobId,
                  'ctx_ddl.sync_index('''||index_name||''');',
                  interval=>'SYSDATE+'||resync_interval||'/1440');
  dbms_output.put_line('Submitted Job#'||jobId);
END;
```

Advanced interMedia

This chapter covers only a small number of features available through interMedia Text. Just to whet your appetite, Here are some of the broader text-searching features of interMedia not covered in this chapter:

More advanced features of the query language

The interMedia query language is extensive and supports Booleans, proximity, stem form expansion, wildcards, thesaurus operations, linguistic-based theme queries, relevance ranking and more. Most of these features can be used in conjunction with WITHIN for powerful XML searching. For instance, a stem form expansion query like:

```
$go WITHIN title
```

would find any of the following:

```
<TITLE>Go</TITLE>
<TITLE>Going Home</TITLE>
<TITLE>Gone With the Wind</TITLE>
<TITLE>The Englishman Who Went Up a Hill</TITLE>
```

Case-sensitive text and substring matching

Remember that when we contrasted the XPath `contains()` and the SQL CONTAINS earlier in this chapter, we noted that two aspects of XPath `contains()` were not mirrored in the SQL CONTAINS. Actually, with proper settings, interMedia can do case-sensitive text and substring searching; they just aren't the default behavior.

Field sections and stop sections

These are different from the zone sections covered in this chapter. Field sections are useful for small, non-overlapping sections like header information. Field sections are more efficient than zone sections for WITHIN queries on large homogenous document sets. Stop sections are used for common XML elements that are not useful for WITHIN searching. They can be added to the autosectioner to avoid indexing them, thereby saving space.

DML processing

Context indexes do not support transactional DML; when a new document is inserted and committed, the document is not searchable right away. Instead, the index must go through a batch update to process changes asynchronously. This batch process can be invoked manually, by the `DBMS_JOB` package, or by a background daemon process called `ctxsrv`.

Datastore support

Your XML documents do not need to be stored in the database. They can be files, web pages, or even virtual XML documents constructed on the fly through PL/SQL.

Language support

interMedia has language-specific technology that allows full-text searching of the major Western European languages, with even more specialized support for German, Dutch, Japanese, Chinese, and Korean. This includes language-specific stemming, base letter transformations, common alternate spellings, compound word decomposition, and Asian language segmentation—all very useful features for foreign-language or multilanguage document collections. Furthermore, all these features can be applied to WITHIN searching, so your XML documents are not limited to English.

And, as they say, much, much more. The interMedia documentation set and the technical overviews available on the Oracle Technology Network provide more in-depth information.

In this chapter:
- *Storing Datagrams in Multiple Tables*
- *Building an XMLLoader Utility*
- *Creating Insert Transformations Automatically*

14
Advanced XML Loading Techniques

In this chapter, we apply a combination of techniques learned in previous chapters to build an `XMLLoader` utility that assists in loading complex XML into multiple tables. We also explore using stylesheets that generate stylesheets for automating the creation of "insert transformations" needed to convert the structure of incoming XML into the canonical `ROWSET/ROW` format for insertion by the XML SQL utility or an XSQL page with an `<xsql.insert.request>` tag.

Storing Datagrams in Multiple Tables

We saw in Chapter 12, *Storing XML Datagrams,* that collection types can be used with object views to handle the automatic storage of XML datagrams containing nested, repeating information. Note that this technique works for any number of *single-level* nested collections, but does not work for *multilevel* nesting of repeating elements. This means that we can use the collection types technique to store `<Department>` datagrams that contain a nested set of `<Employee>`s. We can also use that technique to store `<Department>` datagrams that contain *both* a nested set of `<Employee>`s and a nested set of `<QuarterlyAudit>` entries. In general, any number of single-level repeating elements can be handled with collection types and object views, but if `<Department>`s contain repeating `<Employee>`s, and if `<Employee>`s, in turn, contain repeating `<Dependent>`s, then the technique no longer applies. This situation results from the limitation in Oracle8*i* that collection types cannot contain nested collections.

We need a different technique to handle the two or more levels of nested, repeating elements we'd see in examples of datagrams containing a `<Customer>` with a list of one or more open `<Order>`s, each of which has one or more `<Item>`s, as shown in Figure 14-1.

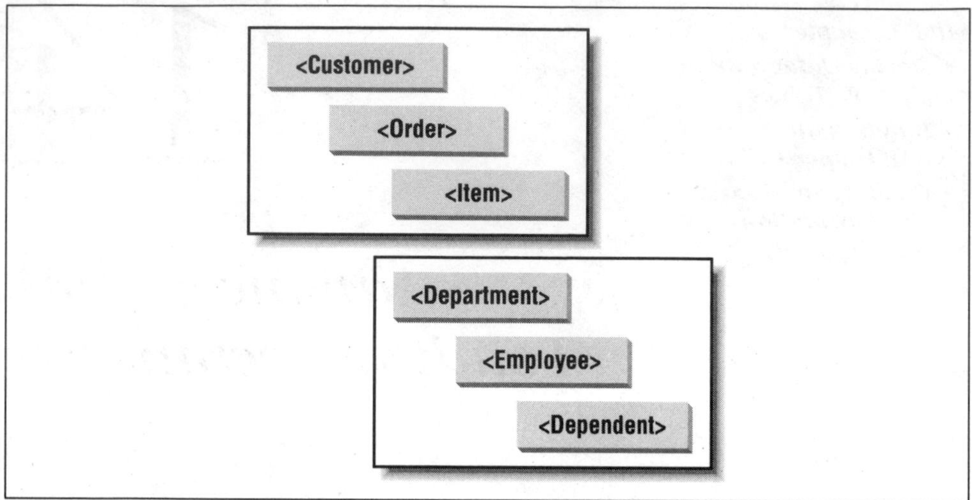

Figure 14-1. Datagrams with more than two levels of nesting

Another example might be a `<Department>` with a list of one or more open `<Employee>`s, each of which has one or more `<Dependent>`s. Let's roll up our sleeves and build an `XMLLoader` utility that exploits all the concepts we've learned earlier in this book but adds a little twist that enables us to handle the automatic insertion of datagrams with any number of nested levels of repeating elements into any number of tables.

We'll start with the XML datagram in Example 14-1, a variation on the `<Department>` and `<Employee>` datagram we worked with in an earlier chapter.

Example 14-1. Multiple Levels of Nested, Repeating Elements

```
<DepartmentList>
  <Department>
    <Id>97</Id>
    <Name>Finance</Name>
    <BudgetPlan>10</BudgetPlan>
    <BudgetPlan>20</BudgetPlan>
    <Employee>
      <Id>111</Id>
      <Name>Ziggie</Name>
      <Salary>1200</Salary>
      <Dependent>
        <Name>Zoe</Name>
      </Dependent>
      <Dependent>
        <Name>Reggy</Name>
      </Dependent>
    </Employee>
    <Employee>
      <Id>193</Id>
```

Example 14-1. Multiple Levels of Nested, Repeating Elements (continued)

```
      <Name>Hubert</Name>
      <Salary>2200</Salary>
    </Employee>
  </Department>
</DepartmentList>
```

The DTD for this datagram appears in Figure 14-2.

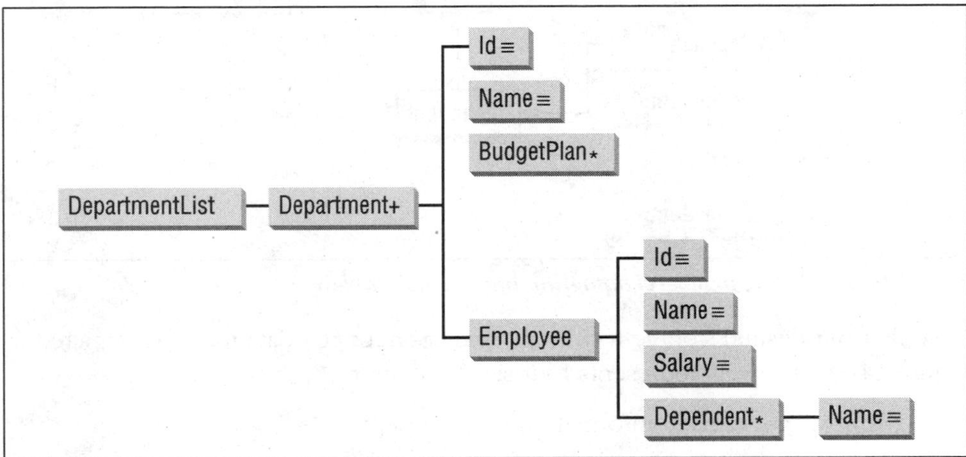

Figure 14-2. Examining the DepartmentList DTD structure

Three aspects distinguish this example from the one we worked with in Chapter 12 (see Example 12-20):

- `<Employee>` elements repeat as direct children of the `<Department>` element, without an enclosing `<Employees>` "container" element.
- `<Department>` has one or more `<BudgetPlan>` element children.
- Each `<Employee>` can have zero or more `<Dependent>` elements.

We want to store this XML datagram into the dept, emp, dependent, and budget_plan_assignment tables, as illustrated in Figure 14-3.

In nearly all previous examples of this kind, we've seen two recurring themes:

- The use of XSLT stylesheets to transform an arbitrary XML datagram into a datagram having the canonical `<ROWSET>/<ROW>` structure for the target table or view
- The use of the Oracle XML SQL Utility's "XML Save" functionality to insert that canonical XML document into the desired table or view

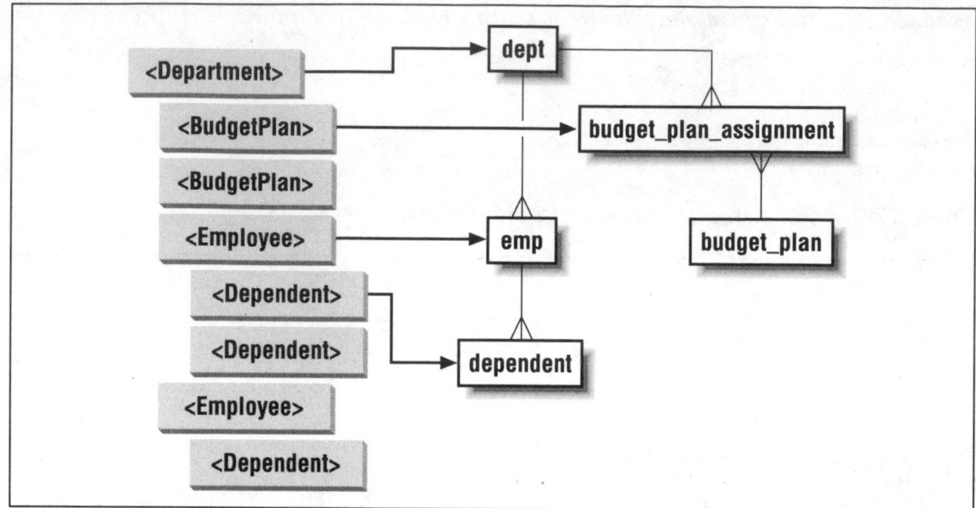

Figure 14-3. Inserting multilevel datagram into multiple tables

Note that our desired storage for the `<DepartmentList>` datagram (as depicted in Figure 14-3) effectively represents four save operations:

- Saving `<Department>` information into the dept table
- Saving `<BudgetPlan>` information into the budget_plan_assignment table
- Saving `<Employee>` information into the emp table
- Saving `<Dependent>` information into the dependent table

We know from previous examples that if we present `OracleXMLSave` with a `<ROWSET>` document full of `<ROW>`s, it can insert the data into a table whose structure matches the element structure of each `<ROW>`. To accomplish the four different save operations into the four different tables, we simply have to:

- Transform the `<Department>` information into a `<ROWSET>` document with the right `<ROW>` structure for the dept table, and use an `OracleXMLSave` object to save it
- Transform the `<BugdetPlan>` information into a `<ROWSET>` document with the right `<ROW>` structure for the budget_plan_assignment table, and use an `OracleXMLSave` object to save it
- Transform the `<Employee>` information into a `<ROWSET>` document with the right `<ROW>` structure for the emp table, and use an `OracleXMLSave` object to save it
- Transform the `<Dependent>` information into a `<ROWSET>` document with the right `<ROW>` structure for the dependent table, and use an `OracleXMLSave` object to save it

We could perform these transformations one step at a time, but it is more efficient to tackle all four transformations in a single stylesheet. If we transform a `<DepartmentList>` into a document that looks like this:

```
<INSERT>
  <ROWSET>
     <!-- Rows to insert into dept -->
  </ROWSET>
  <ROWSET>
     <!-- Rows to insert into budget_plan_assignment -->
  </ROWSET>
  <ROWSET>
     <!-- Rows to insert into emp -->
  </ROWSET>
  <ROWSET>
     <!-- Rows to insert into dependent -->
  </ROWSET>
</INSERT>
```

we can then programmatically loop over each of the four <ROWSET> children and pass each <ROWSET> to an appropriate `OracleXMLSave` object for inserting into the right table. We could hardcode the logic to expect the first <ROWSET> to be for the dept table, the second <ROWSET> to be for the budget_plan_assignment table, and so on. However, in order to make our `XMLLoader` utility generic and reusable for other multitable insert scenarios, we'll adopt the convention of putting the target table name into a `table="`*`tablename`*`"` attribute on the <ROWSET> element. This way, our programmatic logic that processes a multitable insert can work for any set of <ROWSET> elements, targeting any tables necessary.

For this example, we need a stylesheet that will transform the `<DepartmentList>` into a multitable insert document that looks like Example 14-2.

Example 14-2. Skeleton of Canonical Form for a Multitable Insert

```
<INSERT>
  <ROWSET table="dept">
    <ROW>
       <!-- Elements for DEPT columns being inserted -->
    </ROW>
     :
  </ROWSET>
  <ROWSET table="budget_plan_assignment">
    <ROW>
       <!-- Elements for BUDGET_PLAN_ASSIGNMENT columns being inserted -->
    </ROW>
     :
  </ROWSET>
  <ROWSET table="emp">
    <ROW>
       <!-- Elements for EMP columns being inserted -->
    </ROW>
     :
  </ROWSET>
```

Example 14-2. Skeleton of Canonical Form for a Multitable Insert (continued)

```
  <ROWSET table="dependent">
    <ROW>
       <!-- Elements for DEPENDENT columns being inserted -->
    </ROW>
      :
  </ROWSET>
</INSERT>
```

Example 14-3 provides the stylesheet we need.

Example 14-3. Transforming for Multitable Insert

```
<INSERT xsl:version="1.0"
        xmlns:xsl="http://www.w3.org/1999/XSL/Transform">
  <ROWSET table="dept">
    <xsl:for-each select="Department">
      <ROW>
        <DEPTNO><xsl:value-of select="Id"/></DEPTNO>
        <DNAME><xsl:value-of select="Name"/></DNAME>
      </ROW>
    </xsl:for-each>
  </ROWSET>
  <ROWSET table="budget_plan_assignment">
    <xsl:for-each select="Department/BudgetPlan">
      <ROW>
        <DEPTNO><xsl:value-of select="../Id"/></DEPTNO>
        <BUDGETCODE><xsl:value-of select="."/></BUDGETCODE>
      </ROW>
    </xsl:for-each>
  </ROWSET>
  <ROWSET table="emp">
    <xsl:for-each select="Department/Employee">
      <ROW>
        <EMPNO><xsl:value-of select="Id"/></EMPNO>
        <ENAME><xsl:value-of select="Name"/></ENAME>
        <SAL><xsl:value-of select="Salary"/></SAL>
        <DEPTNO><xsl:value-of select="../Id"/></DEPTNO>
      </ROW>
    </xsl:for-each>
  </ROWSET>
  <ROWSET table="dependent">
    <xsl:for-each select="Department/Employee/Dependent">
      <ROW>
        <EMPNO><xsl:value-of select="../Id"/></EMPNO>
        <NAME><xsl:value-of select="Name"/></NAME>
      </ROW>
    </xsl:for-each>
  </ROWSET>
</INSERT>
```

Notice that each of the four <ROWSET> elements in the stylesheet fills in its <ROW> elements by looping over the relevant repeating information destined for that table using `<xsl:for-each>` and an appropriate XPath pattern.

We now have to write the code to handle the processing of this multitable insert document consisting of one or more <ROWSET> elements, each destined for insertion into a table whose name is indicated by the value of its `table="`*`tablename`*`"` attribute.

`MultiTableInsertHandler.java` in Example 14-4 handles the job nicely. Its constructor takes:

- A JDBC `Connection` object to be used for the insert operations
- An `XSLStylesheet` object to transform each document handled into the canonical multitable insert format
- An `ignoreErrors` boolean flag that indicates whether errors in one insert operation should roll back the entire set of inserts performed (default is `false`) or ignore individual errors (default is `true`)

To insert an XML datagram using the `MultiTableInsertHandler`, simply call the `handleDocument()` method to pass the datagram as a DOM `document` and the URL to the datagram (if available; otherwise, pass `NULL`). Internally, `handleDocument()` calls the private `handle()` method to do the real work. This method does the following:

1. Transforms the source XML datagram if necessary. If the source XML datagram is already in the multitable insert canonical format, this transformation can be skipped by passing a `NULL` for the `sheet` parameter of the `MultiTableInsertHandler` constructor.
2. Uses `selectNodes()` to find the <ROWSET> elements in the multitable insert document.
3. Loops over the list of <ROWSET> elements found, and for each one:
   - Creates a new `XMLDocument` `insDoc` containing only the current <ROWSET> element and its child nodes
   - Picks up the target table name from the `table` attribute on the current <ROWSET> element
   - Creates an `OracleXMLSave` object to handle the insertion, passing the JDBC connection and the current target table name
   - Calls `insertXML()` on the `OracleXMLSave` object, passing the current <ROWSET> document

Example 14-4. Handler to Insert Datagram into Multiple Tables

```
import oracle.xml.parser.v2.*;
import org.w3c.dom.*;
import oracle.xml.sql.dml.OracleXMLSave;
import java.sql.*;
import java.net.URL;

public class MultiTableInsertHandler implements XMLDocumentHandler {
  private XMLDocument    categories = null;
  private String         path       = null;
  private String         table      = null;
  private XSLStylesheet  sheet      = null;
  private String         dateFormat = null;
  private int itemsHandled          = 0;
  private int itemsInserted         = 0;
  private boolean ignoreErrors      = false;
  Connection     conn;

  // Provide a JDBC connection and optionally an XSL transformation
  // to be used to transform the XML datagram into multitable insert format
  // If 'ignoreErrors' is true, then individual inserts can succeed even if
  // some fail due to errors. If false, any error on insert does a rollback.
  public MultiTableInsertHandler( Connection conn,
                                  XSLStylesheet sheet,
                                  boolean ignoreErrors ) {
   this.conn         = conn;
   this.sheet        = sheet;
   this.ignoreErrors = ignoreErrors;
  }

  // Process an XML datagram for multitable insertion
  public void handleDocument(Document d, URL u) throws Exception {
    try {
      itemsHandled++;
      handle(d,u);
      conn.commit();
      itemsInserted++;
      System.out.println(formatted(itemsHandled)+": Inserted.");
    }
    catch (oracle.xml.sql.OracleXMLSQLException ex) {
      try { conn.rollback(); } catch (SQLException s) {}
      System.out.println(formatted(itemsHandled)+": Failed, ORA-" +
                         formatted(ex.getErrorCode()));
    }
  }

  // Handle the transformation and multitable inserting
  private void handle(Document d, URL u) throws Exception {
    XMLDocument result = null;
    NodeList    nl     = null;
    // If a transformation has been specified, do the transformation
    if (sheet != null) {
      XSLProcessor  processor = new XSLProcessor();
      DocumentFragment df = processor.processXSL(sheet, (XMLDocument)d);
```

Example 14-4. Handler to Insert Datagram into Multiple Tables (continued)

```
      result = new XMLDocument();
      result.appendChild(df);
    }
    else {
      result = (XMLDocument)d;
    }
    // First check if document element is ROWSET. If present, only one ROWSET
    nl = result.selectNodes("/ROWSET");
    if (nl != null && nl.getLength() == 0) {
       XMLElement e = (XMLElement) result.getDocumentElement();
       // If ROWSET is not Doc Element, Search for ROWSET children elements
       nl = e.selectNodes("ROWSET");
    }
    String table = null;
    int rowsets = nl != null ? nl.getLength() : 0;
    // Loop over all the ROWSET elements we found.
    for (int z = 0; z < rowsets; z++ ) {
      // Create a new document with current ROWSET as doc element.
      XMLDocument insDoc = new XMLDocument();
      XMLElement curElt = (XMLElement)nl.item(z);
      curElt.getParentNode().removeChild(curElt);
      insDoc.appendChild(curElt);
      // Pick up the target tablename from the table attribute of ROWSET tag
      table = curElt.valueOf("@table");
      // If table name was given and ROWSET element has some child elements
      if (table != null && insDoc.getDocumentElement().getFirstChild() != null) {
        try {
          // Create the XMLSave object and pass current ROWSET doc and tablename
          OracleXMLSave xs = new OracleXMLSave(conn,table);
          xs.setCommitBatch(1);
          xs.setIgnoreCase(true);
          if (dateFormat != null) {
            xs.setDateFormat(dateFormat);
          }
          int rows = xs.insertXML(insDoc);
        }
        catch (oracle.xml.sql.OracleXMLSQLException ex) {
          // If we're ignoring errors, then note the error and continue.
          if (ignoreErrors) {
            System.out.println(formatted(itemsHandled)+": Ignoring, ORA-" +
                         formatted(ex.getErrorCode()) + " on table " + table);
          }
          else {
            throw ex;
          }
        }
      }
    }
  }
  public int getItemsHandled() { return itemsHandled; };
  public void setDateFormat(String format) {
    dateFormat = format;
  }
```

Example 14-4. Handler to Insert Datagram into Multiple Tables (continued)

```
  private String formatted(long n) {
    java.text.DecimalFormat df = new java.text.DecimalFormat();
    df.applyPattern("00000");
    return df.format(n).toString();
  }
}
```

The last step is to create a command-line **XMLLoader** utility that makes use of **MultiTableInsertHandler** to let us handle the current task at hand for our **<DepartmentList>** datagram, as well as any future multitable insert scenarios we may need for our more complicated XML datagrams. While we're at it, we'll make sure our **XMLLoader** utility can handle inserting XML datagrams of any size.

Building an XMLLoader Utility

Since many of the XML datagrams you encounter will have been produced by formatting rows of database query results as XML, it will be quite common for the XML datagrams to have a "List of Something" format like this one:

```
<ListOfSomething>
  <Something>
      :
  </Something>
  <Something>
      :
  </Something>
      :
    <!-- repeating potentially thousands of times -->
      :
  <Something>
      :
  </Something>
</ListOfSomething>
```

In the case of our **<DepartmentList>** example in the previous section, we might encounter a **<DepartmentList>** datagram that looks like this:

```
<DepartmentList>
  <Department>
      :
  </Department>
  <Department>
      :
  </Department>
      :
    <!-- repeating potentially thousands of times -->
      :
  <Department>
      :
  </Department>
</DepartmentList>
```

If the <DepartmentList> datagram contains hundreds or thousands of <Department> elements, parsing the document into a tree of nodes in memory can become a problem. This is where our XMLDocumentSplitter class from Chapter 6, *Processing XML with Java*, will come in handy.

Recall that XMLDocumentSplitter uses the stream-based SAXParser to process the XML datagram in question as a sequential stream of tags. It takes a divide and conquer approach to processing large XML documents that have the "List of Something" format by splitting the stream of incoming tags into a sequence of incoming documents based on the tag name of the <Something> element that repeats inside the <ListOfSomething> document element. The net effect is that all of the <Something> "sub-datagrams" are processed and the amount of memory used is only as much as a single <Something> datagram requires.

Since our MultiTableInsertHandler class implements the XMLDocumentHandler interface:

```
import java.net.URL;
import org.w3c.dom.Document;
public interface XMLDocumentHandler {
  void handleDocument( Document d , URL u ) throws Exception;
}
```

we can easily use MultiTableInsertHandler as the document handler that XMLDocumentSplitter will invoke to handle each document it "splits" out of the stream it's processing. Figure 14-4 illustrates how the two classes work in combination when processing a large <DepartmentList> datagram.

For example, if we call the XMLDocumentSplitter class's split() method with the tag name of Department, it will invoke the handleDocument() method on MultiTableInsertHandler for each <Department> subdocument it encounters. As we saw earlier, the MultiTableInsertHandler then handles the details of inserting each individual <Department> document into multiple tables.

Using our ConnectionFactory class from Chapter 6 to pick up named connections from a *Connections.xml* file, we can round out the functionality for the XMLLoader utility in Example 14-5. The utility provides a command-line shell that allows us to apply the combination of XMLDocumentSplitter and MultiTableInsertHandler to any situation we encounter by providing the appropriate command-line options, as shown in Table 14-1.

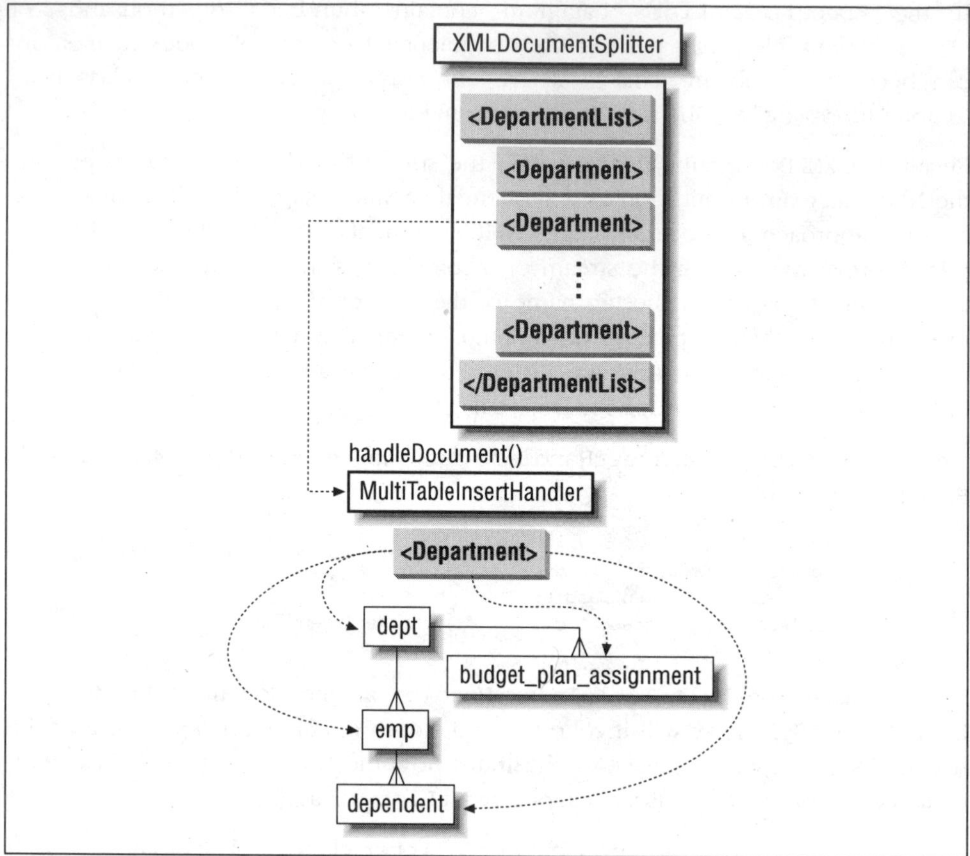

Figure 14-4. How the XMLLoader utility works

Table 14-1. XMLLoader Command-Line Options

Attribute Name	Description
`-file` *`filename`*	Filename of XML source to read.
`-connName` *`connectionName`*	Name of connection to use to connect to the database. Connection definitions are found in the *Connections.xml* file in the CLASSPATH. If no connection is specified, the "default" connection is used.
`-docTag`	Name of the document element comprising the subdocuments you want processed for loading. If no element is specified, the entire file is processed for loading as a single document.
`-ignoreErrors`	If specified, allows individual table inserts to fail with an error (for example, "Row Already Exists") without rolling back the entire set of inserts for the current subdocument being loaded.

Table 14-1. XMLLoader Command-Line Options (continued)

Attribute Name	Description
`-transform` *`stylesheetURI`*	If specified, the XSLT stylesheet with the URI provided will be used to transform each subdocument processed into the multitable `ROWSET/ROW` canonical format for insert.
`-dateFormat` *`datePattern`*	If specified, uses the supplied `java.text.SimpleDateFormat` date pattern to parse values in the insert document destined for insertion into database columns of type DATE.

This means that to load our `<DepartmentList>` datagram from the previous section, we can issue the command:

```
java XMLLoader -file dept-emp-depend.xml
               -transform dept-emp-depend.xsl
               -docTag Department
```

where *dept-emp-depend.xml* is the name of the file containing the `<DepartmentList>` datagram from Example 14-1 and *dept-emp-depend.xsl* is the XSLT stylesheet from Example 14-3. Since this example contains only a single `<Department>` datagram inside it, you'll see:

```
Connecting as <username> at <dburl>
00001: Inserted.
Processed 1 Documents
```

If we want to load a really large `<DepartmentList>` datagram from the *huge-department-file.xml* file containing 5000 `<Department>` datagrams inside it, we issue the exact same command:

```
java XMLLoader -file huge-department-file.xml
               -transform dept-emp-depend.xsl
               -docTag Department
```

The output this time will be:

```
Connecting as <username> at <dburl>
00001: Inserted.
00002: Inserted.
  :
05000: Inserted.
Processed 5000 Documents
```

The full source code of `XMLLoader` appears in Example 14-5.

Example 14-5. Utility to Load Any Size Document into Any Number of Tables

```
import java.net.*;
import java.io.*;
import java.sql.Connection;
import oracle.xml.parser.v2.XSLStylesheet;
import URLUtils;
```

Example 14-5. Utility to Load Any Size Document into Any Number of Tables (continued)

```
public class XMLLoader {

  private static String  dateFormat  = null;
  private static String  docElement  = null;
  private static Connection    conn  = null;
  private static String  connName    = "default";
  private static URL     file;
  private static URL     trans;
  private static boolean ignoreErrs  = false;
  private static XSLStylesheet sheet = null;
  public static void main( String[] args ) throws Exception {
    try {
      processArgs(args);
      conn = ConnectionFactory.getConnection(connName);
      if (trans != null) {
        try {
          sheet = new XSLStylesheet(trans,trans);
        }
        catch (Exception xe) {
          System.err.println("Error loading stylesheet " + trans);
          System.exit(1);
        }
      }
      // Create a multitable insert handler
      MultiTableInsertHandler mtih =
         new MultiTableInsertHandler(conn,sheet,ignoreErrs);

      // Set the date format for the insert handler (null is ok)
      mtih.setDateFormat(dateFormat);

      // Use an XMLDocumentSplitter to handle large documents, passing
      // MultiTableInsertHandler to be used for each "SubDocument" found
      XMLDocumentSplitter splitter = new XMLDocumentSplitter( mtih );

      // Process the input document, splitting it into subdocs to be
      // handled based on the specified docElement.
      splitter.split(file,docElement);

      System.out.println("Processed " + mtih.getItemsHandled() + " Documents");
      conn.close();
    }
    catch(Exception ex) {
      System.err.println("Error: " + ex.toString());
    }
  }

  private static void processArgs(String[] arg) throws Exception {
    int args = arg.length;
    for (int q=0; q<args; q++) {
      String cur = arg[q];
      if (cur.equals("-connName")) {
        connName = q!=args ? arg[q+1] : null;
      }
```

Example 14-5. Utility to Load Any Size Document into Any Number of Tables (continued)

```
      if (cur.equals("-docTag")) {
        docElement = q!=args ? arg[q+1] : null;
      }
      if (cur.equals("-transform")) {
        trans = q!=args ? URLUtils.newURL(arg[q+1]) : null;
      }
      if (cur.equals("-file")) {
        file = q!=args ? URLUtils.newURL(arg[q+1]) : null;
      }
      if (cur.equals("-ignoreErrors")) {
        ignoreErrs = true;
      }
      if (cur.equals("-dateFormat")) {
        dateFormat = q!=args ? arg[q+1] : null;
      }
    }
    if (file == null) {
      System.err.println("usage: XMLLoader -file filename");
      System.err.println("[-connName connectionName]" );
      System.err.println("[-docTag tagname]" );
      System.err.println("[-ignoreErrors]" );
      System.err.println("[-transform stylesheet.xsl]");
      System.err.println("[-dateFormat yyyy-MM-d]");
      System.exit(1);
    }
  }
}
```

Creating Insert Transformations Automatically

In Chapter 12, we learned how to use the **<xsql:insert-request>** element to get posted XML or HTML form data into our database. Recall that the **<xsql:insert-request>** action element has the following syntax:

```
<xsql:insert-request table="targettable" transform="style.xsl"/>
```

where it is the job of the *style.xsl* stylesheet to transform the inbound XML document into the canonical ROWSET/ROW format that reflects the structure of the ***targettable*** table or view. If you're like me, you tire quickly of manually creating these "insert transform" stylesheets and you start thinking of a way to automate their creation. You need look no further than the effective combination of XSQL pages and XSLT to get the data we need and XSLT to produce the "insert transform" for a given table.

Recall that the canonical XML structure required for insert is the same structure that is produced by doing a SELECT * query over the table in question. So let's build a simple XSQL page to do that SELECT * query over a table whose name is a parameter supplied in the request:

```
<?xml version="1.0"?>
<page connname="xmlbook" connection="{@connname}">
  <xsql:query null-indicator="yes" xmlns:xsql="urn:oracle-xsql">
  <![CDATA[
    SELECT *
      FROM {@table}
     WHERE rownum < 2
  ]]>
  </xsql:query>
</page>
```

The FROM clause uses the `{@table}` syntax to refer to an XSQL page parameter and is wrapped in by a `CDATA` section so that none of the characters that occur between the opening `<![CDATA[` and the closing `]]>` need to be quoted; for instance, the less-than sign in our WHERE clause. We use the `WHERE rownum < 2` clause to make sure we only retrieve a single row from the table whose name is passed in as a parameter to the XSQL page request, since we need only a single row to understand the canonical structure. Finally, note that we've included the `null-indicator="yes"` attribute on `<xsql:query>` so that the underlying XML SQL utility produces an element for a column whose value is NULL instead of leaving it out. We'd like to make sure all columns are present in the XML fragment produced by the query. While we're at it, we've also parameterized the named `connection`, and we've provided a fallback attribute named `connname` so that if we're using the `xmlbook` connection name, we don't have to supply a value for the `connname` parameter.

Now that you're seeing more and more XSQL pages in combination with XSLT stylesheets, you might begin to confuse the XSQL Pages syntax for parameter substitution {@*paramname*} and the XSLT syntax for an attribute value template {*XPathExpression*}. Check the file extension of the file you're working on if you have any doubts.

If we use the `xsql` command-line utility to run the preview page above on a table like site_newsstory:

```
xsql GenerateInsertTransform.xsql outfile.xml table=site_newsstory
```

the XML output in Example 14-6 is saved to the file *outfile.xml*.

Example 14-6. One Row of Canonical Output from the site_newsstory Table

```
<?xml version = '1.0'?>
<page connname="xmlbook">
  <ROWSET>
    <ROW num="1">
```

Example 14-6. One Row of Canonical Output from the site_newsstory Table (continued)

```
      <ID>802</ID>
      <TITLE>CommerceOne and Extensibility Partner Around XML Schema</TITLE>
      <URL>http://www.extensibility.com/company/headlines/commerce_one.htm</URL>
      <CATEGORY>1</CATEGORY>
      <DESCRIPTION>CommerceOne and Extensibility have entered into...</DESCRIPTION>
      <TIMESTAMP>1/30/2000 18:54:0</TIMESTAMP>
      <SOURCE>Extensibility.com</SOURCE>
    </ROW>
  </ROWSET>
</page>
```

We need a stylesheet to transform this document into the skeleton of a working XSLT stylesheet that reproduces this same structure but supplies appropriate `<xsl:value-of>` elements to replace the literal text, and `<xsl:for-each>` elements to wrap elements that can repeat, like `<ROW>` or the repeating *`XXX_ITEM`* elements inside an object view's nested table or VARRAY *`column_name`* column.

Writing a stylesheet that produces a stylesheet gets a little tricky because you want to produce elements like `<xsl:for-each>` in the transformed output, but you have to use `<xsl:for-each>` elements in the stylesheet that performs this transformation to process nodes in the source tree. The solution is to use a different namespace prefix to represent the XSLT namespace in the stylesheet that creates a stylesheet. For example, rather than the conventional `xsl` prefix, we can use:

```
xmlns:xslt="http://www.w3.org/1999/XSL/Transform"
```

to define the prefix for the XSLT namespace to be `xslt` instead. Then we can use `xsl` as the prefix for a temporary namespace whose name is any convenient string (like "temp") using the namespace declaration:

```
xmlns:xsl="temp"
```

Then, after screwing our brain on tightly, we proceed to write the stylesheet using elements like:

```
<xslt:stylesheet>
<xslt:template>
<xslt:for-each>
<xslt:value-of>
```

for the "real" XSLT actions, and:

```
<xsl:stylesheet>
<xsl:template>
<xsl:for-each>
<xsl:value-of>
```

as the literal elements they now are, since they are no longer qualified by a prefix for the XSLT namespace.

The last step is to use the special `<xsl:namespace-alias>` action, which we'll need to refer to as `<xslt:namespace-alias>`. The syntax is:

```
<xsl:namespace-alias stylesheet-prefix="xsl" result-prefix="xslt"/>
```

This rewires the namespace associated to elements in the result tree prefixed by `xsl` to be the namespace used by the prefix `xslt` in the stylesheet. That's hard to say in a sentence, but basically it means that instead of creating a result like:

```
<xsl:stylesheet version="1.0" xmlns:xsl="temp">
```

which would not be a valid XSLT stylesheet, it will instead create:

```
<xsl:stylesheet version="1.0"
                xmlns:xsl="http://www.w3.org/1999/XSL/Transform">
```

Example 14-7 shows the source code for the transformation that creates a stylesheet. In addition to `<xsl:namespace-alias>`, it features several interesting XSLT twists we haven't seen before. To make it easier to follow along, we'll list them with the `xslt` prefix they are using in this example:

- A top-level stylesheet `<xslt:param>` allows passing in the `table` name externally.
- `<xslt:strip-space>` with an `elements ="*"` pattern strips any text nodes contained in any element that consist of only whitespace. This can be very convenient when you have a template that matches `text()`, as we do in this stylesheet. Stripping whitespace for all elements means that our template can assume it won't see the carriage returns and indents it doesn't care about.
- `<xslt:comment>` lets our stylesheet construct comments in the result tree.
- `<xslt:copy>` copies the current node to the result tree. The nested content of an `<xslt:copy>` determines which elements or attributes will appear as attributes on and descendent elements of the copied node.
- A clever XPath pattern to match elements that contain elements whose name is the name of their parent element with the suffix `_ITEM` appended to it, like:

  ```
  <SETTLEMENTS>
    <SETTLEMENTS_ITEM>
  ```

Example 14-7. Stylesheet to Create an Insert Transformation for Any Table

```
<xslt:stylesheet version="1.0" xmlns:xsl="temp"
            xmlns:xslt="http://www.w3.org/1999/XSL/Transform">
  <xslt:output method="xml" indent="yes"/>
  <!-- Disregard all whitespace in the source document -->
  <xslt:strip-space elements="*"/>
  <!-- "Rewire" xsl prefix to use xslt prefix's namespace in the result -->
  <xslt:namespace-alias stylesheet-prefix="xsl" result-prefix="xslt"/>
  <!-- Get the tablename as a parameter -->
  <xslt:param name="table"/>
```

Example 14-7. Stylesheet to Create an Insert Transformation for Any Table (continued)

```
<!-- Output an xslt:stylesheet using the temporary prefix xsl -->
<xslt:template match="/">
  <xslt:comment>
    <xslt:text> Created by GenerateInsertTransform.xsl </xslt:text>
  </xslt:comment>
  <xslt:text>&#xa;</xslt:text>
  <xsl:stylesheet version="1.0">
    <!-- Create a comment in the output -->
    <xslt:comment>
      <xslt:text> Transform XXXX into ROWSET for </xslt:text>
      <xslt:value-of select="$table"/>
      <xslt:text> </xslt:text>
    </xslt:comment>
    <!-- Create a root xslt:template in the output using xsl -->
    <xsl:template match="/">
      <xslt:apply-templates select="page/ROWSET/ROW[1]"/>
    </xsl:template>
  </xsl:stylesheet>
</xslt:template>
<!--
 | Match a ROW and create an xsl:for-each in the output. Needs a
 | priority="1" to make more important than template matching *[*] below
 +-->
<xslt:template match="ROW" priority="1">
  <ROWSET>
    <xslt:comment>
      <xslt:text> XPath for repeating source rows </xslt:text>
    </xslt:comment>
    <xsl:for-each select="page/ROWSET/ROW">
      <ROW>
        <xslt:apply-templates/>
      </ROW>
    </xsl:for-each>
  </ROWSET>
</xslt:template>
<!--
 | Match elements that contain other elements or
 | elements that contain text and copy them to the output.
 +-->
<xslt:template match="*[*]|*[text()]">
  <xslt:copy>
    <xslt:apply-templates select="*|text()"/>
  </xslt:copy>
</xslt:template>
<!-- Match text() nodes for column values & output xsl:value-of -->
<xslt:template match="text()">
  <xsl:value-of select="{name(..)}"/>
</xslt:template>
<!--
 | Match an element containing an element whose name is
 | the concatenation of its parent's name and the suffix '_ITEM'
 | This matches object view nested collection columns/attributes
 | whose collection element name <XXX> will contain the items
```

Example 14-7. Stylesheet to Create an Insert Transformation for Any Table (continued)

```
   | in the collection named <XXX_ITEM>.
   | Copy the current element, add a nested comment, and
   | process the *first* <XXX_ITEM> child
   +-->
  <xslt:template match="*[*[name(.)=concat(name(..),'_ITEM')]]">
    <xslt:copy>
      <xslt:comment>
        <xslt:text> XPath for repeating </xslt:text>
        <xslt:value-of select="name(.)"/>
        <xslt:text> items from source </xslt:text>
      </xslt:comment>
      <xsl:for-each select="{name(.)}_ITEM">
        <xslt:apply-templates select="*[1]"/>
      </xsl:for-each>
    </xslt:copy>
  </xslt:template>
</xslt:stylesheet>
```

We edit our *GenerateInsertTransform.xsql* page to associate this *GenerateInsert-Transform.xsl* stylesheet, as well as add a new **<xsql:set-stylesheet-param>** action element to assign the value of the XSQL page parameter named **table** to the XSLT top-level stylesheet parameter named **table**:

```
<?xml version="1.0"?>
<?xml-stylesheet type="text/xsl" href="GenerateInsertTransform.xsl"?>
<page connname="xmlbook" connection="{@connname}">
  <xsql:query null-indicator="yes" xmlns:xsql="urn:oracle-xsql">
  <![CDATA[
    select *
      from {@table}
     where rownum < 2
  ]]>
  </xsql:query>
  <xsql:set-stylesheet-param name="table" value="{@table}"
                             xmlns:xsql="urn:oracle-xsql" />
</page>
```

Now we can try it out to produce a stylesheet to be used when transforming a posted HTML form or XML document for inserting a new news story in the site_newsstory table. We can use the **xsql** command-line utility again:

```
xsql GenerateInsertTransform.xsql NewTransform.xsl table=site_newsstory
```

This produces the following machine-generated XSLT stylesheet in the *NewTransform.xsl* file:

```
<?xml version = '1.0' encoding = 'UTF-8'?>
<xsl:stylesheet version="1.0"
                xmlns:xsl="http://www.w3.org/1999/XSL/Transform">
   <!-- Transform XXXX into canonical ROWSET for site_newsstory -->
   <xsl:template match="/">
```

```
      <ROWSET>
        <!-- XPath for repeating source rows -->
        <xsl:for-each select="page/ROWSET/ROW">
          <ROW>
            <ID><xsl:value-of select="ID"/></ID>
            <TITLE><xsl:value-of select="TITLE"/></TITLE>
            <URL><xsl:value-of select="URL"/></URL>
            <CATEGORY><xsl:value-of select="CATEGORY"/></CATEGORY>
            <DESCRIPTION><xsl:value-of select="DESCRIPTION"/></DESCRIPTION>
            <TIMESTAMP><xsl:value-of select="TIMESTAMP"/></TIMESTAMP>
            <SOURCE><xsl:value-of select="SOURCE"/></SOURCE>
          </ROW>
        </xsl:for-each>
      </ROWSET>
    </xsl:template>
  </xsl:stylesheet>
```

This saves a lot of typing. The only step left after using our new facility to create the skeleton insert transformation is to fill in the right XPath expressions to match the nodes in the source document that need to be inserted, or delete any elements for columns whose values you don't plan to supply in the insert.

III

Oracle XML Applications

This part of the book describes how to build applications using Oracle and XML technologies. It consists of the following chapters:

- Chapter 15, *Using XSQL Pages as a Publishing Framework*, builds on Chapter 8, *Publishing Data with XSQL Pages*, explaining the additional features that make XSQL Pages an extensible framework for assembling, transforming, and delivering XML information of any kind.
- Chapter 16, *Extending XSQL and XSLT with Java*, describes how to extend the functionality of the XSQL Pages framework using custom action handlers and how to extend the functionality of XSLT stylesheets by calling Java extension functions.
- Chapter 17, *XSLT-Powered Portals and Applications*, builds further on Chapter 11, *Generating Datagrams with Java*, and on earlier chapters, describing best practice techniques to combine XSQL pages and XSLT stylesheets to build personalized information portal and sophisticated online discussion forum applications.

In this chapter:
- *Overview of XSQL Pages Facilities*
- *Additional XML Delivery Options*

15

Using XSQL Pages as a Publishing Framework

In Chapter 8, *Publishing Data with XSQL Pages*, we explored the two cornerstone features of Oracle XSQL Pages:

- Assembling an XML data page using one or more parameterized `<xsql:query>` elements
- Transforming that data page for delivery using an associated XSLT stylesheet

However, the Oracle XSQL Pages technology provides many additional features that make it a truly extensible framework for assembling, transforming, and delivering XML information of any kind. In this chapter, we'll get acquainted with its full feature set by studying some simple examples of each feature.

Overview of XSQL Pages Facilities

We'll begin with an overview of how XSQL page processing works, and proceed to explore all of the facilities available to your XSQL pages.

Understanding XSQL Page Processing

At the heart of the XSQL Servlet and the XSQL command-line processor is the XSQL page processor, an engine that uses the Oracle XML Parser, the Oracle XML SQL Utility, and the Oracle XSLT engine to breathe life into your XSQL page template whenever the page is requested. Figure 15-1 illustrates what happens when your web server receives a request for *SomePage.xsql* that contains a reference to the stylesheet *SomeStyle.xsl*.

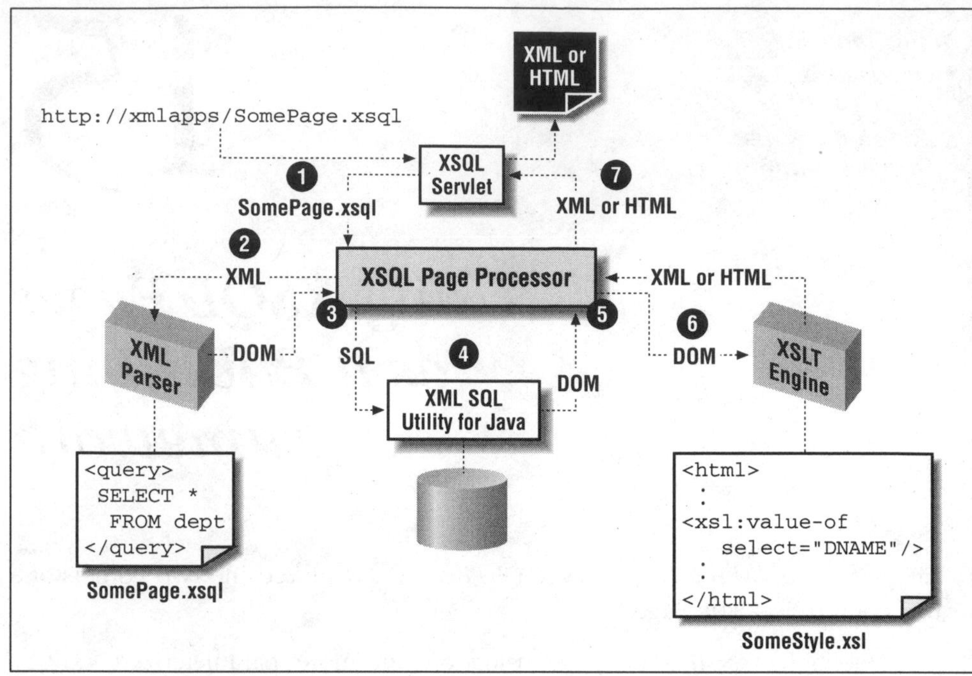

Figure 15-1. Process flow for an XSQL page with a stylesheet

The XSQL page processor:

1. Receives a request from the XSQL Servlet to process *SomePage.xsql*
2. Parses *SomePage.xsql* using the Oracle XML Parser version 2 and caches it for subsequent reuse
3. Acquires an appropriate database connection based on the value of the `connection` attribute on the document element
4. Materializes the XML data page by replacing each XSQL action element of the form `<xsql:xxxx>` with the XML results returned by its built-in action handler
5. Parses the *SomeStyle.xsl* stylesheet and caches it for subsequent reuse
6. Transforms the data page by passing it, together with the *SomeStyle.xsl* stylesheet, to the Oracle XSLT Processor
7. Returns the resulting XML or HTML document to the requester

To make each page request more efficient, the XSQL page processor implements:

- Database connection pooling, growing and shrinking the number of pooled database connections based on load
- Caching of XSQL page templates (instances of DOM `Document` objects) using a "least recently used" (LRU) algorithm to keep the most frequently accessed page templates in memory for fast access

- Caching and pooling of XSLT stylesheets (instances of `XSLStylesheet` objects) to improve throughput by allowing multiple requests to be transformed simultaneously on different threads

Of course, if an XSQL page or XSLT stylesheet changes, the cached copies are thrown away and the new source is read in automatically. All of these features can be tuned with parameters in the XSQL configuration file, which includes lengthy comments describing the use of each parameter. The following list highlights what can be configured in the *XSQLConfig.xml* configuration file:

- The named connection definitions
- The default number of records to fetch per database round trip for `<xsql:query>` actions
- The size (in number of pages) of the LRU cache for XSQL page templates
- The size (in number of stylesheets) of the LRU cache for XSLT stylesheets
- The size (in bytes) of the supplementary output stream buffer to use for the XSQL Servlet (zero to disable if your servlet engine already buffers output)
- The initial and increment size of the connection pool, as well as the timeout threshold (in seconds) for cleaning up connections
- The initial and increment size of the XSLT stylesheet pool, as well as the timeout threshold (in seconds) for cleaning up stylesheet instances
- The MIME types for which to suppress setting character set information
- Whether or not to reload named connection definitions when an unknown connection name is requested
- Whether or not to include per-page and/or per-action timing information in the XSQL page output
- Whether browser-based connection-pool status "dumping" is enabled

With this information under our belts, let's dive into the details of the supporting action elements you can use in your XSQL pages.

Overview of Built-in XSQL Page Actions

The `<xsql:query>` element is just one of many action elements supported in your XSQL page templates. Table 15-1 provides a list of all built-in action elements and a brief description of each.

Table 15-1. Overview of Built-in XSQL Action Elements

Action Element	Description
<xsql:set-stylesheet-param>	Sets the value of a top-level XSLT stylesheet parameter
<xsql:set-page-param>	Sets a page-level (local) parameter that can be referred to in subsequent actions in the page
<xsql:set-session-param>	Sets an HTTP session-level parameter, whose value persists across page requests
<xsql:set-cookie>	Sets an HTTP cookie, whose value is stored in the browser
<xsql:query>	Executes an arbitrary SQL statement and includes its result set in canonical XML format
<xsql:ref-cursor-function>	Includes the canonical XML representation of the result set of a cursor returned by a PL/SQL stored function
<xsql:include-param>	Includes a parameter and its value as an element in your XSQL page
<xsql:include-request-params>	Includes all request parameters as XML elements in your XSQL page
<xsql:include-xml>	Includes arbitrary XML resources at any point in your page by relative or absolute URL
<xsql:include-owa>	Includes the results of executing a stored procedure that makes use of the Oracle Web Agent (OWA) packages inside the database to generate XML
<xsql:include-xsql>	Includes the results of one XSQL page at any point inside another
<xsql:insert-request>	Inserts the XML document (or HTML form) posted in the request into a database table or view
<xsql:insert-param>	Inserts the XML document contained in the value of a single parameter into a table or view
<xsql:dml>	Executes a SQL DML statement or PL/SQL anonymous block
<xsql:action>	Invokes a user-defined action handler, implemented in Java, for executing custom logic and including custom XML information into your XSQL page

We'll examine each action element in more detail in the following sections. Each section presents a simple example to help you understand the common usage scenario.

Working with Parameters

We saw in Chapter 8 how the value of a URL parameter or a parameter supplied on the command line using the XSQL command-line utility can be used inside `<xsql:query>` elements and in the values of attributes on the `<xsql:query>`

element. The XSQL parameter mechanism that supports this facility also supports these features:

- Any XSQL action element or attribute can use parameters in the same way they are used with `<xsql:query>` elements.
- XSQL parameters can reference page-level parameters, HTTP session parameters, and HTTP cookie values in addition to the request-level parameters we saw earlier.

When you reference a parameter like `myParam` inside the content of an XSQL action element, as follows:

```
<xsql:query>
   select name from users where userid = {@myParam}
</xsql:query>
```

or in the attribute value of an XSQL action element, as follows:

```
<xsql:query max-rows="{@myParam}">
   :
</xsql:query>
```

the XSQL page processor determines the value of the parameter by using the following logic:

- If the XSQL Servlet is invoking the page processor to handle the request, the processor checks in the following order to determine if `myParam` is the name of:
  - An XSQL local page parameter
  - An HTTP cookie
  - An HTTP session variable
  - An HTTP request parameter
- If instead, the `XSQLCommandLine` or the `XSQLRequest` classes are driving the XSQL page processor, the processor checks in the following order to determine if `myParam` is:
  - An XSQL local page parameter
  - An XSQL request parameter provided on the command line or passed into the `XSQLRequest.process()` method.

In either case, if none of the attempts produce a matching parameter value, the XSQL page processor looks for a fallback value for `myParam` by searching the current action element and its ancestor elements (that is, the elements that contain it) in order to find an XML attribute of the same name as the parameter. If such an attribute is found, its value is used as the value of `myParam`.

Regardless of the type of parameter, the syntax used to refer to its value is the same. Let's look at each type of parameter and see how to set its value.

All parameter names and references to their values are treated case-sensitively.

Setting private page-level parameters

If you need to retrieve a value from the database and refer to that value in a subsequent action element as a parameter, you can use `<xsql:set-page-param>` to assign the value to a page-level parameter. The basic syntax is:

```
<xsql:set-page-param name="pname">
  <!-- Select statement returning one row and one column here -->
  SELECT Statement
</xsql:set-page-param>
```

The `<xsql:set-page-param>` action performs the SELECT statement and retrieves the *first* row in the result. The value of the *first* column in the SELECT list is assigned to the **pname** page-level parameter. Anywhere parameters are valid, you can refer to **{@pname}** to use the value you retrieved.

The following example illustrates retrieving a user preference from a database table, assigning it to a page-level parameter, then referencing the retrieved value in an attribute of a subsequent query:

```
<page connection="xmlbook" xmlns:xsql="urn:oracle-xsql">
  <!-- Retrieve the value of a page-level param from a query -->
  <xsql:set-page-param name="stories-to-display">
    SELECT headings
      FROM user_prefs
     WHERE userid = {@user}
  </xsql:set-page-param>
  <!-- Use the retrieved parameter value in a subsequent action element -->
  <xsql:query max-rows="{@stories-to-display}">
    SELECT title, url
      FROM latestnews
  </xsql:query>
</page>
```

It's also possible to assign the page-level parameter a value using the syntax:

```
<xsql:set-page-param name="pname" value="val"/>
```

This can be useful to set a page-level parameter to the value of another parameter, the concatenation of other parameters, or a static value. For example, if the value of the **icon** parameter is "star" and the value of the **ext** parameter is ".gif," then the action:

```
<xsql:set-page-param name="image" value="../images/{@icon}.{@ext}"/>
```

results in setting the page-level parameter named **image** to the value **../images/star.gif**. Values of page-level parameters are private to the page in which they are set, so they are not visible to other XSQL pages that might be included in the current page using the **<xsql:include-xsql>** action discussed later.

Setting HTTP session variables

When using XSQL Pages with the XSQL Servlet, you can refer to variables set in the HTTP session. These are variables whose values persist for a single user's session with your web server. If you have not otherwise created the HTTP session, then it is created the first time an **<xsql:set-session-param>** action is encountered. The HTTP session and the variables within it stay alive for a period of time specified by your servlet engine configuration.

To set the value of an HTTP session-level variable, use the syntax:

```
<xsql:set-session-param name="pname" value="val"/>
```

As with any action element attribute, the **value="*val*"** attribute can reference other parameters or be a static value. You can also assign the session-level variable a value retrieved from the database using the syntax:

```
<xsql:set-session-param name="pname">
  <!-- Select statement returning one row and one column here -->
  SELECT Statement
</xsql:set-session-param>
```

For example, the following syntax sets the value of the session-level **shopper-id** parameter to the next value from a database sequence:

```
<!-- Set the value of a session-level param to value from the database -->
<xsql:set-session-param name="shopper-id">
  SELECT shopper_id.nextval FROM DUAL
</xsql:set-session-param>
```

Usually, you want to set a session-level variable only once during the current session. You can ensure that this happens by including the additional **only-if-unset="yes"** attribute on the action element, like this:

```
<!--
 | Set the value of a session-level param to value from the database
 | Only set it if the value has never been set before in this session.
 +-->
<xsql:set-session-param name="shopper-id" only-if-unset="yes">
  SELECT shopper_id.nextval FROM DUAL
</xsql:set-session-param>
```

In addition, you may not want to set the value of the session variable at all if the value to which it is being assigned is a blank or null value. To prevent a session variable from having its value assigned to an empty string, add the **ignore-empty-value="yes"** attribute on the action element, like this:

```
<!--
 | Set the value of the session level variable to 'Yes' if a row is
 | returned from the query. If no row is returned (producing a NULL value
 | to be set) do not set the parameter value.
 +-->
<xsql:set-session-param name="existing-customer" ignore-empty-value="yes">
  SELECT 'Yes'
    FROM customer_table
   WHERE customer_id = {@custid}
</xsql:set-session-param>
```

The same technique applies to the case when the value is set using the **value="*val*"** syntax:

```
<!--
 | Remember the value of the most recently selected menu choice
 | in a session level parameter. Only set the value of "last-menu-choice"
 | to a new value if the "choice" parameter has a non-empty value.
 +-->
<xsql:set-session-param name="last-menu-choice"
                        value="{@choice}"
                        ignore-empty-value="yes"/>
```

You can combine **only-if-unset="yes"** and **ignore-empty-value="yes"** to achieve both effects if desired. As we've seen, session-level variables can be good for remembering values across page requests that are specific to a given user's current session. Note that JavaServer pages or servlets can set session variables programmatically that are visible to your XSQL pages, and your XSQL pages can set session-level variables that can be read by JSPs or servlets executed by the same browser user in the current session.

Setting HTTP cookie values

You can store parameter values across user sessions using HTTP cookies. The **<xsql:set-cookie>** action enables your XSQL pages to set the name and value of the cookie, as well as several parameters that govern its lifetime and visibility. The basic syntax is:

```
<xsql:set-cookie name="pname">
  <!-- Select statement returning one row and one column here -->
  SELECT Statement
</xsql:set-cookie>
```

or:

```
<xsql:set-cookie name="pname" value="val"/>
```

The following additional attributes can be used on an **<xsql:set-cookie>** element:

`max-age="`*`numsecs`*`"`
: Indicates that the cookie value will expire after ***numsecs*** seconds. If no number is specified, the cookie will expire when the user exits the current browser instance.

`domain="`*`servername`*`"`
: Indicates that the cookie value will be readable in the ***servername*** domain. If no server is specified, the cookie will be readable in the full domain name of the current XSQL page being requested.

`path="`*`pathname`*`"`
: Indicates that the cookie value will be readable only for URLs in the ***pathname*** path relative to the cookie's domain or in subdirectories. If no path is specified, the cookie will be readable in the URL path of the current XSQL page being requested.

The **ignore-empty-value="yes"** and **only-if-unset="yes"** attributes may also be used, and will behave the same as for session-level parameters. For example, assume that a user has submitted an HTML login form complete with username and password. You can look up this username/password combination in your registered_users table and set the value of a cookie named **siteuser** if the combination matches. The following XSQL page would handle this:

```
<page connection="xmlbook" xmlns:xsql="urn:oracle-xsql">
  <!--
   | If the username/password combo matches,
   | set a siteuser cookie that will expire in
   | 1 year (= 365 days * 24 hours * 60 min * 60 sec)
   +-->
  <xsql:set-cookie name="siteuser" max-age="31536000"
                   only-if-unset="yes" ignore-empty-value="yes">
    SELECT username
      FROM site_users
     WHERE username = '{@username}'
       AND password = '{@password}'
  </xsql:set-cookie>
  <!-- Other Actions Here -->
</page>
```

Because they are HTTP-specific, session-level parameters and cookies are useful only in XSQL pages that will be requested through the XSQL Servlet over HTTP. If you use the XSQL command-line utility or the **XSQLRequest** class to process an XSQL page containing **<xsql:set-session-param>** and/or **<xsql:set-cookie>** actions, session-level parameters and cookies will have no effect.

Setting XSLT stylesheet parameters

XSLT stylesheets can be parameterized by declaring top-level stylesheet parameters. An example of a stylesheet that declares such a parameter is shown here:

```
<xsl:stylesheet version="1.0" xmlns:xsl="http://www.w3.org/1999/XSL/Transform">
 <!-- XSLT stylesheet parameter "imageDir", overridable default value provided -->
  <xsl:param name="imageDir">/images</xsl:param>
  <!-- XSLT stylesheet parameter "Theme", overridable default value provided -->
  <xsl:param name="Theme">default.css</xsl:param>

  <xsl:template match="/">
    <!-- etc. -->
  </xsl:template>
</xsl:stylesheet>
```

Using the `<xsql:set-stylesheet-param>` action, an XSQL page can assign values to these stylesheet parameters. Following the examples above, the syntax is either:

```
<xsql:set-stylesheet-param name="pname">
  <!-- Select statement returning one row and one column here -->
  SELECT Statement
</xsql:set-stylesheet-param>
```

or:

```
<xsql:set-stylesheet-param name="pname" value="val"/>
```

For example, the following XSQL page sets the values of the `imageDir` and `Theme` stylesheet parameters:

```
<?xml version="1.0"?>
<?xml-stylesheet type="text/xsl" href="SomeSheet.xsl"?>
<page connection="xmlbook" xmlns:xsql="urn:oracle-xsql">
  <!-- Set the stylesheet parameter named imageDir -->
  <xsql:set-stylesheet-param name="imageDir" value="{@subdir}/graphics"/>
  <!-- Set the stylesheet param named Theme by retrieving a user preference -->
  <xsql:set-stylesheet-param name="Theme">
    SELECT selected_theme
      FROM user_prefs
     WHERE userid = {@currentuser}
  </xsql:set-stylesheet-param>
  <!-- Other actions here -->
</page>
```

If you find yourself using `<xsql:set-stylesheet-param>` to set *many* stylesheet parameters to the value of XSQL page parameters, you might consider using `<xsql:include-request-params>`, described later, which includes all request parameters, session variables, and cookies into your XSQL data page in a single action. Once they are part of your data page, they are accessible in the stylesheet via XPath expressions.

Supported Sources of XML Content

In addition to the static XML elements in your XSQL page and the dynamically produced XML content resulting from the `<xsql:query>` action elements, you can exploit several additional options for assembling interesting XML information into your XSQL data page before delivering it or transforming it using XSLT.

Including parameter values

To include the value of any parameter *pname* into your XSQL data page, use the `<xsql:include-param>` action. It takes a single `name` attribute indicating the name of the parameter to include:

```
<xsql:include-param name="pname"/>
```

The `<xsql:include-param>` element is replaced by an element with the same name as the parameter having the parameter value as its text content. Therefore, an action like:

```
<xsql:include-param name="sku"/>
```

produces the element:

```
<sku>1234567</sku>
```

Note that it is possible to use this in combination with `<xsql:set-page-param>` to retrieve a value from the database as a page-level parameter and then insert it into the database. For example:

```
<!-- Retrieve name of sales rep for customer whose id is passed in 'cust'
parameter -->
<xsql:set-page-param name="salesRepName">
  SELECT rep_name
    FROM customer_sales_rep
   WHERE custid = {@cust}
</xsl:set-page-param>
<!-- Insert salesRepName param into the data page -->
<xsql:include-param name="salesRepName"/>
```

produces the XML element:

```
<salesRepName>Jimmy</salesRepName>
```

However, it is more convenient to use `<xsql:query>` directly, in combination with SQL column aliasing and suppressing `rowset-element` and `row-element`:

```
<!-- Insert salesRepName for customer whose id is passed in 'cust' parameter -->
<xsql:query rowset-element="" row-element="">
  SELECT rep_name AS "salesRepName"
    FROM customer_sales_rep
   WHERE custid = {@cust}
</xsql:query>
```

which produces the equivalent single element:

```
<salesRepName>Jimmy</salesRepName>
```

This technique is preferable for including "singleton" database lookup values because it can easily be leveraged to use a single SELECT statement to retrieve multiple lookup values in a single database round-trip. For example, if you need to retrieve not only a sales representative's name, but also the rep's phone number and fax number, you can extend the previous example to look like this:

```
<!-- Insert salesRepName for customer whose id is passed in 'cust' parameter -->
<xsql:query rowset-element="" row-element="">
  SELECT rep_name  AS "salesRepName",
         rep_phone AS "phoneNumber",
         rep_fax   AS "faxNumber"
    FROM customer_sales_rep
   WHERE custid = {@cust}
</xsql:query>
```

and, with a single SQL statement, you add these three elements to the page:

```
<salesRepName>Jimmy</salesRepName>
<phoneNumber>677-899-1001</phoneNumber>
<faxNumber>677-899-1002</faxNumber>
```

If, instead, you used the combination of `<xsql:set-page-param>` and `<xsql:include-param>` you would need three queries to achieve the same effect, since each `<xsql:set-page-param>` assigns only the value of a single parameter from the first column of the SELECT statement. Therefore, `<xsql:include-param>` is most useful for including a single or a small number of request parameters in the data page.

Including all request parameters

If you want to make the entire set of all request parameters, session variables, and cookies available to the XSLT stylesheet in your XSQL page, use the `<xsql:include-request-params>` action. The action element is replaced in the page at page-request time with a subtree of XML elements that represents all of the interesting parameters available to the request. The format of the included XML document fragment when the page is requested through the XSQL Servlet looks like this:

```
<request>
  <parameters>
    <param1>value1</param1>
    <param2>value2</param2>
        :
  </parameters>
  <session>
    <name1>val1</name1>
    <name2>val2</name2>
        :
  </session>
```

```
  <cookies>
    <cookiename1>value1</cookiename1>
       :
  </cookies>
</parameters>
```

When you use the XSQL command-line utility or the `XSQLRequest` class, the `<session>` and `<cookies>` sections are not relevant, so they are not present. The included document fragment in these cases will look like this:

```
<request>
  <parameters>
    <param1>value1</param1>
    <param2>value2</param2>
      :
  </parameters>
</parameters>
```

In contrast with the `<xsql:include-param>`, this technique makes it possible to distinguish whether a parameter is a request parameter, session parameter, or cookie because its value will appear as an element in a child of `request/parameters`, `request/session`, or `request/cookies`, respectively. Using `<xsql:include-param>`, only the value of the parameter is included; and it is not possible to infer whether the value was a request, session, or cookie-based value. For example, in the following XSQL page:

```
<?xml version="1.0"?>
<?xml-stylesheet type="text/xsl" href="SomeSheet.xsl"?>
<page connection="xmlbook" xmlns:xsql="urn:oracle-xsql">
  <!-- Include all request parameters in the data page -->
  <xsql:include-request-params/>
  <!-- Other actions here -->
</page>
```

the associated *SomeSheet.xsl* stylesheet can contain conditional logic to format the page differently if the user is logged in, based on the presence of an HTTP cookie named `forumuser`. A fragment of such a stylesheet would look like this:

```
<!-- If the user is logged in, say hello. Otherwise show login link -->
<xsl:choose>
  <xsl:when test="/page/request/cookies/forumuser">
    <b>Hello, <xsl:value-of select="/page/request/cookies/forumuser"/></b>
  </xsl:when>
  <xsl:otherwise>
    <a href="Login.xsql">Login</a>
  </xsl:otherwise>
</xsl:choose>
```

Using `<xsql:include-request-params>`, the stylesheet can tell the difference between a `forumuser` cookie that it set and a `forumuser` request parameter that a clever user might pass as part of the URL.

Including encapsulated, dynamic queries

When delivering data that must be highly customized by users, or when trying to support an arbitrary query by example on many optional query parameters, even the most clever use of XSQL parameter substitution in your `<xsql:query>`'s SELECT statement is often not right for the job. In these cases, when the *structure* of the query itself must change dynamically, it is possible to handle the job quite easily by using the `<xsql:ref-cursor-function>` action instead of `<xsql:query>`.

As the name implies, `<xsql:ref-cursor-function>` allows you to invoke a database function that returns a reference to a dynamically created cursor and automatically include an XML representation of its query results in your data page. Leveraging Oracle8*i*'s native dynamic SQL feature, your database stored function can literally create any valid SELECT statement in a string, based on any number of decisions your code needs to make, and return a cursor over the query results on that query to your XSQL page. All of the optional attributes supported on the `<xsql:query>` action element with the exception of `fetch-size` are also supported on the `<xsql:ref-cursor-function>` so you have the same degree of control with total flexibility as to the nature of the query being performed.

To return a dynamic query result, your database stored function must exist in a package that declares a weakly typed REF CURSOR type in the package specification to use as the function return value, like this:

```
PACKAGE myDynamicQueryPackage IS
  TYPE myCursorType IS REF CURSOR;
  FUNCTION latestNewsForUser( userid VARCHAR2 ) RETURN myCursorType;
END;
```

In the function body, your code opens a cursor for the dynamic SQL query by using this syntax:

```
-- Open the cursor for the dynamic query
OPEN myCursorVariable
FOR myQueryInAString
USING bindargone,bindargtwo,... ;
-- Return the cursor variable to the caller
RETURN myCursorVariable;
```

As a simple yet complete example, the following package function returns a cursor variable for a query over the dept table if you pass in a number less than 1000 or for a query over the emp table if you pass in a number greater than or equal to 1000. The package specification looks like this:

```
CREATE OR REPLACE PACKAGE DeptOrEmp IS
  TYPE myCursorVariable IS REF CURSOR;
  FUNCTION getInfo(id NUMBER) RETURN myCursorVariable;
END;
```

and the package body looks like this:

```
CREATE OR REPLACE PACKAGE BODY DeptOrEmp IS
  FUNCTION getInfo(id NUMBER) RETURN myCursorVariable IS
    the_cursor myCursorVariable;
  BEGIN
    IF id < 1000 THEN
      -- Open the cursor for a dept query using the id parameter passed
      -- in as the value of the :d bind variable.
      OPEN the_cursor
       FOR 'select * from dept where deptno = :d'
     USING id;
    ELSE
      -- Open the cursor for an emp query using the id parameter passed
      -- in as the value of the :e bind variable.
      OPEN the_cursor
       FOR 'select * from emp where empno = :e'
     USING id;
    END IF;
    RETURN the_cursor;
  END;
END;
```

To test the function, we create the simple XSQL page:

```
<xsql:ref-cursor-function connection="xmlbook" xmlns:xsql="urn:oracle-xsql">
  DeptOrEmp.getInfo({@id})
</xsql:ref-cursor-function>
```

When this page is invoked with the URL:

```
http://xmlapps/enpdept.ssgl?id=7839
```

we get:

```
<ROWSET>
   <ROW num="1">
      <EMPNO>7839</EMPNO>
      <ENAME>KING</ENAME>
      <JOB>PRESIDENT</JOB>
      <HIREDATE>11/17/1981 0:0:0</HIREDATE>
      <SAL>5000</SAL>
      <DEPTNO>10</DEPTNO>
   </ROW>
</ROWSET>
```

However, if we invoke the page with the URL:

```
http://xmlapps/empdept.xsql?id=10
```

we get:

```
<ROWSET>
   <ROW num="1">
      <DEPTNO>10</DEPTNO>
      <DNAME>ACCOUNTING</DNAME>
      <LOC>NEW YORK</LOC>
   </ROW>
</ROWSET>
```

Using Several Bind Variables

If your dynamic SQL statement uses several bind variables, you need to include the correct number of bind variable values in the correct order in the USING clause of the OPEN *cursorVariable* statement. For example, if your query is the string:

```
query := 'SELECT decode(:flag,1,:sal+10,2,:sal+20) AS someval
            FROM some_table
           WHERE id = :id
             AND sal BETWEEN :sal AND :sal*10';
```

you need to provide bind values in the USING clause for all unique bind variable names—`:flag`, `:sal`, and `:id`—in the positional order in which each unique bind variable *first appears* in the query string. In this example, disregarding repeated occurrences, `:flag` appears first in the string, `:sal` appears second, and `:id` appears third, so you would open a dynamic cursor using the syntax:

```
  OPEN myCursor
   FOR query
USING myFlagVariable, mySalVariable, myIdVariable;
```

While the `DeptOrEmp.getInfo()` example is very simple, it clearly illustrates that a single function can return completely different query results based on programmatic logic depending on any number of arguments passed in by the caller—in this case, the XSQL page's `<xsql:ref-cursor-function>` action. Using functions that return ref cursors is also useful for building XSQL pages that do not reveal the queries they are doing in their page source (if, for some reason, developers were not allowed to know what tables were really being accessed to deliver the data). With this technique, only the results of the queries are known.

Including external XML resources by URL

You can use the `<xsql:include-xml>` action to include the contents of any XML-based resource that's addressable by a URL. The URL might refer to a static XML file on another server or, more interestingly, it might be the URL for a web service. The server on the other side of the request may be delivering an XML resource that is a static XML file on its filesystem, or the dynamically created XML from a programmatic resource, such as a servlet, JSP page, Perl program, ASP page, XSQL page, and so on.

To include these kinds of XML-based content in your XSQL page, get the correct URL and make sure that your XSQL configuration file has set your HTTP proxy server properly, if one is required in your environment.

For example, the XSQL page:

```
<page xmlns:xsql="urn:oracle-xsql">
  <ScriptingNewsInfo>
    <xsql:include-xml href="http://scriptingnews.userland.com/xml/rss.xml"/>
  </ScriptingNewsInfo>
  <AirportInfo>
    <xsql:include-xml
    href="http://ws5.olab.com/xsql/demo/airport/airport.xsql?airport={@tla}"/>
  </AirportInfo>
</page>
```

when requested with the URL:

```
http://server/include-xml-example.xsql?tla=XML
```

returns the XML data page shown in Example 15-1.

Example 15-1. Data Page with XML Assembled from External Sources

```
<page>
  <ScriptingNewsInfo>
    <rss version="0.91">
      <channel>
        <title>Scripting News</title>
        <link>http://scriptingnews.userland.com/</link>
        <description>Dave Winer's weblog, covering scripting...</description>
        <language>en-us</language>
        <pubDate>Fri, 07 Apr 2000 07:00:00 GMT</pubDate>
        <lastBuildDate>Fri, 07 Apr 2000 19:10:00 GMT</lastBuildDate>
        <managingEditor>dave@userland.com (Dave Winer)</managingEditor>
        <webMaster>dave@userland.com (Dave Winer)</webMaster>
        <item>
          <title>A win-win solution</title>
          <link>http://www.zdnet.com/pcweek/stories/columns/0,4,0,00.html</link>
          <description>A win-win solution: "The Internet has...</description>
        </item>
        <!-- Lots more <item>s here -->
      </channel>
    </rss>
  </ScriptingNewsInfo>
  <AirportInfo>
    <Ok>
       <Airport num="1">
        <Code>XML</Code>
        <Description>Minlaton, Sa, Australia</Description>
      </Airport>
    </Ok>
  </AirportInfo>
</page>
```

Of course, the results of the XML resource referenced by an `<xsql:include-xml>` element must be well-formed XML; otherwise, an `<xsql-error>` element will be added to your XSQL page instead of the XML you were expecting.

Including dynamic XML from PL/SQL

In Chapter 10, *Generating Datagrams with PL/SQL*, we learned the basic techniques PL/SQL developers can use to serve XML using the Oracle Web Agent (OWA) packages. The generated XML is printed to a PL/SQL page buffer using the routines in the **HTP** package, and the result is pulled from that buffer and delivered to the requester over the Web by any of the following:

- Oracle Internet Application Server 1.0 with **modplsql**
- Oracle Web Application Server 3.0/4.0
- Oracle Web Server 2.1
- WebDB Lightweight Listener

If this style of XML creation is familiar and effective for you, you can use the **<xsql:include-owa>** action in your XSQL page to exploit your OWA-generated XML. The basic syntax is:

```
<!-- Invoke a single stored procedure or packaged procedure -->
<xsql:include-owa>
  StoredProcedureName(args);
</xsql:include-owa>
```

One clever use of **<xsql:include-owa>** is to invoke a PL/SQL stored procedure that validates the arguments passed to it and returns a structured fragment of XML indicating any validation failures that have occurred. If no errors occur, the procedure can perform a DML operation like an insert, update, or delete. As a simple example, consider the following PL/SQL procedure:

```
CREATE PROCEDURE UpdatePrice( sku_to_change VARCHAR2, new_price VARCHAR2 ) IS
  pricenum  NUMBER;
  errors    BOOLEAN := false; -- Assume no errors to begin with
  PROCEDURE show_xml_err(field VARCHAR2, msg VARCHAR2) IS
  BEGIN
    HTP.P('<Error Field="'||field||'">'||msg||'</Error>');
    errors := TRUE;
  END;
BEGIN
  HTP.P('<UpdatePrice>');
  -- Check whether sku_to_change begins with letter 'K'
  IF sku_to_change IS NULL OR SUBSTR(sku_to_change,1,1)<>'K' THEN
    show_xml_err('sku','SKU must be non-null and begin with a K');
  END IF;
  -- Check whether new_price is a positive number
  BEGIN
    IF new_price IS NULL THEN RAISE VALUE_ERROR; END IF;
    pricenum := TO_NUMBER(new_price);
  EXCEPTION
    WHEN VALUE_ERROR THEN
      show_xml_err('price','Price must be a non-null, positive number');
  END;
```

```
    IF NOT errors THEN
      UPDATE product SET price = pricenum WHERE sku = sku_to_change;
      HTP.P('<Success/>');
    END IF;
    HTP.P('</UpdatePrice>');
  END;
```

It generates an **<UpdatePrice>** "statusgram" that contains either a list of one or more **<Error>** elements or the single element **<Success/>** if no validation errors occur. We can call the **UpdatePrice** procedure from an XSQL page like this:

```
<xsql:include-owa connection="xmlbook" xmlns:xsql="urn:oracle-xsql">
   UpdatePrice('{@sku}','{@price}');
</xsql:include-owa>
```

Then, if an HTML form posts (or URL includes) parameters to this XSQL page with values like **sku=J123**, which does not start with a letter **K**, and **price=$10**, which inadvertently includes a dollar sign, the resulting data page will reflect the multiple XML errors in its statusgram:

```
<UpdatePrice>
  <Error Field="sku">SKU must be non-null and begin with a K</Error>
  <Error Field="price">Price must be a non-null, positive number</Error>
</UpdatePrice>
```

An associated XSLT stylesheet could use this error information to render an HTML form that displays the errors in context. A similar validation approach could be performed using Java code in a custom action handler; we'll learn more about this in Chapter 16, *Extending XSQL and XSLT with Java*.

Modularizing reusable XML information content

The ace up our sleeve in this category of **include** elements is the **<xsql:include-xsql>** action. It allows you to assemble one XSQL page by including the results of other XSQL pages. While you'll find this action has 1001 uses, a few of the most common are:

- Factoring a query that occurs in multiple pages into a reusable XSQL page that can be shared by all of them
- Including data from multiple database connections in the same page
- Transforming information using a chain of multiple XSLT stylesheets
- Layering a desired XSLT transformation on top of an existing XSQL data page without modifying the original document

Let's look at some examples. Say you have a *BrowseProduct.xsql* page like the following that retrieves product information for the current product being browsed, along with a list of active promotions going on this hour like this:

```
<?xml version="1.0"?>
<?xml-stylesheet type="text/xsl" href="BrowseProduct.xsl"?>
<page connection="xmlbook" xmlns:xsql="urn:oracle-xsql">
  <xsql:query>
    <!-- Retrieve product information -->
    SELECT sku, price, description,
           decode(qty,0,'Backordered','In Stock') as status
      FROM product
     WHERE sku = '{@id}'
  </xsql:query>
  <xsql:query>
    <!-- Retrieve any active promotions going on this hour -->
    SELECT promocode, blurb, discount
      FROM active_promotions
     WHERE effective_date BETWEEN SYSDATE AND SYSDATE+(1/24)
  </xsql:query>
</page>
```

If you use the "product info" query and the "promotions this hour" query in several different pages, you can create *ProductInfo.xsql* and *PromosThisHour.xsql* to factor these queries into their respective files, as follows:

```
<!-- ProductInfo.xsql -->
<xsql:query connection="xmlbook" xmlns:xsql="urn:oracle-xsql">
  <!-- Retrieve product information -->
  SELECT sku, price, description,
         decode(qty,0,'Backordered','In Stock') as status
    FROM product
   WHERE sku = '{@id}'
</xsql:query>
```

and:

```
<!-- PromosThisHour.xsql -->
<xsql:query connection="xmlbook" xmlns:xsql="urn:oracle-xsql">
  <!-- Retrieve any active promotions going on this hour -->
  SELECT promocode, blub, discount
    FROM active_promotions
   WHERE effective_date BETWEEN SYSDATE AND SYSDATE+(1/24)
</xsql:query>
```

Then you can reuse these files in your original *BrowseProduct.xsql* and any others that need common queries, like this:

```
<?xml version="1.0"?>
<?xml-stylesheet type="text/xsl" href="BrowseProduct.xsl"?>
<page connection="xmlbook" xmlns:xsql="urn:oracle-xsql">
  <xsql:include-xsql href="ProductInfo.xsql"/>
  <xsql:include-xsql href="PromosThisHour.xsql"/>
</page>
```

Notice that when the `<xsql:query>` elements in the original *BrowseProduct.xsql* page are moved to their own files, each becomes an XSQL page in its own right and requires a `connection="`*`connname`*`"` attribute on its document element, as well as an `xmlns:xsql="urn:oracle-xsql"` namespace declaration.

When the XSQL page processor is processing the new, modularized *BrowseProduct.xsql*, it encounters the `<xsql:include-xsql>` elements and recursively processes these nested page requests. All of the request, session, and cookie parameters that are visible to the enclosing *BrowseProduct.xsql* page are also visible to these nested pages. To pass additional parameters or to forcibly override the value of a request parameter for just the nested request, you can tack on parameters to the XSQL page name like this:

```
<xsql:include-xsql href="ProductInfo.xsql?p1=v1&p2=v2"/>
```

The `href` attribute can be any URL; however, relative URLs are the most efficient because the XSQL page processor can cache the XSQL page templates. With a relative URL, you can refer to nested XSQL pages in other directories relative to the one the current XSQL page resides in, like this:

```
<xsql:include-xsql href="../common/ProductInfo.xsql"/>
```

The XSQL page processor is designed to handle these nested page requests efficiently, so using `<xsql:include-xsql>` does not incur additional HTTP requests or additional database connections if the nested pages use the same named connection as the enclosing page.

> If a page like the reworked *BrowseProduct.xsql* page uses `<xsql:include-xsql>` actions and does not include any actions that require a database connection, like `<xsql:query>`, `<xsql:ref-cursor-function>`, or `<xsql:include-owa>`, then technically speaking it does not need a `connection="`*`connname`*`"` attribute on its document element. However, sometimes there is a good reason for leaving the attribute there.
>
> If two or more nested XSQL pages use the same connection, it is more efficient to declare the `connection` on the enclosing page as well. This way, the nested pages will notice that the page including them already has the required database connection, so it will not bother to acquire a new connection from the pool.

Since each of our XSQL pages has its own `connection` attribute, it would be very easy to retrieve the information for the *ProductInfo.xsql* attribute from `connection="inventory"`; the information for the *PromosThisHour.xsql* attribute `connection="marketing"` is obtained by using the right connection name where needed in the nested pages.

If the page included using `<xsql:include-xsql>` is selecting XML-based information that is stored in the database as literal text, you can use the optional `reparse="yes"` attribute to force the text to be parsed and included as *elements* in your including page, instead of just as text.

For example, imagine that you have some B2B XML messages in a queue or in a simple table where you store the XML messages in a CLOB column. You can build an XSQL page to select the text of the XML messages from the table by message ID, like this:

```
<?xml version="1.0"?>
<?xml-stylesheet type="text/xsl" href="Message.xsl"?>
<xsql:query connection="xmlbook" xmlns:xsql="urn:oracle-xsql"
            rowset-element="" row-element="">
  SELECT message as "Message"
    FROM xml_business_messages
   WHERE id = {@id}
</xsql:query>
```

The *Message.xsql* page uses the following *Message.xsl* stylesheet to output the XML text selected from the CLOB column verbatim, without quoting the angle brackets contained in the text as `<` and `>` as would be the default:

```
<!--
 | Message.xsl: includes text of <Message> element *verbatim*
 |              using disable-output-escaping="yes" to avoid turning
 |              angle-brackets in XML text into &lt; and &gt;
 + -->
<Message xsl:version="1.0" xmlns:xsl="http://www.w3.org/1999/XSL/Transform">
  <xsl:value-of disable-output-escaping="yes" select="/Message"/>
</Message>
```

The result is that requesting the message with ID 101 using the URL:

```
http://server/Message.xsql?id=101
```

will produce the document:

```
<Message>
  <Order tracking="123456">
    <Client>99023</Client>
    <Item Qty="4" Sku="1232123">Ticonderoga Yellow Pencil</Item>
  </Order>
</Message>
```

Without the `disable_output_escaping` attribute, the document would have all angle brackets quoted, like this:

```
<Message>
  &lt;Order tracking="123456"&gt;
    &lt;Client&gt;99023&lt;/Client&gt;
    &lt;Item Qty="4" Sku="1232123"&gt;Ticonderoga Yellow Pencil&lt;/Item&gt;
  &lt;/Order&gt;
</Message>
```

You can then include the XML element content of any business message by ID into another XSQL page using **<xsql:include-xsql>** with the **reparse="yes"** attribute. For example, the following page:

```
<page connection="xmlbook" xmlns:xsql="urn:oracle-xsql">
  <xsql:include-xsql reparse="yes" href="Message.xsql?id={@msgid}"/>
  <xsql:query>
    SELECT name
      FROM customer
     where id = {@custid}
  </xsql:query>
</page>
```

can be requested with a URL like:

```
http://server/CustomerMessageProfile.xsql?custid=99023&msgid=101
```

This produces an assembled XSQL data page of:

```
<page&gt;
  <Message>
    <Order tracking="123456">
      <Client>99023</Client>
      <Item Qty="4" Sku="1232123">Ticonderoga Yellow Pencil</Item>
    </Order>
  </Message>
  <ROWSET>
    <ROW>
      <NAME>Neiman Marcus</NAME>
    </ROW>
  </ROWSET>
</page>
```

We saw earlier that if a page included using **<xsql:include-xsql>** has an associated XSLT stylesheet (like *Message.xsql*, which was associated to *Message.xsl*), that stylesheet's transformation is performed before including the resulting XML into the page. If the page that makes use of **<xsql:include-xsql>** has its own XSLT stylesheet, it is processed in the normal fashion to transform the assembled data page before returning it. Figure 15-2 illustrates using this technique to chain stylesheets together or to create pages that style the same underlying XML information in multiple, different ways. The basic steps are as follows:

1. *Emp.xsql* produces the basic XML information for the employee data.
2. *EmpList.xsql* includes *Emp.xsql* and styles it with *EmpTable.xsl* into HTML,
3. *PeopleGroup.xsql* includes *Emp.xsql* and transforms it with *PeopleGroup.xsl* into a hypothetical industry-standard XML format.
4. *PeopleChecklist.xsql* uses a *PeopleChecklist.xsl* provided by the industry-standard group to transform the XML results from *PeopleGroup.xsql* into a standard HTML presentation.

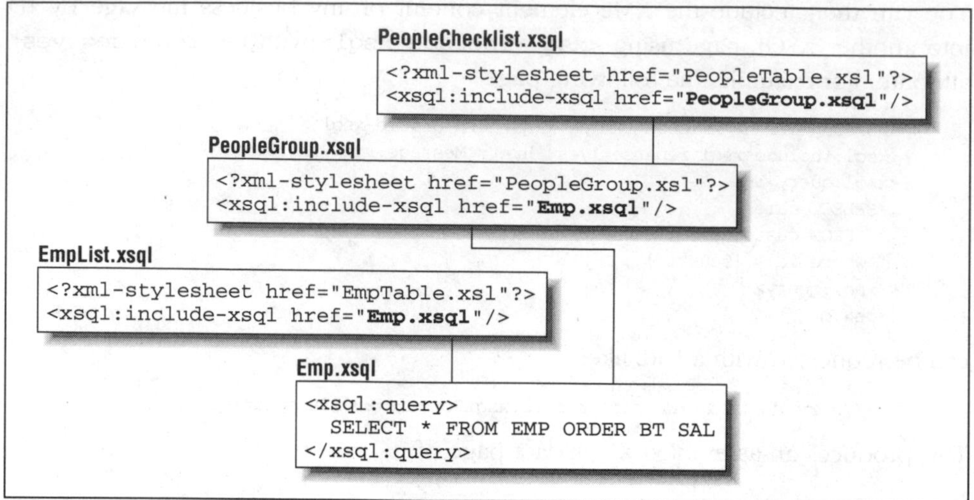

Figure 15-2. Rendering data multiple ways and chaining stylesheets

This shows that, in general, if you already have a *SomePage.xsql* XSQL page, you can apply transformations to it without changing the original page itself to introduce `<?xml-stylesheet?>` instructions. You simply build one or more new XSQL pages that look like this:

```
<?xml version="1.0"?>
<!--
 | Apply SomeNewTransformation.xsl to an existing SomePage.xsql
 | without changing the original page in any way.
 +-->
<?xml-stylesheet type="text/xsl" href="SomeNewTransformation.xsl"?>
<xsql:include-xsql href="SomePage.xsql" xmlns:xsql="urn:oracle-xsql"/>
```

Now that you've seen these examples, I hope it's becoming more clear why users are enthusiastic about the flexibility enabled by `<xsql:include-xsql>`.

Modifying the Database Using Submitted Data

So far, we've seen pages containing actions that set parameters and actions that include XML content. In this section, we briefly describe the actions that allow you to modify database information based on information submitted in the request.

Doing DML or executing PL/SQL

Any time your pages need to update tables, insert information into a table, or invoke stored procedures to accomplish any needed functionality, the `<xsql:dml>` action is your friend. The basic syntax is:

```
<xsql:dml>
  DML Statement
</xsql:dml>
```

or:

```
<xsql:dml>
  BEGIN
    Any valid PL/SQL Statement
  END;
</xsql:dml>
```

For example, to insert the current username stored in a **siteuser** cookie into a page_request_log table, you can do this:

```
<xsql:dml>
  BEGIN
    INSERT INTO page_request_log(page,userid)
      VALUES( 'thispage.xsql', '{@siteuser}');
    COMMIT;
  END;
</xsql:dml>
```

Some users may prefer to always invoke stored procedures instead of including raw DML operations in a page, but both are supported. If the operation is successful, an **<xsql-status>** element is added to your page to replace the **<xsql:dml>** action; it reports the number of rows affected as reported by JDBC:

```
<xsql-status action="xsql:dml" rows="n"/>
```

If the statement returns an error, an **<xsql-error>** element is added to the page to report the problem:

```
<xsql-error action="xsql:dml">
  <statement>update emp set sal = sal * 10</statement>
  <message>ORA-01031: insufficient privileges</message>
</xsql-error>
```

Similar to the **<xsql:query>** example we saw in Chapter 8, the **<xsql:dml>** action can use parameters to represent any part of the DML or PLSQL statement that it will attempt to execute, including the extreme case of using a parameter for the entire statement, like this:

```
<page connection="xmldemo" xmlns:xsql="urn:oracle-xsql">
<xsql:dml>{@statement}</xsql:dml>
</page>
```

While this at first looks very appealing because of its flexibility, be aware that it also allows any user who can request the page to send any DML command to the database named in the connection. For example, the following would dutifully drop your orders table:

```
http://server/dmlpage.xsql?statement=drop%20table%20orders
```

To wield such power responsibly, you can either restrict the database privileges granted to the account named in the xmldemo connection, or use the facilities provided by your web server to password-protect the directory where this page resides.

Handling posted HTML forms and XML documents

You can use the `<xsql:insert-request>` action to insert the data content of posted HTML forms or XML documents into a table or view. If a posted XML document is supplied in a single parameter, the companion `<xsql:insert-param>` action does the job. The basic syntax is:

```
<xsql:insert-request table="table-or-viewname"/>
<xsql:insert-param   table="table-or-viewname"/>
```

You might immediately wonder:

- How does the action know what data I want to insert?
- How does the action know what columns to insert the data into?

The answer is simple: the `insert` action doesn't know the answer to either of these questions on its own. You have to assist in the process by supplying an XSLT stylesheet in the optional `transform="stylesheetname"` attribute that transforms the structure of the posted information into the canonical `<ROWSET>`/`<ROW>` structure for the target table or view. The more typical syntax for this action is:

```
<xsql:insert-request table="table-or-viewname" transform="stylesheetname"/>
<xsql:insert-param   table="table-or-viewname" transform="stylesheetname"/>
```

An additional `date-format="datemask"` attribute is supported to inform the XML SQL utility used under the covers what format to expect for date values. We saw extensive examples of using `<xsql:insert-request>` in Chapter 12, *Storing XML Datagrams.*

Accessing XSQL Pages from JSP

So far we've seen two ways to access XSQL pages, tapping into the services of the XSQL page processor to return the transformed results: the XSQL Servlet and the XSQL command-line utility. In addition to these two mechanisms, it is also possible to access XSQL pages programmatically or from JavaServer Pages (JSPs). A JavaServer page can forward a request to an XSQL page by using the JSP tag called `<jsp:forward>`. The syntax is:

```
<jsp:forward page="relativeURLToXSQLPage"/>
```

This effectively means that the JSP page transfers responsibility to the XSQL page to continue handling the request and return a response. Before doing the `<jsp:forward>`, the JSP page can perform any number of tasks required by using Java scriptlets in the page or by invoking bean methods on a JavaBean.

If you just want to include the results of an XSQL page into a JSP at a strategic point, you can instead use the `<jsp:include>` tag in your JSP. The syntax is:

```
<jsp:include flush="true" page="relativeURLToXSQLPage"/>
```

Note that the `flush` parameter is required by JSP.

Requesting XSQL Pages Programmatically

The `oracle.xml.xsql.XSQLRequest` class allows you to use the XSQL page processor from within your own Java programs. Example 15-2 shows a simple example of using this class.

Example 15-2. Programmatically Requesting an XSQL Page

```
import oracle.xml.xsql.XSQLRequest;
import java.util.Hashtable;
import java.io.PrintWriter;
import java.net.URL;

public class XSQLRequestSample {
  public static void main( String[] args) throws Exception {
    // Construct the URL of the XSQL Page
    URL pageUrl = new URL("file:///C:/foo/bar.xsql");
    // Construct a new XSQL Page request
    XSQLRequest req = new XSQLRequest(pageUrl);
    // Setup a Hashtable of named parameters to pass to the request
    Hashtable params = new Hashtable(3);
    params.put("param1","value1");
    params.put("param2","value2");
    /* If needed, treat an existing, in-memory XMLDocument as if
    ** it were posted to the XSQL Page as part of the request:
    **
    ** req.setPostedDocument(myXMLDocument);
    */
    // Process the page, passing the parameters and writing the output
    // to std out.
    req.process(params,new PrintWriter(System.out)
                      ,new PrintWriter(System.err));
  }
}
```

You can also call `processToXML()` instead of `process()` to return the in-memory XML document that results from processing the XSQL page requested and applying any associated XSLT transformation.

Additional XML Delivery Options

This section describes additional options available to you for delivery of XML in a variety of special cases.

Optimizing Presentation for Requesting Device

It is often desirable to serve the same data differently depending on what kind of program makes the request. For example, you may want to customize the XSLT-based presentation of an XSQL page to specifically optimize for the different capability sets of the Netscape, Internet Explorer, and Lynx browsers. There are many reasons why you might want to differentiate in this way; here are a few of the most common:

- Optimizing an interactive web page for Netscape 4's layer-based dynamic HTML requires coding techniques that are different from those used in optimizing for Internet Explorer's fully dynamic Document Object Model (DOM) in DHTML.
- Internet Explorer 5.0 supports client-side XSLT, allowing the browser to handle the presentation of XML-based information instead of the server,
- Lynx, because it's a character-mode browser, supports only a subset of HTML that it can faithfully display on character terminals.

Luckily, the XSQL page processor makes targeted transformations like this very easy. You can add any number of `<?xml-stylesheet?>` processing instructions to the top of your XSQL page, each of which may specify an optional `media` attribute, as in the following example:

```
<!-- Use "SiteMenu-ie5.xsl" for an IE5 browser -->
<?xml-stylesheet type="text/xsl" media="msie 5.0" href="SiteMenu-ie5.xsl"?>
<!-- Use "SiteMenu-ie.xsl" for an IE browser other than 5.0 -->
<?xml-stylesheet type="text/xsl" media="msie" href="SiteMenu-ie.xsl"?>
<!-- Use "SiteMenu-ns.xsl" for a Netscape browser -->
<?xml-stylesheet type="text/xsl" media="mozilla" href="SiteMenu-ns.xsl"?>
<!-- Use "SiteMenu-lynx.xsl" for a Lynx browser -->
<?xml-stylesheet type="text/xsl" media="lynx" href="SiteMenu-lynx.xsl"?>
<!-- Use "SiteMenu.xsl" as a fallback for any other kind of browser -->
<?xml-stylesheet type="text/xsl" href="SiteMenu.xsl"?>
<website>
   :
</website>
```

By convention, programs requesting resources through HTTP include a user-agent string in their request header to identify themselves. For example:

- Netscape 4.6 on NT sends `Mozilla/4.6 [en] (WinNT; I)`.
- IE 5.0 on NT sends `Mozilla/4.0 (compatible; MSIE 5.0; Windows NT)`.
- Lynx 2.8 on Solaris sends `Lynx/2.8.2rel.1 libwww-FM/2.14`.

The XSQL page processor considers the `<?xml-stylesheet?>` instructions in order and uses the first one whose `media` attribute value matches part of the requesting program's user-agent string. The string match is done case-insensitively so a `media="mozilla"` attribute would match a user-agent value containing "Mozilla" somewhere in the string.

Internet Explorer sends Mozilla/4.0 as part of its user-agent string, so you should include an <?xml-stylesheet?> with a media="msie" to check for an Internet Explorer browser request earlier in the list than one that uses media="mozilla" to test for a Netscape browser.

An <?xml-stylesheet?> that does not include a **media** attribute matches *any* requesting user-agent, so you can include one of these as a fallback to use in case none of the values from the other processing instructions' **media** attribute matches. If none of the <?xml-stylesheet?> processing instructions present are selected, the XSQL page processor behaves as if none were specified in the file.

If your browser supports client-side XSLT transformation, you may wish to deliver the XSQL data page to the client as a pure XML document containing a reference to the stylesheet. You can request this behavior by including the **client="yes"** attribute in the <?xml-stylesheet?> processing instruction whose **media** attribute matches the appropriate browser.

Example 15-3 combines these various <?xml-stylesheet?> options to transform the XSQL data page:

- In the client using *SiteMenu-ie5.xsl* for Internet Explorer 5.0 browsers
- In the server using *SiteMenu-lynx.xsl* for Lynx browsers
- In the server using *SiteMenu.xsl* for all others

Example 15-3. Serving a Format Appropriate to the Requesting Browser

```
<?xml version="1.0"?>
<?xml-stylesheet type="text/xsl" media="msie 5.0" client="yes"
  href="SiteMenu-ie5.xsl"?>
<?xml-stylesheet type="text/xsl" media="lynx" href="SiteMenu-lynx.xsl"?>
<?xml-stylesheet type="text/xsl" href="SiteMenu.xsl"?>
<website connection="xmlbook">
    <xsql:query rowset-element="categories" row-element="category"
                tag-case="lower" xmlns:xsql="urn:oracle-xsql">

      SELECT name, icon, url
        FROM site_category
       ORDER BY pos

    </xsql:query>
</website>
```

For example, requesting the *SiteMenu.xsql* page in Example 15-3 page from an IE5 browser will return the results shown in Figure 15-3.

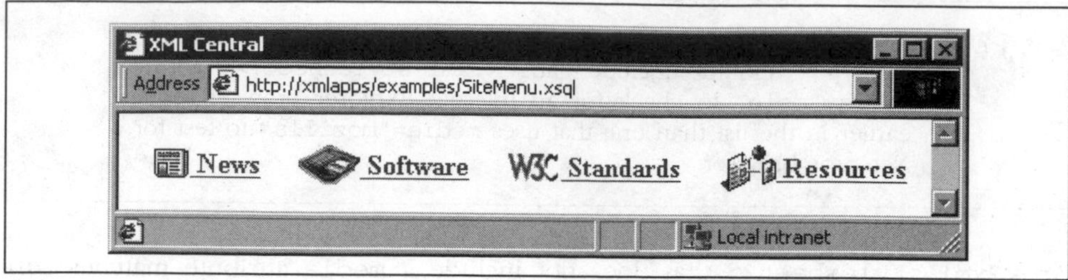

Figure 15-3. HTML results for a site menu bar transformed in the client

This looks the same as the result produced earlier when requested from a Netscape browser in Chapter 8 (in Figure 8-3); however, there is a big difference under the covers. If we select *View Source...* we'll see what's shown in Example 15-4.

Example 15-4. Viewing the XML Source Served Directly to IE5

```
<?xml version = '1.0'?>
<?xml-stylesheet type="text/xsl" media="msie 5.0" client="yes"
  href="SiteMenu-ie5.xsl"?>
<website>
   <categories>
      <category num="1">
         <name>News</name>
         <icon>newspaper.gif</icon>
      </category>
      <category num="2">
         <name>Software</name>
         <icon>software.gif</icon>
      </category>
      <category num="3">
         <name>Standards</name>
         <icon>standards.gif</icon>
      </category>
      <category num="4">
         <name>Resources</name>
         <icon>resources.gif</icon>
      </category>
   </categories>
</website>
```

This confirms that the page is an XML document with an embedded `<?xml-stylesheet?>` processing instruction, rather than the HTML results of a server-side transformation that were returned to a Netscape browser. The browser will retrieve the indicated *SiteMenu-ie5.xsl* stylesheet, and use it to transform the XML page into HTML for display.

Using client-side transformation, you need to make sure to use an XSLT stylesheet that the client's XSLT engine supports. Internet Explorer 5.0 supports the December 12, 1998 Working Draft of XSLT (see *http://www.w3.org/TR/1998/WD-xsl-19981216*), which used a slightly different syntax from the final XSLT Specification (see *http://www.w3.org/TR/xslt*). This doesn't present a problem since we can select a stylesheet with the appropriate IE5-XSL syntax for IE5 browsers when client-side transformation is requested.

At the time of this writing, Microsoft has made available several interim "technology previews" of their updated XSLT Processor, which supports the XSLT 1.0 Recommendation syntax and features, on their MSDN site at *http://msdn.microsoft.com/xml*. Once this technology reaches production quality and is included in a future version of Internet Explorer, the same XSLT syntax and stylesheets will work both server-side and client-side. Hooray! In addition, a client-side XSLT engine will likely be included in a future Netscape browser as well. This will offer developers choices to offload UI styling to the client when appropriate. Using the mechanism described in this section, developers using XSQL Pages can decide based on the user-agent string which browsers should receive results transformed on the server, and which, if any, should perform the final transformation into HTML inside the browser itself.

You may recognize the *SiteMenu-ie5.xsl* stylesheet shown in the next example as a slight modification of the *SiteMenu.xsl* stylesheet from Chapter 8. The key differences between this IE5-specific example and the earlier standard XSLT version are the following:

- The stylesheet has to include the `<xsl:stylesheet>` element, because IE5-XSL does not recognize simple-form stylesheets.
- The URI string defining the `xsl` namespace is different.
- The "shortcut" attribute value template syntax like `src="{icon}"` is replaced by an explicit `<xsl:attribute name="src">` element using an `<xsl:value-of>` to supply the attribute's value from the `<icon>` element in the data page. Attribute value templates were introduced in the XSLT specification after IE5 shipped to customers.

The *SiteMenu-ie5.xsl* stylesheet appears in Example 15-5.

Example 15-5. IE5-Specific XSL Stylesheet for a Site Navigation Bar

```
<xsl:stylesheet xmlns:xsl="http://www.w3.org/TR/WD-xsl">
<xsl:template match="/">
<html><head><title>XML Central</title></head>
 <body>
  <center>
   <table border="0" cellpadding="10">
    <tr>
     <xsl:for-each select="website/categories/category">
      <td>
       <img border="0" align="absmiddle">
        <xsl:attribute name="src"><xsl:value-of select="icon"/></xsl:attribute>
       </img>
       <a>
        <xsl:attribute name="href"><xsl:value-of select="url"/></xsl:attribute>
        <b><xsl:value-of select="name"/></b>
       </a>
      </td>
     </xsl:for-each>
    </tr>
   </table>
  </center>
 </body>
</html>
</xsl:template>
</xsl:stylesheet>
```

If a Lynx browser requests the same URL for the *SiteMenu.xsql* page, then the following *SiteMenu-lynx.xsl* stylesheet will be used for the server-side transformation:

```
<html xsl:version="1.0" xmlns:xsl="http://www.w3.org/1999/XSL/Transform">
<head><title>XML Central</title></head>
 <body>
     <hr/>
     <xsl:for-each select="website/categories/category">
       <a href="{url}"><xsl:value-of select="name"/></a>
     </xsl:for-each>
     <hr/>
 </body>
</html>
```

This Lynx-specific stylesheet avoids the use of HTML tables and images, simply listing the web site category hyperlinks between two horizontal rules. The user of the Lynx browser sees the appropriately simplified view of the site shown in Figure 15-4.

Finally, if you build XSQL pages with user-agent-dependent stylesheets, you can test their output both through the various targeted browsers and through the XSQL command-line utility. To simulate a particular user-agent from the command line, pass an appropriate value for the command-line parameter named `useragent` whose value will be treated by the XSQL page processor as if it were the HTTP request's user-agent string for the purpose of stylesheet selection.

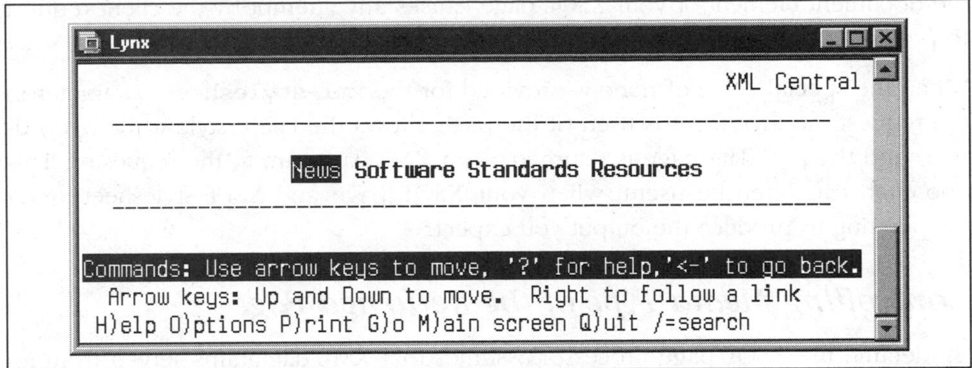

Figure 15-4. Lynx browser showing appropriately simplified HTML page

Supplying a Stylesheet in the Request

In addition to the stylesheets referenced in the `<?xml-stylesheet?>` instructions at the top of your page, a request can directly supply the name of the stylesheet using the optional `xml-stylesheet` parameter. Requesting a URL like:

```
http://xmlapps/SomePage.xsql?xml-stylesheet=SomeOtherStyle.xsl
```

asks the XSQL Servlet to deliver the results of *SomePage.xsql* transformed by the XSLT stylesheet named *SomeOtherStyle.xsl*. This request conceptually adds an equivalent processing instruction to the top of the document, *before* any other `<?xml-stylesheet?>` instructions (if any are present):

```
<?xml-stylesheet type="text/xsl" href="SomeOtherStyle.xsl"?>
```

This parameter causes the stylesheet supplied in the request to override the one that would have been selected for transformation. If the page had no stylesheet specified, the stylesheet parameter causes the page to be transformed using the requested stylesheet rather than returning the XSQL data page as an XML datagram.

The value of the `xml-stylesheet` parameter is treated exactly the same as the value of the `href` parameter in an `<?xml-stylesheet?>` instruction in the page, so it will be interpreted relative to the location of the requested page. In the previous example, the *SomeOtherStyle.xsl* stylesheet would need to exist in the same directory as the *SomePage.xsql* page.

By default, if the request supplies an `xml-stylesheet` parameter, the transformation using the supplied stylesheet is performed on the server. The request may include an additional `transform` parameter which, if set to the value `client`, will cause the transformation to be performed on the client instead.

Since it is not always desirable to allow a client request to override your choice of stylesheets, the XSQL page processor provides a mechanism to disallow this facility on a page-by-page basis. Adding an attribute `allow-client-style="no"` on the document element of your XSQL page causes any attempt by the client request to provide a value for the **xml-stylesheet** parameter to be ignored.

When the special value of **none** is provided for the **xml-stylesheet** parameter in the request, no stylesheet is used (if the page allows the client style to be overridden) and the raw data page is returned as an XML datagram to the requester. This approach can often be useful when your XSQL page and XSLT stylesheet aren't cooperating to produce the output you expect.

Controlling Media Type of the Returned Page

By default, the XSQL page processor assumes that XML datagrams served from an XSQL page containing no **<?xml-stylesheet?>** instructions have **text/xml** as the media type. On the other hand, if your page does include an **<?xml-stylesheet?>** instruction to associate an XSLT stylesheet, the XSQL page processor determines the media type of the result by consulting the XSLT processor. The XSLT processor returns a media type of **text/html** for a transformed document whose document element is **<html>**; otherwise, it returns a media type of **text/xml**.

In order to explicitly control the media type of your XSQL page's output, you exploit the **<xsl:output>** element at the top level of the stylesheet associated with your page. For example, to return a media type of **image/svg**, you would add the following to your stylesheet:

```
<xsl:stylesheet version="1.0" xmlns:xsl="http://www.w3.org/1999/XSL/Transform">
  <!-- xsl:output goes here, at the top-level of the stylesheet -->
  <xsl:output media-type="image/svg"/>

  <xsl:template match="/">
  <!-- etc. -->
```

For a lengthier example, let's consider building XSQL pages to return information to a wireless device that supports the Wireless Markup Language (WML). Your returned documents need a media type of **text/vnd.wap.wml**. WML documents represent a "deck" of display "cards" that a supporting wireless device can receive, present to the user, and enable the user to navigate. To return a valid WML deck, you'll need:

```
<xsl:output media-type="text/vnd.wap.wml"/>
```

at the top of your *SiteMenu-wml.xsl* stylesheet. For a valid WML document, you also need a **doctype-system** and **doctype-public** attribute, so a working example looks like this:

```
<?xml version="1.0"?>
<xsl:stylesheet xmlns:xsl="http://www.w3.org/1999/XSL/Transform" version="1.0">
<xsl:output doctype-public="-//WAPFORUM//DTD WML 1.1//EN"
```

```
            doctype-system="http://www.wapforum.org/DTD/wml_1.1.xml"
                media-type="text/vnd.wap.wml"
                    indent="yes"/>
  <xsl:template match="/">
    <wml xsl:version="1.0" xmlns:xsl="http://www.w3.org/1999/XSL/Transform">
     <card id="top">
       <p>
         <xsl:text>Please choose a news category:</xsl:text>
         <select name="pickcategory">
          <xsl:for-each select="website/categories/category">
            <option value="{name}"><xsl:value-of select="name"/></option>
          </xsl:for-each>
         </select>
       </p>
     </card>
    </wml>
  </xsl:template></xsl:stylesheet>
```

If you associate this with our *SiteMenu.xsql* page, and request the *SiteMenu.xsql* page from your WML-enabled browser, your device will receive the page:

```
<?xml version = '1.0' encoding = 'UTF-8'?>
<!DOCTYPE wml PUBLIC "-//WAPFORUM//DTD WML 1.1//EN"
                     "http://www.wapforum.org/DTD/wml_1.1.xml">
<wml>
   <card id="top">
      <p>Please choose a news category:
        <select name="pickcategory">
            <option value="News">News</option>
            <option value="Software">Software</option>
            <option value="Standards">Standards</option>
            <option value="Resources">Resources</option>
        </select>
      </p>
   </card>
</wml>
```

The returned XML document will have a media type of `text/vnd.wap.wml`, enabling it to be directly "consumed" by a WML-enabled handheld device—for example, a late-model cell phone or a PDA.

Detecting and Formatting Errors

Errors raised during the processing of any XSQL action elements are reported as specific XML elements so that XSL stylesheets can easily detect their presence and optionally format them for presentation if desired. The action element containing the error will be replaced in the page by:

```
<xsql-error action="xxx">
```

Depending on the error, the `<xsql-error>` element will contain a nested `<message>` element and a `<statement>` element with the offending SQL statement.

Here is an example fragment of an XSLT stylesheet that tests for the presence of an `<xsql-error>` element in the document and formats any error it finds for display:

```
<xsl:if test="//xsql-error">
  <table style="background:yellow">
  <xsl:for-each select="//xsql-error">
    <tr>
      <td><b>Action</b></td>
      <td><xsl:value-of select="@action"/></td>
    </tr>
    <tr valign="top">
      <td><b>Message</b></td>
      <td><xsl:value-of select="message"/></td>
    </tr>
  </xsl:for-each>
  </table>
</xsl:if>
```

In this chapter:
- *Developing Custom XSQL Actions*
- *Integrating Custom XML Sources*
- *Working with XSLT Extension Functions*

16

Extending XSQL and XSLT with Java

In this chapter, we examine how Java developers can extend the universe of built-in XSQL action handlers to provide custom actions and information sources and expand the universe of built-in functions in XSLT and XPath for use in stylesheets.

Developing Custom XSQL Actions

Oracle XSQL Pages is an extensible framework. With very straightforward Java code, you can introduce new kinds of actions to perform virtually any kind of custom processing required by your application and to easily incorporate XML information from custom sources. In this section, we'll learn how to write custom XSQL action handlers.

How Action Handlers Work

As we highlighted in Chapter 15, *Using XSQL Pages as a Publishing Framework*, the XSQL page processor processes an XSQL page by looking for action elements from the `xsql` namespace, and invoking an appropriate action element handler class to process each action. An *action handler* is a Java class that handles the runtime behavior of an action element in an XSQL page. Each action handler has full access to the objects it requires:

The DOM object representing the action element in the XSQL page
: Allows the action handler to examine the attributes, nested elements, or text content of the action element to drive the behavior of the action

The XSQL page requesting the context object
: Contains all the parameter values visible in the page, the current JDBC database connection (if any), and other resources available to the current page request

The XML result tree for the action
The root node for the tree of XML element content the action produces, if any

Oracle XSQL Pages ships with a number of built-in action handlers whose functionality we've outlined in previous chapters. Each of the built-in actions is implemented using the same facilities available to you as a developer for building your own actions, so each of the action elements listed in Table 16-1 could have been written by you!

Table 16-1. Built-in XSQL Action Elements and Action Handler Classes

XSQL Action Element	Handler Class in oracle.xml.xsql.actions
`<xsql:query>`	`XSQLQueryHandler`
`<xsql:dml>`	`XSQLDMLHandler`
`<xsql:set-stylesheet-param>`	`XSQLStylesheetParameterHandler`
`<xsql:insert-request>`	`XSQLInsertRequestHandler`
`<xsql:include-xml>`	`XSQLIncludeXMLHandler`
`<xsql:include-request-params/>`	`XSQLIncludeRequestHandler`
`<xsql:include-xsql>`	`XSQLIncludeXSQLHandler`
`<xsql:include-owa>`	`XSQLIncludeOWAHandler`
`<xsql:action>`	`XSQLExtensionActionHandler`
`<xsql:ref-cursor-function>`	`XSQLRefCursorFunctionHandler`
`<xsql:include-param>`	`XSQLGetParameterHandler`
`<xsql:set-session-param>`	`XSQLSetSessionParamHandler`
`<xsql:set-page-param>`	`XSQLSetPageParamHandler`
`<xsql:set-cookie>`	`XSQLSetCookieHandler`
`<xsql:insert-param>`	`XSQLInsertParameterHandler`

Let's study one of our earlier examples. Consider the following XSQL page containing two action elements:

```
<page connection="xmlbook" xmlns:xsql="urn:oracle-xsql">
  <xsql:query max-rows="3">
    SELECT ticker, price
      FROM stock_quotes
    WHERE portfolio_id = {@pid}
    ORDER BY ticker
  </xsql:query>
  <xsql:set-cookie name="portfolio" value="{@pid}"/>
</page>
```

The action handler for that `<xsql:query>` element, the `XSQLQueryHandler` class, contains code that performs the following tasks:

1. Examines the action element attributes, checking for `max-rows`, `skip-rows`, `rowset-element`, etc. The default implementation automatically handles `{@param}` references in the attribute values.

2. Examines the action element text content to retrieve the text of the SELECT statement the action needs to perform. The default implementation automatically handles `{@param}` references in the text.
3. Obtains the current JDBC connection from the XSQL page request context object.
4. Uses the Oracle XML SQL Utility to return an XML document representing the query results.
5. Appends the returned XML document to the action element's XML result tree's root node.

The action handler for the `<xsql:set-cookie>` element performs these steps:

1. Examines the action element attributes, checking for `name`, `value`, `max-age`, and so on.
2. Obtains the `HttpServletResponse` object from the XSQL page request.
3. Sets the cookie of the indicated name to the indicated value.

The following XSQL data page results from processing the previous example:

```
<page>
  <ROWSET>
    <ROW>
      <TICKER>AAPL</TICKER>
      <PRICE>115.48</PRICE>
    </ROW>
    <ROW>
      <TICKER>ORCL</TICKER>
      <PRICE>74.81</PRICE>
    </ROW>
  </ROWSET>
</page>
```

Notice that an XSQL action handler can add XML content to the page (as `<xsql:query>` does), or can simply perform some action without adding any XML content (as `<xsql:set-cookie>` does).

Writing Your Own Custom XSQL Action Handler

Let's get down to specifics so we can start building our own custom action handlers. The only technical requirement of an action handler is that it implement the simple `oracle.xml.xsql.XSQLActionHandler` interface:

```
public interface XSQLActionHandler  {
  /**
   * Initialize the action handler
   *
   * @param  env XSQLPageRequest object
```

```
   * @param   e DOM element representing the Action Element being handled
   **/
  void init(XSQLPageRequest env, Element e);

  /**
   * Handle the action, typically by executing some code
   * and appending new child DOM nodes to the rootNode.
   *
   * The XSQL page processor replaces the action element in
   * the XSQL page being processed with the document fragment
   * of nodes that your handleAction method appends to the rootNode.
   *
   * @param rootNode Root node of generated document fragment
   **/
  void handleAction( Node rootNode ) throws SQLException;
}
```

After the XSQL page processor constructs an instance of your action handler class using the default constructor (no arguments), it performs the following two steps:

1. Initializes the handler by calling its `init()` method, passing in the `XSQLPageRequest` context object and the DOM `Element` representing the action element being handled.
2. Invokes the handler's `handleAction()` method to handle the action, passing in the root node of the action handler's XML result tree.

Any XML nodes appended to the root of the handler's XML result tree are included automatically by the page processor in the resulting XSQL data page.

You can save a tremendous amount of time by extending the base implementation class `oracle.xml.xsql.XSQLActionHandlerImpl`, which provides a default implementation of the `init()` method and a set of many helper methods. In practice, if your action handler extends the `XSQLActionHandlerImpl` base class, you need to provide only a `handleAction()` method that does what you want it to do. As a first example, let's build a custom action handler called `JavaDate` that adds a `<CurrentDate>` element with the value of the current system date to the page.

If you are using JDeveloper 3.1 and have included the XSQL Runtime library in your current project, you can select *File → New...* from the main menu, select the Class icon from the gallery, and fill in the *Class Wizard* dialog as shown in Figure 16-1.

Note that we've selected the `oracle.xml.xsql.XSQLActionHandlerImpl` class to extend for our example `JavaDate` action handler. After clicking on OK, you'll end up with a skeleton Java class with the right `imports` and the correct `extends` clause.

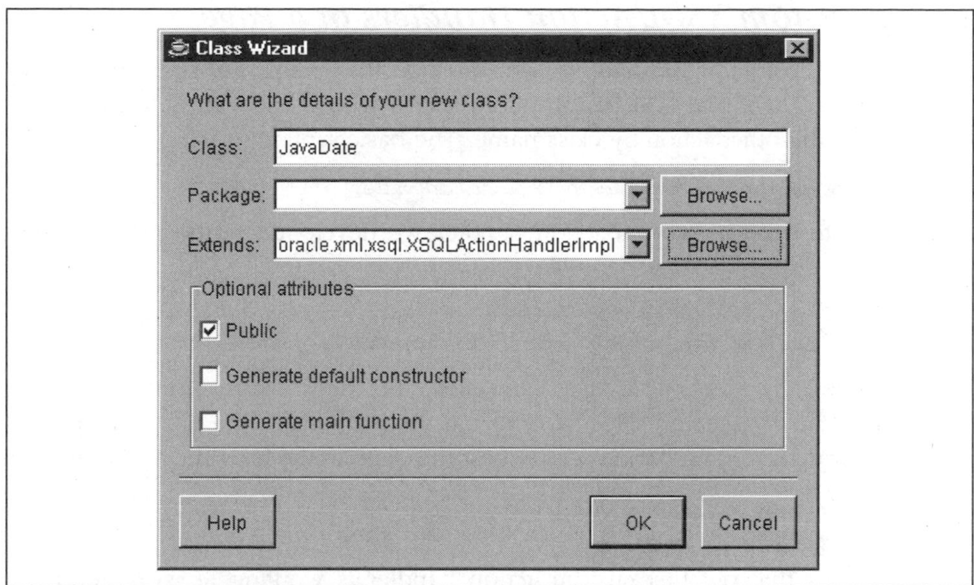

Figure 16-1. Creating a skeleton action handler with the Class Wizard

Next, add the **handleAction()** method to the class like this:

```
import oracle.xml.xsql.*;
import org.w3c.dom.Node;

public class JavaDate extends XSQLActionHandlerImpl {
  public void handleAction( Node root ) {

  }
}
```

Inside the **handleAction()** for this example, we need to append a **<CurrentDate>** element to the root of the XML result tree. The **XSQLActionHandlerImpl** base class provides a useful helper method called **addResultElement** that simplifies this task. In fact, we can accomplish what we need to in a single line of code like:

```
addResultElement(root,"CurrentDate",(new Date()).toString());
```

This means that our first working custom action handler looks like this:

```
import oracle.xml.xsql.*;
import java.util.Date;
import org.w3c.dom.Node;

public class JavaDate extends XSQLActionHandlerImpl {
  public void handleAction( Node root ) {
    addResultElement(root,"CurrentDate",(new Date()).toString());
  }
}
```

Using Custom XSQL Action Handlers in a Page

To invoke a custom action handler, you include the **<xsql:action>** action element in your XSQL page. This is a built-in action whose behavior is to instantiate and invoke any other action by class name. The basic syntax is:

```
<xsql:action handler="yourpackage.YourCustomHandler"/>
```

To quickly test the **JavaDate** action handler we developed in the previous section, we can create an XSQL page like this:

```
<!-- TestJavaDate.xsql -->
<xsql:action handler="JavaDate" xmlns:xsql="urn:oracle-xsql"/>
```

From inside JDeveloper 3.1, we can click the right mouse button on this *TestJavaDate.xsql* page and select *Run* to run the page inside the JDeveloper environment for rapid testing. When we request the page in the browser, we'll see:

```
<!-- TestJavaDate.xsql -->
<CurrentDate>Wed May 03 09:32:26 PDT 2000</CurrentDate>
```

This indicates that our first custom action handler is working. If we extend the **JavaDate** handler to accept an attribute indicating a date format mask, then a user of our action simply adds that new attribute to the **<xsql:action>** element like this:

```
<!-- TestJavaDateWithMask.xsql -->
<xsql:action handler="JavaDate" mask="d/MM/yyyy" xmlns:xsql="urn:oracle-xsql"/>
```

On the code side, we can extend our simple **JavaDate** class to take advantage of the **getActionElement()** and **getAttributeAllowingParam()** methods inherited from **XSQLActionHandlerImpl**. These methods return the DOM **Element** object representing the current action element and the value of an attribute on an element, respectively. We use **getAttributeAllowingParam()** instead of the normal DOM **getAttribute()** method because the former automatically handles the presence of any XSQL parameter values that might be in use as well. The code for **JavaDate** then becomes:

```
import oracle.xml.xsql.*;
import java.util.Date;
import java.text.SimpleDateFormat;
import org.w3c.dom.Node;

public class JavaDate extends XSQLActionHandlerImpl {
  public void handleAction( Node root ) {
    String mask = getAttributeAllowingParam("mask",getActionElement());
    String dateValue = null;
    if (mask != null && !mask.equals("")) {
      SimpleDateFormat sdf = new SimpleDateFormat(mask);
      dateValue = sdf.format(new Date()).toString();
    }
    else {
```

```
      dateValue = (new Date()).toString();
    }
    addResultElement(root,"CurrentDate",dateValue);
  }
}
```

and a quick test of our *TestJavaDateWithMask.xsql* page shows that we get the following document, which is now using our new format mask to format the date:

```
<!-- TestJavaDateWithMask.xsql -->
<CurrentDate>3/05/2000</CurrentDate>
```

To show the value that `getAttributeAllowingParam()` is providing, we can make a quick edit to the *TestJavaDateWithMask.xsql* file to allow the mask to be sent in as a parameter named `format` in the request. We'll also provide a fallback or default value for the format parameter by adding a `format` attribute to the element as follows:

```
<!-- TestJavaDateWithMask.xsql -->
<xsql:action handler="JavaDate" xmlns:xsql="urn:oracle-xsql"
             format="d/MM/yyyy"
               mask="{@format}" />
```

With this edit in place, we can try out a URL like:

```
http://xmlapps/TestJavaDateWithMask.xsql?format=EEEE,KK:mma
```

This produces the date formatted using the requester-supplied format mask:

```
<!-- TestJavaDateWithMask.xsql -->
<CurrentDate>Wednesday,10:07AM</CurrentDate>
```

As we learned in Chapter 6, *Processing XML with Java*, you can quickly reference the JavaDoc for the `java.text.SimpleDateFormat` class, which contains a table summarizing the supported date format mask patterns: press Ctrl-/, type in the full classname, press Enter and click on the *Doc* tab of the code editor.

You might be wondering what happens if the requester passes in a value for the `format` parameter that is not a valid format pattern recognized by the `SimpleDateFormat` class, for example, by requesting the URL:

```
http://server/TestJavaDateWithMask.xsql?format=Q
```

In this case, the requester will see the following error message page in its browser:

```
Oracle XSQL Servlet Page Processor 1.0.0.0
XSQL-017: Unexpected Error Occurred
java.lang.IllegalArgumentException: Illegal pattern character 'Q'
```

The XSQL page processor has built-in error handling to catch unhandled exceptions raised in any phase of the page processing, including unhandled exceptions thrown by your custom action handlers. Obviously, it would be nicer to use a `try...catch` block in our action handler code to catch this problem ourselves and report an error using the standard mechanism that other XSQL action handlers use. We can leverage the `reportError()` method in the `XSQLActionHandlerImpl` base class to do this. Example 16-1 shows an enhanced version of the `JavaDate` action handler that catches the `IllegalArgumentException` and reports the error.

Example 16-1. Action Handler That Catches and Handles Exceptions

```
import oracle.xml.xsql.*;
import java.util.Date;
import java.text.SimpleDateFormat;
import org.w3c.dom.Node;

public class JavaDate extends XSQLActionHandlerImpl {
  public void handleAction( Node root ) {
    // Get the value of the mask attribute
    String mask = getAttributeAllowingParam("mask",getActionElement());
    String dateValue = null;
    if (mask != null && !mask.equals("")) {
      // If we have a non-empty mask, use SimpleDateFormat to format the date
      SimpleDateFormat sdf = new SimpleDateFormat(mask);
      try {
        dateValue = sdf.format(new Date()).toString();
      }
      catch (IllegalArgumentException iax) {
        // If we catch an error, report it
        reportError(root,mask+" is not a valid date format mask");
        return;
      }
    }
    else {
      // Otherwise, just use Date's default string format
      dateValue = (new Date()).toString();
    }
    // Add a <CurrentDate> element to the result with the date value
    addResultElement(root,"CurrentDate",dateValue);
  }
}
```

With this extra error-checking in place, an attempt to request the page again with the illegal value of `format=Q` now produces the document:

```
<!-- TestJavaDateWithMask.xsql -->
<xsql-error action="xsql:action">
   <message>Q is not a valid date format mask</message>
</xsql-error>
```

For our second simple example, we'll build an action handler that interacts with the database to produce its content. We'll create a `Sequence` handler that takes the name of a sequence and returns the next value from the sequence as XML content in the data page. The code appears in Example 16-2.

Example 16-2. Action Handler to Return a Database Sequence Number

```
import oracle.xml.xsql.*;
import org.w3c.dom.Node;

public class Sequence extends XSQLActionHandlerImpl {
  public void handleAction( Node root ) {
    // Get the value of the name attribute
    String seqname = getAttributeAllowingParam("name",getActionElement());
    // Report an error if the attribute is missing since it's required
    if (seqname == null || seqname.equals("")) {
      reportMissingAttribute(root,"name");
      return;
    }
    // Build a select statement to retrieve the next value from the sequence
    String query   = "select "+seqname+".nextval from dual";
    // Retrieve the value of the first column of the first row of the result
    String nextval = firstColumnOfFirstRow(root,query);
    if (nextval != null) {
      // Add a <NextValue> element to the page with the new sequence number
      addResultElement(root,"NextValue",nextval);
    }
  }
}
```

Since what we need to accomplish here can be phrased in terms of a query that returns a single row and a single column, we can leverage the `firstColumnOfFirstRow()` method in the `XSQLActionHandlerImpl` class to do the dirty work of getting the current JDBC connection from the page request context object, executing the query, and returning the result. If you need to do more complicated database interactions, you can use:

```
Connection curConn = getPageRequest().getJDBCConnection();
```

to get access to the live connection from the connection pool that has been assigned to the current page request. If we build a quick XSQL page to test the new `Sequence` handler:

```
<!-- TestSequence.xsql -->
<page xmlns:xsql="urn:oracle-xsql">
  <ID>
    <xsql:action handler="Sequence" name="customer_id_seq"/>
  </ID>
</page>
```

and then run the page from the JDeveloper IDE to test requesting it from our browser, we'll get:

```
<!-- TestSequence.xsql -->
<page>
  <ID>
    <xsql-error action="xsql:action">
      <message>No connection attribute specified on document element.</message>
    </xsql-error>
  </ID>
</page>
```

This happens because we forgot to specify a `connection` attribute on the document element of our page. Our earlier examples using the `JavaDate` custom action handler didn't require a database connection to perform any of the actions on the page, so we didn't see the error earlier. After adding an appropriate `connection` attribute:

```
<!-- TestSequence.xsql -->
<page connection="xmlbook" xmlns:xsql="urn:oracle-xsql">
  <ID>
    <xsql:action handler="Sequence" name="customer_id_seq"/>
  </ID>
</page>
```

we can request again, and we get our desired result:

```
<!-- TestSequence.xsql -->
<page>
  <ID>
    <NextValue>1253213</NextValue>
  </ID>
</page>
```

Note that we're using the `reportMissingAttribute()` method inherited from `XSQLActionHandlerImpl` to report an error condition when a required attribute is missing.

As a simple example of a custom action handler that works with HTTP-specific information, let's build one that retrieves the value of any HTTP header. This might be useful to retrieve the `user-agent` or the `referer` of a page, for example. To illustrate a technique other than getting values from attributes as we've done earlier, we'll let the user enter one or more header names separated by whitespace as the text content of the action element, instead of as one of its attributes.

The XSQL page processor expects to process requests that implement the `XSQLPageRequest` interface. There are three different implementations of this interface:

`XSQLServletPageRequest`
: HTTP-based requests

`XSQLCommandLinePageRequest`
: Command-line requests

`XSQLURLPageRequest`
: Programmatic requests

To exploit a feature that is specific to one of these implementations, you need to code your action handler to first check `getPageRequest().getRequestType()` for the values "Servlet," "CommandLine," or "Programmatic" before casting the `XSQLPageRequest` interface returned by `getPageRequest()` into one of these specific classes. Most frequently, you'll find it necessary only to test for "Servlet" and cast to `XSQLServletPageRequest`, as we do in the `HTTPHeaders` implementation in Example 16-3.

Example 16-3. Action Handler to Return HTTP Header Information

```
import oracle.xml.xsql.*;
import java.util.*;
import javax.servlet.http.*;
import org.w3c.dom.*;

public class HTTPHeaders extends XSQLActionHandlerImpl {
  public void handleAction( Node root ) {
    if (getPageRequest().getRequestType().equals("Servlet")) {
      // If request type is "Servlet" then it's ok to cast
      XSQLServletPageRequest xspr = (XSQLServletPageRequest)getPageRequest();
      // Then we can get the HTTPServletRequest from the XSQLServletPageRequest
      HttpServletRequest req  = xspr.getHttpServletRequest();
      // Create an element using the action element's owning document
      Element e = getActionElement().getOwnerDocument().createElement("Headers");
      // Get the text content of the action element that contains the
      // list of HTTP headers the user wants the values of
      String headerList = getActionElementContent();
      // Use a string-tokenizer to parse the text into
      // the list of whitespace-separated tokens it contains
      if (headerList != null && !headerList.equals("")) {
        Enumeration headerNames = null;
        // If user gave just the name "all", then show all headers
        if (headerList.trim().equals("all")) {
          headerNames = req.getHeaderNames();
        }
        else {
          headerNames = new StringTokenizer(headerList);
        }
        while (headerNames.hasMoreElements()) {
          String headerName  = (String)headerNames.nextElement();
          String headerValue = req.getHeader(headerName);
          // Append the <Name>Value</Name> to the <Headers> element
          addResultElement(e,headerName,headerValue);
        }
      }
```

Example 16-3. Action Handler to Return HTTP Header Information (continued)

```
      // Append the <Headers> element to the XML result root for the action
      root.appendChild(e);
    }
  }
}
```

A few interesting things happen in the implementation of `HTTPHeaders.java`:

- We call the `getActionElement().getOwnerDocument()` method to invoke `createElement()` to construct a new `<Headers>` element to be the parent element of all the elements representing retrieved HTTP header values.
- We use `addResultElement` to add `<Name>Value</Name>` elements as children of the `<Headers>` element instead of directly as children of the XML result root.
- We allow the user to enter the string `"all"` to get all headers and in this case use the `getHeaderNames()` method on `HTTPServletRequest` instead of using a `StringTokenizer` to get the list of header names to iterate over.

To try out our new handler, we might create a test page like this:

```
<!-- TestHTTPHeaders.xsql -->
<page connection="xmlbook" xmlns:xsql="urn:oracle-xsql">
  <xsql:action handler="HTTPHeaders">all</xsql:action>
  <xsql:action handler="Sequence" name="customer_id_seq"/>
  <xsql:action handler="JavaDate"/>
</page>
```

Clicking on an HTML anchor from the *PageReferringToTestHTTPHeaders.html* page that links to *TestHTTPHeaders.xsql* returns the page:

```
<!-- TestHTTPHeaders.xsql -->
<page>
  <Headers>
    <accept-language>en-us</accept-language>
    <host>127.0.0.1</host>
    <cookie>WTGBID=c15k9ixg; siteuser=smuench</cookie>
    <accept>image/gif, image/x-xbitmap, image/jpeg, image/pjpeg, */*</accept>
    <user-agent>Mozilla/4.0 (compatible; MSIE 5.01; Windows NT)</user-agent>
    <referer>http://127.0.0.1/PageReferingToTestHTTPHeaders.html</referer>
    <connection>Keep-Alive</connection>
    <accept-encoding>gzip, deflate</accept-encoding>
  </Headers>
  <NextValue>1253214</NextValue>
  <CurrentDate>Wed May 03 13:57:37 PDT 2000</CurrentDate>
</page>
```

Notice that the value of `page/Headers/referer` reports the name of the page we came from. Since we specified `"all"` as the text content of our `<xsql:action>` element, all header names are displayed. If we change *TestHTTPHeaders.xsql* as follows:

```
<!-- TestHTTPHeaders.xsql -->
<page connection="xmlbook" xmlns:xsql="urn:oracle-xsql">
  <xsql:action handler="HTTPHeaders">

     referer
     user-agent
     {@others}

  </xsql:action>
  <xsql:action handler="Sequence" name="customer_id_seq"/>
  <xsql:action handler="JavaDate"/>
</page>
```

then clicking on a link from a referring page that includes the following URL:

```
http://server/TestHTTPHeaders.xsql?others=accept-language
```

returns the following page:

```
<!-- TestHTTPHeaders.xsql -->
<page>
  <Headers>
    <referer>http://127.0.0.1/PageReferingToTestHTTPHeaders.html</referer>
    <user-agent>Mozilla/4.0 (compatible; MSIE 5.01; Windows NT)</user-agent>
    <accept-language>en-us</accept-language>
  </Headers>
  <NextValue>1253215</NextValue>
  <CurrentDate>Wed May 03 14:24:38 PDT 2000</CurrentDate>
</page>
```

This illustrates how `getActionElementContent()` automatically handles parameter substitution, as `getAttributeAllowingParam()` did in our earlier examples.

In addition to adding XML content to the data page, it is possible for action handlers to set private page-level parameters whose values can be referred to by other actions later in the page. Assume that you have configured your web server to use Basic Authentication to protect a directory containing XSQL pages. This means a user will be prompted for a username/password to authenticate with the web server before being allowed access to request the XSQL pages in that directory. It is definitely useful to be able to refer to the authenticated user's name within your XSQL pages to, for example, query user-specific settings or preferences from tables in your database. The following `SetAuthUserParams` action handler sets the values of the `AuthUser` and `AuthUserHost` page-level parameters:

```
import oracle.xml.xsql.*;
import javax.servlet.http
import org.w3c.dom.Node;
import java.sql.SQLException;
// Capture Basic Authentication username and hostname in XSQL parameters
public class SetAuthUserParams extends XSQLActionHandlerImpl {
  public void handleAction (Node result) throws SQLException {
    XSQLPageRequest xpr = getPageRequest ();
    // If this is a servlet request, then set the private page parameters
```

```
      // named "AuthUser" and "AuthUserHost" to values from the HTTP Request
      if (xpr.getRequestType().equals("Servlet")) {
        XSQLServletPageRequest xspr = (XSQLServletPageRequest)xpr;
        HttpServletRequest      req = xspr.getHttpServletRequest();
        String user = req.getRemoteUser();
        String host = req.getRemoteHost();
        if (user !=null) xpr.setPageParam("AuthUser",req.getRemoteUser());
        if (host !=null) xpr.setPageParam("AuthUserHost",req.getRemoteHost());
      }
    }
  }
```

Then an XSQL page can use the values of the **AuthUser** parameter in a subsequent query like this:

```
<page xmlns:xsql="urn:oracle-xsql" connection="xmlbook">
  <xsql:action handler="SetAuthUserParams"/>
  <xsql:query>
    SELECT favorite_thing AS favorite
      FROM site_user_prefs
     WHERE username = '{@AuthUser}'
  </xsql:query>
</page>
```

Our final example illustrates how to build custom action handlers that invoke built-in action handlers and programmatically augment their results before including the final result in the page. The **CustomInclude** handler in Example 16-4 includes an arbitrary XSQL page by exploiting the **<xsql:include-xsql>** action handler shown in Table 16-1 and performs some custom Java programmatic logic on the result before including it into the invoking page.

Example 16-4. Customizing the Output of a Built-in Action Handler

```
import oracle.xml.xsql.*;
import oracle.xml.xsql.actions.XSQLIncludeXSQLHandler;
import org.w3c.dom.*;
import java.sql.SQLException;

public class CustomInclude extends XSQLActionHandlerImpl {
  XSQLActionHandler nestedHandler = null;
  public void handleAction(Node root) throws SQLException {
    // Create an instance of an XSQLIncludeXSQLHandler
    // and init() the handler by passing the current request/action
    nestedHandler = new XSQLIncludeXSQLHandler();
    nestedHandler.init(getPageRequest(),getActionElement());

    // Rather than passing the default XML result "root" that we're given,
    // we create an empty DocumentFragment and feed *that* to
    // the XSQLIncludeXSQLHandler as its root to work with
    DocumentFragment tmpRoot = root.getOwnerDocument().createDocumentFragment();
    nestedHandler.handleAction(tmpRoot);

    // Custom Java code here can work on the returned document fragment
    // in tmpRoot before appending the final, modified document to the
```

Example 16-4. Customizing the Output of a Built-in Action Handler (continued)

```
    // XML result "root" node we're given by the XSQL page processor
    //
    // For example, add an attribute to the first child
    Element e = (Element)tmpRoot.getFirstChild();
    if (e != null) {
      e.setAttribute("ExtraAttribute","SomeValue");
    }
    // Finally, append the modified tmpRoot fragment as the XML result
    root.appendChild(tmpRoot);
  }
}
```

To test the new handler, we cook up a quick test page like the following:

```
<page xmlns:xsql="urn:oracle-xsql">
  <IncludedStuff>
    <xsql:action handler="CustomInclude"
                 href="TestJavaDateWithMask.xsql?format=EEEE,K:mma"/>
  </IncludedStuff>
</page>
```

Requesting this page through our browser produces:

```
<page>
  <IncludedStuff>
    <CurrentDate ExtraAttribute="SomeValue">Wednesday,4:22PM</CurrentDate>
  </IncludedStuff>
</page>
```

which shows that the *TestJavaDateWithMask.xsql* page was included, correctly picking up the `format` parameter passed in the `href` URL, and that the `ExtraAttribute` attribute was added programmatically.

Even though none of these test pages has included an `<?xml-stylesheet?>` at the top, this is certainly possible. Since all of the built-in action elements are implemented as action handlers in the same way we've just seen, the model does not change a bit when you augment the built-in actions with actions of your own.

Debugging Action Handlers

Inevitably, you'll want to debug your custom action handlers, and luckily, JDeveloper 3.1 makes this a piece of cake. The basic approach is to follow these steps:

1. Run your XSQL page from the JDeveloper 3.1 IDE.
2. Set breakpoints in your custom action handler's Java code.
3. Click on the Debug icon to attach to the running servlet engine that hosts the `XSQLServlet`.
4. Request the page through your browser and step through your code after hitting your breakpoint.

The absolute easiest way to set this up is to use two different JDeveloper projects in the same workspace. The first project contains your action handlers' Java code, while the second project contains the XSQL pages that use and test your custom action handlers.

Figure 16-2 illustrates a simple example of using two projects for some of the custom action handlers we created in the previous section.

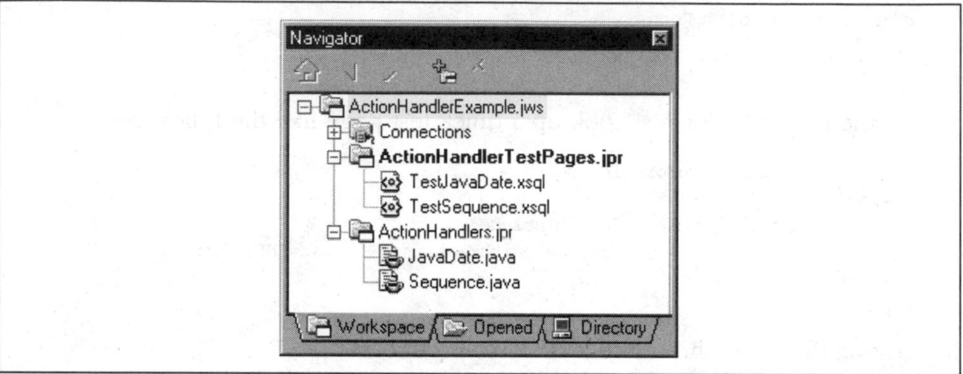

Figure 16-2. Using two projects simplifies action handler debugging

Given a two-project workspace, do the following to prepare for debugging your action handlers:

1. Double-click on the `ActionHandlerTestPages` project containing the XSQL pages to test your handlers to bring up its *Project Properties* dialog.
2. Select the *Run/Debug* tab.
3. Add the `-XXdebugondemand` parameter to the list of Java VM parameters.
4. Make sure the *Debug Files As* list indicates "Normal Java Class", its default setting.
5. Select the *Paths* tab.
6. Make sure *Output Root Directory* is set to the same output root directory as the `ActionHandlers` project to ensure that the compiled class files for your action handlers are automatically included in the CLASSPATH when you run your XSQL pages from this project.
7. Click *OK* to dismiss the dialog.
8. Double-click on the `ActionHandlers` project containing the Java code for your action handlers to bring up *its Project Properties* dialog.
9. Select the *Run/Debug* tab.
10. Select the "Remote Debugging" option from the *Debug Files As* list.
11. Click OK to dismiss the dialog.

At this point, we've configured the `ActionHandlerTestPages` project to run your XSQL pages using the on-demand remote debugging feature. We've also configured the `ActionHandlers` project to enable attaching on demand to the servlet engine running your pages, allowing you to debug your action handlers live as you exercise them through the browser. To start debugging:

1. Click the right mouse button on the desired XSQL page in the `ActionHandlerTestPages` project and select *Run*.
2. Set any initial breakpoints you need in the Java source code for your action handlers in the `ActionHandlers` project.
3. With the `ActionHandlers` project still active in the navigator, click the Debug icon in the toolbar.
4. In the *Remote Debugging* dialog, set the following items:
   - Set *Debugging Protocol* to "Oracle JVM".
   - Set *Hostname* to "`localhost`".
   - Set *Port* to "`4000`", the default debugging.
5. Click the *Attach* button to attach the debugger.
6. Request the XSQL page from your browser.

This will cause your code to run, and when it reaches the first of the breakpoints you set, at that point, you can step through and examine your code to your heart's content.

To stop debugging, click on the Stop icon from the debugger toolbar. This detaches the on-demand debugger from the remotely debuggable servlet engine running your XSQL page. After making any changes to your action handler code to fix the problem, recompile your classes in the `ActionHandlers` project; then repeat the previous steps to debug again.

Selecting to run the XSQL page again will kill the existing, running servlet engine and start a new one. You can explicitly kill a servlet engine at any time by selecting its process name from the *Run* → *Terminate* menu. Figure 16-3 illustrates a running example of debugging our `Sequence.java` action handler using the technique described in this section.

Deploying Custom Action Handlers

When you've built a set of XSQL pages that use custom action handlers, you'll need to deploy the Java classes for your custom handlers in such a way that they can be included in the CLASSPATH of their target servlet environment.

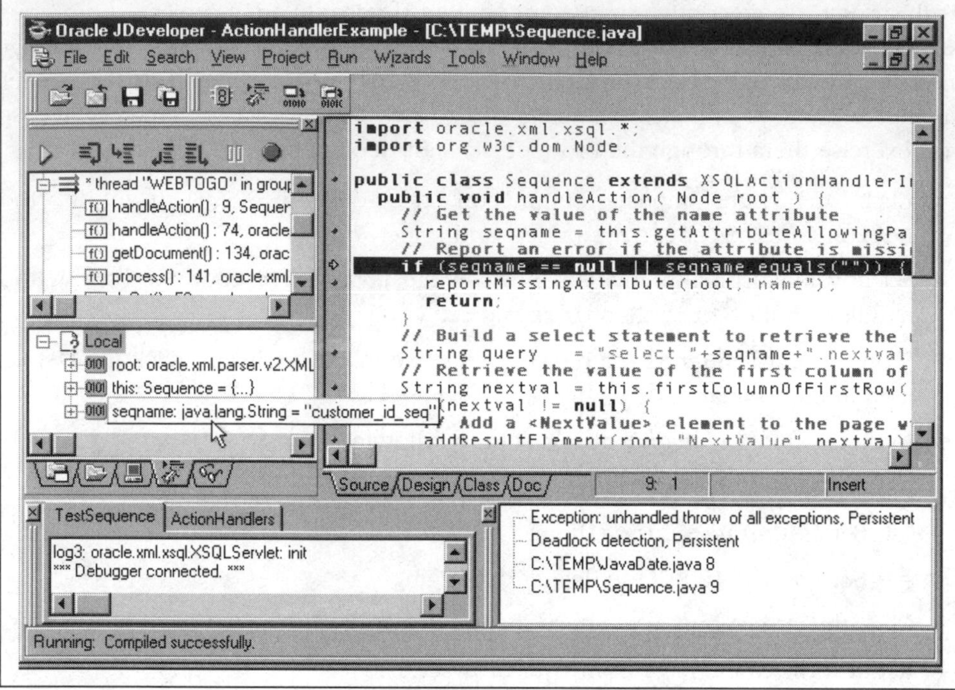

Figure 16-3. Debugging custom action handlers with JDeveloper 3.1

Deploying your classes to a Java archive can be done by hand using the standard *.jar* utility, or it can be automated by creating a simple Java archive-based deployment profile in JDeveloper. For example, to create a deployment profile for the `Sequence` and `JavaDate` handlers from the previous section using JDeveloper 3.1, perform the following steps:

1. Select the `ActionHandlers` project to make it active.
2. Select *New Deployment Profile...* from the right mouse button menu for the project.
3. On the Deployment Profile Wizard's *Step 1 of 3: Delivery* panel, select *Deploy as a Simple archive file.*
4. On the *Step 2 of 3: Project* panel, select the files to include in the archive.
5. On the *Step 3 of 3: Archive* panel, give the archive a name.
6. On the *Finish* panel, give the deployment profile a name and click the *Finish* button.

After creating the deployment profile, you can click on the right mouse button to select the *Deploy* option to redeploy the classes to the archive file at any time. In your production environment, make sure this *.jar* file is included in the server

CLASSPATH and your custom actions will work just like the built-in XSQL page actions on any server.

Integrating Custom XML Sources

In this section, we'll depart from simple examples designed to help understand the technology and provide a real-world example of a custom XSQL action handler that does something really useful. In Chapter 6 we built a class called `JTidyConverter`, which leveraged the freely available `JTidy` JavaBean to convert HTML into a well-formed XML document. Then we wrote some examples illustrating how basic XPath expressions in an XSLT stylesheet could easily extract interesting information like stock quotes from HTML returned by a live request against the Yahoo! Quotes web site. Here we will show a parallel example that illustrates how such useful, dynamic XML information can be adapted into the XSQL Pages framework. Example 16-5 shows the code for this `LiveQuotes` action handler.

As with our more straightforward examples earlier in this chapter, the `LiveQuotes` handler uses `getAttributeAllowingParam` to get the list of ticker symbols from the `symbols` attribute on the action element, then employs the `JTidyConverter` class to retrieve the dynamic HTML page delivered from the Yahoo! Quotes server and return it as an in-memory XML document. Rather than writing code to perform the XSLT transformation ourselves, we take advantage of the XSQL page processor's own `XSQLStylesheetProcessor`, which automatically loads, caches, and pools the *YahooQuotes-to-QuoteStream.xsl* stylesheet. Note that we have to call `getPageRequest().translateURL()` so that the relative URL `YahooQuotes-to-QuoteStream.xsl` is turned into an absolute URL. By calling the `processToDocument()` method instead of just `process()`, we can get back the transformed `<QuoteStream>` as an in-memory XML document.

In order to add the `<QuoteStream>` XML as the result of our `LiveQuotes` handler, we perform these final steps:

- Get the document element of the transformed `<QuoteStream>` document.
- Remove it from the document that currently owns it.
- Append it to the action handler's XML result `root`.

Example 16-5. Action Handler to Include Live XML Quotes from Yahoo! Quotes

```
import oracle.xml.xsql.*;
import oracle.xml.parser.v2.*;
import org.w3c.dom.*;
import java.net.*;
import java.util.StringTokenizer;
import java.sql.SQLException;
import JTidyConverter;
import java.io.IOException;
```

Example 16-5. Action Handler to Include Live XML Quotes from Yahoo! Quotes (continued)

```
public class LiveQuotes extends XSQLActionHandlerImpl {
  private static final String YQUOTES = "http://quote.yahoo.com/q?d2=v1&o=d&s=";
  private static final String YTRANSF = "YahooQuotes-to-QuoteStream.xsl";
  public void handleAction(Node root) throws SQLException {
    XSQLPageRequest req = getPageRequest();
    Element actElt  = getActionElement();
    // Get the list of Symbols from the action element's "symbols" attribute
    String symbolList = getAttributeAllowingParam("symbols",actElt);
    if (symbolList == null || symbolList.equals("")) {
      reportMissingAttribute(root,"symbols");
      return;
    }
    try {
      // Prepare the URL to get quotes from Yahoo! Quotes
      URL yahooUrl = new URL(YQUOTES+symbolList.replace(',','+'));
      JTidyConverter jtc = new JTidyConverter();
      // Convert the dynamically produced Yahoo Quotes page to XML Document
      XMLDocument yahooquotes = jtc.XMLifyHTMLFrom(yahooUrl);

      // Use the XSQL page processor's built-in Stylesheet Processor to
      // have the page processor automatically cache and pool this
      // transformation as needed. Use processToDocument() to get the
      // transformed results as an in-memory XML document.
      Document quoteStream =
         XSQLStylesheetProcessor.processToDocument(yahooquotes,
                                                   req.translateURL(YTRANSF),
                                                   req);
      // Append the quotes to the root of our XML result
      Element docElement = quoteStream.getDocumentElement();
      quoteStream.removeChild(docElement);
      root.appendChild(docElement);
    }
    catch(MalformedURLException mfx) { /* Ignore */ }
    catch(IOException io) {
      this.reportError(root,"Unable to retrieve quotes");
    }
    catch(Exception ex) {
      this.reportError(root,"Unable to retrieve quotes");
    }
  }
}
```

Instant XML stock quotes are now available to any XSQL page we build that needs them. We can throw together a quick *LiveQuotes.xsql* test page:

```
<?xml version="1.0"?>
<page xmlns:xsql="urn:oracle-xsql">
  <!--
   | Include live stock quotes from Yahoo for any symbols
   | includes in the "s" parameter passed in. If no "s"
   | parameter is supplied, we provide a default list
   +-->
```

```
    <xsql:action handler="LiveQuotes"
                 symbols="{@s}"
                 s="ORCL,MSFT,IBM"/>
</page>
```

and request it through our browser with some appropriate ticker symbols in the value of the s parameter:

```
http://server/LiveQuotes.xsql?s=ORCL,MSFT,GE,T,PFE,DIS,CSCO,HLTH
```

As if by magic, our live quotes appear in the browser:

```
<?xml version = '1.0'?>
<page>
  <!--
   | Include live stock quotes from Yahoo for any symbols
   | included in the "s" parameter passed in. If no "s"
   | parameter is supplied, we provide a default list
   +-->
  <QuoteStream time="Wed May 3 7:52pm ET - U.S. Markets Closed.">
    <Quote Ticker="ORCL" Price="75.812"/>
    <Quote Ticker="MSFT" Price="70.562"/>
    <Quote Ticker="GE" Price="156.062"/>
    <Quote Ticker="T" Price="39.812"/>
    <Quote Ticker="PFE" Price="42.688"/>
    <Quote Ticker="DIS" Price="41.250"/>
    <Quote Ticker="CSCO" Price="66.062"/>
    <Quote Ticker="HLTH" Price="18.562"/></QuoteStream>
</page>
```

To prove we haven't forgotten about using XSLT to make our XSQL data page look pretty, we can finish by creating a tiny page as follows:

```
<?xml version="1.0"?>
<!-- LiveQuotesHTML.xsql -->
<?xml-stylesheet type="text/xsl" href="QuoteTable.xsl"?>
<xsql:include-xsql href="LiveQuotes.xsql" xmlns:xsql="urn:oracle-xsql"/>
```

that includes the XML data page from *LiveQuotes.xsql* and applies the *QuoteTable.xsl* stylesheet in Example 16-6 for HTML presentation.

Example 16-6. Stylesheet to Format Live Stock Quotes

```
<html xsl:version="1.0" xmlns:xsl="http://www.w3.org/1999/XSL/Transform">
  <head>
    <style>
       BODY {font-family: Verdana}
       TH {background-color:#cccc99;color:#336699;font-weight:bold;}
      .r1 {background-color: #f7f7e7; color: black}
      .r0 {background-color: #f9f9f9; color: black}

    </style>
  </head>
```

Example 16-6. Stylesheet to Format Live Stock Quotes (continued)

```
  <body>
    <center>
      <h2>Yahoo! Quotes</h2>
      <xsl:value-of select="page/QuoteStream/@time"/>
      <hr/>
      <table>
        <tr>
          <th>Ticker</th>
          <th>Price</th>
        </tr>
        <xsl:for-each select="page/QuoteStream/Quote">
          <xsl:sort select="@Price" data-type="number" order="descending"/>
          <tr class="r{position() mod 2}">
            <td><xsl:value-of select="@Ticker"/></td>
            <td align="right"><xsl:value-of select="format-number(@Price,'0.00')"/>
              </td>
          </tr>
        </xsl:for-each>
      </table>
    </center>
  </body>
</html>
```

Executing this, we instantly see our live quotes in a more presentable manner, as shown in Figure 16-4.

Note some of the interesting XSLT features we're using in *QuoteTable.xsl*:

- We've nested an `<xsl:sort>` element inside our familiar `<xsl:for-each>` loop to cause our live XML quotes to be sorted in descending order by price:

  ```
  <xsl:for-each select="page/QuoteStream/Quote">
    <xsl:sort select="@Price" data-type="number" order="descending"/>
     Content
  </xsl:for-each>
  ```

- We're using an attribute-value template together with the XPath `mod` operator and the `position()` function to alternate between CSS class names `r0` and `r1` achieving the striped coloring of even/odd rows:

  ```
  <tr class="r{position() mod 2}">
  ```

- We're using the XPath `format-number()` function to format the stock quotes to just two decimal places, even though we retrieved them from Yahoo! Quotes with three digits of precision.

So far in this chapter, we've seen that extending the XSQL framework to include custom actions and XML information sources is straightforward, particularly in combination with JDeveloper 3.1 to assist in development, testing, and debugging. In Chapter 17, *XSLT-Powered Portals and Applications*, we'll see how all of the pieces fit together.

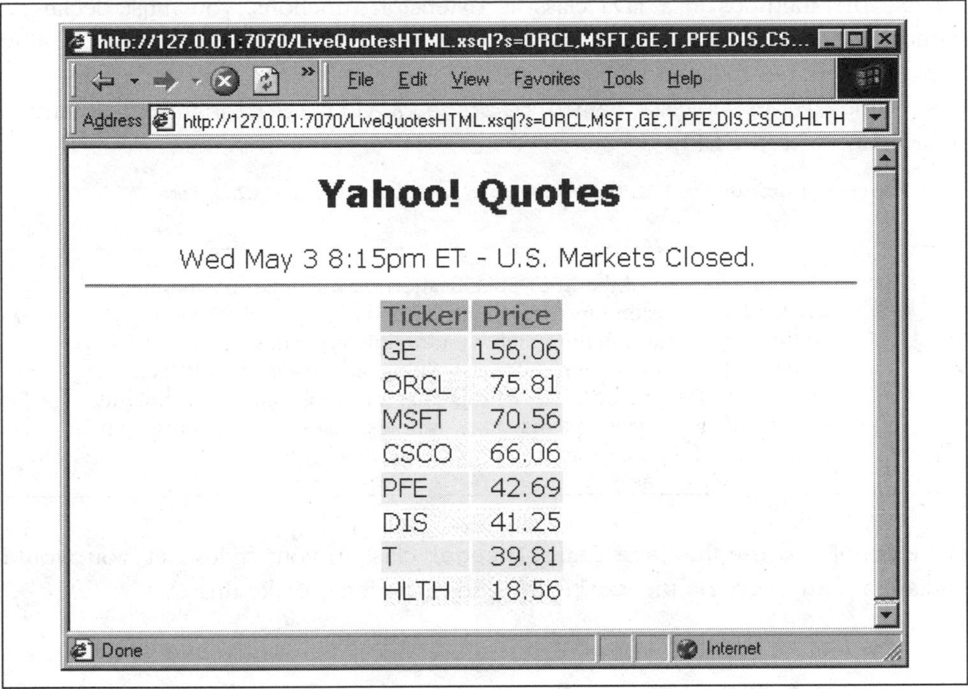

Figure 16-4. Browsing live Yahoo! quote results

Working with XSLT Extension Functions

XSLT and XPath provide numerous built-in functions, many of which we've seen and all of which are listed in the handy XSLT/XPath reference available in Appendix D, *Quick References.* In addition to these built-in functions, XSLT 1.0 defines an extension mechanism that allows user-defined functions to be written in any language. By associating an appropriate XML namespace to an external function or function library, you can use the methods and functions in that external library in your stylesheet.

Vendors are free to provide language bindings for their XSLT processor to enable users to author extension functions in those languages. The Oracle XSLT processor supports the XSLT 1.0 specification for extension functions in Java.

Using Existing Java Classes as Extensions

While building stylesheets, you may run into situations where you cannot find a built-in XSLT or XPath function to do the job, and you may already know that there's a Java class that provides the functionality you want. In these cases, you can use an existing Java class as an extension function to augment your transformation to include virtually anything you can access in Java.

To use the methods in a Java class as extension functions, you must declare a namespace for the Java class in your stylesheet. The namespace prefix can be any convenient name, but the namespace URI for the Java class must be a very specific value. To use a class named *package.qualified.Classname*, declare a namespace with the URI:

```
http://www.oracle.com/XSL/Transform/java/package.qualified.Classname
```

A future version of the XSLT specification may standardize the mechanism for extension functions in particular languages like Java, JavaScript, etc. In the interim, each vendor implementing XSLT 1.0 has picked their own scheme for associating a namespace URI with a Java class. Despite this, later in this chapter we illustrate a technique for building a stylesheet that uses Java extensions *and* works with multiple XSLT processors.

For example, to use the `java.lang.Integer` class in your stylesheet, you would declare a namespace on the `<xsl:stylesheet>` element like this:

```
<xsl:stylesheet version="1.0" exclude-result-prefixes="Int"
    xmlns:xsl="http://www.w3.org/1999/XSL/Transform"
    xmlns:Int="http://www.oracle.com/XSL/Transform/java/java.lang.Integer">
```

The `exclude-result-prefixes` attribute on `<xsl:stylesheet>` or the `xsl:exclude-result-prefixes` attribute on a simple-form stylesheet provides a mechanism to tell the XSLT processor that certain namespaces are only meaningful for use by the stylesheet. Here we've chosen `Int` as the prefix for the `java.lang.Integer` class's namespace, so we include `Int` as the value of `exclude-result-prefixes`. If we do not use `exclude-result-prefixes`, then the processor must dutifully copy the `Int` namespace along into the result document. This would do no harm, but it clutters the result document and could be confusing to someone looking at the result of your transformation.

The easiest kind of method to call is a `public static` method. To invoke a `public static` method like `toHexValue()` on the `java.lang.Integer` class that we've set ourselves up to use, we can simply use the syntax `Int:toHexValue(`*`expr`*`)` anywhere in an XPath expression that functions are allowed. This is the namespace-qualified method name using the `Int` namespace.

As with nearly everything in XML, XSLT, and Java, names are case-sensitive, including the method names used here for invoking Java extension functions.

Although it's not very useful in practice, the following stylesheet imports our *TableBaseWithCSS.xsl* from Chapter 7, *Transforming XML with XSLT*, and provides a template that overrides the formatting of the <SAL> element inside a <ROW> by displaying its salary value in hexadecimal:

```
<!-- EmpHex.xsl: Overide basic ROWSET to table to show SAL in Hexadecimal -->
<xsl:stylesheet version="1.0" exclude-result-prefixes="Int"
    xmlns:xsl="http://www.w3.org/1999/XSL/Transform"
    xmlns:Int="http://www.oracle.com/XSL/Transform/java/java.lang.Integer">
  <xsl:import href="TableBaseWithCSS.xsl"/>
  <xsl:template match="SAL">
    <!-- Invoke public static toHexString() method on current node "." -->
    <td align="right"><xsl:value-of select="Int:toHexString(.)"/></td>
  </xsl:template>
</xsl:stylesheet>
```

We can create a quick *Employees.xsql* page to provide some emp data:

```
<!-- Employees.xsql: Query over emp with dynamic ORDER BY -->
<xsql:query sort="Ename" connection="xmlbook" xmlns:xsql="urn:oracle-xsql" >
  <!--
   | The {@dept}+0 "trick" allows the query to be syntactically
   | correct even when no value for the dept parameter is specified.
   | It has to be {@dept}+0 and *not* 0+{@dept} since if {@dept} is
   | missing, you end up with "+0" or "0+". The former is interpreted
   | as "positive zero", a harmless operation. The latter is invalid
   | SQL since "0+" is missing an operand to add to zero...
   +-->
  SELECT ename, sal
    FROM emp
   WHERE {@dept}+0 = 0
      OR deptno = {@dept}+0
   ORDER BY {@sort} {@dir}
</xsql:query>
```

Then we can reuse the *Employees.xsql* data page inside an *EmpHex.xsql* page that applies our *EmpHex.xsl* stylesheet to the *Employees.xsql* page's data like this:

```
<?xml version="1.0"?>
<?xml-stylesheet type="text/xsl" href="EmpHex.xsl" ?>
<!-- Include datapage from Employees.xsql and style it with EmpHex.xsl -->
<xsql:include-xsql href="Employees.xsql" xmlns:xsql="urn:oracle-xsql"/>
```

Requesting *EmpHex.xsql* in the browser with a URL like:

```
http://server/EmpHex.xsql?dept=20
```

produces a listing like the one shown in Figure 16-5 of the employees for department 20 with salaries in hexadecimal.

Your accountant might not like the look of the hex numbers with lowercase letters, so you can use utility methods on a Java class like `java.lang.String` to fix the problem. In contrast to the `toHexString()` method on `java.lang.Integer` that was `public static`, the `toUpperCase()` method on `java.lang.String`

ENAME	SAL
ADAMS	44c
FORD	bb8
JONES	b9f
SCOTT	bb8
SMITH	320

Figure 16-5. Employees in department 20 with hexadecimal salaries

needs to be called on an instance of a **String** object. This is handled by using XSLT variables.

Using a variable, you can assign the return value of a Java extension function without converting its result to one of the built-in XSLT types: **String**, **Number**, **Boolean**, **NodeSet**, or **ResultTreeFragment**. This means you can invoke one function to return an arbitrary Java object into a variable, and then pass that object as an argument to another function using this variable name. XSLT does not understand or do anything with the arbitrary Java object; it just provides the named variable mechanism to assign a name to an instance of the return value and pass it to another extension function.

When calling instance variables in Java, you invoke the method on an instance of an object like this:

```
String name = "steve";
String upperName = name.toUpperCase(); // Invoke method on instance of String obj
```

In XSLT, to invoke an instance method, you have to pass the instance of the object on which you want the method invoked as the first argument to the function instead. Assuming you've defined the **Str** namespace earlier in the stylesheet with the following syntax:

```
xmlns:Str="http://www.oracle.com/XSL/Transform/java/java.lang.String"
```

you can invoke an instance method like **toUpperCase()** on the **String** class like this:

```
<!-- Assume current node has a child element named <LASTNAME> -->
<xsl:value-of select="Str:toUpperCase(LASTNAME)"/>
```

So the **toUpperCase()** instance method is invoked in XSLT by calling a namespace-qualified function of the same name and passing the instance as the first argument. If the Java instance method takes arguments, you must still pass the instance variable as the first argument to the extension function in XSLT, followed by expression values for the remaining Java method arguments in order.

The following *EmpHexUpper.xsl* stylesheet combines the use of **java.lang.Integer** and **java.lang.String**, invoking a public static method on the former and an instance method on the latter, to produce a list of employees with salaries whose values are uppercased hexadecimal:

```
<!-- EmpHexUpper.xsl: Illustrate calling instance methods -->
<xsl:stylesheet version="1.0" exclude-result-prefixes="Int"
    xmlns:xsl="http://www.w3.org/1999/XSL/Transform"
    xmlns:Int="http://www.oracle.com/XSL/Transform/java/java.lang.Integer"
    xmlns:Str="http://www.oracle.com/XSL/Transform/java/java.lang.String">
  <xsl:import href="TableBaseWithCSS.xsl"/>
  <xsl:template match="SAL">
    <!-- Invoke public static toHexString() method on current node "." -->
    <xsl:variable name="HexSal" select="Int:toHexString(.)"/>
    <!-- Invoke instance method on the String instance returned -->
    <td align="right"><xsl:value-of select="Str:toUpperCase($HexSal)"/></td>
  </xsl:template>
</xsl:stylesheet>
```

Refreshing our browser with the earlier URL, we can add the additional URL parameter *xml-stylesheet=EmpHexUpper.xsl* to quickly test this new stylesheet:

```
http://server/EmpHex.xsql?dept=20&xml-stylesheet=EmpHexUpper.xsl
```

We see that it now produces the uppercased hexadecimal salaries.

If you need to actually construct new instances of Java objects from within the stylesheet, as opposed to invoking public static methods that return an instance that's been constructed inside their Java implementation, you can use the `new()` function qualified by the namespace for your Java class. For example, assuming you've declared a namespace prefix `date` for the `java.util.Date` class, you can do this:

```
<!-- Construct a new java.util.Date instance
  in variable "d" -->
<xsl:variable name="d" select="date:new()"/>
<!-- Call Date's toString() method on the new instance -->
<xsl:value-of select="date:toString($d)"/>
```

or you can combine these two steps into one:

```
<xsl:value-of select="date:toString(date:new())"/>
```

Formatting Rainbow-Colored SVG with XSLT

We'll get a little more creative here and illustrate how to put some simple yet useful Java extension functions to work transforming database query results into scalable vector graphics (SVG). SVG is a W3C standard XML vocabulary for encoding scalable line drawings. It includes XML representations for drawing primitives to do some very amazing things, but we'll confine ourselves to using the SVG elements

<rect> and <text> to draw some rectangles and text on a colorful, dynamic bar chart of employee salary information queried straight out of the database.

Example 16-7 shows a utility stylesheet called *CoolColor.xsl* containing a named template called **Mayura:CoolColor**. Just as element names can be disambiguated using XML namespaces, XSLT allows you to use namespace-qualified template names. This can be very useful if you build stylesheets that include or import templates from other stylesheets, especially stylesheets developed by others. Namespace-qualified template names can help you keep your named templates from accidentally overriding each other due to name clashes.

The **Mayura:CoolColor** template makes use of the **java.awt.Color** class and the **java.lang.Integer** class as extension functions. It declares namespace prefixes for both of these classes, as well as for the **Mayura** prefix used to qualify the **Mayura:CoolColor** template name. All three of these prefixes are added appropriately to the **exclude-result-prefixes** attribute value to avoid being copied into result documents produced by the transformation.

The author of Mayura Draw, an impressive shareware drawing tool for Postscript and SVG available from *http://www.mayura.com*, sent me a "cool colors" algorithm that I turned into the **Mayura:CoolColor** XSLT template for use by stylesheets. The named template handles the job of calculating an eye-pleasing rainbow of cool colors with a parameterized number of colored stripes. Given a particular index number for a stripe in the rainbow, it returns the HTML RGB (Red Green Blue) value for the current color of that stripe in the hexadecimal form RRGGBB. Using some magic cool color constants for saturation and brightness, the template sets a variable to the return value of the public static **getHSBColor()** method to retrieve an instance of a **java.awt.Color** object having the correct hue. Then it passes that object instance using this variable to three instance methods on **java.lang.Color** to retrieve the Red, Green, and Blue RGB values separately. Finally, it uses the public static **toHexString()** method on **java.lang.Integer** to convert the RGB values to hex.

Example 16-7. Template for a Rainbow of Cool-Colored Bars

```
<!-- CoolColor.xsl: Return HTML #RRGGBB color for "cool" color combination -->
<xsl:stylesheet version="1.0" exclude-result-prefixes="Color Int Mayura"
     xmlns:xsl    ="http://www.w3.org/1999/XSL/Transform"
     xmlns:Color  ="http://www.oracle.com/XSL/Transform/java/java.awt.Color"
     xmlns:Int    ="http://www.oracle.com/XSL/Transform/java/java.lang.Integer"
     xmlns:Mayura ="http://www.mayura.com/">
<!--
 | This stylesheet implements a "CoolColor" algorithm that Rajeev, the
 | creator of the shareware SVG editor "Mayura Draw" sent me.
 |
 | Given a total number of colors T and an index N between 1 and T
 | the CoolColor algorithm determines an eye-pleasing color combination
```

Example 16-7. Template for a Rainbow of Cool-Colored Bars (continued)

```
 | for the range of T different colors, and returns the HTML #RRGGBB
 | hex representation of the Nth color in the range.
 +-->
  <xsl:template name="Mayura:CoolColor">
    <!-- Accept a color index and the total number of colors in the range -->
    <xsl:param name="colorIndex"/>
    <xsl:param name="totalColors"/>
    <!-- These are the magic values of saturation and brightness -->
    <xsl:variable name="SAT" select="number(0.6)"/>
    <xsl:variable name="BRT" select="number(0.9)"/>
    <!-- Calculate "r","g","b" values for the 'colorIndex'-th color in range -->
    <xsl:variable name="hue" select="$colorIndex div $totalColors"/>
    <!--
     | Use the public static getHSBColor method on java.awt.Color
     |
     | NOTE: This returns a Java object of the Color class as a return value
     |       into the XSLT variable named "c".
     +-->
    <xsl:variable name="c"   select="Color:getHSBColor($hue, $SAT, $BRT)"/>
    <!--
     | Pass the instance of a java.awt.Color object to three other
     | methods on java.awt.Color to extract the r,g,b values separately
     +-->
    <xsl:variable name="r"   select="Color:getRed($c)"/>
    <xsl:variable name="g"   select="Color:getGreen($c)"/>
    <xsl:variable name="b"   select="Color:getBlue($c)"/>
    <!--
     | Use the public static toHexString() method on java.lang.integer
     | to convert the integer color numbers to Hex for HTML #RRGGBB value.
     +-->
    <xsl:variable name="rs"  select="Int:toHexString($r)"/>
    <xsl:variable name="gs"  select="Int:toHexString($g)"/>
    <xsl:variable name="bs"  select="Int:toHexString($b)"/>
    <!-- If any of r, b, or b values was less than 16, add a leading 0 -->
    <xsl:if test="$r &lt; 16">0</xsl:if><xsl:value-of select="$rs"/>
    <xsl:if test="$g &lt; 16">0</xsl:if><xsl:value-of select="$gs"/>
    <xsl:if test="$b &lt; 16">0</xsl:if><xsl:value-of select="$bs"/>
  </xsl:template>
</xsl:stylesheet>
```

We can immediately put the `Mayura:CoolColor` template to work in an XSLT stylesheet that transforms our familiar <ROWSET> query results from an XSQL page into a rainbow-colored bar chart. We do this simply by creating a transformation that transforms a <ROWSET> like this:

```
<ROWSET>
   <ROW num="1">
      <ENAME>CLARK</ENAME>
      <SAL>2450</SAL>
   </ROW>
   <ROW num="2">
      <ENAME>KING</ENAME>
      <SAL>5000</SAL>
   </ROW>
```

```
    <ROW num="3">
      <ENAME>MILLER</ENAME>
      <SAL>1300</SAL>
    &amp;lt;/ROW>
  </ROWSET>
```

into a document using the SVG vocabulary like this:

```
<?xml version='1.0' encoding='UTF-8' standalone='yes'?>
<!DOCTYPE svg SYSTEM "svg-19990812.dtd">
<svg width="1000" height="1000">
  <desc>Salary Chart</desc>
  <g style="stroke:#000000;stroke-width:1;font-family:Arial;font-size:16">
    <rect x="100" y="55" height="25" width="245" style="fill:#e6975c "/>
    <text x="20" y="73">CLARK</text>
    <text x="355" y="73">2450</text>
    <rect x="100" y="90" height="25" width="500" style="fill:#e6d25c "/>
    <text x="20" y="108">KING</text>
    <text x="610" y="108">5000</text>
    <rect x="100" y="125" height="25" width="130" style="fill:#bee65c "/>
    <text x="20" y="143">MILLER</text>
    <text x="240" y="143">1300</text>
  </g>
</svg>
```

When an SVG-compliant viewer opens a document like this having the MIME type `image/svg`, it renders the shapes in the drawing to produce a scalable vector graphic image. By using a browser plug-in like the Adobe SVG plug-in, your Internet Explorer or Netscape browser becomes an SVG-compliant viewer as well.

You can download the Adobe SVG plug-in from:

http://www.adobe.com/svg/

and the IBM SVG viewer from:

http://www.alphaworks.ibm.com

First, let's attack the job of drawing a single SVG bar with a label in the chart. Each bar is made up of a sequence of SVG elements like this:

```
<text ... /> <!-- Text for label                  -->
<rect ... /> <!-- Rectangle for the "bar"         -->
<text ... /> <!-- Text for the value being charted -->
```

A single row is shown in Figure 16-6.

JAMES 950

Figure 16-6. A single bar in an SVG-based bar chart

Example 16-8 shows the `drawBar` named template, which provides a number of input parameters, some with default values. The `drawBar` template allows the caller to specify values for the following parameters:

`barIndex`
: Picks the desired cool color stripe in the rainbow

`label`
: The text label on the chart; for example, `JAMES`

`value`
: The value to chart with respect to the `maxValue` parameter

`maxValue`
: Scales the current value parameter appropriately

`chartWidth`
: Scales the length of the actual rectangle drawn to fit within the dimensions provided by the caller

`rowCount`
: Calculates the total number of color stripes in the rainbow

The `drawBar` template invokes the `Mayura:CoolColor` template with the current bar's index position and the total number of rows to calculate the appropriate cool color for the current bar.

Example 16-8. Drawing an SVG Bar for a Bar Chart

```
<!-- LabeledSVGBar.xsl: Draw a colorful, labeled rectangle for SVG Bar Chart -->
<xsl:stylesheet version="1.0"
     xmlns:xsl    ="http://www.w3.org/1999/XSL/Transform"
     xmlns:Mayura ="http://www.mayura.com/"
     exclude-result-prefixes="Mayura">
 <!-- Include the stylesheet with the "Mayura:CoolColor" template. -->
 <xsl:include href="CoolColor.xsl"/>
 <!-- Draw a rectangle by creating an SVG <rect> element -->
 <xsl:template name="drawBar">
   <xsl:param name="barIndex"   select="0"/>
   <xsl:param name="label"/>
   <xsl:param name="value"      select="0"/>
   <xsl:param name="chartWidth" select="1000"/>
   <xsl:param name="maxValue"   select="$chartWidth"/>
   <xsl:param name="rowCount"   select="1"/>
   <!-- Set up some constant values to use for calculations -->
   <xsl:variable name="xOffset"   select="100"/>
   <xsl:variable name="yOffset"   select="1"/>
   <xsl:variable name="barHeight" select="20"/>
   <xsl:variable name="gap"       select="4"/>
   <!-- Calculate the "x" and "y" coordinates for the rectangle -->
   <xsl:variable name="x" select="$xOffset"/>
   <xsl:variable name="y" select="$yOffset + $barIndex * ($barHeight + $gap)"/>
```

Example 16-8. Drawing an SVG Bar for a Bar Chart (continued)

```
    <!--
     | Calculate the width of the bar
     |
     | NOTE: division in XPath is done with the "x div y" and not "x/y"
     |       since "x/y" is an XPath pattern that matches <y> elements
     |       when they occur as children of <x> elements.
     +-->
    <xsl:variable name="barWidth"
              select="($chartWidth * $value) div (2 * $maxValue)"/>
    <xsl:variable name="fontHeight" select="18"/>
    <!-- Create SVG <text> element to display the label -->
    <text x="20" y="{$y + $fontHeight}">
      <xsl:value-of select="$label"/>
    </text>
    <!-- Create SVG <rect> element to display the label -->
    <rect x="{$x}" y="{$y}" height="{$barHeight}" width="{$barWidth}">
      <!-- Create the <rect> elements "style" attribute w/ dynamic value -->
      <xsl:attribute name="style">
        <xsl:text>fill:#</xsl:text>
        <!--
         | Call the "coolColor" template to get RRGGBB hex value for
         | a pleasing color combination
         +-->
        <xsl:call-template name="Mayura:CoolColor">
          <xsl:with-param name="colorIndex"  select="$barIndex"/>
          <xsl:with-param name="totalColors" select="$rowCount"/>
        </xsl:call-template>
        <xsl:text> </xsl:text>
      </xsl:attribute>
    </rect>
    <xsl:variable name="x2" select="$xOffset + $barWidth + 10"/>
    <!-- Create SVG <text> element to display the value being charted -->
    <text x="{$x2}" y="{$y + $fontHeight}">
      <xsl:value-of select="$value"/>
    </text>
  </xsl:template>
</xsl:stylesheet>
```

Finally, Example 16-9 shows the stylesheet needed to perform the <ROWSET>-to-<svg> transformation for the simple bar chart. The stylesheet uses an `<xsl:output>` element to set the required serialization options for the resulting SVG document as follows:

- It sets the `standalone="yes"` attribute on the `<?xml?>` declaration.
- It sets the `SYSTEM` URI of the doctype to the required *svg-19990812.dtd* DTD.
- It sets the media type to `image/svg`.

The stylesheet also uses `indent="yes"` to make the result more readable, but this is not an SVG requirement. It includes the *LabeledSVGBar.xsl* stylesheet so it can call the **drawBar** template to draw each bar in the bar chart inside its **<xsl:for-each>** that loops over the **ROWSET/ROW** elements. It also puts to use some of what we learned in Chapter 9, *XSLT Beyond the Basics*, to calculate the values of the top-level stylesheet variables **maxSalary** and **totalEmps**.

Example 16-9. Producing Scalable Vector Graphics with XSLT

```
<!-- SalChart.xsl: Draw a colorful bar chart using SVG-->
<xsl:stylesheet version="1.0" xmlns:xsl="http://www.w3.org/1999/XSL/Transform">
  <!-- Include the stylesheet with the "drawBar" template -->
  <xsl:include href="LabeledSVGBar.xsl"/>
  <!-- Width/Height size of chart area-->
  <xsl:variable name="chartSize" select="1000"/>
  <!-- Select max value of salaries being charted -->
  <xsl:variable name="maxSalary">
    <xsl:for-each select="/ROWSET/ROW">
      <xsl:sort data-type="number" select="SAL" order="descending"/>
      <xsl:if test="position()=1">
        <xsl:value-of select="SAL"/>
      </xsl:if>
    </xsl:for-each>
  </xsl:variable>
  <!-- Select count of number of ROW's -->
  <xsl:variable name="totalEmps">
    <xsl:value-of select="count(/ROWSET/ROW)"/>
  </xsl:variable>
  <!--
  | SVG Viewers expect XML Document with SVG DTD and a Media Type of "image/svg"
  +-->
  <xsl:output standalone="yes" doctype-system="svg-19990812.dtd"
              media-type="image/svg" indent="yes"/>
  <!-- Root Template creates outmost <svg> and <g> graphics element-->
  <xsl:template match="/">
   <svg width="{$chartSize}" height="{$chartSize}">
     <xsl:comment><xsl:value-of select="$maxSalary"/></xsl:comment>
     <desc>Salary Chart</desc>
     <g style="stroke:#000000;stroke-width:1;font-family:Arial;font-size:16">
       <!-- Loop over each ROW in the ROWSET -->
       <xsl:for-each select="ROWSET/ROW">
         <!-- Call the "drawBar" template to draw each bar -->
         <xsl:call-template name="drawBar">
           <xsl:with-param name="barIndex"   select="position()"/>
           <xsl:with-param name="label"      select="ENAME"/>
           <xsl:with-param name="value"      select="SAL"/>
           <xsl:with-param name="chartWidth" select="$chartSize"/>
           <xsl:with-param name="maxValue"   select="$maxSalary"/>
           <xsl:with-param name="rowCount"   select="$totalEmps"/>
         </xsl:call-template>
       </xsl:for-each>
     </g>
   </svg>
  </xsl:template>
</xsl:stylesheet>
```

We can create an XSQL page called *SalChart.xsql* that includes the *Employees.xsql* data page and applies the *SalChart.xsl* stylesheet like this:

```
<?xml version="1.0"?>
<!-- SalChart.xsql -->
<?xml-stylesheet type="text/xsl" href="SalChart.xsl" ?>
<!-- Include datapage from Employees.xsql and style it with SalChart.xsl -->
<xsql:include-xsql href="Employees.xsql" xmlns:xsql="urn:oracle-xsql"/>
```

We can now request our database-driven, XSLT-powered SVG chart in our browser (after installing the Adobe SVG plug-in) using the URL:

```
http://server/SalChart.xsql
```

which returns the chart of the data ordered by `ENAME` as shown in Figure 16-7.

Running your XSQL pages from within JDeveloper 3.1, the IDE automatically makes sure that the CLASSPATH contains any classes in your current project as well as those from any libraries in your project's Library List.

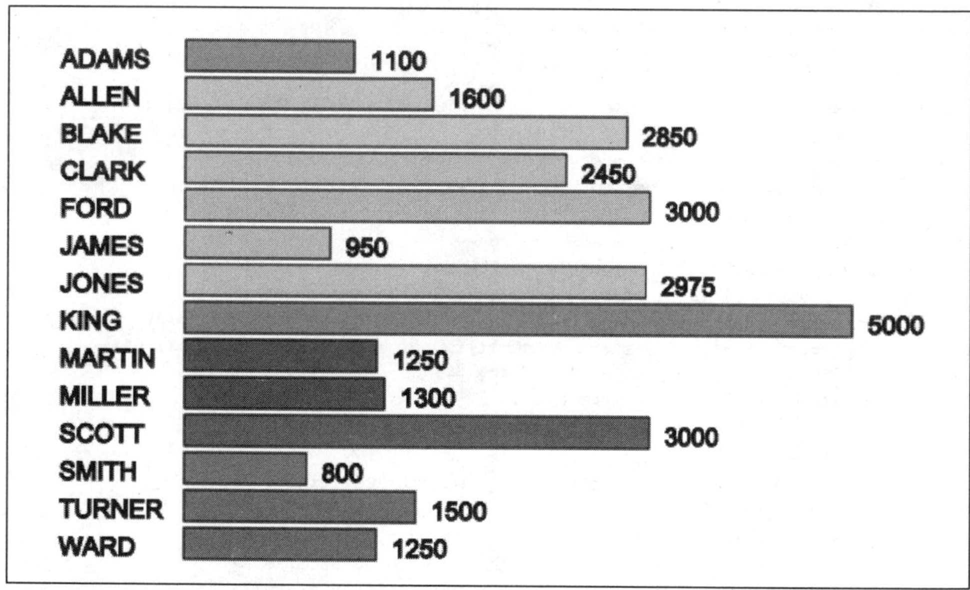

Figure 16-7. Dynamic SVG bar chart transformed from live data

Since the underlying *Employees.xsql* page contained a parameterized ORDER BY clause, we can pass the value `SAL` to the page's sort parameter to sort the data in the data page by salary before it's charted using the *SalChart.xsl* stylesheet with the URL:

```
http://server/SalChart.xsql?sort=sal
```

This produces the chart ordered by the SAL column.

Writing Your Own Java Extension Functions

When you cannot find the function you need among the built-in XPath and XSLT functions, and when no existing Java class does exactly what you need for your transformation, you can write your own Java extension functions and use them in a stylesheet just as we used the Java JDK classes above.

Overloading based on number and type of parameters is supported. The XSLT processor does implicit type conversion between the XSLT types `String`, `Number`, `Boolean`, and `ResultTreeFragment`, and it also performs implicit conversion from a `NodeSet` to a `String`, `Number`, `Boolean`, or `ResultTreeFragment`. Attempting to overload methods based on two types that can be implicitly converted to each other will result in an error.

The following table illustrates the datatype mapping performed between XSLT/XPath types and Java types:

XSLT/XPath Datatype	Java Datatype
`String`	`java.lang.String`
`Number`	`int, float, double`
`Boolean`	`boolean`
`NodeSet`	`oracle.xml.parser.v2.XMLNodeList`, `org.w3c.dom.NodeList`
`ResultTreeFragment`	`oracle.xml.parser.v2.XMLDocumentFragment`, `org.w3c.dom.DocumentFragment`

Example 16-10 shows the `MarkupExtensions` class with its `xmlMarkup()` public static method that we put to use in Chapter 12, *Storing XML Datagrams*. Given any `NodeSet` passed in as an argument, it returns the string representation of that `NodeSet` as XML markup. Techniques to achieve this using pure XSLT are quite messy and difficult to understand. In Java, simply invoke the `print()` method on each node in the node list to serialize that node as XML.

Example 16-10. Extension Function to Write XML as Text Markup

```
import org.w3c.dom.*;
import oracle.xml.parser.v2.*;
import java.io.*;
public class MarkupExtensions {
  public static String xmlMarkup(NodeList nl) throws Exception {
```

Example 16-10. Extension Function to Write XML as Text Markup (continued)

```
    if (nl != null) {
      // Wrap a StringWriter by a PrintWriter
      StringWriter sw = new StringWriter();
      PrintWriter  pw = new PrintWriter(sw);
      int nodes = nl.getLength();
      // Loop over the nodes in the node list. Tell each one to print itself
      for (int z = 0; z < nodes ; z++ ) {
        // Print XML markup for current node
        ((XMLNode)nl.item(z)).print(pw);
      }
      // Return the StringBuffer of the StringWriter
      return sw.toString();
    }
    return "";
  }
}
```

In Chapter 17, we'll see some examples of XSLT named templates that perform string replacement. The technique relies on a named template's recursively invoking itself until there are no occurrences left of the substring you're trying to replace. If you need to replace many different strings by many different other strings, this technique can get messy in a hurry with pure XSLT syntax. A great example of this scenario is creating URLs with illegal characters properly escaped as hex codes.

Certain characters have special meaning in a URL:

Character	Meaning in a URL
?	Separates the base URL from any request parameters
&	Separates multiple request parameters
/	Separates directory names in the URL
Space	Creates gaps in the characters comprising the URL
%	Used to quote illegal characters

The Internet Engineering Task Force (IETF) RFC2396 specification says that these as well as several others should be quoted as two-digit hex values representing their ASCII code equivalents when they occur in a URL. The **`URLEncoder.EncodeURLArgs()`** method in Example 16-11 efficiently handles the substitution of all necessary illegal URL characters by their *xx* hex equivalents.

Example 16-11. EncodeURLArgs XSLT Extension Function

```
import java.util.BitSet;
public class URLEncoder {
  // See http://www.ietf.org/rfc/rfc2396.txt
  private static final String list    = " <>#%&\\/?{}[]|^`\"";
  private static        BitSet escList = new BitSet(256);
```

Example 16-11. EncodeURLArgs XSLT Extension Function (continued)

```
  // Return a string with rfc2396 URL encoding done on it
  public static String EncodeURLArgs( String s ) {
    if (s == null || s.equals("")) {
      return s;
    }
    else {
      StringBuffer b = new StringBuffer();
      int len = s.length();
      for (int z = 0; z < len; z++) {
        char c = s.charAt(z);
        if (escList.get(c)) {
          b.append("%"+Integer.toHexString((int)c).toUpperCase());
        }
        else {
          b.append(c);
        }
      }
      return b.toString();
    }
  }
  static {
    escList = new BitSet(256);
    int len = list.length();
    for (int z = 0; z < len; z++) {
      escList.set(list.charAt(z));
    }
  }
}
```

This allows your XSLT stylesheets to perform the URL encoding on any string value like this:

```
<!--
 | Use the URLEncoder class' EncodeURLArgs method.
 | NOTE: The URLEncode class is not defined in a package, so its
 |       "fully package qualified classname" is just URLEncoder.
 +-->
<xsl:stylesheet version="1.0" exclude-result-prefixes="url"
     xmlns:xsl ="http://www.w3.org/1999/XSL/Transform"
     xmlns:url ="http://www.oracle.com/XSL/Transform/java/URLEncoder">
  <xsl:template match="SomePattern">
    <xsl:variable name="urlVariable" select="SomeExpression"/>
    <!-- Copy the URLEncoded value of the $urlVariable to the result tree -->
    <xsl:value-of select="url:EncodeURLArgs($urlVariable)"/>
    <!-- Copy the URLEncoded value of any XPath expression to the result tree -->
    <xsl:value-of select="url:EncodeURLArgs(AnyExpression)"/>
  </xsl:template>
</xsl:stylesheet>
```

If you need to make your XSLT stylesheets portable across different vendors' XSLT implementations, using Java extension functions can present a problem since each vendor uses a different namespace scheme for specifying Java classes. One way to write a stylesheet that works with any XSLT processor that supports extension functions in Java is to build your stylesheet to include namespace prefixes for all the different namespace URIs that you need to reference, and then use the XSLT function named **function-available()** to test whether a given function in one of the namespaces is available before using it.

The stylesheet in Example 16-12 uses the **URLEncoder** class's **EncodeURLArgs()** method as a Java extension function in a way that will work with Oracle XSLT, Saxon 5.3, and James Clark's XT processor.

Example 16-12. Designing for XSLT Processor Portability

```
<!--
 | PortableURLEncoderTest.xsl: Shows how to use Java extension functions
 | in a way that can work across different vendor's XSLT implementations
 +-->

<xsl:stylesheet version="1.0" exclude-result-prefixes="xtUrl oracleUrl saxonUrl"
     xmlns:xsl       ="http://www.w3.org/1999/XSL/Transform"
     xmlns:xtUrl     ="http://www.jclark.com/xt/java/URLEncoder"
     xmlns:oracleUrl ="http://www.oracle.com/XSL/Transform/java/URLEncoder"
     xmlns:saxonUrl  ="http://anythinghere/URLEncoder">
  <xsl:output method="text"/>
  <xsl:template match="/">
    <xsl:variable name="urlBase">http://foo.com/SomeService</xsl:variable>
    <xsl:variable name="urlArgs" select="'company=at &amp; t / mobilecom'"/>
    <xsl:variable name="quotedUrlArgs">
      <!-- Invoking the xsl:call-template inside  -->
      <xsl:call-template name="escapeURLArgs">
        <xsl:with-param name="text" select="$urlArgs"/>
      </xsl:call-template>
    </xsl:variable>
    <!-- Output the URL as the concatentation of urlBase+"?"+quotedUrlArgs -->
    <xsl:value-of select="concat($urlBase,'?',$quotedUrlArgs)"/>
  </xsl:template>
  <xsl:template name="escapeURLArgs">
    <xsl:param name="text"/>
    <xsl:choose>
      <!-- If xtUrl:EncodeURLArgs is available, then invoke it... -->
      <xsl:when test="function-available('xtUrl:EncodeURLArgs')">
        <xsl:value-of select="xtUrl:EncodeURLArgs($text)"/>
      </xsl:when>
      <!-- If saxonUrl:EncodeURLArgs is available, then invoke it... -->
      <xsl:when test="function-available('saxonUrl:EncodeURLArgs')">
        <xsl:value-of select="saxonUrl:EncodeURLArgs($text)"/>
      </xsl:when>
      <!-- If oracleUrl:EncodeURLArgs is available, then invoke it... -->
      <xsl:when test="function-available('oracleUrl:EncodeURLArgs')">
        <xsl:value-of select="oracleUrl:EncodeURLArgs($text)"/>
      </xsl:when>
    </xsl:choose>
  </xsl:template>
</xsl:stylesheet>
```

This example stylesheet selects a string value for a **urlBase** variable of:

```
http://foo.com/SomeService
```

and a string value for a **urlArgs** variable of:

```
company=at & t / mobilcom
```

which contains some spaces, an ampersand, and a slash. To test this example transformation, you can use any XML file as the source and try the following:

- With James Clark's **xt** XSLT 1.0 processor:

  ```
  $ xt anyfile.xml PortableURLEncoderTest.xsl
  ```

- With Michael Kay's Saxon XSLT 1.0 processor:

  ```
  $ saxon anyfile.xml PortableURLEncoderTest.xsl
  ```

- With the Oracle XSLT 1.0 Processor:

  ```
  $ oraxsl anyfile.xml PortableURLEncoderTest.xsl
  ```

All three processors produce the following identical output:

```
http://foo.com/SomeService?company=at%20%26%20t%20%2F%20mobilecom
```

We can write a stylesheet that refers to extension functions in several different namespaces (only one of which we're expecting to be usable by the current processor at transformation time) because an XSLT 1.0–compliant processor signals errors only if you actually try to *use* the function. By wrapping the extension function in a named template that uses **<xsl:choose>** and **function-available()** to selectively invoke the correct function, we can avoid the situation of ever invoking a function that is not available.

Debugging Your XSLT Java Extension Functions

You will certainly need to debug your XSLT Java extension functions to make sure they are working correctly. Using JDeveloper 3.1, you have two choices for how to do this, both straightforward.

If you are using XSLT in combination with XSQL Pages, you can follow the steps we outlined earlier for debugging XSQL page action handlers. If you set breakpoints in the Java code for your own XSLT extension functions, the debugger will stop at your breakpoint when your function is invoked by the XSLT processor.

If you want to debug from the command line, you can use JDeveloper 3.1 remote debugging support to debug the command-line Oracle XSLT processor. In order to remotely debug the **oraxsl** command-line utility, do the following:

- For the simplest possible experience, make sure you run the **oraxsl** command-line utility using the Java 1.2 VM supplied with JDeveloper 3.1. This VM natively supports remote debugging on Windows NT, where you'll be using

JDeveloper 3.1. If you've installed JDeveloper 3.1 in the *C:\jdev31* directory, for example, the complete path to the Java VM is *C:\jdev31\java1.2\bin\java.exe.*

- Run the **oraxsl** command-line utility using the remote debugging argument to the Java VM. If you are trying to test the transformation of *source.xml* by the *style.xsl* stylesheet that makes use of your extension functions, the exact command will be:

  ```
  java -XXdebug oracle.xml.parser.v2.oraxsl source.xml style.xsl
  ```

  If you run this command with the JDeveloper 3.1 Java VM, you will immediately see the following message on the console:

  ```
  *** Port is 4000 ***
  *** Waiting for debugger connection. ***
  ```

  At this point, the **oraxsl** program is halted and will not proceed to execute until you attach the JDeveloper 3.1 debugger to it.

- In your JDeveloper 3.1 project where the source code for your Java XSLT extension functions resides, make sure that your project is set up for remote debugging. To check this setting, select *Project→ Project Properties* from the main menu, click the *Run/Debug* tab, and set the *Debug As* pop-up list to "Remote Debugging".
- Set your desired breakpoints in your extension function source code.
- Click the Debug icon in the toolbar.
- When the *Remote Debugging* dialog appears, enter **localhost** for the machine name and 4000 for the port, then click *Attach.*

When the debugger attaches to the **oraxsl** process, program execution begins, and you'll hit your breakpoints as soon as the XSLT processor invokes your extension functions.

17

In this chapter:

- *XSLT-Powered Web Store*
- *Building a Personalized News Portal*
- *Online Discussion Forum*

XSLT-Powered Portals and Applications

In this last chapter, we'll work our way through all of the important capabilities of XSLT in the context of building some interesting Oracle XML applications. By the end of this chapter, I predict you will be an incurable XSLT fanatic as its amazing flexibility transforms you into a more productive developer.

XSLT-Powered Web Store

In this section, we'll build a simple site for a web store that offers the basic functionality illustrated in Figure 17-1.

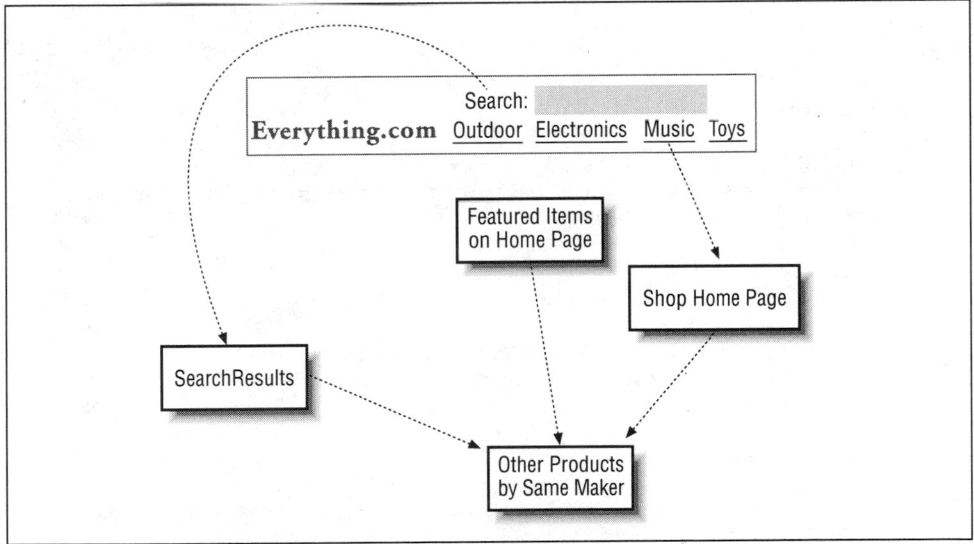

Figure 17-1. Page map of the Everything.com web site

Visitors to the site will be able to see featured items on the home page and can click the name of one of our "shops" to see a home page specific to that shop. They can search the site for a product, and whenever a product appears, they can click a link to see other products by the same manufacturer.

Turning HTML Mockup into an XSLT stylesheet

All product information needs to be displayed consistently across the web store. Our web design team has provided us with an HTML mockup, shown in Figure 17-2, of how each product should look on the site. The HTML file for the mockup is shown in Example 17-1.

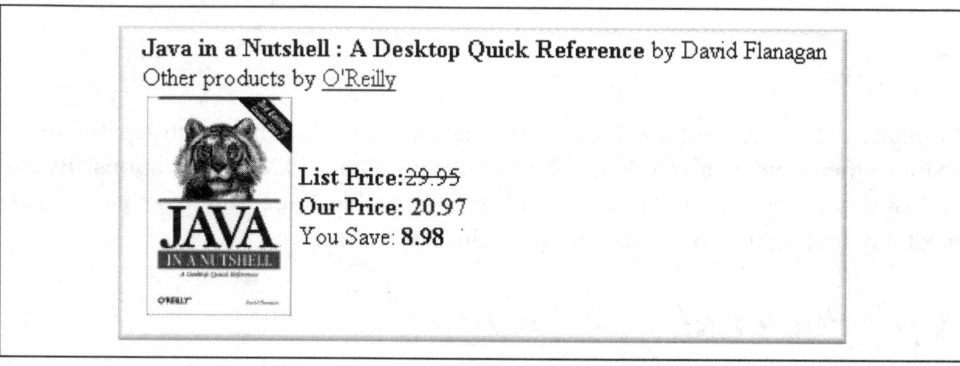

Figure 17-2. Mockup of product display for our web store

Example 17-1. Source for HTML Mockup of Product Information

```
<html>
  <body>
    <center>
    <table border="0">
      <tr>
      <td valign="top">
        <b>Java in a Nutshell : A Desktop Quick Reference</b> by David Flanagan
        <br>Other products by <a href="xxxx">O'Reilly</a>
        <br>
        <table border="0"><tr>
          <td><img src="images/1565924878.gif"></td>
            <td valign="middle">
            <b>List Price:</b><strike>29.95</strike><br>
            <b>Our Price: <font color="blue">20.97</font></b><br>
            You Save: <b>8.98</b>
          </td>
        </tr></table>
      </td>
      </tr>
    </table>
    </center>
  </body>
</html>
```

We'll use Dave Raggett's Tidy tool (described in Chapter 6, *Processing XML with Java*) to convert the web designer's HTML source code into an indented, well-formed XML file that will evolve into an XSLT stylesheet that produces the same look and feel. Run Tidy as follows:

```
tidy -asxml -indent ProductMockup.html > Product.xsl
```

The `tidy` command produces a well-formed XML document in the *Product.xsl* file, shown in Example 17-2, which we can use as a starting point for the XSLT transformation.

Example 17-2. Tidied HTML Mockup in XML

```
<?xml version="1.0"?>
<!DOCTYPE html PUBLIC "-//W3C//DTD XHTML 1.0 Transitional//EN"
    "http://www.w3.org/TR/xhtml1/DTD/xhtml1-transitional.dtd">
<html xmlns="http://www.w3.org/1999/xhtml">
  <head>
    <meta name="generator" content="HTML Tidy, see www.w3.org" />
    <title>
    </title>
  </head>
  <body>
    <center>
      <table border="0">
        <tr>
          <td valign="top">
            <b>Java in a Nutshell : A Desktop Quick Reference</b>
            by David Flanagan<br />
            Other products by <a href="xxxx">O'Reilly</a><br />

            <table border="0">
              <tr>
                <td>
                  <img src="images/1565924878.gif" />
                </td>
                <td valign="middle">
                  <b>List Price:</b><strike>29.95</strike><br />
                   <b>Our Price: <font color="blue">
                  20.97</font></b><br />
                   You Save: <b>8.98</b>
                </td>
              </tr>
            </table>
          </td>
        </tr>
      </table>
    </center>
  </body>
</html>
```

We can easily turn this tidied-up HTML into an XSLT stylesheet that uses a single root template. We just need to wrap the entire content of the document by:

```
<xsl:stylesheet version="1.0" xmlns:xsl="http://www.w3.org/1999/XSL/Transform">
  <!-- For best results with HTML, best not to introduce any extra whitespace -->
  <xsl:output method="html" indent="no"/>
  <xsl:template match="/">
    <!-- Tidied-up HTML document goes here -->
  </xsl:template>
</xsl:stylesheet>
```

We don't need the <!DOCTYPE> and/or <META> for our purposes, so we just delete it. At this point we have a valid, functional XSLT stylesheet that will output the *static* HTML mockup. In order to turn the static template into a page that *dynamically* formats production information from our database, we need to perform two basic steps:

- Build an XSQL page to assemble the dynamic XML data page with all necessary production information
- Replace the static sample information in the XSLT stylesheet with XSLT actions to plug our dynamic XML into the template HTML format.

First things first; we'll start by building the XSQL page.

Building an XSQL Page to Assemble Data

Figure 17-3 illustrates our database schema related to products on the web store.

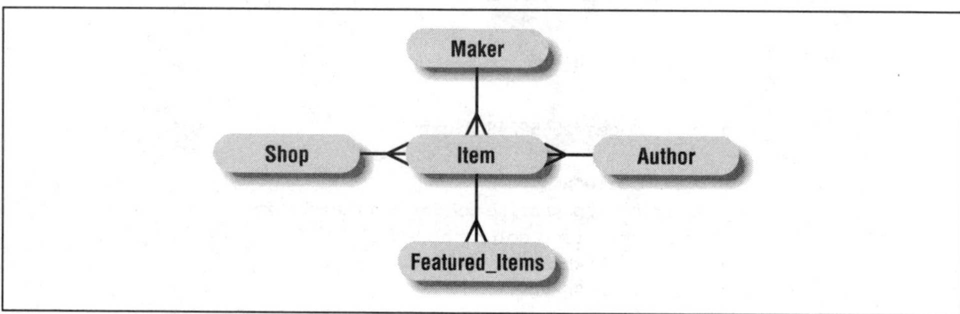

Figure 17-3. Database tables involved in the web store

We create the following *Store.xsql* page to query the product information from the item, author, maker, and shop tables, using an outer join for the optional author information. Note that we've planned ahead and already associated the *Product.xsl* stylesheet we're building to format products for the Web.

```
<?xml version="1.0"?>
<?xml-stylesheet type="text/xsl" href="Product.xsl"?>
<xsql:query max-rows="1" sid="1" connection="xmlbook" xmlns:xsql="urn:oracle-xsql">
```

```
SELECT description,
       author_name,
        maker_name,
        maker.id AS maker_id,
         shop_name,
        list_price,
            price,
        list_price - price AS yousave,
              sku
  FROM item, author, maker, shop
  WHERE item.author_id = author.id (+)
    AND item.maker_id  = maker.id
    AND item.shop_id   = shop.id
    AND shop.id = {@sid}
</xsql:query>
```

Since we'll just be testing the page initially, we add the following two additional attributes on the **<xsql:query>** action element:

max-rows="1"
: Limits the product rows retrieved to a single row

sid="1"
: Produces a default value for the "shop id" parameter **sid** in case none is specified in the request

Requesting the *Shop.xsql* page through our browser, or using the **xsql** command-line utility, we see that this produces the following raw XML datagram:

```
<?xml version = '1.0'?>
<ROWSET>
   <ROW num="1">
      <DESCRIPTION>Manifest Destiny</DESCRIPTION>
      <AUTHOR_NAME>Daisy Dines</AUTHOR_NAME>
      <MAKER_NAME>Fly Rite</MAKER_NAME>
      <MAKER_ID>3</MAKER_ID>
      <SHOP_NAME>Outdoors</SHOP_NAME>
      <LIST_PRICE>13.95</LIST_PRICE>
      <PRICE>11.16</PRICE>
      <YOUSAVE>2.79</YOUSAVE>
      <SKU>0140060898</SKU>
   </ROW>
</ROWSET>
```

With the basic data in place, we turn our attention to evolving the tidied-up HTML mockup, which is now an XSLT stylesheet, into a dynamic data display.

Plugging Dynamic Data into the Stylesheet

We want to design the stylesheet to handle any number of rows of products that might be produced by the query over the product information. For each **<ROW>** element in the **<ROWSET>**, we want to create an HTML table row (**<tr>**) containing the product formatted in the standard way. So we introduce an `<xsl:for-each>` element to wrap the repeating HTML table row, with a `select="ROWSET/ROW"` pattern to select all rows in the dynamic XSQL data page. The contents of the `<xsl:for-each>` element will be instantiated in the resulting page for each `ROWSET/ROW` node selected.

Inside the `<xsl:for-each>` loop, the selected `<ROW>` element is the current node, so any XPath expressions needed to refer to data in the row can use relative patterns. In particular, we do the following, using relative XPath expressions:

1. Replace the static product description:

   ```
   <b>Java in a Nutshell : A Desktop Quick Reference</b>
   by David Flanagan
   ```

   with the dynamic expression:

   ```
   <b><xsl:value-of select="DESCRIPTION"/></b>
   by <xsl:value-of select="AUTHOR_NAME"/>
   ```

2. Replace the static text and hyperlink `href` value in:

   ```
   Other products by <a href="xxxx">O'Reilly</a>
   ```

   with:

   ```
   Other products by <a href="Maker.xsql?id={MAKER_ID}">
                       <xsl:value-of select="MAKER_NAME"/>
                     </a>
   ```

   using an attribute value template `{MAKER_ID}` to substitute the current row's `MAKER_ID` into the `href` attribute value. This will be the `id` parameter passed to the *Maker.xsql* page we'll build later showing all products for a given maker ID.

3. Replace the static `src` attribute's URL:

   ```
   <img src="images/1565924878.gif" />
   ```

   with:

   ```
   <img src="images/{SKU}.gif" />
   ```

4. Replace the static price information:

   ```
   <b>List Price:</b><strike>29.95</strike><br />
   <b>Our Price: <font color="blue">20.97</font></b><br />
   You Save: <b>8.98</b>
   ```

   with:

   ```
   <b>List Price:</b><strike>
                       <xsl:value-of select="LIST_PRICE"/>
                     </strike><br/>
   <b>Our Price: <font color="blue">
                   <xsl:value-of select="PRICE"/>
                 </font></b><br />
   You Save: <b><xsl:value-of select="YOUSAVE"/></b>
   ```

The resulting XSLT stylesheet is shown in Example 17-3.

Example 17-3. Stylesheet to Format Web Store Product Information

```
<!-- Product.xsl: Format Web Store product information -->
<xsl:stylesheet version="1.0" xmlns:xsl="http://www.w3.org/1999/XSL/Transform">
  <!-- For best results with HTML, best not to introduce extra whitespace -->
  <xsl:output method="html" indent="no"/>
  <xsl:template match="/">
    <html>
      <body>
        <center>
          <table border="0">
            <xsl:for-each select="ROWSET/ROW">
            <tr>
              <td valign="top">
                <b><xsl:value-of select="DESCRIPTION"/></b>
                by <xsl:value-of select="AUTHOR_NAME"/><br/>
                Other products by <a href="Maker.xsql?id={MAKER_ID}">
                                    <xsl:value-of select="MAKER_NAME"/>
                                  </a><br/>
                <table border="0">
                  <tr>
                    <td>
                      <img src="images/{SKU}.gif" />
                    </td>
                    <td valign="middle">
                      <b>List Price:</b><strike>
                                          <xsl:value-of select="LIST_PRICE"/>
                                        </strike><br/>
                      <b>Our Price: <font color="blue">
                                      <xsl:value-of select="PRICE"/>
                                    </font></b><br />
                       You Save: <b><xsl:value-of select="YOUSAVE"/></b><br/>
                    </td>
                  </tr>
                </table>
              </td>
            </tr>
            </xsl:for-each>
          </table>
        </center>
      </body>
    </html>
  </xsl:template>
</xsl:stylesheet>
```

Requesting the *Store.xsql* page in our browser with the URL:

```
http://server/Store.xsql
```

uses the default store ID of 1, retrieves the first product row, and transforms it for display, producing the output shown in Figure 17-4.

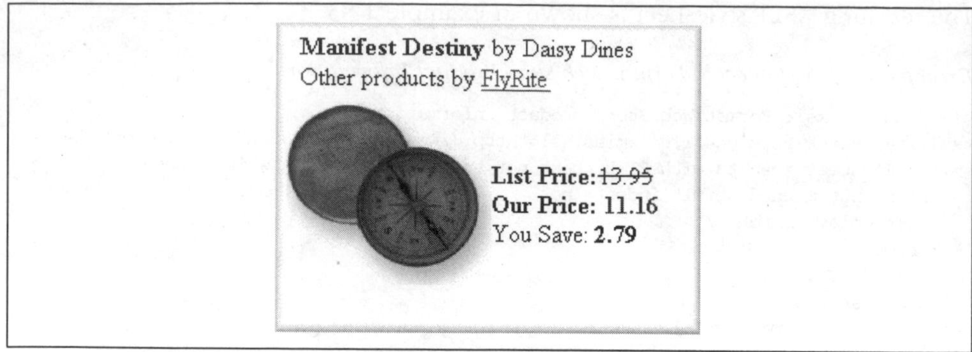

Figure 17-4. HTML output of product from the Outdoors shop

This looks just like what the web designers wanted.

Formatting Numbers and Conditional Formatting

If we request the *Store.xsql* page in our browser, passing a value of `4` for the `sid` parameter to test out an example product in our Toys shop:

```
http://server/Store.xsql?sid=4
```

we get the result shown in Figure 17-5.

Figure 17-5. Same stylesheet formatting product from the Toys shop

We immediately notice a few problems:

- The word "by" appears all alone after the product description because toys don't have authors recorded in our database.
- The "List Price" and "You Save" sections come up blank since we apparently don't record a `list_price` for toys.
- The $6.00 price for the Cymbal Clapping Monkey formats as `6` instead of `6.00`

Let's temporarily turn off the stylesheet processing by adding an **xml-stylesheet=none** to the end of the URL:

```
http://server/Store.xsql?sid=4&xml-stylesheet=none
```

This allows us to see the underlying raw dynamic data page that the XSLT stylesheet is seeing during the transformation:

```
<?xml version = '1.0'?>
<ROWSET>
   <ROW num="1">
      <DESCRIPTION>Cymbal Clapping Monkey</DESCRIPTION>
      <MAKER_NAME>Circus Fun</MAKER_NAME>
      <MAKER_ID>1</MAKER_ID>
      <SHOP_NAME>Toys</SHOP_NAME>
      <PRICE>6</PRICE>
      <SKU>B00000IWIT</SKU>
   </ROW>
</ROWSET>
```

We see that the value 6 is being selected from the database as is, so we'll change our query to format the numbers the way we want them. This will fix one problem:

```
<?xml version="1.0"?>
<?xml-stylesheet type="text/xsl" href="Product.xsl"?>
<xsql:query max-rows="1" sid="1" connection="xmlbook" xmlns:xsql="urn:oracle-xsql">
 SELECT description,
        author_name,
         maker_name,
         maker.id as maker_id,
          shop_name,
         TO_CHAR(list_price,'999999.00')         AS list_price,
         TO_CHAR(price,'999999.00')              AS price,
         TO_CHAR(list_price - price,'999999.00') AS yousave,
               sku
   FROM item, author, maker, shop
   WHERE item.author_id = author.id (+)
     AND item.maker_id  = maker.id
     AND item.shop_id   = shop.id
     AND shop.id = {@sid}
</xsql:query>
```

The other two problems indicate a need to conditionally format information. We want to display the author name if there is one and handle the "List Price" and the corresponding "You Save" sections similarly. We can use the **<xsl:if>** action to wrap portions of the stylesheet template that need to be conditionally included. The **<xsl:if>** element has a required **test="*expression*"** attribute that indicates an XPath expression to be evaluated. If the expression tests **true**, then the content of the **<xsl:if>** is instantiated in the result tree. Otherwise, it is left out.

While any XPath expression is valid to include in an `<xsl:if>` element's test attribute, one of the most common expressions used is a pattern to match an element or attribute. If the pattern matches at least one node, the test evaluates to `true`. If no matches are selected by the pattern, the test evaluates to `false`. For example, to test whether an <AUTHOR_NAME> child element exists for the current node, you can use:

```
<xsl:if test="AUTHOR_NAME">
```

This returns `true` if an <AUTHOR_NAME> child element exists and `false` otherwise. If you need to check that an element exists and that it has a non-empty value, you can use a test like:

```
<xsl:if test="AUTHOR_NAME != ''">
```

We wrap the display of <AUTHOR_NAME>, `<LIST_PRICE>`, and <YOUSAVE> elements with appropriate `<xsl:if>` tests to produce the *Product.xsl* stylesheet in Example 17-4.

Example 17-4. Stylesheet to Correctly Format All Web Store Products

```
<!-- Product.xsl: Format Web Store product information -->
<xsl:stylesheet version="1.0" xmlns:xsl="http://www.w3.org/1999/XSL/Transform">
  <!-- For best results with HTML, best not to introduce extra whitespace -->
  <xsl:output method="html" indent="no"/>
  <xsl:template match="/">
    <html>
      <body>
        <center>
          <table border="0">
            <xsl:for-each select="ROWSET/ROW">
            <tr>
              <td valign="top">
                <b><xsl:value-of select="DESCRIPTION"/></b>
                <xsl:if test="AUTHOR_NAME">
                    by <xsl:value-of select="AUTHOR_NAME"/>
                </xsl:if><br/>
                Other products by <a href="Maker.xsql?id={MAKER_ID}">
                                    <xsl:value-of select="MAKER_NAME"/>
                                  </a><br/>
                <table border="0">
                  <tr>
                    <td>
                      <img src="images/{SKU}.gif" />
                    </td>
                    <td valign="middle">
                      <xsl:if test="LIST_PRICE">
                      <b>List Price:</b><strike>
                                          <xsl:value-of select="LIST_PRICE"/>
                                        </strike><br/>
                      </xsl:if>
                      <b>Our Price: <font color="blue">
```

Example 17-4. Stylesheet to Correctly Format All Web Store Products (continued)

```
                                          <xsl:value-of select="PRICE"/>
                                        </font></b><br />
                          <xsl:if test="LIST_PRICE">
                           You Save: <b><xsl:value-of select="YOUSAVE"/></b>
                          </xsl:if>
                        </td>
                      </tr>
                    </table>
                  </td>
                </tr>
                </xsl:for-each>
              </table>
            </center>
          </body>
        </html>
  </xsl:template>
</xsl:stylesheet>
```

Refreshing the browser page, we see in Figure 17-6 that this now properly handles the missing author and list price.

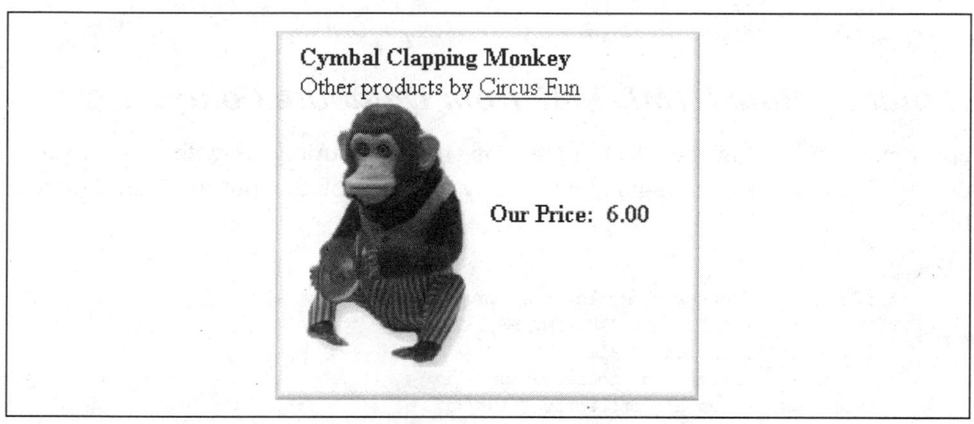

Figure 17-6. Formatting price and handling missing author and list price

Going back to our numerical formatting, when using XSLT to format database query results, there are two strategies for formatting numbers:

- Use the database `TO_CHAR()` function in your SELECT statement to format the number using SQL format masks.
- Use the XSLT `format-number()` function.

The first strategy is easier if you're already familiar with the SQL `TO_CHAR()` function and its format mask language. The latter is better if you need to work with the numerical value of an element within the stylesheet for calculations. For example, if your query includes `TO_CHAR(SAL,'$9,999.00') AS SALARY` in its SELECT list, the corresponding `<SALARY>$2,450.00</SALARY>` will work fine if you are simply including its value verbatim into the transformed result. However, if your stylesheet needs to test if the expression `SALARY > 4500` is `true`, or needs to use the value of `<SALARY>` in a calculated expression, having a `<SALARY>` value from the database that includes a dollar sign and commas will cause problems.

The XSLT `format-number()` function takes arguments for the number and the format mask, but it uses the format masks supported by the `java.text.DecimalFormat` class in the JDK. While other pattern characters are supported, the four key pattern characters of immediate interest are:

`0` A digit

`#` A digit, zero shows as absent

`.` Placeholder for a decimal separator

`,` Placeholder for a group separator

Any character, such as a dollar sign, can appear at the start or the end of a format mask. To format our `<LIST_PRICE>` element using `format-number()` we would use the syntax:

```
<xsl:value-of select="format-number(LIST_PRICE,'0.00')"/>
```

Handling Raw HTML/XML from Database Columns

For some products in the Electronics shop, vendors supply us with a short product blurb in HTML that highlights the key features of the product. An example blurb looks like this:

```
<ul>
  <li>AM/FM and shortwave world-time travel clock radio</li>
  <li>11-band travel radio (AM, FM, SW 1-9)</li>
  <li>LED tuning indicator</li>
  <li>Built-in alarm with snooze button</li>
  <li>Compact design and protective lid</li>
</ul>
```

We can easily add the `BLURB` column to the SELECT list in our *Store.xsql* page, and add another conditional section in our stylesheet:

```
<xsl:if test="BLURB">
  <br/>
  <b><u>Features</u></b><br/>
  <xsl:value-of select="BLURB"/>
</xsl:if>
```

However, if we attempt to request *Store.xsql* on an item in the Electronics shop with a URL like this:

```
http://server/Store.xsql?sid=3
```

we'll see a "Features" section in the browser like that shown in Figure 17-7.

Features
<ul> <li>AM/FM and shortwave world-time travel clock radio</li> <li>11-band travel radio (AM, FM, SW 1-9) </li> <li>LED tuning indicator</li> <li>Built-in alarm with snooze button</li> <li>Compact design and protective lid</li> </ul>

Figure 17-7. Display of HTML markup escaped by XSLT processor

Yikes! This occurs because an XSLT processor is required to escape all illegal characters like angle brackets and ampersands when they occur in text values, so the browser displays the literal angle bracket characters and ampersands as text. We want these literal characters to appear verbatim and unescaped in the output of the transform so the browser will interpret them as HTML tags and not display them as literal angle brackets. For these cases, XSLT supplies the optional `disable-output-escaping="yes"` attribute on `<xsl:value-of>` or `<xsl:text>`. This instructs the processor to disregard the normal escaping mechanism and allows the literal HTML or XML markup to pass through verbatim to the result document. So if we rewrite our `BLURB` section of the stylesheet to look like this:

```
<xsl:if test="BLURB">
  <br/>
  <b><u>Features</u></b><br/>
  <xsl:value-of disable-output-escaping="yes" select="BLURB"/>
</xsl:if>
```

then the products in our Electronics shop will now display correctly, as shown in Figure 17-8.

Serving raw HTML fragments out of database columns directly into web pages can be very useful when you control and trust the content. However, if you are serving information from the database that end users might have entered, there are potential security risks in serving this unverified HTML markup back into the browser. The risks a developer must be aware of are documented at *http://www.cert.org/advisories/CA-2000-02.html*. Although such occurrences are pretty rare, forewarned is forearmed.

Now that we've established the basic product formatting, we need to build these four web site pages:

- Featured Items page
- Search Results page

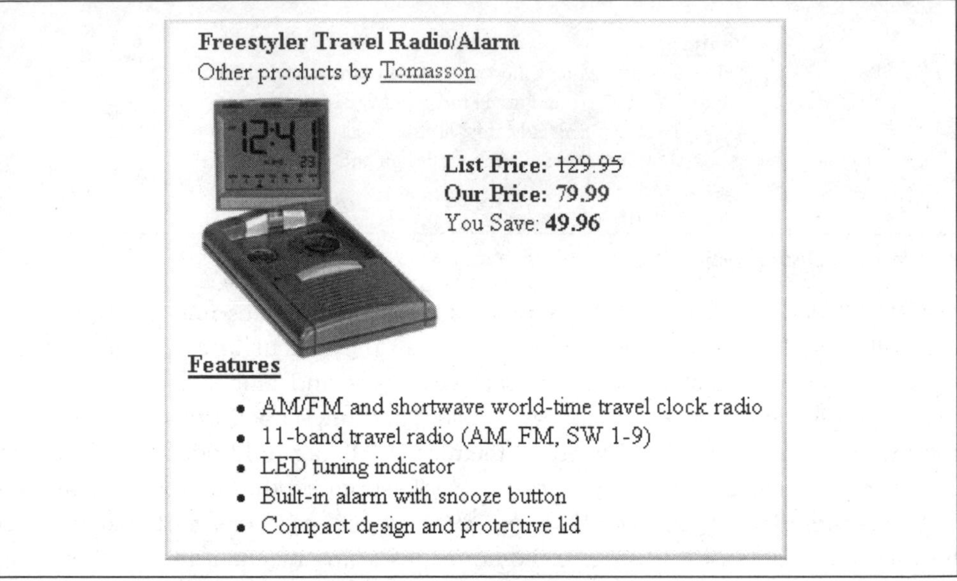

Figure 17-8. Correctly displaying HTML-based product blurb

- Items by Maker page
- Shop Home page

We'll build the four XSQL pages shown in Figure 17-9, leaving *StoreTop.xsql* for later.

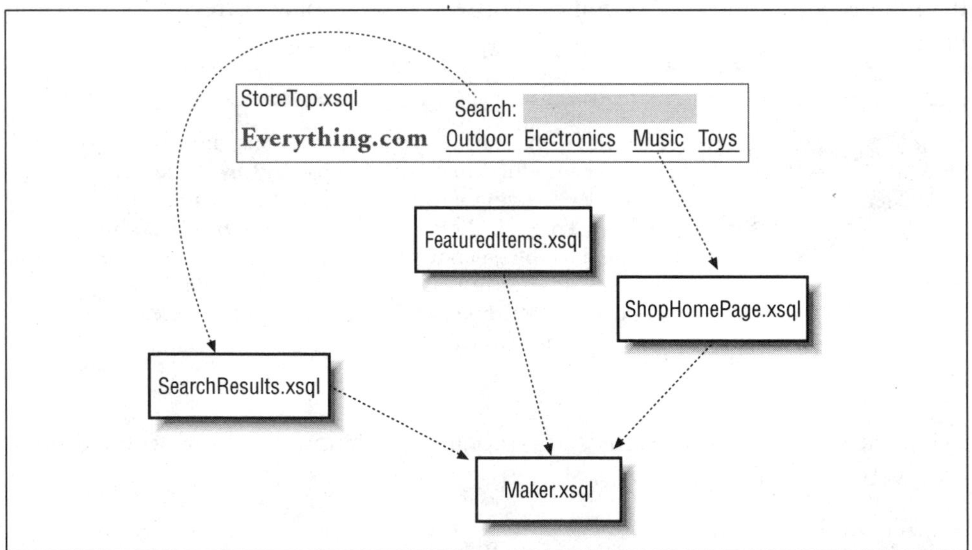

Figure 17-9. Map of XSQL pages to implement the web store

Basically, these pages differ only in the WHERE clauses of their queries. The query in the *FeaturedItems.xsql* page needs to look like this:

```
SELECT description,
       author_name,
        maker_name,
        maker.id AS maker_id,
         shop_name,
             blurb,
        TO_CHAR(list_price,'999999.00')           AS list_price,
        TO_CHAR(price,'999999.00')                AS price,
        TO_CHAR(list_price - price,'999999.00') AS yousave,
               sku
  FROM item, author, maker, shop
  WHERE item.author_id = author.id (+)
    AND item.maker_id  = maker.id
    AND item.shop_id   = shop.id
    AND item.id IN ( SELECT itemid
                       FROM featured_items
                      WHERE sysdate BETWEEN start_date AND end_date )
  ORDER BY description
```

This queries products that appear in our featured_items table where the current date falls between the start_date and the end_date of the featured period for the item. The query in the *SearchResults.xsql* page looks about the same, but has the following WHERE clause:

```
WHERE item.author_id = author.id (+)
  AND item.maker_id  = maker.id
  AND item.shop_id   = shop.id
  AND UPPER(item.description) LIKE UPPER('%{@find}%')
```

The same goes for the *Maker.xsql* page, which shows additional products from the same maker as another product. Its WHERE clause looks like this:

```
WHERE item.author_id = author.id (+)
     AND item.maker_id  = maker.id
     AND item.shop_id   = shop.id
     AND maker.id    = {@id}
```

For the *ShopHomePage.xsql*, we'll use a CURSOR expression to retrieve in a single query the name of the shop, given the shop ID that will be passed in as a parameter as well as the nested set of available products:

```
SELECT shop_name,
       CURSOR( SELECT  description,
                       author_name,
                        maker_name,
                        maker.id AS maker_id,
                         shop_name,
                             blurb,
                       TO_CHAR(list_price,'999999.00')           AS list_price,
                       TO_CHAR(price,'999999.00')                AS price,
                       TO_CHAR(list_price - price,'999999.00') AS yousave,
                              sku
```

```
                    FROM item, author, maker
                    WHERE item.author_id = author.id (+)
                      AND item.maker_id  = maker.id
                      AND item.shop_id   = shop.id
                    ORDER BY shop_name, maker_name
          ) AS items
     FROM shop
    WHERE id = {@id}
```

We could have just selected the shop name and product information in the same flat query, but then we would have ended up with the shop name in every row. XSLT 1.0 does not provide facilities for grouping information containing repeating values to factor out unique groups, so we leverage the database to handle it.

Factoring Reusable Transformation Routines

Finally, we attack the XSLT stylesheets for the four key product pages. All of these pages will be using different queries to display products. We can take advantage of XSLT named templates to factor the product display part of the template we created earlier into a subroutine to be leveraged by multiple stylesheets. After adding another conditional section to avoid displaying "Other products by..." on a page that does not include a `MAKER_ID`, we end up with the named `displayProduct` template in Example 17-5.

Example 17-5. Named Template to Display Web Store Products

```
<xsl:stylesheet version="1.0" xmlns:xsl="http://www.w3.org/1999/XSL/Transform">
  <xsl:template name="displayProduct">
    <b><xsl:value-of select="DESCRIPTION"/></b>
    <xsl:if test="AUTHOR_NAME">
        by <xsl:value-of select="AUTHOR_NAME"/>
    </xsl:if>
    <xsl:if test="MAKER_ID">
      <br/>
      <xsl:text>Other products by </xsl:text>
      <a href="Maker.xsql?id={MAKER_ID}">
        <xsl:value-of select="MAKER_NAME"/>
      </a>
    </xsl:if>
    <br/>
    <table border="0">
      <tr>
        <td><img src="images/{SKU}.gif"/></td>
        <td valign="middle">
          <xsl:if test="LIST_PRICE">
            <b><xsl:text>List Price:</xsl:text></b>
            <strike>
              <xsl:value-of select="LIST_PRICE"/>
            </strike>
            <br/>
          </xsl:if>
```

Example 17-5. Named Template to Display Web Store Products (continued)

```
          <b>
            <xsl:text>Our Price: </xsl:text>
            <font color="blue">
              <xsl:value-of select="PRICE"/>
            </font>
          </b>
          <br/>
          <xsl:if test="LIST_PRICE">
            <xsl:text>You Save: </xsl:text>
            <b>
              <xsl:value-of select="YOUSAVE"/>
            </b>
          </xsl:if>
        </td>
      </tr>
    </table>
    <xsl:if test="BLURB">
      <br/>
      <b><u><xsl:text>Features</xsl:text></u></b><br/>
      <xsl:value-of disable-output-escaping="yes" select="BLURB"/>
    </xsl:if>
  </xsl:template>
</xsl:stylesheet>
```

Now the stylesheets for our XSQL pages can invoke **displayProduct** as a named template to make sure they are all formatting products in a uniform way. Example 17-6 shows the source for the *FeaturedItems.xsl* stylesheet, which includes *DisplayProduct.xsl*, then uses **<xsl:call-template>** to invoke the **displayProduct** template inside its **<xsl:for-each>** loop to format the current <ROW> of product information.

Example 17-6. Calling Reusable Formatting with Named Templates

```
<xsl:stylesheet version="1.0" xmlns:xsl="http://www.w3.org/1999/XSL/Transform">
  <!-- Include the stylesheet containing the "displayProducts" template -->
  <xsl:include href="DisplayProduct.xsl"/>
  <!-- Set the output to not indent so no extra whitespace is introduced -->
  <xsl:output method="html" indent="no"/>
  <xsl:template match="/">
    <html>
    <body>
      <center>
        <h2>Welcome! These Items are featured today...</h2>
        <table border="0">
          <xsl:for-each select="ROWSET/ROW">
          <tr>
            <td valign="top">
              <xsl:call-template name="displayProduct"/>
            </td>
          </tr>
          </xsl:for-each>
        </table>
```

Example 17-6. Calling Reusable Formatting with Named Templates (continued)

```
      </center>
    </body>
    </html>
  </xsl:template>
</xsl:stylesheet>
```

The stylesheets for the other three pages look nearly identical, so these are left as an exercise for the reader.

To build the title frame for the site, we can encapsulate the structure of the store in an XSQL page containing just static XML elements, as shown in *StoreTop.xsql*. Each store and the shops it contains can be represented by **<store>** and **<shop>** elements:

```
<?xml version="1.0"?>
<?xml-stylesheet type="text/xsl" href="StoreTop.xsl"?>
<store>
  <shop name="Outdoors"    id="1"/>
  <shop name="Electronics" id="3"/>
  <shop name="Books"       id="2"/>
  <shop name="Toys"        id="4"/>
</store>
```

The simple-form XSLT stylesheet in Example 17-7 transforms the store structure into a nice-looking banner with a search box and hyperlinks to each particular shop in our store.

Example 17-7. Simple-Form Stylesheet to Handle Web Store Home Page

```
<!-- StoreTop.xsl: format the main homepage of the Web Store -->
<xsl:stylesheet version="1.0" xmlns:xsl="http://www.w3.org/1999/XSL/Transform">
  <!-- For best results with HTML, best not to introduce extra whitespace -->
  <xsl:output method="html" indent="no"/>
  <xsl:template match="/">
    <html>
    <head><link rel="stylesheet" type="text/css" href="Store.css" /></head>
    <body>
       <form target="main" action="SearchResults.xsql" method="post">
         <center>
          <table border="0">
            <tr>
              <td>
                <img src="images/Store.gif"/>
              </td>
              <td>
                <table>
                  <tr>
                    <td>
                      <xsl:text>Search the store:</xsl:text>
                      <input type="text" name="find"/>
                    </td>
                  </tr>
```

Example 17-7. Simple-Form Stylesheet to Handle Web Store Home Page (continued)

```
                <tr>
                  <td>
                    <xsl:for-each select="store/shop">
                      <a target="main" href="ShopHomePage.xsql?id={@id}">
                        <xsl:value-of select="@name"/>
                      </a>
                        
                    </xsl:for-each>
                  </td>
                </tr>
              </table>
            </td>
          </tr>
        </table>
      </center>
    </form>
  </body>
  </html>
 </xsl:template>
</xsl:stylesheet>
```

By tying the *StoreTop.xsql* and the *FeaturedItems.xsql* pages into an HTML frameset with a little *Store.html* document like this:

```
<html>
<head>
<title>XML Book XSQL Sample Site</title>
</head>
  <frameset border="no" rows="90,*">
    <frame frameborder=no noresize name="top" src="StoreTop.xsql">
    <frame frameborder=no name="main" src="FeaturedItems.xsql">
  </frameset>
</html>
```

we end up with the clean, simple site in Figure 17-10 that shows products in a uniform way across the whole site.

Building a Personalized News Portal

In this section, we'll build our second application—a dynamic, database-driven news portal that derives its content from user preference information.

News Category Paging Example

Web-based applications frequently present information to the user in pages. Just consider some sites you might be familiar with. If you perform a search at Amazon.com, WilliamsSonoma.com, or Google.com, you will see your search results a page at a time with a little paging widget that shows you where you are. As

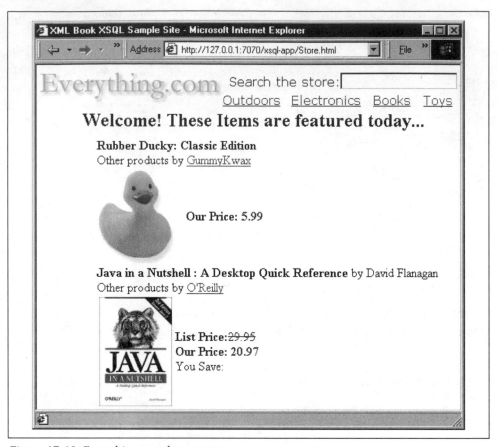

Figure 17-10. Everything.com home page

Figure 17-11 illustrates, each site has a slightly different look to its paging widget, but each one offers the same functionality.

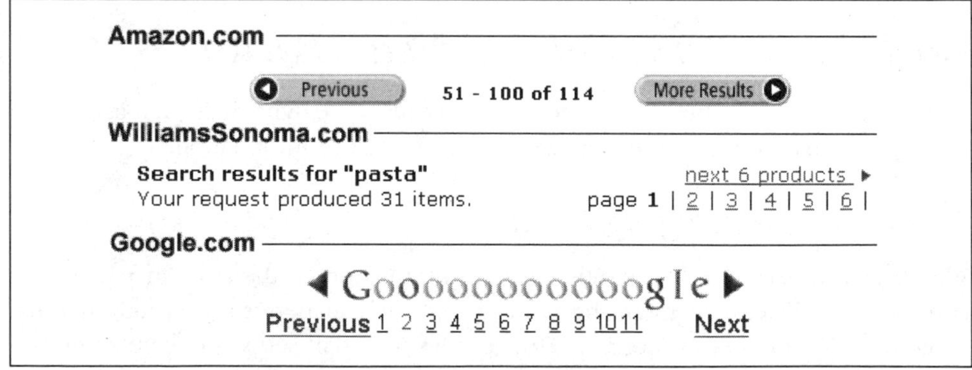

Figure 17-11. Example paging widgets

All of these sites present the results of querying large, relational databases. However, to keep the amount of information on any given page manageable and to keep your response time fast, they all present the results incrementally in pages. A naive technique for scrolling through database query results like this is to open a database cursor, fetch ten records, and keep the cursor open so when the user clicks on the "next page" icon you can fetch ten more pages. However, this technique has many drawbacks:

- Generally, database cursors can only be scrolled forward, so offering a facility to go back to the previous page would be tricky.
- Scrolling backwards or maintaining a current record position in a cursor requires keeping the database cursor open across web page requests. This means you must dedicate a database connection to every single visitor to your site. "Holy maximum-number-of-sessions-exceeded, Batman!" Twenty thousand users querying for web sites, books, or pots and pans would need 20,000 database connections to keep each of their cursors open. And what if users never click on the "next page" button before zooming off to another site to check their stocks? In this case, when do you close the cursor?

It's clear that we need a technique to deliver the query results in a stateless way, so a user can come in, browse some results, and leave without dedicating a database connection to the results and without having to keep track of when to close the results. The stateless paging technique is actually quite simple once you are willing to believe that requerying data you've already queried is not in violation of some database user's moral code.

The trick works like this. Say you have a database query which produces a list of 114 books from your database, like this:

```
SELECT title, description, price, sku, imageurl
  FROM big_table_of_products
 WHERE author like '%THEROUX%'
```

Here's how we can orchestrate the stateless paging through the results:

1. Rather than retrieving all of the rows in the result to determine how many total rows we've found, we instead leverage our powerful database to do it for us with a second query like this one:

   ```
   SELECT COUNT(sku)
     FROM big_table_of_products
    WHERE author like '%THEROUX%'
   ```

   If you're querying and counting columns that are indexed in the database, the answer to this count query can be determined very, very quickly.

2. If we are displaying the first page of results, say with ten rows per page, we fetch just ten rows from the original query, show them to the user, and close the cursor.
3. Later, if and when we're asked to display page number 2, we use the total number of rows per page to calculate how many rows to skip over, and re-execute the same query we did before. This time, to show rows 11–20 we:
   a. Skip 10 rows by fetching them and throwing them away
   b. Fetch the 10 rows for 11–20 and present them to the user
   c. Close the cursor

At first, this skip rows technique sounds slow, but remember that it's the job of the Oracle database engine to keep the most recently accessed data in its buffer caches so that frequently accessed information is accessible super-quickly. Our seemingly inefficient skip-and-query technique actually performs much better than the alternative strategy of leaving lots of database cursors open.

Stateless Paging

Stateless paging through query results can be made even *more* efficient if your query results are ordered by a column value that makes each row distinct. For example, consider a list of employees whose last name is like '%JONES%' that is sorted by user ID. If you remember the value of `userid` that was at the bottom of the current page of results—say '`abjones`'—you can use Oracle8*i*'s powerful top *N* query feature to get the next page of results without requerying rows you've already seen. It merely requires adjusting the WHERE clause of the query like this:

```
SELECT userid, firstname, lastname, phone
  FROM ( SELECT userid, firstname, lastname, phone
           FROM all_emps
          WHERE lastname like '%JONES%'
                 /* This was the orig query critera */
           AND  userid > 'abjones'
                 /* Return matches beyond 'abjones' */
         ORDER BY userid
                 /* Order the inner query by userid */
       )
  WHERE ROWNUM <= 10  /* Get the "top-10", i.e. first 10, rows */
```

This optimizes the "next page" query and avoids the need to query and skip rows, but makes it difficult to support randomly jumping to page *n* of *m*. You can combine the skip-and-query technique with this to achieve a hybrid technique, however.

To implement stateless paging in XSQL Pages-based applications, we can take advantage of the `skip-rows="n"` and `max-rows="m"` attributes on `<xsql:query>` or `<xsql:ref-cursor-function>` to adopt the skip-and-query technique. However, since it's clear from the three examples above that the look of the page navigation display can vary from use to use, it's best if we try to abstract the raw information required for paging and separate it from the presentation. We'll include the raw paging information in our XSQL page and then use an XSLT template to flexibly format it in any look we want.

Given the number of rows per page as an input parameter, the following basic paging information is required to produce a display like those shown previously:

- The total number of rows retrieved by the query
- The total number of pages that this translates into
- The current page number
- If applicable, the previous page number
- If applicable, the next page number

To make the mechanism generic, we also need to add:

- The URL of the current page
- The list of URL arguments to pass to the current page

We're going to use a custom XSQL action handler to take care of all these details for us, so that given a simple action in our XSQL page:

```
<xsql:action handler="Paging" rows-per-page="10" url-params="author title">
  <!-- SQL Statement to Use for Calculating the Total Rows -->
</xsql:action>
```

we will automatically find a `<paging>` information fragment in our data page that will look like this:

```
<paging>
  <total-rows>114</total-rows>
  <total-pages>12</total-pages>
  <current-page>3</current-page>
  <next-page>4</next-page>
  <prev-page>2</prev-page>
  <target-page>BookstoreSearch.xsql</target-page>
  <target-args>author=theroux&title=sea</target-args>
</paging>
```

Given this paging information in our XSQL data page, we can use an XSLT template like the following to control the appearance:

```
<xsl:template match="paging">
  <!-- Elements to govern the visual "look" of the paging display -->
</xsl:template>
```

Example 17-8 shows the code for our custom **Paging** action handler. When invoked by the XSQL page processor in response to encountering an **<xsql:action>** element in the current page, this handler:

1. Retrieves the text of the SQL statement to use as a total row count query by calling **getActionElementContent()**
2. Calculates the total number of rows by passing this query to the **firstColumnOfFirstRow()** method
3. Gets the value of the **rows-per-page** attribute on the action element using the **getAttributeAllowingParam()** method
4. Calls a private method to determine the name of the current page
5. Calculates the total number of pages as well as the next page and previous page numbers based on the value of the current page, which is reflected by the request parameter named **p**
6. Constructs the **<paging>** element and subelements and adds them to the action handler result root
7. Sets the page-private parameters named **paging-skip** and **paging-max** to be used by an **<xsql:query>** or **<xsql:ref-cursor-function>** element later in the same XSQL page to control the appropriate numbers of records to skip to retrieve the records for the current page number

Example 17-8. Custom XSQL Action Handler Simplifies Stateless Paging

```
import oracle.xml.xsql.*;
import oracle.xml.parser.v2.*;
import org.w3c.dom.*;
import java.net.*;
import java.util.StringTokenizer;
import java.sql.SQLException;

public class Paging extends XSQLActionHandlerImpl {
  private static final String PAGE_PARAM_NAME  = "p";
  private static final String ROWSPERPAGE      = "rows-per-page";
  private static final String TARGETPAGEARGS   = "url-params";

  public void handleAction(Node root) throws SQLException {
    XSQLPageRequest req = getPageRequest();
    Element actElt  = getActionElement();
    // Get the count query from the action element content
    String query    = getActionElementContent();
    // Get the number of rows per page, defaulting to 10
    long pageSize   = longVal(getAttributeAllowingParam(ROWSPERPAGE,actElt),10);
    long totalRows  = longVal(firstColumnOfFirstRow(root,query),0);
    long curPage = longVal(variableValue(PAGE_PARAM_NAME,actElt),1);
    // Get the name of the current page to use as the target
    String pageName = curPageName(req);
    // Get any URL parameter names that need to be echoed into paging URLs
```

Example 17-8. Custom XSQL Action Handler Simplifies Stateless Paging (continued)

```
    String pageArgs = getAttributeAllowingParam(TARGETPAGEARGS,actElt);
    // Calculate the total number of pages
    long totalPages = totalRows / pageSize;
    long fract = totalRows % pageSize;
    if (fract > 0) totalPages++;
    // Make sure current page is between 1 and totalPages
    if (curPage < 1) curPage = 1;if (curPage > totalPages) curPage = totalPages;
    // Create the <paging> fragment to add to the "data page"
    Document d = actElt.getOwnerDocument();
    Element e = d.createElement("paging");
    root.appendChild(e);
      addResultElement(e,"total-rows",Long.toString(totalRows));
      addResultElement(e,"total-pages",Long.toString(totalPages));
      addResultElement(e,"current-page",Long.toString(curPage));
      if (curPage < totalPages)
        addResultElement(e,"next-page",Long.toString(curPage+1));
      if (curPage > 1)
        addResultElement(e,"prev-page",Long.toString(curPage-1));
      addResultElement(e,"target-page",pageName);
      if (pageArgs != null && !pageArgs.equals(""))
        addResultElement(e,"target-args",expandedUrlParams(pageArgs,actElt));
    // Set to page-level parameters that the <xsql:query> can use
    req.setPageParam("paging-skip",Long.toString((curPage-1)*pageSize));
    req.setPageParam("paging-max",Long.toString(pageSize));
  }
  // Get the name of the current page from the current page's URI
  private String curPageName(XSQLPageRequest req) {
    String thisPage = req.getSourceDocumentURI();;
    int pos = thisPage.lastIndexOf('/');
    if (pos >=0) thisPage = thisPage.substring(pos+1);
    pos = thisPage.indexOf('?');
    if (pos >=0) thisPage = thisPage.substring(0,pos-1);
    return thisPage;
  }
  // Convert String to long, with a default in case it is blank, null, or not a number
  private long longVal(String longstr, long def) {
    long val = def;
    try {
      if (longstr != null && !longstr.equals(""))
        val = Long.parseLong(longstr);
    }
    catch (NumberFormatException nfe) {}
    return val;
  }
  private String expandedUrlParams(String paramNameList,Element actElt) {
    // Allow comma-separated or space-separated name list
    paramNameList = paramNameList.replace(',',' ');
    StringTokenizer st = new StringTokenizer(paramNameList);
    StringBuffer paramString = new StringBuffer();
    int tokens = 0;
    while (st.hasMoreTokens()) {
      String paramName = st.nextToken();
```

Example 17-8. Custom XSQL Action Handler Simplifies Stateless Paging (continued)

```
      String paramValue = variableValue(paramName,actElt);
      if (++tokens > 1) {
        paramString.append("&");
      }
      paramString.append(paramName)
                 .append("=")
                 .append(paramValue);
    }
    return paramString.toString();
  }
}
```

An XSQL page that makes use of the custom **Paging** action handler should use it at the top of the page. Subsequent **<xsql:query>** or **<xsql:ref-cursor-function>** actions retrieve rows that belong on the *current* page by setting their respective **max-rows** and **skip-rows** attributes to the values of the page-private parameters as follows:

```
skip-rows="{@paging-skip}"
max-rows="{@paging-max}"
```

The following *NewsCategorySimple.xsql* example shows how these parameters are used:

```
<?xml version="1.0"?>
<?xml-stylesheet type="text/xsl" href="NewsCategorySimple.xsl"?>
<page id="1" connection="xmlbook" xmlns:xsql="urn:oracle-xsql">
  <xsql:action handler="Paging" rows-per-page="6" url-params="id">
     SELECT count(id)
       FROM site_newsstory
      WHERE category = {@id}
     ORDER BY TIMESTAMP DESC
  </xsql:action>
  <xsql:query skip-rows="{@paging-skip}" max-rows="{@paging-max}">
     SELECT title as "Title",
            TO_CHAR(timestamp,'Mon DD') as "Date"
       FROM latestnews
      WHERE category = {@id}
     ORDER BY TIMESTAMP DESC
  </xsql:query>
</page>
```

This renders as shown in Figure 17-12.

If we hover over the Next link, we see that it is:

```
http://server/NewsCategorySimple.xsql?p=2&id=1
```

which links to the same XSQL page but passes a **p=2** parameter to request "page 2" of the query results. **id=1** is the current value of the news story category ID that needs to be passed to the page in order to query stories from the right category. This **id** parameter appears in the URL because we included its name in the

Title	Date
IBM Switches to Support SOAP	Apr 27
SOAP Spec 1.1 Released	Apr 26
XSQL Pages / XSQL Servlet Production 1.0.0.0	Apr 26
Oracle to offer Net file system for broader content	Apr 20
First Working Draft of XForms Data Model	Apr 19
Ballmer: It's the tags, stupid	Apr 19

Page 1 of 4 Next - Total 19

Figure 17-12. News stories with a paging display

`url_params` attribute in the `Paging` action handler. If we click on the Next link to go to page 2, and look at its raw data page by tacking on an extra `xml-stylesheet=none` parameter to the URL, we'll see the data page in Figure 17-13.


```
  <?xml version="1.0" ?>
- <page id="1">
  - <paging>
      <total-rows>19</total-rows>
      <total-pages>4</total-pages>
      <current-page>2</current-page>
      <next-page>3</next-page>
      <prev-page>1</prev-page>
      <target-page>NewsCategorySimple.xsql</target-page>
      <target-args>id=1</target-args>
    </paging>
  - <ROWSET>
    - <ROW num="7">
        <Title>Netscape 6 Preview 1 Released</Title>
        <Date>Apr 08</Date>
      </ROW>
    - <ROW num="8">
        <Title>Last Call Drafts of XML Schema Spec</Title>
        <Date>Apr 08</Date>
      </ROW>
    - <ROW num="9">
        <Title>Oracle XML Schema Validation Support</Title>
        <Date>Mar 17</Date>
      </ROW>
    - <ROW num="10">
        <Title>XML Namespaces Myths Exploded</Title>
        <Date>Mar 13</Date>
      </ROW>
    - <ROW num="11">
        <Title>The TwoWay Web</Title>
        <Date>Mar 03</Date>
      </ROW>
    - <ROW num="12">
        <Title>Translate Postscript and PDF to SVG</Title>
        <Date>Feb 28</Date>
      </ROW>
    </ROWSET>
  </page>
```


Figure 17-13. Raw data page for news stories with paging information

Querying page 2 with its normal set of arguments shows that we get the second page of news stories and a paging display, as shown in Figure 17-14, that correctly reflects "Page 2 of 4" with both Previous and Next links.

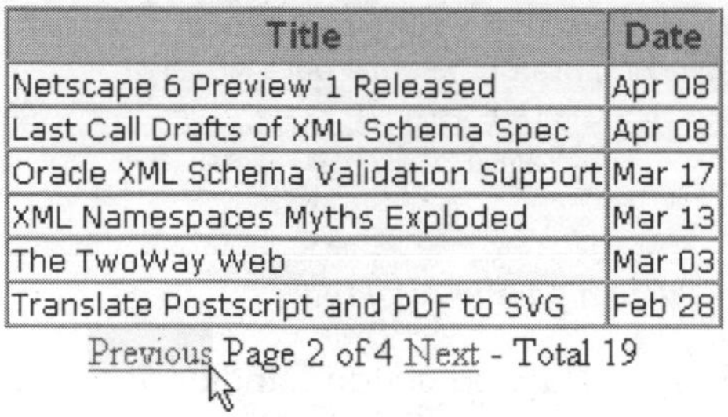

Title	Date
Netscape 6 Preview 1 Released	Apr 08
Last Call Drafts of XML Schema Spec	Apr 08
Oracle XML Schema Validation Support	Mar 17
XML Namespaces Myths Exploded	Mar 13
The TwoWay Web	Mar 03
Translate Postscript and PDF to SVG	Feb 28

Previous Page 2 of 4 Next - Total 19

Figure 17-14. Preview and next links appear when appropriate

How is this magic happening? As with all XML/XSL-based solutions, the answer is that the magic is cleanly separated into data magic and presentation magic. XSQL pages and our custom **Paging** action handler do the data side of the paging magic, which involves:

- Setting up the **<paging>** fragment in the data page, based on the **rows-per-page="6"** attribute and the "row count query" included in the **<xsql:action>** element
- Querying the "window" of rows for the current page by using the **skip-rows="{@paging-skip}"** and **max-rows="{@paging-max}"** attributes on the **<xsql:query>** action element

The look and feel of the page is handled by the following simple stylesheet:

```
<?xml version="1.0"?>
<xsl:stylesheet xmlns:xsl="http://www.w3.org/1999/XSL/Transform" version="1.0">
  <xsl:include href="UtilPaging.xsl"/>
  <xsl:include href="TableBaseWithCSS.xsl"/>
  <xsl:template match="/">
    <html>
      <head>
        <link rel="stylesheet" type="text/css" href="Forum.css"/>
        <title>News By Category</title>
      </head>
      <body bgcolor="#FFFFFF">
        <center>
          <!-- Transform the ROWSET of query results first -->
          <xsl:apply-templates select="page/ROWSET"/>
          <!-- Then transform the <paging> fragment to render "Page N of M" -->
          <xsl:apply-templates select="page/paging"/>
        </center>
      </body>
    </html>
  </xsl:template>
</xsl:stylesheet>
```

Since we're not overriding any templates we're leveraging from other library stylesheets, we can use `<xsl:include>` to include the templates as if they were part of this one. We're including the templates from our *TableBaseWithCSS.xsl* stylesheet in Chapter 7, *Transforming XML with XSLT*, to display the queried rows of data as a table with column headings, and we're including the *UtilPaging.xsl* stylesheet in Example 17-9 to handle the presentation of the paging display. Since we used a CSS stylesheet to separate font and color information from the *TableBaseWithCSS.xsl* transformation, it's easy to use a different *Forum.css* stylesheet here to give the page a new font and color scheme.

Note that the root template controls the order in which the data and paging information is displayed by explicitly using:

```
<!-- Transform the ROWSET of query results first -->
<xsl:apply-templates select="page/ROWSET"/>
<!-- Then transform the <paging> fragment to render "Page N of M" -->
<xsl:apply-templates select="page/paging"/>
```

If we look closely at Example 17-9, we see that the template matching the `<paging>` element is itself factored into a set of `<xsl:call-template>`s to further modularize the way that each part of the paging information is displayed. This lets us override the entire paging display later by importing *UtilPaging.xsl* and providing a new template for `<paging>`. We alternatively can just override the way that the Previous and Next links are rendered by leaving the existing paging template in place and overriding the `previousLink` and `nextLink` named templates. We might do this, for example, to use fancy previous and next page icon buttons like the earlier Amazon.com example instead of the default Next and Previous HTML links.

XSLT supports both `<xsl:include>` and `<xsl:import>` for reusing existing stylesheets in other stylesheets that you build. Use `<xsl:include>` if you want to add all the templates from another stylesheet logically into your current one. Use `<xsl:import>` to include other templates, and set all the templates in the current stylesheet to be considered as more important than the included ones. A rule of thumb is that if you are overriding templates from another stylesheet, use `<xsl:import>`; otherwise, use `<xsl:include>`. Both `<xsl:include>` and `<xsl:import>` can only be used as top-level elements, that is, as immediate children of the `<xsl:stylesheet>` element.

Example 17-9. Reusable XSLT Templates to Format Paging Display

```
<xsl:stylesheet xmlns:xsl="http://www.w3.org/1999/XSL/Transform" version="1.0">
  <!--
   | UtilPaging.xsl: Transform <paging> structural info into HTML
   |                 presentation for "Page N of M" and Next/Prev Links
   +-->
  <xsl:template match="paging">
      <span class="paging">
        <xsl:call-template name="previousLink"/>
        <xsl:text> </xsl:text>
        <xsl:call-template name="currentPageIndicator"/>
        <xsl:text> </xsl:text>
        <xsl:call-template name="nextLink"/>
        <xsl:text> - </xsl:text>
        <xsl:call-template name="totalRowsIndicator"/>
      </span>
  </xsl:template>
  <!-- Display current page indicator "Page N of M" -->
  <xsl:template name="currentPageIndicator">
    <xsl:text>Page </xsl:text>
    <xsl:value-of select="current-page"/>
    <xsl:text> of </xsl:text>
    <xsl:value-of select="total-pages"/>
  </xsl:template>
  <!-- Display total rows -->
  <xsl:template name="totalRowsIndicator">
    <xsl:text>Total </xsl:text>
    <xsl:value-of select="total-rows"/>
  </xsl:template>
  <!-- Display hyperlink to previous page -->
  <xsl:template name="previousLink">
    <xsl:param name="label">Previous</xsl:param>
    <xsl:call-template name="pagelink">
      <xsl:with-param name="pagenum" select="prev-page"/>
      <xsl:with-param name="label" select="$label"/>
    </xsl:call-template>
  </xsl:template>
  <!-- Display hyperlink to next page -->
  <xsl:template name="nextLink">
    <xsl:param name="label">Next</xsl:param>
    <xsl:call-template name="pagelink">
      <xsl:with-param name="pagenum" select="next-page"/>
      <xsl:with-param name="label" select="$label"/>
    </xsl:call-template>
  </xsl:template>
  <!-- Generate correct hyperlink to page 'pagenum' including URL params -->
  <xsl:template name="pagelink">
    <xsl:param name="pagenum"/>
    <xsl:param name="label"/>
    <xsl:if test="$pagenum">
      <a> <!-- This lonesome-looking <a> is an HTML anchor tag -->
        <xsl:attribute name="href">
          <xsl:value-of select="target-page"/>
```

Example 17-9. Reusable XSLT Templates to Format Paging Display (continued)

```
        <xsl:text>?p=</xsl:text>
        <xsl:value-of select="$pagenum"/>
        <xsl:if test="target-args">
          <xsl:text disable-output-escaping="yes">&amp;</xsl:text>
          <xsl:value-of select="target-args"/>
        </xsl:if>
      </xsl:attribute>
      <xsl:value-of select="$label"/>
    </a>
  </xsl:if>
 </xsl:template>
</xsl:stylesheet>
```

So we now have:

- A generic facility for adding stateless paging to any XSQL page
- A library stylesheet to handle formatting the "Page *N* of *M*" display

We'll put both of these to good use in several of the following examples, as we build our simple news story display into a full-fledged, database-driven information portal.

Building Reusable HTML Widgets

Let's learn some cool XSLT tricks to embellish the simple list of news stories presented in Example 17-12. Our web designers have given us an HTML mockup of how they want the news stories on our portal site to look, and have provided us a CSS stylesheet with all their chosen font/color settings to be used across the site. The mockup of the news display is shown in Figure 17-15.

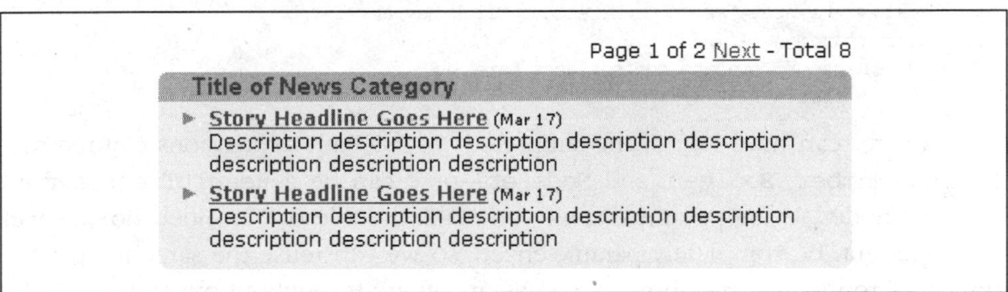

Figure 17-15. HTML mockup for portal news display

The designers tell us "rounded boxes are in!" and inform us that everything on the portal site should be displayed using cool-looking rounded boxes with the title and content inside the box. They have taken the time to figure out the HTML layout and the rounded-corner GIF images required to render the rounded box, so we don't have to figure out that part. Since we're going to need this "TitledBox" widget in many places on our site, our first thought should be to design a reusable XSLT template to represent the box. So, let's do it.

We take the HTML mockup source code and run it through the Tidy utility to turn it into well-formed XML, and we add the necessary `<xsl:stylesheet>` around it. We want the TitledBox widget to be callable from any place we need it, so we make it a named template. We want to be able to pass the title and the box contents to the widget so we can use it to display the rounded box with any title and any content we need inside the box.

Here we can make use of an XSLT feature we haven't used yet: template *parameters*. In Chapter 9, *XSLT Beyond the Basics*, we used top-level stylesheet parameters, but both `match="pattern"` templates and named templates can define template-scoped parameters as well. Parameters are given a name and optionally a default value when they are declared at the top of the template, using the following syntax:

```
<xsl:template name="SomeTemplate">
  <!-- "title" parameter has no default value -->
  <xsl:param name="title"/>
  <!--
   | "list-of-rows" parameter defaults to list of ROW element children of
   | the current node, using the XPath expression ROW
   +-->
  <xsl:param name="list-of-rows" select="ROW"/>
  <!-- "rowname" parameter defaults to the string 'ROW' (note extra quotes!)
  <xsl:param name="rowname" select="'ROW'"/>
  <!-- "otherrowname" parameter defaults to the string 'ROW' as well
  <xsl:param name="rowname">ROW</xsl:param>
  <!-- "content" parameter defaults to a tree of literal result nodes -->
  <xsl:param name="content">
    <b><i><a href="www.somewhere.com">Click Me</a></i></b>
  </xsl:param>
  <!-- Rest of Template content goes here -->
</xsl:template>
```

A parameter can have any of the supported types XPath expressions can return—`String`, `Number`, `Boolean`, and `NodeSet`—or it can be a `ResultTreeFragment` of literal nodes. Using parameters, we can make the title of our Titled Box, as well as its content, be completely parameterized, so we can reuse the same template to do a cool rounded-corner box with a title anywhere throughout our site.

Our *TitledBox.xsl* stylesheet ends up looking like Example 17-10.

Example 17-10. Named Template for a Titled Box with Rounded Corners

```
<xsl:stylesheet version="1.0" xmlns:xsl="http://www.w3.org/1999/XSL/Transform">
  <xsl:template name="TitledBox">
    <xsl:param name="Title"/>
    <xsl:param name="Contents"/>
```

Example 17-10. Named Template for a Titled Box with Rounded Corners (continued)

```
    <table width="100%" cellspacing="0" cellpadding="0" border="0">
      <tr>
        <td width="1%" valign="top" align="left" bgcolor="#CCCC99">
          <img src="images/TL.gif" width="5" height="5" />
        </td>
        <th nowrap="" width="98%" align="left" valign="center" bgcolor="#CCCC99">
          <!--   is numerical character entity for Non-Breaking Space -->
          <xsl:text>  </xsl:text>

          <!-- Put whatever is passed as the Title parameter here -->
          <xsl:copy-of select="$Title"/>

        </th>
        <td width="1%" align="right" valign="TOP" bgcolor="#CCCC99">
          <xsl:text>   </xsl:text>
        </td>
        <td width="1%" valign="top" align="right" bgcolor="#CCCC99">
          <img src="images/TR.gif" width="5" height="5" />
        </td>
      </tr>
      <tr>
        <td width="1%" align="right" valign="TOP" bgcolor="#F7F7E7">
          <xsl:text>   </xsl:text>
        </td>
        <td nowrap="" bgcolor="#F7F7E7" colspan="3">

          <!-- Put whatever is passed as the Contents parameter here -->
          <xsl:copy-of select="$Contents"/>

        </td>
      </tr>
      <tr>
        <td bgcolor="#F7F7E7" width="1%" align="LEFT" valign="BOTTOM">
          <img src="images/BL.gif" width="5" height="5" border="0" />
        </td>
        <td colspan="2" bgcolor="#F7F7E7" height="1" width="98%">
          <img src="images/blank.gif" border="0" height="1" width="1" />
        </td>
        <td bgcolor="#F7F7E7" width="1%" align="right" valign="BOTTOM">
          <img src="images/BR.gif" width="5" height="5" border="0" />
        </td>
      </tr>
    </table>
  </xsl:template>
</xsl:stylesheet>
```

The template defines the two parameters `Title` and `Contents` at the top, and right in the middle of the HTML table that contains the layout and images to achieve the rounded corner effect for the box, we see:

```
<!-- Put whatever is passed as the Title parameter here -->
<xsl:copy-of select="$Title"/>
```

where the title is plugged in and:

```
<!-- Put whatever is passed as the Contents parameter here -->
<xsl:copy-of select="$Contents"/>
```

In addition to the new use of parameters here, we're using a new XSLT action called `<xsl:copy-of>` instead of the familiar `<xsl:value-of>`. The `<xsl:copy-of>` preserves any tree structure that the result of its `select="`*`expression`*`"` attribute might contain by copying that node-set result verbatim into the result tree. In contrast, `<xsl:value-of>` converts the result of its `select="`*`expression`*`"` attribute into a flat string.

To better understand this difference, imagine that the value of the `Contents` parameter is a `ResultTreeFragment` containing the elements for an HTML bulleted list:

```
<ul>
  <li>One</li>
  <li>Two</li>
</ul>
```

The action:

```
<xsl:copy-of select="$Contents"/>
```

copies the `<ul>` element and all its children to the result tree, producing a bulleted list in the final HTML page. In contrast, the action:

```
<xsl:value-of select="$Contents"/>
```

just copies the text `OneTwo` to the result tree, since the value of an element is defined by the concatenation in document order of all of its text node descendants.

Having a result tree fragment containing HTML nodes is different from having a single text element containing the "tags and text" for HTML, as we saw earlier in this chapter with our web store product blurb. In the web store case, we had a text chunk with tags in it that we needed to insert verbatim in the result tree so that the browser would ultimately interpret the angle brackets in the HTML text blurb as tags. In the `<ul>` result tree fragment case here, the processor is working with a tree of nodes and not just a text chunk containing tags. This explains why in the web store example our:

```
<xsl:value-of disable-output-escaping="yes" select="BLURB"/>
```

copies a single text node containing angle brackets and writes the angle brackets verbatim to the output, while:

```
<xsl:value-of select="$Contents"/>
```

flattens the result tree fragment into the string `OneTwo` by concatenating all of the text nodes in the tree fragment.

With our *TitledBox.xsl* stylesheet in place, we can begin creating our news portal. We start by recalling the tables that sit underneath our news portal. We organize our news stories into content categories, so we have a site_newscategory table.

```
CREATE TABLE site_newscategory(
  id   NUMBER,
  name VARCHAR2(80),
  CONSTRAINT site_newscatpk PRIMARY KEY (id)
);
```

and a detail table site_newsstory that holds the information for each story in each category:

```
CREATE TABLE site_newsstory(
  id          NUMBER,
  title       VARCHAR2(100)  NOT NULL ,
  url         VARCHAR2(2000) NOT NULL ,
  category    NUMBER,
  description VARCHAR2(700),
  timestamp   DATE,
  source      VARCHAR2(80),
  CONSTRAINT site_newsstorypk PRIMARY KEY (id),
  CONSTRAINT story_in_category FOREIGN KEY (category) REFERENCES site_newscategory
);
```

Since we're always interested in the latest news, and since in Oracle8*i* views can now contain ORDER BY clauses, we simplify our lives by creating the simple `latestnews` view that sorts the news in descending order by the timestamp of when it was created:

```
CREATE OR REPLACE VIEW latestnews as
  SELECT category,id,title,url,description,timestamp,source
    FROM site_newsstory
   ORDER BY timestamp desc;
```

We create a *NewsCategory.xsql* page to materialize the XML data content for the news story display based on our earlier tables. Note that we're reusing our custom `Paging` action handler since our designers indicated that they want the user to be able to page through the news stories. The query inside the `<xsql:action>` for the `Paging` handler is a row count query that calculates the total number of stories in the news story category whose category ID is passed in the `id` parameter. It uses the same FROM and WHERE clauses as the query in the second `<xsql:query>` action that queries the news stories for the current page. The `<xsql:query>` in the middle of the page looks up the news category name based on the ID that's passed in, and includes the single `<categoryname>` element in the data page by suppressing the `rowset-element` and `row-element` and aliasing the name column to the quoted name "categoryname". The stylesheet can then refer to the name of the current news category using the XPath expression `/page/categoryname`:

```
<?xml version="1.0"?>
<?xml-stylesheet type="text/xsl" href="NewsCategoryBox.xsl"?>
<page id="1" connection="xmlbook" xmlns:xsql="urn:oracle-xsql">
  <xsql:action handler="Paging" rows-per-page="6" url-params="id">
      SELECT count(id)
        FROM site_newsstory
       WHERE category = {@id}
      ORDER BY TIMESTAMP DESC
  </xsql:action>
  <xsql:query rowset-element="" row-element="">
     SELECT name as "categoryname"
       FROM site_newscategory
      WHERE id = {@id}
  </xsql:query>
  <xsql:query skip-rows="{@paging-skip}" max-rows="{@paging-max}">
      SELECT title,url,description,TO_CHAR(timestamp,'Mon DD') as timestamp
        FROM latestnews
       WHERE category = {@id}
      ORDER BY TIMESTAMP DESC
  </xsql:query>
</page>
```

The last step is to give a look and feel to the raw XML information in the XSQL data page by providing the *NewsCategoryBox.xsl* stylesheet in Example 17-11. It includes the *UtilPaging.xsl* library stylesheet to get the "Page *N* of *M*" formatting automatically and our new *TitledBox.xsl* stylesheet for the reusable box widget.

Example 17-11. Stylesheet to Format Detailed List of News Stories

```
<?xml version="1.0"?>
<!-- NewsCategoryBox.xsl: Format detailed news story list for a category -->
<xsl:stylesheet xmlns:xsl="http://www.w3.org/1999/XSL/Transform" version="1.0">
  <xsl:output method="html" indent="no"/>
  <xsl:include href="UtilPaging.xsl"/>
  <xsl:include href="TitledBox.xsl"/>
  <xsl:variable name="i">images/</xsl:variable>
  <xsl:template match="/">
    <html>
      <head>
        <link rel="stylesheet" type="text/css" href="Forum.css"/>
        <title>News By Category</title>
      </head>
      <body bgcolor="#FFFFFF">
        <center>
          <table  border="0" width="600">
            <tr>
              <td width="600">
                <table border="0" width="100%" cellspacing="0" cellpadding="0">
                  <tr>
                    <td colspan="2" align="right" style="font-size:7pt">
                      <xsl:apply-templates select="page/paging"/><br/><br/>
                    </td>
                  </tr>
                </table>
```

Example 17-11. Stylesheet to Format Detailed List of News Stories (continued)

```
            <xsl:call-template name="TitledBox">
              <xsl:with-param name="Title">
                <xsl:value-of select="page/categoryname"/>
                <xsl:text> News in Detail</xsl:text>
              </xsl:with-param>
              <xsl:with-param name="Contents">
                <table border="0" width="100%">
                  <xsl:for-each select="page/ROWSET/ROW">
                    <tr>
                      <td width="3%" valign="top">
                        <img src="{$i}a.gif" width="8" height="9"/>
                        <font color="#FFFFFF">.</font>
                      </td>
                      <td width="97%">
                        <a href="{URL}">
                          <b><xsl:value-of select="TITLE"/></b>
                        </a>
                        <span style="font-size: 7pt">
                          <xsl:text> (</xsl:text>
                          <xsl:value-of select="TIMESTAMP"/>
                          <xsl:text>)</xsl:text>
                        </span>
                        <span class="tr">
                          <br/>
                          <xsl:value-of select="DESCRIPTION"/>
                        </span>
                      </td>
                    </tr>
                  </xsl:for-each>
                </table>
              </xsl:with-param>
            </xsl:call-template>
          </td>
        </tr>
      </table>
    </center>
  </body>
</html>
</xsl:template>
</xsl:stylesheet>
```

Notice several things about the *NewsCategoryBox.xsl* stylesheet:

- Its root template controls exactly where on the page the paging template will include its "Page *N* of *M*" display by simply putting:

  ```
  <xsl:apply-templates select="page/paging"/>
  ```

  at a strategic spot among other literal HTML elements.

- It invokes the `TitledBox` named template using `<xsl:call-template>` and nests inside the `<xsl:call-template>` element two `<xsl:with-param>` actions to pass the appropriate values for the `Title` and the `Contents` parameters.

- The value of the Title parameter is passed by embedding:

```
<xsl:value-of select="page/categoryname"/>
<xsl:text> News in Detail</xsl:text>
```

  inside the <xsl:with-param> element for name="Title". Similarly an entire dynamically constructed <table> whose contents are created using <xsl:for-each> is passed as the value of the Contents parameter.

- As a final touch of class, the *NewsCategoryBox.xsl* stylesheet defines a stylesheet-level variable using <xsl:variable> as the prefix on any image URLs that are created in the page. This way, if we move our images around, we can change the value of the "i" variable to a new value, and all image URLs constructed in the page change accordingly. Remember that variables can be included at the top level of the stylesheet, or within any template and they are scoped to the part of the stylesheet in which they are defined. They behave identically to parameters, except that their values cannot be set from outside.

Finally, we browse our *NewsCategory.xsql* page to check out our work. The results appear in Figure 17-16. 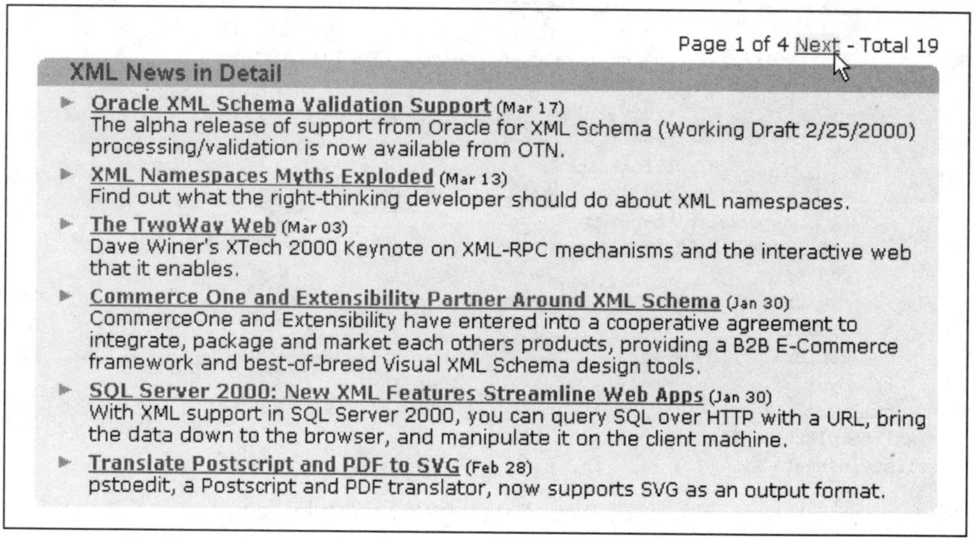

Page 1 of 4 Next - Total 19

XML News in Detail

- **Oracle XML Schema Validation Support** (Mar 17)
  The alpha release of support from Oracle for XML Schema (Working Draft 2/25/2000) processing/validation is now available from OTN.
- **XML Namespaces Myths Exploded** (Mar 13)
  Find out what the right-thinking developer should do about XML namespaces.
- **The TwoWay Web** (Mar 03)
  Dave Winer's XTech 2000 Keynote on XML-RPC mechanisms and the interactive web that it enables.
- **Commerce One and Extensibility Partner Around XML Schema** (Jan 30)
  CommerceOne and Extensibility have entered into a cooperative agreement to integrate, package and market each others products, providing a B2B E-Commerce framework and best-of-breed Visual XML Schema design tools.
- **SQL Server 2000: New XML Features Streamline Web Apps** (Jan 30)
  With XML support in SQL Server 2000, you can query SQL over HTTP with a URL, bring the data down to the browser, and manipulate it on the client machine.
- **Translate Postscript and PDF to SVG** (Feb 28)
  pstoedit, a Postscript and PDF translator, now supports SVG as an output format.

Figure 17-16. Browsing the live news from the XML news category

Since our XSQL page is parameterized, we can rebrowse the URL:

http://server/NewsCategory.xsql?id=2

to see the news from another category if we want, and the automatic stateless paging through the stories works for using Next and Previous to move through the stories in that category too. Pretty darn cool.

Creating a Personalized News Portal

Next, let's build a personalized news portal to offer individual users a list of the news categories they are interested in, as well as a personalized list of stock quotes. To manage the preferences for each user, we'll use a simple schema like the one shown in Figure 17-17.

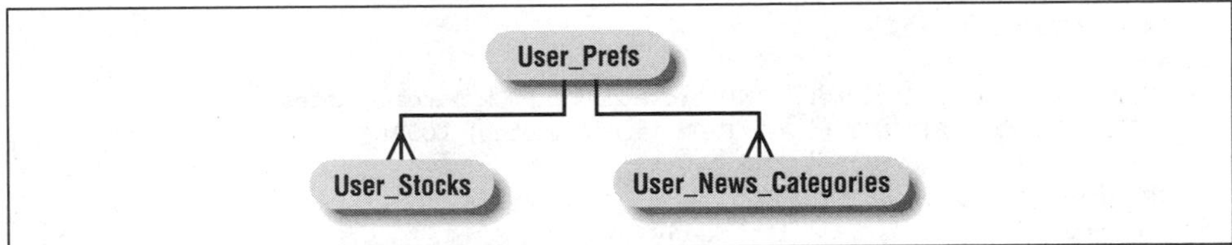

Figure 17-17. Schema for storing user preferences

We can create these tables with the following SQL DDL statements:

```
CREATE TABLE user_prefs (
  userid     VARCHAR2(80),
  headlines  NUMBER,
  CONSTRAINT user_prefs_pk PRIMARY KEY (userid)
);
CREATE TABLE user_stocks(
 userid VARCHAR(80),
 ticker VARCHAR(6),
CONSTRAINT stocks_for_user FOREIGN KEY (userid) REFERENCES user_prefs
);
CREATE TABLE user_news_categories(
 userid VARCHAR(80),
 category NUMBER,
CONSTRAINT categories_for_user FOREIGN KEY (userid) REFERENCES user_prefs
);
```

Every user who visits the site will be able to sign up for a free account, and we'll track that user's user ID with a cookie named `forumuser`, but we need a pseudo-user named `DEFAULT` so we can have some default news categories and stocks to display in case a user has not signed in yet. We insert a row for this `DEFAULT` user in the user_prefs table, and some corresponding default preferences for the user in the user_stocks and user_news_categories tables, like this:

```
INSERT INTO user_prefs VALUES ('DEFAULT', /* Number of Headlines */ 5);
INSERT INTO user_stocks VALUES ('DEFAULT','ORCL');
INSERT INTO user_stocks VALUES ('DEFAULT','MSFT');
INSERT INTO user_news_categories VALUES ('DEFAULT',1);
INSERT INTO user_news_categories VALUES ('DEFAULT',2);
INSERT INTO user_news_categories VALUES ('DEFAULT',3);
```

Our latest stock quotes live in a table called latest_quotes that is populated automatically using a `DBMS_JOB` procedure. The database job executes the `RefreshAllLatestQuotes` stored procedure in Example 17-12.

Example 17-12. Procedure to Refresh Prices of All Stocks

```
CREATE OR REPLACE PROCEDURE RefreshAllLatestQuotes IS
  ------------------------------------------------
  -- Refresh quotes from Yahoo! Quotes for each distinct
  -- ticker symbol in the latest_quotes table.
  ------------------------------------------------
  n           NUMBER := 0;
  tickercount NUMBER;
  curstr VARCHAR2(80);
BEGIN
  SELECT COUNT(DISTINCT ticker) INTO tickercount FROM latest_quotes;
  FOR i IN (SELECT DISTINCT ticker FROM latest_quotes) LOOP
    n := n + 1;
    IF curstr IS NOT NULL THEN
      curstr := curstr ||','|| i.ticker;
    ELSE
      curstr := i.ticker;
    END IF;
    ------------------------------------------------
    -- Use YahooQuotes.StoreLatestQuotesFor to retrieve
    -- live YahooQuotes in XML and store them in the
    -- LATEST_QUOTES table. Do it in batches of 10.
    ------------------------------------------------
    IF n mod 10 = 0 OR n = tickercount THEN
      YahooQuotes.StoreLatestQuotesFor(curstr);
      COMMIT;
      curstr := NULL;
    END IF;
  END LOOP;
END;
```

This leverages the `YahooQuotes.StoreLatestQuotesFor` procedure we created in Chapter 6 to retrieve the quotes in batches of ten from the live Yahoo! Quotes server.

We need to build an XSQL page that queries the requested number of news stories from each category the user has indicated in his or her preferences, and queries the table of 20-minute delayed stock quotes to show the latest prices for the stocks the current user is tracking. Our *News.xsql* page looks like Example 17-13.

Example 17-13. XSQL Page Driving Data Behind the News Portal

```
<?xml version="1.0"?>
<!-- News.xsql: Data page driving the news portal -->
<page connection="xmlbook" xmlns:xsql="urn:oracle-xsql">
  <xsql:query rowset-element="STOCKS">
    SELECT ticker,to_char(price,'999.99') as price
      FROM latest_quotes
      WHERE trunc(day) = (select max(trunc(day)) FROM latest_quotes)
```

Example 17-13. XSQL Page Driving Data Behind the News Portal (continued)

```
        AND ticker IN (SELECT ticker
                         FROM user_stocks
                        WHERE userid = NVL('{@forumuser}','DEFAULT'))
      ORDER BY ticker
  </xsql:query>
  <xsql:query><![CDATA[
    SELECT cat.id,
           cat.name,
           CURSOR( SELECT title,url,description
                     FROM latestnews
                    WHERE category = cat.id
                      AND ROWNUM <= (SELECT headlines
                                       FROM user_prefs
                                      WHERE userid = NVL('{@forumuser}','DEFAULT'))
           ) AS stories
     FROM site_newscategory cat
      WHERE cat.id IN (SELECT category
                         FROM user_news_categories
                        WHERE userid = NVL('{@forumuser}','DEFAULT'))
  ]]>
  </xsql:query>
</page>
```

Notice that we're using the SQL expression:

```
NVL('{@forumuser}','DEFAULT')
```

for the name of the user ID when querying the user_prefs table. This way, if the value of the `forumuser` cookie is not set, the query will execute and get the preferences for the user named DEFAULT as a fallback. We're using our now-familiar CURSOR expression to select the nested detail news stories for each master news category. In the nested CURSOR's SELECT statement, we use the clause:

```
WHERE category = cat.id /* Get the news stories for the current category     */
  /* and retrieve the top 'headlines' number of stories based on user_prefs */
  AND ROWNUM <= (SELECT headlines
                   FROM user_prefs
                  WHERE userid = NVL('{@forumuser}','DEFAULT'))
```

Since the `latestnews` view is ordered, the query engine notices this and uses the `ROWNUM` criteria to efficiently limit the number of rows returned to the "top *N*" rows in that ordered set. In this case, the *N* for the top *N* query is itself determined dynamically by selecting the `headlines` column from the user_prefs table for the current user. Also notice that the WHERE clause in the outer query over the site_newscategory table uses a IN clause, with a subselect to retrieve only the categories indicated by the current user. The resulting raw XSQL data page appears in Example 17-14 for the DEFAULT user.

Example 17-14. Raw Output of the News.xsql Portal Page

```
<?xml version = '1.0' encoding = 'UTF-8'?>
<page>
  <STOCKS>
   <ROW num="1"><TICKER>MSFT</TICKER><PRICE>69.75</PRICE></ROW>
   <ROW num="2"><TICKER>ORCL</TICKER><PRICE>79.94</PRICE></ROW>
  </STOCKS>
  <ROWSET>
    <ROW num="1">
     <ID>1</ID>
     <NAME>XML</NAME>
     <STORIES>
      <STORIES_ROW num="1">
       <TITLE>IBM Switches to Support SOAP</TITLE>
       <URL>http://news.cnet.com/news/0-1003-200-1770721.html</URL>
       <DESCRIPTION>After criticizing a Web technology created by rival
        Microsoft, IBM has changed its mind.</DESCRIPTION>
      </STORIES_ROW>
     <!-- 4 other STORIES_ROW clipped for brevity -->
     </STORIES>
    </ROW>
    <ROW num="2">
     <ID>2</ID>
     <NAME>XSLT</NAME>
     <STORIES>
      <STORIES_ROW num="1">
       <TITLE>SAXON 5.3 Released</TITLE>
       <URL>http://xmlhack.com/read.php?item=427</URL>
       <DESCRIPTION>Mike Kay has announced version 5.3 of his Saxon XSLT
        processor, which delivers significant performance advantages</DESCRIPTION>
      </STORIES_ROW>
      <!-- 4 other STORIES_ROW clipped for brevity -->
     </STORIES>
    </ROW>
    <ROW num="3">
     <ID>3</ID>
     <NAME>B2B</NAME>
     <STORIES>
      <STORIES_ROW num="1">
       <TITLE>Microsoft Banks on the Internet with BizTalk</TITLE>
       <URL>http://www.infoworld.com/articles/hn/xml/00/02/14/000214hnwap.xml</URL>
       <DESCRIPTION>Later in 2000 Microsoft will deliver the second generation
         of its BizTalk tools as well as the BizTalk Server.</DESCRIPTION>
      </STORIES_ROW>
      <!-- 4 other STORIES_ROW clipped for brevity -->
     </STORIES>
    </ROW>
  </ROWSET>
</page>
```

Now we can create the XSLT templates for formatting the news boxes and the stock quotes on the portal home page reusing our `TitledBox` widget from the previous section. For formatting the news stories in the `page/ROWSET/ROW` section of our data page, we create *NewsBoxes.xsl* in Example 17-15.

Example 17-15. Stylesheet to Format News Headlines as Titled Boxes

```
<!-- NewsBoxes.xsl: Format news headlines as TitledBoxes -->
<xsl:stylesheet version="1.0" xmlns:xsl="http://www.w3.org/1999/XSL/Transform">
  <xsl:include href="TitledBox.xsl"/>
  <xsl:template name="NewsBoxes">
    <xsl:if test="not(page/ROWSET/ROW)">
      <xsl:text>You have not selected any news categories...</xsl:text>
    </xsl:if>
    <xsl:for-each select="page/ROWSET/ROW">
      <xsl:call-template name="TitledBox">
        <xsl:with-param name="Title">
          <!-- Title is the category name with link to details -->
          <a href="NewsCategory.xsql?id={ID}">
            <b><xsl:value-of select="NAME"/></b>
          </a>
        </xsl:with-param>
        <xsl:with-param name="Contents">
          <!-- Contents is a list of News Stories -->
          <xsl:for-each select="STORIES/STORIES_ROW">
          <li>
            <a title="{DESCRIPTION}" target="_top" href="{URL}">
              <xsl:value-of select="TITLE"/>
            </a>
          </li>
          </xsl:for-each>
        </xsl:with-param>
      </xsl:call-template>
      <xsl:if test="position() != last()">
        <br/>
      </xsl:if>
    </xsl:for-each>
  </xsl:template>
</xsl:stylesheet>
```

This creates a `NewsBoxes` named template that first uses an `<xsl:if>` to conditionally print a message in case there are no matching `page/ROWSET/ROW` elements. Then, it invokes the `TitledBox` named template, passing an appropriate `Title`:

```
<!-- Title is the category name with link to details -->
<a href="NewsCategory.xsql?id={ID}">
  <b><xsl:value-of select="NAME"/></b>
</a>
```

that provides the category name as a hyperlink to the *NewsCategory.xsql* page we created above, and an appropriate `Contents`. Here the contents are the formatted list of news stories as a bulleted HTML list. Using attribute value templates, we're constructing HTML hyperlinks with:

```
<a title="{DESCRIPTION}" target="_top" href="{URL}">
  <xsl:value-of select="TITLE"/>
</a>
```

So each item in the bulleted list will be a hyperlink to the actual story, displaying the story's `TITLE` in the list and its `DESCRIPTION` in the fly-over help. Notice that we're using the `test="position() != last()"` in an `<xsl:if>` to conditionally add a `<br>` tag after each news story unless it's the last story in the list. The `position()` function returns the current position in the list of `<STORIES_ROW>` nodes, and the `last()` function returns the position number of the last node in the list.

For formatting the stock quotes in the `page/STOCKS/ROW` section of the data page, we create a similar *StockQuotes.xsl* stylesheet, shown in Example 17-16, with a `StockQuotes` named template. It, too, reuses our `TitledBox` template, sets its `Title` parameter appropriately and fills its `Contents` parameter with either a message saying "No stocks selected" or a table of ticker symbols and stock prices.

Example 17-16. Stylesheet to Format Stock Quotes as Titled Boxes

```
<!-- StockQuotes.xsl: Format stock quotes using TitledBoxes -->
<xsl:stylesheet version="1.0" xmlns:xsl="http://www.w3.org/1999/XSL/Transform">
  <xsl:include href="TitledBox.xsl"/>
  <xsl:template name="StockQuotes">
    <xsl:call-template name="TitledBox">
      <xsl:with-param name="Title">
        <!-- Static title of a bolded "Stock Quotes" -->
        <b>Stock Quotes</b>
      </xsl:with-param>
      <xsl:with-param name="Contents">
        <!-- Table of stock quotes is the contents  -->
        <table>
          <xsl:if test="not(page/STOCKS/ROW)">
            <tr><td colspan="2">No stocks selected</td></tr>
          </xsl:if>
          <xsl:for-each select="page/STOCKS/ROW">
            <tr>
              <td><xsl:value-of select="TICKER"/></td>
              <td align="right"><xsl:value-of select="PRICE"/></td>
            </tr>
          </xsl:for-each>
        </table>
      </xsl:with-param>
    </xsl:call-template>
  </xsl:template>
</xsl:stylesheet>
```

We could put both the `StockQuotes` and the `NewsBoxes` named templates in the same stylesheet if we wanted to. However, keeping them separate allows us later to import or include just the templates we need.

To glue the portal home page together, we need a stylesheet like *News.xsl* shown in Example 17-17, with a root template that stitches together these modular pieces in the appropriate spot on the page.

Example 17-17. Stylesheet to Format the News Portal

```
<?xml version="1.0"?>
<!-- News.xsl: Format the news portal page -->
<xsl:stylesheet xmlns:xsl="http://www.w3.org/1999/XSL/Transform" version="1.0">
  <xsl:output method="html" indent="no"/>
  <xsl:include href="StockQuotes.xsl"/>
  <xsl:include href="NewsBoxes.xsl"/>
  <xsl:template match="/">
    <html>
      <head><link rel="stylesheet" type="text/css" href="Forum.css" /></head>
      <body class="page">
        <center>
        <table border="0" width="70%">
          <tr>
            <td valign="top" width="140">
              <xsl:call-template name="StockQuotes"/>
            </td>
            <td width="400">
              <xsl:call-template name="NewsBoxes"/>
            </td>
          </tr>
        </table>
      </center>
      </body>
    </html>
  </xsl:template>
</xsl:stylesheet>
```

Then we add the following at the top of the *News.xsql* portal page to use the new stylesheet:

```
<?xml-stylesheet type="text/xsl" href="News.xsql"?>
```

Now when we browse the *http://server/News.xsql,* we see the assembled and styled portal page for the default user, as shown in Figure 17-18.

All the boxes look uniform, and the contents are fully driven off database-based news story contents and user preferences. We see five news stories in each category, since that was the default number of headings to display for the `DEFAULT` user. Clicking on the dynamically generated headings for a news category, we link to the *NewsCategory.xsql* page we created in the previous section to drill down into the details of the stories in the category and to allow us to page through them at our stateless leisure.

To add a quick Login box to the site, we create a `LoginBox` template that uses `TitledBox` again, as shown in the following code.

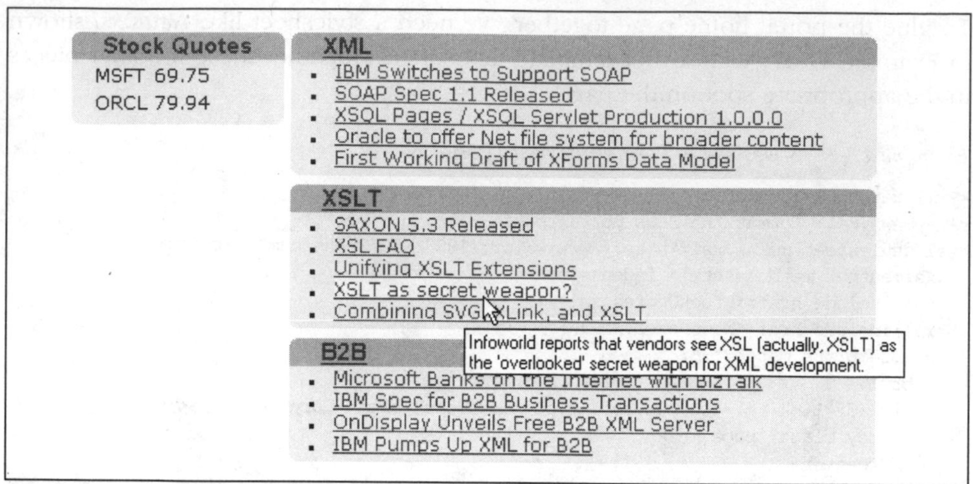

Figure 17-18. Personalized news portal page exploits SQL, XML, and XSLT

```
<xsl:stylesheet version="1.0" xmlns:xsl="http://www.w3.org/1999/XSL/Transform">
  <xsl:include href="TitledBox.xsl"/>
  <xsl:template name="LoginBox">
    <xsl:call-template name="TitledBox">
      <xsl:with-param name="Title">
        <!-- Static title of a bolded "Login" -->
        <b>Login</b>
      </xsl:with-param>
      <xsl:with-param name="Contents">
        <!-- Form goes inside the contents -->
        <br/>
        <form method="post" action="News.xsql">
          <input size="13" type="text" name="youremail"/>
        </form>
      </xsl:with-param>
    </xsl:call-template>
  </xsl:template>
</xsl:stylesheet>
```

Then we add the following three additional XSQL action elements to the top of our *News.xsql* page:

`<xsql:set-cookie>`
: Sets the `forumuser` cookie to the value of the `youremail` parameter submitted from the Login form

`<xsql:set-page-param>`
: Creates a page-level parameter named `forumuser`

`<xsql:include-param>`
: Includes the name of the `forumuser` cookie in the data page so the stylesheet can access it

Once we do this, we end up with the modified *News.xsql* page in Example 17-18.

Example 17-18. Modified News.xsql file that Handles the forumuser Cookie

```
<?xml version="1.0"?>
<!-- News.xsql: Data page driving the news portal -->
<?xml-stylesheet type="text/xsl" href="News.xsl"?>
<page connection="xmlbook" xmlns:xsql="urn:oracle-xsql">
  <xsql:set-cookie name="forumuser" value="{@youremail}"
                   ignore-empty-value="yes" only-if-unset="yes"/>
  <xsql:set-page-param name="forumuser" value="{@youremail}"
                       ignore-empty-value="yes"/>
  <xsql:include-param name="forumuser"/>
  <xsql:query rowset-element="STOCKS">
    SELECT ticker,to_char(price,'999.99') as price
      FROM latest_quotes
      WHERE trunc(day) = (SELECT MAX(TRUNC(day)) FROM latest_quotes)
        AND ticker IN (SELECT ticker
                         FROM user_stocks
                        WHERE userid = NVL('{@forumuser}','DEFAULT'))
      order by ticker
  </xsql:query>
  <xsql:query><![CDATA[
    SELECT cat.id,
           cat.name,
           CURSOR( SELECT title,url,description
                     FROM latestnews
                    WHERE category = cat.id
                      AND ROWNUM <= (SELECT headlines
                                       FROM user_prefs
                                      WHERE userid = NVL('{@forumuser}','DEFAULT'))
           ) AS stories
      FROM site_newscategory cat
      WHERE cat.id IN (SELECT category
                         FROM user_news_categories
                        WHERE userid = NVL('{@forumuser}','DEFAULT'))
  ]]>
  </xsql:query>
</page>
```

Finally, we update our *News.xsl* stylesheet as shown in Example 17-19 to contain a few **<xsl:if>** actions to conditionally invoke the **LoginBox** template if the user has not yet logged in, as well as conditionally show a link to the *Prefs.xsql* page we'll create later in the chapter to edit the user's preferences if he is logged in.

Example 17-19. Stylesheet to Format the News Portal Page

```
<?xml version="1.0"?>
<!-- News.xsl: Format the news portal page -->
<xsl:stylesheet xmlns:xsl="http://www.w3.org/1999/XSL/Transform" version="1.0">
  <xsl:output method="html" indent="no"/>
  <xsl:include href="StockQuotes.xsl"/>
  <xsl:include href="LoginBox.xsl"/>
```

Example 17-19. Stylesheet to Format the News Portal Page (continued)

```
  <xsl:include href="NewsBoxes.xsl"/>
  <xsl:template match="/">
    <html>
      <head><link rel="stylesheet" type="text/css" href="Forum.css" /></head>
      <body class="page">
        <center>
        <table border="0"width="70%">
          <tr>
            <td valign="top" width="140">
              <xsl:call-template name="StockQuotes"/>
              <!-- Show LoginBox if the forumuser in page is blank -->
              <xsl:if test="/page/forumuser = ''">
                <br/>
                <xsl:call-template name="LoginBox"/>
              </xsl:if>
            </td>
            <td width="400">
                <xsl:call-template name="NewsBoxes"/>
            </td>
          </tr>
        </table>
        <!-- Show preferences link if forumuser in page is not blank -->
        <xsl:if test="/page/forumuser != ''">
          <font size="1">
            <a href="Prefs.xsql">
              <xsl:text>Preferences for </xsl:text>
              <xsl:value-of select="/page/forumuser"/>
            </a>
          </font>
        </xsl:if>
      </center>
      </body>
    </html>
  </xsl:template>
</xsl:stylesheet>
```

Requesting the *News.xsql* page again now shows a `Login` box, as illustrated in Figure 17-19.

If we cheat for a moment and use the database directly to insert a user ID and some user preferences for a new user like `smuench`:

```
INSERT INTO user_prefs VALUES ('smuench',/* Number of Headlines */ 4);
INSERT INTO user_stocks VALUES ('smuench','HLTH');
INSERT INTO user_stocks VALUES ('smuench','WEBM');
INSERT INTO user_stocks VALUES ('smuench','ORCL');
INSERT INTO user_stocks VALUES ('smuench','INTC');
INSERT INTO user_stocks VALUES ('smuench','AAPL');
INSERT INTO user_news_categories VALUES ('smuench',2);
INSERT INTO user_news_categories VALUES ('smuench',1);
```

Stock Quotes
MSFT 69.75
ORCL 79.94
Login

XML
- IBM Switches to Support SOAP
- SOAP Spec 1.1 Released
- XSQL Pages / XSQL Servlet Production 1.0.0.0
- Oracle to offer Net file system for broader content
- First Working Draft of XForms Data Model

XSLT
- SAXON 5.3 Released
- XSL FAQ
- Unifying XSLT Extensions
- XSLT as secret weapon?
- Combining SVG, XLink, and XSLT

B2B
- Microsoft Banks on the Internet with BizTalk
- IBM Spec for B2B Business Transactions
- OnDisplay Unveils Free B2B XML Server
- IBM Pumps Up XML for B2B

Figure 17-19. Portal page with additional user login box

and then try to log in by typing **smuench** in the **Login** box and pressing Enter, we'll see the portal snap immediately to show what's in Figure 17-20. It has my stocks and the categories of news I want to see, with the number of headings that my preferences indicate.

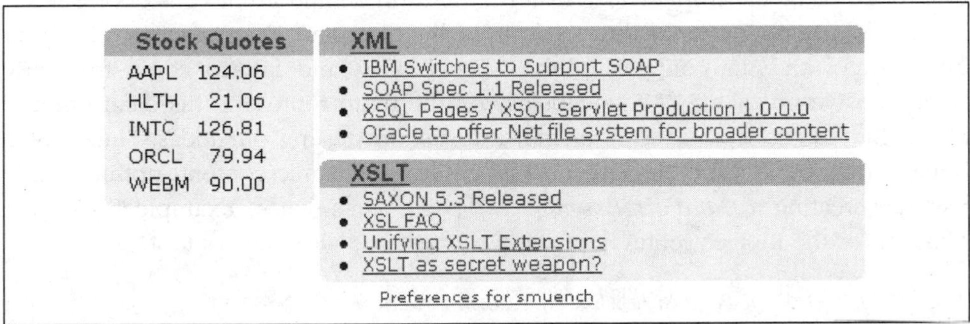

Figure 17-20. Customer portal home page for user smuench

In the next section, we'll see how to use XSLT to built HTML forms in a generic way, allowing us to create a form through which users can edit their preferences.

Separating Structure and Style of Forms

In order to allow users to edit their preferences, we could create an HTML form by hand. However, since this won't be the only form we'll be creating in this chapter, let's step back and see if we can apply XSLT to handle HTML form creation based on some structural information we can include in our XSQL data page.

An HTML form is just a set of items. We'd like to be able to describe the set of items in a more abstract way that allows us to say what kinds of items are in the form and what data should be displayed in the items. The kinds of items that will come in handy for the tasks we'll be doing are illustrated in Figure 17-21.

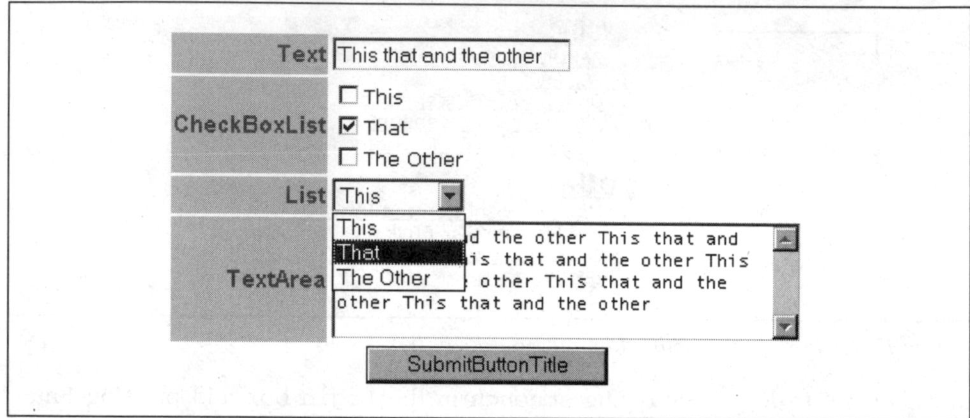

Figure 17-21. Basic data-bound HTML controls

We want to be able to represent a form like the example above in an abstract way, then build an XSLT template to transform the form definition into a working set of HTML form tags. We need the contents of the Text and TextArea to come from any source, and the contents of the CheckBoxList and List to come from any query. So we invent an XML vocabulary on the fly to represent this dataform and we include a set of static XML elements to use for testing our ideas. Since XSQL pages can contain static elements just as easily as dynamic content, nothing stops us from creating a *DataFormExample.xsql* page, as shown in Example 17-20, that consists for the moment entirely of static element and attribute content.

Example 17-20. XSQL Page Builds Example Form Structure

```
<?xml version="1.0"?>
<!-- DataFormExample.xsql: Example page with abstract form stucture def'n -->
<page>
  <dataform target="News.xsql" submit="SubmitButtonTitle">
    <item type="text" name="nameOfTextControl" label="Text">
       This that and the other
    </item>
    <item type="checkboxlist" name="nameOfCheckBoxList" label="CheckBoxList">
      <ROWSET>
        <ROW><VALUE>4</VALUE><DISPLAY>This</DISPLAY></ROW>
        <ROW><VALUE>5</VALUE><DISPLAY>That</DISPLAY><SELECTED>Y</SELECTED></ROW>
        <ROW><VALUE>6</VALUE><DISPLAY>The Other</DISPLAY></ROW>
      </ROWSET>
    </item>
    <item type="list" name="nameOfList" label="List">
      <default>Y</default>
```

Example 17-20. XSQL Page Builds Example Form Structure (continued)

```
      <ROWSET>
        <ROW><VALUE>X</VALUE><DISPLAY>This</DISPLAY></ROW>
        <ROW><VALUE>Y</VALUE><DISPLAY>That</DISPLAY></ROW>
        <ROW><VALUE>Z</VALUE><DISPLAY>The Other</DISPLAY></ROW>
      </ROWSET>
    </item>
    <item type="textarea" name="nameOfTextArea" size="40" label="TextArea">
      This that and the other This that and the other This that and the other
      This that and the other This that and the other This that and the other
    </item>
  </dataform>
</page>
```

We use the most obvious names that come to mind to represent the abstract structural details of our HTML form. For the `text` and `textarea` types of items, we use the text content of the `<item>` element to be the current value of the item. For the `checkboxlist` and `<listitem>`s, we use an embedded `<ROWSET>` to represent the choices in the list and their respective display text.

We can then create an XSLT template to handle the entire `<dataform>` and its contents as shown in Example 17-21. Whenever the template matches a `<dataform>` element, it produces a working HTML form based on the structural information in the form's `<item>`s and the data that needs to be bound to the form. If we use this standard approach to build all forms on our site, then making global changes to how forms work or what they look like happens in a single place.

Here's what's going on in the *UtilDataForm.xsl* stylesheet. The `dataform` template:

1. Creates an HTML `<form>` element with an `action` based on the `target` attribute of the `<dataform>` element using the attribute value template `{@target}`.
2. Processes all the `item[@type='hidden']` nodes, using an `<xsl:for-each>` loop to create an HTML `<input>` element with `type='hidden'` for each one.
3. Processes all `item[@type!='hidden']` nodes, and using an `<xsl:choose>` action, creates the appropriate HTML control for each `dataform/item` based on `dataform/item/@type`.
4. For the `text` and `textarea` item types, uses XPath's `normalize-space()` function on the current node to strip whitespace from the front and back of the text value contained within the `dataform/item` element and replace any sequences of multiple whitespace characters with a single space.
5. For the `checkboxlist` and `list` types, uses a nested `<xsl:for-each>` to process the `ROWSET/ROW` creating the list of items, each with an appropriate value and display text; just outside the `<xsl:for-each>` in both cases, it uses

<xsl:variable> based on the current node so it can reference the value of the variable inside the for-each loop using $*varname*.

6. By combining <xsl:if> with a nested <xsl:attribute>, it conditionally creates a selected attribute on the <option> element for the list, or conditionally creates a checked attribute on the <input> element for a checkbox, (if the element is checked).

Example 17-21. Transforming an Abstract Form Description into HTML

```
<xsl:stylesheet xmlns:xsl="http://www.w3.org/1999/XSL/Transform" version="1.0">
  <!--
   | UtilDataForm.xsl: Transform <dataform> structural info
   |                   into a data-bound HTML Form
   +-->
  <xsl:template match="dataform">
    <center>
      <form method="POST" action="{@target}">
        <xsl:for-each select="item[@type='hidden']">
          <input type="hidden" name="{@name}" value="{normalize-space(.)}"/>
        </xsl:for-each>
        <table>
          <xsl:for-each select="item[@type != 'hidden']">
            <tr>
              <th align="right"><xsl:value-of select="@label"/></th>
              <td>
                <xsl:choose>
                  <xsl:when test="@type='text'">
                    <input type="text" name="{@name}"
                                       value="{normalize-space(.)}">
                      <xsl:if test="@size">
                        <xsl:attribute name="size">
                          <xsl:value-of select="@size"/>
                        </xsl:attribute>
                      </xsl:if>
                    </input>
                  </xsl:when>
                  <xsl:when test="@type='textarea'">
                    <textarea class="code" rows="5" name="{@name}">
                      <xsl:if test="@size">
                        <xsl:attribute name="cols">
                          <xsl:value-of select="@size"/>
                        </xsl:attribute>
                      </xsl:if>
                      <xsl:value-of select="normalize-space(.)"/>
                    </textarea>
                  </xsl:when>
                  <xsl:when test="@type='list'">
                    <xsl:variable name="default" select="default"/>
                    <select name="{@name}">
                      <xsl:for-each select="ROWSET/ROW">
                        <option value="{VALUE}">
                          <xsl:if test="VALUE=$default">
```

Example 17-21. Transforming an Abstract Form Description into HTML (continued)

```
                    <xsl:attribute name="selected"/>
                  </xsl:if>
                  <xsl:value-of select="DISPLAY"/>
                </option>
              </xsl:for-each>
            </select>
          </xsl:when>
          <xsl:when test="@type='checkboxlist'">
            <xsl:variable name="name" select="@name"/>
            <xsl:for-each select="ROWSET/ROW">
              <input type="checkbox" name="{$name}" value="{VALUE}">
                <xsl:if test="SELECTED='Y'">
                  <xsl:attribute name="checked"/>
                </xsl:if>
              </input>
              <xsl:value-of select="DISPLAY"/><br/>
            </xsl:for-each>
          </xsl:when>
        </xsl:choose>
      </td>
    </tr>
  </xsl:for-each>
</table>
<input type="submit" value="{@submit}"/>
</form>
</center>
</xsl:template>
</xsl:stylesheet>
```

To test out our new form creation capability, we create a quick *FormTest.xsl* stylesheet that includes *UtilDataForm.xsl* and defines a root template to create the shell of an HTML form around it before using `<xsl:apply-templates>` with a `select="page/dataform"` to match the included dataform template:

```
<?xml version="1.0"?>
<xsl:stylesheet xmlns:xsl="http://www.w3.org/1999/XSL/Transform" version="1.0">
  <xsl:include href="UtilDataForm.xsl"/>
  <xsl:template match="/">
    <html>
      <head><link rel="stylesheet" type="text/css" href="Forum.css"/></head>
      <body><xsl:apply-templates select="page/dataform"/></body>
    </html>
  </xsl:template>
</xsl:stylesheet>
```

Then we add:

```
<?xml-stylesheet type="text/xsl" href="FormTest.xsl"?>
```

to the top of *DataFormExample.xsql* to associate our stylesheet with it, and request the page in the browser. We see precisely the HTML form illustrated in Figure 17-21. Let's immediately use our new HTML form support to build a page for the user to edit preferences. We create the *Prefs.xsql* shown in Example 17-22.

Example 17-22. XSQL Page to Create/Edit User Preferences

```
<?xml version="1.0"?>
<!-- Prefs.xsql: Create form for displaying/editing user preferences -->
<?xml-stylesheet type="text/xsl" href="Prefs.xsl"?>
<page connection="xmlbook" xmlns:xsql="urn:oracle-xsql">
  <dataform target="News.xsql" submit="Save Preferences">
    <item type="hidden" name="userid">
      <xsql:include-param name="forumuser"/>
    </item>
    <item type="checkboxlist" name="categories" label="News Categories">
      <xsql:query>
        SELECT nc.id AS VALUE,
               nc.name AS DISPLAY,
               DECODE(uc.category,NULL,'N','Y') as SELECTED
          FROM site_newscategory nc,
               user_news_categories uc
          WHERE NVL('{@forumuser}','DEFAULT') = uc.userid (+)
            AND                          nc.id = uc.category (+)
         order by name
      </xsql:query>
    </item>
    <item type="list" name="headlines" label="Headlines Per Category">
      <xsql:query rowset-element="" row-element="">
        SELECT headlines as "default"
          FROM user_prefs
         WHERE userid = NVL('{@forumuser}','DEFAULT')
      </xsql:query>
      <ROWSET>
        <ROW><VALUE>4</VALUE><DISPLAY>4</DISPLAY></ROW>
        <ROW><VALUE>5</VALUE><DISPLAY>5</DISPLAY></ROW>
        <ROW><VALUE>6</VALUE><DISPLAY>6</DISPLAY></ROW>
      </ROWSET>
    </item>
    <item type="textarea" name="stocks" size="40" label="Stocks">
      <xsql:query>
        SELECT ticker||' ' as ticker
          FROM user_stocks
         WHERE userid = NVL('{@forumuser}','DEFAULT')
      </xsql:query>
    </item>
  </dataform>
</page>
```

The page has a `<dataform>` element with `<item>`s of the following types:

`hidden`
: This item is for the `userid` parameter. It gets its value from the text content of the element created in the data page with `<xsql:include-param>`.

`checkboxlist`
: This item displays the set of all available news categories with the current ones checked. It gets its data from the `ROWSET` produced by the `<xsql:query>`.

This is a clever query using outer joins to return the list of available news categories with a letter `Y` or `N` in the selected column depending on whether the current user has selected that category in their preferences. The SQL result looks like this:

```
VALUE DISPLAY    SELECTED
----- ---------- --------
    3 B2B        N
    5 Business   N
    4 Extra      N
    1 XML        Y
    2 XSLT       Y
```

`list`

This item displays the choices for the number of headlines to display. It gets its data from a static <ROWSET> element in the page, since the choices are fixed.

`textarea`

This item lists the stock ticker symbols. It gets its value by producing a <ROWSET> of <ROW>s of <TICKER> elements for the current user's stocks. Note that each value has a space appended at the end. This way, when the dataform XSLT template asks for the value of the content of the item element, it will get the concatenated value of all text nodes with spaces between the ticker symbols.

The stylesheet associated to *Prefs.xsql* is the following simple *Prefs.xsl*, which uses `<xsl:apply-templates>` to cause the `page/dataform` to be transformed:

```
<?xml version="1.0"?>
<xsl:stylesheet xmlns:xsl="http://www.w3.org/1999/XSL/Transform" version="1.0">
  <xsl:import href="UtilDataForm.xsl"/>
  <xsl:template match="/">
    <html>
      <head><link rel="stylesheet" type="text/css" href="Forum.css" />
      </head>
      <body class="page">
        <xsl:apply-templates select="page/dataform"/>
      </body>
    </html>
  </xsl:template>
</xsl:stylesheet>
```

Now when we log in to the portal and click on the "Preferences for smuench" link at the bottom of the page, we see the result of our work: an HTML form dynamically populated with our current preferences from the database, shown in Figure 17-22.

Note that the values displayed in the form reflect the rows we inserted earlier for user ID `smuench`. What happens when we click on the *Save Preferences* button? We need the *News.xsql* home page to handle the posted preferences and update the database with any changes. We'll deal with that in the next section.

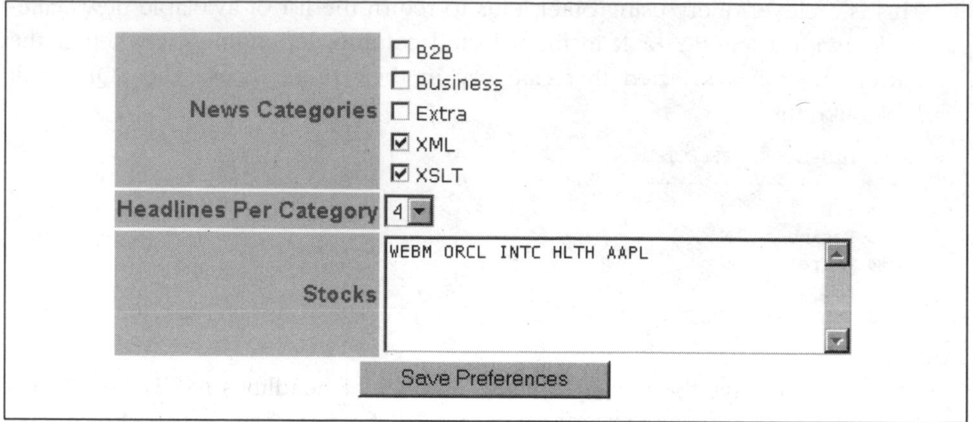

Figure 17-22. User preferences form populated with dynamic data

Updating User Preferences

When the user posts *Prefs.xsql*'s HTML form, the XSQL page processor detects that the MIME type is that of a posted HTML form and materializes an XML document like this:

```
<request>
  <parameters>
    <stocks>WEBM ORCL INTC HLTH AAPL</stocks>
    <headlines>4</headlines>
    <userid>smuench</userid>
    <row><!-- Repeated parameters are row-ified to make processing easier -->
      <categories>1</categories>
    </row>
    <row>
      <categories>2</categories>
    </row>
  </parameters>
  <session>
    <wtgbid>c15k9ixg</wtgbid>
  </session>
  <cookies>
    <forumuser>smuench</forumuser>
  </cookies>
</request>
```

This makes all of the posted form parameters available to the `<xsql:insert-request>` action's `transform` stylesheet for conversion into canonical format for the target table. Here we have information that goes into the user_prefs table, like the number of headlines, information that goes into user_news_categories, like the selected categories, and information that goes into user_stocks. Can we insert it into all three tables simultaneously? Sure. The solution involves creating:

- A view with a structure that is convenient to accept all of the information
- An INSTEAD OF INSERT trigger on the view to programmatically handle the inserted information correctly

We can create a view with a convenient structure like this:

```
CREATE OR REPLACE VIEW user_prefs_view AS
SELECT userid, headlines,
       RPAD('x',200) as stocks,
       RPAD('x',100) as categories
  FROM user_prefs;
```

This selects the **userid** and **headlines** count from user_prefs, adds a VARCHAR2(200) column in the view by selecting the **RPAD('x',200)** expression, and adds a VARCHAR2(100) column in a similar way. Since we're only going to use this view for inserts, we don't really care that a SELECT statement against the view would return 300 letter x's as part of the result. This is just a way to get the database to expect up to 200 characters for the **stocks** column in the view and up to 100 characters for the **categories**. We're going to insert the stocks information as a single string containing the space-separated ticker symbols the user has entered in the preferences form. We'll do the same for the category IDs of any selected categories in the form.

Transforming the materialized request document for insertion according to this strategy is easy. First we use the utility we developed in Chapter 14, *Advanced XML Loading Techniques*, to create a skeleton insert transform for the **user_prefs_insert** view using the XSQL command-line utility (note that all arguments must be on one line, separated by spaces):

```
xsql GenerateInsertTransform.xsql InsertUserPrefs.xsl table=user_prefs_insert
```

This creates the skeleton transformation in the *InsertUserPrefs.xsl* file, as shown in Example 17-23.

Example 17-23. Skeleton Insert Transform for user_prefs_view

```
<?xml version = '1.0' encoding = 'UTF-8'?>
<xsl:stylesheet version="1.0" xmlns:xsl="http://www.w3.org/1999/XSL/Transform">
   <!-- Transform XXXX into canonical ROWSET for user_prefs_view -->
   <xsl:template match="/">
      <ROWSET>
         <!-- XPath for repeating source rows -->
         <xsl:for-each select="page/ROWSET/ROW">
            <ROW>
               <USERID>
                  <xsl:value-of select="USERID"/>
               </USERID>
               <HEADLINES>
                  <xsl:value-of select="HEADLINES"/>
               </HEADLINES>
```

Example 17-23. Skeleton Insert Transform for user_prefs_view (continued)

```
          <STOCKS>
            <xsl:value-of select="STOCKS"/>
          </STOCKS>
          <CATEGORIES>
            <xsl:value-of select="CATEGORIES"/>
          </CATEGORIES>
        </ROW>
      </xsl:for-each>
    </ROWSET>
  </xsl:template>
</xsl:stylesheet>
```

We edit the skeleton transformation to fill in the appropriate **request/parameters** pattern in **<xsl:for-each>**, and change the skeleton patterns to the real names **userid**, **stocks**, and **headlines**, in lowercase. For the value of the **<CATEGORIES>** element, we use a nested **<xsl:for-each>** to loop over all selected categories that have been posted and produce a string that is the value of each **<category>** separated by a space. Finally, we surround the outer **<xsl:for-each>** with an **<xsl:if>** to test that a user ID exists (recall that it was a hidden field in the HTML preferences form). If no **userid** is posted along with the form, then no **<ROW>** elements are created, so no rows are inserted into **user_prefs_view**. The final *InsertUserPrefs.xsl* stylesheet appears in Example 17-24.

Example 17-24. Final Version of the InsertUserPrefs.xsl Stylesheet

```
<?xml version = '1.0' encoding = 'UTF-8'?>
<!-- InsertUserPref.xsl: Insert transform for user_prefs_view -->
<xsl:stylesheet version="1.0" xmlns:xsl="http://www.w3.org/1999/XSL/Transform">
  <xsl:template match="/">
    <ROWSET>
      <xsl:if test="request/parameters/userid">
        <xsl:for-each select="request/parameters">
          <ROW>
            <USERID>
              <xsl:value-of select="userid"/>
            </USERID>
            <STOCKS>
              <xsl:value-of select="stocks"/>
            </STOCKS>
            <HEADLINES>
              <xsl:value-of select="headlines"/>
            </HEADLINES>
            <CATEGORIES>
              <xsl:for-each select="row/categories">
                <xsl:value-of select="."/>
                <xsl:if test="position() != last()">
                  <xsl:text> </xsl:text>
                </xsl:if>
              </xsl:for-each>
            </CATEGORIES>
```

Example 17-24. Final Version of the InsertUserPrefs.xsl Stylesheet (continued)

```
          </ROW>
        </xsl:for-each>
      </xsl:if>
    </ROWSET>
  </xsl:template>
</xsl:stylesheet>
```

We add the following XSQL action element to the top of our *News.xsql* page to handle the posted **preferences** form:

```
<xsql:insert-request table="user_prefs_view" transform="InsertUserPrefs.xsl"/>
```

This uses the stylesheet we just created to transform the posted form information and insert it into the **user_prefs_view**. If the page is requested normally, instead of being the target of a posted HTML form, this action is a no-op. As the very final step, we write the INSTEAD OF INSERT trigger in Example 17-25. The **user_prefs_view** performs the actual insertions and updates into the preferences tables underneath the covers.

Example 17-25. INSTEAD OF INSERT Trigger Handles User Preferences

```
CREATE TRIGGER user_prefs_ins INSTEAD OF INSERT ON user_prefs_view FOR EACH ROW
DECLARE
  debugct       NUMBER;
  stockList     VARCHAR2(200) := :new.stocks;
  catList       VARCHAR2(200) := :new.categories;
  curItem       VARCHAR2(80);
  x             NUMBER;
  temp          VARCHAR2(1);
  userExists    BOOLEAN;
  CURSOR c_userExists(c_userid VARCHAR2) IS SELECT 'x' FROM user_prefs
                                             WHERE userid = c_userid;
BEGIN
  OPEN c_userExists(:new.userid);
  FETCH c_userExists INTO temp;
  userExists := c_userExists%FOUND;
  CLOSE c_userExists;
  IF userExists THEN -- Update existing user
   UPDATE user_prefs SET headlines  = :new.headlines
                     WHERE userid = :new.userid;
  ELSE -- Insert a new user
    INSERT INTO user_prefs(userid,headlines)VALUES(:new.userid,:new.headlines);
  END IF;
  -- Handle Stocks
  DELETE FROM user_stocks WHERE userid = :new.userid;
  WHILE (stockList IS NOT NULL) LOOP
    x := INSTR(stockList,' ');
    IF x > 0 THEN
      curItem := SUBSTR(stockList,1,x-1); stockList := SUBSTR(stockList,x+1);
    ELSE
      curItem := stockList; stockList := NULL;
    END IF;
```

Example 17-25. INSTEAD OF INSERT Trigger Handles User Preferences (continued)

```
    INSERT INTO user_stocks(userid,ticker) VALUES(:new.userid,curItem);
  END LOOP;
  -- Handle Categories
  DELETE FROM user_news_categories WHERE userid = :new.userid;
  WHILE (catList IS NOT NULL) LOOP
    x := INSTR(catList,' ');
    IF x > 0 THEN
      curItem := SUBSTR(catList,1,x-1); catList := SUBSTR(catList,x+1);
    ELSE
      curItem := catList; catList := NULL;
    END IF;
    INSERT INTO user_news_categories(userid,category)VALUES(:new.userid,curItem);
  END LOOP;
END;
```

We're processing a space-separated list of categories and stocks here to simplify the HTML side of the equation. This way, a user just types in quotes as they do on Yahoo!, and the details of parsing the list are handled in the server.

This PL/SQL trigger first uses a cursor to detect if the `:new.userid` being inserted already exists in our user_prefs table. If so, it updates the existing user's headlines preference in user_prefs; otherwise, it inserts a new row in user_prefs for the `:new.userid` with the correct headings selection. Then, in two different WHILE loops, it processes the space-separated stock tickers and news categories. It inserts them into the user_stocks and user_news_categories tables correctly after having first deleted all existing rows in those tables for the current user.

Now is the moment of truth. We exit our browser to clear our existing cookie and restart it. We browse our portal site's URL again at *http://server/News.xsql* and see the opening content for the DEFAULT user from Figure 17-19. We type a new user name like `jcox` into the `Login` box and see what appears in Figure 17-23.

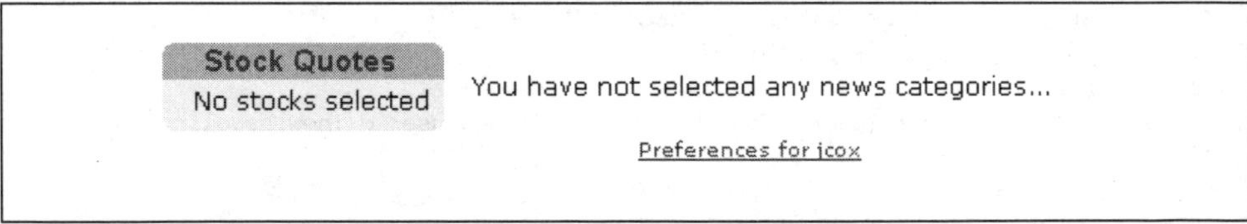

Figure 17-23. Personalized portal page for first-time user

We cross our fingers and click on the preferences link. We get a blank preferences form and click the B2B and XSLT categories, select six headlines per category, and enter the ticker symbols for our favorite stocks as shown in Figure 17-24.

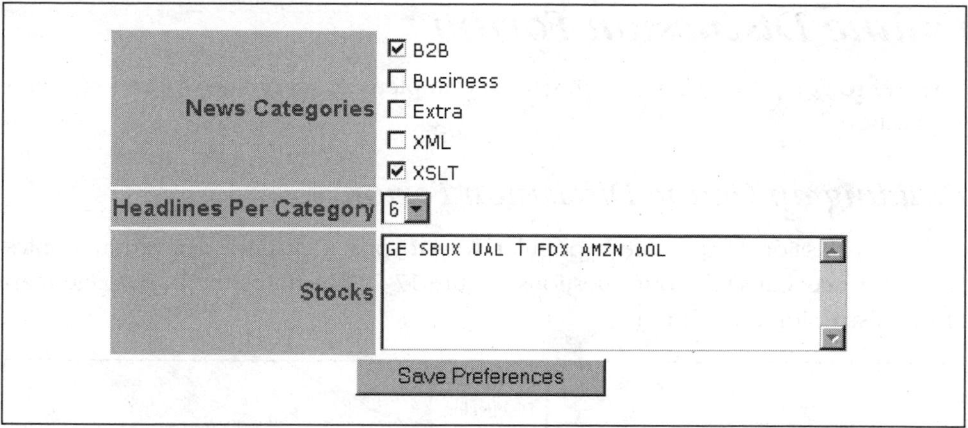

Figure 17-24. Editing preferences for a first-time user

We click *Save Preferences* and instantly see our preferences reflected in the content, as Figure 17-25 shows.

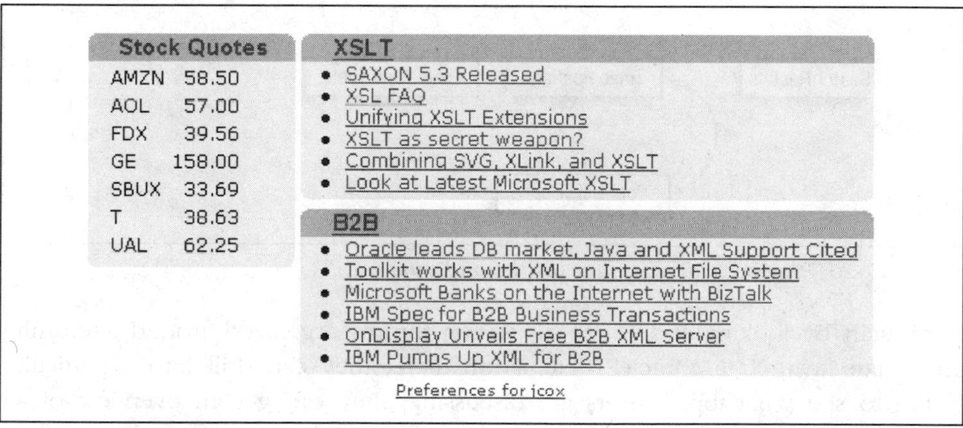

Figure 17-25. Customized portal page for user jcox

If we go to another browser, browse the *News.xsql* page, log in as `jcox`, click on preferences, change our selected categories, alter the ticker symbols, and click, we have successfully edited our existing preferences. If we click on a heading from the portal page, we're brought to the *NewsCategory.xsql* page we built earlier to browse statelessly through all the news stories in that category. The whole site looks consistent, is completely database-driven, and gains all of its power from the combination of XSQL pages and XSLT stylesheets.

Online Discussion Forum

Now we're going to shift into high gear and implement an online discussion forum application.

Building an Online Discussion Forum

Online discussion forums are a popular way to post questions on various topics and have peers answer your questions. Figure 17-26 illustrates the basic page map of the discussion application.

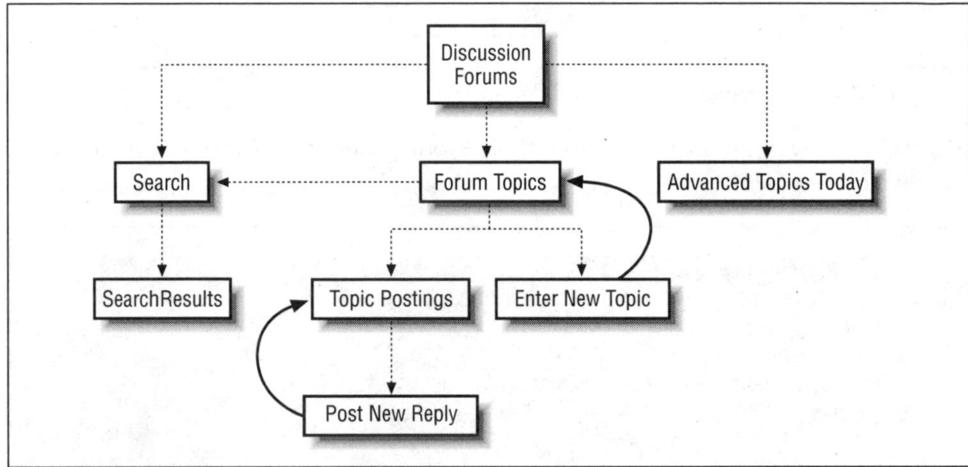

Figure 17-26. Page map for an online discussion forum

Users start by looking at a list of discussion forums organized around interesting areas like Java, XML, Oracle8*i*, etc. From there, they can drill into a particular forum to see what topics users are discussing; they can get an overview of all active topics across all the forums; or they can search for a particular word or phrase and browse through the results. While in a particular forum, users can browse the topics as well as drill in to see what replies have been posted for any topic. In addition, if a user logs in by providing a user ID, they can post new topics and post replies to existing topics.

We'll use this example to illustrate the maximum separation of data from presentation, and the maximum abstraction of our web pages' structure from their appearance. Let's start with the database part of the application. We can keep track of the forums, forum topics, topic postings and replies, and forum users with a straightforward database schema like the one shown in Figure 17-27.

First we create the forum_user table to store our users:

```
CREATE TABLE forum_user(
  userid     VARCHAR2(10),
```

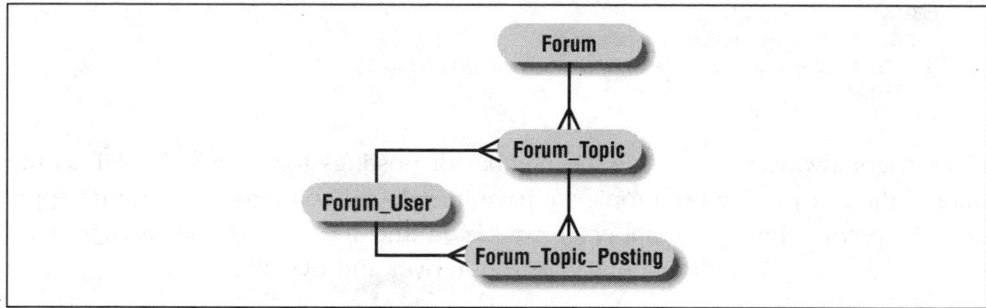

Figure 17-27. Database schema for discussion forum application

```
  email       VARCHAR2(80),
  CONSTRAINT forum_user_pk PRIMARY KEY (userid)
);
```

Next, we create the forum table for storing the forums themselves:

```
CREATE TABLE forum(
  id          NUMBER,
  created     DATE,
  name        VARCHAR2(80),
  CONSTRAINT forum_pk PRIMARY KEY (id)
);
```

To have the database automatically manage the assignment of a unique `id` for each new forum from a sequence, as well as handle the assignment of the `created` date, we create a BEFORE INSERT trigger on the forum table like this:

```
CREATE OR REPLACE TRIGGER forum_id_trig
BEFORE INSERT ON forum FOR EACH ROW
BEGIN
  SELECT forumid.nextval,sysdate
    INTO :new.id,:new.created
    FROM dual;
END;
```

To store the topics in each forum, we create the forum_topic table with a similar BEFORE INSERT trigger to handle `id` and `created` assignment:

```
CREATE TABLE forum_topic(
  id          NUMBER,
  forumid     NUMBER,
  created     DATE,
  title       VARCHAR2(80) NOT NULL,
  userid      VARCHAR2(80),
  postings    NUMBER,
  lastpost    DATE,
  CONSTRAINT forum_topic_pk PRIMARY KEY (id),
  CONSTRAINT topic_in_forum FOREIGN KEY (forumid) REFERENCES forum
);
CREATE OR REPLACE TRIGGER forum_topicid_trig
BEFORE INSERT ON forum_topic FOR EACH ROW
```

```
BEGIN
  SELECT forumid.nextval,sysdate,0
    INTO :new.id,:new.created,:new.postings
    FROM dual;
END;
```

Since users always want to see the number of postings for a topic as well as the date of the last posting on a topic we have introduced columns in the forum_topic table to record the total number of `postings` and the date of the `lastpost` so that we can avoid requerying this information over and over.

Finally, we create the forum_topic_posting table:

```
CREATE TABLE forum_topic_posting(
  id         NUMBER,
  topicid    NUMBER,
  userid     VARCHAR2(30) NOT NULL,
  posted     DATE,
  posting    VARCHAR2(4000) NOT NULL,
  CONSTRAINT forum_topic_posting_pk PRIMARY KEY (id),
  CONSTRAINT posting_for_topic      FOREIGN KEY (topicid) REFERENCES forum_topic
);
```

The BEFORE INSERT trigger on forum_topic_posting handles the ID and `posted` date assignment as we did earlier, but it also updates the values of `postings` and `lastpost` in the forum_topic table by adding one to the `postings` count and updating the `lastpost` to reflect the current SYSDATE:

```
CREATE OR REPLACE TRIGGER forum_topic_postingid_trig
BEFORE INSERT ON forum_topic_posting FOR EACH ROW
DECLARE
  topicid       NUMBER;
  topicpostdate DATE := SYSDATE;
BEGIN
  SELECT forumid.nextval,topicpostdate
    INTO :new.id,:new.posted
    FROM dual;
  UPDATE forum_topic
     SET postings = postings + 1,
         lastpost = topicpostdate
   WHERE id = :new.topicid;
END;
```

The last data problem relates to posting a new topic. When a user starts a new topic by asking the initial question, we want to record a row in the forum_topic table and insert the user's question as the first posting related to that new topic in the forum_topic_posting table. As we did earlier in the chapter, to simplify a case like this, we create a database view for inserting a new topic:

```
CREATE OR REPLACE VIEW forum_new_topic AS
SELECT t.forumid, t.title, t.userid, p.posting
```

```
  FROM forum_topic t,
       forum_topic_posting p
 WHERE t.id = p.topicid;
```

and an INSTEAD OF INSERT trigger that lets us programmatically insert the one logical new topic row into the two physical underlying tables:

```
CREATE OR REPLACE TRIGGER forum_new_topic_ins
INSTEAD OF INSERT ON forum_new_topic FOR EACH ROW
DECLARE
  newTopicId NUMBER;
BEGIN
  INSERT INTO forum_topic(forumid,userid,title)
    VALUES (:new.forumid,:new.userid, :new.title)
  RETURNING id INTO newTopicId;
  INSERT INTO forum_topic_posting(topicid,userid,posting)
    VALUES (newTopicId,:new.userid,:new.posting);
END;
```

This completes the database setup for the application. All the information we need to track is nicely factored into its own table and we've offloaded as much of the data maintenance work as possible onto database triggers, keeping the rest of the application much simpler.

Completely Abstracting Page Structure

Our web designers have gotten even more creative for this discussion forum application, and as a result of extensive usability testing, have concluded that users want our site to:

- Provide a trail of context information on each page to show users where they are and where they've come from. User interface designers call this trail "breadcrumbs."
- Present all available actions a user can perform on the current page in a consistent way.
- Present lists of information in a consistent way throughout the site.
- Allow the user to browse information in small pages, avoiding the need to scroll in the browser.

To implement these requirements, every page on the discussion forum site needs to have the same four structural elements:

- A list of "breadcrumbs"
- A list of "actions"
- The data content of the page
- The paging information for browsing forward/backward through the data

So the abstract information structure of each page on the site, which we'll represent in XML, will look like this:

```
<page>
  <breadcrumbs>
    <!-- Some breadcrumb context information here -->
  </breadcrumbs>
  <actions>
    <!-- Some actions information here -->
  </actions>
  <data>
    <!-- Some ROWSET of data here -->
  </data>
  <paging>
    <!-- Some paging information here -->
  </paging>
</page>
```

Figure 17-28 is the mockup our web designers have provided to show how they want these four consistent structural elements to be rendered for the browser. The graphical elements are:

Breadcrumbs bar
: This bar at the top of the page indicates the current page in the site hierarchy. Previous pages are shown as hyperlinks the user can click to follow the breadcrumb trail back to the home page of the site.

Actions bar
: This bar, which appears just below the breadcrumbs bar, is a simple list of hyperlinks indicating the actions the user can perform from this page.

Data area
: This area presents tabular information in an HTML table with column headings and rows that alternate in color.

Paging area
: This area indicates what page the user is seeing and presents links to navigate forward and backward through the data.

Our basic implementation strategy will proceed as follows:

- We will religiously separate data from presentation. The data required for the structure of each page will be represented by an Oracle XSQL page, and the look of the page will be handled by an XSLT stylesheet.
- We will fully modularize our XSLT presentation strategy. We'll begin with a template for our abstract `<page>` structure, and proceed to implement templates to handle each logical substructure of a page, like `<breadcrumbs>`, `<actions>`, `<data>`, and `<paging>`.

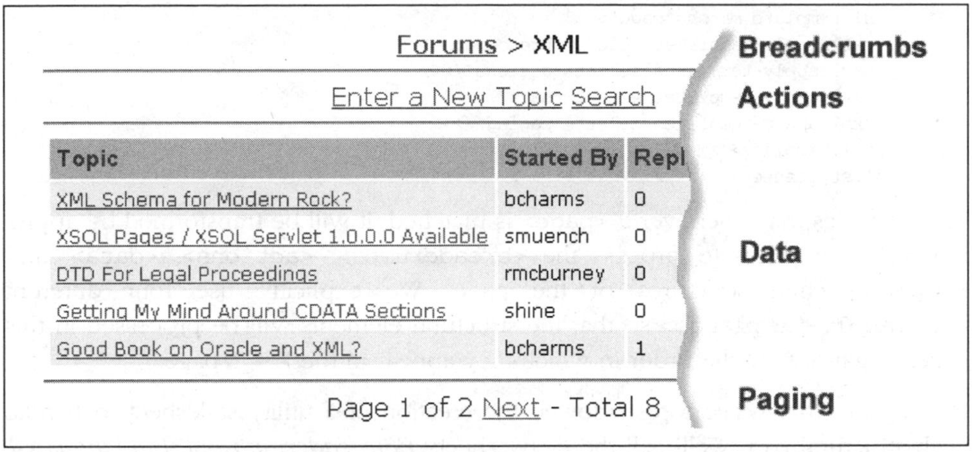

Forums > XML

Breadcrumbs

Enter a New Topic Search

Actions

Topic	Started By	Repl
XML Schema for Modern Rock?	bcharms	0
XSQL Pages / XSQL Servlet 1.0.0.0 Available	smuench	0
DTD For Legal Proceedings	rmcburney	0
Getting My Mind Around CDATA Sections	shine	0
Good Book on Oracle and XML?	bcharms	1

Data

Page 1 of 2 Next - Total 8

Paging

Figure 17-28. Visual mockup for consistent page display

The structure of every page is the same; we endeavor to handle the look and feel of the entire site using a single stylesheet, *ForumStyle.xsl*. It provides a root template that sets up the <html> page, creates a <head> section with a common <title>, handles the <link> to the standard *Forum.css* stylesheet used by every page on the site for font and color information, creates the HTML page <body> element, and processes all children of the root using <xsl:apply-templates>:

```
<!-- ForumStyle.xsl: Main stylesheet for the entire discussion forum site -->
<xsl:stylesheet xmlns:xsl="http://www.w3.org/1999/XSL/Transform" version="1.0">
  <xsl:include href="ForumPageStructure.xsl"/>
  <!-- Single Root Template for Entire Discussion Forum Site -->
  <xsl:template match="/">
    <html>
      <head>
         <title>XML Book Discussion Forum</title>
         <link rel="stylesheet" type="text/css" href="Forum.css"/>
      </head>
      <body><xsl:apply-templates/></body>
    </html>
  </xsl:template>
</xsl:stylesheet>
```

Even before creating the actual stylesheets, we know that every page will be transformed by transforming its contained breadcrumbs, actions, data, and paging sections, in that order. So we can already create the *ForumPageStructure.xsl* stylesheet with the template for page:

```
<!-- ForumPageStructure.xsl: Transform the Abstract Structure of a <page> -->
<xsl:stylesheet xmlns:xsl="http://www.w3.org/1999/XSL/Transform" version="1.0">
  <xsl:include href="UtilBreadcrumbs.xsl"/>
  <xsl:include href="UtilActions.xsl"/>
  <xsl:include href="UtilData.xsl"/>
  <xsl:include href="UtilPaging.xsl"/>
```

```
    <xsl:template match="page">
      <xsl:apply-templates select="breadcrumbs"/>
      <xsl:apply-templates select="actions"/>
      <xsl:apply-templates select="data"/>
      <xsl:apply-templates select="paging"/>
    </xsl:template>
  </xsl:stylesheet>
```

This specifies that whenever a <page> is matched, it will be transformed by applying XSLT templates to process the <breadcrumbs>, <actions>, <data>, and <paging> child structures of the page. We explicitly use four different <xsl:apply-templates> so that the structural elements will be processed in this order, regardless of the order in which they appear in the XSQL page.

Notice, too, that we've foreshadowed the creation of a utility stylesheet to handle each structural part. We'll call these stylesheets *UtilBreadcrumbs.xsl*, *UtilActions.xsl*, *UtilData.xsl*, and *UtilPaging.xsl*. We'll be reusing the *UtilPaging.xsl* library we built earlier in the chapter, so we only have to implement three new main templates to handle our site. In order to iteratively develop the application, we'll create empty stylesheet files for *UtilBreadcrumbs.xsl*, *UtilActions.xsl*, and *UtilData.xsl* that look like this:

```
<xsl:stylesheet version="1.0" xmlns:xsl="http://www.w3.org/1999/XSL/Transform">
  <!-- Todo: Add some templates! -->
</xsl:stylesheet>
```

Let's start at the top of our page map and implement the home page for displaying all the discussion forums. Example 17-26 shows the XSQL page source code for the home page.

Example 17-26. Dynamically Populating Abstract Page Content

```
<?xml version="1.0"?>
<!-- Forums.xsql: Home Page Showing All Discussion Forums -->
<page connection="xmlbook" xmlns:xsql="urn:oracle-xsql">
  <xsql:action handler="Paging" rows-per-page="5">
      SELECT COUNT(id) FROM forum
  </xsql:action>
  <breadcrumbs/>
  <actions>
    <link page="TodaysActiveTopics.xsql" label="Active Topics Today"/>
    <link page="Search.xsql"             label="Search"/>
  </actions>
  <data>
    <xsql:query skip-rows="{@paging-skip}" max-rows="{@paging-max}">
      SELECT f.id as h_id,
             f.name as "Forum",
             to_char(max(t.lastpost),'dd Mon yyyy hh24:mi') AS "Last_Post",
             sum(t.postings) AS "Posts"
        FROM forum f,
             forum_topic t
       WHERE t.forumid = f.id
```

Example 17-26. Dynamically Populating Abstract Page Content (continued)

```
        GROUP BY f.id,f.name
        ORDER BY name
    </xsql:query>
  </data>
</page>
```

Studying this example, we notice the following:

- We're using the custom `Paging` action handler we built earlier to create the `<paging>` section of the data page for us. The query contained in the content of the `<xsql:action>` tag is the count query, which counts the total number of forums.
- The `<breadcrumbs>` section for the home page is empty, since it's the home page.
- The `<actions>` section contains two `<link>` elements defining the pages we can visit.
- The `<data>` section contains an `<xsql:query>` action element to create the nested `<ROWSET>` of information for the page. The query selects the necessary columns from the forum table.

Requesting this XSQL page produces a raw XML output in Example 17-27 as the data page.

Example 17-27. Raw Data Page for the Forums.xsql Page

```
<?xml version = '1.0'?>
<!-- Forums.xsql: Home Page Showing All Discussion Forums -->
<page>
  <paging>
    <total-rows>4</total-rows>
    <total-pages>1</total-pages>
    <current-page>1</current-page>
    <target-page>Forums.xsql</target-page>
  </paging>
  <breadcrumbs/>
  <actions>
    <link page="TodaysActiveTopics.xsql" label="Active Topics Today"/>
    <link page="Search.xsql" label="Search"/>
  </actions>
  <data>
    <ROWSET>
      <ROW num="1">
        <H_ID>3</H_ID>
        <Forum>Business Components for Java</Forum>
        <Last_Post>07 May 2000 23:38</Last_Post>
        <Posts>4</Posts>
      </ROW>
      <!-- etc. -->
```

Example 17-27. Raw Data Page for the Forums.xsql Page (continued)

```
      <ROW num="4">
        <H_ID>1</H_ID>
        <Forum>XML</Forum>
        <Last_Post>07 May 2000 22:47</Last_Post>
        <Posts>12</Posts>
      </ROW>
    </ROWSET>
  </data>
</page>
```

If we add an `<?xml-stylesheet?>` instruction to the top of *Forums.xsql* like this:

```
<?xml-stylesheet type="text/xsl" href="ForumStyle.xsl"?>
```

then request the *Forums.xsql* page again in the browser, we'll see an initial jumble of text like what's shown in Figure 17-29.

```
3Business Components for Java07 May 2000 23:3842Java07 May
2000 22:3854Oracle8i07 May 2000 22:3741XML07 May 2000
22:4712 Page 1 of 1 - Total 4
```

Figure 17-29. Alphabet soup when no templates match data page content

Since the *UtilBreadcrumbs.xsl*, *UtilActions.xsl*, and *UtilData.xsl* stylesheets are initially empty, the only template that is alive is our paging template in *UtilPaging.xsl*. You can see at the bottom of the jumble in Figure 17-29 the phrase "Page 1 of 1 - Total 4", which the paging template contributes to the final output. The rest of the text is produced by the built-in templates we learned about in Chapter 7 that—in the absence of specific templates that match—recurse to child elements and copy text to the output. The page is certainly not very attractive yet, but we're about to change that.

Modularizing the Site Look and Feel

Let's start by formatting the `<ROWSET>` of information in the data section. To handle this, we build a template to match `data` in the *UtilData.xsl* stylesheet, shown in Example 17-28. It is a slight variation on the *TableBaseWithCSS.xsl* stylesheet we built in Chapter 7.

Example 17-28. Formatting ROWSET Data in Tables

```
<?xml version="1.0"?>
<xsl:stylesheet xmlns:xsl="http://www.w3.org/1999/XSL/Transform" version="1.0">
  <!--
   | UtilData.xsl: Transform <data> structural info into HTML table.
   |               Elements in ROWSET/ROW whose name begins with the
   |               prefix 'H_' will be hidden from display in the output.
   +-->
```

Example 17-28. Formatting ROWSET Data in Tables (continued)

```
  <xsl:template match="ROWSET">
    <center>
    <table border="0" cellpadding="4">
      <tr>
        <!-- If there are no ROWs in the ROWSET, print a message -->
        <xsl:if test="not(ROW)"><td>No Matches</td></xsl:if>
        <!--
         | Process child elements of the first ROW whose names do NOT start
         | with 'H_'. This lets user hide column by aliasing it to H_NAME
         +-->
        <xsl:apply-templates select="ROW[1]/*[not(starts-with(name(.),'H_'))]"
                             mode="columnHeaders"/>
      </tr>
      <xsl:apply-templates/>
    </table>
    </center>
  </xsl:template>
  <!--
   | Match ROW and create an HTML <tr> table row. Alternate colors by using
   | attribute value template to toggle between CSS class name r0 and r1.
   +-->
  <xsl:template match="ROW">
    <tr class="r{position() mod 2}">
      <!-- Select all children of ROW whose names do not start with 'H_' -->
      <xsl:apply-templates select="*[not(starts-with(name(.),'H_'))]"/>
    </tr>
  </xsl:template>
  <!-- Match ROW child element -->
  <xsl:template match="ROW/*">
    <td valign="top"><xsl:apply-templates/></td>
  </xsl:template>
  <!-- Match ROW child element and generate column heading -->
  <xsl:template match="ROW/*" mode="columnHeaders">
    <th align="left">
      <!-- Beautify Element Names "This_That" or "This-That" to "This That" -->
      <xsl:value-of select="translate(name(.),'_-','  ')"/>
    </th>
  </xsl:template>
</xsl:stylesheet>
```

We have templates for ROWSET, ROW, ROW/* (child element of a ROW), and ROW/* (child element of a ROW in `columnHeaders` mode).

We've embellished our previous attempt at a generic ROWSET-to-table stylesheet from Chapter 7 by enabling the hiding of columns/elements in the rowset by aliasing their column names to begin with the prefix H_. We've also added an `<xsl:if>` to print out a "No Matches" message if there are no rows to format, and used the XPath `translate()` function to turn element names like `This_That` or `This-That` into the more appropriate column title of "This That".

Now when we refresh our *Forums.xsql* page in the browser, we see what appears in Figure 17-30.

Forum	Last Post	Posts
Business Components for Java	07 May 2000 23:38	4
Java	07 May 2000 22:38	5
Oracle8i	07 May 2000 22:37	4
XML	07 May 2000 22:47	12

Page 1 of 1 - Total 4

Figure 17-30. Table of discussion forums with paging display

If you make edits to XSLT stylesheets that are included or imported by the stylesheet associated to your XSQL page, you won't see the effects of your edits unless you rerun your XSQL page in the JDeveloper IDE or touch the timestamp on the *.xsl* file associated with your page. The Oracle XSQL page processor caches XSLT stylesheets being used by XSQL pages and automatically replaces stylesheets in the cache when it notices that the file timestamp has changed on disk. However, if your XSQL page uses an XSLT stylesheet that `<xsl:include>`s or `<xsl:import>`s other stylesheets, the XSQL page processor cannot keep track of these include/import dependencies.

Notice that in the query we aliased the ID column from the forum table to the column named `H_ID`. Since its name began with `H_`, the `ROWSET`-to-table templates in *UtilData.xsl* leave it out of the output display. The `<data>` and the `<paging>` sections are working correctly now, so let's move on. Working our way up the page, we'll do the `<actions>` section next. We create a template matching `actions` in our *UtilActions.xsl* stylesheet in Example 17-29.

Example 17-29. Library Stylesheet to Handle Formatting of Actions Bar

```
<xsl:stylesheet xmlns:xsl="http://www.w3.org/1999/XSL/Transform" version="1.0">
  <!--
   | UtilActions.xsl: Transform <actions> structural info
   |                  into HTML "action bar" presentations.
   +-->
  <xsl:template match="actions">
    <xsl:variable name="LoginPage" select="'Login.xsql'"/>
    <!-- User is logged in if forumuser cookie is present -->
    <xsl:variable name="LoggedIn"
       select="boolean(/page/request/cookies/forumuser)"/>
    <center>
      <span class="actions">
```

Example 17-29. Library Stylesheet to Handle Formatting of Actions Bar (continued)

```
        <xsl:for-each select="link">
          <a>
            <xsl:attribute name="href">
              <xsl:choose>
                <xsl:when test="@login='yes' and not($LoggedIn)">
                  <xsl:value-of select="$LoginPage"/>
                </xsl:when>
                <xsl:otherwise>
                  <xsl:value-of select="@page"/>
                  <xsl:if test="*">?</xsl:if>
                  <xsl:for-each select="*">
                    <xsl:value-of select="name(.)"/>
                    <xsl:text>=</xsl:text>
                    <xsl:value-of select="."/>
                    <xsl:if test="position() != last()">
                      <xsl:text>&amp;</xsl:text>
                    </xsl:if>
                  </xsl:for-each>
                </xsl:otherwise>
              </xsl:choose>
            </xsl:attribute>
            <xsl:if test="@login='yes' and not($LoggedIn)">Login to </xsl:if>
            <xsl:value-of select="@label"/>
          </a>
        </xsl:for-each>
      </span>
    </center>
    <hr/>
  </xsl:template>
</xsl:stylesheet>
```

To show a different technique here, we're using a single actions template with nested `<xsl:for-each>` loops. We're planning ahead for actions that might require a user login by using an `<xsl:variable>` named `LoggedIn`. This variable tests whether a cookie named `forumuser` has been set by testing for the presence of `/page/request/cookies/forumuser`. XSQL pages with actions requiring a login will need to:

- Use an `<xsql:include-request-params>` to include all the request parameters into their data page for access by the stylesheet
- Use a `login=yes` attribute on their `<link>` element inside the `<actions>` section

The `<xsl:otherwise>` clause of `<xsl:choose>` allows the XSQL page designer to include elements reflecting URL parameters needed for a given action. In our discussion forum application, the parameter will typically be a topic ID, a forum ID, and so on, but we've written the stylesheet in a generic way to run over all child elements of `actions/link` using `xsl:for.each` and formulate a valid URL string with an initial question mark (?) and subsequent ampersands (&) separating parameter names. Notice that the entire `<xsl:choose>` is inside an `<xsl:attribute>` that adds an **href** attribute with a dynamic attribute value to the <a> element. The value for the **href** attribute is determined conditionally with the `<xsl:choose>`.

Refreshing our *Forums.xsql* page now produces a display with actions formatted into a simple action bar as shown in Figure 17-31.

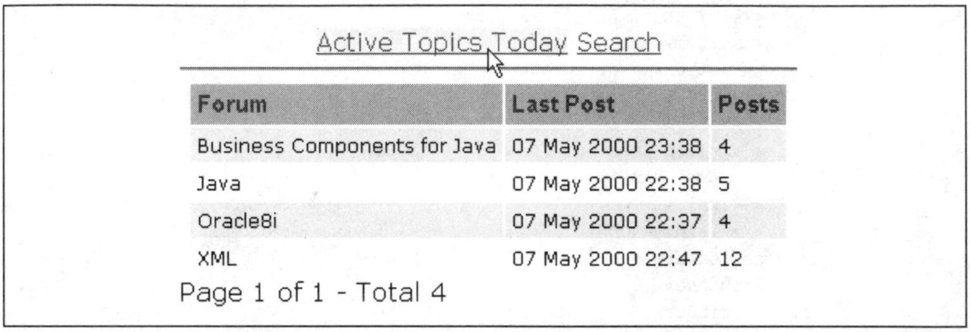

Active Topics Today Search

Forum	Last Post	Posts
Business Components for Java	07 May 2000 23:38	4
Java	07 May 2000 22:38	5
Oracle8i	07 May 2000 22:37	4
XML	07 May 2000 22:47	12

Page 1 of 1 - Total 4

Figure 17-31. Discussion forum display with appropriate action bar

The last step is the **<breadcrumbs>**. Our **breadcrumbs** template appears in Example 17-30 in the *UtilBreadcrumbs.xsl* library stylesheet.

Example 17-30. Library Stylesheet to Handle Formatting of Breadcrumbs

```
<xsl:stylesheet xmlns:xsl="http://www.w3.org/1999/XSL/Transform" version="1.0">
  <!--
   | UtilBreadCrumbs.xsl: Transform <breadcrumbs> structural info
   |                      into HTML breadcrumbs presentation.
   +-->
  <xsl:template match="breadcrumbs">
    <center>
      <span class="breadcrumbs">
        <xsl:choose>
          <xsl:when test=".//forumname">
            <!--
             | Even though we're only expecting one row, this redefines the current
             | node so that XPath's inside can use shorter relative paths
             +-->
            <a href="Forums.xsql">Forums</a>
            <xsl:text> > </xsl:text>
            <xsl:choose>
              <xsl:when test=".//topicname">
                <a>
                  <xsl:attribute name="href">
                    <xsl:choose>
                      <xsl:when test="..//forumname/@url">
                        <xsl:value-of select=".//forumname/@url"/>
                      </xsl:when>
```

Example 17-30. Library Stylesheet to Handle Formatting of Breadcrumbs (continued)

```
                  <xsl:otherwise>
                    <xsl:text>ForumTopics.xsql?id=</xsl:text>
                    <xsl:value-of select=".//forumid"/>
                  </xsl:otherwise>
                </xsl:choose>
              </xsl:attribute>
              <xsl:value-of select=".//forumname"/>
            </a>
            <xsl:text> > </xsl:text>
            <xsl:value-of select=".//topicname"/>
          </xsl:when>
          <xsl:otherwise>
            <xsl:value-of select=".//forumname"/>
          </xsl:otherwise>
        </xsl:choose>
      </xsl:when>
      <xsl:otherwise>
        <xsl:text>Forums</xsl:text>
      </xsl:otherwise>
    </xsl:choose>
  </span>
 </center>
 <hr/>
 </xsl:template>
</xsl:stylesheet>
```

Our breadcrumbs need to look like this:

Forums
: For the home page

Forums > XML
: When the user has drilled down to check out a forum named "XML"

Forums > XML > How do I parse a string?
: When the user has drilled down in a forum to check out a particular topic

Our strategy for the **breadcrumbs** template is based on this three-level idea and uses nested **<xsl:choose>** elements that test for the presence of a **forumname** and a **topicname** to infer what breadcrumbs to display. For each level above the current level, we render the names as hyperlinks to let the user navigate back up to the pages they came from. With this final key template in place, our basic rendering for the entire site is done. Refreshing the *Forums.xsql* page again shows the fruits of our work, displaying the "Forums" root breadcrumb title at the top of the page.

All four key structural elements are in and working. However, the home page is not quite complete. The paging information should be centered like the rest of the elements on the page, and the forum name should be a hyperlink to the *ForumTopics.xsql* page that will show the topics for the given forum.

Overriding Formatting for Certain Columns

Centering the paging information requires us to tweak our *ForumPageStructure.xsl* stylesheet. Let's change:

```
<xsl:template match="page">
  <xsl:apply-templates select="breadcrumbs"/>
  <xsl:apply-templates select="actions"/>
  <xsl:apply-templates select="data"/>
  <xsl:apply-templates select="paging"/>
</xsl:template>
```

to be the following:

```
<xsl:template match="page">
  <xsl:apply-templates select="breadcrumbs"/>
  <xsl:apply-templates select="actions"/>
  <xsl:apply-templates select="data"/>
  <xsl:if test="paging">
    <hr/>
    <center><xsl:apply-templates select="paging"/></center>
  </xsl:if>
</xsl:template>
```

then we can conditionally add a horizontal rule (`<hr/>`) and center the paging information if the page has a `<paging>` element present. Then to make forums appear as hyperlinks, we just need to add a template that matches `ROW/Forum`—that is, `<Forum>` elements when they occur as children of a `<ROW>`—and format the information as a hyperlink instead of the default plain text display. Since we will end up needing a few column-level overrides, let's create a *ColumnOverrides.xsl* stylesheet to contain them. We'll provide templates for `ROW/Forum` as well as `ROW/Topic` while we're at it:

```
<!-- ColumnOverrides.xsl : handle one-off formatting of special cases -->
<xsl:stylesheet xmlns:xsl="http://www.w3.org/1999/XSL/Transform" version="1.0">
  <!-- Anywhere a topic appears in a <ROW>, link to drill-down -->
  <xsl:template match="ROW/Topic">
    <td>
      <a href="TopicPostings.xsql?id={../H_ID}">
        <xsl:apply-templates/>
      </a>
    </td>
  </xsl:template>
  <!-- Anywhere a Forum appears in a <ROW>, link to drill-down -->
  <xsl:template match="ROW/Forum">
    <td>
      <a href="ForumTopics.xsql?id={../H_ID}">
        <xsl:apply-templates/>
      </a>
    </td>
  </xsl:template>
</xsl:stylesheet>
```

The ROW/Forum template overrides the basic ROW/* template in *UtilData.xsl* to format <Forum> elements that occur in a <ROW> specially. Even though the templates for ROW are designed to skip over elements like H_ID to leave them out of the display, our XPath expressions can still access their data. For example, the attribute value template for the <href> attribute on the <a> anchor tag is using id={../H_ID}. This effectively plugs in the value of the current forum's ID for the id parameter in the URL. The ../H_ID refers to the element that is the H_ID child element of the parent ".." of the current <Forum> or <Topic> element.

We make sure to use <xsl:import> instead of just <xsl:include> to import the *ColumnOverrides.xsl* stylesheet into the *ForumPageStructure.xsl.* This will ensure that the imported ROW/Forum and ROW/Topic templates have higher precedence than the imported ROW/*. Since we want the templates in *ColumnOverrides.xsl* to take precedence over the base templates in *UtilData.xsl,* and since XSLT mandates that any <xsl:import> elements must appear at the top of the stylesheet before any other XSLT actions, we've changed *UtilData.xsl* to be imported instead of included and we've moved both of the <xsl:import> statements to the top of the list, in the appropriate order:

```
<!-- ForumPageStructure.xsl: Transform the Abstract Structure of a <page> -->
<xsl:stylesheet xmlns:xsl="http://www.w3.org/1999/XSL/Transform" version="1.0">
  <xsl:import  href="UtilPaging.xsl"/>
  <xsl:import  href="ColumnOverrides.xsl"/>
  <xsl:include href="UtilBreadcrumbs.xsl"/>
  <xsl:include href="UtilActions.xsl"/>
  <xsl:include href="UtilData.xsl"/>
```

Refreshing our *Forums.xsql* page in the browser, we see what's shown in Figure 17-32. The forums are now hyperlinks to the drill-down page we'll create next.

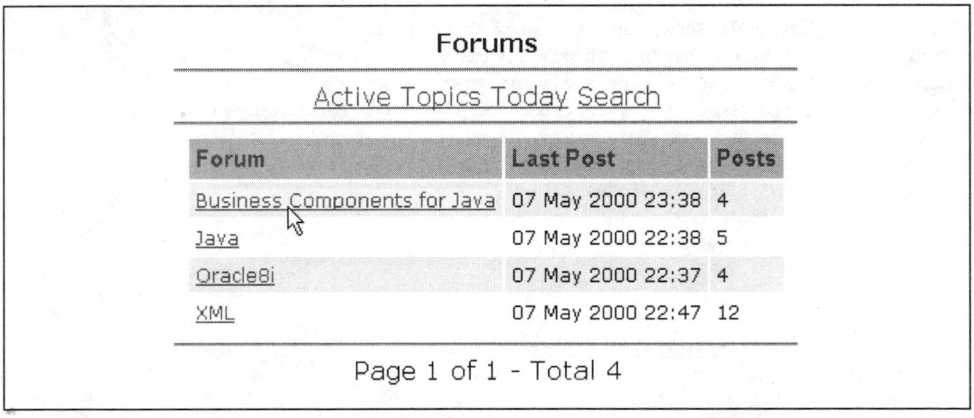

Forums

Active Topics Today Search

Forum	Last Post	Posts
Business Components for Java	07 May 2000 23:38	4
Java	07 May 2000 22:38	5
Oracle8i	07 May 2000 22:37	4
XML	07 May 2000 22:47	12

Page 1 of 1 - Total 4

Figure 17-32. Forum titles show as hyperlinks, paging control is centered

We've now basically done all the hard work to set up the abstract page structure and get an example page styled according to our web designer's specifications. Creating additional pages simply involves coming up with the XSQL page to represent the structure and data for new pages, and possibly introducing additional column-level overrides if we have to do one-off processing. Figure 17-33 illustrates all the pages we will build. One down, seven to go.

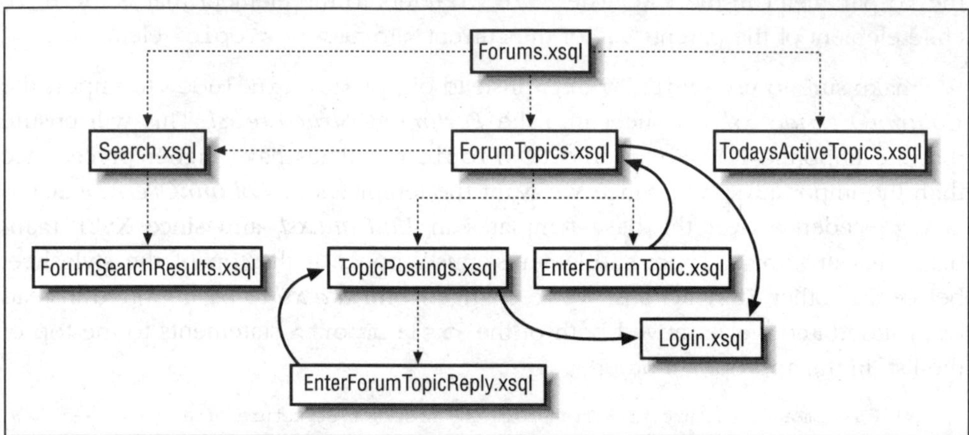

Figure 17-33. Map of XSQL pages to implement discussion forum

To create the drill-down *ForumTopics.xsql* page, we throw together the XSQL page describing its breadcrumbs, actions, data, and paging, and we're done. Example 17-31 shows these four structural parts in a single XSQL data page template.

Example 17-31. XSQL Page to Display List of Topics for a Forum

```
<?xml version="1.0"?>
<!-- ForumTopics.xsql: Show list of topics for a forum -->
<?xml-stylesheet type="text/xsl" href="ForumStyle.xsl"?>
<page connection="xmlbook" xmlns:xsql="urn:oracle-xsql">
  <!-- Include request params so Actions can check for forumuser cookie -->
  <xsql:include-request-params/>
  <xsql:action handler="Paging" rows-per-page="5" url-params="id">
      SELECT COUNT(t.id) AS "total"
      FROM forum_topic t
     WHERE forumid = {@id}
  </xsql:action>
  <breadcrumbs>
    <xsql:query>
      SELECT name AS "forumname", id AS "forumid"
      FROM forum
      WHERE id = {@id}
    </xsql:query>
  </breadcrumbs>
```

Example 17-31. XSQL Page to Display List of Topics for a Forum (continued)

```
  <actions>
    <link page="EnterForumTopic.xsql" label="Enter a New Topic" login="yes">
      <xsql:include-param name="id"/>
    </link>
    <link page="Search.xsql" label="Search">
      <xsql:include-param name="id"/>
    </link>
  </actions>
  <data>
    <xsql:query max-rows="{@paging-max}" skip-rows="{@paging-skip}">
      SELECT t.id                AS h_id,
             t.title             AS "Topic",
             t.userid            AS "Started_By",
             postings-1          AS "Replies",
             to_char(lastpost,'dd Mon YYYY, hh24:mi') as "Last_Post"
        FROM forum_topic t
       WHERE forumid = {@id}
        ORDER BY 5 desc
    </xsql:query>
  </data>
</page>
```

Note a few interesting things about this page:

- It uses `<xsql:include-request-params>` because one of its actions requires a login. Recall that the `actions` template needs to check for the presence of a cookie in the request to detect if the user is logged in.
- The count query inside the `<xsql:action>` handler that creates the paging section uses the `{@id}` to count just the topics in the current forum whose `id` is passed in the URL.
- The `forumname` and `forumid` for the breadcrumbs are queried from the database since only the `forumid` is passed into the page.
- Like every page on our site, it refers to the standard *ForumStyle.xsl* stylesheet.

Now if we click on the "XML" forum name from the *Forums.xsql* page to drill-down to a list of its topics, we see our new *ForumTopics.xsql* page in action as shown in Figure 17-34.

As expected, the breadcrumbs properly reflect where we are in the site; the action bar indicates the actions we can perform; the data is formatted in a consistent tabular format; and the paging display is functional. The column override template for `ROW/Topic` that we created earlier is already doing its job of formatting the `Topic` as a hyperlink to the next-level drill-down page: *TopicPostings.xsql.* Note that since we haven't set our `forumuser` cookie yet, the action bar displays the "Enter a New Topic" link as "Login to Enter a New Topic" with a hyperlink to the *Login.xsql* page as expected.

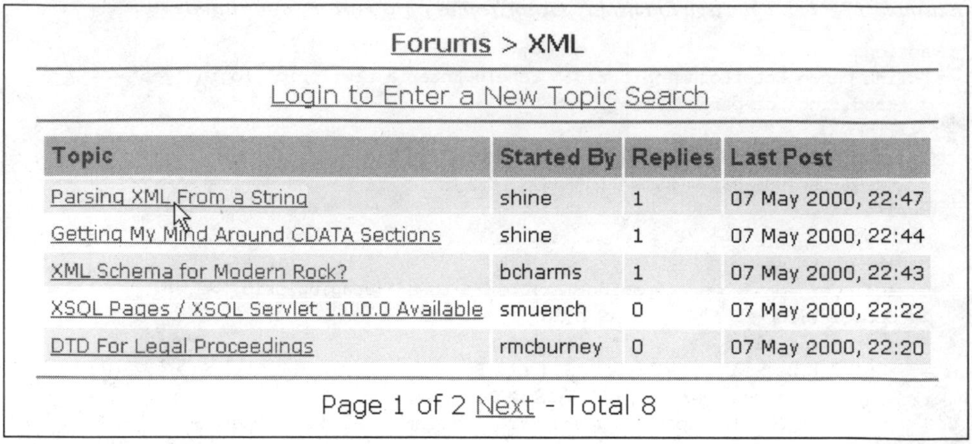

Forums > XML

Login to Enter a New Topic Search

Topic	Started By	Replies	Last Post
Parsing XML From a String	shine	1	07 May 2000, 22:47
Getting My Mind Around CDATA Sections	shine	1	07 May 2000, 22:44
XML Schema for Modern Rock?	bcharms	1	07 May 2000, 22:43
XSQL Pages / XSQL Servlet 1.0.0.0 Available	smuench	0	07 May 2000, 22:22
DTD For Legal Proceedings	rmcburney	0	07 May 2000, 22:20

Page 1 of 2 Next - Total 8

Figure 17-34. Drill-down display of topics for a selected forum

The *TopicPostings.xsql* page appears in Example 17-32.

Example 17-32. XSQL Page to Display List of Postings for a Topic

```
<?xml version="1.0"?>
<!-- TopicPostings.xsql: Show list of postings for a given topic -->
<?xml-stylesheet type="text/xsl" href="ForumStyle.xsl"?>
<page connection="xmlbook" xmlns:xsql="urn:oracle-xsql">
  <!-- Include request params so Actions can check for forumuser cookie -->
  <xsql:include-request-params/>
  <breadcrumbs>
    <xsql:query>
      SELECT t.forumid as "forumid", f.name AS "forumname",
             t.id as "topicid", t.title AS "topicname"
        FROM forum_topic t, forum f
        WHERE t.id = {@id}
          AND f.id = t.forumid
    </xsql:query>
  </breadcrumbs>
  <actions>
    <link page="EnterForumTopicReply.xsql" label="Post a New Reply" login="yes">
      <xsql:include-param name="id"/>
    </link>
  </actions>
  <data>
    <xsql:query>
      SELECT id as h_id,
             userid  AS  "Posted_By",
             posting AS "Posting",
             TO_CHAR(posted,'dd Mon yyyy, hh24:mi') AS "H_Posted_On"
        FROM forum_topic_posting
       WHERE topicid = {@id}
        ORDER BY posted
    </xsql:query>
  </data>
</page>
```

This page does not need a paging section since we want the user to be able to read all the sequential postings in a single page. Again, the breadcrumbs are selected from the database, but this time we're getting information on both the `forumname` and the `topicname`, based on the `topicid` passed into the page.

Using Recursive Named Templates

Clicking from the *ForumTopics.xsql* page on a particular topic name's hyperlink now brings us to a list of all the postings for that topic as illustrated in Figure 17-35.

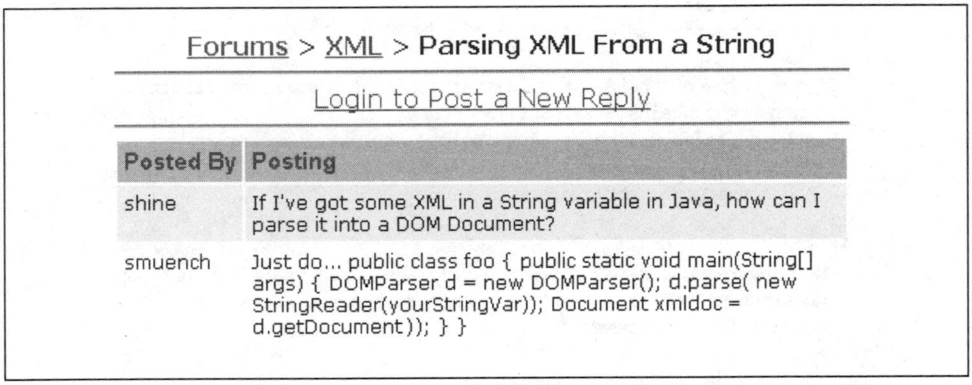

Forums > XML > Parsing XML From a String

Login to Post a New Reply

Posted By	Posting
shine	If I've got some XML in a String variable in Java, how can I parse it into a DOM Document?
smuench	Just do... public class foo { public static void main(String[] args) { DOMParser d = new DOMParser(); d.parse(new StringReader(yourStringVar)); Document xmldoc = d.getDocument)); } }

Figure 17-35. Display of all postings for a particular topic

This looks exactly like what we want; however, the text of the posting is a little jumbled for the Java code example I posted. It would be nice to format the text in a monospaced font and preserve the spacing and carriage returns so that a posted code example could be understood by others reading the postings. It's not as easy as simply formatting the text as an HTML `<pre>` tag, since preformatted text and table cells don't get along so nicely in HTML. The solution involves replacing carriage returns in the text of the posting with an HTML `<br>` tag so that a line break is reflected without using the `<pre>` mode. Preserving indentation is a little tricky too since, in general, whitespace in HTML is generally not treated as relevant, except in the `<pre>` sections that we cannot use here. So, we create the following named template subroutines:

`br-replace`
: Replaces carriage return with `<br>`

`sp-replace`
: Replaces consecutive spaces with non-breaking spaces

The `br-replace` and `sp-replace` named templates in Example 17-33 illustrate a general technique that will likely come in handy for future applications: recursive named templates. We need to use this more elaborate technique for generalized text substitution since the XPath `translate()` function we saw in *UtilData.xsl* only allows one character *x* to be substituted by another character *y*. If we study the `br-replace` template, we see that it accepts a parameter named `text`. This will contain the text passed in by the invoking template for which carriage returns need to be substituted by `<br>` tags.

Example 17-33. Library Stylesheet of Text-Formatting Routines

```
<!-- UtilTest.xsl: Common text formatting routines -->
<xsl:stylesheet xmlns:xsl="http://www.w3.org/1999/XSL/Transform" version="1.0">
  <!-- Replace new lines with html <br> tags -->
  <xsl:template name="br-replace">
    <xsl:param name="text"/>
    <xsl:variable name="cr" select="'&#xa;'"/>
    <xsl:choose>
      <!-- If the value of the $text parameter contains a carriage return... -->
      <xsl:when test="contains($text,$cr)">
        <!-- Return the substring of $text before the carriage return -->
        <xsl:value-of select="substring-before($text,$cr)"/>
        <!-- And construct a <br/> element -->
        <br/>
        <!--
          | Then invoke this same br-replace template again, passing the
          | substring *after* the carriage return as the new "$text" to
          | consider for replacement
          +-->
        <xsl:call-template name="br-replace">
          <xsl:with-param name="text" select="substring-after($text,$cr)"/>
        </xsl:call-template>
      </xsl:when>
      <xsl:otherwise>
        <xsl:value-of select="$text"/>
      </xsl:otherwise>
   </xsl:choose>
  </xsl:template>
  <!-- Replace two consecutive spaces w/ 2 non-breaking spaces -->
  <xsl:template name="sp-replace">
    <xsl:param name="text"/>
    <xsl:variable name="sp"><xsl:text>  </xsl:text></xsl:variable>
    <xsl:choose>
      <xsl:when test="contains($text,$sp)">
        <xsl:value-of select="substring-before($text,$sp)"/>
        <xsl:text>  </xsl:text>
        <xsl:call-template name="sp-replace">
          <xsl:with-param name="text" select="substring-after($text,$sp)"/>
        </xsl:call-template>
      </xsl:when>
      <xsl:otherwise>
        <xsl:value-of select="$text"/>
      </xsl:otherwise>
    </xsl:choose>
  </xsl:template>
</xsl:stylesheet>
```

For convenience, the template selects a literal carriage return character represented by the numerical character entity `
` into a `cr` variable. This variable is used in the `<xsl:choose>` element's clause:

```
<xsl:when test="contains($text,$cr)">
```

which uses the XPath `contains()` function to see if the value of the `$text` parameter contains the value of the `$cr` parameter, that is, if `$text` contains a carriage return. If it contains a carriage return, we select the value of the substring of `$text` located before the carriage return using `substring-before($text,$cr)`. We then create a literal `<br/>` element, followed by a recursive invocation of the `br-replace` template, passing `substring-after($text,$cr)` to see if the remainder of the string has any further carriage returns. In the template's `<xsl:otherwise>` clause, which will be executed when `$text` contains no carriage returns, we simply return the value of `$text`. If `br-replace` has been called recursively, this ends the recursion. The `sp-replace` template is identical to `br-replace` except that it replaces the occurrence of two consecutive space characters with two consecutive non-breaking space characters represented by `  `.

We apply these by adding a third column override template now for the `ROW/Posting` pattern in our *ColumnOverrides.xsl* stylesheet, like this:

```
<!-- Anywhere a Posting appears in a <ROW>, Format it as Code -->
  <xsl:template match="ROW/Posting">
    <td>
      <span class="date">
        <xsl:text>Posted </xsl:text>
        <xsl:value-of select="../H_Posted_On"/>
      </span>
      <hr/>
      <span class="code">
        <xsl:call-template name="br-replace">
          <xsl:with-param name="text">
            <xsl:call-template name="sp-replace">
              <xsl:with-param name="text" select="."/>
            </xsl:call-template>
          </xsl:with-param>
        </xsl:call-template>
      </span>
    </td>
  </xsl:template>
```

`posting` will now show up with its carriage returns and spaces replaced by HTML-savvy equivalents, allowing our `posting` to be displayed in a monospaced font without having to use a `<pre>` element. Now we touch the timestamp on our main *ForumStyle.xsl* stylesheet to cause the XSQL page processor to reload it along with all the stylesheets it includes or imports. We'll immediately see the difference in the display of our posting when refreshing the *TopicPosting.xsql* page as shown in Figure 17-36.

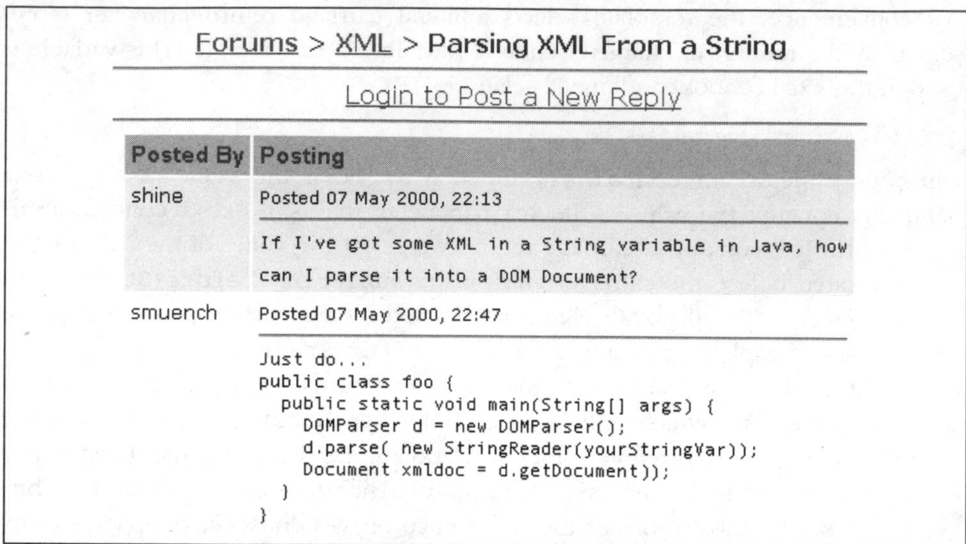

Figure 17-36. User text in postings with nicely wrapped, monospaced font

That looks a lot better! Next, we can knock off the *TodaysActiveTopics.xsql* page by coming up with the right couple of queries in the underlying XSQL page. The page for *TodaysActiveTopics.xsql* is shown in Example 17-34.

Example 17-34. XSQL Page to Display Discussion Topics Active Today

```
<?xml version="1.0"?>
<!-- TodaysActiveTopics.xsql: Listing of topics active today -->
<?xml-stylesheet type="text/xsl" href="ForumStyle.xsl"?>
<page connection="xmlbook" xmlns:xsql="urn:oracle-xsql">
  <xsql:action handler="Paging" rows-per-page="5">
      SELECT count(t.id) AS "total"
      FROM forum_topic t,
           forum f
    WHERE t.forumid = f.id
      AND t.lastpost BETWEEN TRUNC(SYSDATE) AND TRUNC(SYSDATE+1)
  </xsql:action>
  <breadcrumbs>
    <forumname>Active Topics Today</forumname>
  </breadcrumbs>
  <data>
    <xsql:query skip-rows="{@paging-skip}" max-rows="{@paging-max}">
      SELECT t.id              AS h_id,
             t.title           AS "Topic",
             f.name            AS "Forum"
        FROM forum_topic t,
             forum f
       WHERE t.forumid = f.id
         AND t.lastpost BETWEEN TRUNC(SYSDATE) AND TRUNC(SYSDATE+1)
```

Example 17-34. XSQL Page to Display Discussion Topics Active Today (continued)

```
      ORDER BY t.lastpost desc
    </xsql:query>
  </data>
</page>
```

Clicking on the Active Topics Today link from the *Forums.xsql* home page now shows us the list of all topics across all forums that have been updated today as illustrated in Figure 17-37.

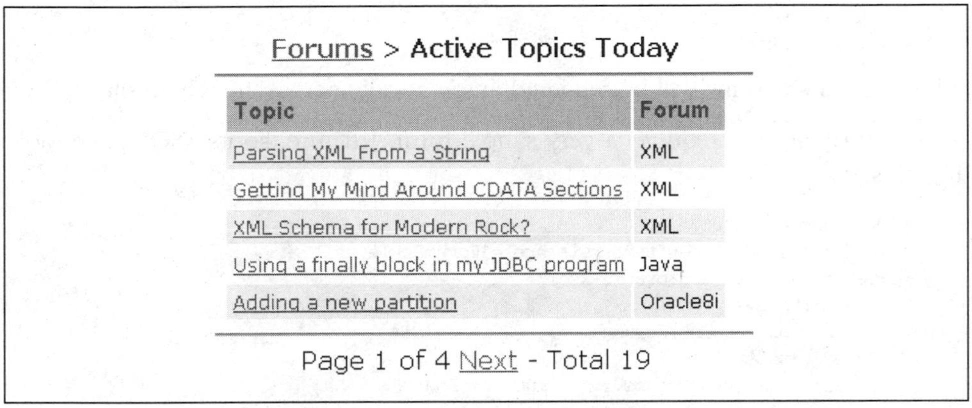

Forums > Active Topics Today

Topic	Forum
Parsing XML From a String	XML
Getting My Mind Around CDATA Sections	XML
XML Schema for Modern Rock?	XML
Using a finally block in my JDBC program	Java
Adding a new partition	Oracle8i

Page 1 of 4 Next - Total 19

Figure 17-37. List of all active discussion topics across all forums

Reusing Templates to Generate Forms

We need to build a few HTML forms based on the tasks for:

- Logging into the forum by providing a username
- Entering a new topic in a forum
- Posting a new reply to an existing forum topic
- Searching the forums

Since we designed the *UtilDataForm.xsl* stylesheet earlier in this chapter with templates to format HTML forms based on a structural description, we can reuse it here. The abstract structure of our page can be enhanced to allow an optional `<dataform>` section. By including the *UtilDataForm.xsl* stylesheet in our *ForumPageStructure.xsl* and adding one additional `xsl:apply-templates` with a `select="dataform"`, like this:

```
<!-- ForumPageStructure.xsl: Transform the Abstract Structure of a <page> -->
<xsl:stylesheet xmlns:xsl="http://www.w3.org/1999/XSL/Transform" version="1.0">
  <xsl:import  href="UtilData.xsl"/>
  <xsl:import  href="ColumnOverrides.xsl"/>
  <xsl:include href="UtilBreadcrumbs.xsl"/>
  <xsl:include href="UtilActions.xsl"/>
```

```
  <xsl:include href="UtilDataForm.xsl"/>
  <xsl:include href="UtilPaging.xsl"/>
  <xsl:template match="page">
    <xsl:apply-templates select="breadcrumbs"/>
    <xsl:apply-templates select="actions"/>
    <xsl:apply-templates select="dataform"/>
    <xsl:apply-templates select="data"/>
    <xsl:if test="paging">
      <hr/>
      <center><xsl:apply-templates select="paging"/></center>
    </xsl:if>
  </xsl:template>
</xsl:stylesheet>
```

all of the HTML forms will be rendered automatically across the whole site.

The *Login.xsql* form requires a very simple form structure, so its XSQL page looks like this:

```
<?xml version="1.0"?>
<?xml-stylesheet type="text/xsl" href="ForumStyle.xsl"?>
<page xmlns:xsql="urn:oracle-xsql">
  <breadcrumbs>
    <forumname>Login</forumname>
  </breadcrumbs>
  <dataform target="Forums.xsql" submit="Login">
    <item type="text" name="userid" label="Your Email"/>
  </dataform>
</page>
```

With this in place, clicking on a link in the action bar like "Login to Enter a New Topic" brings us to a login page like the one shown in Figure 17-38.

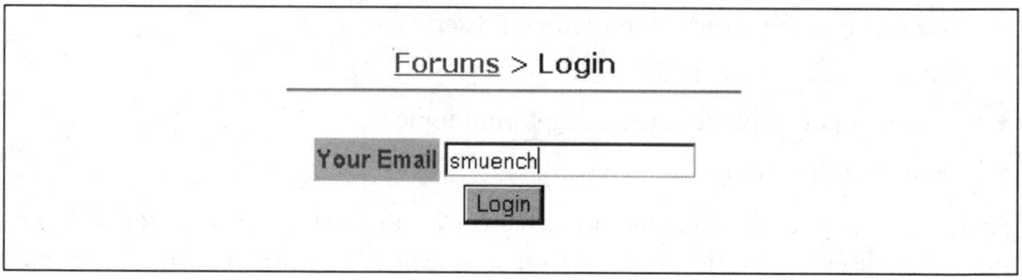

Figure 17-38. Simple login form

Notice that the target attribute indicates that the HTML form submission will be handled by our home page, *Forums.xsql*. We need to add one additional XSQL action element to the top of the *Forums.xsql* page to receive the **userid** parameter and set the **forumuser** cookie with its value:

```
<!-- Added to the top of the Forums.xsql page to set forumuser cookie -->
<xsql:set-cookie name="forumuser" value="{@userid}"
                 ignore-empty-value="yes" only-if-unset="yes"/>
```

Now submitting the login page will set the cookie and show the user the list of discussion forums again. At that point they will now see action links like "Enter a New Topic" and "Post a New Reply" instead of the links asking them to log in.

Example 17-35 shows the *EnterForumTopic.xsql* page to create the form used for entering a new topic in a forum.

Example 17-35. XSQL Page to Enter a New Topic in a Forum

```
<?xml version="1.0"?>
<!-- EnterForumTopic.xsql: Form to enter a new topic in a forum -->
<?xml-stylesheet type="text/xsl" href="ForumStyle.xsl"?>
<page connection="xmlbook" xmlns:xsql="urn:oracle-xsql">
  <breadcrumbs>
    <xsql:query>
      SELECT name as "forumname", id AS "forumid",
             'Enter a New Topic' AS "topicname"
      FROM forum
      WHERE id = {@id}
    </xsql:query>
  </breadcrumbs>
  <dataform target="ForumTopics.xsql" submit="Create Your New Topic">
    <item type="hidden" name="id">
      <xsql:include-param name="id"/>
    </item>
    <item type="text" name="userid" label="Your Email">
      <xsql:include-param name="forumuser"/>
    </item>
    <item type="text" name="title" size="60" label="Topic Subject"/>
    <item type="textarea" name="posting" size="60" label="Your Message"/>
  </dataform>
</page>
```

This defines a dataform with a `hidden` item, a `text` item, and a `textarea`. We indicate that the HTML form should be posted to the *ForumTopics.xsql* page, and add the following extra XSQL action element to the top of *ForumTopics.xsql* to handle the posted HTML form and insert it into the forum_new_topic view.

```
<!-- Added to the top of the ForumTopics.xsql page to handle new posted topic -->
<xsql:insert-request table="forum_new_topic" transform="InsertPostedTopic.xsl"/>
```

When users are just browsing the *ForumTopics.xsql* page, this action element is a no-op.

We need an insert transformation to transform the XML document representing the posted HTML form into the appropriate `ROWSET` structure for the forum_new_topic table. We can generate a skeleton for this automatically by again using our *GenerateInsertTransform.xsql* page with the XSQL command-line utility:

```
xsql GenerateInsertTransform.xsql
     InsertPostedTopic.xsl
     table=forum_new_topic
```

Making a few strategic edits to the skeleton, we fill in the `/request/parameters` pattern as the main loop and fill in the appropriate relative patterns to plug in the right information for the <FORUMID>, <TITLE>, <USERID>, and <POSTING> elements, as shown in Example 17-36.

Example 17-36. Insert Transform for the forum_new_topic Table

```
<!-- Created by GenerateInsertTransform.xsl -->
<!-- InsertPostedTopic.xsl: Insert transform for forum_new_topic table -->
<xsl:stylesheet version="1.0" xmlns:xsl="http://www.w3.org/1999/XSL/Transform">
   <!-- Transform /request/parameters into ROWSET for forum_new_topic -->
   <xsl:template match="/">
      <ROWSET>
         <!-- XPath for repeating source rows -->
         <xsl:for-each select="/request/parameters">
            <ROW>
               <FORUMID>
                  <xsl:value-of select="id"/>
               </FORUMID>
               <TITLE>
                  <xsl:value-of select="title"/>
               </TITLE>
               <USERID>
                  <xsl:value-of select="userid"/>
               </USERID>
               <POSTING>
                  <xsl:value-of select="posting"/>
               </POSTING>
            </ROW>
         </xsl:for-each>
      </ROWSET>
   </xsl:template>
</xsl:stylesheet>
```

Now we can click on "Enter a New Topic" and we'll see our *EnterForumTopic.xsql* HTML form appear. It appears in Figure 17-39.

Forums > Java > Enter a New Topic

Your Email: bcharms

Topic Subject: Job Available for Good Java Programmer

Your Message: Not sure if it's kosher to post this here, but we are looking for a few good Javanauts at our www.clank.com web property.

Create Your New Topic

Figure 17-39. Form to enter a new discussion topic

The current **userid** from the **forumuser** cookie was selected in the XSQL data page as the content of the **dataform/item** element for "Your Email," so this value defaults automatically. Submitting the form now inserts the new posting and shows it at the top of the list of postings for the forum. The database trigger we created on the forum_new_topic view silently does its job of inserting a row into the forum_topic table and a row into the forum_topic_posting table. The database trigger on forum_topic_posting automatically adjusts the number of **postings** and the **lastpost** date for the forum.

The form to enter a reply to a posting should display a form, as well as the history of current replies on the topic so the user formulating a reply can consult the trail of previous users' thoughts. If we include both a **<dataform>** section and a **<data>** section in the XSQL page for *EnterForumTopicReply.xsql*, our overarching *ForumPageStructure.xsl* stylesheet with its **page** template will cause all the ingredients to fall perfectly into place. The *EnterForumTopicReply.xsql* page appears in Example 17-37.

Example 17-37. XSQL Page to Post a Reply to a Forum Topic

```
<?xml version="1.0"?>
<!-- EnterForumTopicReply.xsql: Form to post a reply on a topic -->
<?xml-stylesheet type="text/xsl" href="ForumStyle.xsl"?>
<page connection="xmlbook" xmlns:xsql="urn:oracle-xsql">
  <breadcrumbs>
    <xsql:include-xsql href="ForumTopicLookup.xsql"/>
  </breadcrumbs>
  <dataform target="TopicPostings.xsql" submit="Post Your Reply">
    <item type="hidden" name="id">
      <xsql:include-param name="id"/>
    </item>
    <item type="text" name="userid" label="Your Email">
      <xsql:include-param name="forumuser"/>
    </item>
    <item type="textarea" name="posting" size="60" label="Reply"/>
  </dataform>
  <data>
    <xsql:include-xsql href="TopicPostingsQuery.xsql"/>
  </data>
</page>
```

We need to make changes to *TopicPostings.xsql* similar to what we did for the previous example to handle the posted HTML form and insert it into the forum_topic_posting table. So we add an **<xsql:insert-request>** to the top of *TopicPostings.xsql*:

```
<!-- Added to the top of the TopicPostings.xsql page
     to handle new posted topic -->
<xsql:insert-request table="forum_topic_posting"
     transform="InsertPostedReply.xsl"/>
```

Again employing our handy utility to create the skeleton insert transformation for the forum_topic_posting table, we execute the command:

```
xsql GenerateInsertTransform.xsql InsertPostedReply.xsl table=forum_topic_posting
```

and edit the skeleton stylesheet to produce the *InsertPostedReply.xsl* transformation in Example 17-38.

Example 17-38. Insert Transform for the forum_topic_posting Table

```
<!-- Created by GenerateInsertTransform.xsl -->
<!-- InsertPostedReply.xsl: Insert transform for forum_topic_posting table -->
<xsl:stylesheet version="1.0" xmlns:xsl="http://www.w3.org/1999/XSL/Transform">
  <!-- Transform /request/parameters into ROWSET for forum_topic_posting -->
  <xsl:template match="/">
    <ROWSET>
      <!-- XPath for repeating source rows -->
      <xsl:for-each select="page/ROWSET/ROW">
        <ROW>
<!-- Don't need this one because insert trigger handles its assignment
          <ID>
            <xsl:value-of select="ID"/>
          </ID>
-->
          <TOPICID>
            <xsl:value-of select="id"/>
          </TOPICID>
          <USERID>
            <xsl:value-of select="userid"/>
          </USERID>
<!-- Don't need this one because insert trigger handles its assignment
          <POSTED>
            <xsl:value-of select="POSTED"/>
          </POSTED>
-->
          <POSTING>
            <xsl:value-of select="posting"/>
          </POSTING>
        </ROW>
      </xsl:for-each>
    </ROWSET>
  </xsl:template>
</xsl:stylesheet>
```

Note that since our table's BEFORE INSERT trigger will automatically assign the `ID` and `POSTED` columns, we can comment them out of the insert transformation template or remove these sections completely.

We're ready now to try replying to a posting. Clicking on the "Post a New Reply" link from the *TopicPostings.xsql* page, we'll see our new form, as shown in Figure 17-40.

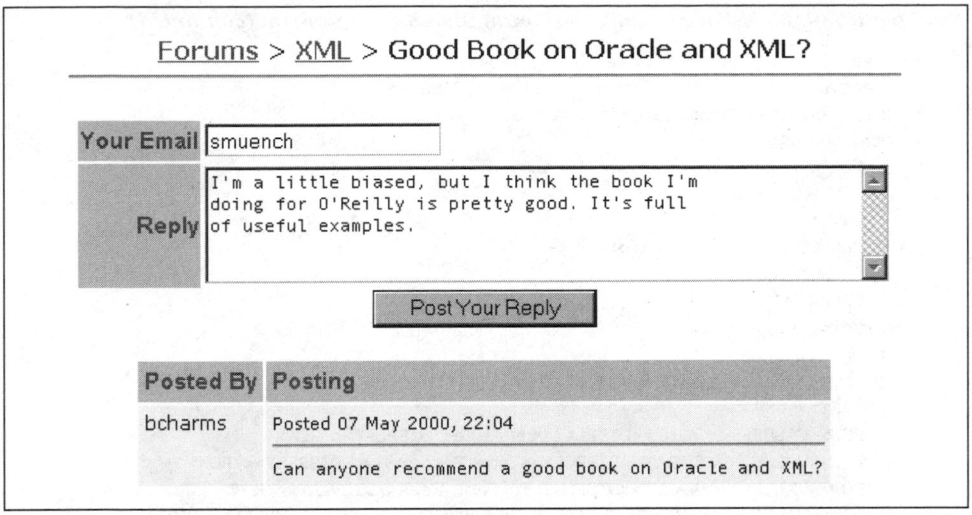

Figure 17-40. Form to let user post a reply on a discussion topic

Notice that our dataform structure from the underlying XSQL page was transformed into the HTML form as desired, and the data section containing the query to produce the list of current postings in date order is formatted by the data template. Since the query produces a `ROW/Posting` element, the `ROW/Posting` template we created in our *ColumnOverrides.xsl* stylesheet formats the `Posting` as HTML-friendly code listings, just as it did on the *TopicPostings.xsql* page.

We're nearly done. The last feature to build is sitewide searching.

Dynamic Queries Using Ref Cursors

We create a *Search.xsql* page in Example 17-39 to display the search form. It uses several list-style items instead of just `text` and `textarea` like the earlier forms.

Example 17-39. XSQL Page to Drive the Forum Search Criteria Form

```
<?xml version="1.0"?>
<!-- Search.xsql: Forum search criteria form -->
<?xml-stylesheet type="text/xsl" href="ForumStyle.xsl"?>
<page connection="xmlbook" xmlns:xsql="urn:oracle-xsql">
  <breadcrumbs>
    <forumname>Search</forumname>
  </breadcrumbs>
  <dataform target="ForumSearchResults.xsql" submit="Search">
    <xsql:set-page-param name="default" value="{@id}"/>
    <item type="text" name="searchFor" size="30" label="Search For"/>
    <item type="list" name="searchIn" label="In">
      <ROWSET>
        <ROW><VALUE>E</VALUE><DISPLAY>Entire Message</DISPLAY></ROW>
        <ROW><VALUE>S</VALUE><DISPLAY>Subject Only</DISPLAY></ROW>
      </ROWSET>
```

Example 17-39. XSQL Page to Drive the Forum Search Criteria Form (continued)

```
    </item>
    <item type="list" name="forum" label="In Forum">
      <xsql:include-param name="default"/>
      <xsql:query>
         SELECT id AS value, name AS display
           FROM forum
         UNION ALL
         SELECT -1, 'All Forums'
           FROM dual
         ORDER BY 1
      </xsql:query>
    </item>
    <item type="list" name="daysAgo" label="By Date">
      <ROWSET>
        <ROW><VALUE>0</VALUE><DISPLAY>Any Date</DISPLAY></ROW>
        <ROW><VALUE>-1</VALUE><DISPLAY>Since Yesterday</DISPLAY></ROW>
        <ROW><VALUE>-7</VALUE><DISPLAY>In Past Week</DISPLAY></ROW>
        <ROW><VALUE>-14</VALUE><DISPLAY>In Past Two Weeks</DISPLAY></ROW>
        <ROW><VALUE>-21</VALUE><DISPLAY>In Past Three Weeks</DISPLAY></ROW>
      </ROWSET>
    </item>
  </dataform>
</page>
```

Two of the `dataform/items` use a static set of nested `<ROWSET>` and `<ROW>` elements to furnish the data for the list "In" and "By Date" lists on the form. We do this because there's no sense in querying the data if it will always be static. On the other hand, the `dataform/items` for the "In Forum" list produces a list of forums by leveraging an `<xsql:query>` with the forum ID passed in as a parameter since new forums might be added at any time. In case no item ID is passed into the *Search.xsql* page, the query also includes a UNION ALL with the statement:

```
SELECT -1, 'All Forums' FROM dual
```

to include that as a default choice in the list.

When clicking the search action from within a forum, the forum ID is passed as a parameter to the *search.xsql* page, and the default behavior is to search for text only within the current forum. If the user clicks on "*SEARCH* from the Forum list," no ID is passed, so the "All Forums" entry we added becomes the default instead.

Our *Search.xsql* form then will look like Figure 17-41.

The *Search.xsql* page targets the *ForumSearchResults.xsql* page so that the search form parameters can be used to query the database and present the search results. What query do we include in the *ForumSearchResults.xsql* page? The query will need to look different depending on what combination of search form parameters the user has set. As we learned in Chapter 15, *Using XSQL Pages as a Publishing Framework*, `<xsql:ref-cursor-function>` handles all the dynamic aspects

Forums > Search

Search For	section
In	Entire Message
In Forum	All Forums
By Date	Any Date

Search

Figure 17-41. Form allowing user to search the discussion forum

inside a stored package function that programmatically determines the query statement, executes that dynamic query, and returns a cursor to the XSQL page to render the results as XML.

Since we want to be able to page through query results, we need to pass the various parameters that affect the query to the stored package function, and have it return us both the actual rows retrieved by the dynamic query and a count we can use as the count query of our `Paging` action handler. Example 17-40 shows the `ForumSearch` package that gets the job done.

Example 17-40. Package to Handle Dynamic Discussion Forum Site Search

```
CREATE OR REPLACE PACKAGE ForumSearch IS
  TYPE ref_cursor IS REF CURSOR;
  FUNCTION Find(forumid   NUMBER   := -1,
               daysAgo   NUMBER   := 0,
               searchIn  VARCHAR2 := 'S',
               searchFor VARCHAR2 := NULL) RETURN ref_cursor;
  FUNCTION Hits(forumid   NUMBER   := -1,
               daysAgo   NUMBER   := 0,
               searchIn  VARCHAR2 := 'S',
               searchFor VARCHAR2 := NULL) RETURN NUMBER;
END;
CREATE OR REPLACE PACKAGE BODY ForumSearch IS
  FUNCTION Query(forumid   NUMBER   := -1,
            daysAgo   NUMBER   := 0,
            searchIn  VARCHAR2 := 'S',
            searchFor VARCHAR2 := NULL) RETURN VARCHAR2 IS
    query  VARCHAR2(2000);
    noCriteriaSupplied  BOOLEAN := LTRIM(RTRIM(searchFor)) IS NULL;
    searchEntireMessage BOOLEAN := UPPER(searchIn)='E';
    restrictToForum     BOOLEAN := forumid > 0;
    restrictByDate      BOOLEAN := daysAgo < 0;
  BEGIN
    query :=
    'SELECT distinct
           t.id              AS h_id,
```

Example 17-40. Package to Handle Dynamic Discussion Forum Site Search (continued)

```
             t.title           AS "Topic",
             t.userid          AS "Started_By",
             t.postings-1      AS "Replies",
             to_char(t.lastpost,''dd Mon YYYY, hh24:mi'') AS "Last_Post",
             f.name            AS "Forum_Name"
        FROM forum_topic t,
             forum_topic_posting p,
             forum f
       WHERE t.id = p.topicid
         AND t.forumid = f.id';
    IF searchEntireMessage THEN
      query := query ||' AND ( CONTAINS(p.posting, '''||searchFor||''')>0 '||
                       ' OR UPPER(t.title) LIKE UPPER(''%'||searchFor||'%''))';
    ELSE
      query := query || ' AND UPPER(t.title) LIKE UPPER(''%'||searchFor||'%'')';
    END IF;
    IF restrictToForum THEN
      query := query ||' AND t.forumid = '||forumid;
    END IF;
    IF restrictByDate THEN
      query := query ||' AND p.posted > SYSDATE + '||daysAgo;
    END IF;
    IF noCriteriaSupplied THEN
      query := query ||' AND 1=2';
    END IF;
    RETURN query;
  END;

  FUNCTION Hits(forumid   NUMBER   := -1,
                daysAgo   NUMBER   := 0,
                searchIn  VARCHAR2 := 'S',
                searchFor VARCHAR2 := NULL) RETURN NUMBER IS
    the_cursor ref_cursor;
    the_count  NUMBER := 0;
  BEGIN
    OPEN the_cursor FOR 'select count(1) from ('||
                        Query(forumid,daysAgo,searchIn,searchFor)||
                        ')';
    FETCH the_cursor INTO the_count;
    CLOSE the_cursor;
    RETURN the_count;
  END;

  FUNCTION Find(forumid   NUMBER   := -1,
                daysAgo   NUMBER   := 0,
                searchIn  VARCHAR2 := 'S',
                searchFor VARCHAR2 := NULL) RETURN ref_cursor IS
    the_cursor ref_cursor;
    my_sal NUMBER := 1;
```

Example 17-40. Package to Handle Dynamic Discussion Forum Site Search (continued)

```
  BEGIN
   OPEN the_cursor FOR Query(forumid,daysAgo,searchIn,searchFor)||
                       ' order by 5 desc';
   RETURN the_cursor;
  END;
END;
```

The package-private **Query()** function figures out the SQL statement based on all the parameters passed in. Notice that if the user has indicated a search not just in the topic title, but in the message body as well, the **Query()** function appends a WHERE clause using an interMedia CONTAINS query to do a text search through the postings.

The public **Find()** function returns the ref cursor of query results returned by the dynamically determined query, while the public **Hits()** function returns the count of the number of rows retrieved by the dynamically determined query.

With all the heavy lifting being done behind the scenes by this database package, the XSQL page in Example 17-41 looks pretty simple.

Example 17-41. XSQL Page to Drive Discussion Forum Search Results

```
<?xml version="1.0"?>
<!-- ForumSearchResults.xsql: Paging display of search 'hits' -->
<?xml-stylesheet type="text/xsl" href="ForumStyle.xsl"?>
<page connection="xmlbook" xmlns:xsql="urn:oracle-xsql">
  <xsql:action handler="Paging" rows-per-page="5"
          url-params="forum daysAgo searchIn searchFor">
      SELECT ForumSearch.Hits({@forum}+0,
                              {@daysAgo}+0,
                              NVL('{@searchIn}','S') ,
                              '{@searchFor}') AS hits

        from dual
  </xsql:action>
  <breadcrumbs>
    <forumname url="Search.xsql">Search</forumname>
    <topicname>Results</topicname>
  </breadcrumbs>
  <data>
    <xsql:ref-cursor-function skip-rows="{@paging-skip}"
                              max-rows="{@paging-max}">
       ForumSearch.Find(forumid   => {@forum}+0 ,
                        daysAgo   => {@daysAgo}+0 ,
                        searchIn  => NVL('{@searchIn}','S') ,
                        searchFor => '{@searchFor}')
    </xsql:ref-cursor-function>
  </data>
</page>
```

The paging handler's count query selects the value of the `ForumSearch.Hits()` function `from dual` to determine the total row count, and the `<xsql:ref-cursor-function>` action element includes the stored package function name with arguments. In order to elegantly handle the case in which no parameter value is passed in, we're using a combination of adding zero to number arguments and the `NVL()` function for string arguments.

We create the functional index to allow us to quickly search the topic headings in a case-insensitive way:

```
CREATE INDEX forum_topic_title_idx ON forum_topic(UPPER(title));
```

and create an interMedia index using the autosectioner we learned about in Chapter 13, *Searching XML with interMedia*, to enable searching on text or XML elements that might be contained in the posting document body:

```
CREATE INDEX forum_topic_posting_idx ON forum_topic_posting(posting)
INDEXTYPE IS ctxsys.contextPARAMETERS ('section group ctxsys.auto_section_group');
```

With that, we're done. We can now click on the Search action link on any page where it appears, enter search criteria using the *Search.xsql* form, and then browse the results of the dynamically determined query in a way that's totally consistent with every other page in the site. Figure 17-42 illustrates browsing the search results.

Forums > Search > Results

Topic	Started By	Replies	Last Post	Forum Name
Using a finally block in my JDBC program	rmcburney	0	07 May 2000, 22:38	Java
Adding a new partition	bcharms	0	07 May 2000, 22:37	Oracle8i
Does a view object break its row into parts?	shine	0	07 May 2000, 22:31	Business Components for Java
Getting My Mind Around CDATA Sections	shine	0	07 May 2000, 22:19	XML

Page 1 of 1 - Total 4

Figure 17-42. Browsing results from a cross-forum search

We've come a long way in a short time. We've directly experienced several examples now of separating data from presentation and pragmatically implementing it using a combination of Oracle XSQL Pages to handle the assembly of the data page and XSLT stylesheets to handle the modular presentation for anything from one page to an entire web site.

Unifying Our News Portal and Discussion Forum

As a final fun project, let's tie together the news portal and the discussion forum we've built with an XSLT-driven tab-page system. Just as we did earlier for the abstract structure of pages, we use a *Site.xsql* page, shown in Example 17-42, to reflect the structure of our site:

Example 17-42. XSQL Page to Drive Tab Set

```
<?xml version="1.0"?>
<!-- Site.xsql: Provide tabset structure for home page -->
<?xml-stylesheet type="text/xsl" href="tab.xsl"?>
<site elt="query" xmlns:xsql="urn:oracle-xsql">
  <!--
   | Pass the values of current "tab" parameter (if passed in explicitly),
   | the "lasttab" cookie (if set), and the name of this page to the
   | XSLT stylesheet that renders the tab bar.
   +-->
  <xsql:set-stylesheet-param name="thispage" value="site.xsql"/>
  <xsql:set-stylesheet-param name="tab" value="{@tab}" ignore-empty-value="yes"/>
  <xsql:set-stylesheet-param name="lasttab" value="{@lasttab}"
                             ignore-empty-value="yes"/>
  <!-- Remember the last tab clicked in an HTTP Cookie -->
  <xsql:set-cookie name="lasttab" value="{@tab}" ignore-empty-value="yes"/>
  <!-- This is static XML that provides the tab structure -->
  <tabs>
     <tab id="News"   name="News"/>
     <tab id="Forums" name="Forums"/>
  </tabs>
</site>
```

We're using some `<xsql:set-stylesheet-param>` elements to pass a few tab-related parameters to the *Tab.xsl* stylesheet in Example 17-43 so the stylesheet can know the currently selected tab. The *Site.xsql* page also uses `<xsql:set-cookie>` to keep track of the latest tab chosen by the user. *Tab.xsl* contains templates to match the site element as well as named templates that match the selected and unselected tabs. Although our site will only have the "News" and "Forums" tabs above, you can easily add more tabs by changing the structural information in the `site/tabs` section of your data page.

Example 17-43. Stylesheet to Render a Set of HTML Tabs for a Frameset

```
<?xml version="1.0"?>
<xsl:stylesheet xmlns:xsl="http://www.w3.org/1999/XSL/Transform" version="1.0">
  <xsl:output method="html" indent="no"/>
  <xsl:param name="tab"/>                     <!-- Allow setting tab externally -->
  <xsl:param name="lasttab"/>
  <xsl:param name="thispage"/>
  <xsl:variable name="i" select="'images/'"/> <!-- Prefix for Image URLs     -->
  <xsl:variable name="cur">                   <!-- Determine the current tab -->
    <xsl:choose>
```

Example 17-43. Stylesheet to Render a Set of HTML Tabs for a Frameset (continued)

```
      <xsl:when test="$tab"><xsl:value-of select="$tab"/></xsl:when>
      <xsl:when test="$lasttab"><xsl:value-of select="$lasttab"/></xsl:when>
      <xsl:otherwise>
        <xsl:value-of select="/site/tabs/tab[1]/@id"/>
      </xsl:otherwise>
    </xsl:choose>
  </xsl:variable>
  <xsl:template match="/">  <!-- ROOT Template -->
    <html>
      <head>
         <link rel="stylesheet" type="text/css" href="site.css"/>
      </head>
      <body bdgcolor="#FFFFFF" leftmargin="0" topmargin="0">
      <xsl:apply-templates/>
      </body>
    </html>
  </xsl:template>
  <!-- Template matching the <site> structure in the XSQL page -->
  <xsl:template match="site">
    <table width="100%" cellpadding="0" cellspacing="0" border="0">
      <tr>
        <td align="LEFT" rowspan="2">
          <a href="../index.html" target="_parent">
            <img src="{$i}banner.gif" width="342" height="69" border="0"/>
          </a>
        </td>
      </tr>
      <tr>
        <td width="98%"> </td>
        <td valign="bottom" align="right">
          <table border="0" cellpadding="0" cellspacing="0">
            <tr>
              <td align="right">
                <xsl:apply-templates select="tabs/tab"/>
              </td>
             </tr>
          </table>
        </td>
      </tr>
    </table>
    <table width="100%" cellpadding="0" cellspacing="0" border="0">
      <tr>
        <td align="right" valign="top" bgcolor="white" height="21" width="100%">
          <img src="{$i}bottom_middle.gif" height="6" width="100%" />
        </td>
      </tr>
    </table>
  </xsl:template>
  <xsl:template match="tab"> <!-- Match a regular tab -->
    <td bgcolor="#B6B687" width="1%" align="LEFT" valign="TOP"><img
    src="{$i}tab_open.gif" height="21" width="13" border="0" /></td>
    <td width="1%" bgcolor="#B6B687">
```

Example 17-43. Stylesheet to Render a Set of HTML Tabs for a Frameset (continued)

```
      <a target="contents" href="{@id}.xsql"
         onclick="location.href='site.xsql?tab={@id}'">
        <font size="-1" face="Arial" color="#000000">
          <xsl:value-of select="@name"/>
        </font>
      </a>
    </td>
    <td bgcolor="#B6B687" width="1%" align="RIGHT" valign="TOP">
      <img src="{$i}tab_close.gif" height="21" width="10" border="0"/>
    </td>
  </xsl:template>

  <xsl:template match="tab[@id=$cur]" priority="10"><!-- Match selected tab -->
    <td bgcolor="#336699" width="1%" align="LEFT" valign="TOP">
      <img src="{$i}ctab_open.gif" height="21" width="18" border="0"/>
    </td>
    <td width="1%" bgcolor="#336699">
      <b>
        <font size="-1" face="Arial" color="#FFFFFF">
          <xsl:value-of select="@name"/>
        </font>
      </b>
    </td>
    <td bgcolor="#336699" width="1%" align="RIGHT" valign="TOP">
      <img src="{$i}ctab_close.gif" height="21" width="12" border="0"/>
    </td>
  </xsl:template>
</xsl:stylesheet>
```

And finally, a little *index.html* page ties the tabs frame and defaults the *News.xsql* page to be the default content in the main section of the page:

```
<html>
  <head>
    <title>XML Book XSQL Sample Site</title>
  </head>
  <frameset border="no" rows="90,*">
    <frame frameborder=no noresize name="tabs" src="site.xsql">
    <frame frameborder=no name="contents" src="News.xsql">
  </frameset>
</html>
```

Figure 17-43 illustrates what the user now sees when logged into the site, with the additional tabs in place. The news portal page is the initial tab displayed.

Clicking on the Forums tab causes *Forums.xsql* to be requested in the main content frame, producing our discussion forum home page on that tab.

And with this final touch of grace, our journey is complete.

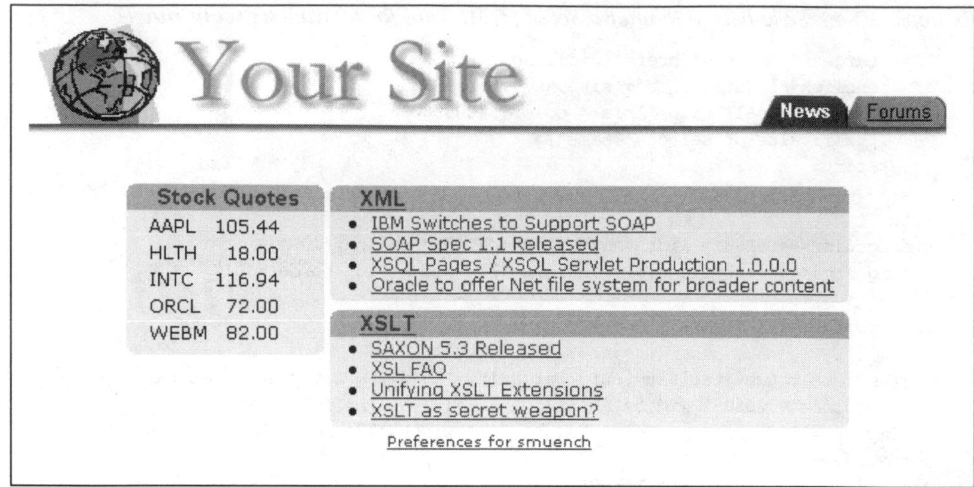

Figure 17-43. Final news portal and discussion application with tabs

In conclusion, we've demonstrated:

- The speed, functionality, and reliability of the Oracle database
- The power of XML as a universal standard for data exchange
- The flexibility of XSLT to transform data into any format required

These factors give us a real leg up in the race to build the next great web application. Throughout this book, we've learned how the powerful features of XML, XSLT, and Oracle8*i*—in combination with Oracle XML technologies like the XML Parser, XSLT processor, XML SQL Utility, and XSQL Pages—allow us to:

- Extract data from a database in XML format
- Search and transform XML data using XSLT and XPath
- Send and receive XML datagrams over the Web
- Store datagrams of any shape and size in the database
- Search efficiently through millions of XML documents
- Assemble XML information and transform it for delivery in any needed format

Now, excited by the opportunities that XML and the Oracle XML technologies enable, all that's left to do is to "go forth and transform!"

IV

Appendixes

This part of the book contains the following reference appendixes:

- Appendix A, *XML Helper Packages*, explains the source code for the PL/SQL helper packages we built in Chapter 3, *Combining XML and Oracle*: `xml`, `xmldoc`, `xpath`, `xslt`, and `http`.
- Appendix B, *Installing the Oracle XSQL Servlet*, describes how to install the XSQL Servlet that you can use with any servlet engine (Apache JServ, JRun, etc.).
- Appendix C, *Conceptual Map to the XML Family*, graphically summarizes the relationships between key XML concepts and the family of XML-related standards that support them.
- Appendix D, *Quick References*, provides cheat sheets on XML, XSLT, and XPath syntax.

XML Helper Packages

This appendix includes the PL/SQL package implementations for the XML helper packages we used back in Chapter 5, *Processing XML with PL/SQL*:

- `xml`
- `xmldoc`
- `xpath`
- `xslt`
- `http`

This appendix also contains instructions on how to install these packages in your Oracle8*i* database.

Installing the XML Helper Packages

To install all of the XML helper packages we used in Chapter 5, follow these steps:

1. Change directory to the *./examples/appa* directory, which contains the files for this appendix.
2. Connect as SYS using SQL*Plus and run the *install_sys_helper_packages.sql*:

   ```
   sqlplus sys/change_on_install @install_sys_helper_packages.sql
   ```

3. Compile `PropertyHelper.java` and use `loadjava` to load it into the database as SYS:

   ```
   javac PropertyHelper.java
   loadjava -verbose -resolve -user sys/change_on_install PropertyHelper.class
   ```

4. Connect as XMLBOOK using SQL*Plus and run the *install_helper_packages.sql* script:

   ```
   sqlplus xmlbook/xmlbook @install_helper_packages.sql:
   ```

Source Code for the XML Helper Packages

The `xml`, `xmldoc`, `xpath`, and `xslt` packages depend on having the Oracle XML Parser for PL/SQL installed. (See Chapter 5 for installation details). In addition, since the Oracle XML Parser for PL/SQL wraps the Oracle XML Parser for Java, one of the following must be true before you can successfully compile and run these packages:

- You must have already:
  - Installed the Oracle XML Parser for Java in your schema
  - Installed the Oracle XML Parser for PL/SQL packages in your schema, and
  - Been granted the JAVAUSERPRIV privilege to execute Java code inside Oracle8*i*
- Alternatively, you must have been granted EXECUTE permission on the Oracle XML Parser for PL/SQL packages installed in another schema.

The xml Package

The `xml` package provides key functionality for parsing XML documents from VARCHAR2, CLOB, BFILE, and URL sources. It uses the Oracle XML Parser for PL/SQL's `xmlparser` package. To use these routines, perform these steps:

1. Call one of the `xml.parse` functions to parse your XML document
2. Work with the returned `xmldom.DOMDocument`
3. Call `xml.freeDocument(`*`yourDoc`*`)` to free the memory used by the parsed representation of your XML document

It is safe to cache the instances of `xmldom.DOMDocument` in PL/SQL package-level variables for parsed XML documents you need to use over and over during the same database session, but remember that the memory they occupy is not freed until you explicitly call `xml.freeDocument`.

Note that if you need to parse an XML document from a URL outside a firewall, or parse any XML document with external references (external entities or DTD, for example) based on URLs outside a firewall, you must call:

```
xml.setHttpProxy('proxyServerName');
```

once in your current database session before using the `parse` functions. The various `parse` functions handle both creating and freeing the `xmlparser.parser` object used to create the in-memory DOM tree representation of your parsed XML file.

Here is the source code for the `xml` package:

```
CREATE OR REPLACE PACKAGE xml AS

  -- Set HTTP proxy server in case you reference documents
  -- or DTDs outside a corporate firewall

  PROCEDURE setHttpProxy(machinename VARCHAR2,
                         port        VARCHAR2 := '80');

  -- Parse and return an XML document

  FUNCTION parse(xml VARCHAR2) RETURN xmldom.DOMDocument;
  FUNCTION parse(xml CLOB)     RETURN xmldom.DOMDocument;
  FUNCTION parse(xml BFILE)    RETURN xmldom.DOMDocument;

  -- Parse and return an XML Document by URL

  FUNCTION parseURL(url VARCHAR2) RETURN xmldom.DOMDocument;

  -- Free the memory used by an XML document

  PROCEDURE freeDocument(doc xmldom.DOMDocument);

END;

CREATE OR REPLACE PACKAGE BODY xml AS
  parse_error EXCEPTION;
  PRAGMA EXCEPTION_INIT(parse_error,-20100);
  http_proxy_host VARCHAR2(200);
  http_proxy_port VARCHAR2(5) := '80';

  PROCEDURE setHttpProxy(machinename VARCHAR2, port VARCHAR2 := '80') IS
  BEGIN
    http_proxy_host := machinename;
    http_proxy_port := port;
  END;

  -- Set HTTP Proxy for Java programs in the current session.
  PROCEDURE setProxy IS
  BEGIN
    IF http_proxy_host IS NOT NULL THEN
      http_util.setProxy(http_proxy_host,http_proxy_port);
    END IF;
  END;

  ------------------------------------------------------------------
  -- Parse functions parse an XML document and return a handle to
  -- the in-memory DOM Document representation of the parsed XML.
  -- Call freeDocument() when you're done using the document returned
  -- by the function.
  ------------------------------------------------------------------
  FUNCTION parse(xml VARCHAR2) RETURN xmldom.DOMDocument IS
    retDoc xmldom.DOMDocument;
    parser xmlparser.Parser;
```

```
BEGIN
  IF xml IS NULL THEN RETURN NULL; END IF;
  setProxy;
  parser := xmlparser.newParser;
  xmlparser.parseBuffer(parser,xml);
  retDoc := xmlparser.getDocument(parser);
  xmlparser.freeParser(parser);
  RETURN retDoc;
EXCEPTION
  WHEN parse_error THEN
    xmlparser.freeParser(parser);
    RETURN retdoc;
END;

FUNCTION parse(xml BFILE) RETURN xmldom.DOMDocument IS
  retDoc xmldom.DOMDocument;
  parser xmlparser.Parser;
  b BFILE := xml;
  c CLOB;
BEGIN
  IF xml IS NULL THEN RETURN NULL; END IF;
  setProxy;
  parser := xmlparser.newParser;
  dbms_lob.createtemporary(c,cache=>FALSE);
  dbms_lob.fileOpen(b);
  dbms_lob.loadFromFile(dest_lob => c,
                        src_lob => b,
                        amount  => dbms_lob.getLength(b));
  dbms_lob.fileClose(b);
  xmlparser.parseCLOB(parser,c);
  retDoc := xmlparser.getDocument(parser);
  dbms_lob.freetemporary(c);
  xmlparser.freeParser(parser);
  RETURN retDoc;
EXCEPTION
  WHEN parse_error THEN
    dbms_lob.freetemporary(c);
    xmlparser.freeParser(parser);
    RETURN retdoc;
END;

FUNCTION parse(xml CLOB) RETURN xmldom.DOMDocument IS
  retDoc xmldom.DOMDocument;
  parser xmlparser.Parser;
BEGIN
  IF xml IS NULL THEN RETURN NULL; END IF;
  setProxy;
  parser := xmlparser.newParser;
  xmlparser.parseCLOB(parser,xml);
  retDoc := xmlparser.getDocument(parser);
  xmlparser.freeParser(parser);
  RETURN retDoc;
EXCEPTION
  WHEN parse_error THEN
    xmlparser.freeParser(parser);
```

```
      RETURN retdoc;
    END;

    FUNCTION parseURL(url VARCHAR2) RETURN xmldom.DOMDocument IS
      xmldoc xmldom.DOMDocument;
    BEGIN
      IF url IS NULL THEN RETURN NULL; END IF;
      setProxy;
      RETURN xmlparser.parse(url);
    END;

    -- Free the Java objects associated with an in-memory DOM tree
    PROCEDURE freeDocument(doc xmldom.DOMDocument) IS
    BEGIN
      xmldom.freeDocument(doc);
    END;

  END;
```

The xmldoc Package

The `xmldoc` package provides three key functions for saving well-formed XML documents to, and retrieving them from, an xml_documents table. A database trigger on the xml_documents table manages a `timestamp` column indicating the last time a new XML document was saved in the table. Each XML document is saved as a CLOB and is accessed by a document name that serves as the primary key for the document. For convenience, you can retrieve an existing document in the table by using:

`xmldoc.get()`
: Retrieves an XML document

`xmldoc.getAsText()`
: Retrieves a string

`xmldoc.getAsClob()`
: Retrieves a CLOB

The `xmldoc.save` method uses the `xml` helper package described in the previous section to `xml.parse` the document being saved, checking it for XML well-formedness in the process. Any well-formedness errors prevent the document from being saved. If the document is well-formed, the code uses the `xmldom.writeToClob` method to save the XML document in the xml_documents table's `xmldoc` CLOB column.

If the documents you are saving contain external references to URLs outside your corporate firewall, you'll need to call `xml.setHttpProxy` once in your current database session before using the `xmldoc` routines.

Here is the source code for the **xmldoc** package:

```
CREATE OR REPLACE PACKAGE xmldoc AS

  -- Save an XML document (parsing it first if necessary) into the
  -- xml_documents table with a given document name.

  PROCEDURE save(name      VARCHAR2,
                 xmldoc    VARCHAR2,
                 docommit BOOLEAN := TRUE);
  PROCEDURE save(name      VARCHAR2,
                 xmldoc    CLOB,
                 docommit BOOLEAN := TRUE);
  PROCEDURE save(name      VARCHAR2,
                 xmldoc    BFILE,
                 docommit BOOLEAN := TRUE);
  PROCEDURE save(name      VARCHAR2,
                 xmldoc xmldom.DOMDocument,
                 docommit BOOLEAN:=TRUE);

  -- Get an XML document by name from the xml_documents table

  FUNCTION  get(name VARCHAR2) RETURN xmldom.DOMDocument;

  -- Get an XML document as a CLOB by name from the xml_documents table

  FUNCTION  getAsCLOB(name VARCHAR2) RETURN CLOB;

  -- Get an XML document as a VARCHAR2 by name from the xml_documents table

  FUNCTION  getAsText(name VARCHAR2) RETURN VARCHAR2;

  -- Remove an XML document by name from the xml_documents table

  PROCEDURE remove(name VARCHAR2, docommit BOOLEAN := TRUE);

  -- Test if a named document exists in the xml_documents table

  FUNCTION  docExists(name VARCHAR2) RETURN BOOLEAN;
END;

CREATE OR REPLACE PACKAGE BODY xmldoc AS

  FUNCTION get(name VARCHAR2, createNew BOOLEAN) RETURN CLOB IS
    c CLOB;
    create_new_clob EXCEPTION;
  BEGIN
    IF createNew THEN
      remove(name);
      RAISE create_new_clob;
    END IF;

    SELECT xmldoc INTO c FROM xml_documents WHERE docname = name;
    RETURN c;
```

```
EXCEPTION
  WHEN NO_DATA_FOUND OR create_new_clob THEN
    IF createNew THEN
      INSERT INTO xml_documents(docname,xmldoc)
           VALUES(name,empty_clob())
      RETURNING xmldoc INTO c;
      RETURN c;
    ELSE
      RETURN NULL;
    END IF;
END;

FUNCTION getAsCLOB(name VARCHAR2) RETURN CLOB IS
BEGIN
  RETURN get(name,FALSE);
END;

FUNCTION  getAsText(name VARCHAR2) RETURN VARCHAR2 IS
BEGIN
  RETURN dbms_lob.substr(getAsCLOB(name));
END;

FUNCTION  get(name VARCHAR2) RETURN xmldom.DOMDocument IS
BEGIN
  RETURN xml.parse(getAsCLOB(name));
END;

PROCEDURE save(name VARCHAR2,xmldoc VARCHAR2,docommit BOOLEAN:=TRUE) IS
  c CLOB := get(name, createNew=>TRUE);
  doc xmldom.DOMDocument;
BEGIN
  doc := xml.parse(xmldoc);
  xmldom.writeToClob(doc,c);
  xml.freeDocument(doc);
  IF docommit THEN commit; END IF;
EXCEPTION
  WHEN OTHERS THEN xml.freeDocument(doc); RAISE;
END;

PROCEDURE save(name VARCHAR2,xmldoc CLOB,docommit BOOLEAN:=TRUE) IS
  c CLOB := get(name, createNew=>TRUE);
  doc xmldom.DOMDocument;
BEGIN
  doc := xml.parse(xmldoc);
  xmldom.writeToClob(doc,c);
  xml.freeDocument(doc);
  IF docommit THEN commit; END IF;
EXCEPTION
  WHEN OTHERS THEN xml.freeDocument(doc); RAISE;
END;

PROCEDURE save(name VARCHAR2,xmldoc BFILE,docommit BOOLEAN:=TRUE) IS
  c CLOB := get(name, createNew=>TRUE);
  doc xmldom.DOMDocument;
```

```
  BEGIN
    doc := xml.parse(xmldoc);
    xmldom.writeToClob(doc,c);
    xml.freeDocument(doc);
    IF docommit THEN commit; END IF;
  EXCEPTION
    WHEN OTHERS THEN xml.freeDocument(doc); RAISE;
  END;

  PROCEDURE save(name VARCHAR2,xmldoc xmldom.DOMDocument,docommit BOOLEAN:=TRUE)
IS
    c CLOB := get(name, createNew=>TRUE);
  BEGIN
    xmldom.writeToClob(xmldoc,c);
    IF docommit THEN commit; END IF;
  END;

  PROCEDURE remove(name VARCHAR2,docommit BOOLEAN := TRUE) IS
    c CLOB := get(name, createNew=>FALSE);
  BEGIN
    DELETE FROM xml_documents WHERE docname = name;
    IF docommit THEN commit; END IF;
  END;

  FUNCTION  docExists(name VARCHAR2) RETURN BOOLEAN IS
  BEGIN
    RETURN getAsCLOB(name) IS NOT NULL;
  END;
END;
```

The xpath Package

The **xpath** package provides four key functions used to exploit XPath expressions on in-memory XML documents:

`xpath.valueOf()`
: Retrieves the value of an XPath expression

`xpath.extract()`
: Extracts the XML markup of nodes matching an XPath expression

`xpath.test()`
: Tests if an XPath expression is true with respect to a node

`xpath.selectNodes()`
: Selects a list of nodes matching an XPath expression

Here is the source code for the **xpath** package:

```
CREATE OR REPLACE PACKAGE xpath AS

  -- Return the value of an XPath expression, optionally normalizing whitespace
```

```
   FUNCTION valueOf(doc        xmldom.DOMDocument,
                    xpath      VARCHAR2,
                    normalize BOOLEAN:=FALSE) RETURN VARCHAR2;

   FUNCTION valueOf(node       xmldom.DOMNode,
                    xpath      VARCHAR2,
                    normalize BOOLEAN:=FALSE)   RETURN VARCHAR2;

   FUNCTION valueOf(doc        VARCHAR2,
                    xpath      VARCHAR2,
                    normalize BOOLEAN := FALSE) RETURN VARCHAR2;

   FUNCTION valueOf(doc CLOB,
                    xpath VARCHAR2,
                    normalize BOOLEAN := FALSE) RETURN VARCHAR2;

   -- Test whether an XPath predicate is true

   FUNCTION test(doc  xmldom.DOMDocument,xpath VARCHAR2) RETURN BOOLEAN;
   FUNCTION test(node xmldom.DOMNode,    xpath VARCHAR2) RETURN BOOLEAN;
   FUNCTION test(doc  VARCHAR2,          xpath VARCHAR2) RETURN BOOLEAN;
   FUNCTION test(doc  CLOB,              xpath VARCHAR2) RETURN BOOLEAN;

   -- Extract an XML fragment for set of nodes matching an XPath pattern
   -- optionally normalizing whitespace (default is to normalize it)

   FUNCTION extract(doc        xmldom.DOMDocument,
                    xpath      VARCHAR2:='/',
                    normalize BOOLEAN:=TRUE)   RETURN VARCHAR2;
   FUNCTION extract(doc        VARCHAR2,
                    xpath      VARCHAR2 := '/',
                    normalize BOOLEAN := TRUE) RETURN VARCHAR2;
   FUNCTION extract(doc        CLOB,
                    xpath      VARCHAR2 := '/',
                    normalize BOOLEAN := TRUE) RETURN VARCHAR2;

   -- Select a list of nodes matching an XPath pattern
   -- Note: DOMNodeList returned has a zero-based index

   FUNCTION  selectNodes(doc xmldom.DOMDocument,
                         xpath VARCHAR2) RETURN xmldom.DOMNodeList;

   FUNCTION  selectNodes(node xmldom.DOMNode,
                         xpath VARCHAR2) RETURN xmldom.DOMNodeList;

   FUNCTION  selectNodes(doc VARCHAR2,
                         xpath VARCHAR2) RETURN xmldom.DOMNodeList;

   FUNCTION  selectNodes(doc CLOB,
                         xpath VARCHAR2) RETURN xmldom.DOMNodeList;

END;

CREATE OR REPLACE PACKAGE BODY xpath AS
```

```
-- "Casts" a DOMDocument as a DOMNode
FUNCTION toNode(doc xmldom.DOMDocument) RETURN xmldom.DOMNode IS
BEGIN RETURN xmldom.makeNode(doc); END;

-----------------------------------------------------------------------
-- Removes extraneous whitespace from a string.
-- Translates CR, LF, and TAB to spaces, then leaves only a single
-- space between characters.
-----------------------------------------------------------------------
FUNCTION normalizeWS( v VARCHAR2 )
RETURN VARCHAR2 IS
  result VARCHAR2(32767);
BEGIN
  result := RTRIM(LTRIM(TRANSLATE(v,CHR(13)||CHR(8)||CHR(10),'   ')));
  WHILE (INSTR(result,'  ') > 0) LOOP
    result := REPLACE(result,'  ',' ');
  END LOOP;
  RETURN result;
END;

-----------------------------------------------------------------------
-- Selects nodes matching an XPath expression and returns the string
-- consisting of the XML serialization of each matching node in
-- document order. Passing an XPath of '/' matches the single root node
-- and so the entire document is serialized to XML markup. If the
-- normalizeWhitespace is set to TRUE (the default) then the string
-- is stripped of extraneous whitespace before being returned.
-----------------------------------------------------------------------
FUNCTION selectAndPrint(doc xmldom.DOMDocument,xpath VARCHAR2,
                        normalizeWhitespace BOOLEAN := TRUE)
RETURN VARCHAR2 IS
  retval   VARCHAR2(32767);
  result   VARCHAR2(32767);
  curNode  xmldom.DOMNode;
  nodeType NATURAL;
  matches  xmldom.DOMNodeList;
BEGIN
  IF xpath = '/' THEN
    xmldom.writeToBuffer(doc,retval);
  ELSE
    matches  := xslprocessor.selectNodes(toNode(doc),xpath);
    FOR i IN 1..xmldom.getLength(matches) LOOP
      curNode := xmldom.item(matches,i-1);
      xmldom.writeToBuffer(curNode,result);
      nodeType := xmldom.getNodeType(curNode);
      IF nodeType NOT IN (xmldom.TEXT_NODE,xmldom.CDATA_SECTION_NODE) THEN
        retval := retval||RTRIM(RTRIM(result,CHR(10)),CHR(13));
      ELSE
        retval := retval||result;
      END IF;
    END LOOP;
  END IF;
  IF normalizeWhitespace THEN
    RETURN normalizeWS(retval);
```

```
  ELSE
    RETURN retval;
  END IF;
END;

--------------------------------------------------------------------
-- The "extract" functions parse the inbound document if necessary
-- and use selectAndPrint to extract the XML markup for the nodes
-- matching the XPath expression passed in. If the normalize parameter
-- is TRUE, extraneous whitespace is removed.
--------------------------------------------------------------------
FUNCTION extract(doc xmldom.DOMDocument,xpath VARCHAR2:='/',
                 normalize BOOLEAN:=TRUE)
  RETURN VARCHAR2 IS
BEGIN
  IF xmldom.isNull(doc) OR xpath IS NULL THEN RETURN NULL; END IF;
  RETURN selectAndPrint(doc,xpath,normalize);
END;

FUNCTION extract(doc VARCHAR2,xpath VARCHAR2 := '/', normalize BOOLEAN:=TRUE)
  RETURN VARCHAR2 IS
  xmldoc xmldom.DOMDocument;
  retval VARCHAR2(32767);
BEGIN
  IF doc IS NULL OR xpath IS NULL THEN RETURN NULL; END IF;
  xmldoc := xml.parse(doc);
  retval := selectAndPrint(xmldoc,xpath,normalize);
  xml.freeDocument(xmldoc);
  RETURN retval;
EXCEPTION
  WHEN OTHERS THEN xml.freeDocument(xmldoc); RAISE;
END;

FUNCTION extract(doc CLOB,xpath VARCHAR2 := '/',normalize BOOLEAN:=TRUE)
 RETURN VARCHAR2 IS
  xmldoc xmldom.DOMDocument;
  retval VARCHAR2(32767);
BEGIN
  IF doc IS NULL OR xpath IS NULL THEN RETURN NULL; END IF;
  xmldoc := xml.parse(doc);
  retval := selectAndPrint(xmldoc,xpath,normalize);
  xml.freeDocument(xmldoc);
  RETURN retval;
EXCEPTION
  WHEN OTHERS THEN xml.freeDocument(xmldoc); RAISE;
END;

--------------------------------------------------------------------
-- The "valueOf" functions parse the inbound document if necessary
-- and use xslprocessor.valueOf to return the value of the matching
-- expression. The semantics of valueOf are the same as <xsl:value-of>.
-- The XPath expression is interpreted with respect to the root
-- element of the document, unless valueOf(node,...) is used in
-- which case the expression is interpreted with respect to the
-- current node.
```

```
----------------------------------------------------------------------
FUNCTION valueOf(node xmldom.DOMNode, xpath VARCHAR2,normalize BOOLEAN:=FALSE)
  RETURN VARCHAR2 IS
BEGIN
  IF xmldom.IsNull(node) OR xpath IS NULL THEN RETURN NULL; END IF;
  IF normalize THEN
    RETURN normalizeWS(xslprocessor.valueOf(node,xpath));
  ELSE
    RETURN xslprocessor.valueOf(node,xpath);
  END IF;
END;

FUNCTION valueOf(doc xmldom.DOMDocument,xpath VARCHAR2,normalize BOOLEAN:=FALSE)
  RETURN VARCHAR2 IS
BEGIN
  IF xmldom.IsNull(doc) OR xpath IS NULL THEN RETURN NULL; END IF;
  RETURN valueOf(toNode(doc),xpath,normalize);
END;

FUNCTION valueOf(doc VARCHAR2,xpath VARCHAR2,normalize BOOLEAN:=FALSE)
  RETURN VARCHAR2 IS
  xmldoc xmldom.DOMDocument;
  retval VARCHAR2(32767);
BEGIN
  IF doc IS NULL OR xpath IS NULL THEN RETURN NULL; END IF;
  xmldoc := xml.parse(doc);
  retval := valueOf(xmldoc,xpath,normalize);
  xml.freeDocument(xmldoc);
  RETURN retval;
EXCEPTION
  WHEN OTHERS THEN xml.freeDocument(xmldoc); RAISE;
END;

FUNCTION valueOf(doc CLOB,xpath VARCHAR2,normalize BOOLEAN:=FALSE)
  RETURN VARCHAR2 IS
  xmldoc xmldom.DOMDocument;
  retval VARCHAR2(32767);
BEGIN
  IF doc IS NULL OR xpath IS NULL THEN RETURN NULL; END IF;
  xmldoc := xml.parse(doc);
  retval := valueOf(xmldoc,xpath,normalize);
  xml.freeDocument(xmldoc);
  RETURN retval;
EXCEPTION
  WHEN OTHERS THEN xml.freeDocument(xmldoc); RAISE;
END;

----------------------------------------------------------------------
-- The "selectNodes" functions parse the inbound document if necessary
-- and use xslprocessor.selectNodes to return a DOM NodeList of
-- nodes matching the XPath expression. To iterate over the node list
-- define "curNode" to be of type xmldom.DOMNode and write a loop like:
--
```

```
--    FOR n IN 1..xmldom.getLength(yourNodeList) LOOP
--      curNode := xmldom.item(yourNodeList, n - 1 );
--        :
--    END LOOP;
----------------------------------------------------------------------
FUNCTION  selectNodes(node xmldom.DOMNode,xpath VARCHAR2)
RETURN xmldom.DOMNodeList IS
BEGIN
  RETURN xslprocessor.selectNodes(node,xpath);
END;

FUNCTION  selectNodes(doc xmldom.DOMDocument,xpath VARCHAR2)
RETURN xmldom.DOMNodeList IS
BEGIN
  RETURN selectNodes(toNode(doc),xpath);
END;

FUNCTION  selectNodes(doc VARCHAR2, xpath VARCHAR2)
RETURN xmldom.DOMNodeList IS
  xmldoc xmldom.DOMDocument;
  retlist xmldom.DOMNodeList;
BEGIN
  xmldoc := xml.parse(doc);
  retlist := xslprocessor.selectNodes(toNode(xmldoc),xpath);
  xml.freeDocument(xmldoc);
  RETURN retlist;
EXCEPTION
  WHEN OTHERS THEN xml.freeDocument(xmldoc); RAISE;
END;

FUNCTION  selectNodes(doc CLOB, xpath VARCHAR2)
RETURN xmldom.DOMNodeList IS
  xmldoc xmldom.DOMDocument;
  retlist xmldom.DOMNodeList;
BEGIN
  xmldoc := xml.parse(doc);
  retlist := xslprocessor.selectNodes(toNode(xmldoc),xpath);
  xml.freeDocument(xmldoc);
  RETURN retlist;
EXCEPTION
  WHEN OTHERS THEN xml.freeDocument(xmldoc); RAISE;
END;

----------------------------------------------------------------------
-- The "test" functions parse the inbound document if necessary
-- and use selectNodes to see if the XPath predicate is true
-- with respect to the current node.
----------------------------------------------------------------------
FUNCTION test(doc xmldom.DOMDocument,xpath VARCHAR2) RETURN BOOLEAN IS
BEGIN
  RETURN xmldom.getLength(selectNodes(doc,'/self::node()['||xpath||']')) > 0;
END;
```

```
  FUNCTION test(node xmldom.DOMNode,xpath VARCHAR2) RETURN BOOLEAN IS
  BEGIN
    RETURN xmldom.getLength(selectNodes(node,'./self::node()['||xpath||']')) > 0;
  END;

  FUNCTION test(doc VARCHAR2, xpath VARCHAR2) RETURN BOOLEAN IS
    xmldoc xmldom.DOMDocument;
    retval BOOLEAN;
  BEGIN
    xmldoc := xml.parse(doc);
    retval := test(xmldoc,xpath);
    xml.freeDocument(xmldoc);
    RETURN retval;
  EXCEPTION
    WHEN OTHERS THEN xml.freeDocument(xmldoc); RAISE;
  END;

  FUNCTION test(doc CLOB, xpath VARCHAR2) RETURN BOOLEAN IS
    xmldoc xmldom.DOMDocument;
    retval BOOLEAN;
  BEGIN
    xmldoc := xml.parse(doc);
    retval := test(xmldoc,xpath);
    xml.freeDocument(xmldoc);
    RETURN retval;
  EXCEPTION
    WHEN OTHERS THEN xml.freeDocument(xmldoc); RAISE;
  END;

END;
```

The xslt Package

The `xslt` package provides five key functions related to XSLT transformations on in-memory XML documents:

`xslt.stylesheet()`
: Creates a new stylesheet object

`xslt.transform()`
: Transforms an XML document to a string

`xslt.transformToDOM()`
: Transforms an XML document to a DOM

`xslt.params()`
: Constructs a parameter list for a transformation

`xslt.freeStylesheet()`
: Frees a stylesheet when you're done using it

It is safe to cache instances of `xslprocessor.stylesheets` in PL/SQL package-level variables for stylesheets that you plan to use over and over during the same database session, but remember that the memory they occupy is not freed until you explicitly call `xslt.freeStylesheet`.

Here is the source code for the `xslt` package:

```
CREATE OR REPLACE PACKAGE xslt AS
  TYPE name_value IS RECORD( NAME VARCHAR2(40), VALUE VARCHAR2(200));
  TYPE paramlist IS TABLE OF name_value INDEX BY BINARY_INTEGER;

  none paramlist;

  -- Return an XSLT stylesheet based on XML document of the stylesheet source

  FUNCTION stylesheet(doc xmldom.DOMDocument) RETURN xslprocessor.Stylesheet;
  FUNCTION stylesheet(doc VARCHAR2)           RETURN xslprocessor.Stylesheet;
  FUNCTION stylesheet(doc CLOB)               RETURN xslprocessor.Stylesheet;
  FUNCTION stylesheet(doc BFILE)              RETURN xslprocessor.Stylesheet;
  FUNCTION stylesheetFromURL(url VARCHAR2)    RETURN xslprocessor.Stylesheet;

  -- Transform an XML Document with an XSLT stylesheet, returning a String

  FUNCTION transform(source xmldom.DOMDocument,
                      style xslprocessor.Stylesheet,
                     params paramlist := none) RETURN VARCHAR2;
  FUNCTION transform(source VARCHAR2,
                      style  xslprocessor.Stylesheet,
                     params paramlist := none) RETURN VARCHAR2;
  FUNCTION transform(source CLOB,
                      style xslprocessor.Stylesheet,
                     params paramlist := none) RETURN VARCHAR2;

  -- Transform an XML Document with an XSLT stylesheet, returning an XML doc

  FUNCTION transformToDOM(source xmldom.DOMDocument,
                           style  xslprocessor.Stylesheet,
                           params paramlist := none)
                           RETURN xmldom.DOMDocument;
  FUNCTION transformToDOM(source VARCHAR2,
                           style  xslprocessor.Stylesheet,
                           params paramlist := none)
                           RETURN xmldom.DOMDocument;
  FUNCTION transformToDOM(source CLOB,
                           style  xslprocessor.Stylesheet,
                           params paramlist := none)
                           RETURN xmldom.DOMDocument;

  -- Return a paramlist to be used for a transformation

  FUNCTION params( n1 VARCHAR2,        v1 VARCHAR2,
                   n2 VARCHAR2:=NULL,v2 VARCHAR2:=NULL,
                   n3 VARCHAR2:=NULL,v3 VARCHAR2:=NULL,
                   n4 VARCHAR2:=NULL,v4 VARCHAR2:=NULL,
                   n5 VARCHAR2:=NULL,v5 VARCHAR2:=NULL) RETURN paramlist;
```

```
    -- Release the memory used by a stylesheet

    PROCEDURE freeStylesheet( style xslprocessor.Stylesheet);

  END;

  CREATE OR REPLACE PACKAGE BODY xslt AS

    -----------------------------------------------------------------------
    -- Reset the parameters on the stylesheet and then set the new
    -- parameter values based on the parameters in the paramlist.
    -----------------------------------------------------------------------
    PROCEDURE setParams(style xslprocessor.Stylesheet, params paramlist) IS
    BEGIN
      IF params.exists(1) THEN
        xslprocessor.resetParams(style);
        FOR i IN 1..params.COUNT LOOP
          IF params(i).name IS NOT NULL AND params(i).value IS NOT NULL THEN
            xslprocessor.setParam(style,params(i).name,'"'||params(i).value||'"');
          END IF;
        END LOOP;
      END IF;
    END;

    -----------------------------------------------------------------------
    -- The "stylesheet" functions create a new stylesheet object from
    -- an XML source. Remember to call freeStylesheet() when you're done
    -- using the stylesheet.
    -----------------------------------------------------------------------
    FUNCTION stylesheet(doc xmldom.DOMDocument) RETURN xslprocessor.Stylesheet IS
    BEGIN
      return xslprocessor.newStylesheet(doc,NULL);
    END;

    FUNCTION stylesheet(doc VARCHAR2) RETURN xslprocessor.Stylesheet IS
      xmldoc xmldom.DOMDocument;
      newsheet xslprocessor.Stylesheet;
    BEGIN
      xmldoc   := xml.parse(doc);
      newsheet := xslprocessor.newStylesheet(xmldoc,NULL);
      xml.freeDocument(xmldoc);
      RETURN newsheet;
    EXCEPTION
      WHEN OTHERS THEN xml.freeDocument(xmldoc); RAISE;
    END;

    FUNCTION stylesheetFromURL(url VARCHAR2) RETURN xslprocessor.Stylesheet IS
    BEGIN
      return xslprocessor.newStylesheet(url,url);
    END;

    FUNCTION stylesheet(doc CLOB) RETURN xslprocessor.Stylesheet IS
      xmldoc xmldom.DOMDocument;
      newsheet xslprocessor.Stylesheet;
```

```
BEGIN
  xmldoc := xml.parse(doc);
  newsheet := xslprocessor.newStylesheet(xmldoc,NULL);
  xml.freeDocument(xmldoc);
  RETURN newsheet;
EXCEPTION
  WHEN OTHERS THEN xml.freeDocument(xmldoc); RAISE;
END;

FUNCTION stylesheet(doc BFILE) RETURN xslprocessor.Stylesheet IS
  xmldoc xmldom.DOMDocument;
  newsheet xslprocessor.Stylesheet;
BEGIN
  xmldoc := xml.parse(doc);
  newsheet := xslprocessor.newStylesheet(xmldoc,NULL);
  xml.freeDocument(xmldoc);
  RETURN newsheet;
EXCEPTION
  WHEN OTHERS THEN xml.freeDocument(xmldoc); RAISE;
END;

-----------------------------------------------------------------------
-- The "transform" functions carry out the transformation described
-- by the XSLT stylesheet object passed-in on the XML document source
-- The resulting target document is returned as a String.
-----------------------------------------------------------------------
FUNCTION transform(source xmldom.DOMDocument,
                   style  xslprocessor.Stylesheet,
                   params paramlist := none) RETURN VARCHAR2 IS
  engine xslprocessor.Processor := xslprocessor.newProcessor;
  out VARCHAR2(32767);
BEGIN
  setParams(style,params);
  xslprocessor.processXSL(engine,style,source,out);
  xslprocessor.freeProcessor(engine);
  RETURN out;
EXCEPTION
  WHEN OTHERS THEN xslprocessor.freeProcessor(engine); RAISE;
END;

FUNCTION transform(source VARCHAR2,
                   style  xslprocessor.Stylesheet,
                   params paramlist := none) RETURN VARCHAR2 IS
  xmldoc xmldom.DOMDocument;
  retval VARCHAR2(32767);
BEGIN
  xmldoc := xml.parse(source);
  retval := transform(xmldoc,style,params);
  xml.freeDocument(xmldoc);
  RETURN retval;
EXCEPTION
  WHEN OTHERS THEN xml.freeDocument(xmldoc); RAISE;
END;
```

```
FUNCTION transform(source CLOB,
                   style  xslprocessor.Stylesheet,
                   params paramlist := none) RETURN VARCHAR2 IS
  xmldoc xmldom.DOMDocument;
  retval VARCHAR2(32767);
BEGIN
  xmldoc := xml.parse(source);
  retval := transform(xmldoc,style,params);
  xml.freeDocument(xmldoc);
  RETURN retval;
EXCEPTION
  WHEN OTHERS THEN xml.freeDocument(xmldoc); RAISE;
END;

------------------------------------------------------------------------
-- The "transformToDOM" functions carry out the transformation
-- described by the XSLT stylesheet object passed-in on the XML
-- document source. The resulting target document is returned as an
-- in-memory XML Document for further processing. Using this function
-- you can "chain" stylesheets together by making the result of one
-- transformation be the source of the next.
------------------------------------------------------------------------
FUNCTION transformToDOM(source xmldom.DOMDocument,
                        style  xslprocessor.Stylesheet,
                        params paramlist := none) RETURN xmldom.DOMDocument IS
  engine xslprocessor.Processor := xslprocessor.newProcessor;
  root   xmldom.DOMNode         := xmldom.makeNode(xmldom.newDOMDocument);
  result xmldom.DOMNode;
BEGIN
  setParams(style,params);
  result := xmldom.makeNode(xslprocessor.processXSL(engine,style,source));
  RETURN xmldom.makeDocument(xmldom.appendChild(root,result));
  xslprocessor.freeProcessor(engine);
EXCEPTION
  WHEN OTHERS THEN xslprocessor.freeProcessor(engine); RAISE;
END;

FUNCTION transformToDOM(source VARCHAR2,
                        style  xslprocessor.Stylesheet,
                        params paramlist := none) RETURN xmldom.DOMDocument IS
  xmldoc xmldom.DOMDocument;
  retdoc xmldom.DOMDocument;
BEGIN
  xmldoc := xml.parse(source);
  retdoc := transformToDOM(xmldoc,style,params);
  xml.freeDocument(xmldoc);
  RETURN retdoc;
EXCEPTION
  WHEN OTHERS THEN xml.freeDocument(xmldoc); RAISE;
END;

FUNCTION transformToDOM(source CLOB,
                        style  xslprocessor.Stylesheet,
                        params paramlist := none) RETURN xmldom.DOMDocument IS
```

```
    xmldoc xmldom.DOMDocument;
    retdoc xmldom.DOMDocument;
  BEGIN
    xmldoc := xml.parse(source);
    retdoc := transformToDOM(xmldoc,style,params);
    xml.freeDocument(xmldoc);
    RETURN retdoc;
  EXCEPTION
    WHEN OTHERS THEN xml.freeDocument(xmldoc); RAISE;
  END;

  ------------------------------------------------------------------------
  -- Construct a paramlist object based on one or more pairs
  -- of 'name','value' parameters.
  ------------------------------------------------------------------------
  FUNCTION params( n1 VARCHAR2,        v1 VARCHAR2,
                   n2 VARCHAR2:=NULL,v2 VARCHAR2:=NULL,
                   n3 VARCHAR2:=NULL,v3 VARCHAR2:=NULL,
                   n4 VARCHAR2:=NULL,v4 VARCHAR2:=NULL,
                   n5 VARCHAR2:=NULL,v5 VARCHAR2:=NULL) RETURN paramlist IS
    p_list paramlist;
  BEGIN
    p_list(1).name := n1; p_list(1).value := v1;
    p_list(2).name := n2; p_list(2).value := v2;
    p_list(3).name := n2; p_list(3).value := v2;
    p_list(4).name := n2; p_list(4).value := v2;
    p_list(5).name := n2; p_list(5).value := v2;
    RETURN p_list;
  END;

  PROCEDURE freeStylesheet( style xslprocessor.Stylesheet) IS
  BEGIN
    xslprocessor.freeStylesheet(style);
  END;

END;
```

The http Package

The `http` package provides support for generic HTTP POST and GET requests on top of the lower-level TCP/IP support found in the `UTL_TCP` package that ships with Oracle8*i*. It differs in two key ways from the `UTL_HTTP` package that also ships with Oracle8*i*:

http
: Handles both GET and POST requests, while `UTL_HTTP` does only GETs

UTL_HTTP
: Supports a `get_pieces` function to return larger responses, while the `http` package assumes that the return is less than 32K

In Chapter 5, we built an `xml_http` package that uses the `http` package as part of its implementation to send and receive XML documents over the Web.

Here is the source code for the `http` package:

```
CREATE OR REPLACE PACKAGE http AS

  -- HTTP POST a document to url and return response

  PROCEDURE post(doc                        VARCHAR2,
                 content_type               VARCHAR2,
                 url                        VARCHAR2,
                 resp                   OUT VARCHAR2,
                 resp_content_type      OUT VARCHAR2,
                 proxyServer                VARCHAR2 := NULL,
                 proxyPort                  NUMBER   := 80);

  -- HTTP GET resource at URL and return response as an XML document

  PROCEDURE get(url                        VARCHAR2,
                resp                   OUT VARCHAR2,
                resp_content_type      OUT VARCHAR2,
                proxyServer                VARCHAR2 := NULL,
                proxyPort                  NUMBER   := 80);

END;

CREATE OR REPLACE PACKAGE BODY http AS

  -- Write data to a TCP/IP connection
  PROCEDURE write(c IN OUT NOCOPY utl_tcp.connection,value VARCHAR2 := NULL) IS
    b PLS_INTEGER; -- Number of bytes written
  BEGIN
    b := utl_tcp.write_line(c,value);
  END;

  -- Write an HTTP Header to a TCP/IP connection
  PROCEDURE write_header(c IN OUT NOCOPY utl_tcp.connection,
                         name VARCHAR2,value VARCHAR2) IS
  BEGIN
    write(c,name || ': ' || value);
  END;

  ----------------------------------------------------------------------
  -- Given an HTTP-based URL, parse the domain, port number, and
  -- path name of the request.
  ----------------------------------------------------------------------
  PROCEDURE setHostPortPath(url VARCHAR2,proxyServer VARCHAR2,
                            proxyPort NUMBER, host OUT VARCHAR2,
                            port IN OUT NUMBER, path OUT VARCHAR2)
  IS
    temp VARCHAR2(400);
    slash NUMBER;
    colon NUMBER;
```

```
BEGIN
  IF proxyServer IS NOT NULL THEN
    ---------------------------------------------------------------------
    -- If a proxy server is set, then TCPconnection is to the
    -- proxy server and the path is the full URL to the actual page
    ---------------------------------------------------------------------
    host := proxyServer;
    port := proxyPort;
    path := url;
  ELSE
    ---------------------------------------------------------------------
    -- If no proxy server is set, then TCP connection is directly to
    -- the host/port specified in the URL.
    ---------------------------------------------------------------------
    temp        := SUBSTR(url,INSTR(url,'http://')+7);
    slash       := INSTR(temp,'/');
    IF slash > 0 THEN
      host := SUBSTR(temp,1,slash-1);
      path := SUBSTR(temp,slash);
    ELSE
      host := temp;
      path := '/';
    END IF;
    colon := INSTR(host,':');
    IF colon > 0 THEN
      port := TO_NUMBER(SUBSTR(host,colon+1));
      host := SUBSTR(host,1,colon-1);
    END IF;
  END IF;
END;

-------------------------------------------------------------------------
-- Read the response back from a TCP/IP connection, checking for
-- an HTTP 200 OK success header and taking notice of the
-- Content-Type: header that might be sent by the server.
-------------------------------------------------------------------------
PROCEDURE get_response_from(c IN OUT NOCOPY utl_tcp.connection,
                            resp OUT VARCHAR2,
                            content_type OUT VARCHAR2) IS
  line      VARCHAR2(32767);
  firstLine BOOLEAN := TRUE;
  header    BOOLEAN := TRUE;
  success   BOOLEAN := TRUE;
BEGIN
  WHILE (success) LOOP
    line := utl_tcp.get_line(c);
    IF firstLine THEN
      IF line NOT LIKE '%HTTP%200%OK%' THEN
        success := FALSE;
      END IF;
      firstLine := FALSE;
    ELSE
      IF HEADER THEN
        IF line = utl_tcp.CRLF THEN
          HEADER := FALSE;
```

```
          ELSE
            IF UPPER(line) LIKE 'CONTENT-TYPE:%' THEN
              content_type :=
RTRIM(RTRIM(RTRIM(LTRIM(SUBSTR(line,14))),CHR(10)),CHR(13));
            END IF;
          END IF;
        ELSE
          resp := resp || line;
        END IF;
      END IF;
    END LOOP;
  EXCEPTION
    WHEN utl_tcp.end_of_input THEN
      NULL; -- end of input
  END;

  ----------------------------------------------------------------------
  -- Perform an HTTP POST request to the specified URL with the
  -- specified 'doc' content in the request body. Return the response
  -- as a String.
  ----------------------------------------------------------------------
  PROCEDURE post(doc                    VARCHAR2,
                 content_type           VARCHAR2,
                 url                    VARCHAR2,
                 resp               OUT VARCHAR2,
                 resp_content_type  OUT VARCHAR2,
                 proxyServer            VARCHAR2 := NULL,
                 proxyPort              NUMBER   := 80) IS
    port      NUMBER := 80;
    host      VARCHAR2(400);
    path      VARCHAR2(400);
    line      VARCHAR2(32767);
    firstLine BOOLEAN := TRUE;
    header    BOOLEAN := TRUE;
    success   BOOLEAN := TRUE;
    c         utl_tcp.connection;
  BEGIN
    setHostPortPath(url,proxyServer,proxyPort,host,port,path);
    c := utl_tcp.open_connection(host, port);
    write(c,'POST '||path||' HTTP/1.0');
    write_header(c,'Content-Type',content_type);
    write_header(c,'Content-Length',LENGTH(doc));
    write(c);
    write(c,doc);
    utl_tcp.flush(c);
    get_response_from(c,resp,resp_content_type);
    utl_tcp.close_connection(c);
  EXCEPTION
    WHEN OTHERS THEN utl_tcp.close_connection(c); RAISE;
  END;

  ----------------------------------------------------------------------
  -- Perform an HTTP GET request to the specified URL and return the
  -- response as a String.
```

```
  ----------------------------------------------------------------------
  PROCEDURE get(url                         VARCHAR2,
                resp                   OUT VARCHAR2,
                resp_content_type OUT VARCHAR2,
                proxyServer             VARCHAR2 := NULL,
                proxyPort               NUMBER   := 80) IS
    port       NUMBER := 80;
    host       VARCHAR2(400);
    path       VARCHAR2(400);
    msg        VARCHAR2(32767);
    c          utl_tcp.connection;
  BEGIN
    setHostPortPath(url,proxyServer,proxyPort,host,port,path);
    c := utl_tcp.open_connection(host, port);
    write(c,'GET '||path||' HTTP/1.0');
    write(c);
    utl_tcp.flush(c);
    get_response_from(c,resp,resp_content_type);
    utl_tcp.close_connection(c);
  EXCEPTION
    WHEN OTHERS THEN utl_tcp.close_connection(c); RAISE;
  END;
END;
```

B

Installing the Oracle XSQL Servlet

This appendix describes how to install the Oracle XSQL Servlet. This servlet can be used with any servlet engine that supports mapping file extensions to a servlet class.

Installing the XSQL Servlet requires just two key steps:

1. Ensure that the following five archives are added properly to your servlet engine's CLASSPATH:
   - *oraclexsql.jar*
   - *oraclexmlsql.jar*
   - *xmlparserv2.jar*
   - *classes111.zip*
   - `<directory containing XSQL Config.xml file>`
2. Map the *.xsql* file extension to the `oracle.xml.xsql.XSQLServlet` servlet class.

Any requests made to your web server with the *.xsql* file extension will then be processed by the XSQL Servlet. Note that the *.xsql* file extension is purely a convention. You can map any file extension (or several different extensions) to the Servlet class without problems.

Supported Configurations

The XSQL Servlet is designed to run on any Java virtual machine, using any JDBC driver, against any database. It has been tested against the most popular configurations. In this section, we document the supported configurations.

Supported Java JDK Versions

XSQL Pages and the XSQL Servlet have been tested using:

- JDK 1.1.8
- JDK 1.2.2

Numerous users have reported problems using XSQL Pages and the XSQL Servlet with JDK 1.1.7, which suffers problems in its character set conversion routines for UTF-8 that make it unusable for processing XSQL Pages.

Supported Servlet Engines

This XSQL Servlet has been tested with the following servlet engines:

- Oracle Internet Application Server 1.0
- Allaire JRun 2.3.3
- Apache 1.3.9 with JServ 1.0 and 1.1
- Apache 1.3.9 with Tomcat 3.1 Servlet Engine
- Apache Tomcat 3.1 Web Server + Servlet Engine
- Caucho Resin 1.1
- NewAtlanta ServletExec 2.2 for IIS/PWS 4.0
- Oracle8*i* Lite Web-to-go Server
- Oracle Servlet Engine in Oracle8*i* 8.1.7
- Sun JavaServer™ Web Development Kit (JSWDK) 1.0.1 Web Server

Supported JSP Implementations

JavaServer Pages can use `<jsp:forward>` and/or `<jsp:include>` to collaborate with XSQL Pages as part of an application. The following JSP platforms have been tested:

- Apache 1.3.9 with Tomcat 3.1 Servlet Engine
- Apache Tomcat 3.1 Web Server + Tomcat 3.1 Servlet Engine
- Caucho Resin 1.1 (with built-in JSP 1.0 support)
- NewAtlanta ServletExec 2.2 for IIS/PWS 4.0 (built-in JSP 1.0 support)
- Oracle8*i* Lite Web-to-go Server with Oracle JSP 1.0

- Oracle Servlet Engine in Oracle8*i* 8.1.7 with Oracle JSP 1.0
- Any servlet engine with Servlet API 2.1+ and Oracle JSP 1.0

In general, JSP should work with any servlet engine supporting the Servlet 2.1 Specification or higher, and the Oracle JSP 1.0 reference implementation or functional equivalent from another vendor.

JDBC Drivers and Databases

The Oracle XSQL page processor has been designed to exploit the maximum set of features against the Oracle JDBC drivers, but gracefully degrade to work against any database with a reasonable JDBC driver. While numerous users have reported successfully using XSQL Pages with many other JDBC drivers, the following drivers have been tested:

- Oracle8*i* 8.1.5 driver for JDBC 1.x
- Oracle8i 8.1.6 driver for JDBC 1.x
- Oracle8*i* Lite 4.0 driver for JDBC 1.x
- Oracle8*i* 8.1.6 driver for JDBC 2.0

At this time, the `<xsql:insert-param>` and `<xsql:insert-request>` action elements depend on the Oracle JDBC driver because they depend on the Oracle XML SQL Utility for Java which, at present exhibits this restriction. A future release of Oracle XML SQL will remove this current restriction.

If you are using the Oracle 8i 8.1.6 driver for JDBC 2.0 (see *http://technet.oracle.com/tech/java/sqlj_jdbc/* in *classes12.zip*) you must download and use the corresponding Oracle XML SQL Utility for JDBC 2.0 (see *http://technet.oracle.com/tech/xml/oracle_xsu/* in *XSU12.zip*) from the Oracle Technology Network.

Prerequisites

Oracle XSQL Pages depends upon:

- Oracle XML Parser V2 Release 2.0.2.7
- Oracle XML SQL Utility for Java
- A web server that supports Java servlets
- A JDBC driver, like Oracle JDBC or Oracle8*i* Lite JDBC

For your convenience, all of these dependent libraries are included with the XSQL Servlet distribution, and all are included with JDeveloper 3.1 on the accompanying CD-ROM.

Downloading and Installing the XSQL Servlet

This section describes in detail how to obtain and install the XSQL Servlet.

Obtaining the XSQL Servlet Software from the Oracle Technology Network (OTN)

You can download the XSQL Servlet distribution by following these steps:

1. Visit *http://technet.oracle.com/tech/xml/xsql_servlet/*.
2. Click on the Software icon at the top of the page.
3. Log in with your OTN username and password; registration is free if you do not already have an account.
4. Select whether you want the Windows NT or Unix download; both contain the same files.
5. Acknowledge the licensing agreement and download the survey.
6. Click on *xsqlservlet_v1_0_0_0.tar.gz* or *xsqlservlet_v1_0_0_0.zip*. Note that if a later version is available, the filenames will reflect the later version number.

Extracting the Files in the Distribution

To extract the contents of the XSQL Servlet distribution, do the following:

1. Choose a directory under which you would like the *.\xsql* directory and subdirectories to go (e.g., *C:*).
2. Change directory to *C:*, then extract the downloaded XSQL archive file. For example, on Unix:

   ```
   tar xvfz xsqlservlet_v1_0_0_0.tar.gz
   ```

   or on Windows:

   ```
   pkzip25 -extract -directories xsqlservlet_v1_0_0_0.zip
   ```

   using the `pkzip25` (see *http://www.pkware.com/shareware/pkzip_cli.html*) command-line tool or the WinZip (see *http://www.winzip.com*) visual archive extraction tool.

3. If you use Windows and will be using the Web-to-go server, start with the next section. If you use Unix or if you use Windows with a different web server (not Web-to-go), skip ahead to the "Setting Up the Database Connection Definitions for Your Environment" section.

Starting the Web-to-Go Server (Windows Only)

The XSQL Servlet comes bundled with the Oracle Web-to-go server, which is preconfigured to use XSQL Pages. The Web-to-go server is a single-user server that supports the Servlet 2.1 API and is used for mobile application deployment and for development. This is a great way to try XSQL Pages out on your Windows machine before delving into the details of configuring another servlet engine to run XSQL Pages.

The Web-to-go web server is part of Oracle's development and deployment platform for mobile applications. For more information on Web-to-go, please visit *http://www.oracle.com/mobile*.

Windows users can get started quickly with XSQL Pages by:

- Running the *xsql-wtg.bat* script in the *.\xsql* directory
- Browsing the URL *http://localhost:7070/xsql/index.html*

If you get an error when you start this script, edit the *xsql-wtg.bat* file to properly set the two environment variables JAVA and XSQL_HOME to appropriate values for your machine:

```
REM ----------------------------------------------
REM Set the 'JAVA' variable equal to the full path
REM of your Java executable.
REM ----------------------------------------------

set JAVA=J:\java1.2\jre\bin\java.exe

set XSQL_HOME=C:\xsql

REM ----------------------------------------------
REM Set the 'XSQL_HOME' variable equal to the full
REM path of where you install the XSQL Servlet
REM distribution.
REM ----------------------------------------------
```

If you install XSQL into a directory other than *C:\xsql* (for example, on another drive like *D:\xsql*), you will also need to edit the *./xsql/wtg/lib/webtogo.ora* file to change the value of the `ROOT_DIR` parameter as follows.

Change:

```
[FILESYSTEM]
TYPE=OS
ROOT_DIR=C:\
```

to:

```
[FILESYSTEM]
TYPE=OS
ROOT_DIR=D:\
```

Then repeat the previous two steps.

If you get an error connecting to the database when you try the demos, you'll need to go on to the next section, then try the previous steps again after setting up your database connection information correctly in the *XSQLConfig.xml* file.

Setting Up the Database Connection Definitions for Your Environment

The demos that accompany the XSQL Servlet download are set up to use the SCOTT schema on a database on your local machine (i.e., the machine where the web server is running). If you are running a local database and have a SCOTT account whose password is `TIGER`, then you are all set. Otherwise, you need to edit the *.\xsql\lib\XSQLConfig.xml* file to correspond to the appropriate `username`, `password`, `dburl`, and `driver` values for the `demo` connection:

```
<?xml version="1.0" ?>
<XSQLConfig>
      :
  <connectiondefs>
    <connection name="demo">
      <username>scott</username>
      <password>tiger</password>
      <dburl>jdbc:oracle:thin:@localhost:1521:ORCL</dburl>
      <driver>oracle.jdbc.driver.OracleDriver</driver>
    </connection>
    <connection name="lite">
      <username>system</username>
      <password>manager</password>
      <dburl>jdbc:Polite:POlite</dburl>
      <driver>oracle.lite.poljdbc.POLJDBCDriver</driver>
    </connection>
  </connectiondefs>
       :
</XSQLConfig>
```

Setting Up Your Servlet Engine to Run XSQL Pages

Unix users and any user wanting to install the XSQL Servlet on other web servers should follow these instructions, depending on the web server being used. There are three basic steps:

1. Include the list of XSQL Java archives as well as the directory where *XSQLConfig.xml* resides (by default *./xsql/lib*) in the server CLASSPATH. For security reasons, make sure the directory where you place your XSQL *Config.xml* file is *not* browsable from your web server.

For convenience, the *xsqlservlet_v1_0_0_0.tar.gz* and *xsqlservlet_v1_0_0_0.zip* distributions include the *.jar* files for the Oracle XML Parser for Java (v2), the Oracle XML SQL Utility for Java, and the Oracle 8.1.6 JDBC driver in the *.\lib* subdirectory, along with Oracle XSQL Pages' own *.jar* archive.

2. Map the *.xsql* file extension to the `oracle.xml.xsql.XSQLServlet` servlet class.
3. Map a virtual directory */xsql* to the directory where you extracted the XSQL files (to access the online help and demos).

Allaire JRun 2.3.3

1. Set up the server CLASSPATH correctly for the XSQL Servlet. This is done by starting the JRun Administrator, clicking on the *General* tab, and clicking on the *Java* subtab, as shown in Figure B-1.

   Append the list of *.jar* files and the directory that need to be in the server CLASSPATH for the XSQL Servlet to the existing value in the Java CLASSPATH field. Assuming that you installed into *C:*, the list looks like this:

   ```
   C:\xsql\lib\xmlparserv2.jar;
   C:\xsql\lib\oraclexmlsql.jar;
   C:\xsql\lib\classes111.zip;
   C:\xsql\lib\oraclexsql.jar;
   C:\xsql\lib
   ```

2. Map the *.xsql* file extension to the XSQL Servlet. To do this, select the *Services* tab in the JRun Administrator and select the appropriate "JRun servlet engine for *XXX*" entry for the servlet engine that corresponds to the web server you are using. In Figure B-2, we'll show how to configure the servlet engine for the (built-in) JRun Web Server (JWS).

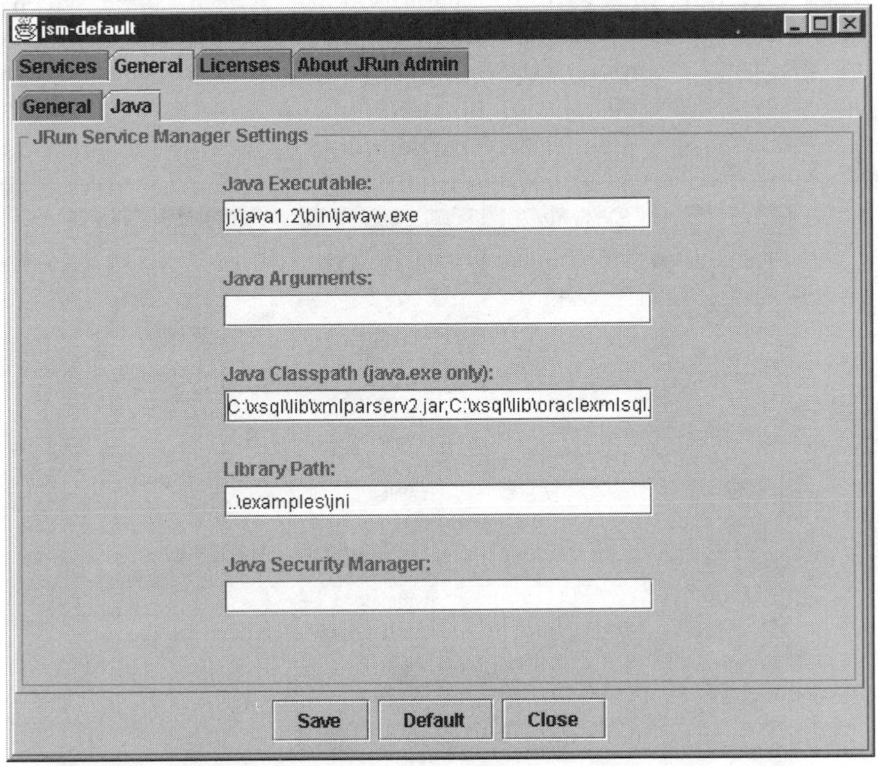

Figure B-1. Setting the JRun Servlet engine CLASSPATH

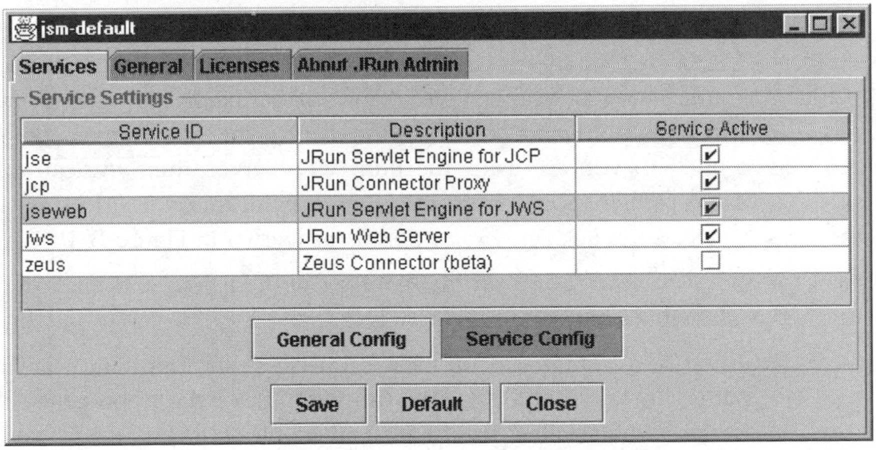

Figure B-2. Select appropriate service to configure for mapping the xsql extension

Then click the *Service Config* button. On the *Service Config* screen (see Figure B-3), select the *Mappings* tab. Click the *Add* button and make an entry for the **.xsql* extension, indicating `oracle.xml.xsql.XSQLServlet` as the servlet to be invoked shown in Figure B-3. Then click *Save* to save the changes, and *Close* to dismiss the dialog.

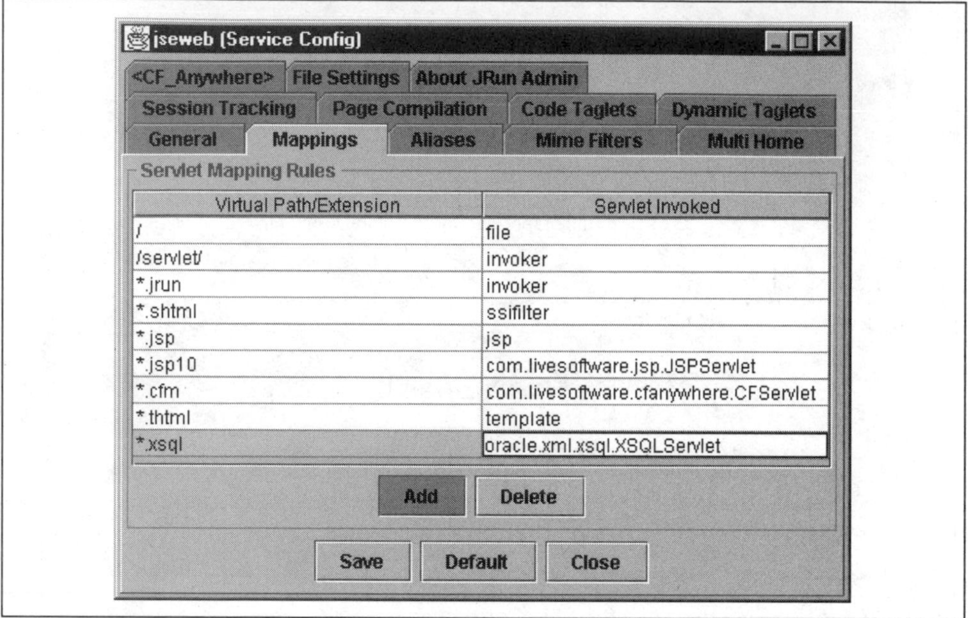

*Figure B-3. Mapping the *.xsql extension to the XSQLServlet class*

3. Map an */xsql/* virtual directory. In this step, we want to map the virtual path */xsql/* to *C:\xsql* (or wherever you installed the XSQL Servlet files). If you are using JRun together with another web server like Apache, IIS, or others, the virtual directory mapping needs to be done using the web server configuration file or utility. If you are using the JRun Web Server, then you can configure this virtual path mapping from the JRun Administrator. To do this, select the "jws" service and click on *Service Config,* as shown in Figure B-4.

   Click on the *Path Settings* tab on the *Service Config* dialog, and click the *Add* button, as shown in Figure B-5.

   Make an entry for a virtual path of */xsql/* (trailing slash important!) that maps to a real path of *C:\xsql* (trailing slash important!), or the appropriate directory into which you installed the XSQL Servlet files. Click *Save* to save the changes, then *Close* to dismiss the dialog.

Restart the JRun server and browse the URL:

```
http://localhost:8000/xsql/index.html
```

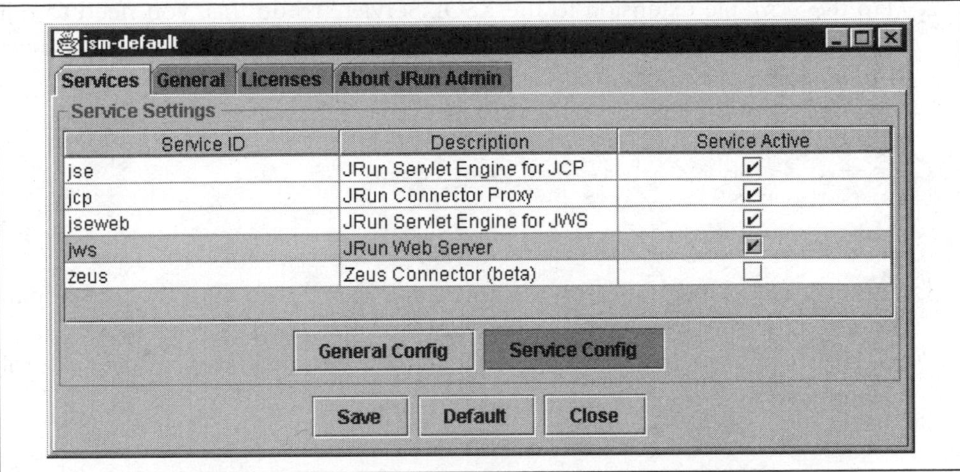

Figure B-4. Selecting the JRun web server service to configure path settings

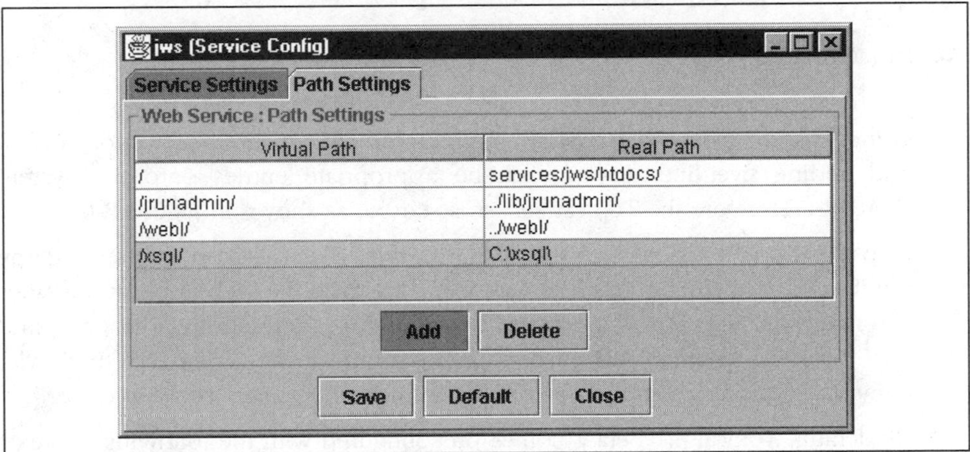

Figure B-5. Adding an /xsql/ virtual path for the XSQL demos

Apache JServ 1.0 or 1.1

1. Set up the server CLASSPATH correctly for the XSQL Servlet. This is done by editing the JServ configuration file *jserv.properties*. Assuming that you installed the XSQL Servlet files into *C:*, you need to add the following entries:

```
# Oracle XSQL Servlet
wrapper.classpath=C:\xsql\lib\oraclexsql.jar
# Oracle JDBC (8.1.6)
wrapper.classpath=C:\xsql\lib\classes111.zip
# Oracle XML Parser V2 (with XSLT Engine)
wrapper.classpath=C:\xsql\lib\xmlparserv2.jar
# Oracle XML SQL Components for Java
wrapper.classpath=C:\xsql\lib\oraclexmlsql.jar
# XSQLConfig.xml File location
wrapper.classpath=C:\xsql\lib
```

2. Map the *.xsql* file extension to the XSQL Servlet. To do this, you need to edit the JServ configuration file *jserv.conf* (in JServ 1.0, this was named *mod_jserv.conf* on some platforms). Add the following line:

```
# Executes a servlet passing filename with proper extension in PATH_TRANSLATED
# property of servlet request.
# Syntax: ApJServAction [extension] [servlet-uri]
# Defaults: NONE

ApJServAction .xsql /servlets/oracle.xml.xsql.XSQLServlet
```

3. Map an /xsql/ virtual directory. In this step, we want to map the virtual path */xsql/* to *C:\xsql* (or wherever you installed the XSQL Servlet files). To do this, you need to edit the Apache configuration file *httpd.conf*, adding the following line:

```
Alias /xsql/ "C:/xsql/"
```

Restart the Apache server and browse the URL:

```
http://localhost/xsql/index.html
```

Jakarta Tomcat 3.1

1. Set up the server CLASSPATH correctly for the XSQL Servlet. This is done by editing the Tomcat startup script named *tomcat.bat* in *./jakarta-tomcat/bin* and adding five lines to append the appropriate entries onto the system CLASSPATH before the Tomcat server is started, as shown in Figure B-6.

2. Map the *.xsql* file extension to the XSQL Servlet. Tomcat supports creating any number of configuration contexts to better organize the web applications your site needs to support. Each context is mapped to a virtual directory path, and has its own separate servlet configuration information. The XSQL Servlet comes with a preconfigured context file to make XSQL Servlet setup easier.

   By default, Tomcat 3.1 Beta 1 comes preconfigured with the following contexts (defined by `<Context>` entries in the *./jakarta-tomcat/conf/server.xml* file):

   — The *root* context

   — */examples*

   — */test*

   — */admin*

   We could install the XSQL Servlet into one of these contexts, but for simplicity we'll create a new context just for the XSQL Servlet that maps to the directory where you installed the XSQL Servlet distribution.

   Edit the *./jakarta-tomcat/conf/server.xml* file to add the following `<Context>` entry with a `path="/xsql"`, as shown in Figure B-7.

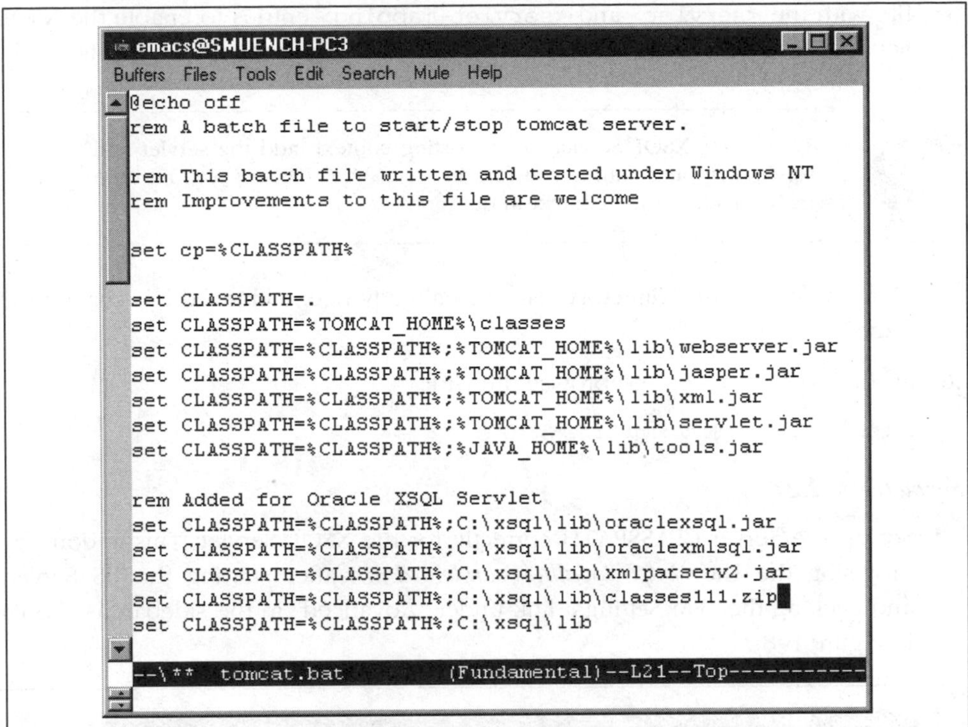

Figure B-6. Setting up the necessary CLASSPATH by modifying tomcat.bat

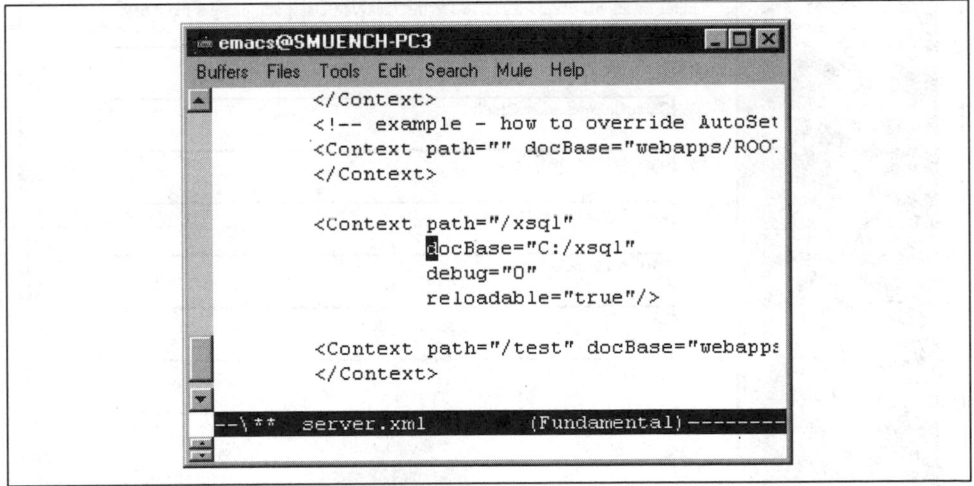

Figure B-7. Adding a context for the xsql root directory

Note that the `docBase="C:/xsql"` points to the physical directory where you installed the XSQL Servlet distribution. Since the XSQL Servlet distribution already ships with a *./xsql/WEB-INF* directory containing the required *web.xml* file with the `<servlet>` and `<servlet-mapping>` entries to enable the XSQL Servlet class to be mapped to the *.xsql* extension, this is the only step needed.

To add the XSQL Servlet to an existing context, add the servlet and servlet-mapping entries you find in *./xsql/WEB-INF/web.xml* into the *web.xml* file for the context in question.

3. Map an */xsql/* virtual directory. This has already been achieved by creating the `/xsql` context.

Restart the Tomcat server and browse the URL:

```
http://localhost:8080/xsql/index.html
```

ServletExec 2.2

1. Set up the Server CLASSPATH correctly for the XSQL Servlet. This is done by browsing the URL *http://localhost/servlet/admin* after starting the IIS Server, and clicking the "VM Settings" link under "Advanced" in the sidebar, as shown in Figure B-8.

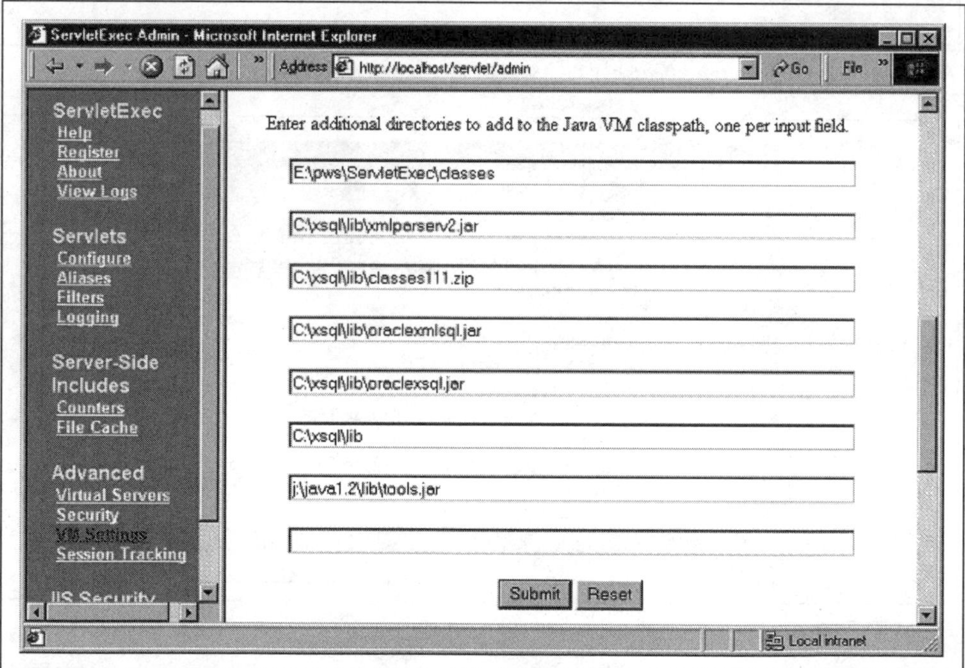

Figure B-8. Adding Java archives to the ServletExec CLASSPATH

Add the four archives and one directory as shown in the figure, by adding them one at a time and clicking the *Submit* button after each new entry.

2. Map the *.xsql* file extension to the XSQL Servlet. Click on *Configure* under the "Servlets" heading in the sidebar to browse the form where you register servlets. Enter a Servlet Name of `oraclexsql` and a Servlet Class of `oracle.xml.xsql.XSQLServlet` into the blank form at the top and click *Submit*. This is shown in Figure B-9.

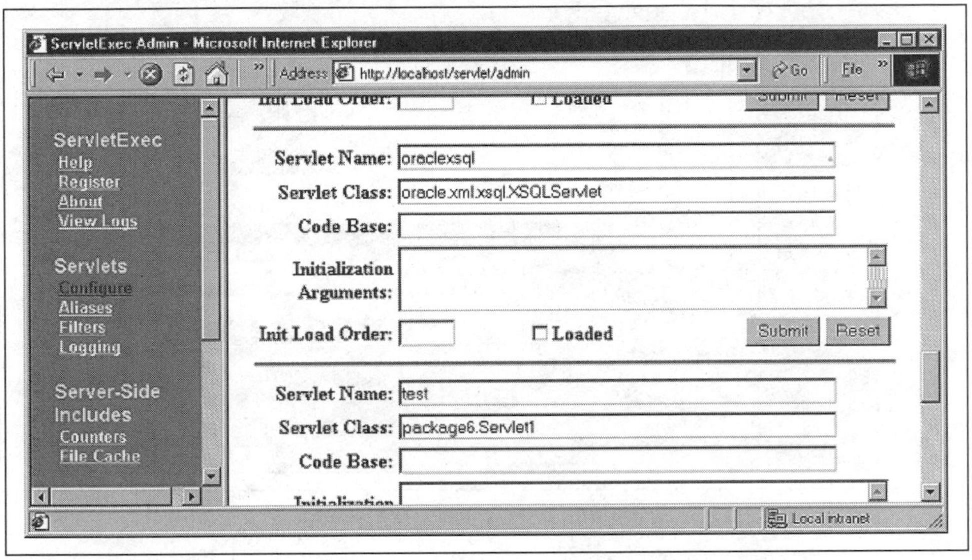

Figure B-9. Defining a named servlet entry for the XSQLServlet class

Click on *Aliases* under "Servlets" in the sidebar. Add an entry as shown in Figure B-10 mapping **.xsql* to the servlet "nickname" `oraclexsql` just defined.

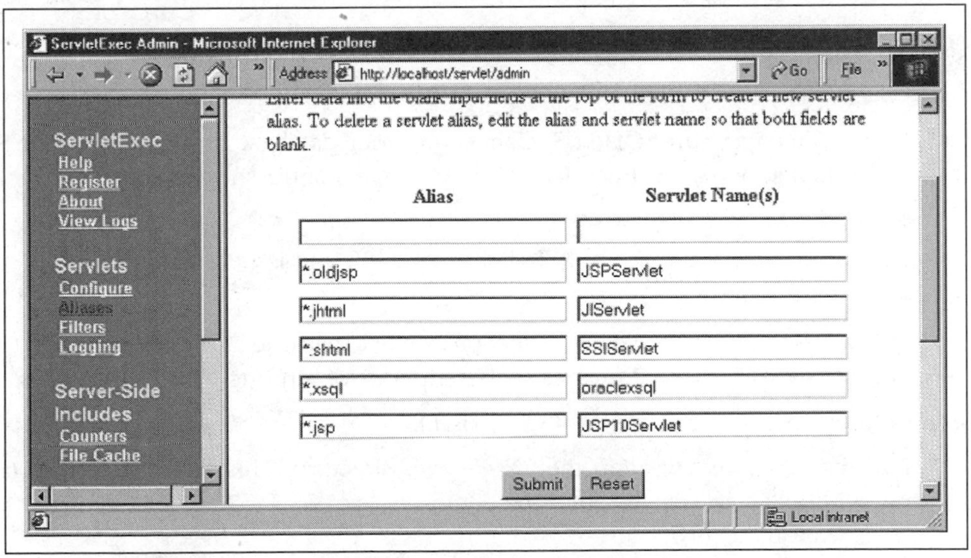

*Figure B-10. Associating the *.xsql extension with the XSQLServlet servlet by name*

3. Map an */xsql/* virtual directory. Use the IIS Admin console to create an */xsql* virtual directory and map it to *C:\xsql* as shown in Figure B-11.

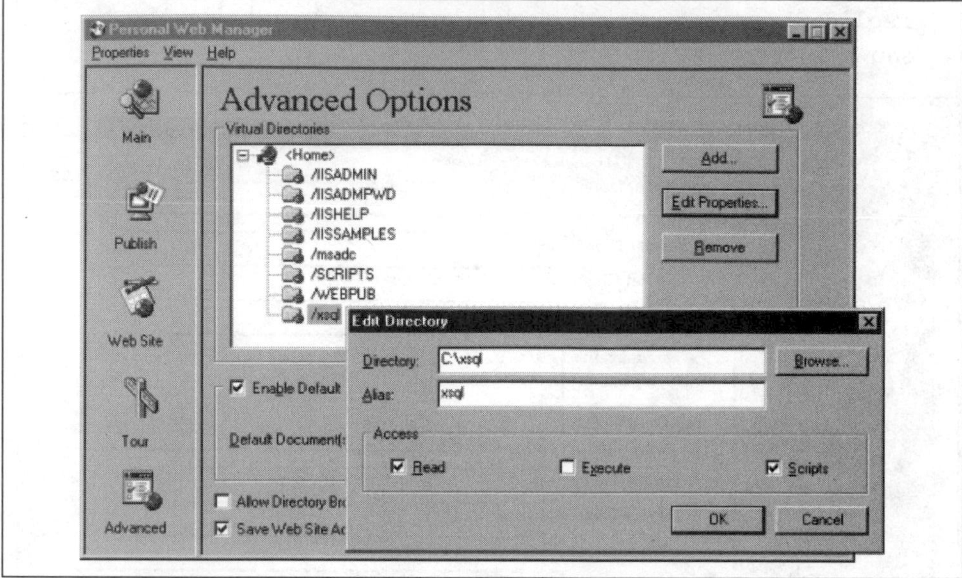

Figure B-11. Creating the /xsql/ virtual directory for the Personal Web Manager

Restart the IIS server and browse the URL:

http://localhost/xsql/index.html

Setting Up the Demo Data

To set up the data for the demos do the following:

1. Change directory to the *.\xsql\demo* directory on your machine.
2. In this directory, run SQLPLUS. Connect to your database as CTXSYS/CTXSYS (the schema owner for InterMedia Text packages) and issue the command:

   ```
   GRANT EXECUTE ON CTX_DDL TO SCOTT;
   ```

3. Connect to your database as SYSTEM/MANAGER and issue the command:

   ```
   GRANT QUERY REWRITE TO SCOTT;
   ```

   This allows SCOTT to create a functional index that one of the demos uses to perform case-insensitive queries on descriptions of airports.

4. Connect to your database as SCOTT/TIGER.
5. Run the script *install.sql* in the *./xsql/demo* directory. This script will, in turn, run all the SQL scripts for all of the demos.

6. Change directory to the *doyouxml* subdirectory, and run the following command:

   ```
   imp scott/tiger file=doyouxml.dmp
   ```

   to import some sample data for the "Do You XML? Site" demo.

C

Conceptual Map to the XML Family

Figure C-1 is a complete conceptual map showing how all of the key XML-related standards discussed in this book fit together.

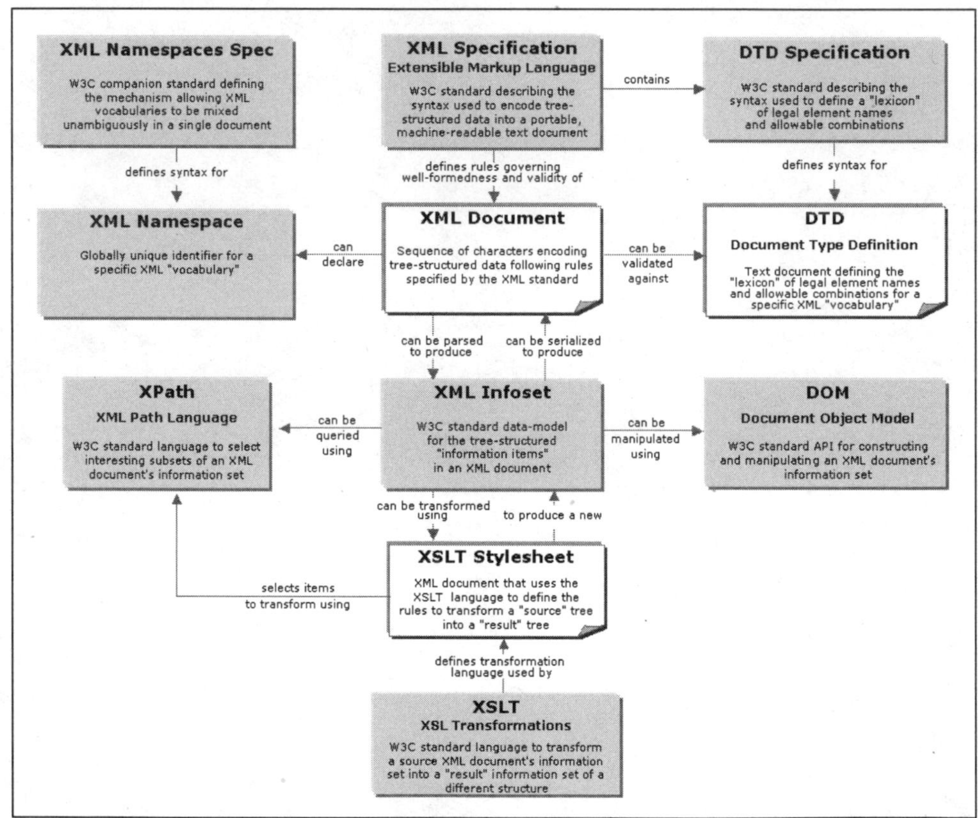

Figure C-1. Conceptual map to the XML family

D

Quick References

This appendix includes compact quick references for XSLT, XPath, and XML. Mulberry Technologies has been distributing these quickrefs for several years, and I use them often. I'm grateful to Mulberry for allowing us to include them in this book. The latest versions are available online at *http://www.mulberrytech.com/quickref/*.

XSLT and XPath Quick Reference

Mulberry Technologies, Inc.
17 West Jefferson Street, Suite 207
Rockville, MD 20850 USA
Phone: +1 301/315-9631
Fax: +1 301/315-8285
info@mulberrytech.com
http://www.mulberrytech.com

Location Paths [XPath §2]

Optional '/', zero or more **location steps**, separated by '/'

Location Steps [XPath §2.1]

Axis specifier, **node test**, zero or more **predicates**

Axis Specifiers [XPath §2.2]

ancestor::	following-sibling::
ancestor-or-self::	namespace::
attribute::	parent::
child::	preceding::
descendant::	preceding-sibling::
descendant-or-self::	self::
following::	

Node Tests [XPath §2.3]

name	node()
URI:name	text()
prefix:name	comment()
*	processing-instruction()
*prefix:**	processing-instruction(*literal*)

Abbreviated Syntax for Location Paths

(nothing)	child::
@	attribute::
//	/descendant-or-self::node()/
.	self::node()
..	parent::node()
/	Node tree root

Predicate [XPath §2.4]

[*expr*]

Variable Reference [XPath §3.7]

$*qname*

Literal Result Elements [§7.1.1]

Any element not in the xsl: namespace and not an extension element

---

XSLT
http://www.w3.org/TR/xslt

XPath
http://www.w3.org/TR/xpath

XSL-List
http://www.mulberrytech.com/xsl/xsl-list/

XSLT Functions [§12, §15]

node-set **document**(*object, node-set?*)
node-set **key**(*string, object*)
string **format-number**(*number, string, string?*)
node-set **current**()
node-set **unparsed-entity-uri**(*string*)
string **generate-id**(*node-set?*)
object **system-property**(*string*)
boolean **element-available**(*string*)
boolean **function-available**(*string*)

Node Types [XPath §5]

Root	Processing Instruction
Element	Comment
Attribute	Text
Namespace	

Object Types [§11.1, XPath §1]

boolean	True or false
number	Floating-point number
string	UCS characters
node-set	Set of nodes selected by a path
Result tree fragment	XSLT only. Fragment of the result tree

Expression Context [§4, XPath §1]

Context node (a node)
Context position (a number)
Context size (a number)
Variable bindings in scope
Namespace declarations in scope
Function library

Built-in Template Rules [§5.8]

```
<xsl:template match="*|/">
    <xsl:apply-templates/>
</xsl:template>
```

```
<xsl:template match="*|/" mode="m">
    <xsl:apply-templates mode="m"/>
</xsl:template>
```

```
<xsl:template match="text()|@*">
    <xsl:value-of select="."/>
</xsl:template>
```

```
<xsl:template
    match="processing-instruction()|comment()"/>
```

Built-in template rule for namespaces is to do nothing

XPath Operators

Parentheses may be used for grouping.

Node-sets [XPath §3.3]

| | *[expr]* | / | // |

Booleans [XPath §3.4]

or **and** **=, !=** **<=, <, >=, >**

Numbers [XPath §3.5]

+ **-** **div** **mod**

XPath Core Function Library

Node Set Functions [XPath §4.1]

number **last**()
number **position**()
number **count**(*node-set*)
node-set **id**(*object*)
string **local-name**(*node-set?*)
string **namespace-uri**(*node-set?*)
string **name**(*node-set?*)

String Functions [XPath §4.2]

string **string**(*object?*)
string **concat**(*string, string, string**)
boolean **starts-with**(*string, string*)
boolean **contains**(*string, string*)
string **substring-before**(*string, string*)
string **substring-after**(*string, string*)
string **substring**(*string, number, number?*)
number **string-length**(*string?*)
string **normalize-space**(*string?*)
string **translate**(*string, string, string*)

Boolean Functions [XPath §4.3]

boolean **boolean**(*object*)
boolean **not**(*object*)
boolean **true**()
boolean **false**()
boolean **lang**(*string*)

Number Functions [XPath §4.4]

number **number**(*object?*)
number **sum**(*node-set*)
number **floor**(*number*)
number **ceiling**(*number*)
number **round**(*number*)

XSLT Elements

Stylesheet Element [§2.2]

<xsl:stylesheet version="1.0" id="*id*"
extension-element-prefixes="*tokens*"
exclude-result-prefixes="*tokens*"
xmlns:xsl="http://www.w3.org/1999/XSL/Transform"> xsl:import*, top-level elements
</xsl:stylesheet>

xsl:transform is a synonym for xsl:stylesheet

Combining Stylesheets [§2.6]

<xsl:include href="*uri-reference*"/>

<xsl:import href="*uri-reference*"/>

Whitespace Stripping [§3.4]

<xsl:strip-space elements="*tokens*"/>

<xsl:preserve-space elements="*tokens*"/>

Defining Template Rules [§5.3]

<xsl:template match="*pattern*" name="*qname*"
priority="*number*" mode="*qname*">
xsl:param* followed by text, literal result elements and/or XSL elements </xsl:template>

Applying Template Rules [§5.4]

<xsl:apply-templates select="*node-set-exp*"
mode="*qname*"/>
<xsl:apply-templates select="*node-set-exp*"
mode="*qname*">
(xsl:sort | xsl:with-param)* </xsl:apply-templates>

Overriding Template Rules [§5.6]

<xsl:apply-imports/>

Named Templates [§6]

<xsl:call-template name="*qname*"/>
<xsl:call-template name="*qname*">
xsl:with-param* </xsl:call-template>

Namespace Alias [§7.1.1]

<xsl:namespace-alias result-prefix="*prefix*|#default"
stylesheet-prefix="*prefix*|#default"/>

Creating Elements [§7.1.2]

<xsl:element name="{*qname*}"
namespace="{*uri-reference*}"
use-attribute-sets="*qnames*">...</xsl:element>

Creating Attributes [§7.1.3]

<xsl:attribute name="{*qname*}"
namespace="{*uri-reference*}">...</xsl:attribute>

Named Attribute Sets [§7.1.4]

<xsl:attribute-set name="*qname*"
use-attribute-sets="*qnames*">
xsl:attribute* </xsl:attribute-set>

Creating Text [§7.2]

<xsl:text disable-output-escaping="yes|no">
#PCDATA </xsl:text>

Processing Instructions [§7.3]

<xsl:processing-instruction name="{*ncname*}">
...</xsl:processing-instruction>

Creating Comments [§7.4]

<xsl:comment>...</xsl:comment>

Copying [§7.5]

<xsl:copy use-attribute-sets="*qnames*">
...</xsl:copy>

Generating Text [§7.6.1]

<xsl:value-of select="*string-expr*"
disable-output-escaping="yes|no"/>

Attribute Value Templates [§7.6.2]

<element attribute="{*expr*}"/>

Numbering [§7.7]

<xsl:number level="single|multiple|any"
count="*pattern*" from="*pattern*"
value="*number-expr*" format="{*string*}"
lang="{*nmtoken*}"
letter-value="{alphabetic|traditional}"
grouping-separator="{*char*}"
grouping-size="{*number*}"/>

Repetition [§8]

<xsl:for-each select="*node-set-expr*">
xsl:sort*, ...</xsl:for-each>

Conditional Processing [§9]

<xsl:if test="*boolean-expr*">...</xsl:if>

<xsl:choose>
<xsl:when test="*expr*">...</xsl:when>+
<xsl:otherwise>...</xsl:otherwise>?
</xsl:choose>

Mulberry Technologies, Inc.

Sorting [§10]

```
<xsl:sort select="string-expr" lang="{nmtoken}"
    data-type="{text|number|qname-but-not-
    ncname}" order="{ascending|descending}"
    case-order="{upper-first|lower-first}"/>
```

Variables and Parameters [§11]

```
<xsl:variable name="qname" select="expr"/>
<xsl:variable name="qname">...</xsl:variable>

<xsl:param name="qname" select="expr"/>
<xsl:param name="qname">...</xsl:param>
```

Using Values [§11.3]

```
<xsl:copy-of select="expr"/>
```

Passing Parameters [§11.6]

```
<xsl:with-param name="expr" select="expr"/>
<xsl:with-param name="expr">...</xsl:with-param>
```

Keys [§12.2]

```
<xsl:key name="qname" match="pattern"
    use="expr"/>
```

Number Formatting [§12.3]

```
<xsl:decimal-format name="qname"
    decimal-separator="char"
    grouping-separator="char" infinity="string"
    minus-sign="char" NaN="string"
    percent="char" per-mille="char"
    zero-digit="char" digit="char"
    pattern-separator="char"/>
```

Messages [§13]

```
<xsl:message terminate="yes|no">
    ...</xsl:message>
```

Fallback [§15]

```
<xsl:fallback>...</xsl:fallback>
```

Output [§16]

```
<xsl:output
    method="xml|html|text|qname-but-not-ncname"
    version="nmtoken" encoding="string"
    omit-xml-declaration="yes|no"
    doctype-public="string" doctype-system="string"
    standalone="yes|no" indent="yes|no"
    cdata-section-elements="qnames"
    media-type="string"/>
```

Key

xsl:stylesheet	Element
version=	Required attribute
version=	Optional attribute
{*expr*}	Attribute value template. Text between any { and } is evaluated as an expression. Attribute value must evaluate to indicated attribute type.
...	Anything allowed in a template
|	Separates alternative values
?	Zero or one occurrences
*	Zero or more occurrences
+	One or more occurrences
#PCDATA	Character data

Attribute Value Types

1.0	Literal value
boolean-expr	Expression returning boolean value
char	Single character
expr	Expression
id	XML name used as identifier
ncname	XML name not containing a colon (:)
node-set-expr	Expression returning a node set
number-expr	Expression returning a number
pattern	XSLT pattern
prefix	Namespace prefix
qname	Namespace-qualified XML name comprising local part and optional prefix
qname-but-not-ncname	Namespace-qualified name comprising local part and prefix
token	Meaning varies with context. See Rec.
uri-reference	Reference to Universal Resource Identifier

XML Syntax Quick Reference

Mulberry Technologies, Inc.
17 West Jefferson Street, Suite 207
Rockville, MD 20850 USA
Phone: +1 301/315-9631
Fax: +1 301/315-8285
info@mulberrytech.com
http://www.mulberrytech.com

Mulberry
Technologies, Inc.

DOCTYPE Declaration

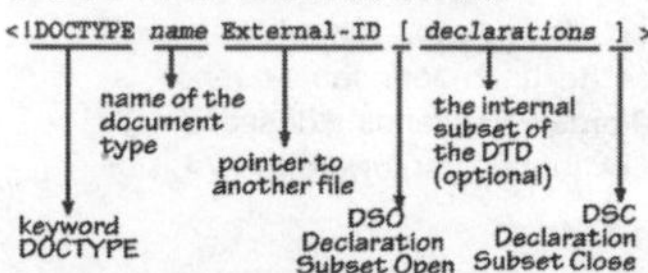
<!DOCTYPE name External-ID [declarations] >
name of the document type
pointer to another file
the internal subset of the DTD (optional)
keyword DOCTYPE
DSO Declaration Subset Open
DSC Declaration Subset Close

Internal Subset

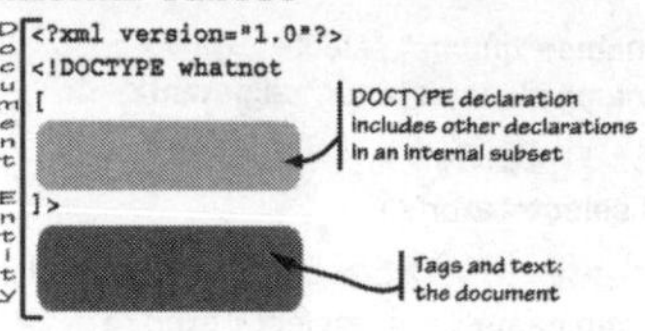
<?xml version="1.0"?>
<!DOCTYPE whatnot
[
]>
DOCTYPE declaration includes other declarations in an internal subset
Tags and text: the document
Document Entity

External Subset

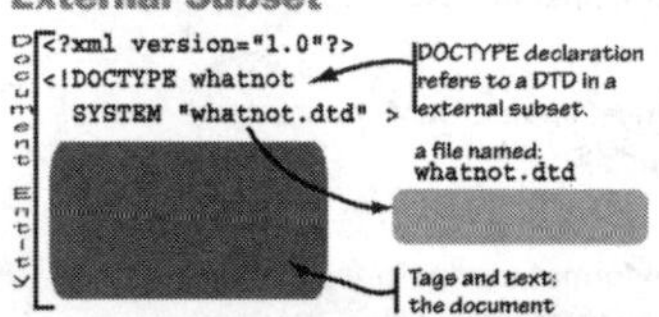
<?xml version="1.0"?>
<!DOCTYPE whatnot
SYSTEM "whatnot.dtd" >
DOCTYPE declaration refers to a DTD in a external subset.
a file named: whatnot.dtd
Tags and text: the document
Document Entity

Internal and External Subsets

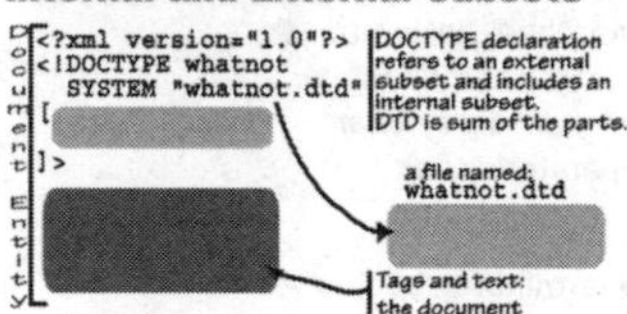
<?xml version="1.0"?>
<!DOCTYPE whatnot
SYSTEM "whatnot.dtd"
[
]>
DOCTYPE declaration refers to an external subset and includes an internal subset. DTD is sum of the parts.
a file named: whatnot.dtd
Tags and text: the document
Document Entity

Conditional Section (DTD only)

```
<![IGNORE[ declarations ]]>
<![INCLUDE[ declarations ]]>
```

External-ID

```
   SYSTEM "URI"
OR
   PUBLIC "Public ID" "URI"
```

Mulberry
Technologies, Inc.

Element Declaration

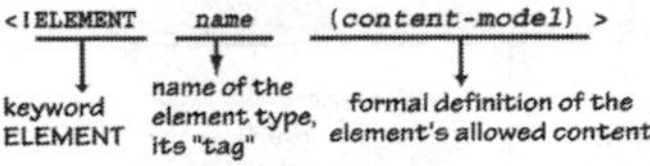

Connectors

,	*"Then"*	Follow with (in sequence)
|	*"Or"*	Select (only) one from the group
Only one connector type per group — no mixing!		

Occurrence Indicators

(no indicator)	*Required*	One and only one
?	*Optional*	None or one
*	*Optional, repeatable*	None, one, or more
+	*Required, repeatable*	One or more

Groupings

(	Start content model or group
)	End content model or group

#PCDATA in Models (first, OR bars, asterisk)

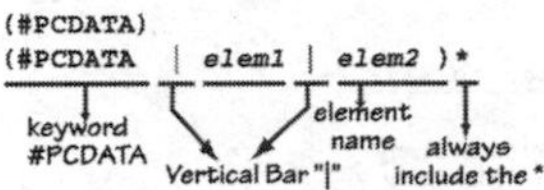

ANY Element Keyword

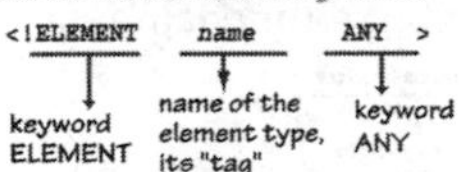

EMPTY Element Keyword

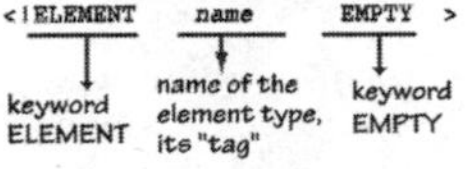

Attribute Declaration

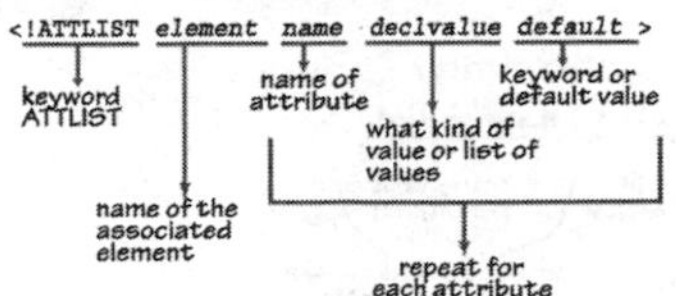

Declared Value Keywords

CDATA	Data character string (default if well-formed)
NMTOKEN	Name token
NMTOKENS	One or more name tokens (spaces between)
ID	Unique identifier for element
IDREF	Reference to ID on another element
IDREFS	One or more IDREFs (spaces between)
ENTITY	Name of an entity (declared elsewhere)
ENTITIES	One or more names of entities

Enumerated Value Descriptions

(a|b|c)	List of attribute values (*Or* between)
NOTATION (x|y)	Names of notations (Requires a list of values as well as the keyword. Values declared elsewhere with NOTATION.)

Attribute Defaults

"*value*"	If attribute is omitted, assume this value.
#REQUIRED	Required. Document is *not valid* if no value is provided.
#IMPLIED	Optional. Not constrained; no default can be inferred; an application is free to handle as appropriate.
#FIXED "*value*"	Fixed value. (Requires a value as well as the keyword.) If the attribute appears with a different value, that's an error.

Reserved Attributes

xml:space	Preserve whitespace or use default
xml:lang	Indicate language of element and that element's attributes and children

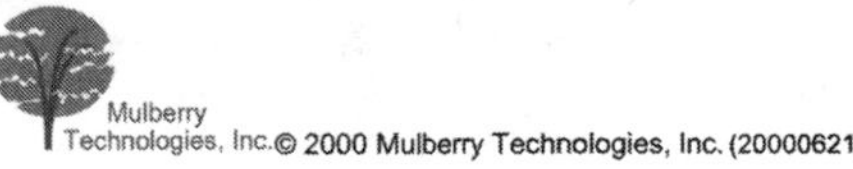

Parameter Entity Declarations

Internal Parameter Entity

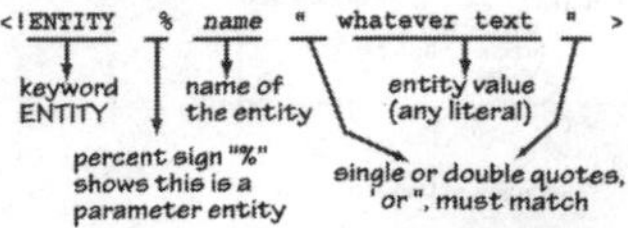

External Parameter Entity

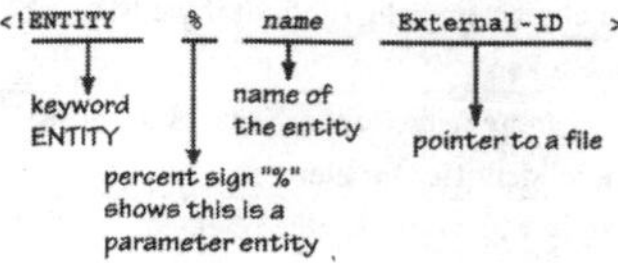

General Entity Declarations

Internal Entity

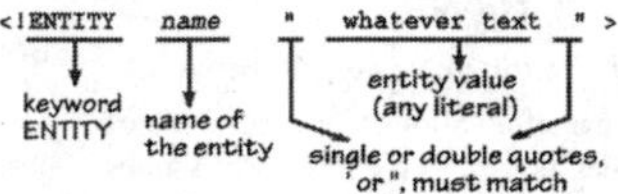

External Unparsed Entity

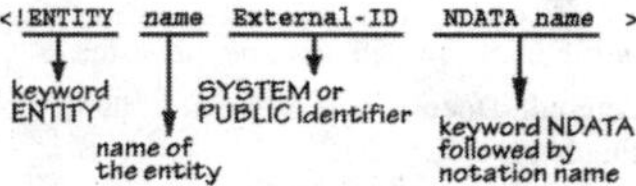

Predefined General Entities

Entity	Displays As	Character Value
`&`	&	`&`
`<`	<	`<`
`>`	>	`>`
`'`	'	`'`
`"`	"	`"`

XML Declaration

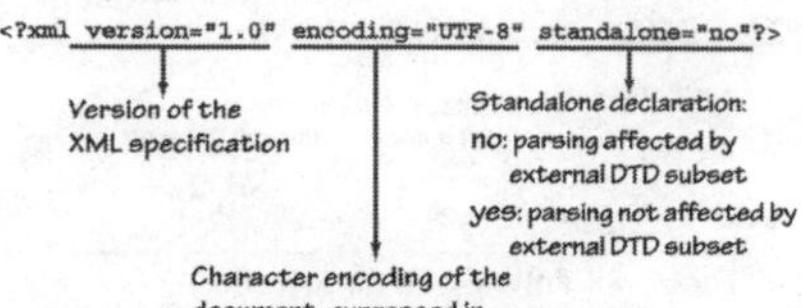

Processing Instruction

```
<?target ***Some Stuff **** ?>
```

Notation Declaration

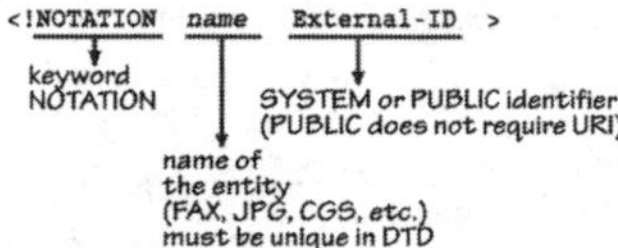

Comment

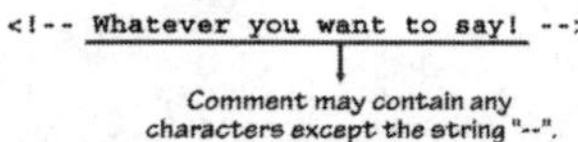

Start Tag with Attribute (in document)

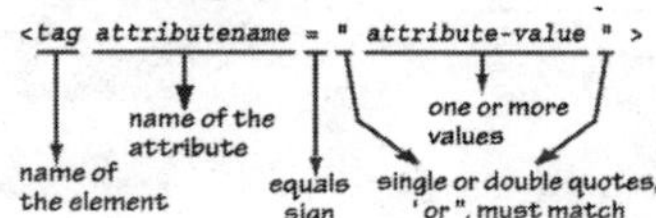

EMPTY Element (in document)

```
<name/>
<name></name>
```

CDATA Section (in document)

```
<![CDATA[ *** Some Stuff *** ]]>
```

Index

Symbols

A

S

T

U

V

W

Z

About the Author

Steve Muench is Oracle's lead XML Technical Evangelist and the development lead for Oracle XSQL Pages. He is Oracle's primary representative to the W3C (World Wide Web Consortium) XSL Working Group, as well as a consulting product manager and developer working on Oracle Business Components for Java, an XML-based business object framework. In his more than ten years at Oracle, Steve has been involved in the support, development, and technical evangelism of Oracle's application development tools and database, and he is a frequent presenter at both Oracle and XML technical conferences. He has been a catalyst in helping development teams across Oracle weave XML and XSLT sensibly into their future development plans.

Colophon

Our look is the result of reader comments, our own experimentation, and feedback from distribution channels. Distinctive covers complement our distinctive approach to technical topics, breathing personality and life into potentially dry subjects.

The animal on the cover of *Building Oracle XML Applications* is a peacock butterfly (*Inachis io*), whose name derives from the prominent blue and black eyespots found on each upper wing. Like the similar markings on peacock feathers, these eyespots contain iridescent areas, which enhance the peacock butterfly's already brilliant coloration. When startled, the peacock butterfly rubs its wings together and spreads them wide, threatening intruders with their vivid patterns, which strongly resemble an owl's visage when seen upside-down.

The peacock butterfly is widespread throughout England, Ireland, and Eurasia, but only vagrant specimens appear in North America. After mating in early spring, female butterflies lay batches of eggs on the underside of leaves of the stinging nettle plant, which provides food for the developing larvae. The new generation of adults takes flight in July, then hibernates over the winter to emerge again in spring, surviving a total of up to eleven months.

Adult butterflies have distinctive red-brown upper wings with bright yellow, blue, black, and white patterning, which span a width of about two inches. When a peacock butterfly folds its wings, the underside is revealed to be dark charcoal in color, allowing the butterfly to blend into the surrounding shrubs during hibernation. Peacock butterflies belong to the large family of *Nymphalidae*, or brush-footed butterflies, so called because their foremost pair of legs is too small for grasping or locomotion and is useful only for cleaning.

Although the peacock butterfly possesses a rare, tropical beauty, the caterpillars draw sustenance from the common stinging nettle, which flourishes both in rural fields and in urban lots, while adult butterflies feast on nectar from the butterfly bush, lilac, and other plants. Peacock butterflies may abound wherever these hardy plants take root, from English nature preserves, to abandoned Welsh mines, to far-flung Siberian settlements.

Ellie Volckhausen designed the cover of this book, based on a series design by Edie Freedman. The cover image is a 19th-century engraving from the Dover Pictorial Archive. Emma Colby produced the cover layout with QuarkXPress 4.1 using Adobe's ITC Garamond font.

Madeleine Newell was the production editor and copyeditor for *Building Oracle XML Applications*. Mary Sheehan and Nancy Kotary provided quality control. Kimo Carter, Nancy Williams, and Molly Shangraw provided production assistance. Brenda Miller wrote the index.

David Futato designed the interior layout based on a series design by Nancy Priest. Mike Sierra implemented the design in FrameMaker 5.5.6. The text and heading fonts are ITC Garamond Light and Garamond Book. The illustrations that appear in the book were produced by Robert Romano using Macromedia FreeHand 8 and Adobe Photoshop 5. This colophon was written by Madeleine Newell.

This book was authored in XML using the DocBook DTD and the SoftQuad XMetal 1.0 XML editor. Drafts of the entire book were transformed directly from the XML source to HTML format using the DocBook XSLT stylesheets and the Oracle XSLT processor.

Whenever possible, our books use a durable and flexible lay-flat binding. If the page count exceeds this binding's limit, perfect binding is used.

More Titles from O'Reilly

Oracle

Advanced Oracle PL/SQL Programming with Packages

By Steven Feuerstein
1st Edition October 1996
690 pages, Includes diskette
ISBN 1-56592-238-7

This book explains the best way to construct packages, a powerful part of Oracle's PL/SQL procedural language that can dramatically improve your programming productivity and code quality, while preparing you for object-oriented development in Oracle technology. It comes with PL/Vision software, a library of PL/SQL packages developed by the author, and takes you behind the scenes as it examines how and why the PL/Vision packages were implemented the way they were.

Oracle Built-in Packages

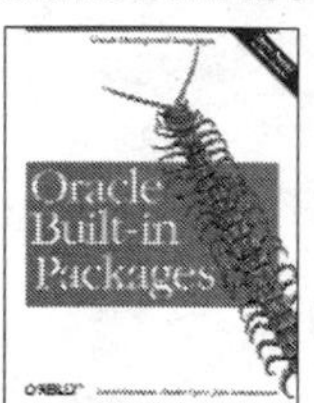

By Steven Feuerstein, Charles Dye & John Beresniewicz
1st Edition April 1998
956 pages, Includes diskette
ISBN 1-56592-375-8

Oracle's built-in packages dramatically extend the power of the PL/SQL language, but few developers know how to use them effectively. This book is a complete reference to all of the built-ins, including those new to Oracle8. The enclosed diskette includes an online tool that provides easy access to the many files of source code and documentation developed by the authors.

Oracle PL/SQL Programming Guide to Oracle8i Features

By Steven Feuerstein
1st Edition October 1999
272 pages, Includes diskette
ISBN 1-56592-675-7

This concise and engaging guide will give you a jump start on the new PL/SQL features of Oracle8i (Oracle's revolutionary "Internet database"). It covers autonomous transactions, invoker rights, native dynamic SQL, bulk binds and collects, system-level database triggers, new built-in packages, fine-grained access control, calling Java methods from within PL/SQL, and much more. Includes a diskette containing 100 files of reusable source code and examples.

Oracle Web Applications: PL/SQL Developer's Introduction

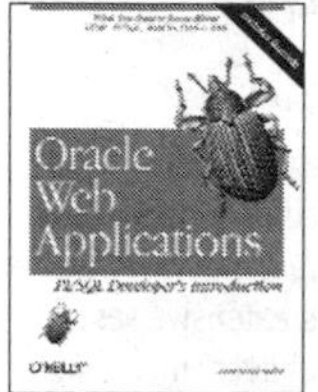

By Andrew Odewahn
1st Edition September 1999
256 pages, ISBN 1-56592-687-0

This book is an easy-to-understand guide to building Oracle8i (Oracle's "Internet database") Web applications using a variety of tools – PL/SQL, HTML, XML, WebDB, and Oracle Application Server (OAS). It also covers the packages in the PL/SQL toolkit and demonstrates several fully realized Web applications. This book provides the jump-start you need to extend relational concepts to Web content and to make the transition from traditional programming to the development of useful Web applications for Oracle8i. Also covers Web development for Oracle8 and Oracle7.

Oracle PL/SQL Programming, 2nd Edition

By Steven Feuerstein with Bill Pribyl
2nd Edition September 1997
1028 pages, Includes diskette
ISBN 1-56592-335-9

The first edition of *Oracle PL/SQL Programming* quickly became an indispensable reference for PL/SQL developers. The second edition focuses on Oracle8, covering Oracle8 object types, object views, collections, and external procedures, as well as new datatypes and functions and tuning, tracing, and debugging PL/SQL programs. The diskette contains an online Windows-based tool with access to more than 100 files of source code.

Oracle PL/SQL Language Pocket Reference

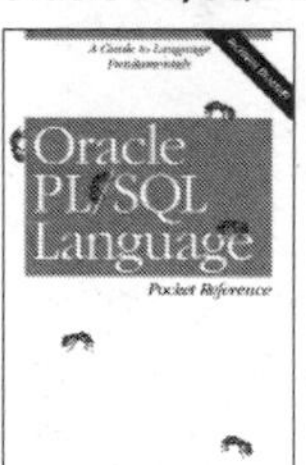

By Steven Feuerstein, Bill Pribyl & Chip Dawes
1st Edition April 1999
104 pages, ISBN 1-56592-457-6

This pocket reference boils down the most vital information from Oracle PL/SQL Programming into an accessible quick reference that summarizes the basics of PL/SQL: block structure, fundamental language elements (e.g., identifiers, declarations, defaults), data structures (including Oracle8 objects), control statements, and use of procedures, functions, and packages. It includes coverage of PL/SQL features in the newest version of Oracle, Oracle8i.

Oracle

Oracle PL/SQL Built-ins Pocket Reference

By Steven Feuerstein, John Beresniewicz & Chip Dawes
1st Edition October 1998
78 pages, ISBN 1-56592-456-8

This companion quick reference to Steven Feuerstein's bestselling *Oracle PL/SQL Programming* and *Oracle Built-in Packages* will help you use Oracle's extensive set of built-in functions and packages, including those new to Oracle8. You'll learn how to call numeric, character, date, conversion, large object (LOB), and miscellaneous functions, as well as packages like DBMS_SQL and DBMS_OUTPUT.

Oracle PL/SQL Developer's Workbook

By Steven Feuerstein with Andrew Odewahn
1st Edition May 2000
592 pages, ISBN 1-56592-674-9

A companion to Feuerstein's other bestselling Oracle PL/SQL books, this workbook contains a carefully constructed set of problems and solutions that will test your language skills and help you become a better developer. Exercises are provided at three levels: beginner, intermediate, and expert. It covers the full set of language features: variables, loops, exception handling, data structures, object technology, cursors, built-in functions and packages, PL/SQL tuning, and the new Oracle8i features (including Java and the Web).

How to stay in touch with O'Reilly

1. Visit Our Award-Winning Web Site

http://www.oreilly.com/

★"Top 100 Sites on the Web" —*PC Magazine*
★"Top 5% Web sites" —*Point Communications*
★"3-Star site" —*The McKinley Group*

Our web site contains a library of comprehensive product information (including book excerpts and tables of contents), downloadable software, background articles, interviews with technology leaders, links to relevant sites, book cover art, and more. File us in your Bookmarks or Hotlist!

2. Join Our Email Mailing Lists

New Product Releases

To receive automatic email with brief descriptions of all new O'Reilly products as they are released, send email to:
listproc@online.oreilly.com
Put the following information in the first line of your message (*not* in the Subject field):
subscribe oreilly-news

O'Reilly Events

If you'd also like us to send information about trade show events, special promotions, and other O'Reilly events, send email to:
listproc@online.oreilly.com
Put the following information in the first line of your message (*not* in the Subject field):
subscribe oreilly-events

3. Get Examples from Our Books via FTP

There are two ways to access an archive of example files from our books:

Regular FTP

- ftp to:
  ftp.oreilly.com
  (login: anonymous
  password: your email address)
- Point your web browser to:
  ftp://ftp.oreilly.com/

FTPMAIL

- Send an email message to:
  ftpmail@online.oreilly.com
  (Write "help" in the message body)

4. Contact Us via Email

order@oreilly.com
To place a book or software order online. Good for North American and international customers.

subscriptions@oreilly.com
To place an order for any of our newsletters or periodicals.

books@oreilly.com
General questions about any of our books.

software@oreilly.com
For general questions and product information about our software. Check out O'Reilly Software Online at **http://software.oreilly.com/** for software and technical support information. Registered O'Reilly software users send your questions to: **website-support@oreilly.com**

cs@oreilly.com
For answers to problems regarding your order or our products.

booktech@oreilly.com
For book content technical questions or corrections.

proposals@oreilly.com
To submit new book or software proposals to our editors and product managers.

international@oreilly.com
For information about our international distributors or translation queries. For a list of our distributors outside of North America check out:
http://www.oreilly.com/www/order/country.html

5. Work with Us

Check out our website for current employment opportunites:
www.jobs@oreilly.com
Click on "Work with Us"

O'Reilly & Associates, Inc.
101 Morris Street, Sebastopol, CA 95472 USA
TEL 707-829-0515 or 800-998-9938
(6am to 5pm PST)
FAX 707-829-0104

International Distributors

UK, Europe, Middle East and Africa (except France, Germany, Austria, Switzerland, Luxembourg, Liechtenstein, and Eastern Europe)

INQUIRIES

O'Reilly UK Limited
4 Castle Street
Farnham
Surrey, GU9 7HS
United Kingdom
Telephone: 44-1252-711776
Fax: 44-1252-734211
Email: information@oreilly.co.uk

ORDERS

Wiley Distribution Services Ltd.
1 Oldlands Way
Bognor Regis
West Sussex PO22 9SA
United Kingdom
Telephone: 44-1243-779777
Fax: 44-1243-820250
Email: cs-books@wiley.co.uk

France

INQUIRIES

Éditions O'Reilly
18 rue Séguier
75006 Paris, France
Tel: 33-1-40-51-52-30
Fax: 33-1-40-51-52-31
Email: france@editions-oreilly.fr

ORDERS

GEODIF
61, Bd Saint-Germain
75240 Paris Cedex 05, France
Tel: 33-1-44-41-46-16 (French books)
Tel: 33-1-44-41-11-87 (English books)
Fax: 33-1-44-41-11-44
Email: distribution@eyrolles.com

Germany, Switzerland, Austria, Eastern Europe, Luxembourg, and Liechtenstein

INQUIRIES & ORDERS

O'Reilly Verlag
Balthasarstr. 81
D-50670 Köln
Germany
Telephone: 49-221-973160-91
Fax: 49-221-973160-8
Email: anfragen@oreilly.de (inquiries)
Email: order@oreilly.de (orders)

Canada (French language books)

Les Éditions Flammarion ltée
375, Avenue Laurier Ouest
Montréal (Québec) H2V 2K3
Tel: 00-1-514-277-8807
Fax: 00-1-514-278-2085
Email: info@flammarion.qc.ca

Hong Kong

City Discount Subscription Service, Ltd.
Unit D, 3rd Floor, Yan's Tower
27 Wong Chuk Hang Road
Aberdeen, Hong Kong
Tel: 852-2580-3539
Fax: 852-2580-6463
Email: citydis@ppn.com.hk

Korea

Hanbit Media, Inc.
Chungmu Bldg. 201
Yonnam-dong 568-33
Mapo-gu
Seoul, Korea
Tel: 822-325-0397
Fax: 822-325-9697
Email: hant93@chollian.dacom.co.kr

Philippines

Global Publishing
G/F Benavides Garden
1186 Benavides Street
Manila, Philippines
Tel: 632-254-8949/637-252-2582
Fax: 632-734-5060/632-252-2733
Email: globalp@pacific.net.ph

Taiwan

O'Reilly Taiwan
No. 3, Lane 131
Hang-Chow South Road
Section 1, Taipei, Taiwan
Tel: 886-2-23968990
Fax: 886-2-23968916
Email: taiwan@oreilly.com

China

O'Reilly Beijing
Room 2410
160, FuXingMenNeiDaJie
XiCheng District
Beijing, China PR 100031
Tel: 86-10-66412305
Fax: 86-10-86631007
Email: beijing@oreilly.com

India

Computer Bookshop (India) Pvt. Ltd.
190 Dr. D.N. Road, Fort
Bombay 400 001 India
Tel: 91-22-207-0989
Fax: 91-22-262-3551
Email: cbsbom@giasbm01.vsnl.net.in

Japan

O'Reilly Japan, Inc.
Yotsuya Y's Building
7 Banch 6, Honshio-cho
Shinjuku-ku
Tokyo 160-0003 Japan
Tel: 81-3-3356-5227
Fax: 81-3-3356-5261
Email: japan@oreilly.com

All Other Asian Countries

O'Reilly & Associates, Inc.
101 Morris Street
Sebastopol, CA 95472 USA
Tel: 707-829-0515
Fax: 707-829-0104
Email: order@oreilly.com

Australia

Woodslane Pty., Ltd.
7/5 Vuko Place
Warriewood NSW 2102
Australia
Tel: 61-2-9970-5111
Fax: 61-2-9970-5002
Email: info@woodslane.com.au

New Zealand

Woodslane New Zealand, Ltd.
21 Cooks Street (P.O. Box 575)
Waganui, New Zealand
Tel: 64-6-347-6543
Fax: 64-6-345-4840
Email: info@woodslane.com.au

Latin America

McGraw-Hill Interamericana
Editores, S.A. de C.V.
Cedro No. 512
Col. Atlampa
06450, Mexico, D.F.
Tel: 52-5-547-6777
Fax: 52-5-547-3336
Email: mcgraw-hill@infosel.net.mx

ORACLE SOFTWARE LICENSE AGREEMENT

YOU SHOULD CAREFULLY READ THE FOLLOWING TERMS AND CONDITIONS BEFORE BREAKING THE SEAL ON THE DISC ENVELOPE. AMONG OTHER THINGS, THIS AGREEMENT LICENSES THE ENCLOSED SOFTWARE TO YOU AND CONTAINS WARRANTY AND LIABILITY DISCLAIMERS. BY USING THE DISC AND/OR INSTALLING THE SOFTWARE, YOU ARE ACCEPTING AND AGREEING TO THE TERMS AND CONDITIONS OF THIS AGREEMENT. IF YOU DO NOT AGREE TO THE TERMS OF THIS AGREEMENT, DO NOT BREAK THE SEAL OR USE THE DISC. YOU SHOULD PROMPTLY RETURN THE PACKAGE UNOPENED.

LICENSE: ORACLE CORPORATION ("ORACLE") GRANTS END USER ("YOU" OR "YOUR") A NON-EXCLUSIVE, NON-TRANSFERABLE DEVELOPMENT ONLY LIMITED USE LICENSE TO USE THE ENCLOSED SOFTWARE AND DOCUMENTATION ("SOFTWARE") SUBJECT TO THE TERMS AND CONDITIONS, INCLUDING USE RESTRICTIONS, SPECIFIED BELOW.

You shall have the right to use the Software (a) only in object code form, (b) for development purposes only in the indicated operating environment for a single developer (one person) on a single computer, (c) solely with the publication with which the Software is included, and (d) solely for Your personal use and as a single user.

You are prohibited from and shall not (a) transfer, sell, sublicense, assign or otherwise convey the Software, (b) timeshare, rent or market the Software, (c) use the Software for or as part of a service bureau, (d) use the Software for or as part of third party training, (e) distribute the Software in whole or in part and/or (f) use the Software in any manner not expressly permitted by this Agreement. Any attempt to transfer, sell, sublicense, assign or otherwise convey any of the rights, duties or obligations hereunder is void. You are prohibited from and shall not use the Software for internal data processing operations, processing data of a third party or for any commercial or production use. If You desire to use the Software for any use other than the development use allowed under this Agreement, You must contact Oracle, or an authorized Oracle reseller, to obtain the appropriate licenses. You are prohibited from and shall not cause or permit the reverse engineering, disassembly, decompilation, modification or creation of derivative works based on the Software. You are prohibited from and shall not copy or duplicate the Software except as follows: You may make one copy of the Software in machine readable form solely for back-up purposes. No other copies shall be made without Oracle's prior written consent. You are prohibited from and shall not: (a) remove any product identification, copyright notices, or other notices or proprietary restrictions from the Software, or (b) run any benchmark tests with or of the Software. This Agreement does not authorize You to use any Oracle name, trademark or logo.

COPYRIGHT/OWNERSHIP OF SOFTWARE: The Software is the confidential and proprietary product of Oracle and is protected by copyright and other intellectual property laws. You acquire only the right to use the Software and do not acquire any rights, express or implied, in the Software or media containing the Software other than those specified in this Agreement. Oracle, or its licensor, shall at all times, including but not limited to after termination of this Agreement, retain all rights, title, and interest, including intellectual property rights, in the Software and media.

WARRANTY DISCLAIMER: THE SOFTWARE IS PROVIDED "AS IS" AND ORACLE SPECIFICALLY DISCLAIMS ALL WARRANTIES OF ANY KIND, EITHER EXPRESS OR IMPLIED, INCLUDING, BUT NOT LIMITED TO, THE IMPLIED WARRANTIES OF MERCHANTABILITY, SATISFACTORY QUALITY AND FITNESS FOR A PARTICULAR PURPOSE. ORACLE DOES NOT WARRANT, GUARANTEE OR MAKE ANY REPRESENTATIONS REGARDING THE USE, OR THE RESULTS OF THE USE, OF THE SOFTWARE IN TERMS OF CORRECTNESS, ACCURACY, RELIABILITY, CURRENTNESS OR OTHERWISE, AND DOES NOT WARRANT THAT THE OPERATION OF THE SOFTWARE WILL BE UNINTERRUPTED OR ERROR FREE.

ORACLE SOFTWARE LICENSE AGREEMENT (cont.)

ORACLE EXPRESSLY DISCLAIMS ALL WARRANTIES NOT STATED HEREIN, NO ORAL OR WRITTEN INFORMATION OR ADVICE GIVEN BY ORACLE OR OTHERS SHALL CREATE A WARRANTY OR IN ANY WAY INCREASE THE SCOPE OF THIS LICENSE, AND YOU MAY NOT RELY ON ANY SUCH INFORMATION OR ADVICE.

LIMITATION OF LIABILITY: IN NO EVENT SHALL ORACLE BE LIABLE FOR ANY DIRECT, INDIRECT, INCIDENTAL, SPECIAL OR CONSEQUENTIAL DAMAGES, OR DAMAGES FOR LOSS OF PROFITS, REVENUE, DATA OR DATA USE, INCURRED BY YOU OR ANY THIRD PARTY, WHETHER IN AN ACTION IN CONTRACT OR TORT, EVEN IF ORACLE HAS BEEN ADVISED OF THE POSSIBILITY OF SUCH DAMAGES. SOME JURISDICTIONS DO NOT ALLOW THE EXCLUSION OF IMPLIED WARRANTIES OR LIMITATION OR EXCLUSION OF LIABILITY FOR INCIDENTAL OR CONSEQUENTIAL DAMAGES SO THE ABOVE EXCLUSIONS AND LIMITATION MAY NOT APPLY TO YOU.

TERMINATION: You may terminate this license at any time by discontinuing use of and destroying the Software together with any copies in any form. This license will also terminate if You fail to comply with any term or condition of this Agreement. Upon termination of the license, You agree to discontinue use of and destroy the Software together with any copies in any form. The Warranty Disclaimer, Limitation of Liability and Export Administration sections of this Agreement shall survive termination of this Agreement.

NO TECHNICAL SUPPORT: Oracle is not obligated to provide and this Agreement does not entitle You to any updates or upgrades to, or any technical support or phone support for, the Software.

EXPORT ADMINISTRATION: You acknowledge that the Software, including technical data, is subject to United States export control laws, including the United States Export Administration Act and its associated regulations, and may be subject to export or import regulations in other countries. You agree to comply fully with all laws and regulations of the United States and other countries ("Export Laws") to assure that neither the Software, nor any direct products thereof, are (a) exported, directly or indirectly, in violation of Export Laws, either to countries or nationals that are subject to United States export restrictions or to any end user who has been prohibited from participating in the Unites States export transactions by any federal agency of the United States government; or (b) intended to be used for any purposes prohibited by the Export Laws, including, without limitation, nuclear, chemical or biological weapons proliferation. You acknowledge that the Software may include technical data subject to export and re-export restrictions imposed by United States law.

RESTRICTED RIGHTS: The Software is provided with Restricted Rights. Use, duplication or disclosure of the Software by the United State government is subject to the restrictions set forth in the Rights in Technical Data and Computer Software Clauses in DFARS 252.227-7013(c)(1)(ii) and FAR 52.227-19(c)(2) as applicable. Manufacturer is Oracle Corporation, 500 Oracle Parkway, Redwood City, CA 94065.

MISCELLANEOUS: This Agreement and all related actions thereto shall be governed by California law. Oracle may audit Your use of the Software. If any provision of this Agreement is held to be invalid or unenforceable, the remaining provisions of this Agreement will remain in full force.

YOU ACKNOWLEDGE THAT YOU HAVE READ THIS AGREEMENT, UNDERSTAND IT, AND AGREE TO BE BOUND BY ITS TERMS AND CONDITIONS. YOU FURTHER AGREE THAT IT IS THE COMPLETE AND EXCLUSIVE STATEMENT OF THE AGREEMENT BETWEEN ORACLE AND YOU.